Forensic Mental Health Assessment
A Casebook

Forensic Mental Health Assessment

A Casebook

Kirk Heilbrun

Geoffrey R. Marczyk

David DeMatteo

OXFORD
UNIVERSITY PRESS

2002

OXFORD
UNIVERSITY PRESS

Oxford New York
Auckland Bangkok Buenos Aires Cape Town Chennai
Dar es Salaam Delhi Hong Kong Istanbul Karachi Kolkata
Kuala Lumpur Madrid Melbourne Mexico City Mumbai Nairobi
São Paulo Shanghai Singapore Taipei Tokyo Toronto

and an associated company in Berlin

Library of Congress Cataloging-in-Publication Data

Heilbrun, Kirk.
    Forensic mental health assessment : a casebook / Kirk Heilbrun, Geoffrey R. Marczyk,
David DeMatteo.
        p.   cm.
    Includes bibliographical references and index.
    ISBN 0-19-514568-2
        1. Psychology, Forensic—Case studies.   2. Mentally ill offenders—Case studies.   3.
Forensic psychiatry—Case studies.   I. Marczyk, Geoffrey R., 1964–   II. DeMatteo, David,
1972–   III. Title.

RA1148 .H452 2002
614'.1—dc21   2001047644

9 8 7 6 5 4 3 2 1

Printed in the United States of America
on acid-free paper

To my parents, Al and Marian. Thanks for everything.

KH

To my family—Charles, Mary Ann, Keith, Brian, Nina, and Helene. Your undying support makes this achievement as much yours as mine.

GM

To my parents, my brother and his family, and my fiancée, Christina.

DD

Preface

There has not yet been a casebook in forensic mental health assessment (FMHA). Given the growth and important development in the forensic specializations of psychology, psychiatry, and other mental health professions, it seemed time to develop one.

We had a number of purposes in constructing the book as we did. One of the most important was to provide the field with case material from forensic reports, which are the most frequently used means of conveying the results of FMHA to attorneys and legal decision makers. We were fortunate enough to persuade a number of psychologists and psychiatrists, each selected for national reputation and specialization, to provide us with case reports from their respective practices. Although these case reports (with one exception) are disguised and altered so they do not come from a single case, they represent "real" case material. They provide legal and mental health professionals, administrators, policymakers, and trainees with a good overview of different kinds of FMHA performed by highly competent forensic specialists.

We also wanted to integrate these forensic case reports with broad principles of FMHA to show how such principles apply to different kinds of forensic assessment. In this sense, the present book was written as a companion to *Principles of Forensic Mental Health Assessment* (Heilbrun, 2001), which describes the derivation and support for 29 broad principles of FMHA. Those interested in how these principles might be applied to FMHA cases can see how we did this in the introduction to each case.

Finally, there are very specific questions about FMHA that cannot be covered well with broad principles. We took a number of questions like this and formulated "teaching points"—particular questions about a substantive or procedural aspect of FMHA—that were addressed following each case. Some of the case report contributors were also kind enough to answer these teaching point questions, providing the reader with a broader overview of perspectives than the three of us could offer.

Our biggest acknowledgment goes to the book's contributors. A number of individuals (Stanley Brodsky, Joel Dvoskin, Bill Foote, Geoff McKee, Reid Meloy, Robert Meyer, Lois Oberlander, Randy Otto, Norman Poythress, Phillip Resnick, Robert Sadoff, David Shapiro, Karin Towers, Herbert Weissman, and Lauren Wylonis) contributed case reports. David Martindale and Michael

Norko contributed excellent reports, which, for reasons unrelated to the quality of the reports, ultimately were not used in the book. Others (Steven Bank, Beth Clark, Gerald Cooke, Margaret Cooke, Dewey Cornell, James Eisenberg, Richard Frederick, Stephen Golding, Leigh Hagan, Stephen Hart, Douglas Mossman, Ira Packer, Robert Prentky, and Kathy Stafford) contributed a case report and wrote a teaching point. Mark Cunningham and Alan Goldstein contributed two case reports and wrote the teaching point for each, while Philip Witt provided two reports and one teaching point. Many of these contributors also offered comments about the book's structure during the 2 years it was being written. Without them the book could not have been done, at least in its present form. We are particularly grateful that these individuals were not only willing to provide case reports but also to perform the additional work of disguising the material and combining elements of different cases to make it ethically acceptable to publish such cases. Thanks to all of you.

Other colleagues have also offered helpful thoughts. Tom Grisso provided a number of useful suggestions during an early phase of our planning. Bruce Sales was instrumental in allowing us to transform the idea for a casebook into a work that would allow us to address the multiple goals of providing case material, modeling reports, illustrating principles, and addressing teaching points. Randy Otto provided useful assistance with the question of potential publishers, and Oxford University Press (particularly Joan Bossert) has done an outstanding job. We are grateful to all of you.

The Villanova/MCP Hahnemann Law-Psychology Program, directed by Donald Bersoff since 1990, has been a stimulating place for research and practice in forensic psychology. The three of us clearly share a passion for this area, but the Law-Psychology Program has allowed us to transform the idea of a casebook into reality over a period of several years. As Dr. Bersoff retires in 2001, we would like to acknowledge the debt that we and the entire field of law-psychology owe him. We hope that others who follow will strive to maintain the high standards he has set.

Finally, we each owe a grateful acknowledgment to our family and friends. Patty and Anna have been very patient with Kirk as he struggled to finish his part of this work. Geff would like to thank his family for the support they provided as he worked on this project. Dave would like to express deep gratitude to his family for their unending support and patience. Finally, Geff and Dave would like to thank Kirk for his continued mentorship and guidance.

Philadelphia, PA   Kirk Heilbrun
April 2001   Geff Marczyk
                                                       Dave DeMatteo

Contents

Teaching Point: Can one ever play more than one role in a single FMHA case?

contributed by Kirk Heilbrun, Geff Marczyk, and David DeMatteo

21 MALPRACTICE, 425

Case 1, 425

Principle: Use multiple sources of information for each area being assessed

case contributed by William E. Foote

Teaching Point: What is the role of the forensic clinician in collecting third-party information?

contributed by Kirk Heilbrun, Geff Marczyk, and David DeMatteo

22 WORKER'S COMPENSATION, 438

Case 1, 438

Principle: Use testing when indicated in assessing response style

case contributed by Kirk Heilbrun, David DeMatteo, and Geff Marczyk

Teaching Point: How does the forensic clinician integrate response style data?

contributed by Kirk Heilbrun, Geff Marczyk, and David DeMatteo

Case 2, 448

Principle: Assess legally relevant behavior

case contributed by Lauren Wylonis and Robert L. Sadoff

Teaching Point: What is the relationship between symptoms and disability in capacity to work?

contributed by Kirk Heilbrun, Geff Marczyk, and David DeMatteo

23 THREAT/RISK ASSESSMENT, 454

Case 1, 454

Principle: Identify relevant forensic issues

case contributed by Kirk Heilbrun, Geff Marczyk, and David DeMatteo

Teaching Point: What are strategies for predicting violent behavior, and others for assessing risk reduction?

contributed by Kirk Heilbrun, Geff Marczyk, and David DeMatteo

Case 2, 462

Principle: Clarify role with attorney

case contributed by Joel Dvoskin

Teaching Point: What are strategies for avoiding dual roles in FMHA?

contributed by Kirk Heilbrun, Geff Marczyk, and David DeMatteo

Case 3, 470

Principle: Use nomothetic evidence in assessing causal connection between clinical condition and functional abilities

case contributed by Stephen D. Hart

Teaching Point: What are the advantages and disadvantages of using actuarial approaches in risk assessment in forensic contexts?

contributed by Stephen D. Hart

Contributors

Steven C. Bank, Ph.D., is Assistant to the Clinical Director at the Center for Forensic Psychiatry in Ann Arbor, Michigan. He is Director of the Postdoctoral Fellowship Program in Forensic Psychology at the Center for Forensic Psychiatry and a consultant to the Michigan Attorney General and the University of Michigan Law School Clinic. He is also past president of the American Board of Forensic Psychology and the Michigan Society of Forensic Psychology. His publications and workshops focus on courtroom communication and ethical and effective expert testimony. Dr. Bank is a Diplomate in Forensic Psychology, American Board of Professional Psychology, and specializes in criminal forensic psychology and forensic mental health administration.

Stanley L. Brodsky, Ph.D., is Professor of Psychology and Coordinator of the Psychology-Law Ph.D. concentration at The University of Alabama. He is a Fellow of APA Divisions 12, 18, 41, and 51. He has been the recipient of the Distinguished Contribution to Forensic Psychology Award by the American Academy of Forensic Psychology and the Distinguished Contribution to Correctional Psychology Award of the American Association of Correctional Psychology. He is author or editor of ten books, including *Testifying in Court* and *The Expert Expert Witness*, both published by the American Psychological Association. He maintains a private practice in forensic psychology and is a frequent leader of workshops on courtroom testimony and on psychotherapy with reluctant clients.

Beth K. Clark, Ph.D., has been in private practice of psychology in Ann Arbor since 1982; her forensic practice is concentrated in civil and family law. Her publications and presentations have focused on psychological testing, child custody, the forensic assessment of children, risk management and ethical practice. Dr. Clark is a Diplomate in Forensic Psychology, American Board of Professional Psychology. She is past president of the Michigan Psychological Association, past-chair of the American Psychological Association's Committee on Legal Issues, and currently president of the American Academy of Forensic Psychology and vice president of the Michigan Society of Forensic Psychology. With her husband, Charles, she is the author of *Law and Mental Health Professionals: Michigan*. She is the 2000 Michigan Psychological Association Distinguished Psychologist.

Gerald Cooke, Ph.D., and Margaret Cooke, Ph.D., are in private practice in Plymouth Meeting, Pennsylvania. Their practice is limited to forensic evaluation, consultation, and testimony, including custody evaluation, personal injury, and other civil matters, as well as criminal forensic assessment. Both have published in professional journals on a variety of forensic issues. He is a Diplomate in Forensic Psychology, American Board of Professional Psychology, and a Fellow of the American Academy of Forensic Psychology.

Dewey G. Cornell, Ph.D., is Professor of Education in the Programs in Clinical and School Psychology of the Curry School of Education and also a Faculty Associate of the Institute of Law, Psychiatry, and Public Policy at the University of Virginia. He has taught personality assessment and lectured on forensic psychology for more than 15 years. He supervises assessment training at the Center for Clinical Psychology Services and maintains a forensic practice with specialization in violent criminal defendants. He has published studies of juvenile homicide, personality assessment, psychopathy, school safety, and related topics.

Mark D. Cunningham, Ph.D., is a clinical and forensic psychologist in private practice with offices in Abilene, Texas. He is a Diplomate in Forensic Psychology (ABPP) and has lectured on capital sentencing evaluations under the auspices of the American Academy of Forensic Psychology. Dr. Cunningham has had extensive involvement in state and federal capital sentencing cases across the United States. His primary research interests and publications are in the areas of violence risk assessment at capital sentencing, death row inmate competencies and characteristics, and antisocial behavior/psychopathy.

David DeMatteo, J.D., M.A., is currently completing a predoctoral internship in clinical psychology at the Medical College of Virginia in Richmond. He received his master's degree in clinical psychology from MCP Hahnemann University and his law degree from Villanova University School of Law as part of the J.D./Ph.D. Program in Law and Psychology. He is anticipating receiving his Ph.D. in clinical psychology from MCP Hahnemann University in the summer of 2002. His primary interests are criminal and civil forensic assessment, psychopathy, and the intersection between public policy and the law.

Joel A. Dvoskin, Ph.D., is Clinical Assistant Professor in the Department of Psychiatry at the University of Arizona. He is a Fellow of the American Psychological Association and the American Psychology-Law Society, and a Diplomate in Forensic Psychology by the American Board of Forensic Psychology. He is Past President of APA Division 18, Psychologists in Public Service. He has previously served as Acting Commissioner of Mental Health for the State of New York and as Associate Commissioner for New York's forensic and correctional mental health system. Dr. Dvoskin serves as a frequent expert witness, trainer, public speaker, and consultant to federal agencies as well as state, local and provincial governments throughout the United States and Canada. Dr. Dvoskin also serves as a consultant to the Threat Assessment Group and is affiliated with Park Dietz and Associates.

James Eisenberg, Ph.D., is Professor of Psychology and Director of the Criminal Justice Program at Lake Erie College in Ohio. For 19 years he served as the Court Psychologist and Associate Director of the Lake County Forensic Psychiatric Clinic in Ohio. He is a Diplomate in Forensic Psychology, American Board of Profes-

sional Psychology. His major work in forensic psychology has been in capital sentencing; he has evaluated numerous capitally charged defendants and has testified in state and federal courts. In 1999 he received a United States Speaker and Specialist grant from the United States Information Agency's Bureau of Information, and was invited to deliver an address to the Honduran National Congress on "The Death Penalty in the United States."

William E. Foote, Ph.D., is currently in the independent practice of forensic psychology in Albuquerque, New Mexico, and is Adjunct Professor, University of New Mexico School of Law. He is a Diplomate in Forensic Psychology, American Board of Professional Psychology, and serves on the Board of ABFP. He has published in the areas of ethics, sexual harassment, and employment discrimination. His professional interests include employment discrimination evaluation, workplace violence, personal injury evaluation, and criminal assessment. He is Past President of the New Mexico Psychological Association and has served on APA Council, the APA Committee on Legal Issues, and the APA Task Force on ABA-APA Relations.

Richard I. Frederick, Ph.D., is currently a staff psychologist at the United States Medical Center for Federal Prisoners in Springfield, Missouri, and Adjunct Professor in Psychology at both Southwest Missouri State University and Drury University, both in Springfield, Missouri. He is a Diplomate in Forensic Psychology, American Board of Professional Psychology. His major research and practice interests include the forensic assessment of criminal defendants and the assessment of malingered cognitive impairment. He is the author of the *Validity Indicator Profile* (1997), a tool for assessing malingered cognitive impairment, and a number of articles in this area as well.

Stephen Golding, Ph.D., is Professor of Psychology and Adjunct Professor of Law and of Psychiatry, University of Utah, a Diplomate in Forensic Psychology, American Board of Professional Psychology, and a Fellow of APA Divisions 12 and 41. He was Clinical Training Director at the University of Utah, 1985–1993; President of Division of Psychology and Law (APA), 1991–1992; and recipient of the Distinguished Contributions to Forensic Psychology Award by the

American Academy of Forensic Psychology in 1994. He was principal author (with Tom Grisso) of the *Specialty Guidelines for Forensic Psychologists*, addressing critical professional and ethical issues at the interface of psychology and the legal system. He maintains an active private practice, as well as teaching, research, and supervision, specializing in professional standards of practice, reforms in expert evidence, professional liability, criminal competencies and responsibility, and child abuse.

Alan M. Goldstein, Ph.D., is Professor of Psychology at John Jay College of Criminal Justice—CUNY. He is a Diplomate in Forensic Psychology, American Board of Professional Psychology, and chairs the Continuing Professional Education Program of the American Academy of Forensic Psychology. He is also a member of the Ethics Committee of the American Board of Professional Psychology, and serves as a member of their Board of Trustees. He is on the editorial boards of *Behavioral Sciences and the Law* and *Criminal Justice and Behavior*. He is editor of *Forensic Psychology*, a volume in *The Comprehensive Handbook of Psychology* (forthcoming). He received the 1997 Distinguished Contribution Award in Forensic Psychology. Dr. Goldstein is in forensic practice in New York.

Leigh D. Hagan, Ph.D., is Affiliate Assistant Clinical Professor of Psychology at Virginia Commonwealth University and in private practice in the greater Richmond, Virginia area. He is a Diplomate in Forensic Psychology, American Board of Professional Psychology, and contributes pro bono service to several judicial and community correctional programs. He has published and presented on ethics in forensic psychology and criminal, civil, and family law matters to mental health professionals and attorneys. His practice includes conducting forensic evaluations on the issues of child custody, psychological damages, risk assessment, and capital sentencing.

Stephen D. Hart, Ph.D., is a professor in the Department of Psychology, Simon Fraser University, Canada, and Visiting Professor in the Faculty of Psychology, University of Bergen, Norway. His primary expertise is forensic assessment and the association between mental disorder and violence. Most of his work focuses on the development, implementation, and evaluation of procedures for assessing violence risk. His

professional practice involves consultation with government agencies, training for mental health and criminal justice professionals, and expert testimony with respect to risk assessment. In 1995, he received the Saleem Shah award for early career research excellence in psychology and law, sponsored jointly by the American Academy of Forensic Psychology and the American Psychology-Law Society/APA Division 41. He serves as President of the American Psychology-Law Society in 2001–2002.

Kirk Heilbrun, Ph.D., is Professor and Chair of the Department of Clinical and Health Psychology at MCP Hahnemann University. He is a Fellow of the American Psychological Association and a Diplomate in Clinical Psychology and Forensic Psychology, American Board of Professional Psychology. He is also past-president of the American Psychology-Law Society/APA Division 41, and of the American Board of Forensic Psychology. He is the author of *Principles of Forensic Mental Health Assessment* (2001) and a number of related articles in the areas of forensic assessment and violence risk assessment.

Geoffrey R. Marczyk, J.D., M.S., M.A., is currently completing a pre-doctoral internship in Clinical and Community Psychology in the Department of Psychiatry at Yale University. He received his law degree from the Villanova University School of Law, and will receive his doctorate in Clinical and Health Psychology from MCP Hahnemann University in the summer of 2002. In addition, he has completed a Master of Arts degree in Counseling Psychology, and a Master of Science degree in Organizational Psychology. His major practice interests include forensic assessment, organizational dynamics, and the application of law and public policy to the mental health sector and its practitioners.

Geoffrey R. McKee, PhD., is currently Clinical Professor in the Department of Neuropsychiatry of the University of South Carolina School of Medicine and was previously Chief Psychologist of the Hall Psychiatric Institute Forensic Psychiatry Service. He is a Diplomate in Forensic Psychology, American Board of Professional Psychology, and past president of the American Academy of Forensic Psychology. Dr. McKee has published extensively in peer-reviewed journals on criminal forensic psychology with empirical studies of competency to stand trial in juveniles, infanticide and filicide by women, and MMPI-2 profiles of pre-trial defendants. He has maintained a private practice in forensic psychology since 1976, and has testified as an expert witness in more than 200 criminal trials, including over 50 death penalty cases.

Reid Meloy, Ph.D., is currently in the independent practice of forensic psychology. He is Associate Clinical Professor of Psychiatry at the University of California, San Diego, Adjunct Professor at the University of San Diego School of Law, and president of Forensis, Inc. He is a Diplomate in Forensic Psychology, American Board of Professional Psychology, and a Fellow of the American Academy of Forensic Sciences; he is also Past President of the American Academy of Forensic Psychology. His primary research interest at present is in the area of stalking; his edited book *The Psychology of Stalking: Clinical and Forensic Perspectives* (1998) received honorable mention for the Manfred Guttmacher Award from the American Psychiatric Association. He received the first National Achievement Award from the Association of Threat Assessment Professionals in 1998.

Robert G. Meyer, Ph.D., is currently Professor of Psychology at the University of Louisville in Louisville, Kentucky. He is a Diplomate in Clinical and in Forensic Psychology, American Board of Professional Psychology, and a Fellow of the American Psychological Association in Divisions 12 (Clinical) and 41 (American Psychology-Law Society). Among his publications are *Preparation for Licensing and Board Certifications in Psychology* (2nd edition, 1995), *The Clinician's Handbook* (4th edition, 1996), and *Practical Clinical Hypnosis* (1992). His professional specializations include personal injury evaluation and treatment, evaluation of trial competency and sanity, and forensic hypnosis.

Douglas Mossman, M.D., is Professor and Director of the Division of Forensic Psychiatry at the Wright State School of Medicine, and Adjunct Professor at the University of Dayton School of Law in Ohio. He previously held faculty positions in the Psychiatry Departments of the Medical University of South Carolina and the University of Cincinnati. In addition to teaching residents, fellows, and upper-level law students, Dr. Mossman maintains a private practice in general, adolescent, and forensic psychia-

try. He has made more than 100 presentations to local, regional, national, and international professional groups, and is the author of more than 80 articles dealing with ethics, forensic psychiatry, medical decision-making, diagnosis and treatment, and statistics. Dr. Mossman is board certified in general and forensic psychiatry, and in 1997 was elected to fellowship in the American Psychiatric Association.

Lois B. Oberlander, Ph.D., is currently a forensic consultant in Massachusetts and was previously Assistant Professor of Psychiatry at the University of Massachusetts Medical School. She is a Diplomate in Forensic Psychology, American Board of Professional Psychology, with professional specializations in adolescent and adult criminal forensic evaluations, and care and protection evaluations. She has published in the areas of ethics, child custody evaluation, child sexual abuse evaluations, and adjudicative competence.

Randy K. Otto, Ph.D., is Associate Professor in the Department of Mental Health Law and Policy in the Florida Mental Health Institute at the University of South Florida. Dr. Otto is a Diplomate in Forensic Psychology, American Board of Professional Psychology. He has previously served as President of the American Academy of Forensic Psychology, and is President-Elect of the American Psychology-Law Society. In 2000, Dr. Otto received the Jerome Fisher Memorial Lecture Award from the Langley Porter Psychiatric Institute at the University California-San Francisco in recognition of his contributions to the practice of clinical psychology and forensic psychology. The second edition of *Law and Mental Health Professionals: Florida*, which he co-authored with John Petrila, will be published in 2002, as will *Adjudicative Competence*, which he co-authored with Richard Bonnie, John Monahan, and Norman Poythress.

Ira K. Packer, Ph.D., is Associate Professor of Psychiatry at the University of Massachusetts Medical School, currently serving both as Director of Forensic Psychology Training and Deputy Director of the Correctional Mental Health Program. He previously served as the Assistant Commissioner of the Massachusetts Department of Mental Health. He is a Diplomate in Forensic Psychology, American Board of Professional Psychology, and is Past President of both the American Board of Forensic Psychology and the American Academy of Forensic Psychology. His research and scholarly interests include the insanity defense, the mentally ill in the criminal justice system, violence risk assessment, and forensic assessment. His practice interests include criminal and juvenile forensic assessment as well as personal injury.

Norman G. Poythress, Jr., Ph.D., is Professor in the Department of Mental Health Law and Policy at the Louis de la Parte Florida Mental Health Institute, University of South Florida. He is a Fellow of the American Psychological Association and Past President of the American Psychology-Law Society. He was the 1990 recipient of the American Academy of Forensic Psychology's Award for Distinguished Contribution to Forensic Psychology. He is co-author of *Psychological Evaluations for the Courts*, and has written extensively in the area of forensic assessment. He was a member of the Criminal Competence Subgroup of the MacArthur Foundation Research Network on Mental Health and the Law between 1989 and 1996.

Robert A. Prentky, Ph.D., is Director of Assessment and Director of Research for Justice Resource Institute in Bridgewater, Massachusetts. He was formerly Chief Psychologist and Director of Research at the Massachusetts Treatment Center for Sexually Dangerous Persons, and has held faculty positions in the Department of Psychiatry, Boston University Medical School, and Department of Psychology, Brandeis University. Dr. Prentky has published and presented widely on juvenile and adult sexual offenders; his research has been supported by 11 federal grants and one state grant. He has also conducted or supervised evaluations of over a thousand juvenile and adult sexual offenders during the last 20 years. He is co-author (with Ann Burgess) of *Forensic Management of Sexual Offenders*, and received the 1998 Significant Achievement Award from ATSA.

Philip J. Resnick, M.D., is Professor of Psychiatry and Director of the Division of Forensic Psychiatry at Case Western Reserve University School of Medicine. He is also an Adjunct Professor at CWRU School of Law. Dr. Resnick directs a fellowship in forensic psychiatry and serves as director of the Court Psychiatric Clinic in the Cleveland, Ohio, area. He served as Presi-

dent of the American Academy of Psychiatry and the Law and sits on the editorial boards of five journals. He has published over 90 articles and book chapters. Dr. Resnick has served as a psychiatric consultant in many civil and criminal cases, including those of Jeffrey Dahmer, Susan Smith, Timothy McVeigh, and Theodore Kaczynski.

Robert L. Sadoff, M.D., is Clinical Professor of Psychiatry at the University of Pennsylvania and in the independent practice of forensic psychiatry in Jenkintown, Pennsylvania. He is Past President of the American Academy of Psychiatry and Law, and a Diplomate in Forensic Psychiatry, American Board of Psychiatry and Neurology. He has published widely on topics related to education in forensic psychiatry, violence, informed consent, malpractice, ethics, the right to refuse treatment, and the assessment of criminal defendants. He is widely sought as a consultant, educator, and a forensic psychiatric expert.

David L. Shapiro, Ph.D., is currently an Associate Professor of Psychology at the Center for Psychological Studies, NOVA Southeastern University in Ft. Lauderdale, Florida. Previously, he was Associate Professor at John Jay College of Criminal Justice, and has also been in the full-time independent practice of forensic and clinical psychology. His professional specializations include competency and sanity evaluation, professional liability, malpractice and ethics. He is a Diplomate in Forensic Psychology, American Board of Professional Psychology. His books include *Psychological Evaluations and Expert Testimony* (1983), *Forensic Psychological Assessment* (1991), and *Criminal Responsibility: A Practice Manual* (1998). In 1986, he received the Distinguished Contribution to Forensic Psychology Award presented at the annual convention of the American Psychological Association.

Kathleen P. Stafford, Ph.D., directs a regional court clinic in northeastern Ohio and maintains a private consulting practice. She is a clinical psychologist and a Diplomate in Forensic Psychology, American Board of Professional Psychology. Dr. Stafford teaches in the Psychology Department at Kent State University and the Department of Psychiatry at Northeastern Ohio Universities College of Medicine. She is currently President of the American Board of Forensic Psychology and Past Chair of the Ethics

Committee of the American Psychological Association.

Karin D. Towers, J.D., Ph.D., is with the University of Massachusetts Medical Center and is a licensed attorney in the state of New Jersey, having recently completed a postdoctoral fellowship in forensic psychology at the United States Medical Center for Federal Prisoners. She received her doctorate in psychology from MCP Hahnemann University and her law degree from Villanova School of Law in the Law-Psychology program at MCP Hahnemann/Villanova in Philadelphia. Her major practice interests are in the forensic assessment of criminal defendants and the treatment of mentally disordered offenders.

Herbert N. Weissman, Ph.D., is in the independent practice of clinical and forensic psychology in Sacramento and San Diego, California, and is Clinical Professor of Psychiatry at the University of California Davis, School of Medicine. He is a Fellow of the American Psychological Association and the Society for Personality Assessment, and a Diplomate in Clinical Psychology and Forensic Psychology, American Board of Professional Psychology. He is also Past President of the American Board of Forensic Psychology, the American Academy of Forensic Psychology, and the California Psychological Association. He has published in the areas of psychological evaluations of stress, trauma, and deception in legal contexts, and also in professional standards in clinical and forensic psychology.

Philip Witt, Ph.D., is a principal in Associates in Psychological Services, P.A. in Somerville, New Jersey, through which he conducts a practice in clinical and forensic psychology. He is a Diplomate in Forensic Psychology, American Board of Professional Psychology, and an adjunct faculty member at Robert Wood Johnson Medical School–University of Medicine and Dentistry at New Jersey and at the Graduate School of Applied and Professional Psychology of Rutgers University. His research and practice interests include the assessment and treatment of sexual offenders, and he served on the New Jersey Attorney General's panel that developed New Jersey's sex offender risk assessment scale.

Lauren Wylonis, M.D., is currently in private practice in Philadelphia, Pennsylvania, serves as Senior Medical Director of Executive Health Resources, and teaches at the Hospital of the University of Pennsylvania. She completed her residency at the Hospital of the University of Pennsylvania and her forensic psychiatry fellowship at Case Western Reserve University Hospitals. She is a Diplomate of the American Board of Psychiatry and Neurology in both general and forensic psychiatry. Her professional interests include psychiatric disability, workplace violence, sexual harassment, and issues of competency and sanity in legal proceedings.

Forensic Mental Health Assessment
A Casebook

Chapter 1

Introduction and Overview

The field of forensic mental health assessment has grown and developed significantly during the past 2 decades. Influenced by a growing body of research and practice literature, the changing health care system, and the rapid expansion of communications technology, interest in forensic psychology and forensic psychiatry appears to be stronger than ever.

The phrase "forensic mental health assessment" (FMHA) is relatively new, having been used by Heilbrun (2001) to describe the process by which certain mental health professionals (psychologists, psychiatrists, and social workers) conduct evaluations for the courts and/or at the request of attorneys. Such evaluations are intended to facilitate better informed legal decision making or assist attorneys by performing evaluations that (depending on their outcome) may be useful for the attorney in representing a client. FMHA is thus a single name for evaluations conducted by individuals of different disciplines, on a variety of questions in civil, criminal, and family law, that share the broad legal context within which they were conducted.

There are various indicators of the development of the forensic field. Professional organizations, such as the American Psychology-Law Society and the American Academy of Psychiatry and Law, have grown steadily since their establishment. A number of journals publish empirical, theoretical, and practice material relevant to FMHA; examples include *Behavioral Sciences and the Law*, *Criminal Justice and Behavior*, *Journal of the American Academy of Psychiatry and Law*, and *Law and Human Behavior*. There are increasing opportunities for the training of individuals in the specialty areas of forensic psychiatry and forensic psychology (Bersoff et al., 1997; Van Zelfde & Otto, 1997; see also the entire issue of *Behavioral Sciences and the Law*, Volume 8, 1990).

One particularly useful way to gauge the status and development of the forensic mental health professions is to consider the books that have been written in this area during the last 20 years. Important recent books in forensic mental health assessment have included *Psychological Evaluations for the Courts: A Handbook for Mental Health Professionals and Lawyers* (Melton, Petrila, Poythress, & Slobogin, 1997, with the second edition updating the 1987 original), the *Handbook of Forensic Psychology* (Hess & Weiner, 1999, updating the Weiner & Hess, 1987 original), *Forensic Evaluation of Juveniles* (Grisso, 1998a), *The Civil Practice of Forensic Psychology: Torts of Emotional Distress* (Greenberg & Brodsky, in press), *Assessing Competence to Consent to Treatment: A Guide for Physicians and Other Health Professionals* (Grisso & Appelbaum, 1998a), *Clinical Assessment of Malingering and Deception* (Rogers, 1997, updating the original 1988 book), *Malingering and Deception in Adolescents: Assessing Credibility in Clinical and Forensic Settings* (McCann, 1998), *Violence and Mental Disorder: Developments in Risk Assessment* (Monahan & Steadman, 1994), *Violent Offenders: Appraising and Managing Risk* (Quinsey, Harris, Rice, & Cormier, 1998), and *The Psychology of Stalking: Clinical and Forensic Perspectives* (Meloy, 1998). These works have expanded on earlier books such as *Evaluating Competencies: Forensic Assessments and Instruments* (Grisso, 1986), *Competency to Stand Trial Evaluations: A Manual for Practice* (Grisso, 1988), *Predicting Violent Behavior: An Assessment of Clinical Techniques* (Monahan, 1981), *Psychological Evaluation and Expert Testimony* (Shapiro, 1984), and *Forensic Psychological Assessment: An Integrative Approach* (Shapiro, 1991).

There are four important sources of authority in FMHA that appear, to varying degrees, in these various works. These sources are *law* (relevant statutes, case law, and administrative code affecting standards and procedure), *ethics* (professional codes guiding the practitioner's conduct in FMHA), *science* (theory and empirical evidence relevant to the questions being addressed), and *standards of practice* (professional literature offering guidelines for good practice in the area). These books also share another common feature. Consistently, they either focus on one area relevant to FMHA (e.g., competence to stand trial, malingering, violence risk assessment), or discuss several areas but treat them distinctly. This is a useful approach to describing FMHA, as there are a number of important distinctions between different kinds of forensic evaluations.

However, there has been less attention to the shared features of different kinds of FMHA. Is forensic assessment an activity that should be considered a collection of numerous different evaluations defined by legal question, or are there common principles that apply to FMHA of different kinds? This question has apparently been addressed in three books: Melton et al. (1997), Greenberg and Brodsky (in press), and Heilbrun (2001). In the first two, this question was discussed in a single chapter, and the authors identified certain principles that would apply to the kinds of FMHA being described in their respective works. However, the Heilbrun book involved a somewhat different approach; the entire book was devoted to identifying and describing broad principles of FMHA and describing their support from sources of authority in law, ethics, science, and standard of practice.

DERIVING PRINCIPLES OF FORENSIC MENTAL HEALTH ASSESSMENT

Melton et al. (1997) included a chapter in which they described recommended procedures in FMHA that are relevant to psychological testing. They began by distinguishing between "therapeutic assessment" (conducted for diagnostic and/or treatment-planning purposes) and "forensic assessment." They described differences in (1) scope (forensic assessment being narrower), (2) importance of the client's perspective (less in forensic assessment), (3) voluntariness (more limited in forensic assessment), (4) autonomy (likewise more limited in forensic assessment), (5) threats to validity (greater risk of conscious, intentional distortion of self-report in forensic assessment), and (6) pace and setting (brisker in forensic assessment due to externally imposed time constraints). The distinction between therapeutic and forensic assessment is not itself a principle of FMHA but provides an important perspective for considering how principles of forensic assessment, distinct from other kinds of mental health assessment, can be identified. This distinction has been described by others as well (e.g., Greenberg & Shuman, 1997; Greenberg & Brodsky, in press; Heilbrun, 1995, 2001).

The recommended procedures in forensic assessment that apply to psychological testing were next described by Melton et al. (1997) as follows. First, testing should be relevant to the specific legal inquiry, with tests selected because they will help to measure behavior or capacities that are related to the legal question before the court. Second, test results should be treated as hypotheses to be verified through other sources, including collateral records and third party interviews. Third, such collateral approaches should be emphasized more strongly than present-state psychological testing in evaluations calling for reconstruction of an individual's thinking, feeling, and behavior at an earlier time. Fourth, tests selected should be face valid—they should *appear* accurate in measuring the indicated capacities, as well as *be* accurate. Fifth, specific kinds of tests and measures—forensic assessment instruments (FAIs; Grisso, 1986) developed particularly to measure the capacities related to a given legal question—are preferable to conventional psychological tests, but only if certain criteria are satisfied for these FAIs. Such criteria include clear directions for administration, objective scoring criteria, quantification of the level or degree of performance, research on reliability and validity, and documentation in a manual. Finally, Melton and colleagues suggested that response style should be assessed in forensic assessment, particularly the potential for exaggeration or fabrication of symptoms of mental illness or cognitive impairment.

Greenberg and Brodsky (in press) have described a "model for forensic examinations" in the civil practice of forensic psychology. The model has a total of 49 guidelines, which are similar to principles but often more specific, for the forensic examiner. These are divided into different areas: basic aspirations, informed consent and initial process, psychometric assessment, specialized testing, interviews of plaintiff, site observation, collateral interviews, results, and reports and testimony. In the area of basic aspirations, they suggest (1) acting in accordance with the Specialty Guidelines for Forensic Psychology, (2) keeping the role as "expert to the court" as paramount, (3) behaving in consideration of the "public nature" of forensic practice, (4) striving for impartiality in attitude and performance, (5) striving for impartiality in assessment, and (6) striving to maintain a reputation for integrity, knowledge, and skill. Under informed consent and initial process, the aspirations include (1) seeking informed consent from the retaining attorney, (2) making all contact with any part or counsel "on the record," (3) conducting an initial discussion of informed consent with each of the parties being examined, (4) providing a written statement to the retaining attorney and the examinee that further explains the examination, (5) using standardized examination procedures, and (6) informing the referring attorney regarding any aspect of the evaluation in which they lack competence. Guidelines in the area of psychometric assessment include (1) using reliable and valid instruments, (2) recognizing human functioning as multidimensional, (3) assuming comparable correlates of test results in clinical and forensic contexts unless there is evidence to the contrary, (4) interpreting test results in light of the particular forensic context, (5) considering test results as hypotheses to be confirmed or disconfirmed, (6) providing examinees with feedback regarding test results, with an opportunity to comment, (7) including only legally relevant interpretive hypotheses in any forensic report, (8) considering both the strengths and limitations of the examinee, and (9) interpreting test results to include both strengths and limitations and incorporate context. For specialized testing, the following are suggested: using specialists as consultants when indicated and interpreting specialized approaches to include both strengths and limitations. With respect to interviewing plaintiffs, they offer aspirations that include (1) showing respect toward the examinee, (2) being considerate of the examinee but impartial regarding the forensic issues, (3) using similar measures across examinations of a similar type, (4) using both structured and unstructured approaches to interviews, (5) avoiding a therapeutic relationship with the examinee, and (6) disclosing significant concerns to the examinee to allow that person to respond. Greenberg and Brodsky also suggest visiting the site of relevant events when possible. Four aspirations are in the area of collateral interviews are offered: (1) conducting collateral interviews with a representative sample of those who have had significant contact with the examinee, (2) selecting collateral interviewees who have first-hand information, (3) obtaining authorization for release of information from the examinee prior to collateral contact with a third party having a privileged relationship with the examinee, and (4) obtaining informed consent from all collateral interviewees. Aspirations relevant to results include (1) generating integrated convergent data, (2) avoiding offering any opinion until adequate data to support (or refute) such an opinion have been considered, and (3) using a standard conceptual organization of results and opinions, suggested by applicable law, across cases. Finally, aspirations are described in the area of reports and testimony: (1) avoiding partial opinions or recommendations until the examination is complete, (2) informing the retaining attorney about findings, opinions, and recommendations to give that person the opportunity to decide whether to use the examiner's services further, (3) including only legally relevant material in reports and opinions, (4) identifying and explaining forensic findings pertinent to impairments in functioning, (5) avoiding pejorative language or interpretations that may unnecessarily or inaccurately pathologize an examinee, (6) avoiding making financial recommendations unless otherwise qualified, or unless such recommendations are psychologically driven, (7) writing at least one substantial paragraph supporting the position of the party against whom the recommendation is made, (8) describing both strengths and weaknesses, (9) avoiding giving opinions about individuals who have not been examined, unless examination has been attempted and supporting data are sufficient to give an (appropriately limited) opinion, (10) presenting all material, even that which is contrary to the recommendation, (11) releasing raw psychological test data only to a mental health professional skilled in the interpretation of such data, and (12) avoiding making public statements about legal proceedings in which they have been involved.

Heilbrun (2001) described the principles of FMHA in more detail, as they were the entire focus of the book. Based on a review of the literature, each principle was described, discussed in terms of the support (or lack thereof) provided by applicable law, ethics, science, and standards of practice, and classified as either *established* or *emerging*. It is these principles that will be applied in the present book, as they have incorporated the principles offered by Melton et al. and Greenberg and Brodsky (in press), just discussed. Each of the 29 Heilbrun principles are described briefly here.

Identify relevant forensic issues. This principle concerns one of the most basic aspects of FMHA: the relevant capacities and behaviors that are to be evaluated as part of the assessment. It distinguishes between the legal question, which is the ultimate matter to be decided by the court, and the relevant forensic issues, which are the capacities and abilities that are included within the legal question. For example, the legal question in a matter of a defendant's competence to stand trial is whether the individual should be adjudicated competent; the forensic issues involve that defendant's capacities to understand his or her charges and the broader adversarial nature of the legal system, assist counsel in his/her own defense through communicating with the lawyer, behave appropriately during a hearing or trial, testify (if necessary) as part of the defense, and consider plea options in a rational way and make a decision regarding plea while incorporating the advice of counsel into this decision. This principle was considered to be *established*.

Accept referrals only within area of expertise. This principle begins with the widely accepted professional tenet that mental health professionals should have sufficient expertise, gained through training and/or experience, to deliver a service well before they ever decide to provide the service. The principle goes on to address the nature of "expertise." It is concluded that expertise in the forensic context has two components: (1) clinical and didactic training and experience with the kind of individual(s) being evaluated, and (2) previous application of this expertise in a forensic context. The principle was classified as *established*.

Decline the referral when evaluator impartiality is unlikely. In roles in which a forensic clinician provides an evaluation and possibly testimony, the impartiality of the clinician is important. This principle identifies influences that can diminish such impartiality and underscores the importance of declining to accept a case when there is something about the clinician's personal beliefs or the circumstances of the case that could unduly interfere with the attempt to remain impartial throughout that particular evaluation. It cites four possible roles for the forensic clinician in the course of a forensic assessment: (1) court-appointed, (2) defense/prosecution/plaintiff's expert, (3) consultant, and (4) fact witness. This principle does not keep forensic clinicians from vigorously defending appropriate conclusions when challenged; it concerns influences that would unfairly skew data interpretation and conclusions. The principle was seen as *established* when the forensic clinician is either court-appointed or a defense/prosecution/plaintiff's expert, but *neither established nor emerging* for a consultant.

Clarify the evaluator's role with the attorney. This principle addresses the problem of multiple roles and the potentially harmful impact of playing more than a single role in a given FMHA case. It uses the roles described in the previous principle. The role of fact witness is recommended whenever there has been a prior professional treatment relationship with an individual being evaluated. This principle emphasizes that it is typically "cleanest" to play only one role among the first three possibilities in a given case. The principle was described as *emerging*.

Clarify financial arrangements. The importance of describing, in advance, the rate or total amount of billing for services is described in this principle, as well as the way in which the fee will be collected. There are some circumstances, such as performing publicly funded evaluations of criminal defendants, in which the payment for services is specified by the jurisdiction, and there is nothing to be clarified. The principle becomes more important when this is not the case, however. It was classified as *established*.

Obtain appropriate authorization. There are two different forms of authorization that can be obtained in FMHA: (1) court order, and (2) permission of attorney and client. The form of authorization that is needed depends on the role being played by the forensic clinician, with the court-ordered role associated with the need for a signed order from the court and the expert for the attorney role requiring the consent of both the attorney and the client. This affects whether the forensic clinician delivers a "notification of purpose" to the individual being evaluated, informing him/her of the relevant nature, purpose, procedures, and limits on confidentiality but not asking for consent or whether the evaluator provides such a notification followed by a request for informed consent. This principle was considered *established*.

Avoid playing the dual roles of therapist and forensic evaluator. Expanding on the description of FMHA roles given in several prior principles, this principle concludes that playing the roles of therapist and forensic evaluator with the same individual creates significant problems and is consistently to be avoided. This principle was classified as *established*.

Determine the particular role to be played within forensic assessment if the referral is accepted. The selection of role within the case, when made in the beginning and retained throughout the case, can prevent problems of various kinds from interfering with the forensic clinician's impartiality and ensure that the expectations of the attorney and the forensic clinician are comparable. There is discussion of a possible exception to the "single role" maxim, involving moving from a role requiring impartiality (e.g., defense expert expected to testify) to a role in which impartiality is not needed (e.g., consultant) *if it is clear from the results of the evaluation that the attorney would not ask for a report or testimony.* However, moving in the opposite direction—from the consultant's role that does not require impartiality to the testifying expert's role that does—would be far more difficult. This principle was considered to be *emerging*.

Select the most appropriate model to guide data gathering, interpretation, and communication. Two broad models of FMHA are discussed: those of Morse (1978a, 1978b) and Grisso (1986). The use of a model can be conceptually valuable in understanding the larger process of FMHA and more specifically useful in an individual case in formulating an assessment plan. This was considered to be an *emerging* principle.

Use multiple sources of information for each area being assessed. This is a very important principle in FMHA. Because of the circumstances under which FMHA is typically conducted, involving some incentive for the individual being evaluated to distort self-report and psychological testing data, it is important to use multiple sources (including collateral records and interviews) to assess the consistency of information across these sources. Agreement across sources makes it more likely that the agreed-upon information is accurate, while inconsistency across sources means that there is inaccuracy in at least one source of information. This principle was classified as *established*.

Use relevance and reliability (validity) as guides for seeking information and selecting data sources. There are two criteria in evidence law that are frequently cited for the admission of expert testimony. The first is relevance to the question(s) before the court; the second is reliability (which, when used in the law, means both psychometric reliability and validity). This principle concerns the use of both criteria when the forensic clinician is deciding which sources of information to use, particularly in selecting third parties to interview and psychological tests to administer. This principle appeared to be *established*.

Obtain relevant historical information. It is virtually always necessary to obtain historical information regarding the individual being evaluated in FMHA, and this historical information is often more extensive than what is needed in a therapeutic evaluation. However, this principle also emphasizes the varying extensiveness of historical information needed in different kinds of FMHA. Some evaluations need a reasonably focused history to provide a context for the evaluation (competence to stand trial, for example), while others require much more breadth (e.g., capital sentencing). This principle appeared to be *established*.

Assess clinical characteristics in relevant, reliable, and valid ways. This principle emphasized the importance of assessing clinical characteristics consistent with at least one model discussed earlier. The choice of which clinical characteristics to assess, and how, is facilitated by the use of the "relevant and reliable" test described earlier. The discussion included the "clinical versus actuarial" debate that has been seen in the literature for nearly half a century and considered how evidence from this debate might be applied toward FMHA. The principle was classified as *established*.

Assess legally relevant behavior. This principle focuses directly on capacities and behavior that are related to the legal question. The criteria of relevance and reliability are applied to determine how to assess these capacities; in some areas, the forensic clinician has the option of using a well-validated forensic assessment instrument. The principle appeared to be *established*.

Ensure that conditions for evaluation are quiet, private, and distraction free. FMHA can be conducted in a variety of environments, some of which are far from ideal. Particularly in settings that emphasize security and may have a limited capacity for mental health evaluation, the forensic clinician may sometimes find that conditions can potentially compromise the validity of the evaluation because they are noisy, allow sensitive material to be overheard, or present other distractions. This principle discusses the balance between reasonable evaluation conditions and other influences (e.g., security, time constraints) and addresses the question of when environmental conditions are sufficiently poor to require the forensic clinician to seek to improve them—and how much to improve such conditions. This principle was described as *established*.

Provide appropriate notification of purpose and/or obtain appropriate authorization before beginning. Whether the forensic clinician provides notification of purpose or obtains informed consent before beginning FMHA depends on the role that is being played and the nature of the associated authorization that was obtained, both of which were discussed in previous principles. Those who are performing a court-ordered evaluation, and have obtained the necessary court order, must provide the individual being evaluated with basic information regarding the nature and purpose of the evaluation, who authorized it, and the associated limits on confidentiality, including how it might be used. In this circumstance, however, participation in such an evaluation is not voluntary, and it would be inappropriate to seek informed consent. By contrast, when a defense or plaintiff's attorney asks a forensic clinician to conduct an evaluation of that attorney's client, the evaluation is voluntary, and informed consent should be obtained before proceeding. This principle was classified as *established*.

Determine whether the individual understands the purpose of the evaluation and associated limits on confidentiality. To be meaningful, a notification of purpose or a notification accompanied by a request for informed consent must be understood by the individual being evaluated. This principle describes how the evaluator can assess whether the information was understood and how the evaluator might proceed if it appears that the information was not well-understood. The principle was described as *established*.

Use third-party information in assessing response style. One of the more important aspects of FMHA is the systematic assessment of response style of the individual being evaluated, particularly the deliberate overreporting or underreporting of relevant deficits or symptoms. This principle considers the use of records and collateral informants in establishing a history from multiple sources and determining whether self-reported information is consistent with other sources and more likely to be accurate. This principle was classified as *established*.

Use testing when indicated in assessing response style. There is an additional approach to assessing response style: psychological testing and the use of specialized measures developed to assess malingering or defensiveness of mental disorder or cognitive impairment. This principle addresses the application of psychological tests and specialized measures for this purpose, describing the available research on the tests and measures that allow them to be used in this way. However, there are relatively few well-validated psychological tests or specialized measures that are available for this purpose. The principle was, therefore, classified as *emerging*.

Use case-specific (idiographic) evidence in assessing clinical condition, functional abilities, and causal connection. This principle describes the first of three ways that science can be applied in FMHA. It involves obtaining information that is specific to the circumstances of the case and present functioning of the individual and making comparisons to that individual's capacities and functioning at other times. The assessment of malingering, for example, should draw on information about whether the individual has ever been diagnosed with a mental disorder or cognitive impairment in the past, and (if so) what symptoms the individual presented at that time. This principle is consistent with the legal goal of individualized justice and is described as *established*.

Use nomothetic evidence in assessing clinical condition, functional abilities, and causal connection. The second way in which science can be applied to FMHA is through the use of empirical data applicable to populations similar to that of the individual being evaluated, and through forensic tools that have been developed and validated on similar populations. When forensic capacities are assessed using norm-referenced tools, the evaluator and the decision maker can consider how similar such measured capacities are to those in "known groups" (such as those who are adjudicated incompetent to stand trial vs. those who are in jail but for whom the issue of trial competence has never been raised). This principle is particularly important for the goal of applying empirical evidence toward informing legal decision making and appeared to be *established*.

Use scientific reasoning in assessing causal connection between clinical condition and functional abilities. When the results of one source of information, such as interview or psychological testing, are considered as "hypotheses to be verified" through further information obtained from multiple sources, then the FMHA is proceeding somewhat like a scientific study. Further, when hypotheses are accepted or rejected depending on how well they account for the most information with the simplest explanation, another important aspect of science is being used. This aspect involves conceptualizing and reasoning rather than data collection, but is as important as the actual data collection itself. This principle was described as *established*.

Do not answer the ultimate legal question directly. There has been a vigorous controversy within the fields of forensic psychiatry and forensic psychology for the past 2 decades concerning whether forensic evaluators ought to communicate their findings by answering the "ultimate legal question" (the legal question to be decided by the court, such as competence to stand trial or the child custody arrangement). When the standards of the field were less clear regarding the importance of relevance, reliability, and thoroughness in FMHA, this debate addressed the potential problem of having an inadequate evaluation conclude by answering the ultimate legal question without allowing the reader of the report to review all the findings or understand the reasoning. The debate is somewhat different at present, with some continuing to observe that many judges and attorneys expect the forensic clinician to offer an ultimate opinion, and (with a few exceptions) that this practice is permitted by evidentiary law. Others counter by stressing the importance of the forensic capacities that are relevant to the ultimate legal question, but adding that the ultimate legal decision includes moral, political, and community-value components that should not play a part in the evaluator's conclusion. This remains an active debate, so this principle was described as *emerging*.

Describe findings and limits so that they need change little under cross-examination. The essence of this principle is that FMHA findings need to be described carefully and thoroughly, supported by multiple sources, and have appropriate limitations explicitly acknowledged. When this is done, the forensic clinician can expect that the results of findings conveyed during cross-examination will not change significantly. In effect, the evaluator has anticipated the potential objections, weaknesses, and alternative explanations for his/her findings and subjected the data analysis and reasoning to careful scrutiny in light of these weaknesses. This principle was classified as *established*.

Attribute information to sources. One of the most important differences between therapeutic and forensic assessment is the nature of the documentation required. By definition, forensic assessment is part of a legal proceeding with an adversarial component. It is crucial, for the evaluator's judgment about what information is consistent across multiple sources and for the opposing attorney or the judge to identify what information came from which sources, to have information carefully attributed by source. This principle was considered to be *established*.

Use plain language; avoid technical jargon. Many of those who use FMHA are either legally trained (judges and attorneys) or typically without training in either the behavioral sciences or the law (jurors). It is important, therefore, to avoid the use of technical jargon as much as possible, or to define technical terms if their use cannot be avoided. This principle is most often applied to report writing, but is applicable as well to expert testimony given in depositions, hearings, and trials. This principle was described as *established*.

Write report in sections, according to model and procedures. It is possible to write the report documenting the FMHA in a way that facilitates the application of various principles described earlier. The different report sections recommended by Heilbrun (2001) include *Referral* (with identifying information concerning the individual, his/her characteristics, the nature of the evaluation, and by whom it was requested or ordered), *Procedures* (the times and dates of the evaluations, the various tests or procedures conducted, the different records reviewed, and the third party interviews conducted, as well as documentation of the notification of purpose or informed consent and the degree to which the information was apparently understood), *Relevant History* (containing information from multiple sources describing areas important to the evaluation), *Current Clinical Condition* (broadly considered to include appearance, mood, behavior, sensorium, intellectual functioning, thought, and personality), *Forensic Capacities* (varying according to the nature of the legal questions), and *Conclusions and Recommendations* (addressed toward the relevant capacities rather than the ultimate legal questions). This principle was classified as *established*.

Base testimony on the results of the properly performed FMHA. There should be a strong relationship between the procedures and findings documented in the report and the expert testimony that is provided based on this evaluation. Almost the entire substantive basis for expert testimony should be documented in the evaluation, allowing the presenting attorney to use the expert's findings more clearly and effectively, the opposing attorney to prepare to challenge them, the judge to understand them, and the expert to communicate them. This principle was considered *established*.

Testify effectively. This principle covers two aspects of expert testimony: substantive and stylistic. The substantive part of expert testimony is addressed by most of the preceding principles, while the stylistic aspect concerns how the expert presents, dresses, speaks, and otherwise behaves to make their testimony more understandable and credible. It is important that both substance and style be strong for expert testimony to be maximally effective. While substantively strong but stylistically weak testimony may have less impact than it should, it is testimony that is substantively weak but stylistically impressive that should be recognized and accorded little influence if the forensic mental health professions are to contribute meaningfully to better informed, legal decision making. Accordingly, this principle is classified as *established* if both substance and style are strong, but *neither established nor emerging* if the basis for the testimony is stylistic strength alone.

THE NEED FOR A CASEBOOK

The field does not presently have a casebook to demonstrate the application of FMHA, although some books (e.g., Melton et al., 1997) have used some case material in illustration. There are three important purposes for a casebook. First, the principles described by various authors in this chapter, if they are to be meaningful, must be applicable to most FMHA cases. Therefore, we have used case material throughout this book to illustrate how such principles can be applied.

Second, it is helpful to see how forensic clinicians, experts in a particular kind of FMHA, actually conduct such assessments. What kinds of data do they collect and from what sources? How do they analyze such information and reason through to conclusions? How do they structure their reports and communicate their results? By using case reports contributed by such experts, this book can answer such questions directly. It is also helpful to consider the details of different forensic assessment cases and debate how the evaluator might have proceeded differently at various points in the evaluation.

Third, specific questions concerning these cases and the application of these principles are discussed at the end of each case. Some of these questions are addressed by the case contributor, presenting a variety of perspectives on FMHA and yielding a good opportunity for teaching some of the detailed procedures involved in FMHA.

APPLYING PRINCIPLES TO FMHA CASES

To combine the principles, cases, and teaching points as we did, it was necessary to take several steps. We began with the assumption that any of the 29 principles described by Heilbrun (2001) should apply to any of the cases in this book. However, some principles are better illustrated by certain kinds of cases; for example, it was difficult to use case reports to illustrate the principles about testimony in any direct way.

We began by dividing the topics into chapters according to legal question. It was important to achieve some balance between criminal/juvenile and civil forensic assessment; we achieved this balance by incorporating legal questions that appeared in the literature as being evaluated in FMHA. Most of the following 23 chapters are divided according to distinct legal questions, with the final 2 (Threat/Risk Assessment and Malingering) being topics that occur across a variety of legal questions.

We then solicited case reports from colleagues who were known for their expertise in forensic assessment in the particular kind of case we were illustrating. Expertise was judged by a number of criteria. These included professional reputation (for practice and teaching), board certification, leadership in the field, and research and scholarship. We carefully considered which principle would be best illustrated by which kind of case. Each of the 29 principles was illustrated once, and some twice, by pairing the principle with a case: The principles that were illustrated twice were those that either needed more discussion or seemed to arise more often in practice. Once a principle and a case report had been matched, the topic of the teaching point was determined by how some specific aspect of the principle was applied in this case.

We asked contributors to begin with genuine case material, but there were ethical and legal limits on how such material could be used in publication. We considered these concerns as described in the next section.

CAUTIONS IN USING CASE MATERIAL

Genuine case material illustrates the richness and complexity of FMHA, accompanied by the problems and limits. Observing how such problems arise in specific cases, the approaches taken by the forensic clinicians in assessing particular capacities under these circumstances, and the style of communicating the results in a report can all be particularly valuable.

However, there are concerns about the privacy of the individual being evaluated in using such case material. There is not the same ethical expectation of confidentiality or legal right to privilege for individuals evaluated in FMHA as there is in therapy, but this difference arises from the distinct purposes of these two activities. A therapy client can reasonably expect that material from treatment will remain private unless it falls under exceptions provided by law (e.g., physical or sexual abuse of a child, or the threat of serious harm to an identifiable third party in some jurisdictions). By contrast, an individual who undergoes FMHA should be notified at the beginning of the evaluation about the purpose and associated limits of confidentiality. In some cases, the FMHA results will be communicated in a report, expert testimony, or both in a hearing or trial that could be open to the public and covered by the media.

Although the individual being evaluated in FMHA should have been informed about these possibilities for how such information might be used, it would be quite unusual to have this individual, his or her attorney, or the presiding judge notified that the material might be used in publication, or to have obtained the consent of appropriate individuals for such use in publication. Further, it may be that using an FMHA report in publication would exceed what is in the public domain, as the report itself (although introduced into evidence) may not have been accessible to the media.

In light of these concerns, there is very little undisguised genuine case material used in this book. We have made exceptions only in one case, in which reports were available for publication or excerpting in the media at the time of the hearing and trial. For all other cases, we have asked the contributors to take two steps before we used these cases in the book. First, we have asked that the reports be *sanitized*, with all potentially identifying information of those involved in the litigation changed to prevent the identification of the case. Second, we asked that the case be combined with elements of another case, a process we called *hybridizing*, to ensure that even sanitized cases could not be identified. We asked contributors to attempt to preserve important data and reasoning from the case but avoid including anything that might increase the risk of case identification. Therefore, we are able to assert with confidence that the cases included in this book preserve some important data and reasoning of genuine FMHA cases, but (with virtually no exceptions) do not represent genuine cases.

HOW TO USE THIS BOOK

There are five levels on which this casebook can be read. First, those interested in considering how broad principles might be applied to FMHA cases can focus on the principle described in the beginning of each case. Second, the reader might attend to a particular approach to applying the principle that is discussed in the teaching point. Third, the question of how the case is evaluated may be considered—how the assessment is structured, how the information is analyzed, the reasoning that leads from results to conclusions, and the way the entire FMHA is communicated. Fourth, any reader interested in observing the particular style of a given contributor can read the case(s) provided by each contributor. Cases can also be considered according to the particular kind of FMHA being performed (civil vs. criminal/juvenile, conventional vs. high profile, child/adolescent vs. adult, or by particular legal question). Finally, any reader interested in the backgrounds of the respective individuals being evaluated in these kinds of reports could go directly to the cases represented and read the book as a collection of cases involving individuals who become involved in litigation and are evaluated as part of that litigation.

Chapter 2

Miranda Rights Waiver

The competence of adult defendants to waive *Miranda* rights (*Miranda v. Arizona*, 1966) is the focus of the two case reports in this chapter. The principle applied to the first case concerns the value of nomothetic data, derived from groups and applied through general laws, to forensic assessment. The teaching point in this case will address the value of forensic assessment instruments (FAIs; Grisso, 1986) that have been developed and validated for a specific kind of forensic assessment. This will serve to highlight one of the important differences between the methodology of behavioral science and that of law: While science emphasizes nomothetic approaches, the law is inclined toward idiographic procedures focused on understanding a particular individual or event. The principle associated with the second case in this chapter—use idiographic evidence in forensic assessment—addresses how the forensic assessment process can also be improved through the use of case-specific information. The teaching point for the second case includes a discussion of the limits on the applicability of FAIs in some cases and of alternatives to using an FAI when such an instrument is not available or applicable.

Case 1

Principle: Use nomothetic evidence in assessing causal connection between clinical condition and functional abilities

This principle concerns the value of applying scientific data gathered with groups to the assessment of domains that are relevant in FMHA. Researchers have gathered scientific data in several areas that are particularly applicable to FMHA. First, studies have provided data on the reliability and validity of various psychological measures, such as psychological tests, structured interviews, and specialized tools, used in FMHA. Second, scientific data provide an estimate of the base rates of relevant behavior (e.g., crime and violence) and the outcomes (e.g., legal decisions on child custody). Such data can be used by evaluators to make empirically grounded judgments regarding the relationship between capacities, behavior, and legal status. Third, the use of measures with known reliability and validity, and the incorporation of empirically derived base rates, can allow the forensic clinician to generate hypotheses that could help answer questions arising in the case being evaluated.

Support for the application of nomothetic data to FMHA can be found in several authoritative sources. In psychology, the *Ethical Principles of Psychologists and Code of Conduct* (*Ethics Code*), published by the American Psychological Association (APA, 1992), contains several sections that are relevant. The *Ethics Code* emphasizes the value of scientifically derived knowledge: "Psychologists rely on scientifically and professionally derived knowledge when making scientific or professional judgments or when engaging in scholarly or professional endeavors" (p. 1600). The *Ethics Code* also emphasizes the importance of research on the applications of various tests or instruments, and it notes that the interpretation of psychological assessment results should be guided by research on the reliability and validity of the procedures used in the assessment (APA, 1992). Additional support for this principle can be found in the *Specialty Guidelines for Forensic Psychologists* (Committee on Ethical Guidelines for Forensic Psychologists, 1991). The *Specialty Guidelines* provides less detailed support for this principle than the *Ethics Code*, but it emphasizes the importance of current scientific information and applying such information to the selection of methods and procedures that are used in FMHA.

Legal support for the use of nomothetic data in FMHA can be found in several important cases. In *Daubert v. Merrell Dow Pharmaceuticals* (1993), the U.S. Supreme Court held that the *Federal Rules of Evidence* are applicable to scientific testimony. In its analysis, the Court's opinion included dicta that offered criteria that could be used at the trial court level to decide whether the "reasoning or methodology underlying the testimony is scientifically valid" (*Daubert v. Merrell Dow Pharmaceuticals*, p. 592) and immediately applicable. These criteria include whether the basis for the opinion is testable, whether it has been tested, the known error rate, and other criteria such as level of general acceptance and indices of peer review. Subsequently, in *Kumho Tire Co. v. Carmichael* (1999), the U.S. Supreme Court held that a *Daubert*-like analysis may also be applied to evaluating experts who testify on the basis of technical or other specialized knowledge (rather than scientific expertise) regarding a matter before the court.

Because accuracy is important in FMHA, the forensic clinician should be able to describe the degree of empirical scientific support that has been demonstrated for a particular FMHA procedure. Accordingly, a forensic practitioner should consider procedures that have an established empirical base. Heilbrun (1992) has offered guidelines on the use of psychological tests in FMHA that underscore the importance of such empirical support. Relevant guidelines include: (1) the test is commercially available and has a manual documenting its psychometric properties, (2) tests with a reliability coefficient of less than .80 would require explicit justification explaining why they are used, (3) the test's relevance to the legal issue or an underlying psychological construct should be supported by validation research, and (4) objective tests and actuarial data combination are preferable when there are appropriate outcome data and a formula exists. Others (Greenberg & Brodsky, in press) have proposed guidelines emphasizing that instruments used in FMHA should be reliable and valid to an extent adequate to the scope of the asserted statements, opinions, and conclusions.

The present case report provides a good example of the application of this principle. The purpose of the evaluation was to assess the individual's ability to make a knowing, intelligent, and voluntary waiver of his *Miranda* rights following his arrest for robbery. The forensic clinician employed several different psychological tools that have an established empirical base. Consequently, the evaluator could describe the degree of empirical support for each of these FMHA procedures if this question arose during testimony.

The tests administered in the present evaluation included a standard intelligence test (Wechsler Adult Intelligence Scale, 3rd edition; WAIS-III), a test of basic academic abilities (Wide Range Achievement Test, 3rd edition; WRAT-3), a test relevant to neuropsychological functioning (Bender Visual Motor Gestalt Test; Bender Gestalt), and a projective personality test (Thematic Apperception Test; TAT). Consistent with this principle, the WAIS-III and the WRAT-3 have established levels of reliability and validity. The reliability and validity of the WAIS-III is firmly established in the field (see, e.g., Kaufman & Lichtenberger, 1999). Similarly, the WRAT-3 has been extensively validated (Wilkinson, 1993), and the Bender Gestalt has a reasonable research base. The TAT, while generally not scored and therefore not measured with respect to reliability, is a test for which a reasonable justification for use could be made on the basis that it can potentially provide information that cannot be obtained from the other tests, interview, or third party information. The use of these tests therefore appears consistent with the guidelines suggested by Heilbrun (1992) regarding the selection and use of psychological tests in FMHA.

Another important aspect of the psychological tests used in the present case concerns their relationship to psychological constructs that are relevant to the forensic issues being addressed. Tests of intelligence (WAIS-III) and basic skills in reading (WRAT-3) have clear relevance to the capacity for making a knowing, intelligent, and voluntary waiver of *Miranda* rights, particularly in their measurement of the individual's ability to read and comprehend written material and understand oral material.

The forensic clinician also administered specialized measures that were specifically designed to assess the capacity of a defendant to make a knowing and intelligent waiver of *Miranda* rights. Specifically, the evaluator administered the Comprehension of *Miranda* Rights (CMR), the Comprehension of *Miranda* Rights-Recognition (CMR-R), and the Comprehension of *Miranda* Rights-Vocabulary (CMR-V; Grisso, 1998b). Because these measures have an established empirical base (Grisso, 1981, 1998b), the evaluator was able to compare the defendant's scores on these tests with the data obtained as part of the test validation process.

Another important aspect of the forensic clinician's use of the CMR, CMR-R, and the CMR-V is their specificity; these tools were developed to measure the functional abilities relevant to the forensic issues included in *Miranda* waiver. The use of psychological tests and specialized forensic tools with an established empirical base, which assess both clinical condition and relevant functional abilities, allowed the use of nomothetic evidence in assessing the causal connection between the individual's clinical condition and his functional abilities related to the waiver of his *Miranda* rights. The use of these empirically supported tools can inform the evaluator's judgment about whether certain kinds of psychopathology or functional deficits are related to the individual's ability to make a knowing, intelligent, and voluntary waiver of his *Miranda* rights. In this case, based partly on the individual's scores on the tests specifically designed to assess his overall comprehension of his *Miranda* rights, the forensic clinician concluded that the individual lacked sufficient understanding of several of his *Miranda* rights.

Alan M Goldstein, Ph.D.
N.Y.S. Certified Psychologist, P.C.
CT. Licensed Psychologist
Diplomate in Forensic Psychology
American Board of Professional Psychology

PRIVILEGED AND CONFIDENTIAL
FORENSIC PSYCHOLOGICAL
EVALUATION

Defendant: Aaron W
D.O.B.: 12/12/78
Age: 19 years
Date of Report: 6/12/99
Indictment No.: 5697/98
Case No.: 586592
Dates Evaluated: 10/14/98, 11/4/98

Aaron W was referred by his attorney, Susan B, Esq., on 9/28/98. At that time, I was informed that her client had been charged with Robbery in the First and Second Degrees related to an incident that occurred on 8/16/98. Mr. W was arrested approximately 1 month following the alleged offense. According to his attorney, Mr. W had been in special education classes throughout his school career. She stated that Mr. W is unable to read and write and has a longstanding diagnosis of Fetal-Alcohol Syndrome. Based on her observations of her client and his reported level of intellectual impairment, she asked that I assess his ability to make a knowing, intelligent waiver of his *Miranda* rights.

The opinions presumed in this report are based on two evaluation sessions conducted with Mr. W at Beekman Correctional Center. During 8 hours of face-to-face contact, I interviewed Mr. W regarding his history and background as well as his recollections of the events that transpired immediately before and during his interrogation by the Westchester County Police Department. I also administered a battery of psychological tests to him. Testing consisted of the following instruments:

- Wechsler Adult Intelligence Scale-III (WAIS-III)
- Wide Range Achievement Test-3 (WRAT-3)
- Bender-Gestalt
- Symbol Digit Modalities Test
- Rey's 15-Item Memorization Test
- Thematic Apperception Test
- Comprehension of Miranda Rights (CMR)
- Comprehension of Miranda Rights-Recognition (CMR-R)

- Comprehension of Miranda Rights-Vocabulary (CMR-V)
- Function of Rights in Interrogation (FRI)

In addition to the above, my opinion is based on my review of copies of the following documents provided to me by Mr. W's attorney:

- Indictment
- Felony Complaint
- Defendant's Prior Record of Disposition of Arrests and Dispositions
- State's Voluntary Disclosure Form
- Defendant's handwritten statement
- School records
- Office of Family and Children's Services records
- Home Assistance report
- Personal Information form
- Mental Health Crisis Team Intervention Report
- Trial Competency Evaluation Reports (11/5/98 & 11/12/98)

In addition, I interviewed the defendant's father by telephone on 11/1/98.

SUMMARY OF RECORDS REVIEWED

According to the Felony Complaint, Mr. W has been charged with Robbery in the First Degree, Robbery in the Second Degree, and Criminal Possession of Stolen Property. It is specifically charged that at the time of the crime, he forcibly stole property and in the course of commission of this act caused serious physical injury to another person. It is alleged that the defendant was aided by another person and that Mr. W knowingly possessed a stolen credit card with intent to benefit from its use. The indictment indicates that Mr. W and his co-defendant choked a seventy-four year-old woman while she was returning home from shopping. It is alleged that the co-defendant knocked this woman to the ground and stole her purse, and the victim suffered a featured hip requiring hospitalization.

Prior to this charge, Mr. W had been convicted of Theft of Services by a plea of guilty (11/20/97). In addition, he plead guilty to a charge of Menacing in the Second Degree and Criminal Possession of a Weapon for which he received a Conditional Discharge based on a plea of guilty.

In Mr. W's handwritten statement (it is noted that while the statement is written in script, the signature line contains a simple, somewhat shaky printed "signature"), he indicated that he had been asked by his co-defendant to serve as a "watch out" because "Frank was going to yoke the old lady." He reported that his co-defendant threw the woman to the ground, took her bag, and that both he and his co-defendant ran from the scene. According to Mr. W, he took two credit cards from the victim's pocketbook.

A review of Mr. W's school records reflects his long history of learning disability and intellectual impairment. In the second grade, he was classified as mentally retarded and placed in special education classes. He was held back in the second and fifth grades. According to the school records, "When given step-by-step directions for simple tasks, Aaron doesn't remember how to proceed." A psychological evaluation conducted when he was age fourteen reports a Stanford Binet IQ of 57 and Vineland Adaptive Behavioral Scale scores ranging from 46 to 54. According to this report, "Aaron can take advantage of situations and manipulate people." He was found to be, "highly distracted, immature, and he had difficulty in focusing his attention." Furthermore, the report states that he "lacks the ability to work with what he has learned and to apply what he has learned to new problems and situations. Aaron has difficulty processing language inherent in such problems."

A psychological evaluation conducted the next year recommended that he "be placed in a highly protective, structured environment designed to deal with his pronounced intellectual deficits." An educational evaluation conducted at the same time reported Verbal Reasoning skills, Auditory Memory abilities, Oral Reading and Listening Comprehension scores ranging from the low first grade to the low second grade levels.

At age seventeen, Mr. W was evaluated through the Office of Family and Children's Services. At that time, the evaluation reported his "severe problems with word recognition, sight vocabulary, as well as his literal comprehension of context." The report reflects his lack of critical thinking skills as well as the need for special educational services to improve his receptive language abilities. Consistent with other records, he was classified as mentally retarded. In addition, diagnoses of Organic Personality Syndrome and Fetal Alcohol Syndrome were reported.

Records from Office of Family and Children's Services indicate that both Aaron's mother and father "are substance abusers and, according to his mother, she regularly ingested alcohol throughout her pregnancy." A home assessment report conducted when he was age seventeen found him to be "low functioning and barely able to read and count his change." At that time, records indicate that Mr. W had been placed on Ritalin in an attempt to control his difficulties with concentration, attention, and what was viewed as a Conduct Disorder. The report also states that he "fluctuates from being passively compliant to behaving in an irrational, non-logical fashion."

Mr. W was interviewed by the Intake Social Worker from the Office of the Public Defender. According to his observations, "Aaron was noncommunicative and did not appear to understand the questions posed to him. To those questions which he was able to give answers, Aaron responded with simple 'yes' or 'no.'" When seen by the Mental Health Crisis Team (approximately 2 weeks before the alleged offense), it was reported that his "Cognitive limitations appear to be considerable, although Aaron could answer simple questions and generate coherent responses."

Trial competency assessments conducted by two psychiatrists found the defendant to be competent to stand trial. One report states that Mr. W "had difficulty performing all but the simplest of calculations and demonstrated poor recognition of letters." Another evaluation indicated that he "has difficulty recognizing letters and reading and performing simple calculations. He has a limited fund of general information. However, Aaron understands things generally when they are explained in simple, uncomplicated terms." Both psychiatrists found Mr. W to be "borderline retarded."

INTERVIEWS OF DEFENDANT

Prior to the start of my initial evaluation gestation, I explained to Mr. W, in the presence of his attorney, that I am a Diplomate in Forensic Psychology of the American Board of Professional Psychology and that my services had been re-

tained by his attorney. Using simple language, I explained to him that the purpose of this evaluation was to acquire information regarding the details surrounding his questioning by the police. I indicated to him that if I were asked to write a report and/or testify, all information he provided to me, as well as any other information I learned about him, might be contained in my report and/or in my testimony. I explained that my notes would be given to his attorney, and under such circumstances his attorney would, under law, be required to turn these notes over to the Office of the Prosecutor. Mr. W was unable to paraphrase this information, stating simply, "You're seeing me to hear what happened." When I again explained this information to him, he stated, "You want to know what took place in the subway." Further attempts to clarify the nature and purpose of this assessment proved to be relatively unsuccessful. Mr. W acknowledged that he understood that, "You're going to write this down." In addition, he stated, "Your job is to go to court and you may write it all down." This evaluation proceeded with authorization from his attorney.

At the start of the second evaluation session, Mr. W was unable to recall my name although he stated that, "I remember you. You're a lawyer, right?" I again indicated the nature of the evaluation and the lack of confidentiality that would exist should I write a report and/or offer testimony. Again, Mr. W was unable to provide informed consent, and the session continued with authorization from his attorney.

Background and History   The information provided by Mr. W during the interviews is relatively consistent with the records I reviewed. Although he had a difficult time sequencing events in his life and there was some confusion regarding details, he did not present information that appeared to be designed to portray himself in an inaccurate light.

Mr. W could not differentiate between his biological parents and his stepparents despite numerous attempts on my part to clarify this issue. He reported that his mother died "of drinking" when he was age 14. According to Mr. W, he has lived with his biological father and stepmother since he was age 7. He could not explain what his father did to earn a living, stating only, "He sells stuff."

Mr. W believed that he attended private school for the earliest grades in his school career. However, he could not recall the names of these schools. He reported that he has been in special education from the start of his school career. When asked to explain why this was the case, he stated, "I was roaming the streets too much." Mr. W left school in the eighth grade. He recalled that prior to this, he had been "left back one or two times because I was slow." He described his reading as "not that good" and his writing as "so so."

Mr. W reported that he has never been employed. He explained, "I can't fill out an application. I never picked up a book and learned how to read." He reported no history of seizures (it was necessary to explain to him what a "seizure" is). He minimized his use of alcohol and denied use of controlled substances at anytime in his life. "It's because of my mother. I mean my stepmother; she didn't let me." Mr. W recalled that at one point in his life, his mother obtained a PINS petition (Person In Need of Supervision) because, "I was running from group homes." However, he claimed he had never heard the term "PINS petition" before.

Recollection of Miranda *Rights Waiver*   According to Mr. W, he was arrested on the night of the crime. However, records show that he was arrested approximately one month later. According to Mr. W, he was approached by the police in the subway. He explained that he initially spoke to the police because "They scared me. They accused me that I robbed her. They also showed a lot of pictures of me and they said that I robbed other people, too."

When asked what rights he had been provided he stated, "They didn't give me none." When asked what rights he should have been provided, Mr. W stated, "the line-up." On closer questioning, Mr. W claimed that, "I don't know about the rights." When pressured he stated, "I'm trying to think. It means to stay out of trouble? Something like that." When asked what the police say on television when someone is arrested, he replied, "You're going to jail." He was unable to spontaneously offer any of the *Miranda* rights.

Mr. W was read the waiver upon which he had printed his name. When asked about the right to remain silent, he stated, "It means the police don't want you to ask them no questions, and they want you to be quiet and say nothing and to just sit down until they're ready for you." As for the use of his statements in court, he stated, "Anything that you say, the lawyer writes it down and he'll tell the judge." When questioned about his right to have an attorney present during interrogation, he stated, "I don't know what that means. It means that you talk to your lawyer and tell him what happened, or you tell the police what happened. Then my lawyer goes to court and he tells the judge what I said or when he calls him on the phone." His right to have an attorney if he could not afford one on his own, Mr. W explained, meant that "If I can't pay for one, somebody will be your lawyer to help you with your case and help you out. The judge gets you a lawyer to talk about your case." Later during the evaluation session, when asked if he could have an attorney present during interrogation, he stated, "No, I don't have that kind of money. I get one in court."

Throughout the evaluation session, Mr. W presented his view that, "The police are there to help you. They talk to you and they tell the judge so they could put you on the right track." Similarly, he consistently expressed the opinion that his lawyer will communicate directly with the judge, failing to recognize the existence of privilege that exists between attorney and client. In this regard, he failed to distinguish between the role of the police and the role of his attorney in terms of the legal representation that would be provided to him. Similarly, throughout the evaluation sessions, Mr. W did not appear to grasp the concept that the right to remain silent meant anything more than remaining quiet until the police were ready to speak with him.

OBSERVATIONS OF BEHAVIOR

Throughout both evaluation sessions, Mr. W appeared to be cooperative. He was friendly, polite, and although he quickly tired, he appeared to almost force himself to remain attentive. Despite these efforts, Mr. W was easily distracted by outside movement and noises. He appeared to be highly anxious and agitated.

No evidence of an underlying thought disturbance was observed during either evaluation session. Mr. W's lack of vocabulary was readily in evidence. In addition to being unable to provide informed consent despite numerous attempts at explaining and reexplaining the nature and purpose of this assessment, Mr. W's thinking was highly concrete and simplistic. He frequently missed the essential nature and purpose of the questions put to him. He had difficulty in presenting a logical sequence of events in his life, and details he did provide were frequently incorrect or incomplete. Rather than attempting to exaggerate the nature of his retardation, the history he provided tended to underestimate the levels of impairment as reported in the records.

RESULTS OF TESTING

On WAIS-III, Mr. W obtained Verbal and Performance IQs of 63 and 59, respectively. These scores fall at or below the first percentile and within the mildly mentally retarded range. His overall or Full Scale IQ of 58 also falls at the first percentile. On the sections that comprise the WAIS-III, Mr. W obtained a Verbal Comprehension Index of 68, a Perceptual Organization Index of 64, a Working Memory Index of 57, and a Processing Speed Index of 68. These scores are consistent with each other and reflect the generalized impairments found across a wide range of intellectual abilities. Mr. W's vocabulary, his common sense or judgment, and his general fund of information fell between the first and second percentiles. Similarly, his attention span fell at the second percentile. He had difficulty defining even simple words such as "penny" ("It is brown").

Mr. W's scores on the WRAT-3 are consistent with his scores on the WAIS-III. He obtained Reading, Spelling, and Arithmetic grade-equivalent scores falling within the first grade and below the first percentile. On the Bender-Gestalt, Mr. W made nine errors that could be scored under the Hutt and Briskin scoring system. A score of five errors or more is generally taken to indicate the possibility of organic impairment. On the Symbol Digit Modalities Test, Mr. W completed 22 items. The completion of 38 items or less for a person his age would strongly suggest the presence of a chronic brain lesion.

Mr. W's TAT stories are consistent with his low level of intellectual functioning. His stories are simple, childlike, and reflect his low level of vocabulary as well as his tendency toward concrete thinking. His stories were often no more than mere descriptions of the pictures shown to him. They reflect his narrow view of the world and his tendency to be puzzled by unfamiliar situations.

Mr. W was administered a number of tests specifically designed to objectively evaluate the ability of a defendant to make a knowing, intelligent waiver of *Miranda* rights. While this test consists of the rights as expressed in the St. Louis County, MO, version of *Miranda* rights, his performance is consistent with scores obtained by those with similar levels of intellectual functioning. In addition, his responses to these instruments are similar to his comprehension of the rights read to him in Westchester County. On an instrument requiring Mr. W to paraphrase each right (CMR), he obtained a score of 1 out of a possible 8. On an instrument designed to evaluate his understanding the vocabulary contained in the St. Louis version of *Miranda* rights (CMR-V; only four of the words are similar to those contained in the Westchester version of *Miranda* rights), he obtained a score of 2 out of a possible 12. On an instrument evaluating his ability to recognize the similarity between each right and three sentences read to him related to these rights (CMR-R), he obtained a score of 8 out of 10. On another instrument in which he is shown pictures and asked a series of questions designed to elicit his understanding of what is occurring (FRI), Mr. W obtained a score of 19 out of a possible 30. With the exception of the test designed to evaluate his recognition of rights, his scores fall significantly below the mean. His scores reflect his lack of comprehension of the right to remain silent, as well as his lack of understanding that he can have a lawyer present during interrogation. In addition, Mr. W did not appear to grasp the concept that what he told the police might be used against him in court. Further, Mr. W did not appear to understand the confidential nature that exists between the communication that occurs between he and his attorney. Although Mr. W stated that he understood a lawyer could be appointed if he did not have money to hire one on his own, when questioned later he stated, "I don't have that kind of money [to get a lawyer during interrogation]."

OPINION

Based on my interviews with Mr. W, his responses to the tests administered, my interview with his father, and my review of the records provided to me, it is clear that the defendant is a mildly mentally retarded, learning disabled individual. Significant impairments are noted in his vocabulary, his ability to express himself, and his overall judgment and reasoning. He has difficulty concentrating and focusing attention. Consistent with his history, screening tests for neurological impairment strongly suggest the presence of an underlying central nervous system dysfunction. Further neuropsychological/neurological testing is necessary to determine the exact nature of this condition.

Mr. W's responses to questions regarding his comprehension of the Westchester County *Miranda* rights as well as his scores on tests designed to objectively evaluate his overall comprehension of *Miranda* rights, indicate his understanding of a number of these rights is lacking. Specifically, Mr. W does not understand the nature of the right to remain silent. He does not comprehend that he could have an attorney present during interrogation, believing that he would be provided one only when he appears in court. Although he grasps the concept that an attorney would be appointed if he did not have the money to pay for one, later questioning revealed his belief that as an indigent individual, he would only be provided with an attorney at such time as he appears in court. In addition, Mr. W does not appear to understand the adversarial nature of the interrogation process. Rather, he believes that the police are "interested in you and want to help put you on the right path." It is Mr. W's belief that both the police and his attorney will report his statements directly to the judge. Consequently, questions are raised as to the impact of his lack of understanding of the confidential nature of attorney and client on his ability to comprehend his *Miranda* rights.

Alan M. Goldstein, Ph.D.
Diplomate in Forensic Psychology
American Board of Professional Psychology

Teaching Point: What is the value of specialized forensic assessment instruments in forensic mental health assessment?

Forensic assessment instruments, such as the *Miranda* tools developed by Grisso that were used in this evaluation, are never the sole basis for an opinion. However, such tools provide significant information for a forensic expert to consider in reaching conclusions. In a sense, FAIs contribute to the expert's determination of the "what" regarding the legal competence question (Is the defendant competent or not competent?), while traditional clinical tests contribute to the expert's understanding of the "why" or the reason for the impairment in competency.

In reading this report, imagine if Grisso's forensic assessment instruments had not been administered to Mr. W. What if only traditional clinical tests, such as the WAIS-III, WRAT-3, Bender Gestalt, Symbol Digit Modalities Test, and the TAT, were given? (Tests such as the MMPI-2 could not be given because of his inability to read.) What effect would this omission have on the opinions reached in this report?

Grisso's *Miranda* instruments are based on the St. Louis County, Missouri, version of the *Miranda* rights. Although *Miranda v. Arizona* (1966) established the content of the warnings to be administered at the time of arrest, the actual wording (vocabulary, reading level, length of sentences, and number of warnings) varies across jurisdictions. It is highly unlikely that the defendant you are assessing would have been administered this version of the warning. However, the inclusion of Grisso's measures adds very significant and relevant information that would otherwise be lacking.

First, these instruments offer a standardized method to assess comprehension of the *Miranda* warnings. The administration of these measures is carefully described in the manual that accompanies these FAIs. Scoring criterion are clearly indicated (along with prompts to clarify unclear or borderline answers). Performance can be expressed in numerical terms. Norms allow comparison of the defendant's scores on various measures with the scores of the norming groups; norms also relate such scores to age, intelligence, and (for adults) offender versus non-offender status. This is valuable information because it provides a base-rate or anchor to which the defendant's scores can be compared. If only an interview were conducted, asking the defendant about comprehension of the rights that were read, there would be no standard to judge whether his or her comprehension is greater than, equal to, or less than those in his demographic category.

Second, data allow examiners to assess consistency across instruments. Scores on Grisso's four measures can be compared with one another. They can also be compared to the defendant's IQ, obtained from an independent measure of his functioning. This information contributes to the assessment of malingering because consistency of performance on independent measures is, in part, one of the criteria used by forensic psychologists in assessing malingering.

Third, by comparing performance on three or four independent instruments of comprehension of each *Miranda* warning, the examiner not only can check for consistency (and therefore malingering) but can also obtain useful information about the specific right or rights the defendant has difficulty grasping. Such information may be valuable to the judge in making a determination of whether the defendant understood each right that was waived.

Fourth, the manual provides a list of court decisions relevant to the admissibility of expert testimony incorporating Grisso's instruments. Opinions and testimony that include data based on objective instruments are likely to be viewed as more credible than those based solely on experience or clinical judgment.

Case 2

Principle: Use case-specific (idiographic) evidence in assessing causal connection between clinical condition and functional abilities

There are a number of important sources of scientific and empirical evidence that can be used to provide relevant information to a variety of legal decision makers. Although reliable and valid empirical evidence is important in FMHA, such evidence should be used in conjunction with scientific reasoning. Such reasoning is particularly important when using an idiographic approach, employing case-specific information, and interpreting it using scientific reasoning (comparable to the single case study design).

Idiographic information is particularly important in assessing relevant domains in FMHA for two reasons. First, an idiographic approach can contribute significantly to the overall accuracy of the FMHA, and accurate information is critical to hypothesis development, testing, and verification. Second, the use of idiographic data enhances the face validity and relevance of the FMHA because of its specificity and applicability to the particular case, making the FMHA more credible to legal decision makers. In addition to enhancing face validity (a particularly important concern in FMHA; see, e.g., Grisso, 1986), the use of idiographic data is important because standards of practice and ethics authority strongly suggest that FMHA should be based on information and techniques that are sufficient to support the conclusions reached in FMHA. Typically, this is accomplished through direct contact with the individual(s) being assessed and the gathering of case-specific information for hypothesis formation and testing. There is also a strong legal justification for using an idiographic approach in FMHA; the enhanced relevance that results from including idiographic data is directly applicable to the admissibility of expert evidence under *Daubert, Kuhmo,* and the *Federal Rules of Evidence.*

The present case provides a good example of the use of idiographic evidence in hypothesis formation and testing. This defendant was evaluated to provide his attorney with information relevant to his competence to waive *Miranda* rights. The case provides an example of the relationship between formally measured intellectual functioning and specific competencies. The idiographic data, obtained through interview and review of case-specific documents, were applied toward describing actual and potential functioning in a variety of domains relevant to the competence to waive *Miranda* rights.

Miranda warnings were designed to protect a defendant's right against self-incrimination under the Fifth Amendment. Under *Miranda,* a defendant enjoys the protections of several rights (the right to remain silent, the right to an attorney, and the right to have an attorney provided if the defendant cannot afford one) and must also show an awareness of the consequences of waiving these rights (the knowledge that any statements made can be used against him or her in a court of law). A defendant must be able to waive these *Miranda* rights in a "knowing, intelligent, and voluntary" manner. Accordingly, the FMHA must consider the specific capacities relevant to a "knowing," "intelligent," and "voluntary" waiver. Further, the primary focus is on the capacities for knowing and intelligent waiver, as a number of courts (e.g., *Miller v. State,* 1986; *Rhode Island v. Innis,* 1980; *United States v. Velasquez,* 1989) have held that the kind of coercion that would typically be evaluated by a mental health professional (e.g., presenting an individual with "hard choices," implying that a sentence will be more severe if the defendant does not waive *Miranda* rights) does not rise to the level of making a waiver involuntary in this context.

The FMHA is primarily concerned with the capacities involved in making such a waiver. The clinical symptoms and cognitive deficits that could limit such capacities, either temporarily (as in acute intoxication) or more permanently (as in severe mental retardation), are also relevant for this assessment. As with other legal questions, the presence of such clinical or cognitive deficits might be described as a necessary but not sufficient basis for a legal decision maker to conclude that waiver was not competently made. The relationship between the clinical or cognitive deficits and the specific relevant capacity must be established. An idiographic approach to this assessment issue would have the evaluator seek to determine what the defendant understood about his or her *Miranda* rights at the time of the confession, how the defendant reasoned in waiving these rights, and whether these capacities for understanding and reasoning were more impaired at the time of the waiver than they are currently.

In the present case, the process of assessing the relevant capacities began with a detailed interview that included a psychosocial history. Relevant idiographic information was obtained when the defendant was informed of the evaluation and the associated limits on confidentiality. Although the defendant, Mr. Doe, appeared to understand the basic purpose of the evaluation, he had some difficulty recalling details related to the evaluation, and he needed to have several parts of the notification repeated. This was the first indication that he might have some deficits in his understanding or recall of information provided to him orally.

Incorporating self-report and collateral interviews, the psychosocial history provided important idiographic information that was relevant to the competencies in question. For example, questioning about Mr. Doe's family history revealed that he had always lived at home with his mother and continued to do so, although he was 41 years old. This suggested that Mr. Doe might not have the skills necessary to live independently, which could suggest deficits in a variety of relevant areas. Similarly, in response to questions about his educational history, he said that he completed fifth grade before dropping out of school at the age of 16, and that he could barely read or write. While both statements required further assessment through independent history-gathering and psychological testing, they were relevant in the present case because of the claim that Mr. Doe had read and understood a standard written *Miranda* waiver.

The psychosocial history also revealed that Mr. Doe was unemployed at the time of the alleged offense and had only held one job in his life—a job changing tires that was given to him by his stepfather. Mr. Doe described his inability to read and write as the primary reason for his limited job history. His difficulty in finding employment and the simple nature of his only job are consistent with cognitive deficits that might be related to his capacities relevant to waiving *Miranda* rights. Mr. Doe did not appear to have a significant mental or medical health history, nor did there appear to be a history of mental illness in his immediate family. Also, Mr. Doe described a substantial history of substance abuse, which included daily use of alcohol. This information was relevant because if Mr. Doe had been intoxicated when he was asked to sign the

Miranda rights waiver, this could have had a significant impact on his ability to waive these rights in a knowing and intelligent fashion.

The interview also yielded information about possible mental illness that could have had adversely affected his relevant capacities. There were no indications, either from the observations of Mr. Doe or from the information he provided, that he suffers from a serious mental illness. However, other important idiographic information was obtained through the clinical interview. For example, Mr. Doe did not respond at length to most questions asked of him without encouragement and further questioning. Also, his responses frequently did not address the question, and he tended to talk about unrelated matters.

Mr. Doe also appeared to give up easily on tasks requiring cognitive effort, a tendency that was particularly apparent during intellectual and academic achievement testing. Mr. Doe was administered the WAIS-R and the WRAT-3 to measure his functioning in these areas. His basic academic skills, as measured by the WRAT-3, showed severe deficits in all three academic areas: Reading and Spelling were measured at a first-grade level, while Arithmetic was measured at a second-grade level. Mr. Doe's performance on the WAIS-R suggested that he would fall in the Borderline Range of intellectual functioning (VIQ = 72, PIQ = 77, FSIQ = 73). These results suggested that Mr. Doe's understanding of written material was limited and provided relevant information in considering the hypothesis that Mr. Doe had reading and understanding deficits, particularly with written material.

Considering this possibility, the evaluators assessed the impact of these deficits on Mr. Doe's specific capacities to knowingly, intelligently, and voluntarily waive his *Miranda* rights. Mr. Doe was asked about each component of his *Miranda* rights. He was also asked to explain his understanding of the meaning and implications of each right. Mr. Doe had difficulty with these requests from the beginning. He said that he did not know "for sure" what a *Miranda* right was, and he had similar difficulty describing the purposes of these rights. Mr. Doe's responses to further questioning suggested that although he had a basic understanding of certain *Miranda* rights, his ability to reason about the advantages and disadvantages of either waiving or refusing to waive such rights was very limited. His knowledge about his *Miranda* rights was superficial, and he quickly became confused in trying to weigh his alternatives. Given his overall level of intellectual functioning as measured by the WAIS-R and his level of reading as measured by the WRAT-3, it seemed likely that his conceptual and verbal skills would not allow him to reason about and communicate material relevant to *Miranda* rights in a meaningful way. This would be particularly applicable if he were presented with *Miranda* rights in written form.

Considering this, it appeared that Mr. Doe could possibly have given a "knowing" waiver of his rights, considered in a very basic sense. However, his capacity to provide an "intelligent" waiver was more limited. The use of various kinds of idiographic information (collateral interviews and records, psychosocial history, clinical interview, and *Miranda* rights vignettes) supplemented the nomothetic information obtained through standardized psychological tests.

How useful would information comparing Mr. Doe's *Miranda*-relevant capacities[1] with those of other criminal defendants have been? What if research allowed us to measure accurately Mr. Doe's "knowledge," "intelligence," or "voluntariness" and assign a percentile value (relative to other criminal defendants) to each measurement? Certainly that would have been helpful in this case. Indeed, the accurate measurement of relevant capacities is one of the strongest arguments for using a good FAI (discussed further in the Teaching Point in this case). Even when such capacities are measured with an FAI, there are important questions that can be addressed by obtaining case-specific information. Are the observed deficits genuine? If so, they should be reflected in other domains, as seen in the defendant's history. How do these deficits affect the defendant's ability to understand, weigh, and communicate information? In this case, because the defendant was reportedly informed of his *Miranda* rights both orally and in writing, and signed a written form indicating his waiver, we assessed both his oral comprehension and his reading skills. Can the observed deficits be managed so that the defendant is able to understand and weigh information meaningfully despite such deficits? In Mr. Doe's case, it was clear that he had extremely limited reading ability, and limited capacity for understanding orally communicated material as well. By using simple language that is repeated and rehearsed, it is possible to improve such capacities somewhat. The question of how much improvement has resulted can be conveyed through descriptive language and quoting the defendant. Whether such interventions were used by interrogating officers can be assessed if there is a transcript or, even better, a videotape of the waiver and confession. Each of these questions can be addressed, at least in part, by idiographic information. Such information clearly makes the assessment results more credible and defensible, both important considerations in FMHA.

FORENSIC EVALUATION

January 26, 1998
Re: John Doe
MC# 1234-5678-09
PP# 123456

REFERRAL

John Doe is a 38-year-old African American male who is currently charged with Attempted Murder, Aggravated Assault, Rape, Kidnapping, False Imprisonment, and related charges. A request for a mental health evaluation to provide the defense with information relevant to Mr. Doe's competence to waive *Miranda* rights, and treatment needs and amenability in the context of public safety, was made by Mr. Doe's attorney.

PROCEDURES

Mr. Doe was evaluated for a total of approximately seven hours on 1-23-98 and 1-26-98 at the Philadelphia City Jail, where he is currently incarcerated. In addition to a clinical interview, Mr. Doe was administered a standard screening instrument for symptoms of mental and emotional disorder (the Brief Symptom Inventory, or

BSI), a standard test of current functioning in relevant academic areas (the Wide Range Achievement Test, 3rd edition, or WRAT-3), and a test of current intellectual functioning (the Wechsler Intelligence Scale for Adults, revised edition, or WAIS-R). In addition, Mr. Doe's mother, Marie Doe, and sister, Joan Doe, were interviewed by telephone on 1-23-98 and 1-25-98, respectively, regarding Mr. Doe's current and past functioning. The following documents, obtained from Mr. Doe's attorney, were reviewed prior to the evaluation:

1. Preliminary Hearing Summary (7-16-97),
2. Trial Transcript, Commonwealth v. John Doe,
3. Philadelphia Police Department Investigation Interview Records (7-11-97),
4. Statement of John Doe (7-11-97, Sex Crimes Unit), and
5. *Miranda* Rights Waiver, John Doe (7-11-97).

Prior to the evaluation, Mr. Doe was notified about the purpose of the evaluation and the associated limits on confidentiality. He appeared to adequately understand the basic purpose of the evaluation, although he had some difficulty recalling details related to the evaluation and needed to have several parts of the notification repeated to him. Mr. Doe reported back his understanding that he would be evaluated and that a written report would be submitted to his attorney. He further understood that the report could be used in his hearing and, if it were, copies would be provided to the prosecution and the court.

RELEVANT HISTORY

Historical information was obtained from the collateral sources described above, as well as from Mr. Doe himself. In addition, historical information was obtained from interviews with Mr. Doe's mother (Marie Doe) and sister (Joan Doe).

John Doe was born on September 26, 1956, to Marie Doe and John Doe Sr. According to Mr. Doe, his mother and father separated and divorced approximately 30 years ago. Mr. Doe indicated that he has not seen his father in a very long time. This is consistent with information provided by Marie Doe, who added that she remarried in either 1981 or 1983. Marie Doe indicated that Mr. Doe was very close to his stepfather and was devastated when he died approximately 10 years ago. Joan Doe confirmed that Mr. Doe had an excellent relationship with his stepfather and added that the family is "very close." Mr. Doe indicated that he has always lived with his mother. He further indicated that he has two sisters, who also live with his mother, and a half-sister, who currently resides in New Jersey with her boyfriend and two children. Marie Doe confirmed the composition of the family. Mr. Doe also stated that he has two children of his own by two different women. Mr. Doe also indicated that he has two male grandchildren, ages 2 and 14 months. Mr. Doe indicated that he has regular contact with his children and grandchildren. He also reported that one of the mothers of his children has a problem with substance abuse and cut him with a broken bottle during an argument over the care of his daughter. Mr. Doe stated that the argument was due to the fact that the mother in question is "never home to take care of things." Marie Doe and Joan Doe confirmed that Mr. Doe has two children and two grandchildren. They also indicated that he sees them on a regular basis and is actively involved in their lives. Mr. Doe denied all forms of abuse at the hands of family members. Marie and Joan Doe also indicated that they were not aware of any kind of abuse that Mr. Doe had suffered from family members.

Mr. Doe apparently has a limited educational history. Mr. Doe reported that he has only completed the fifth grade, and that he was a constant behavioral problem in school and was "thrown out of school for fighting." Marie and Joan Doe indicated that this is accurate. Additionally, Mr. Doe indicated that after he had been expelled from elementary school, he attended the Canto School for approximately 2 years. As described by Mr. Doe and Marie Doe, the Canto School is for children with academic and behavioral difficulties. Mr. Doe reported that he dropped out of school at the age of 16. He was unable to describe his educational activities from approximately fifth grade until his official withdrawal from the educational system. Marie Doe was also unclear on this issue, but did indicate that Mr. Doe did not attend school during this time; rather, he was working in his stepfather's automotive business. Mr. Doe denied all special education involvement. Marie Doe confirmed this but also stated that Mr. Doe can barely read or write.

Marie Doe reported that Mr. Doe does not have any significant medical problems and has never been hospitalized for anything more serious than a broken wrist. Mr. Doe confirmed that he broke his wrist in a moped accident and denied all other medical problems. Marie Doe also indicated that no one in the family has a serious mental disorder and that Mr. Doe has never received treatment (including medication) for any type of mental health problem. Joan Doe responded to the question regarding her brother's mental health history by stating "my brother is not crazy." Mr. Doe initially denied all involvement with the mental health system, but later in the interview indicated that he had seen a psychiatrist twice when he was approximately 17 years old. He could not remember why he was taken to see a psychiatrist.

Mr. Doe reported an extensive history of drug abuse. Specifically, Mr. Doe reported that he has used marijuana, cocaine, syrup, LSD, unspecified prescription drugs, and alcohol in the past. Mr. Doe also indicated that he no longer abuses drugs, claiming to have stopped sometime in 1987. Inconsistent with this, however, he also reported that he still drinks alcohol daily. He also stated that he has committed many of his past offenses to secure money to buy drugs. Although Marie and Joan Doe were aware of Mr. Doe's drug use, they could not supply further details.

Mr. Doe indicated that he is currently unemployed and has only held one job in his life. He indicated that he worked with his stepfather changing tires for approximately 16 years. Mr. Doe was unsure of the dates, but indicated that he began working for his stepfather when he was about 16 or 17 years old. Marie Doe also reported this, as well as stating that Mr. Doe has tried to get a job, but has had difficulty doing so because he can barely read and write. Mr. Doe did not have any clear vocational interests or goals. He indicated that he would "do anything . . . and would like to help" his mother.

An official arrest history was not available at the time this report was written; however, Mr. Doe indicated that he has an extensive criminal history. Specifically, he reported that he has been arrested in New Jersey approximately 35 times.

In addition, Mr. Doe stated that he served 4½ years in Bordentown for robbery, one year in Jamesburg for stealing cars, and 5½ months in Annadale for theft. He was unable to give exact dates. As mentioned previously, Mr. Doe stated that he committed the majority of these offenses in order to supply his drug habit. Mr. Doe also stated that he stole his first car at approximately age 14. The trial transcript reflects a total of 11 arrests outside of this jurisdiction, primarily in New Jersey.

CURRENT CLINICAL CONDITION

Mr. Doe presented as an African American male of below average height with a stocky build, who appeared younger than his stated age. He was dressed in prison garb and was well-groomed when seen for evaluation on 1-23-98 and 1-26-98 at the City Jail, where he is currently incarcerated. Initially, he was cooperative and polite, although somewhat reserved. He remained cooperative and polite throughout the entire evaluation. His speech was clear, coherent, and relevant, although somewhat sparse, and he did not respond at length to most questions without encouragement and further questioning. Frequently, his responses did not address the question asked, and he was inclined to talk about unrelated issues. As a result, questions had to be repeated on a regular basis. He appeared to give reasonable effort to the most of the tasks involved, although he gave up almost immediately on tasks requiring cognitive demands (such as the WRAT-3 and the WAIS-R). When asked about these apparent difficulties, Mr. Doe frequently responded by saying "I don't know." His capacity for attention and concentration appeared adequate, and he was able to focus reasonably well on a series of tasks during the 7-hour evaluation (over 2 days) without becoming visibly distracted. Therefore, it would appear that this evaluation provides a fairly representative estimate of Mr. Doe's current functioning. His mood throughout the evaluation was largely subdued and neutral, and he showed little emotional variability. Mr. Doe was correctly oriented to time, place, and person. Mr. Doe's basic academic skills, as measured by the WRAT-3, showed severe deficits in all three academic areas: Reading (first-grade equivalent), Spelling (first-grade equivalent), and Arithmetic (second-grade equivalent). Each of these areas should be considered in need of remediation. Overall level of intellectual functioning was formally measured with the WAIS-R and was found to be within the Borderline range (VIQ = 72, PIQ = 77, FSIQ = 73). Individuals with such scores are below the fourth percentile, relative to the adult population (in other words, functioning at a lower level than over 96% of adults). Mr. Doe's Verbal IQ score suggests that he has a very poor grasp of verbal and academic skills. Although Mr. Doe's WAIS-R scores reveal few strengths, it should be noted that Mr. Doe appeared to give up easily on numerous items on all subtests of the WAIS-R. Accordingly, Mr. Doe's WAIS-R scores should be interpreted with some caution, as they might provide a slight underestimate of his intellectual and cognitive functioning.

Mr. Doe did not report experiencing any perceptual disturbances (auditory or visual hallucinations), and his train of thought was clear and logical. Mr. Doe also did not report experiencing delusions (bizarre ideas with no possible basis in reality). On a structured inventory of symptoms of mental and emotional disorder (the Brief Symptom Inventory; BSI), Mr. Doe reported the presence of various symptoms. Some of the items endorsed by Mr. Doe involved nervousness, anxiety, difficulty remembering, and symptoms of depression. Mr. Doe denied the presence of suicidal ideation. Mr. Doe indicated that his current symptoms are a result of his current incarceration.

COMPETENCE TO WAIVE *MIRANDA* RIGHTS

Mr. Doe was asked about each respective component of his *Miranda* rights. Each was discussed, and he was asked to explain his understanding of the meaning and implications of each right. Mr. Doe stated that he did "not know for sure" what a *Miranda* right was. When asked about the purpose of *Miranda* rights, he replied that "it's your rights, so I won't get sued or something."

When Mr. Doe was asked to explain the right to remain silent (this question had to be repeated twice), he replied that "I don't have to say nothing." When Mr. Doe was asked about the consequences if he chose to remain silent, he responded "beat me up, I guess." Mr. Doe was then asked if the police could beat him up to make him talk. He replied "yes, they do what they want to do." Similarly, when Mr. Doe was asked if it was legal for the police to beat him up to make him talk, he replied "I don't know . . . nobody did anything about it . . . my momma tell it." Mr. Doe was then asked why he had the right to remain silent; he replied "it's a right ain't it?" He was asked to elaborate on this statement, and responded that it was "not for right or wrong, my right . . . for the court."

Next, Mr. Doe was asked to explain his understanding of the consequences of giving up the right to remain silent—whether he was aware that, if he did so, anything he said could be used against him in a court of law. His understanding of the consequences of giving up his right to remain silent seemed to be clearer. When asked to explain his understanding (this question had to be clarified twice), Mr. Doe replied, "anything I tell them they write down . . . bring it up in court . . . bring it against me."

Mr. Doe was then asked about his right to have an attorney present during questioning; he did not understand this question when it included the term "interrogation." When questioned about his understanding of this right, Mr. Doe replied, "lawyer got to be with me, in charge or something . . . I don't know, never had no lawyer." When asked if he had ever requested a lawyer, Mr. Doe replied "No, I was guilty of my charges before in Jersey." Mr. Doe was then asked whether this would make a difference in whether he asked for an attorney. He replied "don't know . . . don't understand big words." Finally, Mr. Doe was asked if the police could refuse to give him a lawyer until after they had questioned him. In response to this question, he indicated that "bulls can do what they want . . . they didn't give me one when I was there."

Mr. Doe was next asked about his right to have an attorney appointed for him if he could not afford one. He said he had "no money to give 'em . . . PD, right?" When asked if he would get a lawyer if he didn't have enough money, Mr. Doe replied further "I have to have a lawyer when I go to court . . . if I got no money then I don't get one." Mr. Doe was then asked if the police could refuse to get him a lawyer if he didn't have enough money. He said that he "don't know, been locked up for 6 months, haven't seen no one for 4 months."

Finally, Mr. Doe was asked if he remembered signing the *Miranda* Rights Waiver form. He said that the police told him "you're not charged with anything . . . you're going home." Mr. Doe stated that he did not remember if he was read his rights, had given a statement, or signed any forms.

Mr. Doe did not demonstrate an "intelligent" capacity to waive his *Miranda* rights in the following sense: his knowledge was superficial, he quickly became confused, and he showed very little capacity to reason about different circumstances and their applicability to the waiver decision. During the present evaluation, Mr. Doe quickly became confused, even when talking about some of the basic aspects of these rights. First, it was often necessary to repeat and/or paraphrase questions concerning these rights. While Mr. Doe was able to respond on a superficial level concerning the most basic aspects of these rights, it quickly became apparent that he had a very limited awareness of the meaning of these rights. Given his low overall level of intellectual functioning as measured by the WAIS-R (VIQ = 72, in the low Borderline range) and his extremely low level of Reading as measured by the WRAT-3 (Grade 1 equivalent), it seems likely that his conceptual and basic word skills would not allow him to reason about and communicate material relevant to *Miranda* rights at more than a very superficial level. This would be particularly applicable if he were presented with *Miranda* rights in written form; his capacity to understand written material is extremely poor. However, even his capacity to reason through verbal vignettes and hypothetical situations, and their implications for *Miranda* waiver, was very poor.

However, Mr. Doe did seem to have some basic comprehension of certain aspects of his *Miranda* rights, in a sense roughly consistent with his knowing basic facts and procedures that are incorporated into such rights. He was able to indicate that "I don't have to say nothing" as a way of paraphrasing his right to remain silent and that giving up that right could result in statements that had been "written down" being "brought up in court." He could also state that "a lawyer got to be with me . . . in charge, or something," as a way of indicating the meaning of having an attorney present. In other responses as well, Mr. Doe was able to demonstrate a basic familiarity with the elements of *Miranda*.

CONCLUSIONS

In the opinion of the undersigned, based on all of the above:

> Mr. Doe displayed a very superficial understanding of certain basic *Miranda* rights, suggesting that his capacity to "know" basic information was limited but possibly acceptable. However, he quickly became confused and displayed very limited conceptual and verbal abilities, which would impair his capacity to understand anything more complex regarding these rights, to appreciate their importance, or to reason about their applicability to himself under different circumstances. Mr. Doe showed virtually no capacity to understand written material. All these suggested that Mr. Doe did not have the capacity to "intelligently" waive *Miranda* rights at the time of his statement.

Thank you for the opportunity to evaluate John Doe.

Kirk Heilbrun, Ph.D.
Consulting Psychologist

Geff Marczyk, M.A.
Psychology Graduate Student

David DeMatteo
Psychology Graduate Student

Teaching Point: What are the limits of forensic assessment instruments?

It has been recognized that traditional psychological tests and procedures have substantial limitations when applied in a forensic context (Grisso, 1998b; Heilbrun, 1992; Melton et al., 1997; Rogers, 1997). Accordingly, forensic research-ers have developed a variety of forensic assessment instruments that focus di-rectly on the measurement of functional capacities relevant to the larger legal question. The strengths of such FAIs have been discussed in the previous Teaching Point. What are their limitations?

First, the forensic clinician cannot form an opinion based solely on the results of an FAI. Although FAIs provide useful information regarding an indi-vidual's legally relevant functional abilities, there remain several important considerations: context, consistency, and communication. Context is a compo-nent of Grisso's (1986) model of legal competencies:

> The term general environmental context refers to some class of external situations to which a person must respond. Various legal competencies . . . specify widely dif-fering contexts: for example, criminal proceedings (trials), police interrogations, home life, and hospitals. (p. 18)

Context may vary even within the same kind of competence, as evidenced by the potentially different demands on a defendant undergoing a highly publi-cized murder trial, compared with the demands on a defendant in a routine, minor felony trial. Some functions may become more important in certain contexts, and it is the responsibility of the evaluator to consider this and inter-pret the FAI results accordingly.

The second limitation of FAI data concerns the consistency of such data with other sources of information. When the FAI provides impressions that are inconsistent with history, direct observations, and collateral information and observations, this suggests inaccuracy in at least one source. Further, it raises the possibility that a defendant providing responses to an FAI measuring *Mi-randa* waiver capacities, for example, may be malingering or exaggerating deficits in knowledge or reasoning capacity. This could call for a particular focus on the issue of malingering; if this possibility were supported, then the results from the FAI would need to be deemphasized or even discounted.

When FAI results are not communicated effectively, then their value may be reduced. The importance of communicating the results of forensic assess-ment in plain language, free of jargon (Melton et al., 1997), is particularly noteworthy with FAIs, because the obtained scores of the particular defendant may need to be described in the context of the derivation and validation sam-ples, with considerations such as interrater reliability, optimal cutting scores, and the description of the characteristics of individuals falling into groups de-fined by these cutting scores. Such statistical issues are clearly relevant to the value of the FAI, but must be translated for consumers of the evaluation who are not trained in statistics and research design.

A specific example in the context of *Miranda* waiver is useful. Several FAIs have been developed for specific use in the context of a FMHA that is con-ducted to assess an individual's competency to waive his or her *Miranda* rights; one is the Comprehension of Miranda Rights (CMR; Grisso, 1981). The CMR was developed to assess an individual's understanding of *Miranda* rights as they are usually presented in a police interrogation situation. Although the CMR is a useful FAI with strong psychometric properties, it is important to supplement CMR results with case-specific information for several reasons.

First, it is possible that the *Miranda* warnings presented to the defendant differed slightly in their wording from the warnings contained in the CMR. Accordingly, it is important to determine the precise wording of the warnings that were presented to the defendant prior to interrogation. In this case, Mr. Doe's file contained a printed *Miranda* Rights Waiver form that had been presented to Mr. Doe when he was questioned by the police. The evaluators were able to question Mr. Doe using the language in which his rights were presented to him at the time he waived them (assuming that they were read verbatim from the Waiver form, which could not be confirmed because neither video nor audiotape of the interrogation was available). Relying on the warnings given in the CMR or other FAI may reduce assessment accuracy somewhat if the wording of the warnings played a role in Mr. Doe's understanding and subsequent waiver of his rights.

Second, the use of case-specific evidence plays an important role in hypothesis formation and testing. Although the results of testing may suggest a particular explanation or conclusion, case-specific information provides the forensic clinician with relevant information with which to confirm or reject such explanations or conclusions. The CMR is primarily limited to assessing the individual's understanding of the *Miranda* rights. Case-specific information regarding Mr. Doe's academic history, basic academic skills, level of cognitive functioning, and mental health history provided information that allowed the evaluators to offer reasonable explanations for the existence of such deficits.

FAIs can provide the forensic clinician with reliable and valid data on an individual's functional legal capacities. The use of case-specific information can help the evaluator assess the accuracy of self-report, emphasize particularly important capacities in the context of the defendant's circumstances, and communicate more effectively by providing a reasonable explanation for the existence of identified deficits. Case-specific information also enhances the credibility of a given assessment. The use of a relevant, well-validated FAI supplemented by idiographic information from multiple sources would appear to combine the best of both approaches to FMHA.

Note

1. Research in forensic psychology has increasingly moved toward implementing the recommendation made by Grisso (1986) that the measurement of relevant capacities rather than ultimate legal question outcomes is the preferable research strategy for developing and validating FAIs. The usefulness of the ultimate legal determination as an outcome variable is limited by the absence of a "gold standard" (a reliable, valid indicator of the "true" status of a legal competency), a problem first noted by Roesch and Golding (1980).

Chapter 3

Competence to Act as
One's Own Attorney

The case report in this chapter focuses on the competence of criminal defendants to act as their own attorney. The principle to be applied in this case addresses the need to clarify financial arrangements prior to beginning the case, and the teaching point addresses more specifically how the financial arrangements in FMHA can vary under different circumstances. Some of the ways in which such circumstances can vary will depend on whether the forensic assessment is being paid through public or private funds. A contract may be established with a group or agency, as contrasted with an arrangement made with a single practitioner on a specific case. Billing may be done on an hourly basis, or an estimate can be provided for the maximum number of hours that will be spent on a case, with a "cap" established for the total case.

Case 1

Principle: Clarify financial arrangements

This principle addresses the importance of determining who will pay for the forensic clinician's services, the rate at which the services will be billed, and how the fee will be collected. It is customary for independent clinicians and agencies to have either a standard hourly rate or a sliding scale for professional services. The rate and billing arrangements may differ according to the type of service being provided (e.g., forensic evaluation vs. testimony), although billing at a different rate for the various components of FMHA can create significant problems (Heilbrun, 2001).

Under certain circumstances, it is useful to have the fee arrangement addressed in a written document. Although this is typically not necessary when the court is responsible for payment, it may be important when the forensic clinician is privately retained. A written agreement should generally address the following: (1) the nature of services to be provided by the forensic clinician; (2) the estimated number of hours and time period, including provisions if the services cannot be performed within the given estimates; (3) the hourly rate for services, including whether the rate will differ according to the service provided; (4) who will assume responsibility for payment; (5) considerations such as reimbursement for expenses incurred as part of the evaluation; (6) the anticipated products (e.g., verbal consultation, written report, testimony), and (7) when payment will be made (e.g., retainer vs. regular billing vs. billing only on completion of the case).

There are three possible sources of reimbursement for a forensic evaluation: the court (or the jurisdiction it represents), the referring attorney, and the individual being evaluated. Each will be discussed briefly. First, when the court is responsible for payment, compensation is typically authorized by the court when the evaluation is completed. The amount of compensation, and whether it is preestablished, differs between jurisdictions. In some jurisdictions, billing is done according to time rather than for a prescribed total. When this occurs, judges must use their discretion to determine an acceptable range for reimbursement. It may be necessary to obtain advance authorization for exceptional payment in jurisdictions with specifically established fees for particular kinds of FMHA.

The second possible source of funding is the referring attorney. When the attorney is responsible for payment, it is important to address the previously discussed importance of written agreements (whether the agreement with the attorney is written or oral). It is also important that the attorney acknowledge that the responsibility for payment rests with that attorney; it should not become the forensic clinician's responsibility to seek payment from other sources. Payment should be authorized (if a court order is necessary) or deposited in escrow (if the attorney's client is paying for the evaluation) before the evaluation is begun, unless the forensic clinician is confident that the fee will be paid regardless of the results of the evaluation.

For a variety of reasons, it is preferable to avoid the third source of reimbursement (the individual) whenever possible, at least in the sense that payment is provided by the individual directly to the forensic clinician. When the individual provides payment directly, this can strengthen the misperception that he/she is the primary client in the case, which in turn can create misunderstanding about whether the forensic clinician is in a "helping" (as contrasted with a "truth-telling") role. It is preferable, therefore, to have the referring attorney provide payment, even if such payment is in turn obtained directly from the attorney's client.

There is strong ethical, legal, and standard of practice support for this principle (Heilbrun, 2001). Ethical support can be found in the *Ethical Principles of Psychologists and Code of Conduct* (APA, 1992): "As early as is feasible in a professional or scientific relationship, the psychologist and the patient, client, or other appropriate recipient of psychological services reach an agreement specifying the compensation and the billing arrangements" (p. 1602). The *Specialty Guidelines for Forensic Psychologists* (Committee on Ethical Guidelines for Forensic Psychologists, 1991) addresses this principle in two ways. First, during the initial consultation with the legal representative of the party seeking services, the forensic psychologist is obligated to inform the party of several factors that may affect the decision to contract with the psychologist, including "the fee structure for anticipated services" (p. 658). In addition, the *Specialty Guidelines* indicates that forensic psychologists should not "provide professional services to parties to a legal proceeding on the basis of 'contingency fees' " (p. 659).

Legal support for this principle can be found in several sources (Heilbrun, 2001). Fee clarification is typically handled through procedural rules or administrative regulations. In a federal criminal case, for example, Rule 706(b) of the *Federal Rules of Evidence* permits payment of court-appointed experts' fees amounting to "reasonable compensation" in "whatever sum the court may allow." In other federal litigation contexts, however, the court appoints an expert with the expectation that a report and/or testimony may result, with the expert's compensation to be paid by the parties involved in the litigation in a manner directed by the court. In addition, a federal court has the discretion to order a single party to pay in advance the full cost of appointing an expert. Most judges, however, require the parties in civil litigation to split the expert's fee, with the percentage of the fee paid be each party varying with the circumstances of the litigation.

The literature in the area of standard of practice consistently reflects the importance of initial fee clarification (Blau, 1984b; Halleck, 1980). Failure to document the fee arrangement, in writing if necessary, may lead to significant problems in obtaining reimbursement.

COMPETENCY TO STAND TRIAL EVALUATION

Re: Mr. L
April 19, 2000

IDENTIFYING INFORMATION

Mr. L is a 29-year-old male, born on October 7, 1970, who was committed to the Pleasantville State Hospital on March 30, 2000, by the District Court for evaluations of competency to stand trial pursuant to M.G.L. Ch.123 §15b. While on a day pass from Pleasantville State Hospital, he allegedly was disruptive in a bar and became combative when the police were called, at one point lunging to grab a gun from the holster of one of the officers. He was charged with Assault and Battery on a Police Officer.

WARNING ON LIMITATIONS OF PRIVILEGE AND CONFIDENTIALITY

At the beginning of each interview session, Mr. L was informed that I am a psychologist who was assigned to conduct an evaluation on the issue of competency to stand trial. I explained that the evaluations were ordered by the Court and that I would be filing a report with the court, including his statements to me and my observations and

conclusions, and that I might be required to testify in court regarding these matters. He was informed that the information he provided would
not be confidential, therefore. He was also informed that he was not required to answer any
of my questions but that a report would be filed
regardless of his participation. Mr. L indicated his
understanding by paraphrasing the explanation
("You're a psychologist and you can tell the court
everything I say . . . I don't have to talk to you")
and agreed to proceed.

SOURCES OF INFORMATION

This evaluation is based on the following sources
of information:

1. Clinical interviews with Mr. L on April 5,
   April 12, and April 17, 2000, totaling approximately 2 hours and 15 minutes;
2. Psychological testing including the WAIS-
   III (Wechsler Adult Intelligence Scale-
   Third edition);
3. Consultation with his clinician, Ellen
   Jones, MSW;
4. Review of his records from the current
   hospital admission;
5. Review of the discharge review from Pleasantville State Hospital dated 2/1/98;
6. Review of progress notes and discharge summary from Pleasantville State Hospital;
7. Review of a 15A evaluation completed by
   Dr. Robert Jones dated 3/30/00;
8. Telephone conversation on April 3, 2000,
   with attorney Ed Rollins, court-appointed
   to represent Mr. L; and
9. Telephone conversation with Mr. L's
   mother, Sandra L, on April 4, 2000.

RELEVANT HISTORY

Mr. L reported that he is the eldest of three sons
born to his parents. One brother, age 28, is divorced, lives in New Jersey, and is currently unemployed. He has had a history of alcohol abuse
and recently completed a detoxification program.
His younger brother, who is 25, has never been
married, currently resides at home with their
mother, and works at a local factory. Mr. L reported that this brother drinks occasionally but
"he's not an alcoholic." The father, who passed
away 8 years ago from liver disease, was described

by both Mr. L and his mother as an alcoholic.
Although he was often verbally abusive, the father reportedly was not physically abusive to either his wife or children. He moved out of the
home when Mr. L was 10 years old, and they
maintained only occasional contact (birthdays, holidays) until his death. Mr. L described his mother
as his main sources of support, "who has always
been there for me." Recently she was diagnosed
with a heart condition, and this is a significant
source of stress for Mr. L. His mother reported
that after her husband left it was difficult for her
to raise the three boys by herself and that she was
prone to periods of depression and anxiety.

Mr. L did not have problems in school until
his sophomore year, at which time he was often
truant, performed poorly academically, and was
involved in several disciplinary episodes, including two short-term suspensions (related to possession of marijuana in one case and for swearing
at a teacher in the second instance). His mother
reported that he did not have many friends and
spent long periods in his room. He indicated that
he began drinking alcohol at age 11, progressing
to a 6-pack of beer 2 to 3 days a week by the
time he was 16. He also reported that he began
using marijuana at age 12, and estimated that
he smoked one to two joints a day about 3 days
a week by the time he was 16. According to
his mother, he exhibited "tantrums" at home,
screaming at her, threatening her and his brother,
and breaking things in the home. He was psychiatrically hospitalized for 3 weeks at Memorial
Hospital at that time and then placed at Lifelines,
a dual-diagnosis residential program, for 9 months.
At that time he received the diagnoses of Bipolar
Disorder, Alcohol Abuse, and Cannabis Abuse.
After completing the program, he returned home
and was stable for about 6 months, according to
his mother. However, he then began exhibiting
similar problems and dropped out of high school.
Since then he has had sporadic employment in
local convenience stores, at a record store, and
other sales jobs. His longest employment was for
9 months. He has never been married and reported that he has had several brief sexual liaisons, beginning at age 18, but no long-term romantic relationships. He reported having several
male friends and "drinking buddies" but could not
describe any significant friendships.

Mr. L has had six subsequent psychiatric hospitalizations, with his most recent diagnosis being Schizoaffective Disorder. He has received outpatient treatment from the local community mental health center. He has demonstrated a pattern of complying with treatment for several months following discharge from the hospital, but then discontinuing his medications, beginning to drink or use drugs, and having his psychotic symptoms recur. His most recent hospitalization occurred in December 1999, again at Pleasantville Hospital. On admission, he was described as paranoid, claiming that the government was poisoning him with uranium and eavesdropping on his thoughts. He was highly agitated and energetic, sleeping only 2–3 hours a night, and was loud and belligerent on the ward. He also reported auditory hallucinations (i.e., hearing voices) telling him that he was going to be killed. During the early part of the hospitalization he was assaultive toward staff on three occasions. He was treated with the psychotropic medications Lithium and Risperdal, and his symptoms abated. By February 20, 2000, he was considered sufficiently stable to receive day passes, and plans were being made for discharge to a community residential program. However, on one of these passes (March 28, 2000), the current offense allegedly occurred.

As noted earlier, Mr. L's psychiatric problems are often associated with and exacerbated by substance abuse. From all available accounts, he typically will drink 3–4 times a week, usually 6–10 beers a night, accompanied by 1–2 marijuana joints. He has never experienced delirium tremens or withdrawal.

Regarding previous criminal involvement, he was involved in a number of thefts at age 15, which resulted in probation. His adult criminal record includes three previous charges of Assault and Battery. The first of these assaults was against his brother (3–4 years ago), when his brother tried to convince him to go the mental health center. The charge was dismissed as he was psychiatrically hospitalized. The other two assaults occurred with strangers in altercations at bars. On both occasions, Mr. L was intoxicated and threatened the victims with a broken bottle, on one occasion cutting the victim on the arm. He spent 30 days in the County House of Correction awaiting trial on this latter charge but was given probation when the victim did not show up in court.

CIRCUMSTANCES OF ADMISSION

Following his arrest on the current charge, Mr. L was evaluated pursuant to New Jersey General Laws, Chapter 123, §15a by Robert Jones, Ph.D., at the District Court. Dr. Jones noted in his report that:

> Mr. L is a 28-year-old patient at the Pleasantville Hospital with a documented history of treatment for a major mental illness. He was aware of the charges against him and has a reasonably good understanding of the legal process. However, he insists on acting pro se (dismissing his attorney and defending himself) because, he says, his court-appointed attorney refuses to expose the government conspiracy against him. Questions are raised about his competency to serve as his own counsel. A period of further evaluation and treatment at a psychiatric hospital is recommended.

COURSE OF HOSPITALIZATION

On admission to the hospital, Mr. L was frequently observed by various staff members to be inappropriately laughing and appeared to be responding to internal stimuli. Mr. L reported to his clinician during their initial sessions that he believes he hears voices because of his history of drug use and not because he has a mental illness. During the first week of hospitalization, Mr. L was able to participate in a reality-based conversation for about 15 minutes with the attending psychiatrist, but when he was pressed about symptoms of his mental illness he became agitated and expressed the delusional concern that the interview was being bugged via an implant that the government had placed in his body. Nursing notes indicated that he was pacing the floor during the early morning hours and that he slept very little. Over the next 2 weeks it was noted that his energy level decreased, he was sleeping throughout most of the night (waking to use the bathroom but then returning to sleep), and no longer appeared to be hallucinating.

Most recently, he is described in the progress notes as stable: compliant with medications, with sleep, appetite, and activity level within normal limits. He is also described as not aggressive, although occasionally articulating delusional beliefs (e.g., that he is radioactive).

CURRENT MEDICATION

At present Mr. L receives the following medications:

Haldol Decanoate 200 mg IM every 2 weeks;

Lithium Carbonate, 900 mg q hs;

Cogentin 1 mg bid

MENTAL STATUS AND CURRENT LEVEL OF FUNCTIONING

Mr. L is a 29-year-old Caucasian male who was interviewed by this examiner on three occasions. He was cooperative with the interview process and maintained a calm demeanor, even at times when he offered his view that this examiner was part of the larger government conspiracy against him (which will be described in more detail later in this report). On all three occasions he either interrupted or delayed the interview with a request to smoke (since smoking is permitted only at specified times). Although he was persistent in these requests, he did not become agitated when he was told at one point that he would have to wait.

At the beginning of the first interview he announced that "I think this is all a conspiracy," related to the government wanting to use him as an informant. Despite this comment, and other occasional paranoid statements interspersed among the three interviews (e.g., expressing concern that the room, or even his body, had been bugged by the government), he remained cooperative with the interview process. He did not appear to be hallucinating during any of the interview sessions, although he reported occasional experiences of hearing voices of people related to the drug trade talking to him. For example, he stated that these voices tell him that "they're going to torture me." He stated that sometimes he hits himself in the head to get rid of the voices. Although at times he described these experiences as hallucinations, at other times he insisted that they were real and that the doctors in the hospital call them hallucinations as part of an attempt to label him as mentally ill. He alternated between these explanations throughout the interviews.

During the first interview, Mr. L described a number of delusional beliefs, such as claiming that people can change their appearances so he cannot recognize those who are plotting against him. He also expressed the concern that his treating physician and I were part of this conspiracy. By the third interview he no longer spontaneously reported these beliefs. When questioned about them, he stated that "I'm trying to sort out reality from fantasy," acknowledging that he was not sure of the reality of these beliefs. However, he continued to endorse his beliefs about a government conspiracy. It is noted that when he became stressed during the interviews, in response to difficult questions, he tended to react in a paranoid manner, although he was easily returned to a more rational discussion.

Mr. L's mood was stable and he did not appear depressed, manic, or agitated during the interviews. Although his records indicate that he has been suicidal in the past, at present he is not suicidal and has not been displaying symptoms of depression such as disturbances in sleep, appetite, or energy level. The hospital records also confirm no recent evidence of suicidal or self-injurious behaviors or intentions. He was ambivalent in terms of acknowledging his mental illness, as noted above.

Due to his significant history of substance abuse, cognitive testing was administered to Mr. L. He was given the WAIS-III, on which he obtained a Verbal IQ score of 93 (in the Average range), a Performance IQ score 89 (in the Low Average range) and a Full Scale IQ score of 91 (Average range). Of note, his scores revealed significant variability both between and within subtests. For example, on several scales he was able to answer more difficult questions but missed some of the easier ones. He performed particularly poorly on tests of attention and concentration (for instance, he was able to repeat five digits forward but only three backward). His vocabulary scores were within the low average range, with more marked impairments on subtests assessing abstracting ability and social judgment.

Some of his scores were affected by his distractibility and tendency to provide tangential, idiosyncratic responses.

CRITERIA FOR DETERMINING COMPETENCY TO STAND TRIAL

Whether he has sufficient present ability to consult with his lawyer with a reasonable degree of rational understanding and whether he has a rational as well as factual understanding of the proceedings against him.

CLINICAL IMPRESSIONS RELEVANT TO COMPETENCY TO STAND TRIAL

Understanding of the Charges, Verdicts, and Potential Consequences   Mr. L indicated that he is charged with Assault and Battery on a Police Officer. When asked if these charges were serious, he answered, "yeah, they're serious." He understood that the possible outcomes of a trial are guilty, not guilty, and not guilty by reason of insanity, that if he is acquitted he can go home, if he is found NGRI he would be hospitalized, and if found guilty he could be incarcerated or given probation. He explained that being on probation means "see a probation officer, follow rules of probation."

Understanding of the Trial Participants and Process   Mr. L indicated that the prosecutor's role is to "fight for the rights of the Commonwealth," and he would be trying to convict him. He identified a defense attorney's job as "representing the defendant in court . . . he's supposed to do what the client wants," although as discussed below, he indicated a desire to represent himself. When asked who would decide the case, he initially offered that it was the judge. When asked who else, he responded the doctors (apparently referring to the insanity defense) and the jury, which he explained is "a group of people that hears the case, discusses it among themselves, then goes into room and decides if I'm guilty or not, gives their verdict." With minimal prompting, he also indicated that if convicted the judge would sentence him. He identified himself as the defendant and described witnesses who "go in the court and testify on behalf of the plaintiff." He identified pos-

sible witnesses as the police, himself, and other patrons at the bar. Mr. L was able to describe the concept of plea bargain as "when I make a deal with the court take a lesser charge—plead guilty."

Ability to Assist Counsel in Preparing and Implementing a Defense   Mr. L was able to coherently provide his own version of the events and state of mind leading up to the alleged offense. He indicated that he was unwilling to work with his attorney who was pressuring him to pursue an insanity defense. He indicated that he would prefer to represent himself, since he did not have confidence that his attorney would follow his instructions to plead not guilty and focus on the government conspiracy against him. He was able to provide a rationale for his proposed defense, although it is based on paranoid assumptions.

Ability to Make Relevant Decisions   Mr. L discussed the advantages and disadvantages of a guilty versus not guilty by reason of insanity plea. He stated, "now if I plead insanity they could keep me in the hospital as long as they want, this will end up in a commitment." He complained that the government would like to keep him in the hospital to continue their surveillance of him. Although he acknowledged that if he were found guilty he could be incarcerated in the County Jail for a period of several years, which he also found aversive, he indicated that the government would not be able to place bugs in his body there. He was questioned at length about the pros and cons of these different verdicts. Although he was able to indicate his understanding of the possible consequences of the various pleas, he continued to insist that he would not consent to being found not guilty by reason of insanity because it would place him at risk from the government. In a similar vein, he insisted that he would defend himself since his attorney was unwilling to expose the government conspiracy against him.

CLINICAL IMPRESSIONS REGARDING COMPETENCY TO STAND TRIAL

Mr. L appears to understand the charges against him, appreciate their seriousness, and is aware of his plea options and their possible consequences. He understands the roles of the various participants in the trial process, including the role of an attorney. He is also able to provide his own account of the alleged offense. Although there has been some stabilization of the acute symptoms of his mental illness, he continues to harbor delusional beliefs, which affect his ability to weigh rationally the relative merits of various courses of action, including whether to pursue an insanity defense and whether to retain an attorney (versus defending himself). His present decision to represent himself appears to be directly related to his irrational beliefs about a government conspiracy tied to the hospital. As such, his ability to make a rational decision about a defense strategy and whether to defend himself is significantly impaired.

Thus, based on all the above, it is the opinion of this examiner that although Mr. L has a basic understanding of the trial process, his irrational beliefs interfere with his ability to assist in his defense in a rational manner. It is this examiner's opinion that Mr. L's decision to represent himself is based on irrational beliefs and not on a rational weighing of the pros and cons of such a decision. It is therefore recommended that Mr. L be found Incompetent to Stand Trial and not competent to waive counsel at present.

CLINICAL IMPRESSIONS REGARDING NEED FOR CARE AND TREATMENT

Mr. L has a longstanding history of a mental illness, Schizoaffective Disorder, in addition to a history of serious substance abuse, which serves to exacerbate his impairments. Although his mental status has improved over the course of the current hospitalization, he continues to manifest acute symptoms of this disorder, most notably paranoid beliefs. On psychological tests, he demonstrated mild to moderate cognitive deficits, particularly in areas of attention and concentration. However, these deficits appear secondary to a more pronounced thought disorder.

It is the recommendation of this examiner that if Mr. L is adjudicated incompetent to stand trial, that he be committed to Pleasantville Hospital pursuant to applicable state law for treatment and restoration to competency (a petition for his commitment under this section accompanies this report). If the court adjudicates Mr. L competent to stand trial, it is recommended that he be offered the option of remaining in the hospital pending trial. If Mr. L does not agree, it is recommended that he receive treatment and monitoring in the community pending trial. He has a significant history of decompensation in the community, involving becoming assaultive to others. A major risk factor for violence toward others in the community is his continued substance use. Thus, if he were to be discharged directly to the community at present, without adequate safeguards and supports, it is likely that he would pose a risk of harm to himself and others. If this occurs, it is further recommended that this report be shared with the court clinicians who could then evaluate him, pursuant to applicable state law, for acute hospitalization. If he should be reincarcerated, the mental health staff at the correctional facility should be alerted to his presence in order for them to provide close observation and treatment. He has described significant psychiatric difficulties during a previous incarceration.

Respectfully submitted,
Ira K. Packer, Ph.D.

Teaching Point: How do you clarify financial arrangements under different circumstances (e.g., performing an evaluation privately, negotiating a contract, billing hourly vs. a prespecified amount) in forensic assessment?

It is important from both practical and ethical perspectives to be clear at the outset about who is paying for the evaluation, what you will bill for and at what rate, and when payment will be expected. In the case in this chapter, the psychologist was appointed and paid by the court. In such circumstances, the court order serves as the basis for the professional relationship and incorporates the fee structure. In this case, the client and the payor are the same (the court). However, there are circumstances in which the court pays for an independent evaluation for an indigent defendant; in such cases, the payor is the court, but the client is the defense attorney.

When the psychologist is hired by one party in a case, the situation is more complex and requires more planning. Since there is no court order in such cases, it is important to develop a written agreement that clarifies the relationship. It is also advisable to request a retainer as part of this agreement. The amount of the retainer will be determined by an estimate of the amount of time likely required for the evaluation. The attorney should be advised that the cost may exceed the retainer; additional funds would then be requested.

The purpose of the retainer is not simply to ensure payment but also to provide protection from financial pressures or the appearance of pressure. If the forensic clinician has been paid prior to submitting the report, he or she is less likely to be concerned about the financial implications of the opinion (in a worst-case scenario, if the attorney does not like the opinion, the forensic clinician will not be paid at all). Therefore, by the time the report is submitted, it is better if the forensic clinician has been fully paid for all time, including report writing. Furthermore, the agreement should be clear about what is being paid for: *time* to perform the clinical evaluation, collateral contacts, consulting with the attorney, writing a report, and possibly testifying. The agreement should not include language that states or implies that the forensic clinician is being paid for an *opinion*, since this can create the assumption that the opinion will favor the retaining party.

The retainer agreement should also specify who will receive the report. There are some cases in which both sides receive the report although only one party is paying for it. If this is the case, it should be specified clearly in the agreement. Also, it is preferable to be paid directly by the attorney and not the party, although it may be the party who ultimately pays. This helps maintain appropriate boundaries, clarifying that the forensic clinician's client is the attorney, and that opinions and reports will be communicated directly to the attorney, not the party.

The professional services can be billed on an hourly basis or as a flat fee. Either arrangement is legally, ethically, and practically tenable. Some agencies or courts will authorize a specific maximum payment, and it is important to be clear about this at the outset and acknowledge that this fee will constitute total payment for services. In the more typical example of billing on an hourly basis, it is best to provide a general estimate of the range of hours likely to be involved, although allowing some flexibility to cover unusual circumstances.

Chapter 4

Competence to Stand Trial

This chapter focuses on the legal question of competence to stand trial. There are four cases included, as this is a very commonly assessed legal question. The principle for the first case addresses the importance of using plain language and avoiding technical jargon whenever possible in the report and related testimony. The teaching point involves a discussion of how complex information of a scientific and clinical nature can be communicated without technical jargon.

The second case report illustrates the principle of using a model for FMHA. Such a model can be applied toward structuring how the evaluation is conceptualized, the sources of information that are selected, and how the report is structured. Specific ways in which a model can help in such structuring is described in the teaching point.

The value of impartiality for the forensic clinician is addressed by the principle that we have used to illustrate the third trial competence case in this chapter. The particular principle involves declining involvement in a given case when the potential evaluator feels that impartiality would be difficult to achieve. In certain cases, however, such impartiality can be very difficult to maintain for reasons that go beyond the characteristics of the case or the values of the forensic clinician. When the case is highly publicized and there are intense pressures on the attorneys from both sides, there can also be particular pressure on the mental health professional who is involved. Strategies for maintaining impartiality in high-visibility cases is the topic of this case's teaching point.

The final case report in this chapter is linked with the principle involving attribution of information by source. This is one of the most fundamental principles of forensic assessment, which is used in the teaching point to describe how to separate information obtained from two particularly valuable sources: the interview and a structured assessment tool.

Case 1

Principle: Use plain language; avoid technical jargon

This principle concerns the importance of communicating the results of FMHA using language that is easily understood by those who are not mental health professionals. FMHA results can be used in a variety of contexts, and many consumers of such information are not formally trained in medicine, mental health, or the behavioral sciences (Grisso, 1998a; Melton et al., 1997). For example, although many legal and criminal justice professionals (judges, attorneys, administrators, parole officers, case managers, and others) make decisions about individuals with mental disorders on a regular basis, they may have little or no formal training in psychopathology, personality, human development, diagnosis, treatment, or research methodology. To complicate matters further, mental health professionals from different theoretical orientations sometimes attach different meanings to the same terms. Given the nature and implications of the legal decisions of which FMHA is a part, it is important that FMHA results be communicated in a way that avoids confusion and promotes better informed decision making. The best way to establish this common language is to avoid technical jargon and use plain language in communicating results.

One approach to facilitating a shared language is to minimize the use of technical terms that might be misinterpreted by others. When using technical language is essential to conveying accurate information, the terms should be clearly defined. This allows FMHA consumers to integrate relevant behavioral, scientific, and clinical evidence with minimal distortion and optimal understanding and application.

The Ethical Principles of Psychologists and Code of Conduct (APA, 1992) indicates that, "psychologists ensure that an explanation of the results is provided using language that is reasonably understandable" (p. 1604). Although this section refers to "the person assessed," it applies as well to "another legally authorized person on behalf of the client" (e.g., an attorney) and could also apply to judges and opposing attorneys in the context of litigation in which FMHA is used. Similarly, the Specialty Guidelines for Forensic Psychologists (Committee on Ethical Guidelines for Forensic Psychologists, 1991) addresses this point:

> Forensic psychologists make reasonable efforts to ensure that the products of their services, as well as their own public statements and professional testimony, are communicated in ways that will promote understanding and avoid deception, given the particular *characteristics, roles, and abilities of various recipients of the communications.* (p. 663 emphasis added)

These sections emphasize the need for language that is reasonably understandable to the consumer of the evaluation, although with FMHA the primary consumers are typically judges and attorneys rather than the individual who is assessed. Neither the Principles of Medical Ethics with Annotations Especially Applicable to Psychiatry (American Psychiatric Association, 1995) nor the Ethical Guidelines for the Practice of Forensic Psychiatry (American Academy of Psychiatry and the Law [AAPL], 1995) contain anything directly relevant to this principle.

The first case illustrates the application of this principle. The purpose of the evaluation was to provide defense counsel with information relevant to the competence to stand trial of a 35-year-old male charged with armed robbery. The report is written in plain language that would be easily understood by a legal professional without formal training in mental health. In particular, the "Current Clinical Presentation" section of the report provides a good example of how technical concepts can be expressed in plain language.

Although the use of plain language is important in FMHA communication, it is particularly valuable in the clinical presentation section of the report, as the forensic clinician might be tempted to use technical terms to describe the clinical condition of the individual evaluated. For example, the forensic clinician indicates that the individual being evaluated "neither reported or displayed any difficulty with memory for prior events." This same sentence, if written using technical language, might have read "he neither reported nor displayed any indications of impairment in either long- or short-term memory." These two sentences convey information that is comparable in meaning, but the first does not require the assumption that the reader will have formal training in memory, information processing, and cognition.

The present report also provides good examples of the appropriate use of technical language in FMHA, including definitions when indicated. For example, in the "Current Clinical Presentation" section, the forensic clinician states that "his affect during the interview was somewhat *flat*." Standing alone, the term *flat* might convey a variety of meanings other than the absence of appropriate emotional responsiveness. To prevent misinterpretation, the forensic clinician clarifies the meaning of the technical term *flat* by elaborating that "as evidenced by monotonic speech and the minimal use of facial expressions or gestures to accompany or animate his speech." This conveys a reasonably accurate and easily understood description to the reader.

Later in the same section, the forensic clinician refers to "religious/political beliefs judged to be *delusional* in nature." Without further elaboration, the term *delusional* might be misinterpreted or overinterpreted. For example, *delusion* might be confused with *illusion* or *hallucination*. In mental health terminology, a *delusion* is a false belief that cannot be modified by reasoning or demonstration of facts. An *illusion* is a distorted perception, and a *hallucination* is a false perception. By using the term *delusion*, the forensic clinician wanted to describe the presence of unrealistic false beliefs that cannot be modified through reasoning, indicative of certain kinds of severe psychopathology. In this instance, the forensic clinician added clarifying language to convey a more precise meaning: "This complex of religious/political beliefs is judged to be delusional (*unrealistic, and part of a mental disorder*) in nature."

FORENSIC EVALUATION REPORT

Defendant: JT
DOB: 3/13/64
Eval. Date: 5/14/99
Report Date: 6/6/99

REFERRAL

JT is a 35-year-old, single, African American male who was referred for a confidential evaluation of his competence to proceed to adjudication (stand trial) by his assistant public defender, Mr. Henry

Vasey. Mr. T is charged with three counts of armed robbery stemming from incidents that occurred on or about January 4, January 16, and February 11, 1999.

NOTIFICATION

Prior to the evaluation, Mr. T was advised of the purpose and nature of the evaluation. Specifically, he was advised that I was hired by his attorney to conduct an evaluation of his present mental and emotional function as these issues relate to his ability to participate in further legal proceedings. He was told that the evaluation would consist of a clinical interview and, possibly, psychological testing, and that any information gathered in the course of this evaluation would be protected by attorney-client privilege. He was advised that a report would be given to his attorney and that, at his attorney's discretion, I might be subpoenaed to testify at a hearing regarding his competence to proceed. Mr. T indicated that he understood this information and he agreed to participate in the evaluation.

SOURCES OF INFORMATION

The following sources of information served as the primary basis for this report:

- Discovery information, including police reports and interviews with witnesses, relating to the events of January 4, January 16, and February 11, 1999, that led to Mr. T's charges;
- Brief telephone interview with Mr. Vasey on 5/3/99 regarding the nature of his interactions with the defendant and observations that led him to request a competence evaluation;
- Clinical evaluation of Mr. T at the Parker County Jail on 5/14/99, which included a clinical interview and the administration of two psychological measures: The MacArthur Competence Assessment Tool-Criminal Adjudication (MacCAT-CA) and the Structured Interview of Reported Symptoms (SIRS) (3.5 hours);
- Brief interview (approximately 10 minutes) with officer Edward Elliott, who works the

day shift on the unit where Mr. T is housed at the jail;
- Records obtained from the Spring Hill Mental Health Center and from the Central Maryland Psychiatric Hospital, where Mr. T has received psychiatric services on various occasions since 1984.
- Review of psychiatric records on the Mental Health Unit at the Parker County Jail.

BRIEF SOCIAL HISTORY

A brief social history was obtained from Mr. T during the clinical interview on 5/14/99. Mr. T's account of past events was generally consistent with other information contained in prior records.

The defendant was born in Jessup, Md., on 3/13/64. He is the younger of two boys, both of whom were raised by their mother. Mr. T reported that his mother worked as a cook at a high school cafeteria in Jessup. His parents divorced when he was about 4 years old, and he had few memories of his natural father. His mother remarried when the defendant was 9 years old and he referred to his stepfather, Mr. Jordan, as "my dad." He reported a good relationship during his developmental years with both parents.

Mr. T attended school through the tenth grade, dropping out at age 16. He described himself as a poor student, indicating that he repeated the sixth grade twice. He began skipping school at age 14 and described his middle school and high school years as "a series of social promotions. . . . I was bigger than all the other kids, so they just kept on passing me up." He also began using marijuana at age 14 and in later adolescence moved on to other drugs including "speed" and crack cocaine.

Mr. T's first contact with the mental health system occurred in January 1984, when his mother took him in for treatment of "my drug problem." However, he was also diagnosed with schizophrenia by the staff at Spring Hill Mental Health Center, and he was placed on psychotropic medications at that time. Since 1984, he has received both brief inpatient residential treatment at Spring Hill as well as extensive case management services while in the community. There have also been two commitments to the

Central Maryland Psychiatric Hospital (1985, 1997) where his primary diagnosis was also schizophrenia.

The defendant has had no extensive work history, although he has worked in a variety of unskilled positions, usually for brief periods or on a part-time basis. He continued to live with his mother after dropping out of high school, and he began receiving Social Security disability payments in 1986. In 1987, he was convicted of possession of cocaine and served 2 years in the state prison. After his release from prison in 1989, he lived in a psychiatric halfway house but was re-arrested for assault in Jessup in 1990, this arrest stemming from an incident in which he attacked a Baptist minister in the church vestibule after being denied a request to "preach to my people . . . as God's true messenger." He was in prison from 1991 until his release in 1996 and has lived in the Jessup area until his arrest on the current charges, receiving case management and medication followup services through Spring Hill Mental Health Center. His 1997 involuntary admission to the Central Maryland Psychiatric Hospital resulted from a recurrence of delusional thoughts that apparently prompted him to disrupt services at a local church, again claiming that he was a special agent of God.

CURRENT CLINICAL PRESENTATION

Mr. T was interviewed in a quiet, private attorney conference room at the Parker County Jail on the afternoon of 5/14/99. He presented as a tall, heavy-set, African American male who was dressed in standard jail clothing (bright orange jumpsuit and "flip-flop" type sandals). Distinguishing features included a gold tooth (upper, front left) and what appeared to be a jailhouse tattoo of the letters "G-O-D" across the three middle knuckles of his right hand. He wore medium length hair and a mustache, and his personal hygiene appeared to be satisfactory.

Interviewing Mr. T went quite smoothly for the most part. He displayed a friendly, congenial mood and appeared to understand questions posed by this examiner with no difficulty. He responded with relevant and coherent responses throughout the evaluation. There was no indica-tion of defensiveness in responding, and he frequently provided lengthy, well-elaborated answers to questions on a wide variety of topics. He neither reported nor displayed any difficulty with memory for prior events, and he denied any history of head injury or other significant illness.

Although no formal intellectual testing was performed, he appeared to be of at least low-average intelligence, and this clinical impression is consistent with records of prior testing received from Central Maryland Psychiatric Hospital (prior IQ testing yielded an IQ estimate of 89). Mr. T did not endorse or present symptoms of anxiety or depression, and despite the serious legal charges pending against him, he seemed generally optimistic about his future. (As will be described in further detail below, however, this optimism stems from irrational and unrealistic beliefs about his situation that raise significant concerns about his competence.) However, his affect during the interview was somewhat "flat," as evidenced by monotonic speech and the minimal use of facial expressions or gestures to accompany or animate his speech.

The most clinically significant behavior during the evaluation was Mr. T's revelation that "My name is not really JT . . . it is JT Jesus 2000!" He went on to express the belief that he holds special status in the eyes of God and is destined to be "coronated as the chief religious officer for the State of Maryland." He indicated further that his coronation would take place at noon on January 1, 2000, on the steps of the state capital, to be immediately followed by his marriage to the professional singer Vanessa L. Williams. In support of this belief, he produced from his pocket a cover photograph of Ms. Williams that was produced for a music compact disk.

This complex of religious/political beliefs is judged to be delusional (unrealistic, and part of a mental disorder) in nature, and it is a theme that appears repeatedly in records of prior psychiatric evaluations and treatment. However, these records were not available at the time of the evaluation and, therefore, the possibility of malingering existed at the time of the evaluation. To explore this issue, I gathered third-party information in the form of an interview with jail staff (Officer Edward Elliott), obtained records of prior psychiatric evaluation and treatment, and I administered the Structured Interview of Reported Symptoms (SIRS), a clinical tool for the assessment of malingered psychosis.

The data from these three sources were not consistent on the issue of malingering. On the SIRS, Mr. T had moderately elevated scores on the Rare Symptoms scale (which consists of items that occur infrequently in bona fide patients), the Blatant Symptoms scale (which consists of symptoms that untrained people are likely to identify as symptoms of major mental illness), and the Selectivity scale (which suggests somewhat indiscriminant endorsement of psychiatric problems). This combination of elevated scales rarely occurs in clients who respond truthfully to the SIRS but is more characteristic of persons feigning illness. The other sources of data, however, give more credence to Mr. T's presentation as valid symptoms of mental illness. Records from various sources dating back to 1990 note the presence of religious delusions in his clinical presentation. Clearly, these irrational beliefs predate his arrest on the current charges and have not been contrived simply for purposes of manufacturing an "excuse" for his alleged criminal behavior; in fact, these symptoms were not offered in any way as an excuse or justification for the alleged criminal acts.

Therefore, on balance the clinical and historical evidence favors an a finding that Mr. T is not malingering a major mental disorder but, rather, continues to present grandiose delusions that are symptoms of schizophrenia, a disorder of longstanding in this defendant. An additional diagnosis of substance abuse (crack cocaine) is also supported by the defendant's report of recent behavior and history.

EVALUATION OF COMPETENCE TO PROCEED

The relevant test for competence to proceed is whether the defendant has a rational as well as factual understanding of the proceedings against him and is able to adequately assist counsel in the preparation of his defense. Information on these points was gathered from a clinical interview with Mr. T regarding his current legal charges and likely course of the legal process, and the administration of the MacArthur Competence Assessment Tool-Criminal Adjudication (MacCAT-CA).

Factual Understanding of the Proceedings Information gathered in this evaluation suggests no significant impairment in Mr. T's factual understanding of the proceedings. He was able to identify correctly the charges pending against him, and he gave an excruciatingly correct accounting of the possible sentence that could be imposed if he were convicted: "Each case carries a maximum of 15 years, so if they sentenced me to consecutive sentences they could give me as much as 45 years in prison." His score on the Understanding measure of the MacCAT-CA, which assesses familiarity with roles of court personnel, the descriptive parameters of trial versus plea agreement disposition, and other "factual" information about the adjudicatory process, was well above the recommended cutoff score at which concerns about factual understanding are raised. Thus, this evaluation does not suggest significant impairment in his ability to understand factually the nature of the pending proceedings.

Rational Understanding of the Proceedings Mr. T's delusional beliefs about his special religious status appear to compromise his rational understanding of these same proceedings in a number of ways. This was manifest on the Appreciation measure of the MacCAT-CA, where he obtained a score well below the recommended cutoff for raising concerns about rational understanding.

He gave what were judged to be irrational justifications for beliefs that he would be treated "more fairly" and be "less likely to be found guilty" than similarly situated defendants. First, he argued that the judge and/or jury would give him greater leniency in judging his case due to his special religious status. He further elaborated that even if sentenced to the maximum time in prison (45 years), he would serve no more than a few months of his sentence. His justification for this belief was that legal authorities would be forced to release him in time for his "coronation" on January 1, 2000, because failure to do so would incur the wrath of God who would "kill all the white people . . . they won't stand for that." This belief, in turn, related to the defendant's profound indifference to discussing with this examiner the nature and desirability of possible plea agreements that could (hypothetically) be offered in his case.

In summary, despite his rather unimpaired comprehension of the factual nature of the pending legal proceedings, these findings raise serious concerns about his understanding of how the legal process will play out in the particular context of his own case.

Capacity to Assist Counsel   In terms of issues of trust and the cognitive abilities to recall and relate information to counsel that might assist in preparation of a defense, Mr. T is judged to be relatively unimpaired. In the interview with me, the defendant provided a detailed and chronologically organized account of his behavior at the time of the alleged offenses, and he indicated a willingness to disclose and discuss the same information with his attorney, whom he described as "a nice young guy . . . I like him." Further, he was able to provide relevant background information (e.g., prior mental health history) that might be useful in constructing defenses or arguments in mitigation based on mental impairment. His score on the Reasoning measure of the MacCAT-CA was in the range that usually indicates minimal or no impairment in this competence-related ability.

The one concern about assisting counsel that did emerge in the evaluation is one of motivation. While Mr. T displayed adequate abilities to do many of the things anticipated in assisting counsel, his delusional beliefs about special religious status may compromise his motivation to work in his own best interests. In essence, Mr. T speaks about his case as if his special religious status provides him with a "Get-Out-of-Jail-Free Card," effective date January 1, 2000. Thus, he does not appear overly concerned about the severity of his charges and, as noted earlier, displayed no small indifference during this evaluation when discussing some key issues related to possible adjudication—specifically, considering and evaluating possible plea agreement offers. Thus, there are also concerns about his ability to discuss and to reason

adequately about important case issues, and again these concerns stem directly from the impact of symptoms of mental disorder on his thinking.

SUMMARY

The results of this evaluation indicate that Mr. T has a history of major mental disorder, specifically schizophrenia, dating back over 15 years. His symptoms have often included grandiose delusions (irrational and unrealistic beliefs) of a religious nature, and these symptoms are in evidence at present. In the fashion described earlier, these symptoms appear to adversely affect his ability to understand rationally the nature of the pending legal proceedings and potentially to undermine his ability to reason in a rational way about the options (e.g., plea offers) that might be presented to him for consideration. Thus, there is ample clinical evidence on which to raise challenges to the defendant's competence to proceed at this time.

RECOMMENDATIONS

Should the Court determine that Mr. T is incompetent to proceed at this time, it is recommended that he be committed to the Department of Mental Health for restoration services on an inpatient basis at the psychiatric hospital in Baltimore, Md. Mr. T currently displays no insight into the nature of his symptoms nor any inclination to take medication or other treatment on a regular basis ("I've been prescribed medicine before, but I usually take it only when I think I need it"). Prior records indicate that his symptoms have remitted within a period of 4–6 months of inpatient treatment, although his compliance with treatment has been poorer when he has been followed in the community. An inpatient placement will also minimize the chance of his continued use of crack cocaine, which could compromise efforts to restore him to competence through community-based treatment.

Norman G. Poythress Jr., Ph.D.
Licensed Psychologist

Teaching Point: How do you communicate complex scientific material to legal professionals and lay audiences?

Report writing and expert testimony are the most common vehicles for communicating the results of a FMHA. Both require the forensic clinician to document and communicate a variety of observations, clinical characteristics, conclusions, and underlying reasoning that links these domains. Given the specialized and complex nature of this information and reasoning, the forensic clinician must communicate the results of the FMHA in a way that is understandable to both lay audiences and legal professionals.

There are a number of ways that the forensic clinician can communicate the complex observations and reasoning associated with FMHA. When communicating observations, it is helpful to use direct quotations from the individual being evaluated, from third parties, and from other collateral sources of information. Similarly, the forensic clinician can describe observed behavior, whether such behavior was observed by the clinician or by third parties. These approaches can provide lay and legal audiences with clear examples of observations obtained in the course of the evaluation; such observations can provide specific illustrations of relevant aspects of communication and behavior.

The communication of the reasoning and resulting conclusions of a FMHA can be even more complex than the communication of observations. Accordingly, the forensic clinician should attempt to provide the audience with an established framework for conceptualizing and understanding the relationship between clinical observations, reasoning, and the resulting conclusions. For example, a discussion of presenting psychiatric symptoms and related diagnoses could be structured around DSM-IV criteria. This would inform the audience about the features of particular disorders and allow them to compare the relevant clinical characteristics present in the evaluation with those criteria. A comparable approach can be used in communicating functional capacities by using a framework provided by an applicable specialized tool. In addition to their other benefits, a well-validated specialized tool should provide norm-referenced scores that can help an audience quantify level of functioning.

Another approach to effective communication involves the use of contingency statements to explain the relationship between observations, reasoning, and conclusions of a FMHA. A contingency may be given in the form "if x, then y; if not x, then z." Statements of this kind can help the audience understand the links between clinical observations, reasoning, and conclusions that the forensic clinician intends to convey. For example, "If JT receives treatment for his severe depression, then he will present as a lower risk for suicidal behavior; if he does not receive such treatment, his risk may remain high." This contingency statement links clinical observation to reasoning and conclusions in the following way. The clinical observation is that JT is severely depressed. Elsewhere in the report, depression has been described as a risk factor for suicide in JT's case. The conclusion—that treatment for depression will reduce-

John's risk for suicidal behavior, and the absence of such treatment may leave his risk unaffected—allows lay audiences to understand the complex link between mental illness and behavior without needing extensive knowledge in the area.

The use of categories is another effective method for communicating complex scientific information. For example, it is frequently useful to describe the clinical characteristics and their impact on behavior in terms of "unlikely," "possible," or "likely." This categorization should take into account the individual's history, any applicable research, and findings from the current evaluation that consistently describes certain capacities or behavior. Another kind of categorical communication describes the link between clinical characteristics and conclusions as "consistently supported," "mixed evidence," or "consistently not supported." This approach should also incorporate available research and the clinical characteristics of the individual being assessed. In addition to being a valuable method of communicating complex scientific observations and reasoning, categorical approaches allow the forensic clinician to clarify the limits of their findings in terms that lay audiences can understand.

Case 2

Principle: Select and employ a model to guide data gathering, interpretation, and communication

This principle addresses the selection and use of a forensic assessment model to help guide the forensic clinician in gathering and interpreting data, reasoning about results and conclusions, and communicating the entire assessment. A model for FMHA is applicable to several areas of the forensic assessment process. Specifically, a model is relevant to the selection of data sources, the identification of specific legal issues, and the determination of the relationship between clinical symptoms and functional legal deficits. Furthermore, a model can also serve to clarify communication and reasoning.

There is relatively little discussion in the literature of the use of a model in forensic evaluations. In fact, a review of the relevant literature reveals that only two general models exist—one developed in the context of civil commitment (Morse, 1978a, 1978b) and the other constructed to describe different criminal and civil competencies (Grisso, 1986). Some models have been developed, however, for more specific kinds of FMHA (e.g., Bonnie, 1992; APA, 1994). The two general models will be briefly discussed.

Morse's (1978a, 1978b) model is premised on the observation that mental health laws generally focus on three broad questions: (1) the existence of a mental disorder, (2) the functional abilities related to the tasks that are part of the relevant legal question, and (3) the strength of the causal connection between the first and the second areas. Although a detailed discussion of Morse's model is beyond the scope of this chapter, the relationship of the model to the present principle being discussed will be addressed briefly. First, Morse's model describes the implications for data gathering. Specifically, the model emphasizes the need to begin with data about mental health symptoms or intellectual deficits. The model also stresses the importance of capabilities that are relevant to the elements of the legal test. In addition, Morse's model addresses the forensic clinician's reasoning, as the clinician must describe the degree of causal connection between the individual's clinical characteristics and their functional abilities and deficits. Finally, Morse's model facilitates the clinician's task of communicating the results of the evaluation, as it describes the essence of what is being assessed in FMHA. Using this model helps the clinician describe data and reasoning in a more straightforward fashion, whether in a written report or in testimony.

The other general model of forensic evaluations, developed by Grisso (1986), consists of six characteristics that are shared by all types of legal competencies. Grisso termed the six characteristics *functional, contextual, causal, interactive, judgmental,* and *dispositional*. Although a full discussion of Grisso's model is beyond the scope of this chapter, a few highlights will be briefly mentioned.[1] Two elements of Grisso's model—context and interaction—are not found in Morse's model. The context element concerns the influence of the situation in the competence construct, while the interaction element addresses whether the individual's abilities satisfy the demands of the context with which the individual will be faced.

A comparison of the models proposed by Morse and Grisso reveals certain common components. In both models, three elements can be recognized—mental disorder, functional abilities, and the causal connection between the two. Clearly, then, these three elements should be included in any model used in forensic assessment.

The use of a model may assist the forensic clinician in performing a higher quality evaluation as judged by criteria such as those offered by Petrella and Poythress (1983): (1) the examiner used proper legal criteria, (2) an ultimate opinion is clearly stated,[2] (3) an adequate basis for the opinion is stated, (4) clinical characterization of the defendant, (5) psychiatric jargon vs. plain language, (6) information needed to assist the court, and (7) overall quality.

The present report illustrates the application of this principle in the context of a court-ordered evaluation of competence to stand trial. After articulating the legal standard for competence to stand trial under the applicable law (i.e., Michigan law), the evaluator addresses the competence of the defendant (Howard Dudley H) by using a model-consistent approach that combines key features of both the Morse and Grisso models.

The evaluator's discussion of Mr. H's competence to stand trial is organized around the three elements that are shared by the Morse and Grisso forensic assessment models. Specifically, the clinician addresses Mr. H's mental condition, his relevant functional legal capacities (understanding the nature and object of the proceedings against him and ability to assist in the preparation of his defense in a rational manner), and the relationship between mental condition and functional capacities. These are comparable to the components that can be found in the models of forensic assessment described by Morse and Grisso. Each of these three elements will be addressed in the context of the current evaluation.

Regarding Mr. H's mental condition, the evaluator concluded that the defendant warranted a diagnosis of Delusional Disorder, Grandiose Type. Consistent with the models articulated by Morse and Grisso, the evaluator described the clinical characteristics associated with Mr. H's diagnosis. Specifically, the evaluator noted that Mr. H had a delusional belief "that he has developed effective subliminal software that has influenced the behavior of people such as Alan Greenspan and Demi Moore."

The evaluator also addressed Mr. H's awareness of the nature and object of the proceedings against him. Through the use of detailed questioning about various aspects of the proceedings, the evaluator concluded that Mr. H "is aware of the charges pending against him, how those charges arose, and of the possible consequences that may ensue if he is convicted."

Finally, the evaluator addressed the third component of the models—the causal connection between Mr. H's clinical characteristics and his functional abilities to assist counsel in his own defense. The evaluator again used detailed questioning to conclude that Mr. H's clinical symptoms (in particular, his long-term intransigent delusional disorder) would not substantially impair his ability to assist counsel in a rational manner.

Based on this information, the evaluator reasoned that Mr. H "appears to meet the statutory criteria for being found competent to stand trial." Specifically, the evaluator concluded that Mr. H's clinical symptoms did not interfere with his understanding of the nature and object of the proceedings against him. In addition, the evaluator concluded that Mr. H's clinical symptoms would not interfere with his ability to assist in the preparation of his defense in a rational manner.

Returning to the quality criteria suggested by Petrella and Poythress (1983), it may be seen how the application of this model facilitated performing an excellent assessment. First, the evaluator's use of a model in this case ensured that the proper legal criteria would be used, as such guidelines (among other things) directed the selection of functional legal criteria to evaluate. The evaluator also provided sufficient data and reasoning to yield an adequate basis for his conclusion regarding Mr. H's competence to stand trial. The use of a model in the present report ensured that the evaluator would specifically discuss the relationship between Mr. H's clinical characteristics and the functional legal demands. However, the use of a model in this case also encouraged the evaluator to focus on Mr. H's particular clinical characteristics that were potentially relevant to his capacities to understand and assist. The evaluator's use of a model arguably resulted in a better conceptualized and organized process that is directly relevant to the defendant's competence to stand trial.

March 9, 2000

The Honorable Lauren Butler
39th Judicial Circuit Court
Margate County
1355 Morris Avenue
Bronxville, MI 48401

RE: H, Howard Dudley
CFP #: X0059888
Docket #: 00-6342751-FY(M)
Subject: Competency to Stand Trial

Dear Judge Butler:

DEFENDANT IDENTIFICATION AND COURT DATA

This is the first Center for Forensic Psychiatry (CFP) referral for Howard Dudley H, a 30-year-old, divorced, white male, who was born in Madison, Wisconsin, on November 15, 1969. Mr. H is charged with Manslaughter and Fleeing and Eluding under Case Number 00-6342751-FY(M) in the 39th Judicial Circuit Court, Margate County. The defendant was referred to the CFP pursuant to MCL 330.2026(1) on an order for competency to stand trial issued by the Honorable Lauren Butler, Circuit Court Judge, on February 18, 2000.

NOTIFICATION OF PURPOSE

Prior to the interview, and pursuant to MCL 330.1750, the defendant was informed both in writing (the CFP Notification of Rights form) and verbally of the purpose of the evaluation, of the fact that a report would be issued according to legal requirements, and that the examiner might be subpoenaed to testify about the report or other aspects of the examination. The defendant conveyed an understanding of the limits on confidentiality that pertain to this court-ordered examination and participated in the interview. Mr. H stated, "I know that what we talk about you have to tell the court. My lawyer said to cooperate . . . so it's okay with me."

SOURCES OF DATA

Johnston Psychiatric Hospital records

Records of Morris Roger, M.D.

Records of Lenore Cleo, M.D.

Records of Suzanne Gomer, Ph.D.

Rickster City Police Department Incident Report

CFP Defense Attorney Pre-Evaluation Assessment Form

Margate County Jail Transport Form

Phone contact with defense attorney Rodney Aronson

Psychological Testing: Minnesota Multiphasic Personality Inventory-2

CIRCUMSTANCES OF THE EVALUATION

Mr. H was evaluated at the Center for Forensic Psychiatry on March 2, 2000. According to the defendant, and review of the Margate County Jail Transport Form, Mr. H was not receiving any psychotropic medication at the time of the evaluation.

RELEVANT MENTAL HEALTH HISTORY

Available records reveal that the defendant has had contact with three mental health professionals since 1989. From September 1989 until June 1990, Mr. H participated in a therapeutic relationship with Morris Roger, M.D., a psychiatrist in private practice. Dr. Roger's termination note, dated June 7, 1990, states that "Mr. H has a firm delusion that he can influence people by using software that he created. The patient received trials of mood-stabilizing and antipsychotic medications, which did not lessen the delusion. He functions well at work and is socially active. Patient does not wish to continue in therapy because he says he feels fine, and his parents said he could stop therapy if he wants to. The patient has been told that he can contact me anytime in the future if he so chooses. . . . Final diagnosis is Delusional Disorder, grandose (*sic*)."

From February 1994 until October 1994, Mr. H was involved in psychotherapy (and several marital therapy sessions) with Lenore Cleo, M.D., a psychiatrist associated with Johnston Psychiatric Hospital in Bloomington, Michigan. Dr. Cleo's termination summary, dated October 14, 1994, states that "Mr. H's grandiose delusion seems resistant to change . . . displays no other symptoms . . . prognosis for marital issues remains guarded . . . patient is able to acknowledge that other people do not believe that he can control their actions through his software . . . understands that it is not to his benefit to mention his software idea to others and at work."

From May 1998 until November 1998, the patient received psychotherapy from Suzanne Gomer, Ph.D. Mr. H was asked to participate in an employee assistance program due to his recent decreased productivity because he was devoting too much time to developing his "subliminal software." Records indicate that Mr. H was administered Zyprexa (a medication used to treat people with psychotic disorders) by Rachel Joshua, M.D., a psychiatrist associated with the employee assistance program. The Termination of Treatment Note, dated November 13, 1998, and signed by Suzanne Gomer, Ph.D., states that

> Mr. H's diagnosis remains Delusional Disorder, Grandiose Type, Moderate (297.1). The specifier "moderate" was assigned due to Mr. H's recent decreased work productivity. From my review of prior records which address malingering, and from my observations and review of psychological testing, I have ruled out malingering. Currently he is becoming more efficient at work and he remains adequately functional in other aspects of his life. Mr. H's mental condition has remained quite stable over the past 9 years in that his delusion remains fixed and resistant to change yet, with the exception of his recent work problems, he is generally able to function adequately in personal and occupational settings.

From review of the records cited earlier, it does not appear that Mr. Harrrison was ever treated for substance abuse, that his past treatment providers identified substance abuse as a problem, or that he ever asked to be treated for any problems associated with drugs or alcohol.

MENTAL STATUS EXAMINATION (CURRENT CLINICAL PRESENTATION)

Appearance and Behavior   Mr. H entered the interview room willingly, walked with a normal gait, exhibited no psychomotor disturbance (his movements were smooth and not overactive or slowed down), and was cooperative throughout the 130-minute forensic interview. Before sitting down, he looked around the room but soon seemed comfortable and relaxed with this examiner and the surroundings. He had medium length straight black hair, sported a neatly trimmed goatee, wore wire-rimmed glasses, and was attired in an orange jail-issued jumpsuit. Eye contact was good throughout the interview.

Speech and Form of Thought   The defendant's speech was spontaneous, normal in volume, and goal directed. Although his speech was mildly pressured (somewhat accelerated but not difficult to interrupt), he did not demonstrate flight of ideas (abruptly skipping from one related idea to another) or derailment (a rapid shift from one subject to another in an unrelated manner). Mr. H's overall language abilities appeared adequate, as he was able to comprehend what this evaluator said to him and express his thoughts in an organized and goal-directed fashion. He also denied that he had ever experienced racing thoughts.

Mood and Affect   Mr. H described his mood as "not bad under the circumstances" (*mood* refers to an individual's long-term emotional "climate" whereas *affect* refers to someone's short-term fluctuating changes in emotional "weather"). He stated that throughout his life he has not been the type of person who feels particularly elated or particularly depressed, indicating that he's "always been a steady Eddie . . . I always liked my friends and family . . . feel good when I'm working . . . get my 7 hours of sleep and do it all over again." When he was asked how he currently feels he said, "I'm a little nervous . . . considering that I'm in jail . . . I'm alright." His affect was appropriate when discussing the serious nature of his legal situation, and he also displayed a full range of emotional responses that were appropriate to other topics that were discussed (e.g., he enjoyed talking about where he grew up and his childhood friends).

Thought Content and Perceptions Mr. H denied ever experiencing hallucinations (e.g., hearing voices or seeing things that are not there), persecutory ideation (ideas of less than delusional proportions, involving the belief that one is being harassed or persecuted), ideas of reference (the belief that other people or events in one's immediate environment have a particular and unusual meaning), or the belief that others were controlling his thoughts or inserting thoughts into his mind. He did, however, endorse a grandiose delusion (a false belief that is not based in reality and is resistant to change; *grandiose* refers to an inflated appraisal of one's worth, power or knowledge). Specifically, Mr. H claimed that he has "developed a software program that sends subliminal messages to people to make them behave in certain ways." When he was asked to explain how he does this, he replied, "I haven't patented it yet so I'm not explaining it to anyone. From a business viewpoint I have to protect my product." Mr. H was asked how he knows that his software program works, and he stated, "I know what I programmed people to do and then I've seen them do it . . . Alan Greenspan raised interest rates, and before that I got Demi Moore to strip in that movie she made a few years back." When he was asked how he knows that those events happened as the result of his subliminal messages, he responded with a knowing nod and said, "Believe me. These are not coincidences." Mr. H was questioned as to how long he has been using his subliminal software, and he said, "I've been working on it for about 10 years. It's not perfected yet so it doesn't work every single time. Just most of the time. Once I sent a message to President Clinton to tell the truth about Monica (Lewinsky) but it didn't work. . . . You can't reach every mind." The defendant reportedly first thought of subliminal software after he read an article on subliminal advertising about 10 years ago. He has been "perfecting" the program when time allows ever since and plans to market it with the advertising slogan, "Why'd I do that?" Mr. H did not exhibit or endorse any other unusual ideas. The defendant also did not endorse any current homicidal or suicidal ideation, intent, or plans.

Cognitive Functioning On the date of this examination, Mr. H appeared to be well-oriented to person, place, and time. Specifically, he knew his name and that he is currently a defendant undergoing a court-ordered evaluation at the "Forensic Center" in southeast Michigan. He also correctly identified the day, date, and approximate time of day.

Attention and concentration appeared to be within normal limits, as Mr. H was able to calculate simple arithmetic problems and reported that he has no difficulty following the plots of television shows or comprehending magazine articles. Short-term memory, as indicated by Mr. H's ability to recall three words after a few minutes delay, appears within normal limits. Long-term memory, as indicated by the defendant being able to recall social history details, also appears to be within normal limits. The defendant's working memory (the ability to attend and hold information in awareness and manipulate it) also did not seem impaired, as he was able to repeat six digits forward and five digits backward.

Capabilities for abstract reasoning were within normal limits as indicated by his ability to identify the similarity between different objects (e.g., a hammer and a wrench are "tools") and to interpret common proverbs (e.g., Don't cry over spilled milk means, "If something bad happens, move on with your life"). Based on the interview (e.g., fund of information and communication skills) and Mr. H's educational achievement (he graduated community college), and occupational history (e.g., retail sales), he appears to be functioning within the average range of intellectual capabilities.

Insight and Judgment Mr. H demonstrated some limited insight regarding his grandiose delusion. When asked how other people react when he tells them about his subliminal software, the defendant stated, "I know people look at me strange. They don't always believe me . . . but I just go about my business. If they don't want to hear about it, I don't have to talk about it." When he was asked why they don't believe him, he answered, "They could be jealous or maybe they don't believe I'm smart enough to do this. I know some people think I'm a few sandwiches short of a picnic."

When Mr. H was asked if he is certain that his software works, he replied, "I don't have any way to prove it except that I know what messages I send and what happens after I send them." Further questioning revealed that the defendant uses his software "for good" and that he tries not to take advantage of people. When he was asked why it was "good" for Demi Moore to strip in a movie, he answered, "It certainly didn't hurt her career any, and it proved that there's more to her than just being a great actress."

It should be noted that Mr. H is aware that he has been diagnosed as having "grandiose delusions." When he was asked what this meant he said, "That people think what I believe isn't real." When queried about his thoughts regarding what "grandiose" means, he stated, "That you think you have special powers. Like you're supersmart or something. I don't think I'm a genius. I just got a good idea and ran with it."

The defendant's stated responses to potential problems involving social reasoning and judgment were adequate (e.g., if he found a letter in the street, he would take it to the nearest mailbox and deposit it; he would not yell "fire" in a movie theater because it might panic people). Mr. H's operational judgment appears to have been adequate in that he has generally been a responsible employee, has a good driving record, denies ever abusing alcohol or drugs, and has complied with taking psychotropic medications in the past.

PSYCHOLOGICAL TEST RESULTS

On the date of this examination, the defendant was asked to complete the Minnesota Multiphasic Personality Inventory-2 (MMPI-2) in a testing room at the CFP. The MMPI-2 is an actuarial-based, self-report questionnaire that assesses personality and psychopathology. The test consists of 567 statements to which respondents mark each statement as being true or false as it applies to them. When scored, the MMPI-2 yields two types of information. First, the validity scales provide information about how an individual's approach toward taking the test (such as a tendency to exaggerate or minimize psychological symptoms or conditions) may have affected test results. Second, the clinical scales provide a profile of an individual's overall psychological functioning.

Regarding Mr. H, the validity scales indicate that the test results appear to be valid. The defendant appeared to answer test questions in a straightforward, consistent, and nondefensive fashion. The clinical scales are consistent with the clinical impressions derived from the interview in that they portray an individual who is energetic, talkative, enjoys socializing, and endorses some grandiose ideas.

SUMMARY OF CLINICAL IMPRESSIONS

Based on mental health record review, interview, and psychological testing, the clinical picture is that of an individual who exhibits an encapsulated and fixed grandiose delusion that has been resistant to psychotherapy and medication intervention for a documented period of approximately 9 years. Review of mental health records dating from 1989 to 1998 reveal that Mr. H has received trials on an array of psychotropic medications over the years and that such treatment did not eliminate or ameliorate his delusional belief. Mr. H has received the diagnosis of Delusional Disorder, Grandiose Type by each of the mental health professionals who have diagnosed him over the 9-year span. Individuals diagnosed with a Delusional Disorder of the Grandiose Type typically believe that they have some great, but unrecognized, talent, power, insight, or special relationship with a prominent person. In Mr. H's case, he believes that he has developed a software program that can send users a subliminal message that influences their behavior. Although Mr. H's delusional material sometimes intrudes into conversation, he can be easily redirected to return to the topic at hand. Review of the prior mental health records reveals that malingering had been considered and ruled out after being investigated over time during contact with various mental health professionals and through psychological testing. Mr. H does not present with a constellation of symptoms indicative of a formal thought disorder such as schizophrenia (when someone is out of touch with reality and generally exhibits several symptoms such as hallucinations, delusions, and disorganized speech and behavior) or an affective disorder such as Bipolar Disorder (formerly Manic-Depressive Disorder; a disorder of mood that can be manifested by a variety of combinations of elevated mood and/or depression).

LEGAL CRITERIA FOR COMPETENCY TO STAND TRIAL

Concerning the issue of competency to stand trial, MCL 330.2020, Section 1020, states in part that, "A defendant to a criminal charge shall be presumed competent to stand trial. He shall be determined incompetent to stand trial only if he is incapable because of his mental condition of understanding the nature and object of the proceedings against him or of assisting in his defense in a rational manner. The court shall determine the capacity of a defendant to assist in his defense by his ability to perform the tasks reasonably necessary for him to perform in the preparation of his defense and during his trial." Pursuant to MCL 330.2028, Section 1028(2c), the written report to the court "shall contain: The opinion of the center or other facility on the issue of the incompetence of the defendant to stand trial."

COMPETENCY TO STAND TRIAL OPINION

Regarding mental condition, the review of mental health records, the Margate County Jail Transport Form, psychological testing, and the clinical picture presented by the defendant during the interview at the Forensic Center is consistent with the diagnosis of Delusional Disorder, Grandiose Type, which the defendant has received from every mental health professional who has previously diagnosed him. This means that Mr. H is out of touch with reality regarding his belief that he has developed effective subliminal software that has influenced the behavior of people such as Alan Greenspan and Demi Moore. It should also be noted that the defendant's delusion is very speycific and resistant to change but does not pervade the defendant's thinking or impair his daily functioning.

Regarding the nature and object of the proceedings, the review of the Rickster City Police Department Incident Report and the interview at the CFP reveals that the defendant is aware of the charges pending against him, how those charges arose, and of the possible consequences that may ensue if he is convicted. When asked what he is being charged with, Mr. H stated, "Manslaughter and fleeing the police. With everything my lawyer said I could get up to 15 years." The defendant is aware that the main participants involved in a trial are "The judge. You gotta have the judge. The jury . . . and lawyers." When he was asked what he meant by lawyers, he stated, "The prosecutor . . . I think his name is Mr. Heimberg . . . and my lawyer." Further inquiry revealed that Mr. H believes that the prosecutor "wants to find you guilty. To show you did it," whereas the defense attorney "works for me. Wants to prove that I didn't break the law . . . I didn't do it." When he was asked who the defendant is for the case, he replied, "That's me. They're saying I . . . (at this point the defendant provided a narrative of his actions around the time of the alleged offenses) . . . did the crime." The defendant was asked what he knew about "witnesses" and he stated that they "are people that tell what they know about what happened . . . what they say I did." In response to queries about the purpose of a trial, he replied, "They try to convict you." When Mr. H was asked what he meant by "they" try to convict you, he stated, "Actually, the prosecutor. The judge and jury listen to see if you're guilty or not."

The defendant was asked if a jury was always present at a trial and he said, "No. Sometimes it's just the judge." When he was asked when it might be just the judge, he said, "If the lawyer defending you thinks a judge will be fair. A lawyer once told me that if you're guilty, get a jury trial." The defendant is aware that he has a right to a jury trial as indicated by his statement, "If I want to be judged by my peers then they have to give me a jury trial." He reported that if a jury "says you did it, then the judge sentences you to prison for longer or shorter times . . . depending on what he thinks of you." The defendant was then asked if there was a way to avoid a trial and he said, "Don't break the law." Further discussion revealed that the defendant was aware that he could plea bargain and that meant the prosecutor and his attorney would "work out a deal so we didn't have to have a trial . . . I think it means that I would end up with something a lot less than the worst that could happen to me."

Regarding assisting in his defense in a rational manner, the review of the CFP Defense Attorney Pre-Evaluation Assessment Form, the interview at the CFP, and phone contact with the defense attorney, reveals that the defendant is aware that "The court had to give me an attorney" and that his court-appointed attorney is Rodney Aronson. According to the defendant, he has met with Mr. Aronson on one occasion for approximately 45 minutes. He described the meeting as "good . . . he explained stuff to me . . . listened to me, too." When Mr. H was asked if he was worried about his legal predicament he stated, "I don't know if I'm worried . . . that's not going to matter. But I don't want to go to jail . . . I'm planning to help my attorney with anything . . . like cross-examining witnesses."

Further inquiry indicated that the defendant is not minimizing the seriousness of the alleged offenses and possible consequences and that he is motivated to work with his attorney. When he was asked what would happen if he and his attorney disagreed about how to present his case, Mr. H said, "I don't think I'll disagree. He's the lawyer." The defendant did state that he wants to testify but added, "That's not up to me . . . my lawyer might not want me to." The defendant was asked if the prosecutor or judge could force him to testify, and he demonstrated awareness of his right to remain silent by stating, "No. I could take the Fifth like all the others." Regarding his preference for a jury or bench trial, Mr. H said, "That's up to my lawyer." The defendant also indicated that if his attorney wanted to plea bargain, that would be all right "if it makes sense to do. My lawyer and me would need to discuss it . . . it probably would mean a better sentence if the judge wants to be nice."

During this evaluation the defendant was also able to present a detailed version of what occurred in the time period before, during, and after the alleged offenses. He is aware that, in some respects, his version differs from what the police and witnesses say he did. Mr. H also appears able to attend and to concentrate well enough to cogently follow what courtroom participants are saying and asking. Additionally, he indicates a willingness to work with his attorney and to speak up if he hears witnesses say things that "are wrong."

To conclude, based on the aforementioned results, the defendant appears to meet the statutory criteria for being found competent to stand trial. Specifically, Mr. H can participate productively in the courtroom proceedings, including providing a coherent account of the events leading to his arrest, challenging witnesses, and taking his attorney's advice concerning decisions regarding rights, pleas, and defenses. He is aware of the seriousness of the alleged offenses and demonstrates a willingness to defend himself. It must also be noted that the defendant's long-term intransigent grandiose delusion, of his development of subliminal software that can influence those using it, might interfere with trial proceedings. Mr. H does sometimes drift into talking about his delusional material, but he is easily redirected back to the topic being discussed. During the 130-minute forensic interview the defendant needed to be redirected twice. Each time, this examiner asked Mr. H: "Could you please answer the question I asked rather than talk about the subliminal software?" and each time he responded by addressing the original question that was posed.

This examiner had phone contact with the defense attorney on March 6, 2000, for approximately 25 minutes. Mr. Aronson is aware of the potential communication problems with his client. However, he also indicated that his one conversation with Mr. H was productive and that he does not think he would have a problem refocusing his client if he began talking about delusional material. Mr. Aronson also added that he believes the prosecutor and judge would also be able to refocus his client if he began talking about delusional material.

For these reasons, it is the opinion of this examiner that this defendant is capable of understanding the nature and object of the proceedings against him and is also able to assist in the preparation of his defense in a rational manner.

Respectfully submitted,
Steven C. Bank, Ph.D.
Assistant to the Clinical Director
Licensed Psychologist
Consulting Forensic Examiner
Diplomate in Forensic Psychology,
American Board of Professional Psychology

Copies to:
Defense Attorney
Prosecuting Attorney
Court

Teaching Point: How can you use a model to structure the way you write the report?

The following guidelines illustrate how to use a model to structure writing a report:

1. Select the model that is most *relevant* for the referral issue.
2. Include the *content* of the model's elements in the report.
3. Organize report subheadings according to the *chronology* of the model's elements.
4. Modify the model to *fit* the needs of your specific referral.

Relevance. As indicated in the introduction to this case, there are currently only two general models for forensic mental health assessment (although models for specific forensic issues have been developed). If there is no model for the evaluator's specific referral, then the most relevant model available can provide guidance. The appropriate model for Mr. H's case should address Competency to Stand Trial. Grisso's model addresses several different criminal and civil competencies whereas Morse's was developed in the context of civil commitment.

Content. Although Grisso's model was developed from content that is more directly relevant, both of these general models contain the three elements essential for the content of any forensic report: clinical characteristics, legal standards for functional abilities/deficits, and the causal relationship between clinical findings and legal issues. Grisso's six-element model offers more detailed guidelines for the assessment of competence to stand trial, although not all of these elements are represented in separate sections. They may, by contrast, be reflected in the reasoning described in the report. For example, the element of *context* addresses the nature of charges and plea choices, while *interaction* encourages evaluators to consider how the characteristics of a specific defendant and attorney may interact (Is this attorney appropriate for this defendant, given the characteristics of the defendant, the attorney, and the case?).

Chronology. Both models implicitly provide a chronology for report sections: assess mental condition, evaluate functional legal demands, and address the causal connection between mental condition and functional legal demands.

Fit. Evaluators may need to modify either general model to allow it to fit the characteristics of the case. Consider the final elements in Grisso's model: *judgment* and *disposition*. Judgment refers to the decision rendered by the court, while disposition pertains to the legal consequences of adjudicating a defendant incompetent to stand trial. The specific judgment in the case is within the court's domain, which should be acknowledged by the evaluator. The disposition element underscores the importance of the recommendation for treatment for the restoration of relevant deficits (if the evaluator recommends that the individual be considered incompetent to stand trial). It should also be noted that the Grisso and Morse models were not specifically developed as guidelines for structuring reports. This reinforces the importance of modifying models to meet the needs of specific referrals so that the resulting fit works for both evaluators and recipients of reports.

FMHA models can assist the evaluation process in a number of ways: guiding data collection, interpretation, and the communication of results and conclusions. As demonstrated in this case, the relevance, content, chronology, and fit of a model's components can also help evaluators to structure lengthy, detailed forensic reports.

Case 3

Principle: Decline referral when impartiality is unlikely

This principle addresses the nature and value of evaluator impartiality in FMHA, stressing the importance of declining to perform a forensic assessment when impartiality is needed but cannot be achieved. In this context, "impartiality" refers to the evaluator's freedom from significant interference from bias. One kind of bias can result from characteristics or beliefs of the evaluator that may significantly influence the evaluator (e.g., opposition to capital punishment). Another kind of bias refers to situational factors that may influence an evaluator in the direction of a given finding (e.g., a preexisting personal or professional relationship with the litigant).

There are several ways to assess an evaluator's potential impartiality. One test involves the following two-part question, which is structured around the dichotomous outcomes of most legal decisions: (1) what would be the effect on me if the outcome of the case were A, and (2) what would be the effect on me if the outcome of the case were B? Any substantial imbalance in the answers to these two questions suggests that impartiality may be unlikely in the given case (Heilbrun, 2001).

A second test of impartiality uses a fraction termed the "Contrary Quotient" (Colbach, 1981). In the Contrary Quotient, the numerator represents the number of times the evaluator has reached an opinion unfavorable to the referring source, and the denominator is the total number of times an opinion has been requested, yielding a percentage estimate. This ratio is one measure of how well a forensic clinician has managed the pressures that can be exerted by a referring source. However, it can be difficult to interpret without knowing the "true rate" at which an evaluator *should* have reached a contrary finding.

In light of this problem, a third test of impartiality incorporates both the Contrary Quotient and any information regarding available base rates. This two-part test of impartiality can be described as follows: (1) a reasonable balance between favorable and unfavorable results rendered to referring sources, and (2) reasonable consistency with the available base rates.

Support for this principle can be found in several sources of authority. Ethical guidelines applicable to forensic clinicians address impartiality in several ways. The APA *Ethical Principles of Psychology and Code of Conduct* (1992) considers the problems of dual-role relationships and impartiality in the context of forensic assessments as follows:

> In most circumstances, psychologists avoid performing multiple and potentially conflicting roles in forensic matters. When psychologists may be called on to serve in more than one role in a legal proceeding—for example, as consultant or expert for one party or for the court and as a fact witness—they clarify role expectations and the extent of confidentiality in advance to the extent feasible, and thereafter as changes occur in order to avoid compromising their professional judgment and objectivity and in order to avoid misleading others regarding their role. (p. 1610)

The *Specialty Guidelines* (Committee on Ethical Guidelines for Forensic Psychologists, 1991) states that "prior and current personal or professional activities, obligations, and relationships that might produce a conflict of interest" are to be clarified during initial consultation with the legal representative of the party seeking services (p. 658). The *Specialty Guidelines* also addresses impartiality in the context of dual-role relationships, which, according to the *Specialty Guidelines*, forensic clinicians should avoid except in unusual instances: "When it is necessary to provide both evaluation and treatment services to a party in a legal proceeding . . . the forensic psychologist takes reasonable steps to minimize the potential negative effects of these circumstances on the rights of the party, confidentiality, and the process of treatment and evaluation" (p. 659).

There are several distinct roles that can be assumed in forensic assessment, although one role per case is strongly preferred. The value on impartiality varies with each of the roles. In the role of evaluator, impartiality is very important whether the clinician is court-appointed or performing the evaluation at the request of the defense, the prosecution, or the plaintiff. Impartiality is also highly valued when the mental health professional assumes the role of a scientist. In this role, the clinician addresses questions that may be answered by the relevant scientific literature, without reference to the characteristics of the specific litigant. Another possible role that can be played by a mental health professional is that of consultant. As a consultant, the primary purpose of the expert's role is to assist the attorney rather than present information to the court. As such, impartiality is less important and probably not required.[3] A final possible role for a mental health professional is that of fact witness. A fact witness can generally testify regarding direct observations only and cannot offer an opinion or conclusion in the same manner as an expert witness can. If the clinician finds that impartiality is impossible in a particular case (perhaps because of a preexisting professional relationship) and testimony cannot be avoided, one option in some cases involves testifying as a fact witness, thereby avoiding any problems stemming directly from the clinician's lack of impartiality.

In addition to finding support in the relevant ethical guidelines and sources of law, this principle is supported when the standard of practice is considered. Dual-role relationships, and the potential loss of impartiality that may result, are not conducive to high quality forensic assessments. It is difficult or impossible for a forensic clinician to perform an evaluation if the clinician has preexisting inclinations as a result of a dual-role relationship. Therefore, a clinician should avoid performing a forensic assessment in a particular case if the clinician is providing (or has provided) therapeutic services to the individual.

The present case provides an illustration of the importance of declining a referral when impartiality is unlikely. In this case, the forensic clinician was asked by defense counsel to assist in determining whether Mr. Domingo was competent to stand trial under relevant state statutes. The evaluators in this case were in a role in which impartiality is important, given the possibility that the results of this evaluation would be presented to the court in the form of a report and possibly testimony. In such cases, a forensic clinician must not allow personal values or the circumstances of the case to limit impartiality.

In this case, the defendant, Mr. Domingo, was charged in a murder case that had received local and regional publicity. It was not clear at the time of the evaluation whether the prosecution in Mr. Domingo's case would pursue the death penalty, but it remained possible.

The circumstances of such a high-visibility case present the potential for bias of which the forensic clinician must be aware, and decline the referral if reasonable impartiality cannot be maintained. As discussed earlier, the first kind of bias could result from characteristics or beliefs of the evaluator that may significantly influence the evaluator (e.g., vehement opposition to or strong support of capital punishment). The second results from situational factors that may influence an evaluator in the direction of a given finding (e.g., a pre-existing personal or professional relationship with the litigant).

There are a number of situational factors that might influence the impartiality of the forensic clinician in this case. For example, Mr. Domingo had a fairly significant criminal history, and the circumstances of the alleged offense involved an adolescent victim. This combination might create a predisposition toward a certain finding in this case. Other beliefs and characteristics of the forensic clinician could also affect impartiality in this case as well. For example, strong opposition to the death penalty might influence the forensic clinician toward a recommendation that Mr. N was incompetent, making it impossible for him to represent himself at sentencing and possibly preventing the reimposition of the death sentence. A strong belief in the sanctity of all life might lead to a similar conclusion. Conversely, beliefs that chronic offenders, in particular, should be punished severely could lead to the opposite result. The forensic clinician might also have beliefs less related to the specific case that nonetheless might affect impartiality. Over-identification with either the defendant (resulting in the potential minimization of the seriousness of antisocial behavior or the severity of deficits, or the potential exaggeration of the severity or influence of symptoms of mental disorder) or with the victim(s) (possibly resulting in anger and the desire for punishment) can compromise the "emotional balance" that is important for impartiality. Even when such beliefs are attributable to beneficent motives, each has the potential to diminish the reasonable impartiality and balance necessary in FMHA.

FORENSIC EVALUATION

July 1, 1999

Re: Jose Domingo

REFERRAL

Jose Domingo is a 28-year-old Hispanic male (DOB: 10-1-71) who is currently charged with Murder and related offenses. A request for a mental health evaluation to provide the defense with information relevant to competence to stand trial under current New Jersey Code was made by Mr. Domingo's attorney, Sarah Sand, Esquire.

PROCEDURES

Mr. Domingo was evaluated for approximately four hours on 6-1-99 at the Psychiatric Unit of the Corrections Center, where he is currently incarcerated, and again for one hour on 6-22-99 in the official visiting area of the Corrections Center. In addition to clinical interviews on each occasion, Mr. Domingo was administered a standard screening instrument for currently experienced symptoms of mental and emotional disorder (the Brief Symptom Inventory, or BSI). Because Mr. Domingo's command of the English language was unclear prior to beginning the evaluation, Ms. Estelle Thompson provided translation from English to Spanish when necessary during the 6-1-99 part of the evaluation. The following documents, obtained from Ms. Sand's office, were reviewed as part of the evaluation:

1. Notice of Aggravating Circumstances (CP 9809-0569 1/1),
2. Statement of Jose Domingo (9-2-98),
3. Investigation Interview Record of Juan O (9-2-98),
4. Investigation Interview Record of Anna F (9-2-98),
5. Investigation Interview Record of Robert G (9-2-98),
6. Investigation Interview Record of Robert G, Jr. (9-2-98),
7. Investigation Interview Record of David F (9-2-98),
8. Investigation Interview Record of Gil D (9-2-98),
9. Investigation Interview Record of Sam D (9-2-98),
10. Investigation Interview Record of Anna D (9-2-98),
11. Investigation Interview Record of Nelson P (9-2-98),
12. Investigation Interview Record of Wilson C, Jr. (9-2-98),
13. Investigation Interview Record of Jason Q (9-2-98),
14. Investigation Interview Record of Francisco P (9-2-98),
15. Investigation Interview Record of Hector M (9-2-98),
16. Investigation Interview Record of Shelly T (9-2-98),
17. Investigation Interview Record of Miguel D (9-2-98),
18. Investigation Interview Record of Dorothy E (undated),
19. Investigation Interview Record of Mary D (9-2-98),
20. Investigation Interview Record of Lara S (9-2-98),
21. Investigation Interview Record of Maria P (9-2-98),
22. Investigation Interview Record of Officer Kim Z (9-2-98),
23. Investigation Interview Record of Officer Karen Zk (9-2-98),

24. Investigation Interview Record of Officer Sean C (9-2-98),
25. Investigation Interview Record of Officer Delilah C (9-3-98),
26. Investigation Interview Record of Officer Ed M (9-2-98),
27. Investigation Interview Record of Officer Mary S (9-2-98),
28. Camden Police Department Property Receipts (9-2-98),
29. Camden Police Department Incident Reports (9-2-98),
30. Camden Police Department Investigation Report (9-2-98),
31. Correctional Mental Health Services Program Inpatient Discharge Summary (10-19-98),
32. Camden Police Department Mobile Crime Detection Service Report (9-30-98), and
33. Court History (9-24-98).

Prior to the evaluation, Mr. Domingo was notified about the purpose of the evaluation and the associated limits on confidentiality. He appeared to have difficulty understanding the basic purpose of the evaluation and reporting back his understanding that he would be evaluated and that a written report would be submitted to his attorney. He also appeared to have difficulty understanding that the report could be used in his sentencing hearing and, if it were, copies would be provided to the prosecution and the court. The possible reasons for such difficulty will be discussed at length in this report. It should be noted, however, that this notification was delivered several times in Spanish, after Mr. Domingo indicated that he would prefer to converse in Spanish in the beginning of the evaluation.

RELEVANT HISTORY

Historical information was obtained from the collateral sources described above as well as from Mr. Domingo himself. Whenever possible, the consistency of the factual information provided by Mr. Domingo was assessed through the use of multiple sources. In general, Mr. Domingo had significant difficulty providing detailed historical information. He had a tendency to respond very minimally to questions, and often said "I don't know" or "No se" in response to questions that were relatively simple and straightforward. If ad-

ditional collateral information is obtained prior to Mr. Domingo's court date, a supplemental report will be filed.

Jose Domingo was born in Puerto Rico on October 1, 1971. According to Mr. Domingo, he moved to Camden with his family after his father died. Mr. Domingo reported that he has lived in Camden since leaving Puerto Rico. Mr. Domingo indicated that he was approximately 12 years old when his family moved to Camden. Mr. Domingo reported that he has three brothers (ages 27, 26, and 21) and one sister (age 27). Mr. Domingo had difficulty remembering the ages of his siblings and indicated that he was not sure if the ages he provided were correct. According to Mr. Domingo, his mother abuses drugs and alcohol. He also noted that his mother's boyfriend had a "drinking problem" when he resided with the Domingo family.

When Mr. Domingo was asked about his educational background, he reported that he attended elementary school in Puerto Rico. Mr. Domingo denied academic, behavioral, and attendance problems during elementary school. He did note that he stopped attending elementary school after second grade when he was approximately 8 years old. He attributed this to the death of his father. According to Mr. Domingo, he started in sixth or seventh grade after moving to Camden. Although Mr. Domingo reported attending numerous secondary schools, he was unable to elaborate beyond stating that he was enrolled in English as Second Language classes. Mr. Domingo denied all special education involvement. Although Mr. Domingo denied behavioral difficulties during his secondary and high school education, he did admit to truancy and academic problems. Specifically, Mr. Domingo indicated that he rarely attended school. Mr. Domingo also stated that he failed most of his classes and repeated a number of grades. He was unable to elaborate further. According to Mr. Domingo, he attended Kennedy High School for ninth grade when he was approximately 17 or 18 years old, and also indicated that he dropped out of Kennedy sometime in 1991 before completing ninth grade. When Mr. Domingo was asked why he dropped out of high school, he stated that he wanted to "hang out with my friends." Official academic records were not available at the time this report was written.

Mr. Domingo reported a significant psychiatric

history. According to Mr. Domingo, his mother took him to see a psychiatrist at a local mental health clinic at "Y and First streets" shortly after the family arrived in Camden. The Investigation Interview Record of Jose Domingo is consistent with this statement and indicates that Mr. Domingo told police that he was receiving treatment from "a doctor at Y and First cause sometimes I can't sleep." Mr. Domingo stated that he began receiving SSI disability payments because of his "nerves" in 1992, and that he was receiving payments up until his current incarceration. Mr. Domingo was able to provide a limited family psychiatric history. Mr. Domingo reported that his mother was hospitalized approximately 2 years ago in the Psychiatric Unit of Xavier Hospital. He was unable to elaborate further. Similarly, Mr. Domingo indicated that his younger brother takes medication for his "nerves." Again, he could not elaborate further. According to Mr. Domingo, his mother and brother receive SSI disability because of their "nerves."

According to the Correctional Mental Health Services Program Inpatient Discharge Summary (Discharge Summary), Mr. Domingo was referred for admission to the Psychiatric Unit of the Corrections Center on the basis of an involuntary petition completed on 9-12-98. According to the Discharge Summary, the petition for involuntary commitment stated that Mr. Domingo put a sheet around his neck and tied it to the top bunk in an apparent suicide attempt. The Discharge Summary elaborates that Mr. Domingo voluntarily agreed to hospitalization after acknowledging that he had attempted suicide. According to the Discharge Summary, on admission (9-13-98), Mr. Domingo was sad, hopeless, and worried; avoided eye contact; exhibited decreased speech and motor activity; seemed withdrawn, uncooperative, and threatening; demonstrated poor insight and judgement; and reported antisocial attitudes. The Discharge Summary noted that at admission, Mr. Domingo was fully oriented and did not admit to hallucinations or delusions. Initially, Mr. Domingo was placed on suicide precautions and started on the antidepressant Sinequan. According to the Discharge Summary, Mr. Domingo began to admit hearing voices that called his name at night approximately 1 week after his admission. In addition, the Discharge Summary indicates that Mr.

Domingo began to pull hair out of his head after being admitted. The Discharge Summary notes that Mr. Domingo reported that this was not the first time he had pulled hair out of his head. According to the Discharge Summary, Mr. Domingo was placed on Luvox on 9-21-98 to help prevent hair pulling. Similarly, the Discharge Summary indicates that Mr. Domingo's dosage of the antipsychotic medication Haldol was also increased on 9-21-98 because Mr. Domingo continued to complain of hearing voices at night. According to the Discharge Summary, on 10-1-98 Mr. Domingo's antidepressant Sinequan dosage was increased, and his dosage of Haldol was increased again on 10-8-98. The Discharge Summary reports that Mr. Domingo became stable enough to be considered for discharge from the psychiatric unit to protective custody after this final increase in his dosage of Haldol. According to the Discharge Summary, Mr. Domingo's condition had improved in certain regards when he was released into protective custody in the prison on 10-14-98. Specifically, the Discharge Summary indicates that Mr. Domingo was no longer suicidal and was not exhibiting paranoid or assaultive ideation. The Discharge summary indicates that Mr. Domingo was still reporting hearing voices at night when he was discharged into protective custody. The Discharge Summary provides the following discharge diagnosis: Depressive Disorder NOS (296.0), Psychosis NOS, rule out Borderline Personality Disorder, and Marijuana and Alcohol Dependence/Abuse. According to the Discharge Summary, Mr. Domingo is currently taking the following medications: Haldol (10mg/daily), Cogentin (2mg/daily), Sinequan (125mg/daily), and Mellaril (nonformulary version of Luvox 50mg/daily).

Mr. Domingo reported a limited history of substance abuse. He reported that he has used marijuana, alcohol, and Xanax. Mr. Domingo reported that he started using these drugs when he was 24 years old. He reported that he occasionally smoked marijuana with friends and family. When asked to elaborate on the level of usage, Mr. Domingo stated that he would only take "three puffs" approximately once a week. Similarly, Mr. Domingo denied significant alcohol use. He stated that he would share a "forty" with family members approximately once a week. Mr. Domingo also reported that he occasionally used Xanax. He was unable to specify the frequency or quantity of use. Although Mr. Domingo denied a significant history of substance abuse, he indicated that he received court mandated alcohol abuse treatment as a result of a previous arrest.

Mr. Domingo stated that he has never been employed. According to Mr. Domingo, he received welfare until he qualified for SSI disability in 1992. He also reported that his family provided him with financial support. Mr. Domingo was unable to identify any vocational or educational goals.

According to Mr. Domingo, prior to his arrest for the current charges, he had been arrested on two other occasions. He reported that his first arrest, which occurred sometime in 1993, was for theft. Mr. Domingo reported that he served 18 months for this offense. Mr. Domingo reported that his second arrest occurred sometime in 1994 or 1995, when he was charged with mail theft and assault. He similarly reported that he served 18 months and was placed on probation that included participation in an alcohol abuse treatment program. The Court History notes the following arrest history:

1. (5-11-93): Robbery, Theft, Receiving Stolen Property, Criminal Conspiracy, Possession Instruments of Crime, Possession Instrument of Crime—Weapon, Prohibited Offensive Weapon, Reckless Endangerment, Terroristic Threats, Aggravated Assault, Simple Assault.
2. (8-9-93): Theft, Criminal Conspiracy, Receiving Stolen Property.
3. (8-5-94): Reckless Endangerment, Corrupting Minor, Simple Assault.
4. (8-17-95): Robbery, Theft, Receiving Stolen Property, Criminal Conspiracy.

Although there are no details, the Court History suggests that Mr. Domingo received court ordered psychiatric assessments on 3-29-94 and 6-29-93.

CURRENT CLINICAL CONDITION

Mr. Domingo presented on both occasions as a Hispanic male with a medium build who appeared his stated age. He was dressed in prison garb and was well groomed when seen for the evaluation on 6-1-99 at the Psychiatric Unit of the Corrections Center, where he is currently incarcerated, and on 6-22-99, in the official visiting area of the Corrections Center. During the first evaluation, Mr. Domingo at first appeared reluctant to participate in the evaluation; he refused to make eye contact with the evaluators, preferring to stare down at the floor. A bald patch of skin was noted in Mr. Domingo's otherwise full beard. With encouragement and reassurance Mr. Domingo became more cooperative, and he remained cooperative and polite throughout the rest of the evaluation. His speech was clear, coherent, and relevant, but consistently sparse and often insufficient to answer a question. He tended to reply "no se" or "I don't know" fairly quickly, and needed encouragement to respond at greater length. Indeed, Mr. Domingo did not respond at length to most questions asked of him without further questioning and encouragement. Even with such additional questioning and encouragement, Mr. Domingo responded in short, clipped sentences and had difficulty responding to questions beyond simple phrases and yes or no answers. Similarly, Mr. Domingo was unable to provide detailed historical information and frequently indicated that he could not remember or did not know. He appeared to give reasonable effort to the tasks involved. His capacity for attention and concentration appeared limited, but adequate, and he was able to focus reasonably well on a series of tasks during the 4-hour evaluation without becoming visibly distracted.

During the first two hours of the 6-1-99 evaluation, all questioning of Mr. Domingo was conducted by having the question translated into Spanish, and then having his reply translated into English. However, it became clear that Mr. Domingo's tendency to say "I don't know" was less a reflection of his lack of understanding than his very significant suspiciousness toward the evaluators. Mr. Domingo appeared about as likely to say "No se" in response to a question in Spanish as he did "I don't know" to a question posed in English. Therefore, much of the questioning during the third and fourth hours of the 6-1-99 evaluation was done in English, which allowed the evaluators to follow up much more quickly and with greater encouragement to his brief answers. This strategy actually allowed us to obtain somewhat more information than we had previously, so it was clear that Mr. Domingo's English is adequate to allow him to converse in and understand basic important areas related to his case.

During the second (6-22-99) evaluation, we conducted the question without a Spanish interpreter. Mr. Domingo's responding was again sparse and limited, and he again tended to reply by saying "I don't know." He was able to respond differently, or at greater length, to some of the questions when they were repeated and when he was encouraged to respond. However, his tendency toward sparseness and saying "I don't know" was again evident. Under the circumstances, it would appear that these two evaluative sessions may reflect Mr. Domingo's current functioning and capacity for communication in a reasonably good way. It was important to obtain information from other sources on historical matters, however, because Mr. Domingo often did not provide sufficient information when asked about his past.

Mr. Domingo's mood throughout both sessions was largely subdued and neutral, and he showed little emotional variability. He did appear suspicious, particularly in the first part of the initial evaluation session, but seemed to express this through withdrawal and non-responsiveness rather than emotional expressiveness. Mr. Domingo appeared to have only a rudimentary understanding of his own emotional state. He was correctly oriented to time, place, and person. Overall level of intellectual functioning was not formally measured, but appeared to be in the Borderline range.

During the clinical interview, Mr. Domingo at first did not report experiencing any perceptual disturbances (auditory or visual hallucinations), although his train of thought was somewhat muddled and confused at times. Later in the initial evaluation, however, Mr. Domingo indicated that he still sometimes hears sounds or voices when he is by himself in his cell, but could not elaborate. Mr. Domingo also did not report experiencing delusions (bizarre ideas with no possible basis in reality) during the clinical interview. Mr. Domingo also acknowledged a history of auditory hallucinations. According to Mr. Domingo, he began to experience hearing voices when he was relatively young. He was unable to provide an exact age. On a structured inventory of symptoms of mental and emotional disorders (the BSI), Mr.

Domingo reported the presence of various symptoms. Some of the symptoms reported by Mr. Domingo involved nervousness or shakiness inside; feeling others are to blame for most of his troubles; feeling that others cannot be trusted; feeling blue; feeling that people are unfriendly or dislike him; nausea or upset stomach; feeling that he is watched or talked about by others; trouble falling asleep; spells of terror or panic; feeling nervous when left alone; and restlessness. Although Mr. Domingo reported experiencing these symptoms, he had difficulty elaborating on most of the items that he endorsed. He consistently identified nervousness and difficulty sleeping as a source of continuing discomfort. Mr. Domingo also appeared to have difficulty quantifying the level of discomfort that he was experiencing. Further questioning, rephrasing, and encouragement did not help Mr. Domingo provide more detailed information.

COMPETENCE TO STAND TRIAL

Mr. Domingo was questioned in detail regarding his understanding of his current legal situation and his capacity to assist counsel in his own defense on 6-1-99. He indicated that the charge against him is that he "killed someone." His initial response when asked about possible penalties was that he could serve "10 to 20," although he was not able to elaborate on whether he could receive a more serious sentence. His description of the respective roles of judge, jury, prosecutor, and defense attorney in the adversarial context was fairly limited. He reported that the defense attorney is "on my side," but could not elaborate on the responsibilities or roles of defense counsel. He stated that there are "about 12" people on a jury, but did not accurately describe the jury's main functions. He was even more limited in his description of the judge and the prosecutor; when asked a series of questions about the respective roles of each, Mr. Domingo only replied, "I don't know." It would appear, therefore, that Mr. Domingo has some knowledge of his current legal situation that is generally limited to the nature of his charges and their approximate severity. His understanding of the respective roles of the judge and the prosecutor is difficult to judge, but may be significantly impaired; it should be observed that Mr. Domingo was not simply being uncooperative or consistently underreporting all knowledge, since he did offer something about his understanding of the defense attorney and jury. It is important the Mr. Domingo's basic awareness of the roles of court personnel be better, however, to allow him to participate meaningfully in his defense, particularly given the seriousness of his current charges.

There are even more significant limitations on Mr. Domingo's current capacities to assist counsel in his own defense. As described elsewhere in this report, Mr. Domingo's current communication style involves very sparse language and an extreme difficulty in trusting others, both of which appear related to his psychotic disorder. Significant improvements in these areas have been observed during the last 6 months—Mr. Domingo is described by staff as less suspicious, for example—but some problems remain in his capacity to trust his attorney sufficiently to communicate with her as would be needed. Mr. Domingo indicated that he "liked" Ms. Sand, his defense counsel, but could not describe the substance of any of their conversations. Consultation with Ms. Sand indicates that she has experienced significant difficulties in communicating with Mr. Domingo, which she attributed at the time to a low level of intellectual functioning. Mr. Domingo's difficulty in communicating with his defense attorney would also impair his ability to testify in his own behalf, if necessary. It was extremely difficult to get Mr. Domingo to provide the level of detail in a response that would probably be needed in testimony without repeated follow-up questions and encouragement.

Mr. Domingo presented as quiet and withdrawn throughout both evaluative sessions, and would probably behave in a similar fashion during a hearing or trial. He would be unlikely to disrupt the proceedings with outbursts or otherwise unacceptable behavior. However, he also seems unlikely to be able to follow the proceedings and their meaning with much understanding. This is related to a certain ongoing confusion in his thinking, involving both communicating and understanding information, that is a part of his disorder.

Mr. Domingo was not able to spontaneously describe any of his options for plea. When these were provided to him, and he was asked about the meaning of the pleas of guilty, not guilty, no contest, and not guilty by reason of insanity, Mr. Domingo did not accurately identify any component, meaning, or consequence of any of these pleas. It is possible that he would accept a recommendation from his attorney to enter a plea (although this is not certain, given the problems described in the previous paragraph). However, it is also reasonably clear that he does not have even a basic appreciation of what each plea might mean and what its consequences would be. Moreover, it would be impossible for him to rationally consider his options and select a plea that is best for him under the circumstances, given his lack of awareness of the consequences of each of the plea options.

CONCLUSIONS AND RECOMMENDATIONS

In the opinion of the undersigned, based on all of the above, Mr. Domingo

1. suffers from a severe mental disorder characterized by suspiciousness, withdrawal, confused thinking, limited capacity for communication, and auditory hallucinations; this disorder is currently in partial remission;
2. nonetheless, this disorder and its symptoms significantly impair Mr. Domingo's current capacities to understand his legal situation and particularly to communicate with his attorney and make a rational decision about a possible plea.
3. It is recommended that Mr. Domingo be adjudicated incompetent to stand trial, and be committed to a secure inpatient mental health unit where he may receive continued medication and other mental health treatment to address the symptoms of his disorder.
4. It is also recommended that he receive at least twice-weekly counseling from a Spanish-speaking mental health professional focusing on his current legal circumstances, particularly his relevant communication and decision making.
5. Finally, it is recommended that Mr. Domingo be re-evaluated after a period of approximately 3 months to determine whether such treatment has significantly

improved his current deficits in these relevant areas.

Kirk Heilbrun, Ph.D.
Consulting Psychologist

Thank you for the opportunity to evaluate Jose Domingo.

Geff Marczyk, MS, MA
MCP Hahnemann Graduate Student

Teaching Point: What strategies can be used for remaining as impartial as possible in high-visibility cases?

There are a number of strategies that may help the forensic clinician to remain reasonably impartial in high-visibility cases. First, it is important to establish and maintain professional boundaries with the referring attorney. Ideally, interactions should only be for business purposes, with social contact limited or avoided completely. In the courtroom, the forensic practitioner should maintain an appropriate professional demeanor when interacting with counsel and not sit at counsel's table. Finally, the forensic clinician should try to keep from becoming emotionally invested in "winning" the case, instead focusing on presenting his or her own material as effectively as possible.

Maintaining impartiality in communicating the results of the FMHA is also important, and the forensic clinician should avoid various pitfalls. First, the forensic clinician should not provide preliminary opinions; conclusions should be reached and conveyed only after the evaluation has been completed. Second, when communicating the results of the assessment, whether verbally or in writing, the forensic practitioner should avoid emotionally charged language and also stay away from exaggeration (e.g., "absolutely," "unquestionably," "totally," "incredibly," "unbelievably"). Either kind of language can adversely affect the forensic clinician's credibility and perceived fairness, as well as create pressure to exaggerate or otherwise distort other aspects of the evaluation's results.

Media involvement is common in high-visibility cases, and the forensic practitioner may need to take additional steps to ensure the appearance of impartiality when the media are prominently involved. As a general rule, it is prudent to avoid speaking with the media about the case entirely. If offering some kind of statement would present a reasonable alternative to running a gauntlet of cameras and microphones, however, then the forensic clinician may consider an alternative. After testimony has been concluded, a short statement can be prepared and delivered. Such a statement should be relevant to the kind of case at hand but provide no details about the immediate case itself. When a statement like this is delivered, and no subsequent questions are taken, then something is provided for both print and television media, but the forensic clinician does not risk saying something that may later be regretted.

Involvement in high-visibility cases can be very stressful, and the forensic clinician should try to minimize the impact of this stress on his or her professional and personal functioning. Diversions should be used to keep from feeling consumed and overwhelmed by the case. Generally, these diversions could include some form of physical, social, or intellectual activity that has nothing to do with the case. Finally, it is important to retain a larger perspective. As Red Barber once said, whatever "disaster" may occur on one day, the sun will rise right on time the next.

Case 4

Principle: Attribute information to sources

The communication of the results of FMHA is an important step in the forensic assessment process. Whether such communication is written or oral, the value and influence of FMHA is affected by the way in which the results are conveyed. The attribution of information to sources is one of the most important elements of the effective communication of FMHA results. In FMHA, it is important to assess the consistency of factual information across multiple sources of information. However, because legal consumers are understandably interested in the source(s) of such information, it is essential that the forensic clinician cite any sources that provide the basis for the information, impressions, and reasoning presented to the court.

Although this principle is not directly addressed by either of the two major ethics codes for psychology and psychiatry—*Ethical Principles of Psychologists and Code of Conduct* (APA, 1992) and *Principles of Medical Ethics with Annotation Especially Applicable to Psychiatry* (American Psychiatric Association, 1995), respectively—the specialized forensic guidelines for both psychology and psychiatry contain applicable language. The *Specialty Guidelines for Forensic Psychologists* (Committee on Ethical Guidelines for Forensic Psychologists, 1991) emphasizes the importance of detailed documentation in FMHA: "Forensic psychologists have an obligation to document and be prepared to make available, subject to court order or the rules of evidence, all data that form the basis for their evidence or services" (p. 661). Further, when a forensic clinician uses information or data that have been gathered by third parties, the *Specialty Guidelines* emphasizes the importance of citing the source of the information or data: "When a forensic psychologist relies upon data or information gathered by others, the origins of those data are clarified in any professional product" (p. 662). Finally, the *Specialty Guidelines* directly addresses the issue of attribution in this way:

> Forensic psychologists, by virtue of their competence and rules of discovery, actively disclose all sources of information obtained in the course of their professional ser-

vices; they actively disclose which information from which source was used in formulating a particular written product or oral testimony. (p. 665)

The *Ethical Guidelines for the Practice of Forensic Psychology* (AAPL, 1995) also addresses the issue of attribution:

> Practicing forensic psychiatrists enhance the honesty and striving for objectivity of their work by basing their forensic reports and their forensic testimony on all the data available to them. They communicate the honesty of their work, efforts to attain objectivity, and the soundness of their clinical opinion by distinguishing, to the extent possible, between verified and unverified information as well as between clinical "facts," "inferences," and "impressions." (p. 3)

The distinction between "verified and unverified information" cannot reasonably be made without an indication of the source(s) of the information.

No legal authority or empirical research relevant to this principle could be located. There is also relatively little in the standard of practice literature regarding this principle. Still, it is reasonable to consider the attribution of information to sources to be a key element of a well-written report, particularly when the report contains conflicting information obtained from different sources. When this occurs, it is important that the forensic clinician clearly indicate the respective sources of the conflicting information.

The present report is a good illustration of this principle. It describes the results of an evaluation of the defendant's competence to stand trial. The forensic clinician obtained information from numerous sources, including an interview with the defendant, formal testing (the Interdisciplinary Fitness Interview-Revised, the Maudsley Assessment of Delusions Scale, and the Scale for Comprehensive Assessment of Symptoms and History), and collateral documents. Given the numerous sources of information that were considered, it is easy to see the conceptual and practical value of attribution to sources.

Throughout the report, the forensic clinician repeatedly refers to the source(s) of the information being presented. For example, he often attributes information to "Ms. A's self-report," "psychiatric records," "medical records," and "discharge summaries." Where appropriate, he indicates which important records were unavailable when the report was written. It is noteworthy that his attribution of information to third-party sources is consistent with the previously discussed standard for forensic psychologists described in the *Specialty Guidelines* (Committee on Ethical Guidelines for Forensic Psychologists, 1991) regarding the importance of citing the source of the information or data gathered by third parties.

Such attribution helps the court to evaluate the relevance and reliability of the information. It also helps the attorney presenting this evaluation to do so more effectively, and it provides the opposing attorney with a fair opportunity to challenge these findings. Relevance and reliability, two of the cornerstones of evidence law, could not be assessed as readily without attribution of information to sources.

RE: Ms. A

Dear Judge H:

Pursuant to court order, Ms. A was evaluated on 3/24/99 and 4/2/99 at the Mental Health Unit of the Denver Metro Jail. As defined by Colorado Code §77-15-5 *et seq.*, this report details a variety of issues related to Ms. A's competency to proceed. The *Pate*-level doubt as to Ms. A's competency to proceed was raised by her attorney, whose concern was that Ms. A was extremely psychotic, had great difficulty concentrating and remembering aspects of the criminal behavior that is alleged, and appeared unable to appreciate the nature of the mental illness that might be involved in her possible defense. Ms. A was informed of the limited confidentiality of pretrial forensic examinations and was informed (a) that I was not conducting an interview in a therapeutic context, (b) that copies of my report would be sent to defense counsel, the prosecuting attorney, and the judge in this case, and (c) that information that might revealed about the case in the context of this interview could not be entered at trial on the issue of guilt, unless that right was waived by introducing mental state evidence at trial. Ms. A consented to these conditions, and I had previously obtained consent from her attorney to videotape these interviews.

Ms. A was interviewed in the medical conference room of the Mental Health Unit. She was alert and cooperative during both interviews, although it was clear that her psychotic symptomatology was active and intrusive during both interviews. Thus, she was extremely tense and "scared" during both interviews, partially as a function of her situation and partially on account of hallucinatory experiences, especially about the guards outside the room reading her mind, the special meaning that she attached to various noises she could hear, and the voices commenting on me. (As described in detail below, the voices punish her in various ways and also command her to punish others—as I began to establish a level of contact and communication with her, the voices began to urge her to assault me because "you know what's going on.") I terminated my first interview with her early because of her increasing agitation in respect of the commands from the voices to attack me. On account of prior episodes of assaultiveness on the tier, the correctional staff would not unshackle Ms. A, even though I gave my consent. Thus, she was interviewed while wearing both hand and ankle shackles.

SOURCES OF INFORMATION RELIED ON

In conducting this evaluation, I had available to me the following records and reports:

1. Videotape of my interviews, 3/24/99 and 4/2/99
2. Handwritten note by Ms. A with examples of words and phrases spoken to her by her voices
3. UD Emergency Records, 9/19/94; 1/17/98; 12/22/97
4. UA Discharge summary, 1/22/98 and detailed hospitalization records
5. Progress notes, Denver County Jail, various dates
6. Competency evaluation, dated 1/29/97, Dr. G
7. Criminal Information and detailed police reports and discovery
8. East Valley Mental Health records, various dates, 10/21/96–7/21/98

ASSESSMENT TECHNIQUES EMPLOYED AND DATES

I interviewed Ms. A as described above. In addition, the portions of the Interdisciplinary Fitness Interview-Revised (IFI-R), the Maudsley Assessment of Delusions Scale, and the Scale for Comprehensive Assessment of Symptoms and History were administered.

CURRENT CHARGE(S)

Ms. A is charged with aggravated murder and several counts of attempted criminal homicide and aggravated assault related to a series of shootings at WHYY on 2/10/98. The details of those charges were obtained from a comprehensive review of materials supplied to defense counsel.

RELEVANT FORENSIC AND CRIMINAL HISTORY

Ms. A was arrested on 10/7/96 for stalking, disorderly conduct, and assault on a police officer for events that transpired relative to her delusional belief that a local radio station was broadcasting sexual materials about her (see below for other details). Apparently, Ms. A had staked out the radio station for some time, had threatened people at the station, and had refused to leave the vicinity of the station. When the police returned after she came back to the area of the radio station, a fight with the police occurred and she was found to have a knife in her pocket. Ms. A was seen by at least one forensic examiner, Dr. G, who found her to be schizophrenic but "marginally competent" to proceed. Dr. G expressed grave concern about Ms. A and her need for future supervision but opined that she was not currently a danger to herself or others. While records are unclear, it appears that Ms. A was placed on probation following these incidents and followed by East Valley Mental Health. On 12/5/96, Ms. A came to the attention of the University of Denver (UD) because she appeared at their public relations office, was overtly disorganized, and was seeking help with respect to being harassed by Stevie Wonder and a local disc jockey. While this was reported to East Valley, a civil commitment of Ms. A was not deemed appropriate. It is unclear from the available records when, or under what circumstances, Ms. A was no longer deemed to be on probation or under supervision.

In December of 1997, Ms. A was brought to the UD emergency room as detailed below and subsequently committed on 1/2/98, for a period of 90 days for events related to her threatening to kill an FBI agent for not helping her stop the threats and harassment she perceived to be going on against her (see below).

RELEVANT SOCIAL AND DEVELOPMENTAL HISTORY

Ms. A was born in China and moved with her family to the United States at an early age. She reported no known birth complications or eventful medical or psychological problems at an early age. She denied any history of head injury. She has been socialized in American culture and appears to be fluent in English, although she experiences her auditory hallucinations in both English and what she believes to be Chinese.[4]

Ms. A's report of her early childhood mental state implies that her symptoms of being harassed and persecuted began in about the eighth grade when she refused to respond to a note from another student. She believes that this student began to spread rumors about her and that others started to harass and criticize her for her being "a snob" (about interpersonal relationships with the opposite sex). This appears to be the earliest memory she has of the origins of her pattern of thinking about this issue. Ms. A reported[5] that she did quite well in school and liked various topics until about the tenth grade when she began to experience increasing social anxiety and felt increasingly harassed and persecuted at school by her classmates who teased her about her name, placed signs on her back (e.g., "kick me"), and talked about her behind her back. She reported being increasing socially isolated, although she did socialize with members of her own family, and remembers liking sports ("I was a tomboy")—however, she denied taking part in sports with other children, preferring to play with her brother. She denied any memory of early fantasy playmates. The drop in her grades around this time corresponds to her increasing social isolation and fearfulness, as well as distrust of the motives of others. According to her report, Ms. A did graduate from high school.

Ms. A was very hesitant to talk about her sexual development, and it became clear when asked about this that sexual thoughts and feelings are intimately tied to her delusional system, particularly that the voices are spreading her ideas about masturbation "around the country." One of her code words is "master," and this means that the voices are either urging her to masturbate or telling others that she does or that she should "master for the whole nation," that is, masturbate for the whole country or that the whole country knows that she does [or both]. She is very reluctant/unable to speak about some of her internal ideas, both because of intense feelings of privacy and because the voices threaten to punish her if she does.

Ms. A attended university for a short period of time but was forced to drop out because of her increasing feelings of being harassed and stalked by others. She dates her first clear acknowledgment of hearing voices to this time period, but agreed that the thoughts in her head from before had probably been voices for some period of time preceding this. She also briefly worked polishing jewelry but had to stop because of problems with concentration and the increasing intrusiveness of her voices and her concern that others were out to harm her, talk nastily about her, and "threaten and terrorize" her. She went to Los Angeles for a brief period of time to try to escape from the voices; they followed her. It is unclear whether or not her first hospitalization might have occurred in Los Angeles, and this ought to be pursued.

PSYCHOSOCIAL AND MEDICATION TREATMENT HISTORY

On 9/19/94, Ms. A was brought by her mother to the emergency room of UD. She was complaining of derogatory voices, inability to sleep, suicidal ideation, "burning in her head," and concerns that others were talking about her and making fun of her. A referral to East Valley Mental Health was made, and there is a reference to a prior evaluation 5 days before, but no further details. Ms. A reported a long history associated with these symptoms, but no details are given in the record. Records indicate that she was seen from 9/23/94 to 4/24/96 at East Valley Mental Health and treated primarily with Mellaril and an antidepressive medication. During this period of time, she complained about "voices in her head," "burning in her head," feeling that other people were out to get her, depression, and fear that she was going crazy like her sisters. She was discharged from care at East Valley Mental Health when she went to California (Ms. A describes this as an attempt to flee the voices). Her discharge summary indicates some improvement in functioning but is unclear as to level of disturbance at discharge.

In October of 1996, following her arrest for stalking and threatening at the local radio station, she was again seen at East Valley from 10/21/96 until 6/16/97. It is unclear what treatment was provided beyond medication (Zoloft, Trilafon, Mellaril), or what kinds of risk assessments were performed beyond a note that Ms. A admitted to hearing voices telling her to hurt others. It is noted only that Ms. A is schizophrenic, modestly improved, and noncompliant with treatment. The last note entry indicates that Ms. A had been increasingly aggressive over the past week and that her mother intended to take her to the Northern State Hospital where her sister was being treated. No follow-up appears to have occurred. As noted above, on 12/2/96, Valley Mental Health was contacted by the University of Denver about Ms. A, but, beyond a note that commitment did not seem appropriate, there is no indication of further action or supervision.

On 12/22/97, the staff of East Valley Mental Health initiated emergency commitment on Ms. A, following her threat to kill an FBI agent because the FBI was not taking steps to protect her and give her legal services to stop a local radio station disc jockey and Hollywood music stars such as Stevie Wonder from mentally harassing her and talking about her sexually over the airwaves (she apparently had visited the FBI office on a daily basis for several days prior to her threat to harm an FBI agent for not protecting her[6]). She was extremely psychotic and disorganized as well as assaultive in the emergency room, requiring multiple staff to restrain her. She was seen again in the UD emergency room with similar problems on 1/17/98, although it was also noted that the psychotropic medications she had been given in the interim had not stopped the voices or the feelings of being harmed. She reported continuing to feel that various persons were "stalking" her and that her mind was "racing," and that her head felt either "icy" or "burning."

Following a court commitment, Ms. A was hospitalized from 12/22/97 to 1/22/98. She was discharged as somewhat improved over the course of the hospitalization, although it was clear that she still was bothered by voices, which were only "somewhat muted." Her treatment by psychotropic medications was (and is) complicated by a series of side effects involving both anticholinergic and tardive symptoms. During my examination of her, the most prominent effects were agitation and rapid mouth movements. It will be important for future treating psychiatrists to evaluate her tardive symptoms most carefully and to move her away from medications that exacerbate these symptoms as quickly as possible. She will prove, however, to be a very difficult individual to treat because she still shows such signs and symptoms, even though her current medications are much less potent in producing those effects than treatments she has received in the past, and she still shows manifest side effects.

Following her commitment, Ms. A was seen at UD and then again at East Valley Mental Health until July of 1998. Records of exactly when and under what circumstances her commitment was discontinued were not available to me.[7]

CURRENT PSYCHOPATHOLOGICAL STATUS

The current psychopathological status of Ms. A may be best summarized by the following table based on the Brief Psychiatric Rating Scale-Revised:

Domain	Rating	Comment/Observation
Somatic Concern	2	Some concern over dry mouth
Anxiety	7	Very anxious, not only realistically, but also based on psychotic concerns over threats from others around her as well as voices telling her that she will now be executed
Emotional Withdrawal	1	
Conceptual Disorganization	4	While classic thought disorder not demonstrated, she is easily derailed by her internal voices and often misinterprets questions in terms of her delusional system; often distracted in terms of flow of thought by external events
Guilt Feelings	5	Quite concerned, appropriately, about what she did; also voicing indications that she didn't mean to do it, had no choice, it was "her," and so forth
Tension	6	Manifest extreme tension, but complicated by clear side effects from medication and medication history
Mannerisms	1	
Grandiosity	1	
Depressive Mood	6	Extremely tearful and depressed
Hostility	1	
Suspiciousness	5	Repeatedly voices concern over both the hostile intentions of others around her and in recent past
Hallucinations	7	Constant but variable in intensity auditory and command hallucinations (content described elsewhere)
Motor/Speech	1	Except for effects of medication
Retardation Uncooperativeness	1	
Unusual Thought Content	7	Clear manifestations of multiple and extreme delusional system and beliefs; others can read her mind and her thoughts; speak and comment publically about her; harass, threaten her; voices command that she do various things to protect herself; voices instruct her when to hit or beat others to protect herself; voices comment to others about her sexual thoughts and sexual behavior
Blunted Affect	1	
Excitement	1	
Disorientation	4	Difficult concentrating due to distraction from voices

Source: Scale and ratings based on an adaptation of the Brief Psychiatric Rating Scale by the MacArthur Competency Research Project (Woerner, Mannuzza, & Kane, 1988; Golding & Skeem, 1994).

Note: Ratings are: 1 = Not reported; 2 = Very mild; 3 = Mild; 4 = Moderate; 5 = Moderately severe; 6 = Severe; 7 = Extremely severe.

In addition to the other assessment devices and sources of information described above, Ms. A's psycholegal abilities relevant to the issue of competency to proceed were assessed by means of the IFI-R. The IFI-R is a semistructured clinical interview designed to assess the relationship between a defendant's psychopathology and his/her functional psycholegal abilities. In accord with the structure of Colorado Code §77-15-5(4), the IFI-R separately considers a series of specific psycholegal abilities that relate to a defendant's competency to proceed.

PSYCHOLEGAL ISSUES RELATED TO COMPETENCY TO PROCEED

Capacity to Comprehend and Appreciate Charges or Allegations Ms. A understands what she is charged with when it is explained to her and understands, in abstract terms, what murder, attempted murder, and assault mean. She is able to recite back what has been explained to her. However, in the sense of being able to understand what actions she is alleged to have engaged in, she has great difficulties separating what she actually remembers from what seems like a "dream," from what behaviors are alleged.

Degree of Incapacity in This Area:___None/ Mild_×_Moderate___Severe

Specific concerns in this area Ms. A's ability to assist counsel in the sense of comparing the particulars of a charge to her memory and construal of actual events is impaired by the influence of her current psychotic thinking and the influence of her psychotic state on how she processed and stored information at the time of the incident.

Capacity to Disclose Pertinent Facts, Events, and States of Mind. 1. *Ability to provide a reasonable account of own behavior prior to, during, and subsequent to the alleged crime(s).*

Ms. A, consistent with her psychotic state, can provide a disorganized and thought disordered version of events. She can recall that her voices were urging her to "lap" and "bong" (beat and hit) those around her who were stalking her, rioting around her, persecuting her, and so forth. She can recall going to Doug's to obtain a gun on the day of the shooting, but does not recall wearing the

ear protectors continuously from Doug's to WHYY. She has a confused ability to appreciate what happened at WHYY. Her clearest memory is that WHYY had equipment to help others read her mind and that it was the source of others talking over the airwaves about her (particularly about her being a "master" and "master of the world"). She recalls the voices commanding her that she'd get out of trouble if she went to WHYY. She cannot identify anyone in particular that she believed responsible, just "someone there." In her own mind, she describes the events at WHYY as, "we were going to a beautiful island and I was spreading flowers at them, shooting flowers at them." She can vaguely recall some "noises."

2. *Ability to provide an account of behavior of relevant others during the same time period.* Ms. A was acutely psychotic at the time of the incident and cannot provide much in the way of information about the behavior of others at the time of the incident. She can provide some of an account of what she was attending to at the time, by way of the content of what the voices were telling her, and in this sense she can provide a limited account of the behavior of "others."

3. *Ability to provide information about the behavior of the police during apprehension, arrest, and interrogation and comprehension of* Miranda. Ms. A does not recall being Mirandized. She does recall being tackled and held on the floor and has some memory of being interviewed by the police about how she got to WHYY. She does not recall the content of the interview and believed that she did not need to speak to the police because they were reading her mind.

4. *Ability to provide information about state of mind, including intentions, feelings, and cognitions.* Ms. A has a limited ability, consistent with the psychotic state described above.

Degree of Incapacity in This Area:___None/ Mild___Moderate_×_Severe

Specific concerns in this area While Ms. A is able to access some aspects of her mental state at the time of the offense, much of what she can remember and disclose is extremely disorganized and obviously psychotic. Her ability to recall further information after additional treatment is a matter of speculation.

Capacity to Comprehend and Appreciate the Range and Nature of Potential Penalties In the abstract,

Ms. A is aware that she could be executed for her behavior. On the other hand, much of her understanding of this comes from internal voices who, having commanded her to do "what she did" in order to "get out of trouble," now tell her that"she will die." She has no rational understanding of her current situation, nor the options that are available to her.

Degree of Incapacity in This Area:___None/ Mild_x_Moderate___Severe

Specific concerns in this area In my opinion, if Ms. A were to proceed to trial at this point, her decision making would be unduly influenced by her depressive command hallucinations.

Appreciation/Reasoned Choice of Legal Options and Consequences

1. *Appreciation/Understanding of the nature of alternative pleas.* See below
2. *Appreciation/Understanding of the nature of guilty plea or plea bargain.* See below
3. *Capacity to comprehend legal advice.* See below
4. *Capacity to participate in planning legal strategy.* See below
5. *Capacity to appraise likely outcomes.* See below
6. *Capacity to comprehend implications of proceeding pro se.* Not explored. If at some future time Ms. A were to express a wish to proceed pro se, she would need to be reevaluated.
7. *Capacity to engage in reasoned choice of legal strategy without influence of mental disorder.* Ms. A does not believe she has a mental disorder. For her, the voices are real, and she can offer proof that others can read her mind and that her beliefs about others stalking her, harassing her, rioting around her, and causing her harm, fear, and terror are real. She is further convinced that failure to heed the voices will result in being further harmed and terrorized. For this reason, I did not explore her abstract understanding of mental state defenses, plea bargains, and the like. She is not capable, at this point, of any genuine understanding of such options, because, in the first place, she has no genuine understanding of her mental illness. Other problems with her competency to proceed aside, she is currently totally unable to engage in any rational decision as to her legal strategy.

8. *Reasoned choice for treatment.* See above
9. *Other reasoned choice considerations.* Not applicable

Degree of Incapacity in This Area:___None/ Mild___Moderate_x_Severe

Specific concerns in this area This is the principle area of concern with respect to Ms. A. She has a high level of conviction in her delusional beliefs.

Capacity to Appreciate Adversarial Roles and Nature of Proceedings Ms. A is reasonably aware of the roles of court personnel and the nature of proceedings. While she denies that the voices have spoken to her about this area, my clinical opinion is that she would be quite likely to develop a pattern of referential thinking in an actual trial situation. Thus, given her expressed beliefs about the police also being able to read her mind, I would expect that she does have such feelings about others in authority, such as the judge and prosecutor, although she overtly denies this.

Degree of Incapacity in This Area:_x_None/ Mild___Moderate___Severe

Specific concerns in this area None at the present, but given her current mental state, this would need to be reevaluated should an actual trial take place.

Capacity to Manifest Appropriate Courtroom Behavior. 1. *Capacity to track events and witnesses.* Ms. A would not be able to track events adequately. She is greatly influenced by her internal voices, has difficulty concentrating, and often startles in response to stimulation and noises that she construes as threatening.

2. *Capacity to appreciate appropriate behavior and manage emotions.* Ms. A would be unable to manage the internal voices. These have often told her to "lap" and "bong" while she has been on the mental health tier, and in her current state, there is a virtual certainty that she would be unpredictable and explosive in court (particularly when her voices themselves are being discussed).

Degree of Incapacity in This Area:___None/ Mild___Moderate_x_Severe

Specific concerns in this area Obvious problems as detailed above.

Capacity to Testify Relevantly This area is subject to interesting discussion. In a paradoxical fashion, she would be quite able to testify most irrelevantly about what is most relevant to her defense, namely her mental state at the time of the offense. Under an ordinary analysis of the meaning of "relevant," however, she would not be able to track questions, stay on task, and so forth.

Degree of Incapacity in This Area:___None/ Mild___Moderate_×_Severe

Specific concerns in this area   See above.

Quality of Relationship with Attorney.   1. *General relationship with specific attorney, appreciation of attorney's role, appreciation of attorney–client privilege.* Other than a low level of mistrust due to the voices and her general concern with others, Ms. A has a high level of trust in her attorney and others at Legal Aid. She understands their role thus far (but might have difficulty when it came to understanding the implications of a mental state plea). She views her attorney as a father figure who can be trusted.

2. *Specific difficulties with attorney.* None.

3. *Attorney's Pate-level concerns.* All are relevant as detailed above.

Degree of Incapacity in This Area:_×_None/ Mild___Moderate___Severe

Specific concerns in this area   None at the present time.

Necessity of Medication to Maintain Competency and Impact of Current Medication on Demeanor and Participation in Proceedings   This will prove to be a difficult area for Ms. A. She is currently incompetent, even on medication, and has a history of severe side effects with respect to medication. I cannot predict the effects of a future medication regime that might be sufficient to restore her to competency (assuming that is possible). This will need to be carefully re-evaluated in the future.

Degree of Incapacity in This Area:___None/ Mild___Moderate_×_Severe

Specific concerns in this area   See above.

SUMMARY AND INTEGRATED OPINION

While the ultimate opinion in this matter depends on a judicial determination, my profes-

sional opinion is that Ms. A is currently incompetent to proceed. She is severely mentally ill with a probable diagnosis of chronic paranoid schizophrenia. The major areas of psycholegal incapacity have to do with her ability to rationally participate in her defense, her ability to understand the role of her mental illness in that defense, her ability to concentrate, her ability to restrain her aggressive behavior as a consequence of command hallucinations, and her difficulty in accessing realistic memory of her intentions and feelings in and around the time of the offense. She has not responded well to medication in the past, both in terms of reduction of psychopathology and in terms of the development of severe side effects. She will prove to be a most difficult treatment case and will require the attention and supervision of the most skilled and experienced forensic staff at the Colorado State Hospital. It is difficult to opine about the likelihood of her restoration. Given her history, it is quite likely that she will not be restorable. On the other hand, there is no way to assess that at the present time because of the influence of her current situation (jail) on her ability to feel safe. It is possible that, in a more secure and therapeutic environment, she will respond better to both medication and psychotherapy.

I have not been able to complete an evaluation of Ms. A's mental state at the time of the offense, in large part because she is currently so psychotic and reactive (the voices become more aggressive and threatening when "someone understands them"). However, it seems clear that in the future Ms. A will present an interesting challenge to the current Colorado mens rea defense when, and if, she ever regains her competency to proceed. Thus, she presents a rare but classic case of an individual whose ability to intend is severely compromised by both delusions and command hallucinations. Interestingly, the most rational "kernel" of her operating mind attempted to seek help from various authorities (the FBI, ODD) to stop her being harassed and persecuted. By and large, however, it is questionable whether that part of her mind that was in control was Ms. A's mind or the mind of an individual controlled by mental illness. That is, she appears to be suffering from a classic and severe form of mental illness that has been historically described in terms of "made thoughts" (thoughts made by the illness not the person), "made affect" (ditto), passivity symptoms (the person is under the control of the delusions), and "lack of an operating mind" (described above). In order to preserve Ms. A's rights to a fair trial in the future, it will be critical that someone complete her mental state at the time of offense evaluation before too much more time elapses.

Sincerely yours,
Stephen L. Golding, Ph.D.
Professor
Department of Psychology
Adjunct Professor of Law and Psychiatry
Registered Psychologist
State of Utah
Diplomate, American Board
* of Forensic Psychology*

Teaching Point: How does an evaluator separate interview data from structured-test data in analyzing, reasoning about, and communicating the results of FMHA?

While evaluators' report styles may differ substantially, I believe it is essential that the trier of fact have readily available the psycholegal abilities referenced by the relevant statutory and case law, the data on which the evaluator relies in addressing each of these psycholegal abilities, and the critical reasoning that connects data and conclusions, opinions, and implications. This report models that concept. As may be seen in the immediately preceding case report, I routinely use a "boilerplate" form, constructed to reference my jurisdiction's statute and case law, which includes specific clinical symptoms and psycholegal abilities. Other evaluators, working in other jurisdictions, will, of course, need to modify the concept as appropriate.

I came to use this style for several reasons. First, as a matter of experience, I found it difficult to be consistent in my own reports. Thus, the competency domains and issues (i.e., the psycholegal abilities) that form the IFI-R were not always included in my reports. I felt that it would improve both report quality and consistency to start from a boilerplate that prompted me to be more consistent and thorough. More importantly, however, research that I have done over the years, but especially those studies conducted with Dr. Jennifer Skeem, pointed to the conclusion that our essential role as experts—communicating with the trier of fact—would be enhanced by focusing consistently on the range of psycholegal abilities and explaining to the trier of fact the critical reasoning that underlies one's psycholegal conclusions (see generally, Skeem & Golding, 1998; Skeem, Golding, Cohn, & Berge, 1998). Additionally, our research demonstrated that while forensic examiners might tend to "agree" with each other in their final conclusions at a fairly high rate, there were significant and important differences between examiners on which factors they "weighted" and how they combined their weights in reaching their final conclusions.

Finally, Judge David Bazelon's model for how to attend to an expert's evidence (Bazelon, 1975) has always impressed me as cogent and relevant to forensic methods of communication to the trier of fact, as well as professional standards of practice. Thus, the report structure that I use for competency evaluations also includes how I weight the significance of psycholegal abilities strengths and weaknesses.

Jurisdictions differ in the degree to which they require a forensic competency report to address specific underlying psycholegal abilities. I know of no research that directly addresses the issue, but I would wager that report quality and report consistency (between examiners) is higher that require that specific psychological abilities be addressed. I also believe that we ultimately better serve our guild, our clients, and society at large by attempting to counteract, in word and deed, the prejudicial stereotype held by jurists, attorneys, and the lay public that forensic experts are "whores for hire" and correspondingly differ as a function of who the "pimp" was (defense or prosecution; see generally, Golding, 1990). We best do this by developing systematic methods of evaluating types of forensic referrals, identifying the limits and boundaries of our expertise (Committee on Ethical Guidelines for Forensic Psychologists, 1991), and communicating clearly to the trier of fact the logic that connects the data that we have relied on and our opinions, conclusions, and inferences.

Notes

1. For a thorough discussion of Morse's and Grisso's models, see Heilbrun (2001).

2. Although these criteria represent a well-accepted set of standards for forensic practice, it should be noted that there is continuing controversy over whether a clinician should offer an "ultimate opinion." The "ultimate opinion" issue is governed by state law. In the present report, an ultimate opinion was required under Michigan law.

3. Although impartiality may not be required when the clinician assumes the role of consultant, it is still valuable. When assisting an attorney, a consultant is most helpful when he or she maintains a balanced viewpoint. This can help to assist the attorney in anticipating the arguments and challenges that may be raised by opposing counsel.

4. I do not know Chinese. It would be important to have a translator look at her phonetic spelling of various phrases she hears to determine if these are genuine words from Chinese, her own psychotic language, or some blend of the two.

5. I have not yet had an opportunity to review her school records.

6. FBI records of this incident were not available to me, but they would be important to obtain now in anticipation of Ms. A coming to trial at some time in the future.

7. It will be important to obtain the progress notes sent to the civil commitment court as well as the court documentation, including testimony, of Ms. A's discharge from commitment.

Chapter 5

Competence to Be Sentenced

This chapter concerns competence for sentencing. This is a relatively rare issue for forensic clinicians, so there is only one case included. The principle applied to this case involves the use of psychological testing when appropriate to assess response style. A particular kind of malingering—the feigning of cognitive deficits—is discussed in the teaching point.

Case 1

Principle: Use testing when indicated in assessing response style

This principle addresses the value of using psychological and specialized testing to assess response style in FMHA. Response style is an important consideration in FMHA; it refers to the exaggeration, minimization, or accurate reporting of symptoms of mental or emotional disorder. When an individual exaggerates (or even fabricates) symptoms, or when symptoms that are genuinely experienced are minimized or denied, then self-report is less useful and must be deemphasized accordingly. The assessment of response style in FMHA is particularly important because of the incentives that exist in forensic contexts and the perception by judges and attorneys that self-reported information may, therefore, be inaccurate.

Rogers (1984, 1997) has described response style as having four distinct forms: (1) *Reliable/Honest*, in which a genuine attempt is made to be accurate, and factual inaccuracies result from poor understanding or misperception; (2) *Malingering*, involving a conscious fabrication or gross exaggeration of psychological and/or physical symptoms, understandable in light of the individual's circumstances and not attributable merely to the desire to assume the patient role, as in factitious disorder; (3) *Defensive*, in which there is a conscious denial or gross minimization of psychological and/or physical symptoms, as distinguished from ego defenses, which involve intrapsychic processes that distort perception; and (4) *Irrelevant*, involving the failure to become engaged in the evaluation, with responses not necessarily relevant to questions and sometimes made randomly. These four distinct styles provide a useful framework for evaluating response style.

Response style can be assessed through the use of some traditional psychological tests and interviews, as well as by specialized measures that have been specifically designed and developed for this purpose. It is important to note that relatively few psychological tests include any measure of response style, despite the importance of self-report in such tests, and the related assumption that the individual being tested is not deliberately distorting his or her own experience. This was discussed in a recent chapter (Greene, 1997) on the use of several multiscale personality inventories, such as the Minnesota Multiphasic Personality Inventory, 2nd edition (MMPI-2) and the Millon Clinical Multiaxial Inventory-III (Millon, 1994), in assessing malingering and defensiveness. In addition, Rogers (1997) discussed the use of the Structured Interview of Reported Symptoms (SIRS) and its application to malingering. In discussing such tests, it is important to consider both the consistency and accuracy of responding, which encompass underreporting and overreporting. We will describe evidence on item response consistency and the accuracy of responding for the MMPI-2, the MCMI-III, and the SIRS.

Greene (1997) noted that response consistency on the MMPI-2 is assessed through visual inspection for obvious patterns (e.g., TFTFTF, TTFTTF) and by observing the elevation of the F scale. In addition, response inconsistency on the MMPI-2 can be detected through an examination of the Variable Response Inconsistency Scale (VRIN) and the True Response Inconsistency Scale (TRIN), although additional research is needed to provide information regarding the optimal cutoff score for VRIN. With respect to the accuracy of item endorsement, the MMPI-2 contains several scales that are relevant to underreporting or overendorsement of psychopathological symptoms. The results of several recent studies, in which participants were provided with detailed information on the nature of the psychopathology to be faked, suggest that the MMPI-2 validity scales are reasonably effective in distinguishing genuine mental disorders characterized by severe psychopathology, such as schizophrenia, from simulated disorders (Rogers, Bagby, & Chakraborty, 1993). Other research, however, suggests that the MMPI-2 validity scales are less effective in distinguishing between genuine but less severe disorders and faking (Lamb, Berry, Wetter, & Baer, 1994; Wetter, Baer, Berry, Robinson, & Sumpter, 1993).

Greene (1997) noted that response consistency on the MCMI-III is assessed through a 3-item Validity Index that contains nonbizarre items endorsed by less than 0.01% of individuals from clinical populations. The endorsement of one such item suggests caution in the interpretation of the results, while the endorsement of two items indicates an invalid profile (Millon, 1994). The MCMI-III contains a validity scale that is useful in detecting the accuracy of item endorsement. Specifically, the Debasement Scale (Scale Z) of the MCMI-III has been shown to identify college students who were instructed to malinger on the MCMI-II (Bagby, Gillis, Toner, & Goldberg, 1991).

The SIRS (Rogers, 1992), a 172-item structured interview with eight primary scales, was developed specifically for assessing the feigning of psychopathology. Research with the SIRS suggests that it is effective in discriminating between feigners and genuine patients (Rogers, 1997). The SIRS is limited, however, by its inability to detect a malingerer who falsely reports a single symptom and fails to respond meaningfully to a number of questions. In addition, the SIRS provides limited information regarding the "partial malingerer"— the individual who experiences genuine symptoms but who also selectively reports, exaggerates, or fabricates some symptoms depending on the circumstances.

This principle appears to be well supported on ethical, empirical, and standard of practice dimensions. It is important, however, that forensic practitioners select the few tests that meet the appropriate criteria for relevance and empirical support. Toward this end, Heilbrun (1992) offered guidelines that include the explicit assessment of response style through the use of tests, such as the MMPI-2, that have demonstrated empirical support for this application. There are also several interview strategies that can help the forensic practitioner in assessing response style. For example, asking specific and detailed questions, recording the responses, and asking the questions again later in the evaluation can help the forensic practitioner to assess consistency. Finally, when assessing an individual's response style, it is important for the forensic practitioner to employ multiple measures. The use of multiple measures, such as psychological tests, structured interviews, and collateral information, provides additional support for conclusions regarding the individual's response style.

The present report illustrates the application of this principle in the context of a court-ordered evaluation of competence to enter a plea and to be sentenced. Because the referral question involved the cognitive capacity of the defendant to understand his current situation, the evaluator was concerned with obtaining an accurate representation of the defendant's cognitive functioning. Therefore, an accurate assessment of the defendant's response style was necessary. Because the evaluator was skeptical about the accuracy of the self-reported psychopathological symptoms, he addressed the possibility of the defendant's malingering.

The determination of malingering was made through the use of interview strategies and psychological testing. As part of the evaluation, the defendant was administered several psychological tests, such as the SIRS and the MMPI-2, that have demonstrated empirical support in detecting malingering. This selection of tests is consistent with the guidelines offered by Heilbrun (1992) regarding the assessment of response style by using tests with empirical support for that purpose. Because the evaluator suspected that the defendant was malingering, the defendant was administered psychological tests on three occasions in an effort to assess consistency of responding.

The results of the first administration of the SIRS suggested that the defendant was misrepresenting himself as mentally ill; his responses were consistent with those of someone intending to feign a psychotic disorder. Specifically, he endorsed an excessively high number of unusual symptom combinations. Because the defendant was exaggerating his psychopathological symptoms, his response style would be characterized as malingering (Rogers, 1984, 1997). The defendant scored in the "Definitely Malingering" range on one scale, and in the "Probably Malingering" range on four others. After the evaluator spoke with the defendant regarding the possibility that the defendant was feigning mental illness, the defendant was readministered the SIRS. The results indicated that the defendant substantially modified his report of psychopathological symptoms. On the second administration, the defendant scored in the "Probably Malingering" range on only two scales. As such, the SIRS provided one effective means of assessing malingering in this case.

The defendant was also administered the MMPI-2. He consistently endorsed items reflecting psychopathology, with the number of items endorsed far exceeding the number of items usually endorsed by patients. The MMPI-2 VRIN, TRIN, and F scales reflected scores consistent with a pattern of responding often seen in individuals trying to feign mental disorder. When the MMPI-2 was readministered, the defendant's response style would be classified as irrelevant (Rogers, 1984, 1997).

Based on the results of the psychological testing, the evaluator concluded that the defendant presented with a malingering response style. By using psychological tests with demonstrated empirical support for the evaluation of response style, the evaluator was able to more accurately assess the defendant's response style. The defendant's pattern of responding on the SIRS and MMPI-2 was consistent with the performance of individuals who are attempting to feign mental illness by exaggerating psychopathological symptoms. The evaluator concluded that the defendant was malingering psychopathology, motivated by his expectation that a diagnosis of schizophrenia might contribute to a reduced sentence. Based on the results of the evaluation, which included a thorough assessment of the defendant's response style, the evaluator concluded that the defendant was competent to proceed with the plea agreement and subsequent sentencing.

FORENSIC REPORT[1]

Dates of Evaluation: July 29 to August 30, 1999
Date of Report: August 30, 1999

REFERRAL

DV is a 36-year-old, single Black male who was referred to the U.S. Medical Center for Federal Prisoners by the U.S. District Court for the Western District of Missouri pursuant to Title 18, U.S. Code, Section 4241 and 4247(b). According to the documents provided by the U.S. Attorney assigned to the case, DV was charged with Possession of a Firearm by a Convicted Felon.

The referring Court directed that a mental health professional at the Medical Center examine DV and provide an opinion regarding his competency to enter a plea and to be sentenced. Prior to beginning the initial interview, DV was informed that the usual psychotherapist/patient relationship did not exist and that the information obtained from the evaluation was not confidential. He was also informed that a report would be prepared and submitted to the referring Court and then be distributed to both the defense and prosecuting attorneys. DV acknowledged and appeared to understand these conditions and was periodically reminded of the conditions as the evaluation progressed.

SOURCES OF INFORMATION

This evaluation was conducted in the Mental Health Evaluation Unit of the U.S. Medical Center for Federal Prisoners. During his stay at the facility, DV was regularly observed by clinical and correctional staff. He participated in additional clinical interviews with the undersigned evaluators. Additionally, the medical staff completed a routine physical examination of DV. Other sources of information included psychological testing, including:

1. Validity Indicator Profile
2. Rey 15-Item Memory Test
3. Rey Auditory Verbal Learning Test
4. Dot Counting Test
5. Rey Word Recognition Test
6. Test of Nonverbal Intelligence-2
7. Structured Interview of Reported Symptoms
8. Minnesota Multiphasic Personality Inventory-2
9. Shipley Institute of Living Scale

Documents reviewed included prior medical records, and criminal investigative materials, including:

1. Order for Psychiatric Examination of Defendant, United States District Court for the Western District of Missouri, dated July 14, 1999.
2. United States Government Memorandum dated May 5, 1999.
3. United States Government Memorandum dated May 4, 1999.
4. Plea Agreement, United States District Court for the Western District of Missouri, dated April 26, 1999.

5. DV Proffer, undated.
6. Indictment, United States District Court for the Western District of Missouri, dated March 31, 1998.
7. Report of Investigation, dated February 12, 1998.
8. Springfield Police Department Statement Form, dated January 27, 1998.
9. Offense-Incident Report, Springfield Police Department, dated January 27, 1998.
10. Complaint/Arrest Affidavit, undated.

DEFENDANT'S PERSONAL HISTORY

DV's personal history was obtained through self-report and review of criminal investigative materials.

DV stated that he lived at home with his mother, father, and two brothers until the age of 8, when his mother was killed in a car accident. DV stated that after his mother's death, he began living with an aunt, who raised him until he left home at the age of 14. He stated that when he was 14 years old he moved to Missouri, where he initially lived with his older brother.

According to DV, he attended school through the eighth grade. He stated that he was expelled from school after the eighth grade, partly because of his poor attendance and partly because of his involvement in two fights. He reported repeating the eighth grade once due to his poor attendance. DV stated that his grades were mostly Bs, Cs, and Ds. He described school as being difficult for him because he never had any family support. He stated that after his mother died, nobody really cared whether he went to school. He denied ever attending special education classes or being diagnosed with a learning disability.

DV stated that he began smoking marijuana as a teenager and has continued to use it throughout adulthood. He reported that prior to his arrest, he used marijuana on a daily basis. He stated that he drinks alcohol much less frequently, primarily on the weekends or when it was available. He stated that selling illicit drugs has been his primary source of income through the years.

DV stated that he has two sons. He reported having a close relationship with his 10-year-old son, who lives in another state. He reported having little to no contact with his 13-year-old son, who lives in yet another state. He reported a series of brief relationships with women, never having sustained a relationship for longer than 6 months.

DV stated that he has been arrested at least 20 times throughout adolescence and adulthood. He has been incarcerated in state prisons twice, both for felony convictions. According to DV, the only previous mental health treatment he has received was during his incarceration in a state prison. He stated that he had been experiencing nervousness, tremors, and what he referred to as "depression." This "condition" was reportedly treated with antipsychotic medication for a period of 6 months. His reports of past mental health symptoms were vague, and he indicated that he has never sought mental health treatment when out of prison.

HOSPITAL COURSE

DV was admitted to the Mental Health Evaluation Unit on July 29, 1999. On admission, he was housed in a locked ward, as is standard policy. Initially, DV was cooperative but guarded. He gave a vague and unconvincing report of hearing voices and stated that he experienced difficulty sleeping. He reported receiving treatment in the past with antidepressant medication for "depression."

On arrival at the Medical Center, DV was receiving thioridazine (an antipsychotic medication, 200 mg at bedtime). This medication had recently been prescribed in the county jail based on a brief interview, and was discontinued by the staff psychiatrist after the initial interview. He received diphenhydramine (50 mg at bedtime, as needed) throughout the study period to help him sleep.

By August 5, DV had displayed no evidence of problems from the discontinuation of medication. He was cooperative, and he was deemed suitable for transfer to an unlocked unit. He was allowed to go unescorted throughout the institution to various activities. He managed his daily routine in the institution with full capacity to care for himself. Hygiene and personal grooming were satisfactory. DV interacted appropriately with staff members and other inmates. He intermittently complained of difficulty sleeping. No disturbance in appetite was noted.

During formal interviews, DV was initially uncooperative with the evaluators. He was non-disclosing and pretended not to understand what was asked of him. He was strongly encouraged to cooperate with the evaluation. After a period of observation and initial psychological testing, we explained to him that his report of experiencing auditory hallucinations was unlikely to be true. We informed him that we did not believe he had any mental disorder. DV ostensibly changed his attitude and agreed to cooperate with us. He told us that he was not mentally ill, but he seemed to want to continue to present himself as somewhat impaired. He also agreed to recomplete some of the psychological testing that had previously been administered to him. Because his performance on tests in the second administration did not substantially improve, we met with him again and reemphasized the importance of answering test items truthfully and to the best of his ability. He insisted that he had done his best. We took the position that perhaps he had not understood the directions for the testing and reexplained how to complete the tests. He was then tested a third time and improved substantially.

MENTAL STATUS AT THE PRESENT TIME

DV was alert and oriented to person, place, time, and situation. His speech was clear and coherent, although low in volume and slowly delivered. Psychomotor movements were slow. There was no evidence of thought disorder. His thinking was linear, relevant, coherent, and organized, and showed no evidence of delusional content. DV's mood was euthymic. He displayed a limited range of emotional expression. He demonstrated no apparent psychosis. He denied any current suicidal or homicidal ideation or intent.

PSYCHOLOGICAL TEST RESULTS

DV was administered psychological testing on three separate occasions. Initial test results clearly revealed that DV intended to represent himself as mentally ill and confused. He was presented with our conclusion that he had been feigning mental illness. He claimed he had not and agreed to be retested with some of the tests. His performance on the second attempt did not suggest active feigning, but he did not appear engaged in giving an accurate portrayal of his abilities. After further counseling, he was readministered two tests, which he appeared to complete in a cooperative fashion.

DV's responses on a structured interview of symptoms of mental illness were consistent with those of someone intending to feign psychotic mental illness. He endorsed an excessively high number of unusual symptom combinations. He tended to report that he had experienced almost any type of unusual psychotic experience with a high degree of impairment.[2] When this test was readministered, he substantially modified his report of problems but still endorsed an unusually large number of psychological problems with significant levels of impairment. This pattern of responding was not as clearly similar to that of individuals who malinger mental disorder.[3]

On a self-report inventory of personality characteristics, DV's responses were consistent and reflected a good comprehension of the test items. He consistently endorsed items obviously related to psychopathology. He endorsed a significant number of items infrequently endorsed by chronic mental health patients. Additionally, the number of mental health symptoms he endorsed far exceeded the number of items typically endorsed by mental health patients.[4] This pattern of responding is typically seen among individuals who wish to feign mental disorder. When this test was readministered, his responses appeared to be irrelevant to content and too inconsistent to interpret. It was likely that he responded without paying close attention to the test statements.[5]

DV's performance on several tests of memory was also consistent with that of someone who is feigning cognitive impairment. For example, he presented with a greater ability to recall words for memory than to recognize them. This finding is typically restricted to individuals who are feigning memory impairment.[6]

His first efforts on tests of cognitive ability resulted in estimate of ability in the range of Mild Mental Retardation. Measures of motivation and effort, however, indicated that he was motivated to respond incorrectly or to give minimal effort.

When these measures were readministered in the second testing session, they continued to indicate that he was only providing token effort to respond correctly, and tests of cognitive ability were not administered. In the third testing session, he responded with much greater effort. Repeat administration of tests of cognitive ability indicated he had at least Low Average ability in nonverbal reasoning, word knowledge, and verbal comprehension.[7]

DIAGNOSTIC FORMULATION

DV does not manifest a mental disorder. Over the period of this evaluation, DV's behavior was observed on a daily basis. He demonstrated excellent hygiene and organization in daily behavior, but he appeared to make an attempt to malinger mental illness. He actively reported to nursing and correctional staff that he was hearing voices. He acted confused when they questioned him about his complaints. When evaluated by the examiners in formal interviews, however, these complaints appeared feigned.

His initial performance on psychological tests was consistent with that of individuals who feign mental illness. In addition to exaggerating commonly experienced symptoms of mental illness, DV reported experiencing an abundance of unbelievable and unlikely symptoms. Not only was his test performance unbelievable it was also inconsistent with his daily behavior. When he was told that his presentation was not believable, he promptly ceased portraying himself as mentally ill.

Although DV stopped actively feigning mental illness, and in fact told us that he was not mentally ill, he nevertheless continued to underrepresent his cognitive abilities on psychological tests. As we continued to emphasize the need to cooperate with testing, he gradually became more cooperative, and his performance improved. His gradual improvement supports the conclusion that it was his approach to evaluation rather than genuine deficits that was responsible for his initially poor performance on tests of memory and cognition.

DV reported receiving antipsychotic medication while incarcerated in a state prison. He stated that he was treated for what he referred to as depression, but it is unlikely that he has ever experienced a clinical depression. DV's report of past symptoms of depression and psychosis was vague and unconvincing. Based on a brief interview, he recently received a diagnosis of schizophrenia in the county jail. This conclusion was probably the result of undetected malingering.

DV appears to have been malingering in a halfhearted fashion. He was apparently aware that his recent diagnosis of schizophrenia might contribute toward a reduced sentence, even beyond the reduction gained in his plea agreement. When faced with the prospect of having us report to the court that he was malingering, however, he clearly changed his report of confusion and psychotic experience. He claimed he had no mental disorder and eventually chose to reveal his true abilities on psychological testing. He is not currently malingering.

DV does not manifest a mental disorder. He does manifest a personality style and behavior pattern that is characterized by antipathy toward authority and violation of social norms and laws. He is persistently irresponsible in relationships and personal commitments. He has abused marijuana throughout his adolescence and adulthood. His personality style does not generally constitute a mental illness.

DIAGNOSES

According to the criteria set forth in the *Diagnostic and Statistical Manual of Mental Disorders*, Fourth Edition (American Psychiatric Association, 1994), DV is diagnosed as follows:

Axis I: Malingering (resolved)
          Cannabis abuse
Axis II: Antisocial personality disorder
Axis III: None

OPINION CONCERNING COMPETENCY TO PROCEED

DV was aware of the terms and conditions of his plea agreement. He recognized the consequences of a guilty plea and was able to articulate rational and coherent reasons for entering such a plea. He demonstrated an awareness of the potential benefits of accepting a plea agreement, as well as the possible consequences of violating te terms of the

agreement. He accurately and completely related the circumstances of the offense to which he has pled guilty. He fully described the process of making a plea. DV knew he has the choice to stand trial, and he believes that entering a plea provides a better outcome. He knew that the current adjudication constitutes his third felony conviction, and he knew the sentencing mandates associated with a third felony conviction. That is, DV was aware that he could have received a very lengthy sentence for his third conviction and knew his plea carried the probability of a relatively short sentence. He knew that his plea agreement called for his full cooperation in the resolution of his case. When we indicated that we thought he was not cooperating with the evaluation sought by the court by actively misrepresenting his true mental state, he became very concerned and substantially modified what he told us about his mental state. His thinking evidenced no irrational reasoning or delusional content. His conduct throughout the course of his hospitalization, especially in interview with us, demonstrated that he is quite capable of communicating effectively with his attorney. He knew that the sentence he was anticipating was based on an agreement with the prosecutor, was not binding on the court, and was intended to punish him for his behavior. He expressed confidence in his attorney and related several instances of cooperation with his attorney in reaching the plea agreement.

Based on these considerations, it is our opinion that DV is competent to proceed with his case. He is aware of the nature and potential consequences of the charge against him and he is able to properly assist his attorney in this matter. He has a rational and factual appreciation of the circumstances relating to his potential sentence. He does not manifest a mental disorder that would interfere with these abilities.

Comment   The determination of malingering in this case was initiated by a skepticism about symptoms reported by the defendant. His report of depression was inconsistent with the application of antipsychotic medications. It is not unusual, however, for individuals with psychosis to sometimes misunderstand or underreport prior psychotic episodes, misrepresenting them as "depression" or "nervous breakdowns." In the case of

DV, when asked to describe his episode of depression, he reported that he had heard voices, and he reported nothing more. We chose not to question the examinee about a list of possible experiences, preferring instead to ask open-ended questions and evaluating the completeness of his response. Because of our advantage of inpatient evaluation, with individuals under constant observation, we can safely observe individuals over time without medication to see if they demonstrate a coherence of symptomatology that would suggest a mental disorder. DV demonstrated symptoms of mental disorder only in conversations with direct care staff and not in interactions with other defendants or with secondary administrative staff.

Initial psychological testing was quite helpful to direct our attention to the likelihood he was faking a mental disorder. Engaging DV in an open discussion of what was happening was more difficult. Based on the SIRS, MMPI-2, and VIP results, we were rather confident that DV was misrepresenting his true mental state. When we told him that we did not believe he had a mental disorder and was faking symptoms, his response was to claim that he had not been faking, did not have a mental disorder, and had responded truthfully to testing. When he was retested, he did not perform well, continuing to report some problems on the SIRS and responding randomly on the MMPI-2. He made only a token effort to perform well on the VIP. Given the importance of his cognitive capacity to know what was happening in his case, we were most concerned with obtaining a valid representation of his thinking skills. DV was no longer actively feigning a psychotic disorder, but he was unwilling to reveal his true cognitive abilities. Our strategy was to reapproach him for testing, allowing him to "save face." We suggested the possibility that we had not given clear instructions on how to complete the test and re-explained them in excessive detail. With this basis for explaining his previous poor performance, he was free to respond correctly, and did so.

Karin Towers, J.D., M.A.
Psychology Intern

Richard Frederick, Ph.D.
Diplomate in Forensic Psychology, ABPP

Teaching point: How do you assess feigned cognitive deficits?

Consistent with Heilbrun's (1992) exhortation to use tests with demonstrated empirical support for identification of invalid response styles, Van Gorp and colleagues (1999) found that tests that specifically assess malingering classified invalid response styles more accurately than some recommended posttest analyses of standard neuropsychological procedures. When cognitive impairment is potentially at issue in a forensic examination, I routinely have examinees complete a number of procedures and tests that specifically assess the reliability of their presentation. I follow Rogers's (1997) guidance to gather convincing evidence of malingering and to understand the motives of the test taker before concluding that malingering exists. Convincing evidence of malingering includes instances of improbability in testing and clinical presentation. Examiners should look at all the evidence, including clinical presentation, test findings, the case history, and potential gain for misrepresentation of abilities, to make sense of all the information.

Courts are often interested in the capacity of criminal defendants to reason, attend, concentrate, track proceedings, and remember salient details. Courts, compensation boards, and juries must determine whether civil plaintiffs have suffered compensable impairment in functional cognitive capacities, intellect, or memory ability. Psychologists and neuropsychologists have developed a number of tests to identify impairments in these capacities but relatively few evaluate response style. The VIP is the only commercially available test that has been developed and validated to directly evaluate the believability of presentation of ability in reasoning, intellect, and word knowledge (Frederick & Crosby, 2000). Some other tests and procedures have been reported for this purpose but are not routinely available or well validated.

By contrast, there are a number of procedures available to assess memory impairment. The Portland Digit Recognition Test (PDRT; Binder, 1990) and the Test of Memory Malingering (TOMM; Tombaugh, 1997) have a extensive literature establishing their validity. The TOMM, in particular, has identified performance characteristics for a number of clinical conditions involving brain impairment (e.g., Ress, Tombaugh, Gansler, & Moczynski, 1998). Currently, the primary strategy of identifying suspicious performance for these tests is to identify the range of errors that are likely for individuals with genuine memory impairment and to establish that as the lower boundary of acceptable performance. The PDRT requires a relatively long time (up to an hour) to present 5-digit strings for memorization and recognition, but the TOMM can be administered much more quickly, in as little as 5 to 10 minutes. It uses simple line drawings. Some of the drawbacks of the PDRT have been eliminated with the development of the Victoria Symptom Validity Test (VSVT; Slick, Hopp, Strauss, & Thompson, 1997), a test that administers 5-digit strings for memorization and recognition by computer. The VSVT provides a useful analysis of errors and response time. The manual is quite helpful in interpreting the meaning of recognition errors.

I like to use a number of procedures developed by Andre Rey, a neuropsychologist in Geneva from the 1930s to the 1960s. These include the Word Recognition Test (WRT), the Auditory Verbal Learning Test (AVLT), and the 15-item Rey Memory Test (RMT, known by a number of slightly dissimilar names). Rey's procedures are not well established as malingering detection techniques, although they have received more examination on malingering detection than any other technique in the professional literature. The Rey techniques were primarily introduced to the United States through Lezak's 1983 book on neuropsychological assessment. When read in the original French, however, it appears that Lezak did not accurately report Rey's test procedures and instructional sets, or fully communicate Rey's approach to malingering detection. Rey (1958) clearly stated that his techniques were merely "signs" and cautioned against overinterpretation, noting that the presence of a single positive sign should not cause the evaluator to reach a conclusion of malingering. These techniques and their various instructional sets have been described (Frederick, 1997), and the applicable literature reviewed (Frederick, Crosby, & Wynkoop, 2000).

The Rey 15-Item Memory Test (RMT) presents 15 items on a sheet of paper for visual memorization. Failure to reproduce nine items is generally considered predictive of malingering, unless severe impairment is present or possible. Frederick (2000a) demonstrated that the RMT is especially useful in criminal forensic evaluations (which are not primarily neuropsychological) in identifying malingering. Greiffenstein, Baker, and Gola (1996) examined a number of methods of evaluating memory complaints. They found that comparing performance on Rey's recognition and recall memory techniques was useful in identifying malingered memory impairment. Given that recognition memory should be much stronger than recall memory, performances in which recall appears stronger than recognition require close scrutiny (see also Frederick, 2000b).

It is possible to evaluate complaints of amnesia by developing a recognition test that is individually tailored to the information the patient claims not to know (Frederick, Carter, & Powel, 1995; Frederick & Denney, 1998). I have found that such assessment of claimed amnesia has much greater sensitivity than indirect assessment by available malingering tests.

Making sense of the presentation means integrating information from history, testing, clinical presentation, and the incentive for malingering to form hypotheses about the patient. In evaluating evidence relevant to these hypotheses, it is sometimes useful to confront the patient with concerns that their testing performance does not reflect their best abilities and to ask to retest them. In the example we presented, there was clear evidence that we could not trust results of the first testing, nor could we support hypotheses that considered the results of this testing to be accurate.

Notes

1. Identifying information about this individual, including initials, certain demographic information, some case characteristics, and the referring court have all been disguised to protect his identity.

2. On the first administration of the SIRS he scored "Definitely Malingering" in the Severity category, and "Probably Malingering" in the Blatant, Subtle, Selectivity, and Symptom Combination categories.

3. On the second administration of the SIRS, he scored "Probably Malingering" in the Subtle and Severity categories.

4. On the MMPI-2 first administration, $VRIN = 6$, $F = 37$, $Fb = 22$, and $F(p) = 8$.

5. On the second administration of the MMPI-2, $VRIN = 10$, $F = 28$, $Fb = 13$, $|F - Fb| = 15$, $F(p) = 3$.

6. He recalled six words on the Rey AVLT first trial. On the Rey WRT, he correctly recognized five words and misrecognized five words. On the Rey 15-item test, he reproduced six items correctly. One row of the two reproduced was a combination of sticks and a circle.

7. On the first administration of the VIP, his performance were classified as "irrelevant," with a total score of 55/100 on the nonverbal subtest and 39/78 on the verbal subtest. On the second administration of the VIP, his performances were classified as "careless," with a total score of 54/100 on the nonverbal subtest and 49/78 on the verbal subtest. For the third testing session, only the nonverbal subtest was administered. His performance was classified as "compliant," with a total score of 74/100.

Chapter 6

Competence to Be Executed

This chapter's case concerns the competence of a death-sentenced defendant to be executed. The principle involves attributing information to the source(s) from which it was obtained. In the teaching point, there is a more specific discussion of attribution—how to attribute information and the justification for doing so.

Case 1

Principle: Attribute information to sources

Because this principle is discussed in chapter 4, we now demonstrate how it can be applied to this chapter's case report.

The report can be used as a particularly good illustration of this principle. In this report of the evaluation of the defendant's competence for execution, the forensic clinician obtained information from numerous sources, including an interview with the defendant, interviews with third parties, psychological testing of the defendant, and more than 30 records from various sources. Given the complexity of the issue and the numerous sources of information that were considered, it was essential that the information contained in the report be attributed by source.

Throughout the report, the forensic clinician refers to the source(s) of the information being presented. For example, he often attributes information to "self-report," "psychiatric records," "medical records," "interviews with . . . ," and "affidavits of third parties." This attribution of information to sources helps the court in evaluating the relevance and reliability of the information being presented. It also helps the attorney presenting this evaluation to do so more effectively and provides the opposing attorney with a fair opportunity to challenge these findings. Relevance and reliability, two of the cornerstones of evidence law, could not be readily assessed without attribution of information to sources.

To some extent, the different headings used throughout the report reflect the source of the information being presented. For example, the heading "Knowledge of Execution" clearly indicates that the information being presented was obtained directly from the defendant. Similarly, the heading "Third Party Observations of Mr. H's Understandings" reflects collateral sources for the information provided in this section. It is also noteworthy that the evaluator's attribution of information to third party sources adheres to the previously discussed standard for forensic psychologists described in the *Specialty Guidelines for Forensic Psychologists* (APA Committee on Ethical Guidelines for Forensic Psychologists, 1991): When a forensic practitioner uses information or data gathered by third parties, the practitioner should cite the source of the information or data.

The attribution of information to sources in this report is particularly noteworthy in the "Summary" section. Throughout this section, the author clearly indicates the bases from which his conclusions were drawn. For example, he indicates that "residual aspects of [the defendant's] psychotic disorder remain as demonstrated in Mr. H's mental status, psychological testing, and family descriptions." This type of attribution of information to sources, even in the report's summary section, facilitates the accurate and effective communication of the evaluation's results.

EVALUATION OF COMPETENCY TO BE EXECUTED

Re: Ex Parte John H, in the 42nd State District Court
Defendant: John H
Defendant's Date of Birth: 6-20-61
Date of Report: 6-02-99

Dates and Techniques of Evaluation

4-22-99 Clinical and forensic interview of John H, 275 minutes

4-22-99 Psychological Testing of John H, including Minnesota Multiphasic Personality Inventory-2 (MMPI-2) and Personality Assessment Inventory (PAI)

4-22-99 Interview of Sgt. Stan Jones (State Department of Corrections, Death Row Unit), 35 minutes

4-22-99 Observation of John H's cell at Death Row

5-06-99 Clinical and forensic interview of John H, 215 minutes

5-11-99 Telephone interview of Steve M (friend), 43 minutes

5-11-99 Telephone interview of Elizabeth L (friend and spiritual advisor), 37 minutes

5-11-99 Telephone interview of Cindy J (friend), 28 minutes

5-11-99 Telephone interview of Keith H (brother), 32 minutes

5-12-99 Telephone interview of Julia S (friend), 70 minutes

5-12-99 Telephone interview of Jack L (stepbrother), 40 minutes

5-12-99 Telephone interview of Carla J (exwife and mother of sons), 12 minutes

Records Reviewed

- Petition for Writ of Habeas Corpus filed with court 3-16-99 (9 pages)
- Memorandum and Order filed with court 4-5-99
- Health records from 1994–1999 including Clinic Notes, State Department of Corrections, Psychiatric Center Death Row Individual Treatment Plan dated 6-17-91, and

Psychiatric Center Death Row Treatment Plan Review dated 6-17-91

- State Department of Corrections Disciplinary Summary 1991–1997
- Affidavit of Brian F. Fallon dated 3-16-99
- Affidavit of Margaret B. L (mother) dated 3-16-99
- Affidavit of Edward C. L (stepfather) dated 3-16-99
- Affidavit of Jacob H (brother) dated 3-16-99
- Affidavit of Larry P. R (cousin) dated 3-16-99
- Affidavit of Glenn Ray S dated 3-16-99
- Affidavit of Jack L (stepbrother) dated 3-16-99
- Petition for Clemency and Request for Reprieve Supplement
- Petition for Clemency and Request for Reprieve regarding James H
- Pictures of James H
- Journal of James H: A Personal History
- Birth Certificate of James H
- Certificate of Death for Clarence B (James's father)
- Journal Entry—Legal Change of Name
- School Records of James H (Westview High School and Central High School 1976 to1979)
- Military Records including letter from John Rothwell, Colonel, U.S. Army, dated 9-24-79
- Original Petition for Divorce
- Letter from Margaret L (mother) to Carl Strong, attorney, in 1984
- Metro Police Department Crime Report dated 8-12-87
- Certified Copy of Indictment dated 11-24-87
- Margaret L's trial court testimony in 1988
- Margaret L's trial court testimony in 1992
- State documents copies from District Attorney files in 1996 including notes and information from Drs. John G, Ann B, and list of doctors
- Certified Copy of Jury Verdict, Judgment, and Sentence
- Death Warrant and Order Setting Execution
- Newspaper Articles
- University Medical Center Records, August 1978
- U.S. Army Medical Records, including Report of Medical Examination dated

12-18-79, Clinical Record Cover Sheets, Hearing Conservation Data Sheet, Reference Audiogram, Dental Records, and Chronological Record of Medical Care from 5-2-80 to 3-29-81

- Woods Memorial Hospital Records (1983), including Discharge Summary dated 11-13-83
- Glenhaven Psychiatric Hospital Records (1983), including Discharge Summary dated 12-11-83, Admission Evaluation dated 11-20-83, and various Progress Notes and Nurses Notes
- Veterans Administration Medical Center Records dated 12-11-83 to 1-11-84
- William A, M.D., Evaluation dated 6-6-84
- John F, D.O., Evaluation dated 6-15-84
- Paul D. W, Ph.D., Evaluation (Affidavit dated 4-19-96) and various tests and progress notes attached
- State Department of Corrections Medical Records (1988 to present)
- Robert C, DO, MA, Vitae and Evaluation (undated)
- Letters in Support of Clemency for James H
- Petitions in Support of Clemency for James H

REFERRAL

Examination and evaluation of John H's competency to be executed was ordered by the Honorable Jackson Smith, State District Court, on 4-21-99. I was nominated to evaluate Mr. H by defense counsel. Another expert, whose interviews, records review, and findings were entirely independent of my own, was nominated by the State. The definition of competency to be executed was considered as per Article 26.03 of the State Code of Criminal Procedure as follows: "Defendant is incompetent to be executed if the defendant does not understand that he or she is to be executed and the execution is imminent; and the reason he or she is being executed."

I conducted two examinations of Mr. H in the infirmary of the Death Row Unit of the State Department of Corrections. An office affording both privacy and freedom from distraction was utilized for these interviews. At the outset of the examination, Mr. H was informed of the purpose of the evaluation, the associated statutory parameters, and that a report of my findings would be made available to the court, defense counsel, and state's attorney. He was able to paraphrase his understanding of these provisions and agreed to proceed. Additionally, records were reviewed and third party sources were interviewed. These procedures are reasonably relied on by forensic psychologists in coming to reliable expert opinions.

FINDINGS

History of Psychological Disorder Mr. H is the second of three children from a marriage that ended in divorce when he was age four. His mother remarried when he was approximately age six. He had infrequent contact with his biological father, who died 15 years ago. Mr. H's mother, Margaret L, described that across childhood he was generally well adjusted and displayed no significant conduct problems until age 12 (5-23-84, correspondence to Carl Strong, attorney). His psychological and behavioral difficulties were subsequently characterized by antisocial behavior, drug abuse, mood disorder, and psychotic symptoms.

More specifically, early adolescent conduct disorder symptoms included disruptive behavior in school with associated grade deterioration. These behavioral problems escalated in mid-adolescence to truancy, repeated runaways, shoplifting, theft, and drug abuse. Mr. H made an initially positive adjustment to U.S. Army training, but was subsequently discharged after 10 months in lieu of facing disciplinary charges. Mr. H described being involved in multiple sexual relationships, both consecutive and concurrent with each other. These were principally with females, but eventually included a homosexual relationship with one of his murder victims. He described moving in with and subsequently marrying a woman who worked in a topless bar. Mr. H described subsequently divorcing and marrying for a second time but could not sustain a stable and responsible marriage interaction secondary to heavy drug abuse. He noted that his second marriage resulted in two sons, although he had little contact with these children following the divorce. He also described his employment history was unstable, adding that he was jailed for hot check charges. He described pulling an "insurance scam" on the job by falling off a pallet and pretending to be hurt in order to collect workmen's compensation and insurance settlement. He also described selling methamphetamine.

Mr. H's self-report, as well as psychiatric records, detailed an extensive history of drug abuse from early adolescence. Medical records variously described him as beginning to sniff glue at age 12 (Glenhaven Psychiatric Hospital progress record 11-29-83) and at age 15–16 (Woods Memorial Medical Center consultation report dated 11-13-83). Mr. H described on interview beginning to drink alcohol in eighth grade, escalating to a widely variable pattern when in the Army ranging from little to sufficient intoxication to pass out. He described beginning to abuse marijuana in junior high as often as he could obtain it, increasing to several times weekly by high school. He described that he would subsequently use marijuana daily, if available, as well as hashish and concentrated powder THC. Mr. H described extensive abuse of psychedelics, most heavily during his high school years. This included a self-report of 50 to 100 hits of LSD between the ages of 16 and 24 and experimentation with hallucinogenic mushrooms, peyote, and mescaline. He described using Quaaludes on 5 to 10 occasions. He described periodic use of synthetic narcotics (including Talwin®, Percodan®, and Dilaudid®). Glenhaven Psychiatric Hospital records additionally describe Mr. H as having abused PCP.

Mr. H described first abusing methamphetamines in the Army. He described graduating to shooting speed in week-long runs. This is consistent with his mother's report (5-23-84 correspondence) of discovering needle-related paraphernalia in their home. Mr. H described that his heavy chronic abuse of I.V. methamphetamines continued until the spring of 1987. It is probable that Mr. H's drug abuse was implicated in his psychological deterioration in late 1983 and early 1984, which culminated in his psychiatric admissions. Specifically, Mr. H described heavily abusing methamphetamine and hallucinogenics across the time period prior to his psychiatric admissions. Additionally, the discharge summary of Glenhaven Psychiatric Hospital dated 12-11-83 identified that Mr. H had taken an "excessive amount of LSD" two days prior to his 11-14-83 admission to that facility. Mr. H described his psychotic symptoms as intensifying when he used methamphetamines and hallucinogenics. Chronic heavy methamphetamine abuse is associated in the research literature with precipitating a methamphetamine-induced psychosis that is quite similar in presentation to paranoid schizophrenia and that may persist even after methamphetamine abuse is discontinued.

Psychotic Experience   There is a genetic predisposition to a number of mental illnesses, including affective disorders (mood) and schizophrenia. Mr. H has a positive family history of both affective disorder and/or schizophrenia, including his paternal great grandfather, paternal great uncle, uncle, maternal grandmother's cousin, maternal great uncle, and four maternal cousins. Additionally, a sibling has been diagnosed with Bipolar Disorder (manic-depressive) and Schizoaffective Disorder. There are reports that Mr. H's biological father suffered from mental illness (unspecified) as well. Thus Mr. H would be viewed as having biological vulnerability to both mood and psychotic symptomatology.

As described above, Mr. H's initial psychological symptoms took the form of acting out in adolescence. According to his mother (5-3-83 correspondence), Mr. H first exhibited psychotic symptoms on his return to their home following his discharge from the Army in 1981. At that time, he erected a wooden pyramid to sleep under, professing bizarre beliefs about the advantages that would accrue to him from this practice. Potentially demonstrative of the interactive aspects of his methamphetamine abuse and genetic psychotic vulnerability, his family discovered drug paraphernalia for "shooting up" in the bathroom that he utilized (5-23-84 correspondence).

Mr. H's (interview, mother's 1984 correspondence) employment and relationship pattern was unstable across the subsequent 2 years. Both he and his mother described a marked break in his psychological perceptions and functioning occurring in the fall of 1983. In her correspondence, Ms. L noted that in October 1983 Mr. H began expressing vague paranoid ideation toward his roommates and girlfriend, as well as exhibiting symptoms of depression. Mr. H indicated that on Halloween 1983 he experienced a "premature awakening of kunbalini [life force]." The experience he described appears to have been an acute

psychotic break with a continuing delusional perception that he had leapt into the air and was struck by a bolt of lightning. He asserted that the associated transfer of energy exploded a car down the street. Mr. H also reported that he experienced thought insertion, thought broadcasting, and acute paranoia at that time. Ms. L, in her correspondence, described his 11-12-83 telephone call to her as exhibiting floridly psychotic delusional symptoms.

Mr. H was subsequently taken by his family to the Woods Hospital Emergency Room on 11-13-83, where he was admitted for 24 hours before being transferred to Glenhaven Psychiatric Hospital. Review of admission and discharge summaries associated with this admission reveal diagnoses of Schizophrenia, probably paranoid type with acute decompensation, and Multiple Drug Abuse.

Mr. H was subsequently treated at Glenhaven Psychiatric Hospital from 11-14-83 to 12-11-83. Diagnostic impression on admission was Acute Paranoid Schizophrenia. The diagnosis was revised midhospitalization to Depressive Reaction and Acute and Chronic Drug Use. On discharge, the diagnoses were as follows: Borderline Personality Disorder and Drug Abuse. These revised diagnostic impressions were apparently secondary to a conclusion that Mr. H's drug abuse had been integral to precipitating his psychotic experience.

Mr. H was admitted to the Veterans Administration Hospital on 12-12-83 with an initial diagnostic impression of Schizophrenia and Drug Dependence—LSD, methamphetamine. Mr. H was apparently treated in the VA for approximately 1 month. An effective transition to outpatient follow-up and outpatient medication maintenance did not occur.

Mr. H denied receiving any subsequent psychiatric intervention prior to the capital offense, though he noted that he was in a halfway house program for a period of time. As described earlier, he indicated that his psychological status varied with the intensity of his drug abuse. Conclusions regarding the severity of psychological disorganization occurring during the days and weeks prior to the capital offense vary depending on whether one relies on the May 1988 interviews described by Dr. Frost or the autobiographical account of his psychological deterioration entitled "Journal of James H: Personal History," apparently written by Mr. H in 1991. Certainly, aspects of the two murders had bizarre and disorganized elements consistent with psychotic experience, particularly in the face of Mr. H's previously nonviolent history. The issue is further complicated by Mr. H's fluctuating and inconsistent attempts to deny and minimize perceptions of himself as currently or previously psychotic. This tendency was variously exhibited during his interview and is also described in his psychiatric records and by family members; it may have been operative during the interview with Dr. F.

Psychological Status Since Incarceration Review of medical records reveals the occurrence of two suicide attempts while Mr. H was confined pretrial in the Harrison County Jail. These involved a self-inflicted laceration on 10-9-87 and a drug overdose on 12-27-87. These suicidal behaviors would be consistent with experience of a depressive disorder, particularly given depressive symptoms noted in the Glenhaven Psychiatric hospitalization of 1983 and the family history of affective disorder.

Mr. H has received only intermittent psychological/psychiatric support since his arrival at Death Row in 1988. Mr. H apparently first requested psychological services in July 1990 as he sought psychological testing relative to a writ that he was preparing to file with the courts. He was subsequently described by Richard F, Ph.D., Correctional Psychologist at the Death Row Unit, as being "personable," "verbal," and "able to relate well." Mr. H was additionally described as "doing well psychologically and experiencing no difficulties that were apparent" (8-19-90). Dr. F did note the following month, however, that Mr. H displayed some "paranoid mentation" in response to the interpretation of the MMPI that he had been given.

In October and November of 1990, Mr. H was described in the Death Row Unit Mental Health Records as being friendly, verbal, and appearing to do well. In early 1991, though, Mr. H began to report markedly exacerbated symptoms, including auditory hallucinations and feelings that he could read negative thoughts emanating from others. Skepticism was voiced in the progress note, however, as the report of these symptoms followed soon after Mr. H was informed that his sentence had been reversed and he would be re-

tried. In February 1991, Mr. H described auditory and tactile hallucinations involving "space beings" that he believed sometimes interfered with his thinking. Mr. H was described as finding these symptoms similar to those that he experienced in 1982 and 1983. At the same time, he was observed to be alert, oriented, cooperative, articulate, and without depressive or suicidal ideation. He was further described in contemporaneous progress notes as being in no acute distress.

Apparent continued exacerbation of psychotic symptoms was described in progress notes of 5-1-91 as Mr. H reported

> ideas of reference from TV and radio, and feels he can read other people's thoughts. Thinks maybe he has a special mission from God. MMPI showing profile consistent with schizoid personality or bipolar illness. Thought processes clean. Mood mildly depressed. No formal thought disorder. Impression Atypical Psychosis—Rule Out Paranoia Schizophrenia. Plan: Stelazine [an antipsychotic medication] 5mg at night for 30 days.

A subsequent note on 5-18-91 detailed continuing ideas of reference from the television with increased paranoia and complaints that the Stelazine was not effective. The medication order was modified to Thorazine [an antipsychotic medication], 100 mg in the morning and in the evening for 30 days.

Establishing whether or not Mr. H's symptom complaints across 1991 were bonafide is complicated by the mental health clinic note of 1-11-93 by Mr. Rice:

> Clinic Note: SCR. Have known inmate for several years. Admittedly used his drug history as pretext for "not guilty by reason of insanity" on retrial. He received another conviction and death sentence. Now in no distress and not in need of inmate services.

Subsequent clinic note of 9-25-94:

> inmate escorted to clinic saying he wants to talk specifically to Mr. R about several issues, primarily because he feels Mr. R might be helpful regarding a classification hearing. States he has no "psychological problems" at this time and would rather wait for Mr. R.

Mental status reveals good orientation, memory, affect. No sign of thought disorder, no suicidal/homicidal ideation noted. Inmate pleasant, talkative, appearing well-(illegible).

Subsequently on October 23, 1994, mental health notes reflect: "In no distress, oriented, calm, alert, not delusional, paranoid, or depressed." Subsequent clinic notes in 1995 and 1997 described Mr. H as continuing to be calm and in no apparent distress.

Inferences regarding Mr. H's psychological status across his death row incarceration can also be made from his participation in inmate activities. Mr. H indicated that for 6–7 months prior to his 1991 retrial, he worked on the paint crew 4 hours daily, 5 days a week. He stated that he was out of his cell most of the day during this time, interacting with other death row inmates. He described returning to this job for approximately 9 months following his retrial until he was removed from this position for engaging in a group inmate protest. He described subsequently becoming involved, along with other inmates, in writing and editing a death row newsletter entitled *Fortitude*. Mr. H described an intervening period of time where he was kept on lockdown because of refusing to cut his hair. When he relented regarding this grooming issue he returned to a more open wing and became involved with another newsletter: "Death Row Journal." Mr. H described returning to the paint crew in 1996 and 1997. He subsequently worked as a porter and tier janitor for approximately 1 year until he was removed from this position for transporting tobacco.

The absence of more intensive and continuous mental health intervention, as well as his participation in inmate work roles, suggests that thought disorder symptoms, if occurring, were sufficiently encapsulated or controlled to present no gross disturbance of his reality testing or capacity to appropriately modulate his behavior.

Interviews and affidavits of third parties reflect widely differing perceptions of Mr. H's psychological status on death row prior to and up to his 3-23-99 execution date (for which he received a stay). Specifically, affidavits of Brian F (Clemency Counsel), Margaret L (mother), Edward L (stepfather), Jacob H (brother), Larry R (cousin),

Glenn S (friend), and Jack L (stepbrother) detail various delusions and mental aberrations that Mr. H has exhibited to them involving pyramids, astral travel, atomic or telepathic powered flutes, communication with the dead, an inability to die, and use of quasi-religious constructions to explain and disguise delusional thought processes. Some of these affiants also described that such delusional beliefs were routinely interspersed with other instances in which Mr. H would seem logical, lucid, and reality oriented.

Telephone interview of family members also reflected their perception that Mr. H exhibited significant symptoms of mental illness. Jack L, his stepbrother, described Mr. H's past statements reflecting delusions that he had already died, could time-travel to past lives, had been killed by two aborigines with spears in a past life, associated this to their reincarnation as his two victims, had been physically restrained by God from killing others as part of his offense, and experienced astral projection. He further described Mr. H as conversationally preoccupied with his Sant Mat (derivative of Sikh tradition) religious beliefs.

Carla J, ex-wife and mother of Mr. H's two adolescent sons, described receiving letters from Mr. H that were full of strange ideas that made little sense. She described that many of these letters were sufficiently disorganized and illogical that she could not follow the thought processes. She added that the logic and clarity of Mr. H's thought processes, as reflected in his conversation, has fluctuated widely depending on the degree of emotional stress that he is experiencing. She described instances in which he was quite relevant and appropriate when relaxed, as contrasted with instances when he was under stress, struggled to form sentences, and "spaced off" to the extent that she was unsure whether he was still aware of her presence.

Keith H, Mr. H's brother, indicated that Mr. H has expressed beliefs that he can time-travel and more recently believed that he was traveling via astral projection to visit with Elizabeth L. He further asserted that Mr. H believes that in the course of these visits he has impregnated Elizabeth L and is the father of the baby she is carrying. Mr. H further noted that the look in Mr. H's eyes was also an indication of his underlying delusional experience.

By contrast, longstanding friends and correspondents of Mr. H do not perceive this same degree of psychological disorder. Steve M described himself as an ordained minister who also has a master's degree in counseling. He described having known and visited Mr. H for 10 years. He stated that while he believes Mr. H was mentally ill and psychotic at the time of the offense, he has observed no evidence of this psychosis in 10 years. He added that Mr. H has not tried and is not attempting to appear mentally ill. He observed that across the 10 years of their acquaintance, Mr. H has grown steadily calmer. He reported that he had never seen him as delusional. He indicated that they have discussed a wide range of issues, and while he does not agree with all of his beliefs, he has not considered them to be reflective of thought disorder.

Elizabeth L described a close relationship to Mr. H and his family for many years. She described that in a single conversation approximately 5 years ago, Mr. H made a comment that she perceived as "diabolical" and that frightened her. She described that otherwise Mr. H has consistently been "completely lucid." She described him a competent man who had experienced a past psychotic episode associated with drug use and whose psychological faculties were now unremarkable. She described him as a well-loved and well-respected inmate who has been a peacemaker and mediator with other inmates.

Cindy J described beginning to correspond with Mr. H approximately 7 years ago, with face-to-face meeting 4 to 5 years ago, and a series of telephone conversations approximately 4 years ago. She related that in his correspondence Mr. H had related dreams and "visions" that he has had that some might regard as fantastic or crazy. At the same time, she found him to be very articulate in his writing and expression, and did not perceive him as "round the bend."

Glenn S identified himself as an ordained minister with some training as a chaplain. Mr. H had given him consent to speak to me. Mr. S reported that he had known Mr. H for 3 to 4 years and had talked to him at length on approximately six or seven occasions for 2 to 4 hours each. He described that across these conversations he had not identified anything unusual about Mr. H's mental status. Specifically, Mr. S noted that he had detected no disorientation, confusion, delusions, or hallucinations. Mr. S expressed his opinion that Mr. H had a very serious psychological disorder at one time and had unsuccessfully attempted to get help prior to his capital offense. He described that Mr. H is no longer in the psychological state that he was at that time.

Sgt. Jones, State Department of Corrections, Death Row Unit, was interviewed on the Death Row Unit. He described that he had worked on death row since February 1998. During that time he could not recall Mr. H behaving in a bizarre or grossly disturbed fashion. He observed that Mr. H appeared to be a relatively bright inmate who did not attract a lot of attention. He said that Mr. H occasionally asked relevant and appropriate questions about how a particular policy might apply to him. Review of Mr. H's disciplinary record from November 1991 to February 1999 with Sgt. Jones revealed 10 disciplinary infractions, none of which appeared to reflect a disorganized pattern of behavior.

Current Mental Status   Mr. H was interviewed at length on two occasions, separated by approximately 2 weeks, so that comparative information could be obtained regarding his mental status. His presentation and mental status were virtually identical from one interview to the next. Mr. H presented as an alert male who appeared his stated age. His manner was cooperative, and he exhibited no unusual mannerisms or behavior. Hygiene was good, and no body odor was detected. Eye contact was consistent but not intimidating. Speech was clear and coherent. He was fully oriented to time of day, day of the week, date, month, and year. Additionally, he was oriented to being incarcerated on death row and that the interview was taking place in the infirmary. He could identify and recall my name and function both within and across the interviews. Mr. H appeared to be bright and verbally articulate. This observation is consistent with limited intellectual assessment performed by Richard F, Ph.D., in 1991 demonstrating verbal intellectual abilities in the 90th percentile and nonverbal intellectual abilities in the 80th percentile. Concentration as reflected in serial 7's and digit span was good. He subtracted backward from 100 by 7 rapidly and without error.

Recent and remote memory appeared to be intact. He could repeat six digits forward and five reversed. He could recall three colored objects, both after initial verbal presentation and after 10-minute delay. He could recall in detail his two capital trials and various activities in which he had been involved on death row. Additionally, he provided a history that was consistent with, although more detailed than, his records. Proverbs were well abstracted and desymbolized. He accurately performed simple arithmetic calculations. Mood was euthymic and affect appropriate to content of speech. Mr. H described his mood as being somewhat depressed following his stay of execution, as he had prepared himself for this event. Suicidal ideation was denied. Thoughts were generally logical and goal directed, with no evidence of tangentiality, circumstantiality, or loosened associations. Regarding his experience across the last several months, he denied hallucinations, paranoia, ideas of reference, thought insertion, or having a special mission in life.

While his general presentation was appropriate and realistic, there were indications of underlying, if well-encapsulated, delusional thought processes. Specifically, he denied that he had recently had the experience of broadcasting his thoughts to others, but indicated that he thought he could do so if he chose. When asked why he did not engage in such thought broadcasting, he explained that it would be an intrusion on the privacy of others and thus disrespectful. Additionally, Mr. H appears to have little observing ego regarding his psychotic breaks in 1982 and 1983. He appears not to recall the most disorganized aspects of his behavior at that time. Other aspects, such as jumping in the air and being met by a bolt of lightning, have been integrated into his religious beliefs as reflecting an actual event associated with the premature release of life force energy. Similarly, he now regards his disorganized and homicidal conduct at the time of the capital offense as not the product of a schizophrenic disorder or chronic drug-induced psychosis, but rather his responsiveness to and misinterpretation of communications and influences of destructive souls that he had relied on. Mr. H seems not to have logically and consistently integrated these experiences. In addition to reflecting on underlying residual thought disorder symptoms, Mr. H's failure to logically tie up these loose ends may also be associated with the "relative diffuse and generalized neurological impairment" described by Dr. F in 1991. Mr. H thus seems to have encapsulated his thought disorder vulnerability and integrated it with his religious beliefs, allowing his behavior to be broadly well organized and reality based and providing a vehicle for him to maintain an intact self-perception.

It is emphasized that Mr. H did not volunteer these delusional perspectives and even made every effort to present himself as normal and psychologically intact. These delusional beliefs were revealed only after continued probing.

To obtain additional information about Mr. H's current functioning, I observed the contents of his cell. There was a blanket rolled up at the top of his bed and a towel spread over a small storage chest. Socks and rags hung on a line on the wall of the cell. Newspapers and neatly stacked books were visible under the bed. The cell generally appeared to be neat and well ordered, with no clutter, filth, odor, or obviously bizarre writings or drawings. Mounted on the wall were a calendar, a picture of an Indian guru, and a printed color chart apparently of a Sant Mat spiritual pathway. At his sink were toothbrush, shampoo, Vaseline, and shaving brush. A paperback novel, *Conqueror's Pride* by Timothy Zahn, was visible.

Mr. H's responses to MMPI-2 personality testing revealed a profile pattern almost identical with that he obtained 12 years ago (contained in the Petition for Clemency and Reprieve, Section 29, Dr. Paul W's evaluation). The only significant discrepancy between the two is indication of more pronounced depressive symptomology, which is not surprising given Mr. H's more extended tenure on death row and his recent experience of a stayed execution date. This profile pattern also points to the psychological vulnerabilities of his history: antisocial trends, alcohol/drug abuse, and psychotic thought processes. Mr. H's responses to the Personality Assessment Inventory were quite consistent with the MMPI profile pattern, as he displayed trends toward psychotic thought processes and antisocial personality traits as well as substance abuse. Personality testing thus provides additional support for the presence of underlying or encapsulated thought disorder.

KNOWLEDGE OF EXECUTION

Mr. H stated that at his initial capital trial and his retrial, he was sentenced to death by lethal injection. When asked how that procedure would be carried out, he responded that he would be placed on a gurney and strapped down. I.V.s would be placed in both arms. He would then be given a combination of three different drugs: sodium pentathol, potassium chloride, and another that he could not identify. He reported that one of these drugs anesthetizes, another one stops the heart, and the third shuts down the respiratory center. He reported that the procedure is supposed to be painless, but he is uncertain of that, as no one has been back to make a report. Mr. H described that the procedure would take only a few minutes and that in most of the executions, the executed individual has been pronounced dead in less than five minutes. Mr. H indicated that an autopsy would be performed subsequently, and the body would then be released to relatives or whomever had been designated to pick it up. He reported that if this designation was not made, the inmate would be taken to a "potter's field" in the county where they would "plant your body in the ground." Mr. H thus expressed a clear understanding of the mechanisms of execution and inferentially its finality, as he pointed out that no one had been back to inform us regarding the subjective experience of it.

When questioned regarding what he expected would subjectively occur in his own execution, he responded that normally the spirit or soul is spread out all over the body, and in death attention is withdrawn from the limbs to the trunk, and then subsequently to the heart and the throat. As breath stops, he said, awareness goes into the head, and the rest of the body becomes numb. Consciousness then permanently departs the body.

When questioned about what would happen to his body following the execution, he said that it depended on whether the body was cremated or buried. If cremated, he said, since 75% to 80% of the body was water, it would be absorbed and the solids would return to the elements from which they came—earth, wind, and fire. He additionally explained that if cremated, he would be burned up and all of the atoms in his body would go to another form. When questioned what would occur if he were buried, he explained that it was the same process, but slower—decomposition would also involve heat, though at a lower temperature, and eventually his body would go back to the earth.

When questioned whether he expected to reanimate his body or come back to life, he replied that normally one doesn't reanimate one's body and that the way people come back is to reincarnate through a process of birth. He allowed that Jesus was described as being resurrected from the dead, so the phenomena is perhaps possible, but he did not expect that to happen to him.

When specifically questioned regarding whether there was any reason why he would not die at a scheduled execution, Mr. H responded, "Only if a miracle happens." When I inquired whether he is anticipating that a miracle will occur, he responded that he was not expecting a miracle to occur and would not hope for one even if that were a possibility. He described that he hopes not to even be reincarnated, as he would prefer to subsequently exist on a spiritual plane rather than be tied to the limitations of physical time and space.

When questioned regarding past statements that had been attributed to him that he could not die, he explained that he had apparently been misunderstood. He described that he had been speaking on a spiritual level. Specifically, he described a belief that his physical body could be killed and would decompose, but his spirit was everlasting and would be liberated by his death. When questioned regarding statements that had been attributed to him that he had already died, he explained that most of the experience of his life had been taken away by his prison confinement on death row. Additionally, he described that in the experience of meditation and dreams one withdraws consciousness from the body and may even travel as spirit consciousness outside of the prison. He described that he had thus had partial experience with the phenomena of withdrawing consciousness from his body with the critical difference being that in meditation consciousness returns to the body, while in death consciousness is unable to reanimate the body. Mr. H described that "physical death is irreversible."

Knowledge that His Execution Is Imminent   Mr. H described that his 3-23-99 execution date had been stayed in order to assess his competency to be executed. He described that a hearing would be scheduled shortly to address this issue. He anticipated being found competent to be executed and that a new execution date would be set for the near future. There is no indication that Mr. H's mental status has materially changed since 3-23-99. Accordingly, his perceptions and responses to that execution, which came within hours of being carried out, are considered to provide reliable inferences regarding his understandings. Mr. H reported that he had been well aware of the approach of this 3-23-99 scheduled execution date. Of greater significance, he described engaging in activities that provide some inference regarding his knowledge of the impending execution. Specifically, Mr. H described that much of his activity on death row has been oriented toward preparing himself to die. He described that he had read and studied comparative religions. He had most intensively studied the traditions of Sant Mat, a derivative of the Sikh tradition, and had become an "initiate" (disciple) within this religious group. He described establishing correspondence with a teacher or "Master," as well as other Sant Mat initiates.

Mr. H described his longstanding practice of meditation as oriented toward growing spiritually and preparing himself for death. He described that as a result he has come to a personal spiritual perspective of no longer being afraid to die. He explained that there is nothing to fear in death if you understand that death is only a transition, a doorway to a higher level of consciousness. He described that from this perspective, death is something to look forward to. He described a recognition that some would find his posture toward death difficult to understand. He explained that many people are quite attached to family, job, and possessions that they don't want to be separated from, and thus death is quite frightening for them. Mr. H described that because he had prepared himself and was ready to die in mid-March, he was disappointed and upset by the stay. He described, however, a perspective that these events are in God's time and that there is apparently a higher purpose involved in the delay. Mr. H additionally asserted that he did not desire for his religious beliefs regarding the role of the spirit or his understanding of the hereafter to be put on trial.

Regarding specific preparations for his March 23, 1999, execution date, Mr. H described that he began partial fast about a month before, drinking juices, milk, and a few nachos. He described that this was a process of cleansing and purifying his body for death and making it easier for his consciousness to separate from his body as it would not be involved in digesting food. Mr. H described that in the week prior to the scheduled execution, he meditated extensively and listened to Sant Mat religious tapes and music tapes. He said that for several days before the execution he did not sleep. He explained that he did not set out to stay awake; rather, he could not sleep as he was looking forward to going home and being with God and felt the presence of his guru. Mr. H further described fasting and sleep deprivation as being associated with vision quests such as those described by Native American Indian traditions. He described that he talked at length to death row inmate friends, one of whom had an execution date soon after Mr. H's.

Mr. H described that he had special, extended visits with his family, as well as his designated spiritual advisor (Elizabeth L) in anticipation of his execution. He explained that he had modified his visiting list to include individuals that he desired to invite as witnesses to his execution. He described primarily designating Sant Mat initiates as his witnesses so that their meditation could both provide support and create an ambiance that would facilitate the departure of his spirit from his body. Mr. H described saying goodbye to his physical family as his scheduled execution time approached. He reported that his family cried and were quite distressed. He reported that while he understood their grief, he saw his death as a cause for celebration as his spirit would be liberated. He described that his spiritual family of fellow Sant Mat initiates better understood this liberation and so responded to him more calmly and positively.

Mr. H described writing letters in anticipation of his impending execution. He described that some of these letters were directed toward individuals who had been corresponding with him, encouraging them not to cry for him, explaining that he was going home, and testifying to what the Master had done in his life. He acknowledged that the purpose of these letters was to give comfort to these individuals and to direct them toward what he regarded as a spiritual path of enlightenment. Mr. H described writing another letter to the families of his victims, asking for their forgiveness so that they would come to know the peace that he has.

Mr. H also demonstrated his awareness of the impending execution date in mid-March by giving away his possessions. He described that he had given his books the week before to Elizabeth L and had given other possessions to other inmates who were initiates.

Mr. H described that approximately 2 weeks before the execution date he met with Sgt. Jones, discussing and completing a form regarding the designation of witnesses, distribution of property, disposal of the remains, clothing worn to the execution, request for a last meal, and other final arrangements. According to Sgt. Jones, Mr. H responded to each of these inquiries in a considered, relevant, and rational fashion.

Understanding of the Reason He Is Being Executed
In response to inquiry, Mr. H described in detail the sequence and events associated with the murders of his two victims. He identified these victims by name and approximate age. He subsequently described his apprehension and charge for these offenses. As described above, he outlined the essential sequence and main events of both trials with accompanying critique of the performance of his attorneys. He described plausible hypotheses for his capital juries arriving at their determinations of guilt and sentence at each trial. He opined that the jury was likely fearful of his potential for future violence. He described an awareness and recognition that the sentence of death was specifically related to his conviction of capital murder. He further recognized that this sentence was scheduled to be carried out on 3-23-99. He reported that any future execution date established would represent a continuing effort to carry out the sentence of the jury.

Mr. H's recognition of the nexus between execution and the sentence of the court in this case is inferentially expressed by his autobiographical statement penned in 1986, as well as a letter to "Becky" dated 3-6-92. Mr. H described taking an active role in advising his attorneys of how the retrial could be pursued more effectively. This participation also supports an inference that Mr. H appreciated the relationship of his conviction to his sentence. Indeed, in his letter to Becky, Mr. H described the alternatives that might result from the retrial as including a return to Death Row or confinement in prison or a psychiatric hospital.

In this same letter, Mr. H demonstrated partial awareness at the time of the correspondence for the wrongful nature of his conduct as he described: "I regret what happened because those people died by my hand whereas I should have left them to their own karma." This is the same sentiment that he expressed during my recent evaluation interviews with him. He also acknowledged having had insufficient regard for human life at the time of the offense, as he denied his victims the opportunity to "realize God in this lifetime and obtain liberation from the cycle of birth and death."

Interestingly, in this correspondence to Becky, Mr. H identified that the processes of his mind prior to the capital offense may be of use to psychologists in the treatment of mental illness, noting the mental illness he had suffered and the delusions that he had operating under. At the same time, Mr. H's thought processes through the letter evolve toward notions of karma, destiny, and inevitability. Similarly, in my interviews with him he acknowledged how heavy drug abuse disrupted the rationality of his thought processes, while in the same discussion pointing to explanations of karma and the probability that he and his victims had been in some adversarial position with each other in a past life. In this sense, he expressed a belief that his behavior may have been an expression of justice for their offenses against him in a past life. He continues to express a belief that he and his victims converged through some expression of destiny / karma / synchronicity or other spiritual mechanism. As has been described earlier in this report, his integration of his religious beliefs into the psychological disorganization of his offense behavior appears to be the product of persistent residual psychotic thought process. Also noted previously, his explanation lacks logical integration and is thus inconsistently expressed.

Considerations of Mr. H's views of the underlying offense and whether these are adversely affected in their rationality by his psychological disorder are relevant to whether he understands "the reason he or she is being executed" as per Article 26.03. Specifically, the issue of whether Mr. H understands the reason that he is to be executed may be interpreted to mean that he understands that his execution is in response to a conviction and sentence for a specific charged act. It is troubling, though, that the statute in this regard employs the term "understand" rather than a more limiting term such as "know." "Understanding" of the reason that he is to be executed could be more broadly interpreted as whether he possesses a rational understanding of his own moral culpability for the capital offense (compromised by beliefs in karma, addressing past life injustices, acting with pure motives), the profound irreversible gravity of the act for the victims (compromised by belief in reincarnation), the ongoing risk of future violence (compromised by lack of insight regarding his psychotic disturbance), the demands of justice (compromised by belief in karma and trans-lifetime retribution), the hope of deterrence (compromised by belief in destiny and inevitability), and the horror of society (compromised by judgments that others are overattached to the temporal and physical), all of which arguably represent the fundamental reasons for the existence of a penalty of death and hence an execution.

A corollary issue when there is an irrational perspective regarding the underlying capital offense, involves whether such a mentally ill or mentally impaired defendant can come to terms with himself or make peace with his Maker prior to being executed. The reasonable, rational exercise of these self-examination and self-accountability / reconciliation to God functions would seem to require a rational view of the capital offense.

I emphasize, however, that I humbly regard the statutory interpretation of the extent of understanding of the reason for execution to be a matter of judicial determination and not psychological expertise. Accordingly, in this evaluation I have endeavored to provide data relevant to the extent and rationality of Mr. H's concrete and more abstract understandings of the reasons for execution. Generally, the view of his friends and fellow Sant Mat initiates reflected a more con-

crete interpretation of whether he associated his execution with his capital offense—hence their perception that he understands the reasons for his execution. His family, by contrast, expressed concern that he suffers from continuing delusional distortions of the capital offense and fails to recognize it as a tragic embodiment of his mental illness. These differences in perspective underscore the different interpretations of the meaning of "understand the reason for his execution" and will be illustrated in the section that follows.

Third Party Observations of Mr. H's Understandings   Third parties who interacted with Mr. H in close proximity to his March 23, 1999, scheduled execution date were interviewed. Because Mr. H's mental status appears to have been relatively stable since March 23, the observation of these individuals can provide useful information for inferring his understanding that he was to be executed, that the execution was imminent, and the reason for the execution.

Sgt. Stan Jones, State Department of Corrections, Death Row Unit, described completing the preexecution questions with Mr. H. He described informing Mr. H that the condemned man could designate five persons as execution witnesses, in addition to selecting a spiritual advisor. Sgt. Jones reported that Mr. H determined that he would remove some individuals from his visitors' list so that additional persons could be added to the witness list. Sgt. Jones described Mr. H as demonstrating a recognition that he was selecting friends who were coming to witness the execution. Sgt. Jones reported that Mr. H designated a spiritual advisor, who would have extended visits 2 days before and the day of the execution. He indicated that Mr. H did not want a will, as he had no substantial outside property, instead stating that he was going to give everything he had to his brother. Sgt. Jones said that Mr. H anticipated that he would spend the remaining funds in his inmate trust account or direct it to his brother or another individual.

In response to Sgt. Jones's inquiry regarding disposition of Mr. H's property on Death Row, he described Mr. H as indicating his intention to pack his property and give it to a visitor who was associated with his religious beliefs. Sgt. Jones explained to Mr. H that if he sent his property off the unit he could not get it back at a later time, though he could retain possession of it if he took it with him to the walls and his execution were then stayed. Mr. H was described as acknowledging his understanding of this provision. Sgt. Jones reported requesting the name and location of an attorney who could be in easy contact during the 36 hours before the execution, should some contact need to be made, and Mr. H designated the attorney who was handling his appeals. Sgt. Jones described discussing with Mr. H the disposition of remains, which would be necessary within 48 hours after the death sentence was carried out. Sgt. Jones could not recall specifically who Mr. H designated but believed that it was his brother or Mr. M. Sgt. Jones could not recall Mr. H's response to his request for a last meal. Mr. H informed me during the interview that he had not intended to take a last meal, as he wanted his digestive system to be empty and purified.

Sgt. Jones described asking Mr. H what clothing he wanted to wear to the execution and recalled that Mr. H elected to be executed wearing his prison uniform. Sgt. Jones noted that Mr. H appeared to be well aware of the realities of the pending execution, with no indication of lack of awareness of what was occurring or why these procedures were being followed. He described Mr. H as exhibiting no abnormal displays or expressions. He observed that Mr. H's responses seemed considered and well reasoned regarding election of individuals for his visiting and witness list and disposition of his property. As Sgt. Jones recalled, Mr. H appeared to have already made arrangements for disposition of his remains. He commented that Mr. H also had prepared a list of 12 inmates he wanted to see prior to his execution, a privilege that was extended to inmates whose death sentences are imminent.

When interviewed by telephone, Steve M, minister and 10-year friend of Mr. H, stated that Mr. H had taken him off of his visitation list with his approval so that he could put out of town family and friends on his list. He described him as requesting cremation, as he wanted Elizabeth L, his spiritual advisor, to take his ashes to India. Mr. M stated that Mr. H had initially asked her to take charge of the memorial service and funeral arrangements. Mr. M added that Mr. H gave away all of his possessions, including his stamps

and any remaining funds on his books. He indicated that Mr. H also gave away his typewriter but with an understanding that he could get it back if his execution were stayed. Mr. M reported that Mr. H wanted to see him the day of his scheduled execution to say goodbye, although they had spoken on many occasions of seeing each other in the next life. He described Mr. H as perceiving that he had done a "stupid" thing by telling two psychologists that he could not die when he knew they would "take it wrong" and assume that he meant physically and not spiritually. Mr. M stated that Mr. H exhibited knowledge that he would be executed, noting that he explained that one medication put him to sleep, another stopped his breathing, and a third one stopped his heart. Mr. M added that Mr. H absolutely recognizes that they are executing him for his capital offense of conviction.

Mr. M said that Mr. H was relatively certain that he would be executed on 3-23-99, and was reconciled to it. He described Mr. H as having reconciled himself to a spiritual realm and feeling shocked to have this aborted and to find himself still in his body. He reported that Mr. H retains a sense of self-preservation and does not want to die, but at the same time is not against the state for killing him for what he did. Mr. M observed that Mr. H's death preparations involved the presence of the Sant Mat fellow initiates who were assisting him with that process. He said that Mr. H wanted to have Sant Mat adherents present to assist him with the death process. He described Mr. H as having fasted for several days prior to the scheduled execution date to cleanse his body in preparation for the spirit leaving the body. Mr. M also observed that Mr. H was attempting to have closure with everyone that he could. According to Mr. M, Mr. H described his family as angry and conflicted, and was attempting to reconcile them with each other. Mr. M noted that Mr. H had spoken to him of wanting to write something that would facilitate reconciliation with the families of his victims. He described Mr. H as fully discussing with him the steps of execution and sequence of his body being picked up by the local funeral home as well as the subsequent disposition. He described Mr. H's awareness of conflicts that his mother had with his disposition desires; she wanted to have his ashes to spread at the family cemetery, while he wished that his ashes would be spread in India. Mr. M described Mr. H asking him to help protect his wishes.

Elizabeth L, designated spiritual advisor, described arriving the week before the 3-23-99 execution date with two 4-hour special visitations on 3-16-99 and 3-17-99. She observed that on the Monday prior to the execution date, she was there for 8 hours. She described Mr. H's awareness that his execution was imminent, as evidenced by his writing and notifying her when he received an execution date. She stated that he had informed her of the preexecution procedures of the prison, including extended visitation policies, necessary visitor identification, and other information that she needed to visit within the prison. She commented that the prison chaplain subsequently briefed the witnesses but that Mr. H had already comprehensively covered this information with her. She described Mr. H as being concerned that she be prepared for what she might see during the actual execution. She noted that he explained in detail the specific process of execution, including the sequence of injection by three different drugs and the effects that each would have on his body. He also described to her the potential side effects of the execution drugs, including convulsing, shaking, urinating, and seizures.

Elizabeth L described Mr. H as expressing the desire that his body be cremated and his ashes divided into two portions—some for his mother and the remainder for Elizabeth. She described his desire to have his ashes sprinkled at a Retreat Center of the Sant Mat community. She explained that there is a burial ground there where Mr. H's spiritual teacher had once visited. Elizabeth commented that Mr. H had originally wanted her and his mother to take the ashes to India and meet his teacher's successor. As a result of more extended discussions, she said, Mr. H was convinced that it would be more practical, given the expense of such travel and his mother's age, to have his mother distribute that portion of this ashes on the Pacific coast rather than India.

Elizabeth L said that Mr. H had been building up to the execution and that he and most of the other initiates sat and meditated together for approximately an hour before he was led out to the actual death chamber unit. Mr. H had asked to be anointed prior to his execution, she indicated, but the prison administration had denied this request. She added that anointing was not part of the Sant Mat tradition but was Mr. H's way of attempting to gain closure with his body. Regarding the Sant Mat witnesses, she commented that he wanted all of them to be silent with him in meditation, as he expressed an anticipation of taking some comfort from others in the room being "on the same wavelength." This is a belief system that she shares, as she indicated that if someone knew that he was going to be ejected from the body, it was nice to have supportive people around him.

Elizabeth L also described Mr. H as fasting solidly for 14 days prior to the scheduled execution and not sleeping much at the end. She further described him as wanting to maintain his dignity even in death and his desire to avoid defecating on the execution table. He had given her his entire library as well as letters from his spiritual teacher, legal documents, and artwork, she reported, and released two large bags of property to her just prior to the execution date.

Regarding Mr. H's understanding of the reasons for his execution, she said that she and Mr. H had discussed over a period of years that he was going to be executed because of his crime. She described possessing many letters that express an understanding of the reason that he is in this predicament and that she has had no communication before or since that deviates from this. Elizabeth L was unable to identify any communication or behavior of Mr. H that would lead her to believe that he did not understand the reality of his execution, the imminent nature of it, or the reason for it.

Elizabeth L reported that Mr. H was quite depressed following the stay of execution, as he had given away everything he owned and thus was taken back to an empty cell. She reiterated his belief system that Sant Mat initiates don't regard death as evil but rather as a reunion with the Divine. She described Sant Mat as a small and somewhat obscure derivative of the Sikh tradition that it is not a very large movement in the United States. She also stated that Mr. H had expressed concern that Sant Mat not be placed on trial in his case.

Cindy J, one of the designated witnesses for the stayed 3-23-99 execution, described arriving on 3-21-99 and leaving on 3-24-99. Mrs. J said that she had previously offered to be present at his execution and had heard of the Mr. H's execution date through mutual friends. She described writing him and again offering to be present, adding that he wrote back and said that he would like for her to be there. She described conversing with Mr. H on 3-22 and 3-23 for a couple of hours each day, as this time was also shared with the family. She described Mr. H as being aware of the date and time of the execution and added that she saw his associated emotional turmoil stemming from multiple simultaneous visitors exhibiting a wide range of emotional responses. She said that Mr. H was quiet and mostly let others talk to him, adding that he always showed an awareness that he was in prison, appeared to recognize visitors even though some had not been to see him in prison, and was quite patient in letting others tell him whatever they needed. She reported that when she was with him she saw no evidence of hallucinations. Mrs. J is also a Sant Mat initiate and indicated that others might think their perception of God was bizarre or delusional—particularly the belief that someone could look forward to and embrace death rather than being afraid of it. She said that because Mr. H was so calm, others who were present regarded this as bizarre. She reported that his family was quite emotional and expected him to be as well.

Mrs. J recalled that Mr. H spoke to Elizabeth L about the disposition of his remains. Mrs. J recalled that another minister had asked Mr. H what he wanted done with the remains and that he had described his desire to be cremated. Mrs. J could not identify any communications or behaviors with Mr. H that would suggest that he did not understand the reality of his execution, it imminent nature, or the reason for it. Mrs. J also described Mr. H as being confused and upset when the execution was stayed, as he had been looking forward to being free. She said that he had written to her prior to the scheduled execution that he was looking forward to being "released" (spiritually) soon.

Mr. Glenn S (minister) indicated that he had arrived in the Death Row area on 3-20-99, and

left on Thursday 3-25-99. He described conversing with Mr. H on Monday 3-22-99 and Tuesday 3-23-99. He also described Mr. H's belief in the hereafter—that his physical body could be killed but his spirit would live on, and that dying was "going home." He thought that Mr. H was prepared to die, at least as prepared as one can be. He noted that Mr. H was doing everything that he could to prepare for the moment when his body and soul would separate, including fasting, meditation, prayer, and restitution efforts toward the family members of his victims. Mr. S described Mr. H speaking to him of a letter that he was preparing for this latter purpose.

Mr. S described Mr. H as giving most of his musical instruments, books, and writings to Elizabeth L to distribute. He said that Mr. H had shown a desire for his sons to have some of the things that were important to him, including the flute. Mr. S described Mr. H as seeking closure with a number of people as his execution date neared, and characterized the entire preceding weekend as a process of goodbye. He described Mr. H's preparation of the last hours as involving meditation so that he could maintain the clarity of mind and focus in the moment of death, and his perception of the process of silent meditation as a mechanism to begin separating from the body and moving to the spiritual realm. He observed that Mr. H was almost looking forward to this, not in a suicidal fashion or without self-preservation, but as a process of preparing to die. He described Mr. H as having a profound faith in letting go, adding that Mr. H considered God to be ultimately in control.

Mr. S described Mr. H as wanting to be cremated and wanting his mother, Mr. S, and Elizabeth L to take his ashes to India. He described Mr. H as acceding to the wishes of his mother to divide his ashes so that some could be placed at the family cemetery. He described their discussion of the spiritual implications of separating his ashes, with him ultimately concluding that it would be acceptable to divide them. He described him as expressing empathy with his mother's experience of the tragedy of having a son about to be executed.

Mr. S described Mr. H as being quite aware that his execution had been scheduled for Tuesday, 3-23-99, and that all of the activities of the preceding weekend had pointed toward that execution. He further observed that Mr. H had asked that they meditate as part of the preparation for his execution at 6:00 p.m. Tuesday, and displayed no confusion or disorientation regarding the presence of friends and fellow initiates or the rationale for this meditation activity.

Mr. S described Mr. H as having expressed his recognition of the reason for the execution—that he had been convicted of killing two people and had been given the death sentence. In response to my question about whether Mr. S could provide any information that might suggest that Mr. H did not understand that he was to be executed, that his execution was imminent, or the reason for his execution, Mr. S said that he could not.

Mr. H's family expressed greater reservations regarding his psychological status and relevant capacities for understanding at the time of his 3-23-99 stayed execution date. Jack L, Mr. H's stepbrother, described arriving on 3-19-99 and returning to his home on 3-24-99. Mr. L described having visitation with Mr. H on Friday, Saturday, Monday, and Tuesday, with most of these visits being about 2 hours long. Mr. L stated that on the preceding Saturday he had spoken to Mr. H about a flute that he had built that he described as being powered by mental telepathy and operating with perpetual motion. During his last two visits, Mr. L indicated that Mr. H appeared to be in a trance-like state, not saying very much and simply looking blankly from one person to another. He described Mr. H's verbalizations as being limited to "yes," "no," or "can you feel the love?" Mr. L described a few other instances in which Mr. H responded that he could feel the Master standing behind him. At the same time, Mr. L acknowledged that Mr. H had given his personal property to Elizabeth L and was writing a letter to the family members of his victims. When I asked why he had given his possessions away, Mr. L replied "because he [Mr. H] thought he was going to die." Mr. L went on to explain, however, that at times Mr. H said that he was already dying and that at other times would say that he couldn't die. Mr. L reported that Mr. H had stopped eating and sleeping for several days, as Mr. H said he no longer needed to eat—that activity was simply a physical thing.

Mr. L said that Mr. H had spoken to his (Mr. H's) mother over the years about his desire to be cremated and have his mother fly to India and sprinkle his ashes over the area where his teacher's ashes had been spread. Mr. L added that in the last days before the scheduled execution, Mr. H changed his plans and said that Elizabeth L should get the ashes. When I asked her why Elizabeth L was to get the ashes, Mr. L explained that Elizabeth L is pregnant and Mr. H believes that she is pregnant with his child, through which he would be reincarnated as the new Sant Gi or teacher. When I inquired as to whether he had explicitly stated this, Mr. L described that it had been "sort of alluded to" as Mr. H had smiled and said "I know" when told of Elizabeth L's pregnancy. Mr. L described Mr. H's awareness of some discussion about whether their mother would get some of the ashes.

When I inquired regarding any steps Mr. H might have made to have a sense of closure or say goodbye, Mr. L indicated that the last day the family was visiting, Mr. H had gazed at each of them for about 10 minutes without blinking, seemingly as a way of saying goodbye.

When I asked Mr. L whether he had seen anything from Mr. H that might suggest he did not understand the reason for his execution, Mr. L replied only that Mr. H believes that what happened is his karma and he was destined for death row—and that the offenses therefore had to happen. Mr. L indicated that while Mr. H knows on one level that he is being executed because two people were killed, he relates that offense to another reason that has nothing to do with the murder—karma and destiny.

Mr. L described Mr. H as being aware of the pending execution as far as Mr. L could tell, although Mr. L added that they did not talk about the execution during the last few days. He said that in their earlier conversations that weekend, Mr. H had talked to him about their life together growing up. By contrast, during the last 2 days before the scheduled execution, Mr. L indicated that Mr. H appeared to believe that they were communicating telepathically.

Keith H, Mr. H's older brother, arrived in the area on 3-22-99 and left on 3-24 or 3-25. He described being able to have two visits with Mr. H, the second being shared with a number of other people. He described the visits as lasting 2 to 3 hours. Keith described Mr. H as participating in saying goodbye to him, talking to him about their growing up and how much he loved him and appreciated things he had done for him, looking to meet him on the other side. Keith said that on the day of the scheduled execution, Mr. H didn't speak much. Keith said he thought that it was unnatural that Mr. H didn't break down, but added that he knew his brother was aware that the family could not handle witnessing the execution. Keith described Mr. H as giving away his possessions to other inmates on death row, with his personal papers going to Elizabeth L. Keith further described Mr. H as fasting for a period of time in preparation for the execution, as Mr. H believed that if he fasted the death process would be easier. Keith discussed his perception of Mr. H being delusional during these final visits based on "the look in his eyes." He indicated that he observed no evidence of overt hallucinations but found it strange that the Sant Mat initiates would look at one another and nod and smile, with one commenting that they did not need to talk as they knew each other's thoughts. Mr. H recognized the family members and evidenced no surprise or confusion as to why they were there, according to Keith, who added that he believes that Mr. H knows he is to be executed and that this will result in his departing his physical body. He further described Mr. H having expressed awareness that he has been convicted of capital murder by the court and that this is the reason for his execution.

SUMMARY

The following expert opinions are offered with a reasonable degree of psychological certainty.

There are historical indications of severe psychotic disturbance of a schizophrenic, drug-induced, and/or combination etiology. Encapsulated or residual aspects of this psychotic disorder remain as demonstrated in Mr. H's mental status, psychological testing, and family descriptions.

Diagnostic Impression
- Schizophrenia, Paranoid type, Episodic with mild interepisode residual symptoms (DSM-IV #295.30)
- Rule out: Psychotic Disorder Not Other-

wise Specified, Hallucinogen and Amphetamine Induced, with Hallucinations and Delusions, mild residual symptoms (DSM-IV #298.9)
- Rule out: Diffuse mild neuropsychological deficits (by history and prior testing)
- Substance Dependence, in remission secondary to controlled environment (by history)

Despite the presence of these residual symptoms, Mr. H's behavior and interaction pattern has been sufficiently well compensated in the structured environment of prison that his symptoms, with brief exceptions, have not been obvious to State Department of Corrections mental health clinicians, correctional staff, or friends with whom Mr. H has maintained longstanding acquaintance.

No data were made available to me to indicate that Mr. H, at any time across his tenure on death row, has failed to recognize that he is physically confined on death row and facing execution.

He is able to describe the process and mechanism of execution in detail as well as the subsequent destruction of the physical body and irreversibility of physical death. His recognition of the imminent nature of his execution as displayed within the last 2 months when his 3-23-99 execution was stayed is reflected in his verbalized reports. This awareness of the imminent nature of his execution is demonstrated in a series of behaviors including giving away property, making plans for the disposition of his remains, seeking emotional closure with family and friends, preparing correspondence to the families of his victims, engaging in a pattern of intensive fasting and meditation, and assembling a group of witnesses to assist his spiritual exit.

Mr. H exhibited a concrete understanding of the reasons for his execution in that he described the capital offense and associated victims; provided a relatively detailed and insightful account of his two capital trials, their shortcomings and rationales for their outcome; and expressed a recognition that his execution would be the enactment of the death sentence imposed by his capital jury.

Mr. H further exhibited partial awareness of the moral implications of his capital offense and the future dangerousness concerns of the jury. He does not regard his execution as a miscarriage of justice.

It is probable, though, that Mr. H's understanding of his personal culpability and other abstract foundation reasons for the imposition of a death penalty for his capital offense of conviction is disturbed and compromised by encapsulated underlying psychotic thought processes that have become integrated with his religious beliefs. Whether an "understanding of the reason for execution" extends to a fully rational appreciation of broader and more abstract execution justifications as opposed to a more concrete recognition of the execution being the sentence of the court for a given crime is a matter of judicial determination.

Respectfully submitted,
Mark D. Cunningham, Ph.D.
Clinical and Forensic Psychologist
Diplomate in Forensic Psychology
American Board of Professional Psychology

Teaching Point: Why and how do you attribute information to sources in forensic mental health assessment?

Attributing information to specific sources in a forensic mental health assessment is done for the following four primary purposes:

1. Identifying the source of the data allows the parties in the litigation to confirm the information through investigation, produce and review these records, and/or call these individuals as witnesses at trial. Both direct and cross-examination are better informed when the source of the data is made explicit. Additionally, the trier of fact is better able to compare the representations of the report with the testimony of particular witnesses.
2. By specifying the source of the data, both of the parties to the litigation, as well as the trier of fact, are informed of the nature of the relationship between the source and the individual being evaluated. Any potential bias of the source is thus more transparent.
3. Disclosure of the presence or absence of redundant reports provides data regarding the corroboration of evidence.
4. Identification of the sources of information allows independent appraisals of the comprehensiveness, neutrality, and reliability of the evaluation.

As with many issues, the "how" of source attribution is less straightforward and more problematic than the "why." For example, in a complex case with extensive records, identification of every document reviewed and subsequent detailed attribution to it could become prohibitively lengthy. Similarly, detailed description of each third party's report could bog down rather than assist the understanding of the trier of fact. There is a place for shorter reports and more limited testimony. It is important, however, to consider the purpose of the report; whether it will later be supplemented by more detailed testimony; whether records and sources are already listed in other discovery; what detail promotes scrutiny, accuracy, and fairness; and what data are needed by the trier of fact to avoid abdicating its role to the expert.

In the preceding report on competence for execution, the balance leaned toward the more detailed source attribution. There were a number of reasons for this decision to draft a report of highly specific source attribution:

1. The determination before the court was one of extraordinary gravity.
2. It was unlikely that there would be opportunity to supplement the report with oral testimony.
3. Discrepancies in the observations of family and other third parties were most accurately conveyed through their own descriptions. Additionally, by identifying these third parties and their relationship history with the death row inmate, the frequency/quality of their observations, as well as any bias in their perceptions, could more easily be scrutinized.
4. Anecdotal descriptive detail provided the most transparent basis for understanding and critiquing the analysis of the data in the report.
5. The report was intended to be informative and analytical, but not conclusory with respect to the ultimate legal question.

Of course, even in this example involving more specific source attribution, not every detail was included. Specific categories of records were detailed, but not every document within those categories. Records, interview, testing, and third-party reports were edited to include only information deemed relevant to the psycholegal determination before the court. For additional consideration, see the *Specialty Guidelines for Forensic Psychologists* (1991) VII.E., VI.B., VI.F.1, VI.F.3, VII.B., and VII.D.

Chapter 7

Criminal Sentencing

This chapter has four case reports on criminal sentencing. Although FMHA on criminal sentencing may be conducted for a variety of charges (for example, see Chapter 12 for an example of a federal criminal sentencing evaluation), all four reports in this chapter are capital sentencing evaluations. We have focused on this kind of FMHA because capital sentencing evaluations are among the most detailed and demanding forensic assessments that are performed. The principle applied to the first case involves the nature of notification or informed consent that is applicable in FMHA, while the teaching point elaborates on this issue in the context of capital sentencing evaluations. The principle associated with the second case—obtain relevant historical information—addresses the importance of history in FMHA broadly considered, while the teaching point again contains a more specific elaboration on the application of this principle in capital sentencing cases. The principle applied to the third case involves the importance of impartiality in FMHA and the need to decline certain referrals when impartiality does not appear possible for the forensic clinician. This is a particularly important consideration in capital sentencing cases, which often involve heinous acts; the teaching point involves the perspective of the contributing forensic clinician on "cases that I won't take—and why." Finally, the principle regarding the importance of history is again applied to the fourth case, reflecting the particular relevance of historical information on defendants undergoing capital sentencing evaluations. The teaching point addresses the accuracy of third-party information that contributes to the development of an appropriately comprehensive history in this kind of FMHA.

Case 1

Principle: **Provide appropriate notification of purpose and/or obtain appropriate authorization before beginning**

This principle concerns the information about the evaluation conveyed to the individual being assessed, and the nature of the authorization needed, before the evaluation begins. This can vary depending on whether the context of the evaluation calls for providing the evaluee with relevant information (notification of purpose), or providing this information and also obtaining informed consent. This distinction is important because it suggests that while informed consent is needed in some forensic assessments, it is not in others—and need not be requested in the same way.

Evaluations that are authorized by court order generally do not require informed consent.[1] FMHA on competence to stand trial or involuntary civil commitment are examples. For such evaluations, it is appropriate to begin with a notification of purpose. For other types of FMHA that are not conducted under court order, typically cases that are referred by the individual's attorney, the forensic clinician must obtain the informed consent of the individual being assessed.

In either instance, the forensic clinician should identify himself/herself, describe the evaluation to be conducted (its purpose, who requested or authorized it, how it might be used, and how the results will be conveyed), and indicate that the evaluation is not part of a therapeutic or treatment relationship. Generally, the information should be conveyed in clear, basic language appropriate to the individual's capacity for understanding written or spoken language. A reasonable guideline is that such information should be conveyed at a comprehension level no higher than necessary to take a standardized objective test such as the MMPI-2. The information should be provided at an even more basic level if the individual has significant intellectual and/or verbal comprehension deficits. It is also important to assess how well the individual has understood this information.

Much of the information provided to the individual being evaluated will be comparable under both the informed consent and notification of purpose/ limits on confidentiality conditions. However, there may be differences between the information provided under each condition in the following areas: (1) the purpose of the evaluation; (2) who has authorized the evaluation; (3) how the evaluation will be used; (4) the expected and possible limits on confidentiality; (5) whether the individual can exercise discretion over how and when the report will be used; and (6) who will receive the results of the evaluation.

Elaboration of this approach to notification of purpose and informed consent can be found in the *Criminal Justice Mental Health Standards* (American Bar Association [ABA], 1989) and the *Guidelines for Child Custody Evaluations in Divorce Proceedings* (American Psychological Association [APA], 1994). The *Criminal Justice Mental Health Standards* indicates that both the evaluating forensic clinician and the defense attorney have obligations to provide a defendant with a clear explanation of the purpose and nature of the evaluation, the potential uses of any disclosures made during the evaluation, the conditions under which the prosecution will have access to information obtained and reports prepared, and the consequences of the defendant's refusal to cooperate with the evaluation. The *Guidelines for Child Custody Evaluations in Divorce Proceedings* recommends that informed consent be obtained from all adults, participants, and as appropriate, child participants, and that all participants be informed about the limits of confidentiality and the disclosure of information.

Additional support for providing appropriate notification of purpose and/ or obtaining informed consent before beginning the FMHA can be found in several sources of authority. The American Psychological Association's *Ethical Principles of Psychologists and Code of Conduct* (APA, 1992) addresses this principle as follows:

> When psychologists provide assessment, evaluation . . . or other psychological services to an individual, a group, or an organization, they provide, *using language that is reasonably understandable* to the recipient of those services, appropriate information beforehand about the nature of such services and appropriate information later about results and conclusions. (p. 1600; emphasis added)[2]

In addition, the *Ethics Code* clearly describes the importance of this type of notification:

> Psychologists discuss with persons and organizations with whom they establish a scientific or professional relationship (including, to the extent feasible, minors and their legal representatives) (1) the relevant limitations on confidentiality, including limitations where applicable in group, marital, and family therapy or in organization consulting, and (2) the foreseeable uses of the information generated through their services. (p. 1606)

The *Specialty Guidelines for Forensic Psychologists* (Committee on Ethical Guidelines for Forensic Psychologists, 1991) elaborates on the distinction between notification and informed consent and the appropriate procedure when the latter is needed but not obtained:

> Unless court ordered, forensic psychologists obtain the informed consent of the client, or party, or their legal representative, before proceeding with such evaluations and procedures. If the client appears unwilling to proceed after receiving a thorough notification of the purposes, methods, and intended uses of the forensic evaluation, the evaluation should be postponed and the psychologist should take steps to place the client in contact with his/her attorney for the purpose of legal advice on the issue of participation. (p. 659)

The *Specialty Guidelines* also refers specifically to the importance of informing the individual of his or her relevant legal rights:

> Forensic psychologists have an obligation to ensure that prospective clients are informed of their legal rights with respect to the anticipated forensic service, of the purpose of the evaluation, of the nature of the procedures to be employed, of the intended uses of any product of their services, and of the party who has employed the forensic psychologist. (p. 659)

The *Principles of Medical Ethics with Annotations Especially Applicable to Psychiatry* (American Psychiatric Association, 1995) indicates that

> Psychiatric services, like all medical services, are dispensed in the context of a contractual arrangement between the patient and the treating physician. The provisions of the contractual arrangement, which are binding on the physician as well as on the patient, should be explicitly established. (p. 4)
>   A physician shall respect the rights of patients, of colleagues, and of other health professionals, and shall safeguard patient confidences within the constraints of the law. (p. 5)

Although this language is less explicit than that in the *Specialty Guidelines*, there is an emphasis on two similar points. The first involves the understanding about the nature of the relationship, which is explicitly established, and the second involves a respect for confidentiality rights under the law. This is described even more explicitly when the *Principles of Medical Ethics* addresses services that are more similar to FMHA than many described in this document:

> Psychiatrists are often asked to examine individuals for security purposes, to determine suitability for various jobs, and to determine legal competence. The psychiatrist must fully describe the nature and purpose and lack of confidentiality of the examination to the examinee at the beginning of the examination. (p. 6)

As with the other sources of ethics authority, the *Ethical Guidelines for the Practice of Forensic Psychiatry* (American Academy of Psychiatry and the Law [AAPL], 1995) emphasizes the importance of establishing the limitations on confidentiality at the beginning of the evaluation. They note that

> An evaluation of forensic purposes begins with notice to the evaluee of any limitations on confidentiality. Information or reports derived from the forensic evaluation are subject to the rules of confidentiality as apply to the evaluation and any disclosure is restricted accordingly. (p. 1)

In several places, the *Ethical Guidelines* also allude to the distinction between informed consent and notification of purpose:

> The informed consent of the subject of a forensic evaluation is obtained when possible. Where consent is not required, notice is given to the evaluee of the nature of the evaluation. If the evaluee is not competent to give consent, substituted consent is obtained in accordance with the laws of the jurisdiction. (p. 2)

The distinction between circumstances involving the need for informed consent versus those requiring notification is again made:

> It is important to appreciate that in particular situations, such as court ordered evaluations for competency to stand trial or involuntary commitment, consent is not required. In such a case, the psychiatrist should so inform the subject and explain that the evaluation is legally required and that if the subject refuses to participate in

the evaluation, this fact will be included in any report or testimony. (AAPL,1995, p. 2)

In addition, the importance of emphasizing that the clinician is playing a forensic role, rather than providing treatment, is underscored:

> The forensic situation often presents significant problems in regard to confidentiality. The psychiatrist must be aware of and alert to those issues of privacy and confidentiality presented by the particular forensic situation. Notice should be given as to any limitations. For example, before beginning a forensic evaluation, the psychiatrist should inform the evaluee that although he is a psychiatrist, he is not the evaluee's "doctor." The psychiatrist should indicate for whom he is conducting the examination and what he will do with the information obtained as a result of the examination. (p. 2)

The forensic clinician should provide information about the evaluation that is accurate in the context of the individual's legal circumstances and consistent with applicable statutes, administrative code, and case law. It should be communicated in plain, simple language. If written notification is provided, then the required reading level should not be greater than that necessary to take a standard psychological test such as the MMPI-2. Whether this information is provided orally or in writing, the evaluator should check to determine how much of the information was understood by asking that the major elements be recalled and, if necessary, paraphrased.

The importance of disclosure as part of notification of purpose and informed consent, in the context of FMHA, was highlighted in *Estelle v. Smith* (1981). In *Estelle*, the U.S. Supreme Court affirmed the lower court's decision to prohibit the use of the results of a trial competence evaluation in a subsequent sentencing proceeding in which the defendant was not notified that the results of the FMHA could be used in both proceedings.[3]

The present case report provides an example of the application of this principle. The purpose of the evaluation was to provide the defense with information relevant to the capital sentencing of a 21-year-old man charged with murder. More specifically, the report indicates that the evaluation was conducted because the defense attorney wanted the jury to understand the defendant's history of antisocial behavior in the context of the possible presence of neuropsychological dysfunction. Given the death penalty context and the defense-requested status of the evaluation, informed consent is clearly an important issue in this case.

Because the defendant appeared to have neuropsychological deficits, it was particularly important that the forensic clinician ensured that the defendant understood the relevant information. Accordingly, such information would have been provided at a very basic level.

The defendant in this case, Jimmy M., was charged with aggravated murder in the shooting death of a police officer in November of 1997. Mr. M has an extensive criminal record and a history consistent with an antisocial personality disorder. The question often raised by defense attorneys in such a case is whether to introduce such evidence to the jury or to avoid any mention of such a disorder. Antisocial personality disorder is not usually considered to be a mitigating factor.

In this case, the defense attorneys felt that the jury should be educated about the disorder and given a complete history of this defendant in order to explain why Mr. M acted the way he did. In addition to the antisocial personality disorder, Mr. M had suffered from a serious head injury, resulting in the request for a neuropsychological evaluation. Therefore, the following report contains a mitigation report, which includes a separate report from a consulting neuropsychologist.

PSYCHOLOGICAL REPORT

Re: State of Ohio v. Jimmy M
Preliminary Psychological Evaluation

Jimmy M is a 21-year-old African American male referred to me for a psychological evaluation. He is currently charged with aggravated murder, with death penalty specifications. Mr. M was interviewed on the following dates for a total of approximately 14 hours:

- December 24, 1997
- December 31, 1997
- January 30, 1998
- February 12, 1998
- February 22, 1998
- April 30, 1998
- May 28, 1998

In addition to the clinical interview, the following materials were reviewed and taken into consideration in the preparation of this report:

1. Leroy School Records
2. Thompson School Records
3. Leroy General Hospital Records coverings periods of treatment from 9/21/76–9/24/76, 12/22/76, 2/12/77, 3/26/77, 6/28/77, 8/1/77, 8/20/77, 10/28/77, 12/16/77–12/19/77, 3/16/85, 6/9/85, 8/20/85, 9/14/88, 9/15/88, 3/22/89, 8/11/89, 9/16/94, 8/10/97, and 8/12/97
4. Records from Leroy Clinic
5. Metro Life Flight & Hospital
6. Superior County Jail Medical
7. Juvenile Court Summary
8. Youth Detention Center Summary
9. Probation Summary
10. Jail Records Summary
11. Child Support Summary
12. Superior County Youth Detention Center
13. Presentence Report, Case #xxxxx
14. M Docket, Case #xxxxx
15. Employment Summary and records from Mag-Nif, Inc., Borg-Warner, and Royal Plastics, and
16. Darlene M Docket Summaries: 2/85 trial digest Docket CR #xxxxx, Docket CR #xxxx, Docket CR #xxxxx.

CREDENTIALS

I am a Board Certified Forensic Psychologist and a Diplomate of the American Board of Professional Psychology, and am licensed to practice psychology in Ohio. I am Professor of Psychology at Lake Erie College and Director of their Criminal Justice Program. I am also the Associate Director for the Lake County Forensic Psychiatric Clinic and have worked there for the past 17 years performing evaluations for the Lake County Court of Common Pleas. My private practice includes both clinical and forensic psychology. I have evaluated well over 5,000 adult criminal defendants, including approximately 175 charged with capital offenses.

SOCIAL HISTORY

Jimmy M reported that he was born to Darlene M (who was 15 years old when she got pregnant) and apparently Bob Hoover on September 21, 1976. He indicated that he has only seen his father twice, once when he was in the fifth or sixth grade and a second time last year while he was incarcerated. He indicated that he was primarily raised by Martha Washington as his foster grandmother; Ms. Washington was Jimmy's mother's foster parent. Ms. Washington raised a number of foster children. Records indicate that Darlene M was a drug addict and alcoholic who was arrested and spent time in jail and prison before dying of a drug overdose in 1989. On one occasion, when Mr. M was eight years old, according to court documents, Darlene and her codefendants used Mr. M to hide stolen money. Mr. M's records indicate significant behavioral problems following his mother's death. He subsequently had numerous contacts with juvenile authorities and was placed with the Department of Youth Services on several occasions. He reported numerous conflicts with his grandmother, and records indicate that Ms. Washington was often unwilling to assume custodial care, although on other occasions she would request custody. Mr. M stated that they remain close today.

According to Thompson and Leroy school records, Mr. M attended three different elementary schools in Leroy and Youngstown. He attended Leroy High School through the 11th grade. He was sent to the Cuyahoga Hills Boys School and obtained his GED in August of 1994.

He reported that when he was 14, about a year after his mother died, he joined the 59th and Hoova gang, a sect of the Leroy Crips. He considers the gang to be part of his family, since several of his relatives are members. He added that he is not particularly active in the gang at present.

Mr. M has fathered two children, he said. He has a five-year-old daughter by Jane Callow; a second child, born to Betty Hard, died at two months. Prior to his arrest, Mr. M reported, he had been seeing Karina Smith.

MEDICAL HISTORY

Mr. M was diagnosed with asthma when he was 10 years old. He underwent neurosurgery in 1994 after he was attacked with a hammer by Ron Hall, according to Leroy Hospital records. These records indicate that he was unconscious for several days. Mr. M recalled that he experienced at least one seizure following his hospitalization. Due to the serious nature of this injury, a thorough neurological and neuropsychological evaluation is indicated to determine if there is any lasting neurological impairment. Mr. M has had numerous visits to the emergency room for a variety of ailments throughout much of his life. (Please refer to the enclosed time line.)

SUBSTANCE ABUSE HISTORY

Mr. M describes himself as a social drinker. He stated that he used marijuana daily and denies use of cocaine.

LEGAL HISTORY

Mr. M's juvenile records indicate that his first offense was for shoplifting in 1992. Other offenses include trespassing, curfew violations, attempted arson stemming from a wastebasket fire at Leroy High School, disorderly conduct, and truancy. He also has a felony drug possession and a misdemeanor firearm violation. On five occasions he was confined to the Leroy County Youth Detention Center.

Mr. M's adult records includes convictions for felonious assault and carrying a concealed weapon. He reported that he assaulted Ron Hall, who had previously beaten him unconscious, requiring neurosurgery. Mr. M was incarcerated from June 1996 to April 1997.

PSYCHOLOGICAL TESTING

On the Wechsler Adult Intelligence Scale-Revised (WAIS-R), Mr. M obtained a Verbal IQ of 92 (30th percentile), a Performance IQ of 82 (11th percentile), and a Full-Scale IQ of 86 (18th percentile). This places him in the Low Average range of intelligence. The WAIS-R is a standard measure of intellectual functioning and reflects an individual's ability to think rationally, act purposefully, and deal effectively with his environment. The difference between Verbal and Performance IQ scores is suggestive of possible neuropsychological impairment. Mr. M should therefore be evaluated for such impairment.

In responding to the test and during the interview process, it became clear that Mr. M is surprisingly intelligent and articulate. His abstract thinking capacity is quite high, and he demonstrates a sophisticated understanding of some complex issues.

The Minnesota Multiphasic Personality Inventory-2nd edition (MMPI-2) is a test designed to assess a number of the major patterns of personality and emotional disorders. Mr. M produced a number of internally inconsistent and unusual responses. The resulting profile is therefore not valid according to the usual criteria for validity assessment.

Neuropsychological Assessment (performed by John Riley, Ph.D., ABPP)

Date of Examination: 5/15/98

Date of Report: 6/1/98

Referral Question and Issues Prompting the Referral: The defendant, Mr. M , was referred for evaluation by his co-counsels, Robert Tillick and David Dipple, in order to determine the presence, nature, and extent of brain dysfunction secondary to a reported assault with the claw end of a hammer on 9/16/94.

Sources of Information

Leroy Board of Education

Leroy County Medical Center Emergency Department (ED).

Metro Health Medical Center

Summary of medical and schooling records provided by Mr. M's counsel.

MMPI-2 profile provided by Dr. James Eisenberg.

WAIS-R test protocol provided by Dr. James Eisenberg.

Clinical interview and testing of Mr. M by this examiner (5/15/98).

Neuropsychological Test Battery Paced Auditory Serial Addition Test (PASAT); Trigram Recall Test; Stroop Test; Rey Complex Figure Test and Recognition Trial (RCFT); Recognition Memory Test; Wechsler Memory Scale III (WMS-III); Wechsler Adult Intelligence Scale-III (WAIS-III);

Porteus Maze Test; Wisconsin Card Sorting Test (WCST); Boston Naming Test; Controlled Oral Word Retrieval Test (FAS); Category Instance Generation Test (CIG); Finger Oscillation Test; Wide Range Achievement Test-3rd edition (WRAT-3: Reading subtest); Beck Depression Inventory (BDI).

Years Education Mr. M said he went to school up to the 11th grade and subsequently obtained his GED. He described his school performance as follows: "I never really applied myself." He also reports a history of frequent truancies and school suspensions. According to the Leroy Board of Education records, his grades declined as he progressed through school and became increasingly truant. When questioned as to why he had been so frequently suspended, he replied, "tardiness."

Psychiatric Mr. M reported a history of depressed mood beginning at the age of 13 when his mother died, following which he "started withdrawing from people and stayed to myself." He also reported an increase in irritability following the 9/16/94, assault. He further noted that, at the time of the acts leading to his arrest on the current charges, this irritability had increased, "because many family members were in jail for a long time." He stated, "I was facing a robbery charge and I didn't want to go to jail." Mr. M expressed paranoid beliefs "that the police department hates me and my family and they are all conspiring; my lawyers and the judge are all conspiring against me." He stated that the onset of these beliefs was in 1992. Mr. M's MMPI-2 profile dated 2/13/98, while only marginally valid, did show very severe paranoid trends, which are consistent with what he had reported during the interview with me on 5/15/98. There is no apparent history of mental health treatment.

Current Medications None.

Substance Abuse History Cannabis abuse from the age of 14 years.

Medical History Relevant to Referral Question Mr. M was assaulted with the claw end of a hammer on 9/16/94. He reported a loss of consciousness (LOC) of three days duration, stating that he was unconscious until he awoke from surgery. The summary provided by Mr. M's counsel stated that the EMS report indicated that he was confused and disoriented and that he had been conscious when they had arrived at West 30th and Superior Avenue in Leroy, Ohio. This same summary reported that Mr. M had a grand mal seizure shortly after arrival in Leroy County Medical Center's ED and had to be intubated. This was confirmed in the records from Leroy County Medical Center, as was the fact that he had been "assaulted with a hammer and beaten up in the face and head multiple times." He was also described as having received superficial knife wounds. These same records state that Mr. M was conscious, although not talking on arrival at the ED. He was described as alert and oriented to time, place, and person.

It is not clear whether Mr. M is confusing a loss of consciousness with posttraumatic amnesia or a period of confusion following the trauma. Mr. M's final diagnoses at Leroy County Medical Center were as follows:

Rule out intracerebral bleed

Extensive head injury

Fracture mandible

Fracture nasal bones

Open fracture right little finger

Grand mal seizure activity

According to Leroy County Medical Center records, Mr. M was life-flighted to MetroHealth Medical Center, where his condition was listed as critical. The Metro Life Flight nursing note dated 9/16/94, indicated that, prior to intubation, Mr. M was moving all four extremities purposefully, indicating that he was conscious. While his Glasgow Coma Scale (GCS) was only 9 at Leroy County Medical Center, this was apparently due to his having been chemically paralyzed with neuroconium to facilitate intubation, because he was seizing. This procedure is conducted in order to prevent the swallowing of the tongue and to maintain an open trachea. Subsequent to intubation, his GCS reading was 15, and he was described as alert and oriented, indicating that he was conscious. Sprinkled throughout the MetroHealth records is the unresolved issue of whether there was any loss of consciousness (e.g., ALOC, "no loss of consciousness"). Even if there was a loss of consciousness, it does not appear to have been prolonged.

Despite this, however, Mr. M appears to have sustained significant acute insult to the brain as indicated by the head CT scan data showing the following:

9/16/94—Depressed, communited (crushed into small pieces) left parietal skull fracture and associated epidural (outside of the dura mata, which is the outermost and most fibrous of the three membranes covering the brain just underneath the skull) hematoma (collection of blood, usually clotted); subarachnoid hemorrhage bilaterally.

9/17/94—Status postcraniectomy with small amount of blood in the left parieto-occipital region of the skull; small amount of blood in the interhemispheric fissure; small area of contusion (bruise) in the region of the depressed fracture.

According to Mr. M, the Dilantin he was prescribed following the postassault seizure was supposed to be continued for two years (presumably as a prophylactic). However, he discontinued taking it after six months, "because I felt I wasn't going to have seizures, and I read about the side effects and didn't want that either." He indicated that he never actually experienced side effects or any subsequent seizures.

Cognitive Complaints   Mr. M reported an approximate 25%–33% reduction in concentration and memory as a result of the head injury sustained on 9/16/94. The impact of this decline in cognitive functioning being reported by Mr. M includes difficulty initiating activities, remembering directions, remembering what others have communicated to him after a period of time has elapsed, and keeping track of conversations. In particular, he reports difficulty remembering, "when the sentences are too long; when people started using long sentences in court."

Assessment Results   Mr. M's performance on neuropsychological tests, including screening procedures for detecting malingering of memory impairment, very clearly indicates that he is not malingering impaired cognitive test performance. For example, his scores on a recognition memory challenge were well outside the range of those instructed to exaggerate memory disturbance or where there is external evidence of a powerful incentive to malinger. Further evidence arguing against a diagnosis of malingering is the fact that he performed within expected limits on most clinical measures of brain functioning, the exception being divided attention/speed of processing. The comparable level of performance on current and premorbid measures of IQ argues against a global deterioration in overall brain functioning, as does his normal range performance on dementia-sensitive language measures, that is, confrontation naming and generative naming.

Mr. M's ability to lay down and retain newly acquired material of both a verbal and visuospatial nature appears to be intact. Thus, he was well able to learn and retain a list of shopping items, the details and gist of narrative material, and the details of a previously copied complex design. The fact that his Average range WMS-III memory indexes (range 103–130) were not significantly lower than his Average range WAIS-III IQ measures (range 98–103) also suggests that there has been no deterioration in the ability to encode, consolidate, and retrieve new information.

Unstructured problem solving requiring flexible adaptation to changing environmental demands also appears to have been spared, as has the planning and organizational aspect of executive functions. Evidence for the absence of dysfunction in executive functioning involves his having used categorical clustering strategies when retrieving material from remote memory. Mr. M's systematic approach to copying a design also indicated a relative sparing of executive functioning, as does his implementing a plan of action while drawing lines to the exits of visually complex mazes. Impaired performance on this maze task is conceptualized as measuring the planning and organizational aspect of executive functions. Performance on this task is also sensitive to disruption by visuospatial and working memory deficits, neither of which were evident in Mr. M's performance.

Intact visuospatial functioning is indicated by Mr. M's being able to accurately judge the angular orientation of radiating lines, copy a complex design, or assemble blocks by visually matching their designs to sample patterns.

The major residual cognitive sequelae to the 9/16/94 head trauma are speed of processing, divided attention, and immediate span of attention. Low span and divided attention capacity were particularly evident when attempting to repeat in reverse order orally presented numbers or taps on randomly arrayed blocks. Divided attention/speed of processing deficits were also quite evident when attempting to sum aloud randomly presented numbers, adding each number to the immediately preceding one under speed-demanding conditions. Finally, the speed of processing index of the WAIS-III, as represented by the scale score of 4 on the Digit Symbol-Coding subtest, is the lowest of all the WAIS-III indexes. A discrepancy of this magnitude occurs in less than 1% of the normative sample.

Opinion and Etiology The overall pattern of test results indicates significant residual speed-of-processing/divided deficits due to the 9/16/94 head trauma. These are common lingering sequelae to the type of injury sustained by Mr. M. There also appears to have been an increase in irritability following this injury, another common sequela to head trauma. Such information deficits produce an increased vulnerability to irritability due to an individual's information processing resources becoming overloaded. This, coupled with his paranoia, would tend to trigger aggressive outbursts. The fact that there does not appear to have been a sustained loss of consciousness does not rule out residual brain dysfunction, especially as there was evidence of acute brain insult on the CT scans and he had a seizure.

Taken together, these findings indicate a diagnosis of Cognitive Disorder B Not Otherwise Specified. In addition, by history and current presentation, he would qualify for a diagnosis of Antisocial Personality Disorder with Paranoid Features.

Considering the results of the neuropsychological evaluation just described, as well as the other findings by Dr. Eisenberg, the undersigned would offer the following:

Diagnostic Impressions

Antisocial Personality Disorder

Cognitive Disorder B Not Otherwise Specified.

Cannabis Abuse

The evidence for a diagnosis of antisocial personality disorder for Mr. M is overwhelming. The essential feature of Antisocial Personality Disorder is a pervasive pattern of disregard for, and violation of, the rights of others that begins in childhood or early adolescence and continues into adulthood. What is of particular significance is the effect of parental influence on this disorder. Antisocial Personality Disorder is seen more frequently in the first-degree biological relatives of those with the disorder than it is in the general population, and the risk to biological relatives of females with APD tends to be higher than the risk to biological relatives of males with APD (American Psychiatric Association, 1994).

DISCUSSION

Mr. M's personal history is consistent with individuals who demonstrate features of an antisocial personality disorder and an attachment disorder. An attachment disorder is conceptualized as a condition of profound insecurity with extreme vacillations between a desire for proximity and attachment and a dread and avoidance of engagement. The subsequent pathology reflects traumatic attachment experiences beginning early in life. Prolonged disruption of the bonding/attachment process leads to detachment. The child is apathetic and stops bonding to others, becomes increasingly self-absorbed, is preoccupied with nonhuman objects (material goods), and does not display emotion. These attempts at emotional detachment become the precursors of an eventual pattern of adult antisocial behavior. Violence and anger help break a cycle of ambivalence, although the cycle repeats itself.

The antisocial behavior exhibited by Mr. M is a direct result of his highly dysfunctional family, the lack of effective role models, the absence of male bonding, and the enabling by an equally antisocial and drug dependent mother. His behavior reflects his survival instincts, and his personality reflects the lack of effective empathy and moral development. Mr. M's mother was 15 when she was pregnant and 16 when he was born. Given her own drug, alcohol, and legal problems she was clearly unable to provide adequate parenting. His foster grandmother was, at best, inconsistent in her ability to provide for Mr. M and the other children within her care, who included Mr. M's mother. Following his mother's death, Mr. M's behavior showed clear signs of deterioration, and he joined the local gang.

As a result of Mr. M's early childhood experiences, he has bonded to no one, has little capacity for empathy, and has shut off his emotions from the rest of the world. Only under conditions of strict supervision, such as with the Department of Youth Services, has he demonstrated some ability to accomplish tasks at hand, such as completing his GED.

Sincerely,
James R. Eisenberg, Ph.D.
Diplomate, American Board of Professional
*   Psychology (Forensic)*

Teaching Point: How do you obtain informed consent in capital cases?

In some ways, informed consent in capital cases is no different than in noncapital cases. However, in a capital context, the defendant is consenting to an evaluation that is part of a process that could result in the imposition of the death penalty. In addition, there are as many as nine opportunities for an appeal, and an assessment may be requested throughout the course of the trial and appellate process. Such potential appellate issues include pretrial (*Miranda* issues, voluntary confessions), trial (competency to stand trial, sanity at the time of the offense), direct appeal (additional evaluations), appeal to the state supreme court, postconviction relief (new round of evaluations), return to the state courts on postconviction issues, federal habeas, federal appeals court, and U.S. Supreme Court, with the additional possibility of evaluating a defendant's competency to be executed (see *Ford v. Wainwright*, 1986). For these reasons, forensic psychologists should clearly communicate to the defendant (see *Estelle v. Smith*, 1981) that he or she is consenting to an evaluation that is not confidential and that the information obtained may be subject to both direct and cross-examination throughout the course of the trial and posttrial period. Such testimony could convince a jury to impose the death penalty (and for other courts to uphold the sentencing), even if the psychologist is retained by the defense or appointed to assist the defense.

Several problems arise in capital cases that are different from noncapital cases. A defendant may deny his involvement in the alleged criminal offense, and the psychologist may be placed in the difficult position of testifying in front of a jury that has already convicted the defendant. With properly prepared mitigation this is not necessarily a problem. Many defendants deny their guilt, or at least deny elements of the offense that would be considered as aggravating factors. Informed consent or notification of purpose needs to be obtained or provided so the defendant understands the specific role of the expert psychologist. The psychologist is neither the factfinder nor responsible for sentencing. The defendant should clearly be informed that the psychologist will often be testifying following a guilty verdict.

Testimony in capital cases is usually linked to specific mitigating factors. Those factors often exist regardless of a defendant's admission or denial of culpability. For example, a defendant's denial would not contradict testimony concerning the defendant's relationship with co-defendants. Perhaps he was not the primary offender, although still eligible for the death penalty. Testimony regarding the defendant's role in the offense in relation to his co-defendants, and his broader tendency in social interaction to be a leader or a follower, could be relevant in such cases. Even if the defendant is found to be the principal offender, a neuropsychological evaluation may give the jury sufficient grounds for recommending a life sentence over the death penalty. Consider the following mitigating factors found in many jurisdictions:

1. Whether the victim of the offense induced or facilitated it;
2. Whether it is unlikely that the offense would have been committed but for the fact that the offender was under duress, coercion, or strong provocation;
3. Whether, at the time of committing the offense, the offender, because of a mental disease or defect, lacked the substantial capacity to appreciate the criminality of his conduct or to conform his conduct to the requirements of the law;
4. The youth of the offender;
5. The offender's lack of a significant history of prior criminal convictions or delinquency adjudications;
6. If the offender was a participant in the offense but not the principal offender, the degree of the offender's participation in the offense and the degree of the offender's participation in the acts that led to the death of the victim;
7. The act of the defendant was not the sole proximate cause of the victim's death;
8. It is unlikely that the defendant will engage in further criminal activity that would constitute a continuing threat to society;

9. Mental retardation (some states automatically exclude the mentally retarded from execution); and
10. Any other factors that are relevant to the issue of whether the offender should be sentenced to death.

Expert testimony may be used to establish most (if not all) of these mitigation factors regardless of the defendant's denial of wrongdoing. However, testifying to numbers two or three may pose a problem when the defendant is adamant about his innocence. If the theory of mitigation rests with residual doubt about the defendant's legal guilt, then testimony as to the defendant's state of mind at the time of the criminal acts would clearly undermine such a strategy. Yet in most cases, with proper voir dire and trial strategy, a defense attorney can walk the fine line between maintaining residual doubt and establishing certain factors that might result in mitigation. By this point in the trial the jury has already returned a guilty verdict, but they may still want an explanation (although not an excuse) for the defendant's conduct. Perhaps the only way to accomplish this is through expert testimony that can be posed as a hypothetical. Most courts give wide latitude during mitigation hearings and permit such testimony. The attorney's job is to weigh the prejudicial versus probative value of introducing such testimony.

In most cases, defendants will provide informed consent when the role of the psychologist is clearly stated. Liebert and Foster (1994) have proposed standards of practice for mental health evaluations in capital cases. If such standards were followed, then informed consent provided by the defendants would be part of a larger process that would likely yield better-informed sentencing decisions by the trier of fact.

Case 2

Principle: Obtain relevant historical information

This principle concerns what constitutes "relevant" historical information and how to obtain such information in a particular case. In forensic assessment, the range of potentially relevant domains is much greater than in therapeutic assessment. For example, when conducting FMHA, in addition to gathering historical information about the social, medical, mental health, and family functioning of the individual being evaluated, it may be important to obtain further information about the individual's criminal, military, school, sexual, and/or vocational histories, depending on the nature of the evaluation.

Historical information is particularly important for several reasons. These include the value of behavior, the importance of response style, and the accuracy of self-reported factual information, as well as characteristics and symptoms, and the obvious need for information about the relevant thoughts, feelings, and behavior of the individual at a certain time when a reconstructive evaluation is being conducted. In addition, accurate historical information can strengthen the basis for predicting future outcomes (e.g., violent behavior, treatment response) that are part of some kinds of FMHA.

There is reasonably strong support for the importance of history in FMHA from ethical, legal, empirical, and standard of practice sources of authority. In general, ethics sources of authority emphasize that history is an integral part of mental health evaluation within accepted clinical and scientific standards. For example, the *Ethical Principles of Psychologists and Code of Conduct* (APA, 1992) indirectly addresses the important of historical information:

> Psychologists' assessments, recommendations, reports, and psychological diagnostic or evaluative statements are based on information and techniques (including personal interviews of the individual when appropriate) sufficient to provide appropriate substantiation for their findings. (p. 1603; also p. 1610 under Forensic Activities)

Further, the *Specialty Guidelines for Forensic Psychologists* (Committee on Ethical Guidelines for Forensic Psychologists, 1991) notes that:

> [F]orensic psychologists have an obligation to maintain current knowledge of scientific, professional, and legal developments within their area of claimed competence. They are obligated also to use that knowledge, consistent with accepted clinical and scientific standards, in selecting data collection methods and procedures for an evaluation, treatment, consultation or scholarly/empirical investigation. (p. 661)

Neither the *Principles of Medical Ethics with Annotation* (American Psychiatric Association, 1995) nor the AAPL's *Ethical Guidelines* (1995) address this principle.

Legal support for this principle can be found in several sources. Generally, relevant legal standards emphasize the application of history to various legal questions. The *Criminal Justice Mental Health Standards* (ABA, 1989) indicates that the contents of a written report should include the "clinical findings and opinions on each matter referred for evaluation" as well as the "sources of information and . . . factual basis for the evaluator's clinical findings and opinions" (p. 109). Although the *Criminal Justice Mental Health Standards* does not indicate specifically that historical information must be obtained, it can be reasonably inferred that it is important to describe an individual's history in adequate detail when information from the individual's history serves as either a source of information or a factual basis for "clinical findings and opinions."

Case law provides some additional support for the importance of relevant historical information, particularly in cases in which the forensic issues are broad or when the legal decision can have very serious consequences for the individual being evaluated. For example, in capital cases, the defense is entitled to psychiatric assistance to provide mitigating evidence (if applicable) at sentencing and to counter prosecution evidence of future dangerousness (*Ake v. Oklahoma*, 1985). History is relevant to both future dangerousness and adjustment to incarceration, which are among the aggravating and mitigating criteria for capital sentencing in many jurisdictions.

The application of history to FMHA may also be valuable in establishing a pattern of behavior that can serve as a context for the forensic issue(s) being assessed and for using historical information to suggest and test hypotheses. The importance of history in establishing a pattern of behavior, including serving as a source of information about the probability of certain types of future behavior, is particularly apparent when addressing forensic issues that involve prediction. Making and testing hypotheses regarding forensic issues can be facilitated when a detailed history is obtained, as the likelihood that a given hypothesis may account for relevant legal behavior (e.g., "he shot a stranger because he experienced command auditory hallucinations instructing him to do so") may depend on both previous experience (e.g., the prior frequency of experienced command hallucinations) and behavior (e.g., the prior frequency of compliance with such command hallucinations).

Although historical information is part of virtually every form of mental health assessment, whether therapeutic or forensic, the scope of the needed information varies according to the type of evaluation being conducted. When the forensic issue is narrow and focuses primarily on the individual's present state, there is less history that is relevant. By contrast, when the forensic issue is broader, or if potentially serious consequences may result, than the breadth of the relevant history may expand accordingly.

The present report provides an example of the application of this principle. It focuses heavily on the presentation of relevant historical information. The forensic clinician consulted numerous sources of information in an effort to obtain as much historical information regarding the defendant as possible. In doing so, he was able to offer a more comprehensive picture of the defendant's history. This historical information was presented primarily to establish a pattern of behavior that could serve as a context for the forensic issue(s) being addressed. For example, one consideration in sentencing involved the likelihood that the defendant would engage in future acts of violence. Accordingly, the report focused on the defendant's history of violent behavior in an effort to establish a pattern of behavior.

J. Reid Meloy, Ph.D., A.B.P.P.
Clinical and Forensic Psychology

Diplomate, Forensic Psychology
American Board of Professional Psychology
Fellow, Society for Personality Assessment

June 3, 1998
The Honorable Richard P. Matsch
Chief Judge
United States District Court for the
District of Colorado
RE: United States of America v. Terry Lynn Nichols

Dear Judge Matsch,

I am writing to you in response to the letter sent by Alexander Fleming, M.D., concerning your sentencing of Terry Lynn Nichols tomorrow, June 4, 1998. I have been retained by the United States Government as an expert consultant and potential mitigation rebuttal witness since January 1997, in the federal prosecution of Terry Nichols.

DATABASE

The findings and opinions I offer are based on my studying of a voluminous amount of material provided to me by the U.S. Attorney's Office and the FBI in the prosecution of Terry Nichols. This material included approximately 8,000 pages of 600 different documents (including videotapes, audiotapes, and books read by Mr. Nichols), which also contained both defense and prosecution interviews of 185 individuals that had personally known Mr. Nichols over the course of his life. These individuals ranged from family members, neighbors, acquaintances, and employers who knew him primarily in Michigan, Nevada, and Kansas, to individuals who knew him during his tenure in the U.S. Army from 1988–1989. Although I would have liked to have interviewed people that knew him most intimately, such as his son, David, and his ex-wife, Susan Dever, my efforts to conduct such interviews were met with vehement resistance by the defense and did not succeed. In addition to these data sources (which were preceded and complemented by a careful study of 12,000 pages of documents during the prosecution of Timothy McVeigh), I also downloaded and read the entire trial transcript in the case of *U.S. v. Terry Nichols* from November 3, 1997, to January 7, 1998. The trial included the testimony of approximately 85 prosecution and 94 defense witnesses, many of whom knew Terry Nichols personally, and was able to shed further light on his personality, behavior, history, and motivations. I was unable, however, to interview Mr. Nichols directly, and my findings and opinions should be viewed with this limitation in mind.

FINDINGS AND OPINIONS

1. I agree with Dr. Fleming's opinion that Mr. Nichols is a very quiet, private, and self-reliant individual. The evidence clearly describes an introverted, isolated individual who preferred his own company, particularly during periods of stress in his interpersonal relationships. Introversion is a part of one's temperament and appears to be largely inherited. In Mr. Nichols's case, this introversion contributed to a personality that was described by others and Dr. Fleming as a "loner . . . reclusive, even suspicious . . . reticent, if not isolated" (p. 6). I also agree with this perception of Mr. Nichols and find it quite consistent with what we would expect in a bomber.

In the course of the McVeigh and Nichols trials, I and my assistant, Joseph McEllistrem, M.A., conducted an exhaustive review of all the known research on the personality and motivations of bombers (we searched through eight English language computer databases). One of the characteristics that has been documented throughout the research of the past 50 years is that bombers are often introverted, isolated, and suspicious loners who tend to hold their emotions inside and do not express them in any direct way (amply documented in the case of Mr. Nichols). They choose, instead, a *passive-aggressive* mode of expressing hostility, a technical term I will elaborate on below.

2. I agree with Dr. Fleming's opinion that Mr. Nichols is intelligent. In fact, I was able to closely study the results of the vocational testing taken by Mr. Nichols during his enlistment in the U.S. Army in April 1988. Intelligence is a very stable trait, and we can confidently assume that it was the same in 1988 as it was at the time of the bombing 7 years later. Test results from the Armed Services Vocational Aptitude Battery indicate Mr. Nichols produced scores that were at least one, and in some cases close to two, standard deviations above the average of his entire unit's score. This means that on all of the subtests, he scored better than most of the men who joined the army at that time, and this vocational battery roughly corresponds to IQ. I conclude that Mr. Nichols's IQ is in the superior range.

3. I agree with Dr. Fleming that Mr. Nichols formed very close attachments to his family members, his ex-spouse, and his children, including children that were not his biological offspring. There is no question that this is a positive attribute, and Dr. Fleming emphasizes Nichols's loy-

alty to these people and the similarity between his relations with his co-defendant and his two wives and mother (p. 4). One of the very stable characteristics attributed to Mr. Nichols by many different people who have known him is his devotion to others (and eventually to a political belief that no entity, including local, state, and federal government, had jurisdiction over him), and his caretaking of his children as best he could.

In many ways Dr. Fleming is describing an individual with many *dependent* personality characteristics. Mr. Nichols, when he does attach to others, forms very close attachments, will remain loyal to them, and will actively participate in the relationship. A dependent personality is very active and is not passive.[4] This is a central aspect of Mr. Nichols that goes to the heart of his active participation in the bombing of the Murrah building. Individuals with dependent personalities are fearful of the loss of their few relationships and will go to great lengths to never express hostility or anger, a normal emotion felt in all relationships at times, directly toward the other person. This absence of anger or hostility *in his personal relationships* is a stable and robust finding throughout Mr. Nichols's life. In fact, I could find virtually no incident in the entire body of evidence I reviewed where Mr. Nichols expressed anger directly and openly toward someone about whom he cared.

What Mr. Nichols did, instead, was to shift his anger, hostility, and frustration onto other people and entities with whom he did not have a personal relationship. The first recorded event of this pattern occurred when he renounced his voter registration card in February 1992, in Evergreen Township, and proceeded through a series of jurisdictional renunciations and declarations that he was an "expatriate absolute," including his renunciation of his U.S. citizenship 2 years later. Mr. Nichols ranted against authority because he could not risk expressing anger in his personal life. The most striking illustration of this absence of anger was his welcoming of his second wife, Concita, into the United States after she informed him that she had been impregnated by her former boyfriend while she remained in the Philippines after their marriage. The most striking illustration of his hostility against people and entities he did not personally know was the bombing of the Murrah building.

4. Terrorist bombing is a political act that involves meticulous planning and preparation. In the case of the Oklahoma City bombing, Mr. Nichols was the strategist. Throughout the records there are numerous descriptions of Mr. Nichols's ability to carefully plan, consider his options carefully, focus on details, and as Dr. Fleming writes, "think(ing) things through on his own" (p. 2). There was also little risk that he would reveal the bomb-making plans to others, given his privacy and secrecy, a finding confirmed in the testimony of Concita Nichols at trial (testimony Dec. 11, 1997). He was part of what militia researchers have described for several years as "a leaderless cell": no identified leader, no formal association with a hierarchy, and lethally mobile. Mr. Nichols provided the long distance, stable anchor for the conspiracy to unfold.

5. Although Dr. Fleming did not comment on this specifically, it is my opinion that Mr. Nichols's absence from Oklahoma City on the day of the bombing is exactly what we would expect from an individual who avoids conflict, has done so all his life, yet is intensely loyal to ideas and close relationships. This illustrates another central characteristic in Mr. Nichols that also emerges from the bombing research: Most bombers are *passive-aggressive* and do not express their hostility, anger, and alienation in a direct manner. Bombing (along with firesetting) is the quintessential passive-aggressive criminal act: the perpetrator does not have to be there, no actual violence is directly witnessed, no empathic feelings for the victims will get in the way, yet the ideational and emotional gratification is enormous. Killing from a great distance is efficient, effective, low risk, and especially palatable to an individual who has avoided direct conflict all his life.

6. It appears from the records that Mr. Nichols's alienation from the government had a variety of causes, including his experiences with other farmers in the Decker, Michigan, area, his experience in the army, and his association with his brother, James, and his co-defendant. It is important to note, however, that the first evidence of his renunciation of legal authority over him, February 25, 1992, *pre-dates* both Ruby Ridge and Waco. It appears that Mr. Nichols's alienation and hostility, again only expressed toward people and objects he does not personally know, was deep and profound.

7. Dr. Fleming talks extensively about the defense of "denial" in Mr. Nichols. I don't quite understand his thinking, other than to conclude that Dr. Fleming somehow believes that Mr. Nichols was not consciously aware of his activity and its purpose from September 1994 until April 1995. Denial is an important psychological defense, most apparent in young children, and Dr. Fleming attempts to link it to Mr. Nichols by addressing denial and its use among alcoholics (Mr. Nichols's mother was arguably alcoholic). For several reasons, I find his argument fundamentally flawed. First, denial as a psychological defense is impossible to infer without a clinical interview, and Dr. Fleming does not indicate he ever interviewed Mr. Nichols. Second, denial is very difficult to measure from a scientific perspective. Third, it is a changeable, dynamic state, rather than an enduring trait. Finally, any data in this case suggesting that Mr. Nichols intentionally attempted to conceal evidence (of which there are ample) would contradict Dr. Fleming's theory.

8. Mr. Nichols is a true believer. He believes that all the frustrations and disappointments in his life are caused by others. He believes that there is only hope in loyalty to close friends and family, and that all government is fundamentally corrupt. Unfortunately and tragically, his true beliefs were not without hope for sudden, radical change, and they found expression in a terrible act. As Eric Hoffer wrote in *The True Believer* in 1951: "For there is often a monstrous incongruity between the hopes, however noble and tender, and the action which follows them. It is as if ivied maidens and garlanded youths were to herald the four horsemen of the apocalypse" (p. 11).

Thank you for your time and attention.

Sincerely,
J. Reid Meloy, Ph.D., ABPP

Teaching Point: Role of history in sentencing in forensic mental health assessment

The criminal law has a rich history of considering the mental status of the offender in determining criminal responsibility and appropriate sentencing. The role of punishment in the criminal justice system supports leniency for criminal offenders suffering from mental illness and/or diminished mental capacity. Specifically, two theories of criminal punishment, culpability and deterrence, support leniency when the defendant's volitional conduct is affected by mental illness and/or diminished mental capacity. Generally, in both capital and noncapital cases, federal and state jurisdictions consider the impact of mental illness and/or mental retardation on sentencing and penal sanctions, and the presence of serious mental illness or retardation is usually considered a mitigating factor (*Criminal Justice Mental Health Standards*, Standard 7-9.3; ALI Model Penal Code § 210.6[4][c], ABA, 1999). For example, the U.S. Sentencing Guidelines provide for downward departure due to diminished mental capacity (United States Sentencing Guidelines § 5k2.13). In the state of Pennsylvania, the presence of extreme mental or emotional disturbance is a potential mitigating factor in capital sentencing cases (42 Pa. C.S.A. § 9711 [a][2]).

Given the importance and complicated nature of the issue, forensic clinicians are frequently called on to address sentencing issues as they relate to mentally ill defendants. Typically, sentencing evaluations fall into three broad categories: (1) treatment needs and amenability; (2) information bearing on the offender's culpability; and (3) future dangerousness (Melton et al., 1997). Historical information obtained through FMHA is one important component that can be used to address both the broad and specific issues involved in these aspects of sentencing. In an assessment addressing treatment needs and amenability, historical information can be useful in identifying the success of past treatment attempts and the deficits that should be targeted for intervention. For example, academic records and a detailed employment history provide the basis for identifying deficits in formal education and vocational training. Similarly, numerous relapses and unsuccessful interventions might lead to different treatment recommendations for a chronic substance abuser. In an evaluation of the offender's criminal culpability, psychiatric records might provide a historical perspective on the development of symptoms and presenting problems associated with mental illness. Finally, factors such as social history, psychiatric hospitalization history, and arrest history are essential components for the assessment of risk for violence. Accordingly, historical information plays an important role in FMHA sentencing evaluations. By gathering historical information related to the relevant functional capacities and deficits, the forensic clinician can address the impact of mental health issues on a variety of sentencing issues.

Case 3

Principle: Decline referral when impartiality is unlikely

Because this principle is discussed in Chapter 4, we now demonstrate how the present report illustrates the application of this principle. The present case provides an illustration of the importance of declining a referral when impartiality is unlikely. The forensic clinician in this case was retained at the request of defense counsel regarding mitigation of the death penalty; he had previously evaluated Mr. R to assess his mental status at the time of the offense. Early in the report, the forensic clinician describes the circumstances of the original evaluation and notes that testimony was not given in the case, so the jury did not consider the results of the evaluation in their deliberations regarding the death penalty. This disclosure is important because it clarifies that the forensic clinician did not play a dual role in this case.

Although retained by the defense, the forensic clinician was still acting in a role in which impartiality is important to accurate and informed legal decision making. Accordingly, the forensic clinician had to keep personal values or the circumstances of the case from adversely affecting his impartial stance.

The defendant, Mr. R, was sentenced to death for committing two murders. The Supreme Court of New Jersey set aside the death penalty and ordered a new penalty phase because the original jury had been defectively charged on the aggravating factor involving torture or aggravated battery. The current evaluation was conducted to evaluate Mr. R for potential mitigating factors that might be presented at new penalty phase of the trial.

Evaluator bias can arise in cases like this. The forensic clinician must be aware of the influences that can create such bias and decline the referral if impartiality cannot be maintained. As noted earlier, one kind of bias could result from characteristics or beliefs of the evaluator that may significantly influence the evaluator (e.g., vehement opposition to or strong support of capital punishment). The second kind of bias could be created by situational factors that may influence an evaluator in the direction of a given finding (e.g., a pre-existing personal or professional relationship with the litigant). There are a number of situational factors that might influence the impartiality of the forensic clinician in this case. For example, the facts surrounding the murders suggested that Mr. R also engaged in torture that had a sexual component. The heinous nature of these offenses might create a predisposition toward a certain finding in this case. However, strong opposition to the death penalty might influence the forensic clinician toward a recommendation in the opposite direction.

ALAN M. GOLDSTEIN, PH.D.
N.Y.S. Certified Psychologist, P.C.
Ct. Licensed Psychologist
Diplomate in Forensic Psychology
American Board of Professional Psychology

PRIVILEGED AND CONFIDENTIAL
FORENSIC PSYCHOLOGICAL
EVALUATION

Defendant: Steven R., Jr.
Date of Birth: 9/10/56
Age at Initial Evaluation: 28 years
Dates Evaluated: 2/9/85, 2/22/85, 3/1/86,
    9/3/91, 10/18/94
Date of Report: 1/13/93

Tests Administered

WAIS-III
TAT
Rorschach
Rotter Incomplete Sentences Blank (Adult
    Form)

Human Figure Drawings
Three Wishes
MMPI (Independently scored and interpreted)
Rogers Criminal Responsibility Assessment Scale
Hare Psychopathy Checklist

Steven R Jr., a 35-year-old African American male, was initially referred for a forensic psychological evaluation in January 1985 by his attorneys, Carl Brine and Michael Philby, Office of the Public Defender of the Croton Adult Region. Mr. R has been charged in a 13-count indictment with crimes allegedly committed on 7/19/84. Specifically, he was charged with having purposely or knowingly murdered Walter Jamison and Maria Jamison, two counts of felony murder, two counts of burglary in the third degree, unlawful possession of a weapon, unlawful possession of weapon with a purpose to use it unlawfully against another person, obstruction of justice, attempted murder of Ginny Calones, aggravated arson or arson in the third degree, sexual assault, and assault. I was asked to evaluate Mr. R's mental state at the time of the offenses, addressing state statutes 2C:4-1 and 2C: 11-3.

On the basis of my evaluation of Mr. R, a report was prepared at the request of his attorneys. Reference is made to this report (2/21/85), a copy of which has been provided to both defense counsel and to Mr. Steven Stanton, Assistant Prosecutor for the State. I was not asked to provide testimony in this case, nor was my report considered by the jury. The jury found Mr. R guilty of purposeful or knowing murder, felony murder, burglary, and hindering prosecution. He was found not guilty of aggravated arson. During the penalty phase of this trial, the State contended that: Mr. R's conduct was outrageously or wantonly vile, horrible, or inhumane and involved torture, depravity of mind, or aggravated battery to the victims; he committed these murders to escape detection of a previous crime; and these crimes were committed while he was engaged in the commission of felony. Defense counsel argued for the presence of three mitigating factors: Mr. R's actions occurred while under the influence of extreme mental or emotional disturbance; that his capacity to appreciate the wrongfulness of his conduct or to conform his behavior to the requirements of the law was significantly impaired as the result of mental disease or defect or intoxication; and that the defendant's character or record of the circumstances of the offense were relevant factors to be considered in mitigation of the death penalty. The jury found all three aggravating factors and the mitigating factors of "extreme emotional disturbance" and the "character" factor. In addition, they found that two of the aggravating factors individually outweighed the mitigating factors, and, accordingly, Mr. R was sentenced to death.

The Supreme Court of New Jersey set aside the death penalty and ordered a new penalty phase of this trial. Specifically, the Court opined that the jury had been defectively charged on the aggravating factor involving torture or aggravating battery.

I was contacted on 6/12/91, by Ms. Lisa Bennett, Esq., and Steven Rosen, Esq., of Bennett and Rosen, Mr. R's present counsel. I was asked to reevaluate Mr. R with regard to the presence of mitigating factors as they might relate to the penalty phase of his trial.

Prior to the preparation of this report, I reviewed copies of the following documents provided to me by his attorneys:

DISCOVERY MATERIAL RELATED TO THIS OFFENSE

Arrest Reports (9/20/84)

Police Accident Report (7/24/84)

Police Investigation Report (9/20/84, North Patterson)

Prosecutor's Office Preliminary Report (9/20/84)

Medical Examiner's Report of Autopsy (9/19/84) of Walter Jamison

Medical Examiner's Report of Autopsy (9/19/84) of Maria Jamison

Police Report (8/19/84) listing evidence taken

State Police Evidence Log (9/19/84)

Defendant's Record of Prior Arrests and Dispositions

Transcript of Grand Jury Proceedings (10/14/84)

Supreme Court Decision (State v. R)

Interview of William Eislin by Carl Brine, Esq. (10/25/84)

STATEMENTS

Voluntary Statement of Shirley R (9/10/84)

Voluntary Statement of Ginny Calones (9/19/84)

Voluntary Statement of Mary Wells (9/19/84)

Signed Miranda Rights Waiver of Defendant (9/20/84)

Voluntary Statement of Defendant (9/20/84)

Voluntary Statement of Sara Calones (9/20/84)

Voluntary Statement of Lisa Paul (9/24/84)

Voluntary Statement of Douglas Paul (9/24/84)

FIRE DEPARTMENT RECORDS

Administrative Submission (9/21/84)

Fire Department Fire Record Card (9/18/84)

Division Report (8/18/84)

Emergency Police Call (9/19/84)

CROTON COUNTY JAIL RECORDS REGARDING THIS INCIDENT

Sheriff's Department Form (9/21/84)

Clinic Appointment—College Hospital (4/3/85)

Medical Department Memo (3/18/85)

SCHOOL AND PSYCHIATRIC RECORDS

Board of Education, Division of Child Guidance Records:
Psychological Report (6/27/69)
Referral to Psychiatrist (6/11/73)
Learning Disabilities Teacher—Consultant Report (5/4/73)
Consulting Psychiatrist's Report (6/14/73)
Psychological Test Report of Robert Clark, Ph.D. (2/28/86)
Psychological Report of Lawrence Miller, Ph.D. (3/6/85)

MISCELLANEOUS RECORDS

Military Records (3/20/74–2/2/78)

Prior Incident, Continuation, and Arrest Reports (9/15/78–8/30/84)

Sheriff's Department Forms (10/15/78, 12/30/80, and 1/28/84)

MEDICAL RECORDS OF GINNY CALONES

Laboratory Report (5/11/84)

Walk-in Clinic—University Hospital Report (5/11/84)
General Pediatrics Records (5/11/84 and 5/16/84)

1972–3/85 DEFENDANT'S MEDICAL RECORDS

Hospital Records—Emergency Department Records (10/4/72–5/11/73)

Hospital Records—Admissions/Discharge Record (7/8/73–8/14/73)

University Hospital Admissions Record (3/28/85)

In addition to my review of the above documents, I also conducted the following interviews:

Ms. Shirley R (2/22/86 and 3/1/86)
Ms. Christine Canton (2/20/86)
Donald Billington (5/1/86)

It should be noted that I first attempted to re-interview Mr. R at the request of his attorney on 2/17/92 at Owens State Prison. Mr. R refused to leave his cell block and declined to be interviewed at the time.

At the start of each evaluation session, I explained thoroughly to Mr. R that I am a psychologist whose services were retained through the offices of his attorney. I indicated my role in his case and the lack of confidentiality that would exist if I were requested to prepare a written report and/or testify. He was aware that a second penalty phase had been ordered and that he was entitled to present mitigating factors at that time. Mr. R was told that I am a Diplomate in Forensic Psychology of the American Board of Professional Psychology, that I would make notes based on his answers to my questions during the interview, and that his responses would be used, in part, in the formation of an opinion. He was further informed that I would, at his attorney's request, prepare a thorough, balanced report that might contain information detrimental to his case. My nonadvocacy role was explained to him, and he acknowledged that he understood the lack of confidentially involved in this evaluation. Thus, the evaluation was conducted with Mr. R's informed consent. At the time of preparation of this report, I have spent approximately 20 hours with Mr. R.

SUMMARY OF ABOVE DOCUMENTS

I have reviewed copies of the documents cited above, and, because of their extensive nature, they will not be summarized in detail. The exception is those documents that relate directly to Mr. R's actions and the events leading to these actions of 9/19/84.

According to the Board of Education records, Mr. R attended Allen Avenue School and was referred for Psychological Evaluation on 2/27/69. At that time, Mr. R was approximately 12½ years of age. He was referred for evaluation because of aggression to his peers. It is reported that his mother had come to school and physically punished him in front of others. Mr. R was found to be "anxious all the time" and demonstrated signs of anxiety, instability, and insecurity.

Mr. R was again referred for psychiatric/psychological evaluation when he was approximately age 16½. According to the records (6/11/73), Mr. R was found to be fighting, hostile to girls, belligerent, and having a severe stutter as a child. It is reported that he had been raised by his grandmother in North Carolina. According to the Psychiatric Report (6/14/73), Mrs. R indicated that she had no relationship with her son, claiming that they rarely spoke. She described him as being moody and a loner, and reported that her common-law husband had unexpectedly left their home to marry another woman. Mr. R indicated that he found girls "ugly by the way they act." He was diagnosed as being "an emotionally disturbed child."

Mr. R entered the United States Marine Corps on 3/25/74, and was officially separated from the service on 11/13/77 under Honorable Conditions. The records indicate that he received the Good Conduct Medal and the National Defense Service Medal. While stationed in Japan, Mr. R was convicted by Japanese civil authorities for attempted rape in the course of a robbery and sentenced to 4½ years. A review of the records indicates that it was the opinion of the U.S. military that it was, "not clear as to efforts put forth to verify or research claims of respondent." Statements made by the victim and key witnesses were found to "appear suspect."

Prior to 9/19/91, Mr. R had been involved in a number of incidents that led to arrests. For the most part, allegations focused on loss of control of his temper resulting in verbal outbursts or throwing objects. On 9/9/78, Mr. R had been accused of forcing a mentally retarded girl to have sexual intercourse with him, allegations that Mr. R denied. Other incidents involved verbal threats, fighting, and criminal mischief, possession of marijuana, possession of a knife, threatening another individual, and driving his automobile into a ditch filled with water.

On 7/10/84, Maria Jamison indicated to the police that Mr. R had broken down her front door, but she refused to sign a complaint. On 7/18/84, the Police Incident Report indicates that Ms. Brennan had slapped her daughter, at which time Mr. R again kicked in her door and "punched complainant repeatedly in her face." Ms. Jamison indicated that she believed Mr. R to be the father of her daughter's unborn child. Again, Ms. Jamison refused to sign a complaint against Mr. R. A review of the medical records of Ginny Calones (5/11/84) indicates that although Mr. Jamison believed her daughter to be pregnant, she was determined not to be pregnant on medical examination.

According to Police Department arrest reports (9/20/84), Mr. R was placed under arrest at approximately 3:40 a.m. for a crime he committed at approximately 2 a.m on 9/19/84. The victims were found dead in their apartment, and Mr. R was initially charged with homicide and burglary. The records also indicate that he had committed the crime of arson of 9/18/84 at approximately 11:30 p.m. Prior to this date (8/24/84), the Police Accident report indicates that a car driven by Mr. R had jumped the sidewalk and sideswiped a building, causing extensive damage to both the car and the building. The driver had fled the scene of the incident.

The Police Department Continuation Report (9/20/84) indicates that the front door of the Jamison's apartment had been forced open. A 2-year old baby was found unharmed on the bed. Walter Jamison's body was found in the kitchen, and Maria Jamison's body was found in the bedroom. Both had been beaten and stabbed and their throats cut. A baseball bat was found partially inserted in Maria Jamison's vagina. It is reported that Ginny Calones, the 13-year old daughter of the victims, had indicated that her "parents had several disputes with her former boyfriend, one Steven R. . . . he was a [sic] adult and she was a juvenile and they didn't like the idea of him seeing her." This report indicates that a male had called the police indicating that he had killed two people and that a baby was alive in the apartment. This report also indicates that a fire had been discovered in the defendant's apartment on August 18 and that Mr. R's mother indicated that her son had told her of the arson and the killings.

The report of the medical examiner found that Walter Jamison's injuries indicated stab wounds to the chest and abdomen, assault to the head with a blunt instrument, lacerations of the head, fractured skull, hematoma, contusions of the brain, and internal hemorrhage. Maria Jamison was found to have been assaulted by a blunt instrument and had a fractured skull, a massive contusion of the brain, and slash injuries to the neck.

According to the Voluntary Statement of Ms. Shirley R (9/19/87), she last saw her son at 3:30 a.m. on that date but had spoken to him three times since then. She indicated that her son said that he had killed the Jamisons. Ms. R recalled that he was accompanied by a friend, "Keena," who also indicated that she had been involved in the killings. Mr. R allegedly told his mother that Maria Jamison had pressed rape charges against him and that he had set his apartment on fire because his wife had left with their baby son, Ginny had been taken from him, he would have to go to jail, and "his life was over." He indicated in a series of approximately 12 telephone calls that he was going to kill three other individuals as well.

According to the Voluntary Statement of Ginny Calones (9/19/84), Mr. R had been her boyfriend; she had known him for over 2 years and he had argued with her parents beginning in June. She indicated that she had gotten an abortion in July. She had refused to go out with him and he had hit her because of this. The Voluntary Statement taken from Ms. Mary Wells (9/illegible/84) indicates that Ms. Wells is a Special Police Officer with the Police Department. She had seen Mr. R and a younger girl at approximately 3:00 a.m. on 9/19/87; at that time, Mr. R indicated that he had killed two people. He told her that his mother was upset because he had told her about this, and he asked Ms. Wells to talk to her to calm her down. He also indicated to her that he would be dead within a week. Ms. Wells did not file a report with the police because she did not believe Mr. R. She recalled that earlier in the week, the defendant's mother indicated that her son had wanted to take Ms. Wells's service revolver.

I reviewed Mr. R's signed waiver of Miranda rights (9/28/84) and his statement to the police (9/20/84). He indicated that he kicked the door to the Jamison's apartment open at approximately 2:00 a.m. He grabbed Walter Jamison,

asking him, "Why was they trying to hurt me. . . . I only tried to help you." He recalled that he hit Mr. Jamison across the throat, stabbed him, and then hit him with a baseball bat. He then went into the bedroom of Maria Jamison but could hear Keena hitting Mr. Jamison with a baseball bat. According to Mr. R, Keena entered the bedroom with a baseball bat and Mr. R moved the baby, who had been sleeping in the bed with Ms. Jamison, out of the way. Keena hit Ms. Jamison with a bat, and Mr. R hit her with a cinderblock, then with a baseball bat. He inserted the bat into Ms. Jamison's vagina, stating, "That's for having Ginny." He then went to his mother's house and later notified the police about the baby who had been left on the bed. He also indicated to the police that he had started a fire in his apartment on 9/18/84 because, "I was trying to burn up all the memories in the house." He further indicated that he had wanted to kill Ginny and his wife's (Betty's) parents. He blamed Ginny for the fact that Betty left with his infant son and blamed Betty's parents because they had reportedly talked his wife into leaving him.

Ginny Calones gave a Voluntary Statement on 10/7/84. She claimed to have had an abortion in June, when she was 4 months pregnant. When Mr. R learned about the abortion, she said, he hit her in the mouth, and they broke up 2 weeks later. She recalled four altercations between Mr. R and her parents. During the last incident, he said to them before he left, "I'll get you and Maria one way or another." Ms. Calones recalled that her mother had told Mr. R about filing a complaint of statutory rape.

Fire Department records (9/18/84) indicate they responded to a call of a fire at Mr. R's residence. The fire had been confined to a bed and the immediate surrounding area. According to the report, men's clothing, papers, and baby bottles were in the vicinity of the fire.

According to the Grand Jury proceedings (10/14/84), Detective John Beverly testified that a call was received from an unidentified male indicating that he had killed two people and that a baby would be found alive in the Jamison's apartment. The voice was identified by Ginny Calones as Mr. R's.

A review of the County Jail record indicates that Mellaril had been prescribed for Mr. R

(3/21/85). He was described in a memo as "upset and acting strangely." Mr. R reported that he had taken 60 pills in a suicide attempt. Records (University Hospital 3/28/85–4/3/85) indicate that Mr. R was found unconscious, apparently having taken a number of pills following an argument with another inmate. He was brought comatose to the hospital. He was discharged and returned to the County Jail on 4/3/85.

A social worker at the Billington Mental Health Center was interviewed by an investigator from the Office of the Public Defender on 10/7/84. According to the records, Mr. R voluntarily came to the Center seeking treatment. He spoke to the worker in the waiting room for approximately 5 minutes, and she recalled that Mr. R indicated that he "was tired of trying to kill himself." He reported that he had crashed his car into a brick wall in an attempt to take his life. She directed him to the first floor where an appointment could be made; she did not know whether he followed through in establishing an appointment. No record was found of Mr. R seeking treatment.

According to an interview conducted with William Easley (10/25/84), he is 20 years older than Ms. R and had been her common-law husband and had "acted as a father" to Mr. R. He indicated that Shirley R "was a hooker," whom he met when she was working at a bar. After she brought her children to live in New Jersey from North Carolina, he recalled that she continued to work as a prostitute. He believed that Mr. R and his brother had seen their mother bringing men to their apartment. "I was mostly her protector. I didn't let anyone bother her. . . ." He then added spontaneously, "I was not like a pimp or anything of that sort. . . ." About the time Mr. R started to attend Jay Street School, Mr. Easley left his common-law wife and her children, indicating, "I found myself another gal and I liked her a little better and I just left the house." He indicated that following this, he did not see Mr. R on a regular basis.

I have reviewed the initial transcript, a copy of which was provided to me by Ms. Bennett. Ginny Calones testified that Mr. R had gotten along well with her parents and that they had been friends. Ms. Betty R testified that she left Mr. R in early

July 1984, having lived with him since August 1983. He told her that the Jamisons threatened to press charges of statutory rape of their daughter against him. Her husband drank with Jamison, and she recalled that he indicated that he fought with them previously because of the possibility of pending charges.

According to a friend, Mr. R had driven his car at a high rate of speed into a wall sometime in July 1984. He indicated to him that, "Damn it, I can't even kill myself." According to the testimony of Ms. Carol Crescent, a social worker at Croton Medical Center, she met the defendant in May 1984 when his son was born 9½ weeks premature. She indicated that Mr. R was appropriately anxious, concerned, and supportive of his wife. Mr. R appeared to "bond" with the baby and was very caring in his relationship with his son.

Shirley R testified as to her son's early history. She reported that she had brought him to North Carolina to live with her mother and sister. She had argued with her sister, who later placed a hot plate on her son's face. Later, his aunt cut Ms. R's 2-year-old son's face with a razor blade. She left the defendant to live with her mother and returned 2 years later, bringing her son back to Newark. At the time, Ms. R was living with William Easley. She reports that Mr. Easley would beat her son and at times would beat her, frequently in the presence of her children. Ms. R recalled that while attending school, her son tried to jump off the roof of Madison Street School, and an appointment was made to see a psychiatrist or psychologist at Central Hospital. Her other son, Scott, was thrown to his death off the Garden State Parkway approximately 3 years before the trial, reporting that "Steve was broken up" over this.

Ms. R recalled that her son was very upset when his son was born weighing three pounds, indicating that Mr. R would cry about the baby. On one occasion, he brought a music box to the hospital for his baby to hear "so he wouldn't hear the machines." She described her son's concern of having to tell Betty about Ginny's pregnancy and the possibility of a rape charge being brought against him. When his wife left him, "he let himself go—crying, calling, . . . he couldn't be still. Like a wind-up—talks, rattling about something else."

She indicated that her son went to the mental health clinic seeking treatment because, "he said he thought he was losing his mind." Although Mr. R expressed a desire to admit himself to a psychiatric hospital, she advised him against it because "they never let you out." Instead, Ms. R testified that she brought her son to a "root doctor" who "works magic." Her son was given oils, candles, pills, told to recite the Twenty-Third Psalm, and to place oil on Betty's clothing. She indicated that Mr. R was unable to sleep, having lost Betty, Ginny, and his brother. She recalled her son stating, "I have nothing to live for." On the night of September 18, he and Keena indicated that they burned his apartment. Later, they indicated that they killed the Jamisons and needed $40 for a place to sleep. Both were "high." She reported that her son was both frightened and anxious about the Jamison's accusations of statutory rape. On cross-examination, Ms. R indicated that she had not told the police or the Grand Jury that her son appeared high. She said that her son stated that he would, "not go to jail for some rape because he didn't rape anyone." Later, she explained that he had burned his apartment because he was "burned memories."

According to David Walters, he observed Mr. R in his apartment in early September 1984 on two occasions. He found the apartment to be black, candles were burning, and Mr. R was chanting. He recalled that Mr. R had received "something from a witch doctor" and had kicked in the screen of his television set. Mr. R was found staring at his son's empty crib.

INTERVIEWS OF OTHER PARTIES

Ms. Christine Canton was interviewed by me at the Office of the Public Defender on 2/20/86. She described Mr. R as a man who would "flirt with other girls in front of his wife," yet he did not want her to leave. The defendant "was a good-hearted person inside. He would go to the store for me . . . he'd offer me money." She described Mr. R as a person whose "feelings would be hurt quickly . . . he was like a kid. He'd become sad, not angry. He would just walk away like a kid. He would do anything for you if you need it." She recalled Mr. R telling her that he had driven his car into a wall, stating, "I feel like killing myself." "He started to act strange," a change noted when Mr. R claimed that Betty's "mother and father sent my wife away from me to South Carolina." She believed that Mr. R attempted to send money to her to pay for her return to New Jersey, but "they [her parents] wouldn't give him the address. He was going to kill himself and would say, 'Nobody had ever liked me.'" According to Ms. Canton, "Steve really was cracking up." Prior to his automobile accident, "he was depressed . . . he'd get goofier when was more depressed. He drove his car into a wall, talked of jumping off the roof, burning himself up. He got real serious." Because of the deterioration in his behavior, Ms. Canton "told him a couple times to see a psychiatrist." She told him this on at least two occasions; she first made the suggestion when Mr. R spoke about "running his car into a wall."

Shirley R, the defendant's mother, was interviewed by me on two occasions, both at the Office of the Public Defender. These interviews occurred on 3/22/86 and 4/1/86. According to Ms. R, her son was "a happy baby." She left her son in North Carolina with her mother when he was approximately 3 years of age, and she returned to New Jersey. When her son was ready to attend school at age 5, she returned to her home state with him. She recalled that at the time, "He knew who I was, but he called my mama Mama." Her sister had been angry at her and "she put a hot plate on him. I beat my sister up and she [my mother] put me out for about 2 weeks." On another occasion, her sister, "cut him with a razor. . . . She loved him to death." On yet another occasion, Ms. R recalled, she and her sister "got in another argument and she grabbed my baby. I walked to her and she cut him on the face. My mother put me out again."

Ms. R indicated that her son attended Madison Street School. On one occasion, she recalled, "girls one day put lipstick and rouge all over his face. The kids would always chase him home, and Bill and I went downstairs and we made Steven fight. I was always at the school; he was always doing something. I was told he was overactive and was given a prescription for pills to keep him down a little. It made him very tired." At this school, she indicated, her son "went up on the roof. Someone did something to him and he went on the roof and was going jump off the roof. I took him to a psychiatrist for a few months and we talked together. . . . "

When questioned closely about her prior activities as a prostitute, Ms. R expressed extreme resistance at revealing this in Court. She stated, "There's the fear of bringing up my being a prostitute. I'm worried about losing my job; I work around kids in a cafeteria in school. I had to do it; Bill did shit—I had to put money in their little pockets. I never left them; I had to keep them clean; I had nothing left. The friend I lived with would throw me out." She stated, "I'll do anything for Steve," although her refusal to discuss her past in Court is inconsistent with this statement.

Ms. R recalled that her son "came to me after [the crime]. He was hyped up, like a wild person. It was around two o'clock in the morning and he looked scared. He called me first and told me, but I didn't believe it until Keena said, 'I got my first body.' " Ms. R spontaneously remembered that her son would say, "Mama, why can't I hold on to nobody?"

When interviewed on 4/1/86, Ms. R remembered her apartment on Main Street, her residence when she returned from North Carolina with her son. There was a "coal stove; addicts moved in, women had track marks and were selling drugs, and there were prostitutes. There was drinking in the street and addicts came into the building and started fires in the hallway, shooting-up, and Steve would see women with different men and inviting men in." Ms. R stated

> prostitutes would bring clients to my house. Steven and his brother were home, and I would charge each [prostitute] two dollars for the room. It was a different part of my house, and there would be four different girls, seven days week; I only used it on Friday night and sometimes Saturday. Bill was there as the "protector" for the other girls, too. There were fights a couple of times as he threw out customers. I had a gun in the house and Bill would be in the closet. Once, a guy put a knife around my neck. Bill threw someone down the stairs. He wouldn't let me go out of the room. The boys would be

home. Steve seen Bill beat me a number of times with a belt because I didn't want to go out on the corner . . . the boys saw it.

INTERVIEWS WITH DEFENDANT

Mr. R was evaluated by me on four occasions while incarcerated in the County Jail (2/9/85, 2/22/86, 3/1/86, and 10/17/94) and once while awaiting a retrial on the penalty phase at State Prison (9/3/91). According to Mr. R, he met his father on one or two occasions. He described him as an alcoholic who died of cancer. At the time he was conceived, "my mother was in a youth house and met my father there. She got pregnant just to get out of the Youth House. She was a kid having a kid. She told me that when I was little. . . . I remember everything derogatory she told me when I was little." He stated, "When I was little, she was a prostitute. She would bring clients home. . . . we didn't say anything, but the other kids knew [about it]." He described his mother as a person who, "did what she had to do; whatever we needed, we got." However, he added, "I paid a mental price. Everyone knew what she was doing."

According to Mr. R, Bill Easley moved in with his mother and was both her lover and her pimp. Mr. Easley was "all right; he didn't care for me. He didn't like me. I was the kid who stayed in trouble, played hooky. He raised us and didn't realize things were wrong." Mr. R indicated that on one occasion, "he tried to kill me. I hit him with a mop, and he tried to stab me in the chest." He continued, "He treated me like I wouldn't amount to shit. . . . If not for him, my mother wouldn't be turning fucking tricks. . . . He shit on the family, screwing my mother's best friend." He indicated that, "I got to love him; but he was piece of shit." According to Mr. R, he discovered that Mr. Easley "was married when he took us to his house. It was a big pretty, white house, and he brought me there to mow the grass."

Mr. R stated that he spent his initial years raised by his grandmother in North Carolina. He remained there until he was approximately age 5 or 6. He stated, "I thought she [my grandmother] was my mother." He said that he was surprised to discover that wasn't true when his mother returned to pick him up, "she told us she was our mother. I said, 'No, she wasn't.' She got my brother and bribed us into the car with a cookie. My grandmother told us to go." When he returned home, he recalled, he felt like "an outside kid. I talked country and there was teasing." He was beaten by his mother and Mr. Easley "because I wouldn't fight back [when teased]. I'd be beaten with belts, once with an extension cord. My mother would throw plates." Mr. R remembered an incident while in junior high school in which his parents "got rid of my dog. He was gone when I got home [from school]." He was told that the dog was "kicked out on the turnpike. It was the only way she [my mother] could get to me." He also recalled an incident in which a group of girls teased him, applying lipstick and rouge to his face. On another occasion, Mr. R recalled, he went to the roof of his school building wanting to commit suicide because he had been harassed by other children. He indicated that the school principal found him there and notified his mother.

Mr. R recalled his days in North Carolina. When he was approximately 2 or 3 years old, he said, his mother's sister "went to cut me with a straight razor. She put her arm back and cut me in the face. I never forgot it." On another occasion, he recalled, "I was under a chair; she came in and saw me playing. She put a hot plate on top; I looked up and she put it right on my face. She dropped the hot plate." He recalled that his mother beat up his aunt for cutting him with a razor and that his aunt "burned me to get even."

When Mr. R returned to Warren, he attended the Madison Street School and later, Foster Place Junior High School. He described himself as having been "an odd kid. They could do things to me, and I wouldn't talk to you. I was different; I was scared of people. I didn't belong, couldn't belong, and couldn't approach people."

Until December 1973, Mr. R worked for a roofing company. Following his military service, he held a position driving a sanitation truck in the evenings. Prior to this, he had held position as a welder.

Mr. R indicated that he enlisted in the U.S. Marine Corps in February 1974. He stated that he was discharged in December 1977 with "an Honorable Discharge." He denied that any conditions were attached to his discharge. He stated that while in Japan, he was tried on charges of

attempted rape in the course of committing a robbery: "I didn't understand too much of it; it was in a Japanese court."

According to Mr. R, he and Betty lived together for approximately 2 years. "She used to leave when she felt like leaving; her family didn't care for me." He indicated that his son was born in May 1984. At the time, he "weighed 2 pounds." Mr. R remembered that, "I was upset and would stay all night at the hospital." His son was discharged from the hospital in July 1984. When he brought his son home, "I felt proud . . . he was in the hospital until he weighed about 5 pounds." He believed that Betty's attitude toward her son was "she didn't give a shit. I stopped going to work when the baby was discharged. . . . I stayed home with the baby for fear she'd take the baby."

According to Mr. R, he told Betty of Ginny's suspected pregnancy. "I tried to clean up my mistakes. I told her I messed up and I needed help. I trusted her . . . I wanted her to know . . . there was nothing to hide." He describe his distraught state when his wife left. He telephoned her on numerous occasions but said that her parents would not permit him to speak with her. He also "threw out all of her clothing and shit. She left behind my son's birth certificate, a check, and I burned up the stuff." Although Mr. R claims to have 10 children, he viewed this child as "special." He indicated, "the mothers had kids, and then they just vanished with them." Again, he emphasized that "the baby almost died. I was the only one there; no one there; no one gave a shit [about him] but me." About his other children, Mr. R indicated, "I fed them, clothed them, and then they vanished on me. I was left with nothing."

Mr. R recalled meeting the Jamisons in January 1984. He indicated that he met them through a neighbor in their building. "No one wanted to help them. I helped them—bought them a TV, towels, house stuff; that's the way I am. They appreciated it. . . . I fed them for a month." He described his relationship with Maria as "fine." He saw the Jamisons as people who were "both on welfare and just didn't care about nothing; as long as they got something to drink, they were satisfied." He recalled that there was a fire in their apartment, and in July 1984, "they moved out with their family, and I took them to find another apartment and gave him money for a cab when he had to work."

He described their daughter, Ginny, as someone who "was screwing everything that walked and had a penis. She accused me of being the father [of her child] and they made her get an abortion. They found out she was messing with all the other little boys. She burned me." Mr. R indicated, with some indignation, that "I caught crabs from her—not from a 13-year-old girl; I'm not dirty. I was shocked—a 13-year-old. She was telling everyone she was pregnant by me. She told my girlfriend who was pregnant and my wife who was pregnant. She wrote letters, telling everyone. I told my wife about her." He described his relationship with Ginny as "something stupid; it was over and goodbye. That was it." He had indicated to her that "I'd take care of it [the baby]." He claimed that her parents knew that he had been sexually involved with her and "they condoned it. They knew it because I was in her room and Mr. Jamison told her that I couldn't spend the night in his house." He described two episodes in which he was involved in verbal and physical altercations with both Walter and Maria. On one occasion, he recalled, "I kicked in the door because she was hollering. There was no reason for her being beaten. I took her to her father's." He indicated that on a prior occasion, the Jamisons had called the police; he recalled that he "hit him, not hard, I tapped him on the leg. They'd run off at the mouth when they were drunk."

Mr. R indicated that the Jamisons had threatened him with statutory rape. "They were mad because their booze supply was cut off." He claimed to have ended his relationship with Ginny and "stayed away for about 1½ months." Nonetheless, he would see the Jamisons "because I play basketball. I didn't speak to them." When asked about having threatened them, Mr. R indicated, "You say stupid shit when you're angry. It was no more than that. I might have said it, but I don't remember. When you're mad and angry, you can say anything."

Mr. R reported that on one occasion, 2 weeks before the crime, he attempted to "kill myself." He recalls driving his car into a wall, but "there is a very high side walk and it hit it. I was doing about 80 mph; the car hit the curb, and it flew and slammed into the side. The car just spun, and

the side crushed in and bounced off the wall." He indicated that he left before the police arrived.

Mr. R stated that he felt his emotional state was deteriorating and had asked his mother to take him to the County Mental Hospital a week prior to the crime, "because I was getting high. They said they didn't take walk-in cases." He then indicated that, "Mama got off work. She took me to see a voodoo doctor. She could see that something was wrong with me . . . she [the "root doctor"] gave me candles and pills, but it didn't help. I did it, stuff with Satan, Bibles, and pills. Also, the Twenty-Third Psalm—the Lord is my Shepherd—seven times, and the candles seven times, and powered incense."

Mr. R described a gradual deterioration in his emotional state, beginning with his wife's decision to leave him, taking their son with her. When she left, "I had a lot of phone bills to get her back. I lived on the phone." He indicated, "I started getting high when Betty left in August, not before. I went to my mom for money for a ticket to get her back. She made you owe her if she gave you something and my mom didn't care about her; she didn't give me the money; I didn't have a picture of my own damn son." On one occasion, "I tore up my mother's room after they left in August. She said she wasn't coming back and I stopped doing everything . . . my mom didn't care. She hoped I'd die because I tore up her room. I was getting high then—on dust; it was the first time [I ever tried it]. Coke-basing, all shit I didn't do; crack. . . ." He indicated that he also had been drinking "every day for a month. I borrowed money for it; I sold my TV and stereo and tools."

Mr. R reported that he placed his son's birth certificate and a check in a frying pan, burning them "to give up the memories." He left and called the Fire Department. In another interview, Mr. R indicated that "I set the crib on fire and Keena set the bed on fire. . . . I was burning up memories in the house, in the crib."

Mr. R was questioned in detail during each interview about the events on 9/19/84. On 2/9/85, he stated that he initially had been going to visit his mother with Keena because "I needed money and maybe I was a little high [to buy] coke." He recalled that on that day, "I had been drinking heavily—vodka and beer; I was drinking before this, 40-ounces of Old English 800 malt liquor. I was smoking reefers all day and dust at 7:00 p.m. I had mescaline earlier, about 3:00 p.m." When asked how this affected him, Mr. R stated, "The honest truth, I can't tell you. I don't know. I may have been high but I didn't realize it. I can't explain how I felt. I wanted more and I didn't want to stop."

He stated

we passed Ginny's house and I saw Walter in the bedroom window, and he saw me. Walter and I were talking, we both were high, and words passed about a fire in the house they used to live in. I said I'd kick his ass. I went in the hallway and kicked down the door. I was between knowing it was wrong and not caring it was wrong; I guess I knew it was wrong, but I said to myself, I didn't care. Keena kept saying, "go ahead, go ahead." I kicked it open and ran in at Walter, wrestled and fighting on the floor. He fell back; by this time, I didn't know what was going on. I was tired. She handed me the knife.

He stated, "I was out of it. I can't explain it. I heard her say something to Walter." He indicated that, "he [Walter] was on top of me. Blood started falling . . . I had the knife and blood was on it. She said, 'Wipe the blood on the bed. . . .'" Mr. R stated that he then went into the hallway, and he heard Keena "call me and told me he was dead. He wasn't dead before I walked out. I was out of it. I was gone. . . . " He then indicated he heard a sound coming from the bedroom, and "Keena was cutting the woman's throat. . . . I went in to pick up Mike on the bed and said to myself, 'No.'" Regarding the bat, Mr. R claimed, "I didn't know about the bat. I had no knowledge of it. I just saw her cutting her throat."

When Mr. R left the Jamison's apartment, he indicated that he called the police because "I thought about Michael." He stated, "I called 911, and she connected me . . . a cop came on the phone and said who he was and I said two people are dead. I killed them and a baby is in the house."

Throughout all interviews, Mr. R remained resistant to describing and revealing his inner thoughts and feelings. He was consistently mildly depressed, indirectly expressing suicidal ideation.

At times, feelings of despair and hopelessness would be expressed. There were times when Mr. R was unable or refused to elaborate, but this occurred with respect to exploring his feelings rather than revealing details about his criminal acts. He sometimes appeared to be overly concerned about what I thought of him and what others would think about him should they learn of the details of his life. He appeared to be highly sensitive to even subtle cues that would indicate to him that he was, in some way, being "judged." His marked ambivalence about important people in his life was apparent in each evaluation session. Similarly, he demonstrated changes of mood throughout each session. He consistently expressed his disappointment in people, feeling let down and abandoned. At other times he was resistant to acknowledging negative feelings, especially toward his mother. Although no evidence for an active thought disorder was found during the interviews, he would sometimes ramble in a somewhat disjointed fashion. His level of insight appeared to be poor, and his understanding of his motives, thoughts, and feelings somewhat superficial.

RESULTS OF PSYCHOLOGICAL TESTING

Mr. R is functioning within the Low Average range of intelligence on the WAIS-III. His Full-Scale I.Q. of 87 falls at approximately the 19th percentile. His Verbal I.Q. of 85 falls within the Low Average category. His Performance I.Q. of 94 falls within the Average range. On the subtests that comprise the WAIS-III, Mr. R's scores range from Low Average to High Average; most cluster around the Low Average range. Only one score falls within the High Average category. Mr. R indicated that he had been administered a battery of psychological tests, including the WAIS-III, 1 week before my initial appointment with him. Since practice effects on these tests are significant, primarily affecting scores on the Performance section of the WAIS-III, it is not surprising that he obtained his highest score on a subtest most susceptible to the effects of practice. When considering the effects of practice, it is most likely that his "true" Performance I.Q. falls closer to his

Verbal I.Q. than was indicated on the day of testing by me.

The most noteworthy feature of his WAIS-III test record is the degree of intratest variability observed. Since each subtest is arranged in order of increasing difficulty, those without an active thought disorder tend to respond correctly to easy test items and give incorrect responses to move difficult questions. To a moderate degree, Mr. R's answers to test questions appeared to be somewhat unrelated to their degree of difficulty. Thus, he might give an incorrect response to an easy test item while responding correctly to a considerably more difficult question. While on some subtests this pattern may represent an unevenness in intellectual development, the nature of his responses, both correct and incorrect, and his answers on other subtests suggest the presence of a thought disorder. Mr. R tends to fade in and out of awareness. There is a lack of predictability in his overall judgment and cognitive skills. For the most part, he can focus in on the tasks at hand and weigh what he sees and hears in arriving at a judgment or answer that is expressed clearly and precisely. However, at other times he becomes confused. His indecisiveness and lack of focus were most apparent on the Picture Arrangement subtest. This subtest requires the examinee to rearrange a series of pictures so that they tell a sensible story in chronological sequence. Mr. R thought aloud as he rearranged the pictures. He was unable to focus on the cues present, which would have assisted him in establishing cause-and-effect relationships. Rather, he showed considerable indecisiveness, changing his mind, finding it very difficult to establish a temporal sequence. He was seemingly unaware of this difficulty, responding incorrectly to relatively easy test items and at other times, demonstrating the ability to focus, analyze, and react appropriately. The considerable variation in his level of thinking was apparent on the following comprehension test question: "Why do people who are born deaf have trouble learning to talk?" He responded to this question as follows: "They can't see so they can't hear. They have to adjust mentally. No. The mind has to be in contrast to the voice; they read lips." Such variability in his thinking suggests an underlying thought disorder

when taken in conjunction with other responses during the evaluation.

Mr. R's overall judgment or common sense falls within the Average range. Again, however, there is considerable variability in his level of response. In a non-test situation, the degree to which his behavior or responses would be appropriate and focused remains unpredictable. If the situation proves to be emotionally charged for him, his thinking may tend to deteriorate, and his responses would lack focus and would be inconsistent with general, everyday behavior.

An analysis of his Performance subtests score does not suggest the presence of a central nervous system dysfunction. It is likely that a number of subtests were artificially inflated due to practice effects. He had considerable difficultly in perceiving cause-and-effect relationships. Mr. R found it difficult to focus on cues that would allow him to establish a temporal sequence. He became confused but remained relatively unaware of such confusion, responding at a relatively low level inconsistent with his overall functioning.

Mr. R's self-image is a poor one. He is preoccupied with feelings of inadequacy. While his present situation may serve to exacerbate these feelings, his responses to the tests suggest that his overall lack of confidence is longstanding. Mr. R is unsure of himself, indecisive, and lacking a sense of direction. Life has been unrewarding and empty for him. Such feelings appear to have their basis in reality. His life is marked by lack of completion: his failure to complete school on schedule; his failure in the military; his inability to hold a job; his incomplete college career; and the absence of a long-term heterosexual relationship. Consequently, Mr. R's needs for love, belonging, and respect remain unmet, and he anticipates failure at every turn.

Perhaps the one area of his life in which he presents a façade of "success" is his relationship with many women. As a result, he tends to feel comfortable in their presence. Yet even these feeling are accompanied by self-doubts. Beneath this superficial, narrow front, Mr. R anticipates rejection. In a sense, he believes that no one needs him and that his life serves no purpose. His tendencies to anticipate rejection in all situations lead him to feel easily hurt and unappreciated.

He is overly sensitive to signs that others have found his faults and would reject him for them. In fact, Mr. R may encourage others to reject him, in a sense serving to confirm his worst fears.

Mr. R has yet to resolve his strong needs for love and acceptance from his mother who, according to the tests administered to him, is seen as an unforgiving, rejecting, non-nurturing person. Mr. R hungers for her affection but receives virtually none. Consequently, he has a strong sense of deprivation, feeling ignored as a child and unappreciated as an adult. Early feelings and thoughts of family focus on the lack of support or encouragement he received. Such feelings have been generalized to a hypersensitivity to rejection by all women. Mr. R sees women as insincere, unworthy of trust, and out for themselves only, a generalization of feelings toward his mother. He is, therefore, quick to feel jealous or rejected. Such feelings exacerbate this underlying rage and are likely to take over his behavior so that he is prone to act in an impulsive, vague, poorly organized, detached manner. Affect may be lacking when his anger is vented. Feelings toward his father are equally ambivalent. Anger toward his father is generalized to other adults who were seen as being in a superior position to him. When feelings of being unappreciated, slighted, hurt, or rejected are touched on, Mr. R may become more likely to act out these feelings in an explosive yet detached manner. Under such circumstances, his indecisiveness and ambivalence increases. His thinking is likely to become disorganized, while his affect becomes more detached. His behavior tends to lack a sense of planning, focus, or direction.

On the MMPI, questions are raised regarding the possibility that his profile may be invalid because of some combination of overstatement of symptoms due to panic, intentional exaggeration, difficulties in reading or comprehending the items, carelessness, or errors in entering his responses on the answer sheet. A serious vulnerability to a psychotic decompensation is indicated. Anger may be expressed through both irritability and passivity, with unexpected outbursts alternating with absence of involvement. Distrust and emotional estrangement from his family and friends are likely to be major, current difficulties for him if not chronic problems. Mr. R may demonstrate

emotional inappropriateness or flatness along with looseness of associations. Patients with a similar patterns have often expressed feeling of unreality, and they have shown unusual thought processes, emotional flatness, and apathy and, in a few cases, delusions or hallucinations. In addition, feelings of hopelessness are suggested. His general level of ego strength and self-sufficiency appears very poor and seriously diminished. Chronic dependency on alcohol or drugs is suggested on the basis of this evaluation. Mr. R's responses to the MMPI and his pattern of scores has been associated with the diagnoses of borderline psychotic state and with incipient and overtly schizophrenic reaction. A history of mood fluctuations is also suggested by this profile.

Based on Mr. R's background history, his behavior during the interviews, and on the tests administered, and also on my review of the records cited in this report, the diagnostic impression is of Borderline Personality Disorder (301.83). At times, when Mr. R feels threatened, his tenuous controls fail him and his behavior may deteriorate, resulting in Brief Reactive Psychosis (298.80).

SUMMARY AND FORENSIC OPINION

Mr. R relates as an insecure individual filled with feelings of inadequacy. He is overly concerned as to the impression he makes on others, quick to feel he is being judged poorly or that he is being criticized. His strong need for acceptance and the mood swings he demonstrated through the sessions are consistent with the diagnosis of Borderline Personality Disorder. Affect tended to be blunt, and at times, his thoughts would ramble. On the WAIS-R, his demonstrated considerable variability within a number of subtests suggests a cognitive process in which he tends to fade in and out of awareness. In addition, some confusion was evidenced in his thinking, as well as with Mr. R's tendency to misinterpret cues and to respond in an unpredictable, inconsistent fashion. His thinking tends to affect his overall judgment, such that his inner emotion may substantially impair his cognitive controls and his ability to reason. He tests as being somewhat socially shy, reflecting his underlying feeling of inadequacy. Mr. R's only source of positive identification is in his sexuality, feeling comfortable in relating to women on a sexual, albeit superficial level. He tests as being hyperalert to criticism and to signs that he may be rejected or betrayed. He possesses extremely strong needs for love, belonging, respect, and acceptance, and when these needs are not met, feelings of emptiness and panic may overwhelm him. His level of insight into these dynamics is extremely poor. His responses to the tests suggest that under such circumstances, he is likely to experience a sense of disorganization and a decompensation. On such occasions, his controls are likely to fail him, and the deterioration in his judgment and in his ability to modify his behavior may result in a psychotic deterioration consistent with a Brief Reactive Psychosis. The ingestion of alcohol and drugs is likely to further loosen his sense of controls. On the MMPI, his responses indicate high levels of fear and anxiety, with marked tendencies to be overwhelmed by his ruminations over such fears. The report indicates a serious vulnerability to psychotic decompensation and unusual thought process, as well as the likelihood of a loss of control over his actions. The diagnosis of both Borderline Personality Disorder and Schizophrenic Disorder are possible based on this profile.

A review of Mr. R's life history suggests the roots of his personality disorder, as well as his marked tendencies to quickly feel betrayed and abandoned. His self-image is based on his perception that his birth was merely a ticket for his mother to be discharged from youth house where she had been remanded by the Court. At an early age, he was brought to North Carolina by her and left there to be raised by his grandmother and aunt. Ms. R's lack of concern regarding her son's welfare (including his physical well-being) is evidenced by the fact that she willingly left him following episodes in which her sister burned her son's face with a hot plate and slashed him in the face with a razor. Rather than leaving with her son, Ms. R physically attacked her sister, resulting in being expelled from her mother's home. Ms. R returned to her mother's house when she believed it was time for her son to go to school. His memories of leaving are marked by the image of unwillingly being enticed into her car by the promise of a cookie. At the time, Mr. R indicated, he believed his grandmother to be his "mama."

Upon returning to Croton, Mr. R developed a self-image of being an outsider. He spoke with a strong southern drawl, which served to separate him for his peers. In addition, records indicate that he also demonstrated a very severe stutter. Serving to further diminish his self-image and to separate him from his peers, was his knowledge that his mother was employed as a prostitute—a fact that Mr. R claims to have been known throughout his neighborhood. Furthermore, his mother would bring clients home on a regular basis, engaging in sexual activity in the family's apartment, an activity acknowledged by his mother who stated that she did so only 2 days a week. In addition, his mother indicated that she regularly rented rooms to at least four other prostitutes for $2 a client, 7 days a week.

Ms. R began to live with her common-law husband, a man who resided in the family's apartment for 10 years. Mr. R's relationship with him was ambivalent. This man functioned as Ms. R's "protector," defensively stating, "I'm not pimp or anything." Both Mr. R and his mother indicated that Mr. Easley would hide in a closet with a gun while his mother and the other women serviced their clients. At times, Mr. R witnessed Mr. Easley physically attack clients, and at other times Mr. Easley would act out his rage against Mr. R. In addition, Mr. R would witness Mr. Easley physically beat his mother.

At school Mr. R's hyperactivity resulted in the need for psychotropic medication. On one occasion he was attacked by a group of young girls who applied rouge and lipstick to his face. On another occasion, following a disagreement with another student, he went to the roof of the school building where he was found by his principal, who notified his mother and referred him to a psychologist or psychiatrist. Mr. R was evaluated by the Board of Education at age 12½. At the time, signs of instability were noted. An evaluation performed at age 16½ by the Board of Education found Mr. R to be an "emotionally disturbed child." Mr. R's reluctance to defend himself in the face of teasing and physical beatings by his peers would result in physical beatings administered by Mr. Easley and his mother. When Mr. R was 15, Mr. Easley abandoned his "family," deserting them when he "found a gal I liked better." Mr. R recalled learning about Mr.

Easley's "other family" when he brought Mr. R to his other home to mow the lawn. Mr. R's relationship to his brother was also marked by considerable ambivalence, feelings that intensified upon Scott's death.

In the weeks preceding the crimes of which Mr. R was convicted, a marked deterioration is noted in his level of functioning. Sources for this deterioration are readily apparent and numerous. They serve to build upon his defective personality structure, leading to a significant breakdown in his controls. He experienced considerable resentment and anger at Ginny Calones for a variety of reasons. These include her telling others about her pregnancy, her reputation for sexual involvement with "little boys," her unilateral decision to have an abortion, his belief that she exposed him to "the crabs," and her role in ending his marriage to Betty. Mr. R had enjoyed what he believed to be a highly positive, close relationship with Walter and Maria Jamison. He had attempted to ingratiate himself to them, a common pattern in his life, by loaning them money, helping them move when their apartment was burned, and driving them in his car when they needed to go shopping. Characteristic of Mr. R's Borderline Personality Disorder, he was quick to feel unappreciated and insulted by them. He experienced an intense sense of betrayal regarding the Jamisons' threats to file a complaint of statutory rape against him.

Mr. R appeared to have been appropriately concerned over the premature birth of his son. Records indicate the he had "bonded" with his son, spending a considerable period of time with him in the hospital. Mr. R identified with this weak, small, different child, a child whose mother, in Mr. R's eyes, did not care about him. After his son's discharge from the hospital, Mr. R anticipated that his wife would leave with their son, resulting in Mr. R's decision to remain home from work to prevent this from occurring. On 8/6/84, Betty did, in fact, leave him, taking their son with her. Mr. R was quick to feel a sense of abandonment, emptiness, and panic over this "desertion." In part, he felt that his life had ended because of the loss of his son.

This began a noticeable, marked deterioration in Mr. R's mental state. His sense of abandonment and emptiness, as well as his sense of loss, resulted in a large number of desperate calls to

Betty's parents in an attempt to entice her to return. She refused to accept his collect calls. According to his mother, Betty's parents could be heard laughing at him on the telephone. They refused to give him information and threatened to physically harm him should he appear at their home. Mr. R began to drink and abuse drugs, including cocaine, crack, and angel dust, in a desperate attempt to self-medicate. Mr. R, in an unfocused frenzy, destroyed his mother's apartment. Consequently, his mother refused to talk to him, withdrawing what little emotional and financial support she had given him. This further rejection served to increase his sense of abandonment and panic, leading to increased confusion and disorganization.

On 8/24/84, Mr. R indicated, he drove his car into a wall in an attempt to end his life. His failure to succeed ironically resulted in increased feelings of ineptitude. Mr. R sought help at a community mental hospital, but his lack of patience to wait for an appointment made his efforts futile. As he deteriorated further, he possessed some awareness of his decreased ability to control his behavior and act in a focused, rational fashion. Mr. R asked his mother to take him to a mental hospital, but the records indicate that his mother discouraged him, expressing the belief that one is never discharged from a mental hospital. Rather than seeking professional help for her son, she brought him a "root doctor." Treatment for Mr. R's mental problems consisted of lighting candles, taking "pills," sitting in darkness, and chanting the Twenty-Third Psalm in front of his son's empty crib. In addition, he was advised to place oils on his wife's clothing. When efforts did not work, he was again advised to return to the root doctor for a follow-up appointment. My interview with a friend of Mr. R, as well as sworn testimony, confirms Mr. R's efforts to follow the prescribed treatment plan.

Mr. R's emotional deterioration is documented in my interview with Christine Canton. She described him as a person who was easily hurt and offended. She clearly reported a mental deterioration consistent with a brief reactive psychosis. She described Mr. R as initially depressed, withdrawn, and "acting strange." As his behavior deteriorated, his unkempt appearance reflected his decompensation. On four occasions prior to the murders of the Jamisons, he told her that he would set himself on fire. She described him as "cracking up" and "acting looser." His disturbed behavior led her to recommend on at least three different occasions that he see a psychiatrist.

Prior to the crimes, Mr. R had told both Ms. Canton, as well as his mother, of his thoughts of killing "five people." According to his mother, her son's "mind was racing." He had also indicated to his mother his desire to steal the weapon of Special Police Officer Wells.

On 9/18/84, Mr. R, in a disorganized, idiosyncratic, purposeless action, burned his son's birth certificate and other documents, including a check. He did so to "get rid of the memories." He then called the Fire Department to report the fire. Shortly after this act, Mr. R and Keena arrived at the Jamisons' apartment, and he committed acts that resulted in the deaths of Walter and Maria Jamison.

Based on my extensive interviews with Mr. R, his responses to a comprehensive battery of psychological tests, my interviews of others who were familiar with Mr. R at the time of the crime, and my review of the documents cited in this report, it is my opinion that on 9/19/84, Mr. R's criminal actions were a product of his underlying emotional disturbance. His actions at the time reflection a brief reactive psychosis in an individual with a Borderline Personality Disorder. His actions are marked by a significant loss of control of his impulses, resulting in a disorganized, poorly focused, frenzied acting out of his underlying sense of range and betrayal. A significant impairment existed in both his judgment and in his impulse controls, his actions representing a culmination of feeling directed at all those who have abandoned him and betrayed him in the past. His ability to reason, judge, and modify his behavior was overwhelmed by his underlying feelings, such that a significant impairment occurred in his ability to control his conduct. Mr. R's ability to focus his thoughts and attentions on the nature of the injuries he inflicted on his victims was severely impaired. His emotional state was such that he was cognitively unaware of the severity of the pain he was inflicting on the Jamisons. In addition, his loss of control of his inner rage was such that his ability to control his actions was significantly impaired. Similarly, the alleged postdeath mutilation that occurred to the body of Maria Jamison reflects his brief reactive psychosis and is a product of his mental disturbance. His actions lacked focus and reflect an acting out of his emotions rather than of his thoughts and intentions. His mental state was such that it is reasonable to conclude that Mr. R lacked the ability to recognize both the pain he was inflicting on her, as well as to note the fact that she had died.

Alan M. Goldstein, Ph.D., P.C.
New York State Certified Psychologist
Diplomate in Forensic Psychology –
American Board of Professional Psychology

Teaching Point: What kinds of cases do you avoid accepting because they would make it too difficult for you to remain impartial?

In this case, the crime was particularly brutal. Two people were killed, the means of death allegedly involved torture that took place over an extended period of time and the insertion of a baseball bat into the vagina of one of the victims. This alleged behavior was heinous. Yet I believed that I could conduct an objective assessment of the defendant, free from the effects of interference from the repulsive details of this capital crime. Why did I believe this?

When I was contacted by the first attorney in this case, the aggravating factor of torture and depraved indifference to human life were claims of the prosecution and not "facts" established by the jury. Mr. R was entitled to the presumption that these aggravating factors did not exist. In addition, he (and all defendants) should have access to experienced experts who do not judge, but rather assess. My personal views on capital punishment, which fluctuate somewhat over time, are such that they would not interfere with my performing an objective assessment in capital cases. If the U.S. Supreme Court finds execution for a capital crime constitutional, I believe that there are, indeed, individual cases that call for the death penalty. (I do have questions about the means by which capital cases are identified by prosecutors, the "luck of the draw" as to the experience and dedication of the attorneys in the case, the composition of the jury, and the availability of experienced experts in all fields.) Yet I have testified for the defense in at least one case in which I personally believed that the aggravating factors outweighed the mitigating factors (despite the jury's view to the contrary following deliberations). I have also conducted assessments in which I could not find mitigating factors—a reality check on the evaluator's impartiality over a number of cases.

Would I evaluate a defendant in a capital case for the prosecution or conduct a competency to waive the penalty phase or competence to be executed assessment? Although I have not done so, I believe that I would participate in such assessments. Regardless of who retains the expert, the findings should be identical. It is my view that the defendant would have an honest chance at an impartial, objective opinion, independent of the side that retained my services. However, since I have not conducted such assessments to date, I cannot conclude that if my testimony had been part of the information considered by the judge or jury that led to the execution of a defendant, I would continue to participate in such evaluations with emotional detachment.

Several years ago, within a period of 2 months, I conducted three independent sentencing evaluations of men accused of molesting young children. By the end of the third evaluation, I began to feel anger and disgust over what appeared to be their consistent attempts to rationalize their actions and blame their young victims (statements consistent with research on this topic). In light of my feelings about these crimes, I decided to take a "sabbatical" from cases involving sexual abuse of children. I believed that I could no longer remain emotionally detached from what was told to me by such defendants. I questioned my ability to conduct these evaluations in an unbiased manner. Only within the last year have I resumed evaluating defendants accused of such crimes, believing that the cumulative effects of these three cases having significantly diminished.

Experts should never conduct assessments when dual relationships exist. Any prior contact with the defendant, victim, or others related to the defendant or involved in the case should remove the expert for participating. By chance, I had learned that a friend's child had been a student of a murdered fifth grade teacher. When the prosecutor contacted me to conduct an assessment of the defendant's mental state at the time of the crime, I declined to do so. My awareness of how the victim's death had effected the children in her class, and this child in particular, led me to conclude that my ability to remain objective had been contaminated.

I have turned down other cases for reasons other than issues related to objectivity. For example, in one case I was asked to evaluate a defendant accused of terrorist activities. It was my belief that I had been chosen, in part, because I am Jewish and that perhaps a jury would be more likely to see me as credible should I offer testimony favorable to the defendant. In a sense, I felt the lawyer was using me for reasons unrelated to my expertise. In another case, it became apparent to me that my involvement, ostensibly to assess issues related to insanity, was requested in order to have me introduce evidence (in the form of data I had relied on) to the jury that they otherwise would not have heard. In another, although my opinion was only tangentially related to the proposed defense, it was the lawyer's hope that I would present the defendant's version of the crime to the jury without exposing the defendant to the cross-examination he would have faced had he testified.

Experts must be sensitive to a wide range of situations in which their impartiality may likely be impaired or questioned. In addition, if the proposed testimony appear to be "off topic," experts must question whether their involvement serves some motive other than to educate the trier-of-fact as to the forensic issues in the case.

Case 4

Principle: Obtain relevant historical information

This principle has been discussed in detail earlier in this chapter. Therefore, we will move directly to demonstrating how the present report illustrates the application of this principle. The current report provides a good example of what constitutes relevant historical information and how to obtain it in the context of a capital mitigation evaluation. The "Dates and Techniques of Evaluation" and "Records Reviewed" sections of the report describe the sources of information used in this evaluation. Relevant historical information was collected from a variety of sources, including clinical interviews, collateral interviews, and self-report. Historical information covering a variety of relevant domains, such as the social, medical, mental health, and family history of the individual being evaluated, is presented. Because this is a capital mitigation evaluation, it was also important to obtain detailed information about domains specifically related to statutorily defined mitigation factors.

The first section of the report identifies the mitigating factors in this jurisdiction as follows: (1) formative events or experiences that adversely affected the defendant's emotional welfare, moral development, socialization, judgment, impulse control, substance abuse vulnerability, and other developmental and/or psychological processes; (2) positive characteristics, relationships, and behaviors displayed by the defendant (in spite of these adverse experiences); and (3) effects of the defendant's execution on his children (if any). Although information addressing these factors might be uncovered through a broader history, the nature of the legal decision in this case clearly underscores the importance of these specific historical components. Based on current risk-relevant literature, the first section identifies a broad range of risk and protective factors that bear on the issue of mitigation. With these factors identified, the clinician can then describe relevant historical information that specifically addresses each factor.

For example, the first risk factor discussed is "multigenerational family system dysfunction and corruptive influence." In this section, there is extensive historical information, derived from a number of sources, that directly addresses the dysfunctional environment in which the defendant was raised. A similar pattern is seen in the next section, "paternal corruptive influence and abandonment." Because the issue involves family relationships, the clinician collected historical information from the defendant and from collateral interviews with other family members. Later in the report, when the clinician addressed "untreated Attention Deficit Hyperactivity Disorder," the clinician used collateral interviews of former teachers to gather relevant historical information.

By integrating self-report with information obtained from collateral sources, the forensic clinician was able to provide historical information in the areas specifically relevant to the legal question. This approach to gathering historical information can be seen throughout the report, which consistently integrates information obtained from collateral sources with self-report. Finally, using this approach allowed the clinician to address a relatively broad forensic issue in an organized and easily comprehensible manner.

CAPITAL SENTENCING EVALUATION

Re: *People v. JJ*
Defendant: JJ
Defendant's Date of Birth: 10-4-81
Date of Report: 7-25-00

DATES AND TECHNIQUES
OF EVALUATION

6-3-00	Clinical and forensic interview of JJ, 273 minutes
6-4-00	Clinical and forensic interview of JJ, 320 minutes
6-4-00	Interview of JA (ex-girlfriend, have a daughter together)
6-4-00	Interview of FJ (cousin)
6-8-00	Interview of WJJ (older brother)
6-8-00	Interview of SN (maternal aunt by marriage)
6-8-00	Interview of WW
6-9-00	Interview of LJ (aunt by marriage)
6-9-00	Interview of DJ (mother)
9-9-00	Interview of WA (father)

6-9-00 Interview of SW (younger half-sister)
6-9-00 Interview of JAJ (paternal cousin)
6-10-00 Interview of SA (older half-sister)
6-11-00 Interview of DW
6-11-00 Interview of WW (maternal aunt)
6-22-00 Interview of FJ (3rd grade teacher)
6-22-00 Interview of SAA (4th grade teacher)
6-24-00 Interview of MW (neighbor)
6-28-00 JA (Captain at County Jail)
6-28-00 GM (Correctional Officer at County Jail)
6-28-00 WH (Correctional Officer at County Jail)
6-28-00 SS (Correctional Officer at County Jail)
7-14-00 Interview of WA, Jr. (brother) in U.S.P. Beaumont

RECORDS REVIEWED

Charity Hospital records of DJ dated 2-6-78 through 12-11-93

Community Hospital records of DJ dated 7-30-91 through 12-4-92

Birth records regarding JJ

Charity Hospital records regarding JJ

Social Service records regarding JJ

School records regarding JJ

Juvenile detention records regarding JJ

State Death Penalty Statute

Discovery regarding pending capital charges including police reports, statements, autopsy reports, and crime scene photographs

County Jail Rules and Regulations for Inmates

County Sheriff's Department Initial Classification Assessment of JJ of 12-18-99

Summary of Disciplinary Violations at County Jail

CAPITAL OFFENSE

JJ and two co-defendants are charged with two gang-related capital murders on 12-13-99.

REFERRAL

I was contacted by defense counsel for JJ regarding my willingness to serve as a forensic psychology expert on capital sentencing determination issues. At the outset of the evaluation, JJ was advised that while retained as an agent of the defense, I remained an independent evaluator. Accordingly, my findings might not prove favorable to him. He was further advised that any information he provided to me, as well as my findings and conclusions regarding my review of records and interviews of third parties, would remain within the attorney-client privilege until my report was released by the defense or I was called by the defense to testify. At that point, any information I had obtained from any source, as well as any opinions or conclusions based on that information, could be subject to release to the State or testimony in open court. Defense counsel was present while these provisions were explained, and counsel advised JJ not to respond to any questions about the time period of the alleged capital offense or about any past unadjudicated offenses. JJ executed a release of information and informed consent to evaluation based on the above provisions.

The following sections detail historical information regarding JJ's life history, psychological research references, and associated psychological conceptualizations relevant to capital mitigation. Section 1 outlines aspects of JJ's history, character, and background that may be important with respect to mitigation. Each factor is accompanied by a discussion of the mitigating implications of the factor and, in many cases, associated research. Section 2 reviews the violence risk assessment (future dangerousness appraisal), which details essential violence risk-assessment methodology and data that should be presented to the jury to reduce the likelihood of error in their determination.

SECTION 1: MITIGATING FACTORS

For purposes of this evaluation, mitigating factors are considered to be:

- Formative events or experiences that adversely affected the defendant's emotional welfare, moral development, socialization, judgment, impulse control, substance abuse vulnerability, and other developmental and/or psychological processes;
- Positive characteristics, relationships, and

behaviors displayed by the defendant (in spite of these adverse experiences); and

- Effects of the defendant's execution on his children (if any).

The experience of being adversely shaped or limited by forces not personally chosen, or chosen as a minor, is critical to considerations of moral culpability—a concept at the heart of mitigation. To this end, it is important to differentiate mitigation (the primary psycholegal issue at the sentencing phase) from criminal responsibility (a primary psycholegal issue at the guilt phase)—that is, moral culpability (choices shaped by forces he did not choose) vs. criminal responsibility (wrongful awareness/absence of compulsion). In other words, the choices exercised by a defendant in an alleged capital offense may have been shaped by the formative influences of multiple profoundly adverse developmental experiences.

Presented in the following sections are adverse developmental factors identified through an interview with JJ, interviews of family members and other third parties, a review of records, and a review of relevant research. These sources and types of data are reasonably relied on by clinical and forensic psychologists in coming to conclusions on relevant issues in this area.

The necessity of separately delineating the various adverse developmental factors and their impacts rests on two premises. First, it is unlikely that a lay population, such as a jury, would be aware of the individual and combined effects of these adverse developmental factors. Unless informed by broad and comprehensive expert testimony about these factors, the jury lacks a sound basis for giving them weight as mitigators. Second, the risk of violent criminal outcome increases as the number of adverse life factors increases. Thus, the cumulative saturation of risk factors can be critical to the outcome.

In addition to cumulative saturation, the research literature identifies that outcome is a function of the interaction of risk, vulnerabilities, and protective factors. Research describes the broad interaction of risk and protective factors in terms of the following:

- Trauma (sexual, physical, psychological, neglect);
- Predisposing and contextual factors (ge-

netic, neurological, and physical vulnerabilities, troubled interpersonal relationships, accidents of the environment); and

- Protective factors (secure attachments in infancy and early childhood, supportive relationships, awareness of childhood pain, supportive confidant).

The analysis of risk, vulnerabilities, and protective factors in the etiology of criminal violence is quite similar to explanations of who gets cancer—that is, carcinogen exposure, predisposing factors, and protective factors. All of the children growing up in a neighborhood built on top of a toxic waste dump do not get cancer; rather these children as a group experience a markedly increased incidence of cancer as compared with children from more benign settings. Similarly, a history of profoundly adverse developmental experiences does not invariably result in a criminally violent outcome, only an increased likelihood of such an outcome. Everyone need not totally succumb to the toxic exposure for it to be implicated.

Research sponsored by the U.S. Department of Justice regarding the precursors of serious and chronic delinquency, as well as youth violence, identified the following risk factors (odds ratios in parentheses) and protective factors:

Individual Factors

- Hyperactivity, concentration problems, restlessness, and risk taking ($\times 2$–5)
- Aggressiveness ($\times .5$–6)
- Early initiation of violent behavior ($\times 6$)
- Involvement in other forms of antisocial behavior
- Beliefs and attitudes favorable to deviant or antisocial behavior.

Family Factors

- Parental criminality ($\times 0$–3.8)
- Child maltreatment
- Poor family management practices ($\times 2$)
- Low levels of parental involvement
- Poor family bonding and family conflict
- Residential mobility ($\pm$)
- Parental attitudes favorable to substance abuse and violence ($\times 2$)
- Parent–child separation

School Factors

- Academic failure
- Low bonding to school
- Truancy and dropping out of school
- Frequent school transitions
- High delinquency rate schools

Peer-Related Factors

- Delinquent siblings
- Delinquent peers
- Gang membership (× 3–4)

Community and Neighborhood Factors

- Poverty (× 2)
- Community disorganization (crime, drug selling, gangs, poor housing)
- Availability of drugs and firearms
- Neighborhood adults involved in crime
- Exposure to violence and racial prejudice

Situational Factors

Protective Factors

Individual Characteristics

- Female gender
- Intelligence
- Positive social orientation
- Resilient temperament

Social Bonding to Positive Role Models

- Family members
- Teachers
- Coaches
- Youth leaders
- Friends

Other Protective Factors

- Healthy beliefs and clear standards for behavior, including those that promote nonviolence and abstinence from drugs.
- Effective early interventions

As will be demonstrated in the discussion that follows, JJ had many of the risk factors and none of the protective factors that have been identified in this research. JJ experienced the following adverse developmental experiences:

1. Multigenerational family system dysfunction and corruptive influence
2. Paternal corruptive influence and abandonment
3. Maternal neglect, emotional abuse, and corruptive influences
4. Home instability and frequent relocations
5. Inadequate supervision
6. Sexual abuse
7. Family violence and physical abuse
8. Observed community violence
9. Family victimization
10. Gang socialization
11. Untreated Attention Deficit Hyperactivity Disorder
12. Learning disability and academic failure
13. Neuropsychological deficits
14. Predisposition to alcohol and drug abuse
15. Immaturity

MULTIGENERATIONAL FAMILY SYSTEM DYSFUNCTION AND CORRUPTIVE INFLUENCE

Both of JJ's parents were damaged themselves. WA, father of JJ, was abandoned by his own mother while he was in diapers. He subsequently saw her three times during his childhood. WA's father was irresponsible and unstable. He married at least six times. When the children were in his care, he moved frequently, often leaving the children in the care of others. WA recalled being placed in four different foster homes and the County Home, as well as residing with three different aunts and his paternal grandparents for periods of time. WA noted that he went out on his own at age 12. He reported involvement in the criminal justice system from age 9. As a youth, he was affiliated with a street gang and was arrested for burglary and armed robbery. He was confined to juvenile institutions four times, including one lasting for 1 year. WA reported continued fights, drug dealing, and other criminal activity across his adulthood. WA subsequently had 13 children by 5 or more women. He abandoned JJ and his siblings for years, despite knowledge of the profound neglect by their mother and instability of their foster placements.

DJ, mother of JJ, is one of 12 children born to her parents. Her father was a physically and verbally abusive alcoholic. DJ displayed marked psychological instability and behavior problems from childhood. DJ repeatedly ran away. She was placed in foster care at age 11, as her parents could not control her. She spent much of her school years in various state schools and girls' homes. At age 16, she was found to be a delinquent ward of the State. DJ began drinking alcohol at age 17 or 18, and she subsequently maintained a pattern of severe alcohol dependence across her adulthood. She lived a transient lifestyle and recurrently supported herself through prostitution. There is an extensive history of alcoholism in her extended family system. DJ has had six children by five different partners.

JJ intermittently spent time during his childhood living with his maternal grandparents. SA, JJ's older sister, described their grandfather as "wild," "crazy," and frequently drunk.

Most of JJ's uncles and cousins were gang members and involved in criminal activity. JAJ, JJ's paternal cousin, stated: "Most of the males in our family are either dead or in prison. My father is in prison, along with my cousins. . . . My uncle was murdered on the street, along with one of my cousins."

WA Jr. noted that at least one of JJ's uncles had been a high-ranking gang member until his death. One uncle was described as a having a leadership position in the Vice-Lords. JJ reported having been quite close to this uncle because they had spent much time together, and JJ perceived him as looking out for him and helping him. The uncle was reportedly shot to death when JJ was 11 or 12. SN, part of JJ's extended family network, confirmed these events, stating that the uncle had been abducted and executed by other young men who were supposed to be his friends. His body was found in a car that had been set afire behind a nearby housing project.

All four of JJ's brothers have had substance dependence problems, gang involvement, and criminal outcomes. Three of his brothers are currently in prison on charges ranging from drug distribution to attempted murder. JJ's older sister, SA, does not have a criminal record but has been

heavily identified with gang activities. She first became pregnant at age 14, and she had three children by age 17. SA has been treated in drug rehabilitation and is currently in recovery.

Implications Family history is critically important to character and background. There are several reasons for this. Some personality characteristics, behavior patterns, and social vulnerabilities are genetically transmitted. Of specific relevance, there is evidence of genetic predisposition to antisocial personality traits and substance dependence.

Other characteristics and behaviors are generationally transmitted by family scripts. Family scripts are broad outlines of behavior and life sequence that are conveyed both verbally and, more importantly, by example in the lives of parents, grandparents, siblings, and extended family. School dropout, early pregnancy, early marriage, criminal activity, gang involvement, domestic abuse, substance abuse, and many other maladaptive behaviors may be extensively represented in a family system from one generation to the next. In JJ's childhood, adverse family modeling included gang involvement, criminal activity, gun possession, irresponsibility, rejection, anger, violence, perverse sexuality, and substance abuse.

Other maladaptive behaviors, including criminal activity and violence, may be the result of sequential emotional damage. In other words, individuals who have been significantly emotionally damaged in childhood come into adulthood with limited emotional resources and, as a result, may not parent their own children humanely or effectively. The children may be emotionally damaged themselves and thus at a greater risk for adverse adult outcomes, including substance dependence, criminal activity, and violence.

PATERNAL CORRUPTIVE INFLUENCE AND ABANDONMENT

JJ is the product of a relationship between his father, WA, and DJ, who never married but cohabitated until JJ was approximately age 5. JJ is the fourth of six children of his mother, but only he and his older brother, WA Jr., share the same father. LJ, JJ's aunt by marriage, noted that WA occasionally attempted to deny that JJ and WA Jr. were his children. She stated that "DJ would have to find WA and argue with him to come see the boys."

WA and DJ were described by multiple family members as selling marijuana out of the house. JJ was approximately age 5 when WA was arrested and subsequently imprisoned on drug charges. JJ was described as having been quite disturbed by the incarceration of his father, and he reportedly refused to visit WA while he was incarcerated. WA subsequently moved to another state and did not maintain visitation or financial support of the children. LJ described WA's departure as affecting JJ very negatively: "He never mentioned his father after he left, and seemed angry and hurt—as if he had been abandoned."

Implications of Paternal Corruptive Influences and Abandonment Parental criminality and parental attitudes favorable to substance abuse and violence are significant risk factors in the development of serious youth delinquency and violence. This makes intuitive sense. The value systems and behavior patterns of children are strongly impacted by the behaviors and attitudes of family members, particularly older males and/or father figures who represent role models to them.

Developmental research literature identifies father absence as a potentially substantial developmental hazard. Fatherless children are much more likely to grow up in poverty. Fifty-seven percent of African-American children living with only mother are in poverty, compared with 15% living with married parents. The low supervision of adolescents frequently found in father-absent homes, though, was more often the cause of delinquency than poverty. Boys from father-absent homes are more likely to commit a school crime. The likelihood that a young male will engage in criminal activity doubles if he is raised without a father and triples if he lives in a neighborhood with a high concentration of single-parent families. Seventy percent of the juveniles in state reform institutions grew up in single- or no-parent situations. Seventy-two percent of adolescent murderers grew up without fathers. In summary, fatherless children are at a dramatically greater risk for drug and alcohol abuse, mental illness, suicide, poor educational performance, teen pregnancy, and criminality.

MATERNAL NEGLECT, EMOTIONAL ABUSE AND CORRUPTIVE INFLUENCES

JJ's mother, DJ, was described as never working and instead relying on prostitution, public assistance, other family members, a series of men, or her children for financial support. She lived with a series of alcohol- and drug-abusing men, including JJ's father. It is unclear whether she was abusing alcohol or drugs during her pregnancy with JJ. Family members noted that, at the very least, DJ was abusing drugs within months after JJ was born.

WA Jr. stated that there were times when public aid was cut off and they might go without food for 1 or 2 days. DJ was described by other family members as being emotionally neglectful as well, extending little time or attention toward the children. DJ repeatedly left the children in the care of her parents or siblings for months at a time.

DJ reported that much of this neglect was associated with being addicted to alcohol and cocaine until August 1997. There is some external corroboration of her substance abuse problem. Notes from the Charity Hospital emergency room dated 9-18-91 described DJ as "heavily intoxicated" on her presentation to the emergency room after being hit by a car while crossing the street. Even following the purported cessation of substance abuse, DJ continued to display a tenuous emotional equilibrium, including attempting suicide on several occasions. The most recent suicide attempt occurred several days before the alleged capital offense, and it represented a substantial source of instability and turmoil for JJ.

Implications of Maternal Neglect, Emotional Abuse, and Corruptive Influences JJ's childhood was characterized by a chronically unstable attachment to his mother. DJ repeatedly abandoned JJ, only to return for varying intervals when she attempted to reassert parental relationship. These physical abandonments were only a part of the attachment instability of this mother–child relationship. DJ's cocaine dependence almost certainly resulted in erratic and unpredictable behavioral responses, as well as emotional detachment. These markedly interfered with her capacity to provide a maternal relationship when she was present. DJ's cohabitation with drug-abusing men added a further element of instability to parenting interactions with JJ.

Psychological research unequivocally demonstrates that normal child development depends on a stable relationship with a caring adult. A secure attachment to a parental figure is crucial to healthy psychological development. Because children are more vulnerable than adults to changes in their environment, relationship continuity and structure are quite important. Traumatic disruptions in the parent-child relationship may cause immediate emotional distress and bewilderment, as well as severe lasting psychological harm. Adverse impacts of disruptions in the emotional bonds of a child with a parent or other primary attachment figures include damage to identity, lowered self-esteem, psychological disorders, intellectual and academic deficits, impaired capacity to trust and care for others, and deficient identification with social ideals. Any of these effects may lead to behavior problems.

This nexus of disordered family and violent offending is not a matter of personal conjecture. Career investigators from the Behavioral Science Unit of the FBI have asserted that the quality of the attachment to parents and other members of the family during childhood is central to how the child will relate to and value other members of society as an adult.

INSTABILITY OF HOUSEHOLD AND FREQUENT RELOCATIONS

As a result of DJ's irresponsibility and chaotic lifestyle, the children endured frequent relocations of residence and living circumstance. These moves were between JJ's maternal grandparents, maternal relatives, men DJ was involved with, housing projects, and various apartments. JJ explained that they often moved because of problems with the rent, the place "might not be right," or they were just staying with people for a few days or weeks. SN stated that "DJ was a drifter and moved around a lot."

Implications of Residential Instability and Mobility Residential mobility is one of the delinquency risk factors identified by Department of Justice research. This is not surprising. Household instability has a destabilizing impact on a child's life. Because children require structure and stability for healthy emotional and social development, residential instability and mobility may undermine this basic need. This is particularly salient in a family setting such as that of JJ's childhood, which was chaotic and internally destabilized by substance abuse, neglect, and violence. Residential instability would also interfere with stable peer relationships and school stability, which could undermine the child's attempts to establish islands of security in these arenas.

INADEQUATE PARENTAL SUPERVISION

As described previously, JJ's father was minimally involved with him in early childhood and left altogether when JJ was age 5. His mother was repeatedly absent and his care was abdicated to others. Across JJ's childhood, his mother was alcohol- and substance-dependent. DJ was described as exhibiting an attitude that, by age 12, the boys were grown and required no ongoing support or supervision. SN, part of JJ's extended family network, stated: "When JJ was around 11 or 12, DJ asked me to take JJ and let him live with me. I told her that I was too busy with my own children. She told me, 'JJ ain't no child. He is grown.'" DJ's attempts at disciplining JJ were inconsistent and frequently abusive. She made no attempts to supervise or set limits on him while he was an adolescent.

Implications of Inadequate Parental Figure Supervision and Structure Healthy child development requires not only a stable and secure relationship with a parent, but also limit setting and guidance through discipline. In the absence of either of these fundamental parenting factors, there is a grave risk to psychological health and positive socialization. Quite simply, lack of parental discipline contributes to aggressiveness and predisposes an individual to violence in the community. While JJ's physical needs were attended to, he otherwise raised himself as a child of the streets without guidance, supervision, or discipline. DW was too ineffectual to exercise these functions, and CJ was too drug-dependent to structure her own life, much less JJ's life.

SEXUAL ABUSE

While JJ denied being sexually abused, his sister, SA, stated that both she and JJ had been sexually abused in each other's presence by one of their mother's live-in boyfriends across a 6-month period of time when JJ was approximately age 6. WA Jr. independently confirmed that he had been aware of this abuse, but felt helpless to prevent it. JJ reported that when he was 8 years old, a 16-year-old female cousin exposed herself to him and engaged him in mutual fondling on a number of occasions over a 3-month period. He reported that this sexual contact progressed to mutual oral-genital stimulation and simulated intercourse. JJ also reported that his mother was indiscrete in her sexual liaisons with men, so that he was disturbed by the noises of her sexual encounters in the next room. JJ stated that his older brothers kept sexually explicit videos in the home, which he surreptitiously watched with neighborhood peers. Other family members verified the presence of these sexually explicit videos. JJ reported that when he was selling drugs at age 12 and 13, women who were over age 30 would interact sexually with him in exchange for drugs. Even though these experiences had a seemingly consensual quality, they were not developmentally benign.

Implications and Relevant Research Regarding Sexual Abuse Research has identified four broad traumatic impacts of being sexually abused as a child. Traumatic sexualization may occur as the child's sexuality is inappropriately shaped by the abuse experience. Being sexually abused represents a profound betrayal, because the perpetrator is often someone the child was dependent on. This may subsequently be associated with relationship distrust, feeling unlovable, interpersonal dependency, and retaliatory aggression. The child experiences a profound sense of powerlessness in the face of sexual abuse, because his will and sense of control are overwhelmed. This may re-

sult in continuing feelings of incompetence, depression, anxiety, and adult victimization or domination. The sexually abused child may experience a significant sense of stigmatization as badness, shame, and guilt become incorporated into the child's self-image. This may result in low self-esteem, anticipation of rejection, poor relationship choices, or promiscuity. Other sexual exposures during childhood that are psychologically damaging include precocious exposure to adult sexual exchange, perverse family atmosphere, perverse and/or promiscuous parental sexuality, inappropriately sexualized relationships, observed sexual abuse of another, and premature sexualization.

A history of childhood sexual victimization appears to be associated with equal levels of later psychological dysfunction in both male and female clinical subjects. These psychological dysfunctions include dissociation, anxiety, depression, anger, sleep disturbance, and post-sexual abuse trauma. Interestingly, males displayed as much psychological disturbance as females, though reporting less extensive and less extended abuse. This suggests one of two hypotheses: (1) there is an equivalent impact of sexual abuse for males or females regardless of any differences in its severity or duration between the sexes, or (2) sexual abuse is more traumatic for males since lower male abuse levels were associated with symptoms that were equal to that of more severely abused females.

A number of factors may negatively affect the recovery of males from sexual abuse, including reluctance to seek treatment, minimizing the experience of victimization, difficulty accepting shame and guilt, exaggerated efforts to reassert masculinity, difficulties with male intimacy, confusion about sexual identity, power/control behavior patterns, externalization of feelings, vulnerability to compulsive behaviors, greater difficulty in adjusting to stress, and difficulty in expressing and communicating affect.

Sexual abuse creates unique disclosure problems for male victims. In other words, males tend not to disclose their complaint about the sexual abuse experiences as readily as females. Boys are sexualized with a male ethic of self-reliance, which inhibits disclosure of the victimization. Disclosing same-sex abuse to peers or parents might threaten a boy's developing masculinity or pose a risk of being labeled a homosexual. Additionally, disclosure may result in a loss or curtailment of the boy's greater independence and freedom.

Initial effects on males following sexual abuse usually involve behavioral disturbances, including aggression, delinquency, and non-compliance. Other problematic initial effects may include emotional distress; displays of guilt, shame, and negative self-concept; psychosomatic symptoms; confusion regarding sexual identify and sexual preference; problematic sexual behaviors; and vulnerability to juvenile sexual offenses. Long-term effects of sexual abuse include increased risk for depression, somatic disturbance, and self-esteem deficits; difficulty maintaining intimate relationships; problems with sexual adjustment; alcohol and substance abuse; and sexual offending.

FAMILY VIOLENCE AND PHYSICAL ABUSE

As discussed previously, JJ's maternal grandfather was prone to outbursts of physical abuse when drinking. WA, JJ's father, was described as being prone to fits of rage. JJ's clearest recollection of domestic violence involved his mother's boyfriend/common-law husband who resided with them for a period of time. JJ reported that WA and DJ fought frequently. JJ also reported seeing his mother with black eyes, and he stated that WA "messed up one of her legs real bad jumping on her."

DJ was abusive in her discipline of the children. WA Jr. stated that his "[m]other would whip us with an extension cord that had knots tied into it. You would be beaten if you messed up—this could be as often as every day or not so often—it depended on how often you 'messed up.'" JJ reported that his mother disciplined them with a belt or an extension cord when they were younger but that after age 11 or 12, his mother would discipline them by hitting them with her fist in the chest or arm.

Implications and Relevant Research Regarding Abuse in Childhood JJ's history included routine physical abuse at the hands of his mother and periodic abuse from his maternal grandfather. It is notable that JJ experienced extensive parental neglect in addition to the abuse he experienced. Abused children may show a variety of initial and long-term psychological, emotional, physical, and cognitive effects, including low self-esteem, depression, anger, exaggerated fears, suicidal feelings, poor concentration, eating disorders, excessive compliance, regressive behavior, health problems, withdrawal, poor peer relations, acting out, anxiety disorders, sleep disturbance, lack of trust, secretive behavior, excessively rebellious behavior, and drug or alcohol problems. In addition, research suggests the following broad conclusions:

1. Child abuse and neglect can seriously affect a person's physical and intellectual development and can lead to difficulty in self-control.
2. Abused and untreated children are more likely than non-abused children to be arrested for delinquency, adult criminal behavior, and violent criminal behavior.
3. When abused children are not given appropriate treatment for the effects of the abuse, the lifetime cost to society for an abused child is very high.
4. Children who are exposed to parental violence, even if they are not targets of this violence, have reactions similar to those of children exposed to other forms of child maltreatment.

OBSERVED COMMUNITY VIOLENCE

The inner-city neighborhood where JJ grew up was characterized by drug dealing, gang activity, and extensive violence. JJ and his family described hearing gunfire occurring in the surrounding community almost nightly. JJ reported that in his neighborhood, many of his peers carried handguns. He noted that when they played basketball, several of the youths would lay their guns down beside the basketball court. At other times, he would observe handguns in waistbands. LJ, widow of JJ's uncle, described the southside area where JJ grew up as follows:

This community has nothing to offer. It is a dangerous place to live. People in the neighborhood shoot at each other, and you cannot sit on the porch at night because there is always something going on. I was terrified to walk around the neighborhood and would never walk to DJ's house after dark because she lived near the underpass, which was considered an especially dangerous area. The neighborhood was violent at the time JJ was growing up. I never liked going over into that area because someone was always getting shot.

SN stated

I usually had no qualms about riding the bus to get around the city, but I refused to ride the bus to the southside projects because it just was not safe . . . the projects were a very dangerous place, and there was a murder there almost every day when JJ and his family lived there . . . JJ liked coming to my house because I lived in a safer community, and he could play outside and just act like a child and not have to worry about the dangerous elements that infested the Roosevelt Project.

JAJ, JJ's first cousin, stated: "I know the southside was a dangerous place. It was too dangerous for me to walk alone in certain areas, especially near the underpass. As children we learned that we had to be extremely cautious or we could get hurt. We were taught at school to never walk alone."

Regarding the southside housing projects, WW reported

JJ's family lived in the southside projects for several years. Their apartment was in a tall, overcrowded building about 14 stories high. Each floor had a long ramp area that looked like a cage, because there was a railing and a high fence to keep residents from falling over the edge. The elevators did not work at least half of the time, and JJ's family lived on the 12th floor. This meant not only hiking up 12 flights of stairs, this also meant entering a danger zone every time you went to and from the home. You had to be on guard because the stairwells and elevators could be dangerous. People were robbed, raped, and beaten in these common areas.

JJ reported that one of his early recollections of observed community violence was not long after they moved to the southside housing proj-

ects when he was approximately age 7. He described playing in a playground area characterized by benches and a little grass. He stated that one man got into an argument with a second man who was sitting on a bench. The man left, but soon returned and began shooting at the second man at close range. JJ reported that the victim tried to run and fell over the bench. JJ stated that he observed this scene from approximately 15 feet away. He recalled the victim bleeding and his own sense of shock.

The second shooting JJ observed in childhood occurred when a fight broke out while a group of older boys were playing ball. He described the assailant as shooting the victim, who reportedly kept running and trying to get away. At age 9, he observed his cousin being pistol whipped after JJ had been ordered off the building steps by a mentally disturbed neighbor and his cousin attempted to intervene.

JJ reported that when he was 11 years old, he looked out the window to observe someone on the porch below being shot repeatedly while begging the assailant to stop. At age 12 he heard gunshots in the hallway and found two bodies on top of each other. At age 13 he observed a young man get beat with bats and then shot in the stomach with a .22. The young man lay bleeding against the side of a building until an ambulance arrived.

WA Jr. stated that at age 15, he and JJ were talking to an acquaintance when an ex-boyfriend assaulted her, chased her down, and shot her six times. JJ subsequently held her as she lay dying, while WA Jr. called for an ambulance. When JJ was age 16, a longstanding adult friend of his mother's was shot outside an adjacent building. JJ stated that he observed her lying in a pool of blood from 15–20 feet away.

JJ reported other instances of seeing females fighting with each other and, on several occasions, seeing one stab the other. He described an instance of observing one girl bite a piece of another girl's ear off in a fight. He stated that he observed men fighting and one hitting another with a baseball bat.

JJ described that women were routinely raped in the elevators or stairwells of various buildings making up the Roosevelt projects. He described hearing reports of rapes at a frequency of about twice weekly. JJ and his older sister described an instance of a woman being raped outside of their apartment door. They did not go to her aid because they feared what would happen to them if they opened the door.

JJ reported that on approximately 10 occasions, he heard shots in the courtyard and found a crowd gathered around a body. He had been acquainted with some of the victims. JJ reported that following a shooting, the coroner's office would pick "stuff off the ground that looked like macaroni [brains] and putting it in a sack."

Further, both JJ and his family described a number of his peers who had been well known to the family who became casualties of gun-related violence.

Statistical data provide additional support for JJ's childhood experience of traumatic violence exposure. For example, of 22-25 local municipal districts, from 1987 to 1994, JJ's neighborhood ranked 8th–12th in population, but 2nd–5th in violent criminal offenses. In 1994, when the southside area ranked 12th among the districts in population, it was 2nd in number of reported rapes. The direct contrast with other neighborhoods in the city is perhaps more illustrative. In 1994, when JJ's neighborhood suffered 40 homicides per 100,000 population, Highland Park experienced .5 homicides per 100,000 population—an 80-fold difference in their respective murder rates.

JJ's mother and older sister, SA, described him as initially disturbed by the violence he observed. They reported that he exhibited nervousness and restlessness, intrusive memories of and preoccupation with the shootings, feelings of personal vulnerability that this "could happen to me," sleep disturbance, and trouble concentrating. In time, however, they noted that he seemed hardened to this experience and even seemed to deliberately place himself in danger.

Implications and Relevant Research Regarding Chronic Violence Exposure During Childhood Research has been conducted on inner-city high-density public housing project zones similar to the one JJ grew up in. For example, during the 1980s, Chicago's largest public housing project—Robert Taylor Homes—had a rate of murder and aggravated assault 20 times that of the city as a whole. More than half the murders and aggravated assaults in the entire city took place in a few high crime "war zones." The experiences of American children growing up in these high crime housing projects has been compared by researchers with those of children growing up in the war zones of Mozambique, Cambodia, and the Middle East.

Grief and loss reactions in response to chronic violence exposure may be particularly problematic, and the violent death of a parent or other significant caretaker is most devastating. As previously discussed, when JJ was approximately age 11, his uncle, who he had looked up to as a father figure, was murdered by gunshot. Research suggests that the accompanying grief of children may not be resolved and may be complicated by rage and retaliation. Sustained disruption in their experience of trust, predictability, safety, and competence may occur. In addition, children who experience or witness life-threatening situations may develop serious difficulties in concentration and performance in school.

Moreover, exposure to chronic violence during childhood negatively impacts on moral development. Associated stunting of moral development may include inadequate self-control, reduced regard for self or others, perceptions of others as hostile, deficient moral reasoning, attitudes that view aggression as normal and appropriate, development of a distorted view of maleness, and reduced sense of community identification. Chronic exposure to violence may result in an unhealthy adaptation to this violence. In addition, chronic exposure to violence may result in an increased risk to defend against the anxiety of this experience by employing "identification with the aggressor" as a psychological survival mechanism. Simply stated, the frightened child feels safer when he imitates and identifies himself with those who created the danger. JJ's offenses of incarceration are reenactments of the violence he observed, which often occurred to members of his family. Finally, witnessing recurrent violence may result in Posttraumatic Stress Disorder (PTSD), emotional distress and behavioral problems, increased fighting, weapons carrying, gang involvement, school failure, school suspension, and substance abuse. Again, a number of these are evident in JJ's behavior pattern.

FAMILY VICTIMIZATION

JJ's cousin was shot and killed by a gang in the neighborhood. WA Jr. stated: "The guys who shot him also shot up the family cars and house. Shootings also took place in and around our grandparents house on 46th and Greely. Gang members would come by and shoot up the house. I really did not feel safe anywhere, because there was always somebody shooting."

JJ reported other instances of family victimization. His older sister, SA, was robbed and carjacked at gunpoint, and his mother was struck in the head with a 2 × 4 in a purse snatching, while standing at a phone booth on the next block.

JJ also reported experiences of being personally victimized. For example, he stated that he was beaten and robbed of his jacket at age 15 by a group of 10 teenage males only two blocks from his house. JJ recalled multiple incidents of being present with a group of peers when a car would drive by and someone inside would open fire. He described observing sparks as the bullets ricocheted off the pavement. At age 14, the ex-boyfriend of a girl that he was seeing pointed a handgun at him in a threatening fashion. On two occasions, he experienced superficial gunshot wounds, one creasing his shoulder and another hitting his calf.

Relevant Research Regarding the Effects of Childhood Psychological Trauma JJ's life history is characterized by traumatic experiences from multiple sectors of his life. These include precipitous paternal abandonment, maternal abuse and neglect, observed domestic violence, physical abuse, sexual abuse, observed community violence, and family and personal victimization. These traumatic experiences can be expected to have long-term effects. Traumatic stress in childhood is widely described in the literature as being central to the development of a spectrum of subsequent psychological disorders. In addition, traumatic childhood experiences can skew expectations about the world, the safety and insecurity of interpersonal life, and the child's sense of personal integrity. These altered expectancies in turn alter the child's inner plans of the world, shape concepts of self and others, and lead to forecasts

about the future that could have a profound influence on current and future behavior. In addition, experiencing severe stress in childhood is associated with the later development of PTSD. Factors that appear to guard against PTSD and shorten its course include a rapid engagement of the victim in treatment with the active sharing of emotions, early and ongoing social support, reestablishment of a sense of community and safety, involvement in a therapeutic setting with others who have been equally traumatized, avoidance of retraumatization, and avoidance of activities that prevent or interrupt treatment. JJ received none of these ameliorating experiences.

GANG SOCIALIZATION

JJ reported being involved in a gang throughout his entire life. He also reported that most of his family—brothers, cousins, uncles—were involved in a gang. Gang membership and/or affiliation was pervasive in JJ's extended family. Early in his childhood, before being formally initiated into the gang, JJ described receiving some protection from gang members who would not let older kids meddle with him. This protective action, combined with his hunger for older male role models, significantly increased his identification with the gang. JAJ stated that "Gangs were a part of everyday life in the Englewood community. The younger kids looked up to the older gang members as role models." JJ described looking up to his uncles, characterizing them as "strong" and respecting them because they "took care of themselves and their family." He described beginning to throw up gang signs at age 8 or 9. JJ stated that if any member of the family were in a fight and he was out there, then he was involved and thus indirectly associated with the gang. JJ described being "jumped" in the Vice-Lords at age 13. Practical survival seemed to be an element in JJ's early gang affiliation, as well. SN stated that "Gangs are prevalent in the southside area. If you are not in a gang, you are harassed by the gang members. You cannot live safely in this neighborhood unless you are in a gang."

With JJ's gang affiliation came drug trafficking. He stated that he started selling drugs at age 12 or 13 for an older gang member. He reported that as this trafficking developed and grew, his economic capability, self-respect, and social standing all increased. He explained that in school, the teachers already had an attitude toward him because his family name was known and "labeled." Additionally, he reported that he did not have the "right clothes" to wear to school and felt humiliated at having to go to school to eat breakfast. He described the household instability and chaotic violence-filled neighborhood as making it difficult to focus on school. He reported that he did not have the feeling of "being somebody" at school. JJ indicated that when he began selling drugs he felt like he was somebody. He stated that he could then help his mother. He no longer had to worry about what they were going to eat the next day. He could buy clothes for his siblings. He could take his auntie shopping. He could take care of his cousins. He could buy food and distribute it to other gang members or kids in the neighborhood whose mothers were on drugs. Women became interested in him because he had a car, clothes, and money.

JJ reported that most of the males from his neighborhood were in the Vice-Lords and that most of these young men are "locked up or dead." He reported that he now perceives that higher gang members use the younger ones. He explained that the younger ones take the risk and sell the drugs, while the higher ups "sit back" and "have a life for their family." When questioned about why he didn't leave the gang, or permanently run and begin another life somewhere else, he responded with a surprising degree of insight. He stated: "Where are you going to run to? You never been anywhere. You are uneducated. It was not until I came to jail that I started reading books. You don't know how to survive out there. You don't have any skills to get a job. You're not allowed to leave if you're high enough to know things. If you're too young you know nothing else."

Implications of Gang Socialization JJ also reported that the gang provides a sense of collective security. He described gang members assisting each other with food, clothing, and financial support, as well as providing a collective response to external aggression. He stated, however, that a reciprocal obligation was incurred to the gang and its members. Specifically, he stated that when "you're in a gang, if another guy gets jumped on, you are obligated to assist them or you are at risk from the gang." He described this obligation as being enforced whether on the street or incarcerated. JJ's alleged capital offense quite obviously involved a gang-motivated response to perceived aggressive act by another gang.

UNTREATED ATTENTION DEFICIT HYPERACTIVITY DISORDER (ADHD)

ADHD is characterized by a triad of symptoms: excessive motor activity, inattention, and impulsivity. The disorder is thought to be the result of insufficient activity of inhibitory or "braking" neurons in the brain. JJ was described as exhibiting a high degree of motor activity and physical restlessness as a child. He was noted to be extremely fidgety and constantly on the go throughout his childhood. Between the ages of 5 and 7, he was unable to sit still for more than 5 minutes, even when watching television. School records indicate that he was constantly out of his seat. He could rarely be persuaded to sit through supper. Consistent with the excessive motor activity that is characteristic of ADHD, he had much difficulty in falling asleep at night. Distractibility was evident at both home and school. At home he quickly lost interest in toys. At school he was described as highly distracted by other students and extraneous noises. JJ was further described as having difficulty completing assignments unless given one-on-one support. Some indication of impulsiveness was evident in minor behavior problems in elementary school. Impulsivity was certainly evident in early adolescent misconduct at school and in the community. There were suspicions that he suffered from ADHD (interview of FJ, third grade teacher; interview of SAA, fourth grade teacher). Despite these suspicions and strong evidence of ADHD, JJ was not formally assessed or treated for this disorder.

Implications of Untreated ADHD Untreated, ADHD is a broad risk factor for disturbed peer relationships, academic failure, juvenile delinquency, alcohol and drug abuse, and adult criminal activity. JJ received neither counseling nor medication for his symptoms. By early adolescence, JJ was failing in school, experiencing repeated school suspensions for misconduct, abusing substances, making negative peer identifications, and beginning to engage in illegal activity. All of these were precursors of the capital offense, which itself appears to have been quite impulsive and poorly conceived in planning, execution, and aftermath. Testimony at the sentencing phase identifying this disorder and describing JJ's symptoms across childhood and adolescence, had obvious mitigating significance—particularly as an additional bridge tying school misconduct and failure, drug abuse, delinquency, and other impulsive acts to the capital offense. Quite commonly, there is the comorbid presence of a behavior disorder, such as Oppositional Defiant Disorder or Conduct Disorder. Academic difficulties are also common among children with ADHD. Finally, ADHD teens are at an increased risk for behavioral problems in school.

When hyperactivity is combined with Conduct Disorder, the risk for substance abuse increases substantially. Adults with a history of ADHD are more likely to develop conduct disorders, alcoholism, and sociopathy. Relatives of individuals with ADHD are more likely to suffer ADHD, antisocial behaviors, and mood disorders. Individuals with a history of childhood hyperactivity are 7 times more likely to suffer from an antisocial personality disorder or drug abuse problem. Childhood hyperactivity has a significant relationship with alcohol problems and violent offending. The combination of ADHD and Conduct Disorder was a strong risk factor for adult criminality. A childhood history of ADHD and/or conduct disorder is commonly observed among male prison inmates.

LEARNING DISABILITY AND ACADEMIC FAILURE

JJ exhibited marked deficiency in academic progress and achievement prior to the onset of truancy and behavioral difficulties. Both his third and fourth grade teachers reported that JJ had been identified as learning disabled. They noted, however, that only very limited special education services were available in the school system. Ac-

cess to these services was compromised by repeated school transfers secondary to residential moves. School records indicate that JJ received special education programming for reading and math in fifth grade. In sixth grade, JJ was in a special class for students who were overage, slow learners, or were repeating a grade. Later testing in 1993, during seventh grade, revealed broad academic deficits reflected by the following grade level scores: Vocabulary 4.3, Reading Comprehension 3.5, Spelling 3.2, Capitalization 3.8, and Punctuation 3.1 (described in P.S. 113 records). That same year, JJ failed the reading and writing portions of the Literacy Passport Test. JJ's seventh grade teacher at P.S. 113 reported that JJ's academic difficulties were not the result of lack of effort. She noted that in spite of his difficulties, JJ tried very hard and was pleased when he was able to accomplish something. This is consistent with most evaluations of JJ's conduct across his elementary years, as reflected in the limited retrievable educational records. JJ's behavior deteriorated as the academic demands of his curriculum increased. The response of the school system involved limited special education instruction in elementary school and limited special education services in seventh grade. Thereafter no remedial services were offered, and the focus was on JJ's truancy and school misconduct—principally through suspensions.

Implications of Learning Disability and Academic Failure The chronic frustration and failure associated with learning disabilities result in these deficits being a strong risk factor for disruptive school behavior and eventual dropout. It is not terribly surprising that with academic capabilities three grades or more below grade placement, JJ lost motivation, became truant and disruptive in his school behavior, and subsequently dropped out. This sequence also propelled him toward identification with marginal peers as he was out of the structure of a school setting and on the streets. While the school system was obviously attempting to maintain order through the suspensions of JJ, they responded to a minor who did not have the skills to structure himself by removing him from the only real structure of his life—school. The structure of the streets filled the vacuum.

NEUROPSYCHOLOGICAL DEFICITS

JJ experienced a number of neurologically significant events. At 11 months he was treated for a fever of 105.4 degrees. There was ongoing consideration across JJ's early adolescence regarding whether he suffered from a psychomotor seizure disorder. EEG testing on 2-18-93 indicated the following: "Mildly abnormal awake record with excessive posterior slowing, slightly more on the right. No clear focal abnormalities or epileptiform activity seen." A repeat EEG that was sleep deprived on 3-10-93 described an impression of "[m]oderately abnormal record with possible left mesial temporal spike activity." For a period of time, JJ was treated with phenobarbital and/or Dilantin, but this was administered inconsistently by his mother. Multiple head injuries are also reflected in JJ's medical records. Seizure activity in JJ was additionally described by his sister, SA, who reported that his body would seize up and get rigid. JJ would spit or drool and get a thick foamy mucus at his mouth. He would drop to the ground, if not in bed, and would bite his lip. DJ also reported that JJ would get blinding headaches accompanied by nausea.

Additionally, JJ was described as exhibiting periodic outbursts of rage, which were out of proportion to the provoking stimulus. While it is conceivable that these emotional outbursts may have been in response to the chaotic family and life context that JJ experienced, these responses may also have reflected central nervous system dysfunction.

Neuropsychological consultation, including medical records review and evaluation, was performed in February 2000. The report stated that JJ exhibited multiple risk factors for organic impairment, including possible prenatal exposure to alcohol and drugs, spiked fevers in excess of 105 degrees at a young age, abnormal EEG findings on occasion, seizures and treatment with anticonvulsants, alcohol and drug abuse, and repeated head injuries with loss of consciousness. On neuropsychological testing, JJ demonstrated mild deficits with respect to attention, naming, and executive functions/reasoning. The evaluator concluded that these impairments likely reflected the effect of cumulative head injury and that his findings were suggestive of organic impairment.

EEG testing and neurological evaluation are pending.

Implications and Relevant Research Regarding Neuropsychological Deficits and Aggression   The presence of brain dysfunction is a risk factor for multiple adverse outcomes that may increase the likelihood of criminal conduct or violent offense. These adverse effects include academic frustration and failure, impulsivity, judgment deficits, emotional dyscontrol, and behavioral disturbance. There is a growing body of psychological, psychiatric, and neurological literature that reports that brain damage is present in disproportionately high amounts among violent offenders.

PREDISPOSITION TO ALCOHOL AND DRUG ABUSE

Alcohol and substance abuse were reported to be rampant in JJ's extended family. Family members who were alcohol or substance dependent included his father, mother, brother, paternal uncles, and maternal grandfather. Additionally, there was extensive modeling of substance abuse in front of JJ by family members, community members, and peers. JAJ, first cousin of JJ, stated that "JJ grew up watching many of our relatives abuse drugs and alcohol, including JJ's mother." JJ reported that he began to abuse alcohol at age 13, with rapid escalation to getting drunk two nights each weekend. By age 15, he was drinking regularly through the week, as well as heavy consumption on weekends. He described alcohol-related blackouts and increased tolerance. He stated that he began to use marijuana at age 12, smoking one joint twice weekly. Between the ages of 14 and 18, his marijuana use escalated to smoking heavily on a daily basis.

Implications   Primary risk factors for alcohol and/or drug dependence include genetic predisposition, modeling of substance abuse, and developmental trauma. All of these risk factors are present in JJ's history.

First, JJ's inheritance of a predisposition for substance dependence is consistent with research. Second, alcohol and drug dependence were modeled by other family members, gang associates, and peers. Finally, the third risk factor for substance dependence of developmental trauma is evidenced by JJ's history of multiple traumatic stressors. Among individuals with histories of developmental trauma, substance abuse can be conceptualized as an attempt at analgesic self-medication of the associated anxiety spectrum symptoms.

In addition to these risk factors for alcohol and substance abuse, JJ's ADHD was another risk factor for substance dependence, because research points to an increased incidence of substance dependence among adolescents and young adults with ADHD. There is also evidence in the school records and teacher interviews that JJ suffered from learning disabilities. Academic frustration and failure contribute to early school dropout and negative peer affiliations, which are additional risk factors for substance abuse in adolescence. The absence of effective parental supervision or limit setting across adolescence was a further risk factor for substance dependence. With all three primary substance abuse risk factors present, as well as ADHD, learning disabilities, and inadequate supervision, JJ was at markedly increased risk to initiate a pattern of alcohol and substance dependence in early adolescence. Substance dependence in adolescence significantly disrupts and blocks the developmental tasks of this stage, including growth in maturity and coping capabilities, adaptive socialization, and responsible achievement.

Of critical importance, substance dependence and intoxication are risk factors for violence in the community and thus have a direct nexus to JJ's alleged involvement in the capital offense of conviction, as he is described as having consumed over 17 beers in the 2 hours prior to the offense. A number of research studies identify a frequent intersection of alcohol/substance abuse and criminal violence. JJ was thus affected by redundant substance-dependence risk factors in early adolescence that subsequently disrupted a healthy developmental trajectory and markedly increased his risk of criminal violence, including the alleged capital offense.

IMMATURITY

It is significant to note in mitigation that JJ was only 18 when arrested on the capital case.

Implications of Immaturity   Brain development of the frontal lobes continues to age 25. Executive functions associated with frontal lobe functioning include insight, judgment, impulse control, frustration tolerance, and recognition of consequences. Significant age-related growth in these capabilities, conventionally referred to as "maturing" or "growing up," occurs between the ages of 18 and 25 in all individuals. All 18-year-olds are thus "immature" in brain development and psychological functioning.

There is reason to believe that JJ was somewhat more immature at age 18 than most other 18-year-olds. Symptoms of ADHD suggest additional mild nervous system immaturity or deficiency in attention and impulse control processes. His intellectual capability as measured in 1989 was Low Average at best—Full-Scale IQ = 83, which indicates that 87% of same age peers had greater intellectual capability. When the error range of the WAIS-R is considered (Standard Error of Measurement, 95% confidence level = ±6), his true IQ score could fall into the Borderline range of intellectual functioning, or as low as the sixth percentile. As the limit-setting, discipline, guidance, and modeling functions of parenting are integrally related to the development of moral reasoning, social judgment, and impulse control, the marked neglect of JJ's mother could be expected to result in general immaturity in socialization. As described above, adolescent drug dependence also acts as a strong impediment to psychological and social maturity. All of these factors point to JJ at age 18 as being less mature than his age mates.

In addition, there is a clear association between youthfulness and violence risk. The association of youthfulness with violence risk likely implicates immaturity, impulsivity, poor judgment, peer and gang susceptibility, poorly established male identity, and other developmental vulnerabilities of adolescence. JJ's age, when combined with his multiple risk vulnerabilities, was an obvious factor in his criminal aggression.

CONCLUSION

JJ's experience was part of a family system that normalized gang activity, drug trafficking, gun carrying, and violent aggression, encouraged aberrant social attitudes, propelled him toward criminal activity and gang involvement, created a harsh, hostile, violent view of the world, and placed him at gravely higher risk to perpetrate or become a victim of violent homicide. The surrounding marginal community had an additional corruptive influence and also worked to instill gang activity and violence as a way of life. His experience of rejection and parental neglect within his immediate family can be identified as markedly increasing his vulnerability for psychological disorder, delinquency, and sense of belonging provided by a gang. His recurrent traumatic experience of physical and sexual abuse appears to have additionally propelled him toward interpersonal distrust, anger, and aggression. It is likely that these experiences of neglect and abuse resulted in significant unresolved trauma responses and rage.

JJ's experiences of recurrent relocation and chaotic living situation are likely to have undermined opportunities for corrective emotional experiences that might otherwise have occurred through stability or fortuitous positive mentoring from the community. JJ's exposure to domestic violence served to reinforce models of aggression as well as prompt additional trauma responses. His extensive observation of community violence was a profoundly traumatic and injurious life experience with multiple adverse impacts on his adjustment and, combined with other influences, placed him at marked increased likelihood of significant aggression in the community. Given the instability of his home, the multigenerational corruptive influence of family, and dangers of his neighborhood, it is not surprising that JJ identified with a gang as a mechanism to secure belonging and to ensure practical survival, however short term. The presence of neuropsychological deficits and/or seizure disorder would have represented an additional impediment to academic progress in childhood and adolescence and likely would have acted as an underlying disinhibiting factor in aggressive responses.

Multiple significant adverse developmental events are evident in JJ's history, which both separately and, more importantly, collectively provide some explanation of the defendant's involvement in gang activity, his associated weapons carrying, and life trajectory culminating in the alleged capital offense. As described above, these developmentally adverse experiences include:

1. Multigenerational family system dysfunction and corruptive influence
2. Paternal corruptive influence and abandonment
3. Maternal neglect, emotional abuse, and corruptive influences
4. Home instability and frequent relocations
5. Inadequate supervision
6. Sexual abuse
7. Family violence and physical abuse
8. Observed community violence
9. Family victimization
10. Gang socialization
11. Untreated ADHD
12. Learning disability and academic failure
13. Neuropsychological deficits
14. Predisposition to alcohol and drug abuse
15. Immaturity

Analyzing JJ's development as outlined through the above mitigating experiences finds many risk factors for delinquency. Below is a list of relevant risk factors (the risk factors that are present in JJ's development are in italics):

Conception to Age 6

- Perinatal difficulties
- Minor physical abnormalities
- *Brain damage*
- *Abuse and maltreatment*
- *Family history of criminal behavior and substance abuse*
- *Family management problems*
- *Family conflict*
- *Parental attitudes favorable toward, and parental involvement in, crime and substance abuse*
- *Early antisocial behavior*
- *Academic failure*

Age 6 to Adolescence

- *Extreme economic deprivation*
- *Community disorganization and low neighborhood attachment*
- *Transitions and mobility*
- Availability of firearms
- Media portrayals of violence
- Family management problems

- Family conflict
- Parental attitudes favorable toward, and parental involvement in, crime and substance abuse
- Early and persistent antisocial behavior
- Academic failure
- Lack of commitment to school
- Alienation and rebelliousness
- Association with peers who engage in delinquency and violence
- Favorable attitudes toward delinquency
- Early initiation of delinquent and violent behaviors
- Constitutional factors (e.g., low intelligence, *hyperactivity, and attention-deficit disorders*)

The redundancy of risk factors was in the simultaneous absence of any of the protective factors that might have inhibited the development of delinquency:

- Individual characteristics (female gender, intelligence, positive social orientation, and resilient temperament).
- Social bonding to individuals (prosocial family members, teachers, coaches, youth leaders, and friends) and institutions (schools and youth organizations).
- Healthy beliefs and clear standards for behavior, including those that promote nonviolence and abstinence from drugs.

SECTION 2: VIOLENCE RISK ASSESSMENT

There is conceptual and research literature regarding assessment of violence risk. Research literature describes actuarial (group statistical) and anamnestic (past pattern of behavior) approaches as being most reliable in assessing likelihood of violent behavior. Multiple actuarial studies indicate that the majority of individuals convicted of capital murder will not represent a disproportionate risk of violence while confined in prison. In addition, research suggests the following:

1. Past community violence is not strongly or consistently associated with prison violence
2. Current offense, prior convictions, and escape history are only weakly associated with prison misconduct.

3. Severity of offense is not a good predictor of prison adjustment.

Similarly, JJ's history of antisocial behavior and attitudes in the community is not considered to be informative regarding his risk of violence in prison. Neither Antisocial Personality Disorder (APD) nor psychopathy (as measured by the PCL-R) has been demonstrated as predictive of violence in prison. This is likely a function of both base rates (75% of prison inmates can be diagnosed with APD) and the different contingency structure of prison. It is also important to note that the rate of inmate violence falls rather dramatically as the seriousness of that violence increases. Moreover, and particularly relevant to JJ's risk of serious violence in prison across his lifespan, there is a good deal of research indicating that rates of disciplinary infractions and violence tend to decline with age in both the community and prison.

Based on this research, there is a 20–30% likelihood that a capital offender would commit an act of violence at some time during his capital prison term. The likelihood that he would seriously injure another inmate is substantially lower, and the likelihood of seriously injuring a staff member is quite remote. The probability of his killing another inmate is at 1% or less. Assuming a 40-year life expectancy, the probability of his killing a staff member is well below .0001. There is an approximately 8–10% likelihood that he would present a more chronic violence problem, although it should be noted that chronic violence could be contained by administrative segregation/detention or supermaximum forms of custody.

In particularizing a violence risk estimate to JJ, there are a number of factors that would serve to modestly increase his risk above the group base rates:

- JJ will be 19 at entrance to a capital life prison sentence.
- JJ has a history of juvenile detention and jail misconduct, including activities that might give rise to inmate violence such as gambling and drug use.
- JJ was repeatedly cited in past incarcerations for making threatening statements to staff when angry, as well as being intimidating to other inmates.

- JJ has a long-term personal and family affiliation with a street gang that also functions as a prison gang. He has held a position of leadership in that street gang.

Violence Risk Management/Prevention Measures
Violence risk is virtually always a function of context. Therefore, a risk assessment should include an evaluation of what risk management variables and what contextual factors might be modified to reduce the likelihood of violence. In other words, if JJ were identified as representing a serious and disproportionate risk of assaultive violence in prison, could that risk be reduced by any modifications in the context of his prison custody? The answer is an unequivocal yes. The Department of Corrections has policies, procedures, and facilities for reducing opportunities that predatory inmates or gang leaders might otherwise have to behave in a violent or assaultive manner or to disrupt the orderly operation of the prison system. These mechanisms include single celling, segregation, administrative segregation (some with steel doors and/or steel-plated walls), and lockdown, as well as Super-Max confinement. The Department of Corrections maintains a 400-bed Super-Max facility.

Standard Super-Max protocols at the most restrictive level involve the following:

1. confinement to a single cell for most of each 24-hour period;
2. sharply limited contact with both staff and other inmates;
3. limited duration and severely curtailed activity for out-of-cell recreation, either individually or in small groups;
4. severely limited (or no) inmate telephone access;
5. no contact visits;
6. shackling before removal from cell and double staff escorts; and
7. other security provisions, such as consumption of meals in the cell and the careful monitoring of mail.

Therefore, the Super-Max facility would provide removal and isolation of the most difficult to manage inmates, rehabilitation of the institutional behavior of many of these disruptive inmates, and deterrence for the entire inmate population.

Higher violence risk inmates can thus be controlled by associated increased restriction, supervision, and isolation, so that any opportunity they might have to be assaultively aggressive is substantially negated, resulting in a subsequent marked decline in base rates of serious institutional violence and death system wide. If JJ were identified as a substantial risk of violence in prison, administrative segregation or Super-Max confinement would result in substantially reduced opportunities to cause injury to others.

Respectfully submitted,
Mark D. Cunningham, Ph.D.
Clinical and Forensic Psychologist
Diplomate in Forensic Psychology
American Board of Professional Psychology

Teaching Point: How do you evaluate the accuracy of different sources of third-party information?

Forensic mental health professionals have an ethical and professional obligation to base their findings on data that is as reliable as possible (see *Specialty Guidelines of Forensic Psychologists* (1991) VI.F.1, 3). This necessarily entails consideration of the accuracy of third-party reports. While there is no simple answer to this question, analysis of the credibility of third-party information in a forensic mental health assessment can be assisted by considering several issues.

1. To what extent is the report independently corroborated? The more individuals who have independently described observing the same history or events, the stronger the likelihood of credibility and accuracy. For this reason, extensive record review and interview of multiple third parties is typically undertaken in forensic mental health assessments. It is preferable to interview third parties individually and separately to increase the independence of their reports.

2. What motivation might the third party have to misrepresent a report? Reports from education, social service, and medical sources are given greater credibility, as these observers have the least personal investment in the outcome of the forensic mental health evaluation. Reports that predated the instant litigation are less likely to biased by it. Neighbors and co-workers represent a somewhat more invested position, but are still relatively detached. Former in-laws and ex-spouses are also less likely to give overly positive reports. Law enforcement and/or correctional personnel are ideally independent, but can have a punitive personal bias or can experience pressure from co-workers or supervisors to favor the prosecution.

The potential bias of friends and family members is more problematic. Because of their attachment to the individual being evaluated, they understandably have some investment in the disposition. At the same time, they may be the only observers of certain aspects of history and behavior—such as personal or parental substance abuse, family violence, sexual abuse, or other traumatic experience. Also, even when the stakes for the defendant are very high (e.g., potential death sentence), reluctance to acknowledge having perpetrated maltreatment and/or taboos against disclosure of "family secrets" may be more powerful than their desire to spare their loved one. Indeed, it has been my routine experience in capital sentencing evaluations that some or most family members deny dysfunctional behavior in the family, even in cases where the abuse/neglect are confirmed in social service records.

3. Is the report consistent with known patterns of behavior or verifiable aspects of the historical context? This question involves placing the specific report in a larger context. For example, when parental alcoholism has been confirmed, reports of associated parental inconsistency, neglect, or abuse become more credible. When repeated observation of community violence is described, the confirmed residence of the defendant in an inner-city public housing project across childhood markedly increases the credibility of the report. When a third party describes her own experience of maltreatment at the hands of a given perpetrator, reports that the defendant experienced similar abuse at the hands of the same perpetrator are more credible.

4. Is the report in personal terminology and accompanied by congruent affect? Descriptions that are consistent with the speech and developmental/social perspective of the individual making the report are more likely to represent an independent recollection. The presence of emotional discomfort in describing painful events also contributes to source credibility.

With these considerations in mind, it is important to underscore that a forensic mental health assessment involves the communication and analysis of data, not determinations of fact. In other words, the obligation of the forensic mental health professional is to comprehensively collect and analyze the data. That includes presentation and analysis of discrepant or inconsistent data, discussion of alternative hypotheses, and rationale for credibility considerations. It is for the trier of fact to make the final accuracy determination and apply that determination to the ultimate issue.

Notes

1. There may be other reasons to obtain informed consent in some court-ordered evaluations, however. See the Teaching Point for Case 1, Chapter 11 for a discussion.

2. The ethical demand in therapeutic assessment for an explanation of results after completion of the evaluation, as expressed in this standard, does not necessarily apply in forensic assessment. See Standard 2.09 (APA, 1992).

3. Legal support relevant to informed consent and notification of purpose for FMHA may also be contained in the statutes and administrative code of a given jurisdiction, which should be consulted for jurisdiction-specific guidance.

4. In one study conducted by the FBI and published in September 1992, the second most frequent personality disorder in a sample of offenders who had murdered law enforcement officers was dependent personality disorder (23%; Pinizzotta & Davis, 1992).

Chapter 8

Juvenile Commitment

This chapter focuses on the legal question of the disposition of juvenile cases. It is called "commitment" because the commitment to a state department of juvenile justice for residential placement is one of the options before the juvenile court if there is a finding of "not innocent." Other options typically include community placement or some form of probation, whether intensive or standard. The principle for this case involves accepting referrals within one's area of expertise. The teaching point addresses more specifically the training and experience important for a forensic clinician to attain expertise in juvenile forensic assessment.

Case 1

Principle: Accept referrals only within area of expertise

This principle concerns the importance of forensic clinicians having sufficient expertise and experience to perform a FMHA competently. Because FMHAs are conducted for a wide range of individuals in legal contexts, the clinician must consider a variety of individual factors, such as age, racial and ethnic background, disorders in mental, emotional, cognitive, and developmental functioning, substance use disorders, physical problems, and the impact of incarceration. Given these diverse influences, it is important that the clinician have sufficient training and experience with individuals in the specific population of which the individual being evaluated is a part. It is also important to have training and experience in forensic areas: knowledge of relevant law and procedures, an awareness of the differences between forensic and clinical psychology and psychiatry, and a working knowledge of the techniques and tools that are applicable in such evaluations.

Support for performing FMHA only within an area of expertise can be found in several sources of authority. In psychology, the *Ethical Principles of Psychologists and Code of Conduct* (APA, 1992) emphasizes the importance of professional competence:

Psychologists strive to maintain high standards of competence in their work. They recognize the boundaries of their particular competencies and the limitations of their expertise. They provide only those services and use only those techniques for which they are qualified by education, training, or experience. Psychologists are cognizant of the fact that the competencies required in serving, teaching, and/or studying groups of people vary with the distinctive characteristics of those groups. In those areas in which recognized professional standards do not yet exist, psychologists exercise careful judgment and take appropriate precautions to protect the welfare of those with whom they work. They maintain knowledge of relevant scientific and professional information related to the services they render, and they recognize the need for ongoing education. Psychologists make appropriate use of scientific, professional, technical, and administrative resources. (p. 1599)

The *Specialty Guidelines for Forensic Psychologists* (Committee on Ethical Guidelines for Forensic Psychologists, 1991) elaborates on competence for forensic practice, indicating that services are provided "only in areas of psychology in which [forensic psychologists] have specialized knowledge, skill, experience, and education" (p. 658). Further, the *Specialty Guidelines* notes that there is a responsibility for a fundamental and reasonable level of knowledge and understanding of the legal and professional standards that govern experts in legal proceedings and "an obligation to present to the court, regarding the specific matters to which they will testify, the boundaries of their competence, the factual bases (knowledge, skill, experience, training, and education) for their qualifications as an expert on the specific matters at issue" (p. 658). A similar position can be found in the *Principles of Medical Ethics with Annotations Especially Applicable to Psychiatry* (American Psychiatric Association, 1995). A "psychiatrist who regularly practices outside his/her area of professional competence should be considered unethical" (p. 4). Further, the *Ethical Guidelines for the Practice of Forensic Psychiatry* (AAPL, 1995) notes that "expertise in the practice of forensic psychiatry is claimed only in the areas of actual knowledge and skills, training and experience" (p. 4). Clearly, these ethical standards define the boundaries of competence by knowledge, skill, experience, and education/training, and provide no exceptions to the need for competence in an area of practice.

Legal support for accepting referrals only within an area of expertise can be found in Rule 702 of the *Federal Rules of Evidence*, under which an expert can offer evidence in scientific, technical, or other areas of specialized knowledge. Further, the prospective expert must have acquired special knowledge, skill, experience, training, or education that would allow the individual to address the issues within their areas of expertise that are before the court.

The question of when a forensic clinician is sufficiently "expert" to perform a forensic assessment has also been addressed by the American Bar Association's *Criminal Justice Mental Health Standards* (1989). Under Standard 7-3.10, no professional should be appointed by the court to evaluate a person's mental condition unless their qualifications include:

(a) sufficient professional education and sufficient clinical training and experience to establish the clinical knowledge required for the specific type(s) of evaluation(s) being conducted; and (b) sufficient forensic knowledge, gained through specialized training or an acceptable substitute therefor, necessary for understanding the relevant legal matter(s) and for satisfying the specific purpose(s) for which the evaluation is being ordered. (p. 130)

Regarding minimum professional education and clinical training requirements for evaluators and expert witnesses, the *Standards* notes that necessary and desirable education and training requirements differ according to the subject matter of the evaluation and the specific legal issue. For example, it is suggested that an evaluation concerning a person's present mental competence could be conducted by a variety of mental health providers at different levels of training. However, for an evaluation concerning a person's mental condition at the time of an alleged offense, or a person's future mental condition or behavior when these issues arise as part of a sentencing proceeding or special commitment proceeding, the *Standards* suggests that the clinician should be a psychiatrist or a doctoral-level psychologist.

Heilbrun (1995) proposed a two-step process for conceptualizing and evaluating the question of expertise in the context of forensic assessment based on the above sources of authority. The first step is determining whether the clinician has *substantive expertise* with a given population; the second involves whether this expertise has been *applied in forensic contexts*. Substantive expertise involves formal training and experience (both supervised and independent) with a given population. The second step involves demonstrating how specialization, formal training, supervised experience, advanced certification, and related professional activities can be demonstrated in forensic applications. Pertinent questions include the extent to which the clinician has applied substantive expertise with a particular population to issues arising in the course of litigation, and how often the clinician has applied this expertise in the course of litigation.

There is clear agreement within the ethical standards of psychology and psychiatry about the importance of providing services only within areas of competence. In addition, some sources of legal authority provide definitions of expertise in the forensic context, stressing the importance of education, training, and experience in the practice of FMHA. The available literature in the area of standard of practice strongly supports the principle of providing services only in areas of competence, with more recent literature offering a better delineation of levels of competence in both substantive areas and forensic applications (Bersoff et al., 1997; Heilbrun, 1995).

The present case report provides a good example of the application of this principle. The purpose of the evaluation was to determine a 15-year-old juvenile's mental state at the time of the offense and to identify factors in his psychological adjustment and personal history that would be relevant to sentencing. As suggested in the *Criminal Justice Mental Health Standards* (ABA, 1989), the forensic clinician in this case was a doctoral-level psychologist. The clinician also had substantive education, training, and experience in FMHA, and has a particularly strong background in juvenile issues. The report reflects awareness of the criteria for the legal decisions on insanity and mitigation. The evaluator also showed an understanding of forensic practice by using a variety of data sources, including psychological testing, clinical interview, collateral interviews, and collateral document review. Finally, the forensic clinician demonstrated a substantive knowledge of adolescent psychopathology by assessing a variety of domains relevant to the DSM-IV diagnostic criteria for depression.

PSYCHOLOGICAL EVALUATION
CONFIDENTIAL

Subject: Delbert Smith
Birthdate: 5/5/85
Case: State v. Delbert Smith
      Johnson County Circuit Court
Examiner: Dewey G. Cornell, Ph.D.
Report date: November 1, 2000

PURPOSE OF EVALUATION

Delbert Smith is a 15-year-old boy charged with the murder of his high school principal, Randolph Jones, on June 2, 2000. This evaluation was conducted at the request of Defense Counsel for the purpose of determining Delbert's mental state at the time of the offense and to identify factors in his psychological adjustment and personal history which would be relevant to sentencing. Delbert is being tried as an adult in Circuit Court.

I interviewed Delbert for the first time on August 4, 2000, and informed him of the purpose of this evaluation. He read and signed my evaluation consent form. Delbert was advised that the results of the evaluation would not be confidential if, in consultation with Defense Counsel, he decided to use the evaluation at trial or sentencing. Delbert expressed understanding of the nature and purpose of the evaluation and agreed to proceed. His parents also agreed to the evaluation.

SOURCES OF INFORMATION

Interviews

1. Delbert Smith on 8/4/00 (4 hours); 8/5/00 (8 hrs); 10/7/00 (3 hrs)
2. James Smith (father) on 8/6/00 (2 hrs)
3. Georgia Smith (mother) on 8/6/00 (3 hrs, including home visit) and 9/15 (30 minutes, by telephone)
4. Abe Abernathy (school psychologist) on 8/29/00 (1.5 hrs)
5. Joseph Morgan (assistant principal) on 8/29/00 (1 hr)
6. Alice McIntire (language arts teacher), Julia Johnson (science teacher) and Robert Montgomery (band director) on 8/29/00 (1 hr)
7. Jonathan Atkins (classmate) and father Jeff Atkins on 8/27/00 (1 hr)
8. Daniel Dennis (Detention Center Supervisor) on 8/4/00 (1 hr) and 10/15 (20 minutes, by telephone)
9. Dr. Deborah Arnold (psychiatrist) on 8/15/00 (40 minutes, by telephone) and 9/25 (30 minutes, by telephone)

Psychological Testing

10. Millon Adolescent Clinical Inventory (MACI) administered on 8/4/00
11. Rorschach Inkblot Test administered on 8/5/00
12. Wechsler Intelligence Scale for Children, Third Edition (WISC-III) administered on 8/5/00
13. Trail-Making Test A and B, administered on 8/5/00
14. Bender-Gestalt and Rey Complex Figure Drawing Tests, administered on 8/5/00

Information Forwarded from State's Attorney

15. Grand Jury Indictment, offense report, citation forms, and other court documents and orders (25 pages)
16. Transcript of preliminary hearing (45 pages)

17. Police investigation reports including summaries of interviews with Adam Conner and 14 other high school students, 5 teachers, 3 office staff members, school custodian, bus driver, school resource officer
18. Coroner's report (15 pages)
19. Transcript and videotape of police interview with Delbert Smith on 6/2/00 (28 pages)
20. Report of psychiatric and psychological evaluation for State's Attorney conducted by Elizabeth Henson, M.D., and Clarence Schiflet, Ph.D., dated October 5, 2000 (24 pages)

Information Forwarded from Defense Counsel

21. Medical records from pediatrician, Dr. Josiah Jones (22 pages)
22. Medical records from Johnson County Hospital (5 pages)
23. School records from Johnson County Public Schools (26 pages)
24. Information from Delbert's parents, including papers and school assignments from Delbert's bedroom (35 pages), letters from Detention Center (10 pages), and lists of his video games, movies, compact disks, and other belongings (12 pages)

FAMILY BACKGROUND AND DEVELOPMENTAL HISTORY

Delbert Smith was born in Leeville on May 5, 1985, the third child of James and Georgia Smith. Mr. Smith, age 50, is a sales manager for a Leeville automobile dealership, and Ms. Smith, age 46, is a nursing assistant. The two older children no longer reside at home. Jessica Smith, age 19, attends a state college, and Barbara Smith Lawson, age 22, is married and resides in a nearby town. The Smiths were divorced in 1980. The children lived with Ms. Smith and visited their father on alternate weekends.

According to Ms. Smith, she filed for divorce from her husband because of his chronic drinking and associated marital conflict. She does not report episodes of physical violence in the home but describes weekly arguments associated with periods of drinking when Mr. Smith would become verbally abusive. Mr. Smith acknowledged a history of heavy drinking but reports that

through attendance at Alcoholics Anonymous he has maintained 3 years of sobriety.

Mrs. Smith described what she termed a "normal, close" relationship with her son. She had few occasions to discipline him and generally permitted him to spend his free time as he wished. She maintained a strict rule that Delbert complete his homework immediately after school and that he notify her when he had an upcoming test. The most serious misbehavior Ms. Smith could recall was a year ago when she found Delbert had experimented with drinking some wine he found in the refrigerator. This prompted a discussion of Mr. Smith's drinking problem that Ms. Smith felt was effective in persuading her son not to experiment further with drinking.

Mr. Smith described his relationship with his son as an "okay relationship, I was waiting for him to get a little older so we could do more together, more father and son stuff. He didn't like sports too much." Mr. Smith saw his son once or twice a month and they usually spent their time together attending a movie and eating at a restaurant. Mr. Smith purchased a hunting rifle for Delbert on his thirteenth birthday. His father stated that he had not taken his son hunting but emphasized that he had twice taken him to a shooting range to teach him "gun safety."

Medical History History of Delbert's early development was obtained from his parents and medical records. Delbert was a full-term baby with a normal delivery and birth weight of 9 pounds, 2 ounces. His mother denied any use of alcohol, tobacco, or other drugs during pregnancy. Delbert reached normal developmental milestones such as walking and toilet training on time. His growth charts were within normal limits. He had frequent ear infections and his speech was not well developed at age 4; as a result, he received speech therapy for approximately 6 months. By all accounts, Delbert was a relatively quiet child and posed few behavioral problems. No serious illnesses or traumatic experiences were reported. His most significant injury was a dislocated finger sustained in a fall from a tree at age 5. There is no report of serious head injury or loss of consciousness.

School History Information on Delbert's school history was obtained from his parents, school records, and interviews with school personnel. School personnel interviewed for this evaluation included an assistant principal, a school psychologist who evaluated Delbert for special education services, and two recent teachers. In second grade Delbert was identified with reading problems and placed in a resource room for learning disabled children. He often seemed disinterested in classwork, and although he was regarded as generally quiet and well-behaved, he was sometimes reprimanded for off-task behavior. An evaluation for attention deficit disorder in third grade was negative, and his behavior problems were regarded as based on "low motivation for school work." The school psychologist reported that Delbert's teachers expressed concerns that he was troubled by his home life, but this issue was not pursued. According to Ms. Smith, during this time period in Delbert's life, Mr. Smith was involved in several drunk-driving incidents. After a school presentation by Mothers Against Drunk Driving, Delbert expressed worry that his father would be killed in an accident, as well as occasional fears to ride in the car with his father.

In the fourth grade Delbert obtained grade-level scores on the Comprehensive Test of Basic Skills (CTBS), a well-known standard achievement test. At his triennial evaluation in fifth grade, it was noted that his reading achievement (standard score 85) was not significantly discrepant from his intellectual aptitude (Wechsler Verbal IQ 95), and as a result his resource room services were discontinued.

In middle school, Delbert's grades were uneven, ranging from B+ in band to Ds in language arts and science. Delbert recalled that he was frustrated to make low grades in middle school, particularly in comparison with his sister, Jessica, who made excellent grades and was placed in the gifted program. During the seventh and eighth grades, Delbert began to feel that none of the other kids liked him, and he got into trouble for doing things to attract attention, such as clowning and talking in class.

Starting high school in the ninth grade, Delbert recounted that he began the year resolved to earn good grades like his sister but became discouraged when he earned three Bs and a C the first grading period. During the remainder of the year his grades were consistently Bs or Cs. Delbert joined the school chess club but did not play well enough to make the team and eventually dropped out of the club. Delbert played in the marching band, but as a ninth grader who was relatively less skilled than other band members, he was assigned to the reserve section of students who did not march in band competitions.

Bullying at School Delbert reported numerous experiences of being harassed and humiliated by peers at school. In middle school he often refrained from going to the rest room because larger boys would push him around or fling water on him. He had the impression that everyone disliked him and enjoyed teasing him because of his small stature and appearance. According to Delbert, students habitually called him "Dopey Delbert" and put signs on his locker with this name and a cartoonish drawing of a dwarf. Apparently this name originated in middle school when Delbert brought to school a Snow White lunch box that had belonged to his older sister. Delbert had hoped that when he moved on to high school in the ninth grade that the name-calling would cease, but found that it continued.

According to Delbert and school personnel interviewed for this evaluation, new members of the band were informally "initiated" by older students during their first few months of the school year. Older students referred to initiates by derogatory names and expected them to perform small favors for them such as filling their water bottles or carrying their musical instruments to the practice field. The school band director acknowledged that initiation was permitted as a longstanding tradition that preceded his coming to the school. He maintained that the students took the experience in good fun and that no one ever complained to him about initiation. According to Delbert, he was singled out for harsh treatment by several older boys because he refused to clean and polish their instruments. Over a period of months, Delbert's relationship with the older boys deteriorated, and they reportedly pushed and shoved him, hid his instrument from him, and called him abusive names. On one occasion Delbert challenged one of the boys by calling him a name, whereupon the boy struck him in the mouth, causing his lip to bleed and preventing him from participating in band practice. The boy threatened Delbert and told him not to tell the band director about the incident.

Delbert also reported episodes of bullying in the hallways and cafeteria at school. The boy using the adjoining locker frequently pushed Delbert aside, and when Delbert shoved the boy back one day, the boy grabbed Delbert around the neck and threatened to choke him to death. After this incident, Delbert stopped using his locker and either carried his belongings with him or placed them in the band storage room. Delbert recalled other instances when larger boys would mock him or tease him at school, making fun of his appearance, dress, or behavior. Boys would take food from his tray in the cafeteria or intentionally spill his drink on his food. The few instances when Delbert attempted a retort, the boys laughed and made fun of his comment, so he soon learned to remain quiet and turn away.

Delbert usually did not challenge kids who harassed him and passively accepted the abuse. He was afraid of getting into a fight. Delbert resented these experiences and could not put them out of his mind. He stated, "I got mad all the time, but I didn't do anything. I just had to figure out how to get even, how to get 'em back." When asked why he did not go to school authorities, Delbert related that he did not feel the teachers liked him and that he feared the boys would retaliate. He commented, "Telling on other kids is the worst thing you can do at this school." Similarly, Delbert did not tell his mother about his abusive experiences at school because "She would have just hit the roof, gone into the school and yelled at them all and made it worse."

According to investigation records, students interviewed by the police confirmed that Delbert was often subject to teasing at school. Students witnessed Delbert being called names and saw cartoonish drawings entitled "Dopey Delbert the Dwarf" on his locker. Two students recalled that some boys would take his food or spill his drink in the cafeteria. Student band members confirmed that ninth grade students underwent an initiation period, but none of them recalled Delbert receiving more severe treatment than other classmates. None of these students witnessed any instances of physical aggression directed against Delbert. One student interviewed for this evaluation, Jonathan Atkins, sat next to Delbert in band

and was friends with him. Jonathan did recall Delbert coming to band practice with a "fat lip" and being unable to play his instrument, and that Delbert told him that another band member had struck him. Jonathan observed at least one incident when a band member shoved Delbert and also witnessed the choking incident at Delbert's locker.

Friendships   For approximately one year prior to the shooting, Delbert felt alienated and increasingly distant from his friends and other peers. He expressed resentment toward the students who bullied him and the onlookers who watched and laughed. He apparently abandoned relationships with students he had known in the eighth grade and stopped attending the church youth group where he previously had a small circle of friends.

Delbert's closest friendship was with another ninth grader, Jonathan Atkins, a boy of similar short stature who reportedly experienced similar mistreatment by other boys. Delbert and Jonathan spent considerable time together playing violent video games (such as the "Doom" series) that involved shooting imaginary characters. In these games, the two boys imagined that they shot at boys in the school who mistreated them. The boys also enjoyed going to an amusement center where they could play laser tag, a game that involved firing laser guns at other participants. In this setting, the boys enacted fantasies such as taking over the school or overcoming an attack by teachers, a theme stimulated by a movie they had seen.

During the spring of 2000, Delbert became attracted to a group of students who described themselves as "goths" and dressed in black clothing and jewelry adorned with satanic symbols. The leader of this group, Jim Kane, had long black hair and wore white make-up that gave him a witch-like appearance. According to students interviewed by the police, Jim attracted a great deal of attention with his odd dress and with statements he would make about sensitive topics like religion and homosexuality. He was outspokenly critical of the school administration and gained considerable status in the eyes of many students for defying school authorities and speaking out against school rules. According to school personnel, Jim's parents had supported him in a successful challenge to the school's dress code, and he took pride in wearing a long black trench coat to classes. Delbert emphasized that the members of Jim's gothic group never teased or belittled him, and they seemed immune to the reactions of other students.

Delbert began spending time with Jim and his group but did not adopt their style of dress. According to Delbert, Jim told him that he had to earn the right to join their group by completing a "quest" and "defeating a dragon." As part of this quest, Delbert carried out a series of "missions" that included shoplifting CD's and magazines for the boys and spray-painting gothic graffiti on a building. Like many ninth grade students, Delbert was vulnerable to being manipulated by this group because they were older and he wanted to impress them and win their approval. Because Delbert felt rejected by his classmates, the opportunity to associate with a group of students who seemed unaffected by peer pressure was appealing.

Delinquent Behavior Adolescent delinquency typically involves a constellation of behavior problems beginning in early childhood. Based on all available information, Delbert did not have the typical early childhood behavior problems associated with delinquency. He did not exhibit early problems in getting along with other children, or a pattern of aggressive or disruptive behavior. He was not oppositional or defiant with his parents or teachers. He did not get into trouble for lying, stealing, or destroying property. His school records and report cards do not indicate persistent discipline problems, although he was identified as having learning and motivational problems in the primary grades.

Adolescent delinquents typically begin a pattern of alcohol and drug use early in their teenage years. Delbert denied alcohol or drug use, and with the exception of a single incident reported by his mother, no one interviewed for this evaluation reported substance use.

Delbert did disclose several episodes of shoplifting and spray-painting graffiti on a building after he began associating with a new group of peers in the second semester of ninth grade. He also admitted taking money from his mother's purse on two occasions in the past year.

Family Psychiatric History According to information obtained from Delbert's parents, his family has a significant history of psychiatric disorder. Delbert's father has a history of alcohol abuse, as does a paternal uncle and paternal grandmother. Delbert's mother reports two episodes of depression for which she received psychiatric medication and counseling. A maternal uncle with a history of depression committed suicide in 1982. These observations are noteworthy because a genetic predisposition to severe depression can be inherited. A predisposition to alcohol abuse can also be inherited and may be associated with clinical depression.

ACCOUNTS OF THE OFFENSE

Shooting Delbert gave accounts of the shooting to this examiner on 8/4/00, 8/5/00, and 10/7/00. These accounts were compared to accounts Delbert gave on three other occasions:

> Police interrogation on 6/2/00
> Interview by Drs. Elizabeth Henson and Clarence Schiflet on 9/10/00
> Interview by Dr. Deborah Arnold on 9/23/00

There is consistency across these accounts on many points: Delbert acknowledged that he took a loaded handgun from his father's apartment on the weekend prior to the shooting. He hid the gun under the mattress of his bed in his mother's home until Friday, June 2, when he carried the gun to school in his backpack. Upon getting off the bus at school, Delbert walked among a crowd of students moving toward the front entrance of the school. The school principal, Randolph Jones, was in front of the entrance of the school, where he typically stood and greeted students as they entered the building. Delbert set his backpack on the ground approximately 10 yards in front of Mr. Jones, removed the handgun, and fired one shot into the air. Delbert then pointed the gun in the direction of Mr. Jones and fired two shots in rapid succession. Both shots struck Mr. Jones in the chest, resulting in his death before emergency personnel arrived at the scene. Delbert was tackled by another student, 18-year-old Adam Conner, a senior and member of the football team. Delbert dropped the gun and remained pinned to the ground by Adam until the school resource officer arrived at the scene. Delbert was arrested by local police and gave a videotaped statement later that day.

Although Delbert's account of his behavior was generally consistent across interviews, over time Delbert provided more information about his thoughts and motives concerning the offense. Delbert told me that he was unable to give a complete account of his thoughts and feelings because it was so difficult to talk about. He stated, "I did a terrible thing and I can't think about it anymore."

Peer Knowledge of the Shooting In his statement to the police at the time of his arrest, Delbert claimed sole responsibility for the shooting. He denied that anyone had encouraged him to bring a gun to school or to shoot the school principal. However, in the course of my interviews with Delbert, he acknowledged that a group of students had sometimes talked about using guns to take over the school or to shoot persons at school. This group included Jim Kane and several other boys he identified as members of the gothic group. Delbert stated that Jim Kane "hated Mr. Jones because Mr. Jones had it in for him. Jim was always talking about getting even with Mr. Jones." Delbert recalled that "Jim and the other guys was always talking about taking over the school. I said I would help 'em do it, I guess. I just wanted them to include me in the plans, but they kept saying I was too young or I wouldn't be able to handle a gun."

Delbert related that the boys in the gothic group had similarly told him he would not be able to shoplift CDs from a local music store. "They told me I couldn't do it, but then I got them exactly what they asked for."

When asked specifically if anyone had told him to shoot the principal, Delbert replied, "No one told me to do it, I just knew Jim wanted it done, and I wanted to show him what I could do. He said I couldn't do it, but I wasn't chicken. It sounds stupid now, but that is what I was thinking."

Jim Kane was unavailable to be interviewed for this evaluation, on advice of his attorney. According to police investigation reports forwarded from the State Attorney's office, Jim also declined to participate in an interview with police investigators. The police investigation reports include interviews with two students who belonged to the gothic group, Michael Jamison and Dennis McCurdy. Both boys admitted that Jim Kane had talked about getting even with the school principal, and both reported that Jim had told Delbert, "This job is too big for you." Both students denied encouraging Delbert to shoot Mr. Jones and maintained that they had no knowledge that he intended to do so.

Two other students, Jonathan Atkins and Marion Sparks, told police investigators that Delbert had hinted about the shooting to them. According to Jonathan, on the day prior to the shooting, Delbert had told him, "Tomorrow is payback time. You won't want to miss it." Jonathan denied that he knew Delbert had obtained a gun or that he had planned to shoot anyone. He admitted that he and Delbert had often made up fantasies of shooting persons they knew while playing video games, but insisted that the two of them had never discussed actually shooting someone. Marion Sparks reported to the police that Delbert had approached her in the school hallway during lunchtime the day before the shooting. He had said to her, "Keep away from the principal tomorrow, I don't want you getting hurt." She asked him what he was talking about, but he walked away without responding.

Motivation Over the course of three interviews, Delbert emphasized different motives for the shooting. In his initial account on August 4, he said that he did not know why he shot the principal, that he "must have blanked out" and that "it seemed like a dream, like I wasn't really there." Delbert appeared to be defensive and unwilling to disclose his thoughts and feelings to someone he had never met before. On August 5, Delbert seemed more willing to talk about the offense and acknowledged that he had thought about shooting someone at school for approximately 1 month prior to the offense. He had considered shooting several of the students who had mistreated him. He described intense feelings of resentment and anger toward these students and the student body as a whole. He stated, "they made me feel like a piece of sh—, excuse me, like I was no good. Always calling me names and making fun of me. I had to show them I was somebody. I had to make them leave me alone."

Delbert also related plans to shoot himself. He thought about shooting himself the day after he took the gun from his father's apartment. He reported that he loaded the gun and aimed it at his head the evening prior to the shooting but was unable to bring himself to pull the trigger.

During his interview on October 7, Delbert stated that he knew he would be "in serious trouble" for shooting someone and that he expected to be sent to "jail." He stated, "I really didn't care what happened to me. I couldn't shoot myself, so I guess this was the next best thing, just get it over with and go to jail."

According to the written report by Drs. Elizabeth Henson and Clarence Schiflet, Delbert stated that he had planned the shooting for 3–4 weeks, and that after shooting the principal and several students, he imagined himself fleeing the scene and stealing a car. Delbert then planned to drive to Florida and go to Disneyworld.

In his interview with Dr. Deborah Arnold on 9/23/00, Delbert stated that he did not go to school intending to shoot the principal. Instead, he planned to show off the gun and intimidate several students who had teased him. Once he arrived at school, he changed his mind because it seemed to him that the principal was laughing at him. He stated, "I know it's stupid, but I just had the idea that if I shot the principal for laughing at me, all the older guys would leave me alone. It's all like a dream. It seemed like slow motion."

DIAGNOSTIC FORMULATION

Mental Status Exam Delbert is a 15-year-old Caucasian boy who was interviewed at the Johnson Juvenile Detention Center on 8/4/00 (4 hrs), 8/5/00 (8 hrs), and 10/7/00 (3 hrs). Delbert spoke in a clear and coherent manner. He was alert, oriented to his surroundings, and understood the nature and purpose of the evaluation. He was responsive to questions, even though some topics made him uncomfortable and he often required repeated questions to elaborate his answers. As with most adolescents incarcerated for serious crimes, Delbert was initially restrained and somewhat inhibited in his presentation. He tended to deny feelings of distress and talked in a rather flat and unemotional tone. He was unwilling to discuss his more personal thoughts and feelings, and at first gave minimal answers to questions. Over time, he became more responsive

to questions and displayed an appropriate range of emotions, including feelings of guilt and remorse for his actions.

Depression Although initially Delbert was unwilling to acknowledge feelings of distress or depression, during the second interview he communicated more of his private thoughts and feelings. Delbert was clearly remorseful about the offense and cried about it during the interview, stating that he deserves punishment for committing murder. Delbert's feelings of self-criticism are so painful that he does not want to think about them; when he does think about them, he becomes suicidal and thinks about ways to kill himself. I alerted the Detention Center psychologist to evaluate him for suicide risk.

Delbert has classic symptoms of clinical depression, including depressed mood and feelings of guilt, difficulty falling asleep and difficulty sleeping through the night, and lack of energy. He engages in some recreational activities, such as watching television and playing cards, but his sense of enjoyment is diminished and short-lived. He frequently gives up his recreational time and returns to his cell. Delbert reports trouble concentrating, particularly when reading. Delbert said he does not have a diminished appetite, but this symptom of depression is often not present in adolescents. Delbert's chart indicates that he has gained 2 pounds since his incarceration.

Delbert's history of suicidal ideation dates to the seventh grade when he began to think that no one liked him. He felt teased and put down by other kids and thought about different ways to kill himself. His reactions seemed out of proportion to the events he described with his peers and indicated a distorted perception of how others felt about him. In the spring of 2000, he became seriously suicidal. He took a rope from the garage and experimented with different ways of making a hangman's loop. He also considered jumping out of a large building in his home town.

Paranoid Thinking Delbert did not describe pervasive, grossly unrealistic beliefs that would clearly qualify as paranoid delusions. He did not endorse classic paranoid delusions involving mind control, supernatural persecution, contamination or poisoning, or thought broadcasting. However, Delbert did reluctantly report a number of paranoid fears, which are abnormal and symptomatic of disturbed thinking. Delbert described ideas of reference that his classmates were watching him and laughing about him. Sometimes when riding the school bus Delbert felt that everyone on the bus was talking about him and making fun of him. These experiences were sufficiently troubling that Delbert repeatedly asked his mother to drive him to school. Delbert also felt uncomfortable in the school cafeteria. After going into the cafeteria to purchase a drink, Delbert looked for a secluded place to eat elsewhere in the school building. His teachers confirmed that Delbert was found eating his lunch in the custodian's storage room.

Prior to the shooting, Delbert did not describe hearing voices, seeing visions, or other false sensory experiences that could be considered full-blown hallucinations. However, there were indications of less severe, but symptomatic, disturbances in his perception of reality. For nearly a year, Delbert has imagined that others were talking about him, calling him names, or saying that he was stupid. At times when he was home alone, Delbert thought he heard a voice calling him "dopey."

According to his parents, Delbert was unusually concerned about privacy and security. He complained that the curtains in his bedroom did not adequately cover the windows and often kept the shades down, even during the day. At night, Delbert insisted on closing curtains in the family room before he would watch television, and he often checked to make sure all of the doors to the house were locked.

Evaluation for Antisocial Characteristics Delbert does not have the typical history of a youth who is developing antisocial personality characteristics. The available data indicate that he did not display early childhood behavior problems associated with Conduct Disorder or Oppositional Defiant Disorder. He does not have a pattern of alcohol or substance abuse. He does not have a history of violent behavior prior to the offense. His most significant delinquent behavior occurred during the 6-month period immediately prior to the offense. This period of delinquent behavior was atypical of his previous functioning and appears to have taken place largely, if not entirely, in association with an older group of boys who exerted a negative influence on him. Delbert was

evaluated for the presence of psychopathic personality characteristics using criteria of the Hare Psychopathy Checklist (Youth Version), generally regarded as the most serious antisocial syndrome with the poorest prognosis for treatment. Notably, Delbert does not demonstrate characteristics near or above the level associated with psychopathy.

Psychological Testing Delbert was administered the Wechsler Intelligence Scale for Children-III (WISC-III), the Millon Adolescent Clinical Inventory (MACI), and the Rorschach Inkblot Test. On the WISC-III, Delbert obtained a Full Scale IQ of 120, which corresponds to the 91st percentile of his age group. (The margin of measurement error for this test generates a 95% confidence interval of 114–124).

It is noteworthy that Delbert's intelligence test scores are consistent with the most recent achievement test scores found in his school records; his overall score on the Stanford Achievement Tests in the seventh grade placed him at the 85th percentile. This level of intelligence and achievement test performance is inconsistent with the below average grades Delbert earned in school. This inconsistency raises the possibility that motivational or emotional factors prevented Delbert from performing in school at a level commensurate with his abilities. It should also be noted the Delbert was diagnosed with a learning disability in his early elementary years but improved sufficiently so he no longer met the school's standards for special services. However, Delbert might retain milder limitations in reading or learning. Students with Delbert's high level of intelligence often develop compensatory learning strategies that reduce, but do not eliminate, the effects of learning disabilities on academic performance.

MACI The MACI is a standard, objectively scored test of personality adjustment that contains scales to measure tendencies toward personality disorders and psychological problems such as depression, impulsivity, and delinquency. Delbert's responses indicated a high level of distress and emotional turmoil, consistent with his clinical presentation during the interview. He obtained very high scores on Introversive and Inhibited scales. This personality profile characterizes an adolescent who is highly introverted, emotionally inhibited, and lacking in a sense of social competence and confidence. Delbert also reported high levels of depression and endorsed items associated with suicidal tendencies. Notably, Delbert did not register a high score on scales measuring a delinquent or antisocial predisposition.

Rorschach The Rorschach Inkblot Test is a projective personality test that can be reliably administered and scored using Exner's Comprehensive System. Delbert's test scores indicated serious deficits in coping ability and the presence of significant depression. His profile did not indicate deficits in his perception of reality or the presence of formal thought disorder that would indicate a psychotic state. Nevertheless, his profile reflects longstanding weaknesses in his ability to cope with interpersonal conflicts and emotional challenges. His perception of social interactions tends to be idiosyncratic and prone to distortion, but his responses are not consistent with an antisocial or psychopathic profile. Overall, the results of Rorschach testing are consistent with findings from the MACI and support the conclusion that his current presentation reflects longstanding social inhibitions and deficiencies in his social competence and sense of emotional well-being.

Diagnosis Delbert reported of periods of depression throughout the past 2 years, with the most severe period starting approximately 1 month prior to the shooting. Prior to the shooting his depressive symptoms included depressed mood and lack of energy, diminished interest in pleasurable activities, social withdrawal, and sleep difficulties. On at least two occasions Delbert considered suicide. Despite his periods of depression, Delbert was at times cheerful and active and at other times irritable and argumentative, which might give the impression that he was not depressed. Particularly in children and adolescents, depression is sometimes difficult to recognize and may be masked by other behavior problems. On the basis of these findings, Delbert meets diagnostic criteria (*Diagnostic and Statistical Manual of Mental Disorders, Fourth Edition* or *DSM-IV*, APA, 1994) for Major Depressive Disorder prior to the offense. Delbert described depressive feelings of worthlessness and inadequacy accompanied by paranoid thoughts that his peers disliked him and ridiculed him. His paranoid thoughts are a significant symptom but do not appear to be of sufficient severity to indicate the presence of Psychotic Features to his depression.

FORENSIC OPINIONS

Mental Illness According to state code, "mental illness" is defined as "a serious emotional disturbance that significantly impairs perception of reality, judgment, or rational behavior. Mental illness does not include conditions manifested primarily by repeated criminal or antisocial conduct." The legal definition of mental illness does not translate into specific diagnostic categories used by mental health professionals. Ultimately, the judge or jury must interpret this definition and decide if Delbert meets criteria for mental illness. In this examiner's opinion as a clinical psychologist, with a reasonable degree of certainty, Delbert is seriously emotionally disturbed, meeting diagnostic criteria for Major Depression. His judgment regarding his social relations and behavior are substantially impaired. His behavior is grossly maladaptive, and he has experienced significant depression, paranoid fears, and distortions in his perceptions of himself and others. His mental disorder was present at the time of the offense, and there is evidence that his mental state had declined during the weeks preceding the shooting.

Insanity According to state code, "insanity" means that "a person is not responsible for criminal conduct if, as a result of mental illness, the person lacks substantial capacity either to appreciate the wrongfulness of his conduct or to conform his conduct to the requirements of the law." Ultimately, the judge or jury must interpret this definition and decide if Delbert meets criteria for insanity. In this examiner's opinion as a clinical psychologist, with a reasonable degree of certainty, Delbert was aware that the shooting he committed was criminally wrong, and he did not lack the capacity to control his conduct and refrain from committing the crime.

Mitigation In this examiner's opinion, there are significant factors in Delbert's background and the circumstances of the offense to merit mitigation of his sentence.

1. Delbert suffers from serious emotional disturbance, which rendered him mentally ill

at the time of the offense. Major Depression is a severe form of depression that distorts the individual's thinking, generating intense feelings of despair and hopelessness that cloud judgment and perspective on the future.

2. Delbert's criminal behaviors were substantially motivated by the abuse and ridicule he experienced in school, and he was especially susceptible to this mistreatment because of his mental condition.

3. Delbert was substantially influenced in his criminal actions by older peers. Adolescents are highly susceptible to peer influences, and it is unlikely he would have committed the offense without their encouragement.

4. Delbert is amenable to treatment and rehabilitation. He is remorseful for his actions and would benefit from an opportunity to examine his motivations and intentions in the context of a therapeutic relationship. He has the intellectual and emotional capacity to undertake meaningful therapeutic work and to develop and mature. He does not manifest a psychopathic or antisocial personality, as commonly found among serious criminal offenders.

Disposition

1. As a 15-year-old boy, Delbert should be incarcerated in a facility with persons of similar age. He is vulnerable to abusive treatment by other incarcerants. He should not be exposed to adult incarcerants while he is a juvenile.

2. Delbert should be treated with psychological therapies including individual psychotherapy addressing his responsibility for his crime.

3. Delbert should be treated for his depression and paranoid fears with psychotropic medication, with continuous monitoring of his medication level and response to determine the appropriate course of treatment. His risk of suicide should be monitored.

4. Delbert has well above average capacity for educational achievement. He should be assigned to an educational program appropriate to his learning potential so as to facilitate his rehabilitation, maturation, and adjustment to incarceration.

5. Delbert has adjusted well to incarceration and has not posed a substantial risk for aggressive behavior. His risk of violent behavior should be periodically reevaluated and considered in the context of his current mental state and environmental stresses, but at the present time his prognosis is good.

Respectfully submitted,
Dewey G. Cornell, Ph.D.
Clinical Psychologist

Teaching Point: What training and experience in forensic and mental health areas are needed for juvenile forensic expertise?

The ideal forensic examiner for a juvenile should be a mental health professional who is experienced in clinical work with adolescents and who has knowledge of the forensic issues germane to juvenile proceedings. Excellent overviews can be found in Grisso's (1998a) *Forensic Evaluation of Juveniles* and Schetky and Benedek's (in press) *The Comprehensive Textbook of Child and Adolescent Forensic Psychiatry*.

Capable forensic examiners who work with adults should be cautious about evaluating a juvenile without adequate training or supervision. It is possible to conduct a seemingly competent evaluation but fail to obtain the data necessary to construct a complete picture of the developmental and familial context for the youth's clinical presentation and delinquent behavior. Interview styles and techniques that work well with adults may elicit limited or even misleading information from youths, resulting in an incomplete or inaccurate case formulation. Adolescent defensiveness, mistrustfulness, and difficulty in tolerating painful feelings makes some youths appear cold and remorseless when the opposite may be true. Adolescent egocentrism, sensitivity to shame, or intense counterdependency may lead some youths to refuse to disclose information important to their defense, such as a history of physical or sexual abuse. Examiners must broaden the scope of the evaluation to include information from parents and schools and must use psychological tests and measures appropriate to this age group (Hoge & Andrews, 1996). In all cases, examiners must be vigilant about the possibility of malingering or dishonesty and seek corroboration for the adolescent's statements.

There are multiple challenges to assessing the presence of both mental disorder and delinquency among juvenile offenders. The prevalence of mental disorders in delinquent populations is relatively high, but serious psychopathology may be overlooked in children and adolescents because the symptoms and signs of disorder may be clouded by developmental limitations and variations in clinical presentation not commonly seen among adults. Youthful impulsivity and experimentation, moodiness and emotional outbursts, transient family conflicts, and negative peer influences may or may not account for seemingly disturbed reasoning and behavior.

A further complication is that delinquent behaviors are commonplace in the general adolescent population, so it is difficult to assess the likelihood that an adolescent's offense reflects an established antisocial trajectory. Grisso (1998a) pointed out that many clinicians misunderstand the relation between Conduct Disorder and Antisocial Personality Disorder, and often fail to recognize that most youths who engage in delinquent behavior, including those who meet criteria for Conduct Disorder, will desist in this behavior as adults.

The examiner must have specialized knowledge of juvenile forensic issues and delinquency research. Juvenile forensic issues include waiver of *Miranda* rights, adjudicative competence, transfer to adult court, rehabilitative potential, and risk of harm to others (Grisso, 1998a). Although many of these issues are familiar to adult forensic clinicians, legal standards for juveniles are less well defined, and the weight to be given to developmental immaturity remains largely unspecified. Moreover, even mental health clinicians experienced in treating youths may not be familiar with the large, multidisciplinary body of literature on juvenile delinquency or the specialized literatures on topics such as juvenile sex offenders, firesetting, and youth gangs.

Finally, the clinician must actively delineate his or her professional role in conducting a forensic evaluation. It should be distinguished from a treatment relationship, and the clinician should adhere to the ethical standards and practice guidelines of his or her profession, assiduously striving to remain as objective as possible.

Chapter 9

Juvenile Competence to Stand Trial

This chapter focuses on juvenile competence to stand trial. The principle illustrating the first case addresses the importance of considering both relevance and scientific reliability and validity in considering how to seek information and select data sources in forensic assessment. Following the report, the teaching point discusses the selection of tools that might be used in evaluating juvenile trial competence. The second case begins with the principle that addresses the importance of evaluation conditions that are quiet, private, and distraction-free. The teaching point following the second case discusses how an evaluator can determine whether assessment conditions are "good enough" to proceed.

Case 1

Principle: Use relevance and reliability (validity) as guides for seeking information and selecting data sources

This principle concerns how obtaining information and selecting different sources of such information in FMHA should be guided by relevance to the forensic issues and the reliability (in the language of science, both reliability and validity) of the different sources. FMHA can involve many potential sources of information. To the extent that any such source is inaccurate, it cannot increase the overall accuracy of the evaluation; most likely, it will decrease overall accuracy, particularly if given too much weight. The forensic clinician must, therefore, be selective about the data sources that are used in the FMHA. Relevance and reliability, two important components of evidence law, can serve as useful guides for determining which sources of information should be considered.

Relevance can be established by describing the logical basis for a connection between a mental health construct (e.g., severe mental illness) and the relevant forensic issue(s) (e.g., capacities to consider information in a knowing and intelligent way). It can also be described by citing empirical evidence about the strength of the relationship between these constructs in research studies.

The concept of reliability can also be applied to FMHA through the legal constructs found under the *Federal Rules of Evidence* and *Daubert* (*Daubert v. Merrell Dow Pharmaceuticals*, 1993; *Fed. R. Evid.* 702; Heilbrun, 2001). One particular criterion for "reliability," a term used by the U.S. Supreme Court in *Daubert* to connote both scientific reliability and validity, involves the "error rate" of the measure. To obtain an error rate, there must be existing research with a "correct" outcome against which the accuracy of a particular measure can be calibrated. Given the difficulty in operationalizing such a "true" outcome in legal settings, such data are rarely available.

Sources of ethics authority address the issue of validity and relevance in a number of ways. The APA's *Ethical Principles of Psychologists and Code of Conduct* (1992) notes that psychological test construction should incorporate "scientific procedures and current professional knowledge for test design, standardization, validation, reduction or elimination of bias, and recommendations for use" (p. 1603). Further, caution should be exercised when testing special populations: "Psychologists attempt to identify situations in which particular interventions or assessment techniques or norms may not be applicable or may require adjustment in administration or interpretation because of factors such as the individuals' gender, age, race, ethnicity, national origin, religion, sexual orientation, disability, language, or socioeconomic status" (p. 1603). Finally, it is emphasized that forensic assessments, recommendations, and reports should be "based on information and techniques . . . sufficient to provide appropriate substantiation for their findings" (p. 1610).

The *Specialty Guidelines for Forensic Psychologists* (Committee on Ethical Guidelines for Forensic Psychologists, 1991) addresses the issue of legal reliability by stressing the importance of using "current knowledge of scientific, professional and legal developments" in selecting data collection methods and procedures for an evaluation (p. 661). Regarding "relevance," it is noted that "forensic psychologists avoid offering information from their investigations or evaluations that does not bear directly upon the legal purpose of their professional services and that is not critical as support for their product, evidence, or testimony, except where such disclosure is required by law" (p. 662). This language underscores the importance of relevance in both the selection and the communication stages of the evaluation process—the forensic clinician should select approaches and tests whose results allow communication of data relevant to the forensic issue(s) underlying the evaluation's legal question.

Consistent with these sources of ethics authority and Rule 702 of the *Federal Rules of Evidence*, the U.S. Supreme Court emphasized the importance of relevance and reliability as criteria for acceptance of scientific evidence in federal jurisdictions (*Daubert*, 1993). The Court in *Daubert* considered Rule 702 in terms of relevance—there must be "a valid scientific connection to the pertinent inquiry as a precondition to admissibility"—and reliability—the expert's assertion must be based on scientific evidence and "supported by the appropriate validation" (p. 2795). The focus is on the evaluation of particular methods or measures, which may allow a court to go beyond the general acceptance of a method to consider its scientific base (Thames, 1994).

The present case report provides an example of the application of relevance and reliability to the selection of data sources in the context of juvenile competence to stand trial. The application of relevance in a FMHA context can be established qualitatively and quantitatively. Qualitatively, relevance to the forensic issue can be addressed by describing the logical basis for a connection between the mental health construct and the relevant forensic issues(s). In this case, the forensic clinician was asked to assess the competence to stand trial of a 14-year-old defendant. There are a variety of mental health constructs and historical data that might be relevant to this legal question, with some data sources being more relevant than others when the forensic issues are considered.

For example, in the report, the forensic clinician chose data sources that are directly relevant to the forensic issues being assessed. Under South Carolina law, the defendant must have the "capacity to understand the proceedings against him and to assist in his own defense." Accordingly, the forensic clinician incorporated data sources that could be relevant to these capacities.

In this case, the forensic clinician chose quantitative data sources (the Georgia Court Competency Test-Mississippi State Hospital Revision, or GCCT-MSH, and the MacArthur Competency Assessment Tool-Criminal Adjudication, or MacCAT-CA) to assess the defendant's capacity to understand the nature of the proceedings against him and the ability to assist in his own defense. More specifically, these instruments were used to assess the defendant's reasoning abilities and factual knowledge of court matters as they pertain to the criminal justice system. Although neither instrument is normed for adolescent populations, the possibility of confinement and transfer of charges to adult criminal court necessitated the assessment of the defendant's competence to stand trial in the context of adult defendants. On the GCCT-MSH, the defendant's score just barely exceeded the score for the group of adult defendants considered competent to stand trial by forensic clinicians. Similarly, the results of the MacCAT-CA suggested minimal to mild impairment in the defendant's factual and rational understanding of the nature of the proceedings and his ability to assist his attorney in his own defense, respectively.

Related to the legal construct of competence are intellectual, cognitive, and academic capacities. Deficiencies or impairment in these areas could directly affect an individual's ability to understand the nature of the proceedings against him or her and the ability to assist legal counsel in mounting an adequate defense. In this case, the forensic clinician again used quantitative methods to assess these domains. Specifically, the forensic clinician used the Wechsler Intelligence Scale for Children-3rd edition (WISC-III) to assess intellectual and cognitive functioning, and the Wide Range Achievement Test-3rd edition (WRAT-3) to assess academic achievement.

Results of the WISC-III suggested a Full-Scale IQ in the Low Average range, with specific deficits in vocabulary, fund of information, and abstract reasoning. Similarly, the defendant's performance on the WRAT-3 suggested a sixth-grade reading level, reflecting below average word recognition skills. Deficits in reading and vocabulary development could have a direct bearing on the defendant's ability to communicate effectively with defense counsel and/or understand related written material and is, therefore, valuable information for this evaluation.

Mental state and the presence of severe psychopathology can also affect an individual's competence. To assess this domain, the forensic clinician used both a clinical interview and a more quantitative approach: the Million Adolescent Clinical Inventory (MACI). The results of the MACI, in conjunction with the clinical interview, helped rule out the presence of major mental disorders and symptoms (such as psychosis, bipolar disorder, hallucinations, delusions, and paranoia) that might adversely affect the defendant's ability to assist in his own defense. A connection between mental health construct and the relevant forensic issues is needed. In this case, the forensic clinician makes this connection in the "Opinion" section of the report by integrating the results of quantitative assessment into a final conclusion that the defendant was minimally competent and had many deficits that should be the focus of intervention.

Re: Conrad S.

Your Honor:

Pursuant to your June 17 appointment of me upon the stipulation of Ms. Rx, Conrad's defense attorney, and case prosecutor, Mr. Dx, I saw this 14-year-old Caucasian male for a forensic psychological evaluation to assess his current mental state, diagnosis, and "capacity to understand the proceedings against him and to assist in his own defense" (44-23-410, S.C. Code Ann. [Law Co-op. 1984 & Supp. 199x]).

At the time of the evaluation, Conrad was in his second week of detainment in the Juvenile Unit of the Rxx County Detention Center, awaiting adjudication on charges of two counts of first degree criminal sexual conduct against his eight-year-old female neighbor, allegedly occurring this year on June 1 and 2. Conrad allegedly engaged in digital penetration of the girl's vagina inside her clothing while they were alone on the back porch of Conrad's home. According to police reports, the girl told her mother on the evening of June 2, and Conrad was arrested by police on June 3. Conrad was detained at the Rxx County Detention Center, where he has remained following mandatory weekly detention hearings conducted by Family Court Judge M. on June 10 and Your Honor on June 17. This is the first time that Conrad has been involved with the Family Court system. Concerns regarding Conrad's competency to stand trial were raised by his attorney when it was learned that Conrad is currently two grades behind his classmates, after repeating both kindergarten and first grade because he was "not ready" for school, and that he receives special assistance (Resource Room) in reading.

In addition to clinical interviews on June 21, 22, and 23, I administered to Conrad the Wechsler Intelligence Scale for Children-3rd Edition (WISC-III), the Wide Range Achievement Test-Revision 3 (WRAT-3), the Developmental Test of Visual Motor Integration (VMI), the Millon Adolescent Clinical Inventory (MACI), the Georgia Court Competency Test-Mississippi State Hospital Revision (GCCT-MSH) and the MacArthur Competency Assessment Tool-Criminal Adjudication (MacCAT-CA).[1]

I reviewed numerous documents supplied by the prosecution and defense, including the police incident reports, the alleged victim's statement, the juvenile petitions for each count, and Conrad's educational records from kindergarten to sixth grade. On June 21, I interviewed his employed, high school graduate, single-parent biological mother, Mrs. S, who gave consent to the evaluation on consultation with Conrad's lawyer. On June 21 and 23, I observed case-related discussions between Conrad and his attorney, the specific content of which, under attorney–client privilege and previous agreement of all parties, will not be disclosed within this report.

Prior to the start of the evaluation, and in the presence of his mother and attorney, I informed Conrad that I would be asking him questions and giving him certain psychological tests, that I would be making a written report of the evaluation's results, and that I might testify in court about my findings. I informed him that he could refuse to answer any specific question, though answering others, and could stop the evaluation at any time. Although his mother had consented to the evaluation just prior to my first contact with Conrad, I wished to assess his capacity to independently agree to the evaluation. When asked to explain his understanding of the examination, he stated: "I can answer your questions and take some tests if I want to. You'll make a report to the judge. You might talk in court about me." He answered in a similar manner at the beginning of each subsequent evaluation session. It is my opinion that Conrad understood the reasons for the evaluation and was able to independently consent to the examination. Although his attorney remained during clinical assessment of attorney–client interactions and to advise Conrad whether (but not how) to answer any case-specific questions, neither Conrad's mother nor attorney were present during psychological testing to ensure standardization of test administration procedures.

CLINICAL IMPRESSIONS AND MENTAL STATUS

For each session, Conrad entered the examination room without incident, displaying normal gait and posture. He was neat and clean and appeared to show adequate concern for his personal appearance and hygiene. He was alert and oriented, and was able to exert sufficient attention and concentration to interview questions and assessment tasks. His answers to questions were relevant, well associated, and goal directed. There was no evidence of delusions or obsessions, although he reported constantly thinking about his charges. He denied ever experiencing auditory or visual hallucinations. There were no signs of psychosis during any evaluation session. His mother confirmed his report that he has not suffered a closed head injury, seizure, or loss of consciousness. She further corroborated his report that neither he nor any member of his family has received inpatient or outpatient psychiatric or other mental health care. He denied a history of alcohol or drug use and denied present or past thoughts or plans to harm himself or others.

His intellectual functioning as measured by the WISC-III falls within the Low Average range (FSIQ = 88; 21st percentile), with deficits relative to his age mates in vocabulary, fund of information, and abstract reasoning. His performance on the VMI (23rd percentile) did not suggest significant deficits in visual-motor integration and was consistent with his level of intellectual functioning. His WRAT-R Reading level at the sixth grade reflects his below-average word recognition ability; his Arithmetic performance at the eighth-grade level is more consistent with his expected placement.

Throughout each evaluation session, Conrad's affect was appropriate though constricted, apparently partly because he was apprehensive about his current legal situation. He rarely smiled, did not openly express humor or laughter, and was often tearful. His mood was depressed and anxious; he reported frequently crying in his cell, disturbance in his sleep patterns, diminished appetite, and recurrent thoughts about being arrested and possibly remaining in jail. His performance on the MACI was valid, although slightly biased toward minimizing psychological conflicts and emotional difficulties.

Adolescents with MACI results similar to Conrad's are described as dependent, unassertive, somewhat avoidant persons who are often subject to the influence of others and may exhibit impulsive, poorly thought-out acts. Such juveniles rarely display bizarre or unusual behaviors or highly fluctuating moods suggestive of a major mental disorder (e.g., psychosis, bipolar affective disorder). A history of delinquency or repeated conflict with authority (e.g., parents, teachers, police) is unlikely in adolescents with Conrad's MACI results. Notably, Conrad's score on the Sexual Discomfort scale of the MACI was consistent with male youth who have recurrent concerns regarding sexual impulses and who have higher anxiety and tension than their peers over issues of a sexual nature.

DIAGNOSTIC IMPRESSION

Axis I: Adjustment disorder with mixed anxiety and depression, acute Reading disorder

Axis II: No diagnosis

Axis III: Deferred

Axis IV: Problems related to interaction with the legal system (arrest/detention)

Axis V: 61–70 mild to moderate symptoms

COMPETENCE TO STAND TRIAL

To establish an initial screening of Conrad's trial competency, the GCCT-MSH was administered on June 21. Following clinical evaluation of competency, the MacCAT-CA was administered on June 23 to assess his reasoning abilities in addition to his factual knowledge of court matters. Although neither instrument has norms for adolescents, the possibility of involuntary confinement and/or waiver to General Sessions Court necessitates the assessment of Conrad's competency against the standard of normal adult defendants. On the GCCT-MSH, Conrad's score just barely exceeded the cutoff score for adults considered competent by their examiners.

Understanding of Legal Proceedings During the June 23 clinical assessment of competency to

stand trial, Conrad was generally unable to cite and define the charges against him. He stated that he'd been accused of "having sex" with a neighbor girl, but he was unable to indicate the specific criminal charge or explain the differences between first and second criminal sexual conduct and the lesser charge of lewd act on a minor under age 14. He was not sure how long he might be confined at the Department of Juvenile Justice (DJJ), but knew that it could be for "many years" (maximum penalty to age 21 with placement in adult corrections at age 18). He knew the roles and responsibilities of the judge ("he listens to both sides and sees who is lying and sentences people to jail"), defense attorney ("he tries to get you out of trouble in court"), and witnesses ("they tell what happened"), but was less clear about the duties of the prosecutor ("I don't know, asks you questions?") and the jury ("they listen to the judge"). He knew the difference between pleas of guilty ("you did it") and not guilty ("you didn't do it"), but was unable to define the pleas of not guilty by reason of insanity (NGRI) and guilty but mentally ill (GBMI), which would be available in his case if he were to be waived to adult court. He knew that while in court he needed to control his behavior and not be disruptive to the proceedings ("I'll sit and be quiet") but did not know he could alert his lawyer if he knew a witness was lying during testimony. He is aware of the seriousness of the proceedings against him ("I'm scared, I'm in a lot of trouble"). Conrad's low average intellectual functioning, receptive vocabulary, and abstraction ability will make it difficult for him to independently understand what is said in court, though he should be able to understand the testimony of the alleged victim if she were to testify at his hearing.

Assist in His Defense In response to careful, patient questioning, Conrad was able to relate the specific facts of his case to me but was less able to express what he was thinking and feeling prior to, during, and after contact with the girl ("I don't know, kind of excited I guess"). He was very apprehensive and ashamed of having to tell his female attorney what had happened and was terrified of having to face his mother ("Could you tell her what happened?"). While he understood that he could ask his attorney questions about legal matters and his case, observation of his contacts with Ms. Rx indicated that his embarrassment about the charges and his generally passive, dependent personality style resulted in Conrad remaining silent, except to respond "OK" or "yes, ma'am" when his attorney would ask for confirmation that he understood a particular point of strategy. He stated that he likes Ms. Rx and thinks she is doing "a good job" for him, but he was unable to cite examples of her assistance to him so far (Ms. Rx was retained by his mother on June 8, 2 days before his first detention hearing). Conrad's limited reading ability will make it difficult for him to independently consider written legal material provided to him (he could not read and explain in his own words the two juvenile petitions in his case), but he was able to understand the document when it was verbally explained by his attorney. Although Conrad was able to learn the basic elements of plea arrangements as applied to his case ("I won't go to DJJ as long if I say I'm guilty of just touching her" [lewd act on minor under 14]), he was unable to retain possible advantages and disadvantages of other case strategies (e.g., pleading not guilty and having a trial in Family or General Sessions Court; pleading guilty to assault and battery of a high and aggravated nature to avoid registry as a sex offender). He has a self-protective interest in the outcome of his case ("I want to go home or be on probation like my friend was") but was also realistic about the possibility of confinement ("I'll probably be sent to DJJ"). His embarrassment, anxiety, and limited verbal skills may be a barrier to his providing effective testimony in court.

On the MacCAT-CA norms for competent adult defendants, his scores in the 60th percentile on Understanding, 14th percentile on Appreciation, and 10th percentile on Reasoning suggest that Conrad has minimal to mild impairment in his factual and rational understanding of the procedures and ability to assist his attorney, respectively. Notably, Conrad's score on Understanding was relatively higher, because the test provides for instruction when an item is initially failed. His relatively lower scores on Appreciation and Reasoning were due to his limited abilities to explain his thinking and judgment for the answers he gave items in those sections.

OPINION

Pursuant to 44-23-420 (2), it is this examiner's opinion that Conrad is presently minimally capable of understanding the proceedings against him and assisting his attorney in his defense. He displays many deficits that require attention, as cited in the Recommendations section below.

RECOMMENDATIONS

1. Given the deficits indicated within this report, Conrad's attorney is encouraged to teach and check his understanding of court proceedings in each contact with him.
2. Reexamination of Conrad with the MacCAT-CA during the week prior to his delinquency hearing (currently scheduled for August 24) is recommended to affirm his retention of trial competency matters.
3. Twice-weekly counseling with an adult male licensed psychologist or social worker is recommended to help reduce his anxiety and help him cope with his current legal situation.
4. If Conrad's current symptoms persist or worsen, a psychiatric consultation for the utility of antidepressant medication is recommended as an adjunct to his twice-weekly counseling.
5. Ongoing pre-hearing assessment and monitoring of Conrad's suicide risk is recommended given his age, the nature of his charges, his fears of being assaulted at DJJ as a child molester, and the duration of his possible confinement until age 21. It is recommended that if he is adjudicated delinquent, the DJJ correctional and sex offender treatment staff continue to monitor Conrad for suicide risk.

Geoffrey R. McKee, PhD, ABPP
Diplomate in Forensic Psychology
Clinical Professor, Department of Neuropsychiatry & Behavioral Science
University of South Carolina School of Medicine

Teaching Point: How does a forensic clinician decide on tools to use in
                  evaluating juvenile competence to stand trial?

The first step in selecting tools to use in evaluating juvenile competence to
stand trial involves considering the context of the evaluation. Although the
legal standard (understand the nature of the charges and assist counsel in
mounting an effective defense) is the same under *Dusky*, competence to stand
trial evaluations in juvenile court may require the forensic clinician to consider
unique competencies and developmental issues. These unique issues can be
found in both clinical and psycholegal domains.

Regardless of context, in the clinical domain, the forensic practitioner should
use the guides of relevance and reliability for measuring juvenile psychopathology,
intellectual functioning, and (at younger ages, such as 13 and below) developmental maturity. In the psycholegal domain, the forensic clinician should consider
whether there is an available assessment tool (e.g., the MacArthur Competence
Assessment Tool for Criminal Adjudication; Poythress, Monahan, Bonnie, &
Hoge, 1999) that has been derived in relevant areas, measured for reliability and
different kinds of validity in multiple samples, is commercially available, and accompanied by a supporting manual. In the absence of such an instrument, which
is currently unavailable for juvenile competence to stand trial, it is best to use
semi-structured interviewing and relevant psychological testing that incorporates
various elements of competence to stand trial that are most applicable to the
context. In conjunction with this approach, it is also helpful to gather information
through multiple sources to address the individual's capacities in competence-
related areas. In this case, if the referral had involved evaluating Conrad for competence to stand trial in juvenile court only, then neither the GCCT nor the
MacCAT-CA would have been appropriate for use. As explained in the report,
however, the possibility of disposition of this charge in criminal court meant that
it was appropriate to consider Conrad's capacities relative to adult criminal defendants. If the evaluator had concluded that Conrad had deficits that suggested very
significant problems for trial competence in criminal court, and if there were
some reasonable possibility that disposition could occur in juvenile court, it would
also have been helpful for the evaluator to comment (in this report, or in a separate one) on Conrad's relevant capacities for juvenile trial competence.

Case 2

Principle: Ensure that conditions for evaluation are quiet, private, and
             distraction free

This principle describes the degree of quiet, privacy, and freedom from distraction that are important in FMHA. Providing a private and distraction-free envi-

ronment initially seems so basic as to be a truism: It is always important to ensure that administration conditions are reasonably good in any type of evaluation setting. In a forensic context, however, there may be certain problems that are encountered more frequently than they might be in other kinds of mental health assessment. Individuals undergoing FMHA are evaluated in a variety of settings, ranging from jails, prisons, detention centers, and secure hospitals to outpatient clinics and private offices. When FMHA is performed in criminal or juvenile cases, the defendant is often incarcerated or hospitalized in a secure setting. Forensic clinicians must be careful to respect security needs, but must also be clear about the minimally acceptable conditions under which the evaluation can be meaningfully performed.

What are appropriate conditions for conducting FMHA? Relatively little attention is paid to this question in testing manuals and basic texts on mental health interviewing, perhaps because it seems so obvious. The same is true for empirical research; except for the influence of environment on performance in psychological testing, the impact of such influences has rarely been studied. Based on research on the influence of assessment conditions on psychological test performance, Anastasi (1988) recommended that the evaluator should (1) follow standardized procedures in detail, (2) record unusual testing conditions, however minor, and (3) take testing conditions into account when interpreting test results. She observed that the assessment room should be free from undue noise and distraction, and provide adequate lighting, ventilation, seating, and working space for test takers. Similar considerations have been stressed for clinical interviewing and mental status examination (Nurcombe & Gallagher, 1986).

Ideally, FMHA would be conducted in a private, comfortable, and distraction-free environment. Unfortunately, ideal assessment conditions are often not possible in FMHA, particularly when the evaluation is conducted with an individual who is incarcerated. For example, the present evaluation took place in the somewhat chaotic environment of the juvenile "holding area" of a family court house. The evaluators were first given a private conference room in which to conduct the evaluation, a setting that was quiet, private, and distraction free. While the evaluation was in progress, however, it was necessary to change rooms because the conference room had been scheduled for a meeting. The second setting was noisier and offered less privacy, requiring a move to a partitioned conference area that still offered less than optimal privacy. The alternative was to return to complete the assessment another time, which could have required additional authorization (in the form of a letter from the referring attorney or an order from the court) and resulted in significant delay. The question of when such conditions were no longer "good enough" was important, therefore, with potentially adverse consequences resulting from the decisions to continue or stop, respectively.

There are two aspects to "good enough" conditions in FMHA. First, the evaluator must respect the individual's need for privacy because of the areas being assessed, many of which are potentially very sensitive. This is particularly important when such information could be used in a legal proceeding. When information is overheard by an inappropriate party, it might be used to the detriment of the individual being evaluated. In cases such as the sexual abuse of a minor, for example, it could also put the individual at risk for harm when they are returned to population. It is essential, therefore, that the evaluation be conducted in an environment that allows the individual being examined to communicate information that will not be overheard.

In the present case, the individual was asked about past psychiatric difficulties, family problems, substance abuse, past criminal behavior, and a variety of other areas of a sensitive nature. The adolescent being evaluated in this case was charged with a sexual offense; without appropriate privacy, he might not have been willing to answer questions relevant to such alleged conduct.

The second aspect of "good enough" conditions in FMHA concerns an environment that is as free from distraction as possible. This is important because visual or auditory distractions might adversely affect the individual's ability to concentrate and respond in a way that reasonably represents their capacities. It becomes even more important when the evaluation requires the individual to focus on a variety of related and possibly difficult tasks over an extended period of time.

In this case, the individual was evaluated to address capacities relevant to three separate legal questions: competence to stand trial, competence to waive *Miranda* rights, and amenability to treatment in the context of public safety. To assess these capacities, we evaluated the individual over a 5-hour period of time and administered a variety of tests aimed at addressing the relevant capacities and risk factors. The assessment included a clinical interview, a structured screening instrument for adolescent symptoms of mental and emotional disorder (the Massachusetts Youth Screening Inventory, or MAYSI), a standard test of current functioning in relevant academic areas (the Wide Range Achievement Test, 3rd edition, or WRAT-3), and a test of current intellectual functioning (the Wechsler Intelligence Scale for Children, 3rd edition, or WISC-III). A distraction-free environment was especially important in this case, given that the individual was 13 years old and frequently impatient with the length of the evaluation and the extensive testing. Without distractions during the assessment, it is easier to determine an individual's capacity for attention and concentration under optimal circumstances. This also yielded a more accurate evaluation of symptoms and relevant behavioral characteristics that would not have been possible when significant external stimulation was present. In this case, the individual had a documented history of Attention-Deficit/Hyperactivity Disorder and also showed behavioral characteristics suggesting that he currently met DSM-IV criteria for ADHD. The testing environment was important to determine how he might respond over an extended period without significant distractions and then (for a short period) in the face of such distractions. The evaluators commented on the change in environment during the evaluation, and noted its potential impact on the administration and results of the WISC-III, the test that was administered after the change in the testing room.

FORENSIC EVALUATION

July 28, 1998
Re: John Doe
P.P. # 123456
Juvenile # 12345678

REFERRAL

John Doe is a 13-year-old African American male who is currently charged with Rape, Involuntary Deviate Sexual Intercourse, Indecent Assault, Indecent Exposure (two counts), Aggravated Indecent Assault, Incest, Recklessly Endangering Another Person, Sexual Assault, and Statutory Sexual Assault. A request for a mental health evaluation to provide the defense with information relevant to John's competence to stand trial was made by John's attorney.

PROCEDURES

John was evaluated for approximately 5 hours on 7-27-98 at the Pittsburgh Family Court (Juvenile Division), where he was seen for purposes of this evaluation. (John was transported from the Wilderness Challenge Program for purposes of this evaluation.) In addition to a clinical interview, John was administered a structured screening instrument for adolescent symptoms of mental and emotional disorder (the Massachusetts Youth Screening Inventory, or MAYSI), a standard test of current functioning in relevant academic areas (the Wide Range Achievement Test, 3rd edition, or WRAT-3), and a test of current intellectual functioning (the Wechsler Intelligence Scale for Children, 3rd edition, or WISC-III). Attempts to contact John's father were unsuccessful. The following documents, obtained from John's attorney, were reviewed as part of the evaluation:

1. Pittsburgh Police Department Complaint or Incident Report (dated 6-23-98),

2. Pittsburgh Police Department Investigation Report (dated 6-27-98),
3. Pittsburgh Police Department Investigation Interview Record (dated 6-23-98),
4. Pittsburgh Police Department Investigation Interview Record (dated 6-23-98),
5. *Miranda* Rights Waiver Form (dated 6-23-98),
6. Pittsburgh Police Department Investigation Interview Record of John Doe (dated 6-23-98),
7. Pittsburgh Police Department Biographical Information Report (dated 6-23-98),
8. Juvenile History Inquiry of John Doe (dated 7-23-98),
9. Common Pleas Court-Pittsburgh (Juvenile Branch) Report (dated 6-25-98),
10. DHS/CYD Investigation Reports (dated 5-10-96 and 7-3-98),
11. Academic History Profile of John Doe from Thomas Jefferson Middle School (dated 7-3-98),
12. Attendance History Profile of John Doe from Thomas Jefferson Middle School (dated 7-3-98),
13. Student Credit Profile of John Doe from William Allen School (dated 5-10-96),
14. Attendance History Profile of John Doe from William Allen School (dated 5-10-96),
15. School District of Pittsburgh Psychological Report (conducted on 2-19-96),
16. Court Reviews from Oakbrook, Inc. (dated 8-11-97 and 12-12-97),
17. Discharge Summary from Oakbrook, Inc. (1-12-98),
18. Wilderness Challenge Confidential Psychological Evaluation (7-2-98),
19. Wilderness Challenge Psychiatric Evaluation (7-3-98),
20. School District of Pittsburgh, Division of Special Education, Individualized Education Program (dated 2-28-95),
21. School District of Pittsburgh Student Evaluation Records (dated 11-2-92, 2-17-94, and 3-10-94),

22. Pittsburgh Court of Common Pleas (Family Court, Juvenile Branch) Delinquent Petition (dated 10-26-95),
23. Pittsburgh Police Department Complaint or Incident Report (dated 10-25-95),
24. Pittsburgh Police Department Investigation Report (dated 10-25-95),
25. Pittsburgh Youth Advocate Programs P.H.I.S. Court Reports (dated 12-20-95 and 1-19-96),
26. Social Summary for Forensic Evaluation (7-23-98),
27. Adjustment Summary Report for John Doe from the Franciscan Aftercare Program (dated 3-30-98),
28. Psychological Summary (1-30-96), and
29. Social and Psychological Services File Notes (dated 5-31-96).

Prior to the evaluation, John was notified about the purpose of the evaluation and the associated limits on confidentiality. Initially, he had some difficulty reporting back his understanding of the purpose of the evaluation. After further explanations and repeated questioning, however, he appeared to understand the basic purpose of the evaluation, reporting back his understanding that he would be evaluated and that a written report would be submitted to his attorney. He further understood that the report could be used in his pre-trial hearing and, if it were, copies would be provided to the prosecution and the court.

RELEVANT HISTORY

Historical information was obtained from the collateral sources described above, as well as from John himself. Because John appeared to be a relatively poor historian, it was particularly important to assess the consistency of the factual information provided by John across multiple sources. If additional collateral information is obtained prior to John's court date, a supplemental report will be filed.

John Doe was born to Jane and John Doe Sr. John reported that his parents never married. According to the Social History (7-23-98), John is the fifth of eight children born to Jane Doe and John Doe Sr. John reported that he has one brother and six sisters. John also reported that he had twin brothers who died when he was about four years old. John indicated that his youngest sister currently lives in Pittsburgh and that his other siblings live with relatives in California. According to the Social History, John's siblings have been living with their paternal aunt and paternal grandmother in California since being sent there by John's mother in the summer of 1997. According to the Wilderness Challenge Psychological Evaluation (7-2-98), John was unable to explain why he was not sent to California with his siblings. According to the Social History, John's father reported that John was not sent to California because John receives SSI income and John's mother wanted the financial support. John reported that he was raised by both parents until they ended their relationship when he was about 9 or 10 years old. John reported that he lived with his mother from the time his parents separated until June 1, 1998. According to the Wilderness Challenge Psychological Evaluation, John also lived with his maternal grandmother after his parents separated. John reported that he lived with his maternal aunt and his three cousins from June 21, 1998, until his arrest for the current charges on June 23, 1998.

According to the Psychological Report from the School District of Pittsburgh (2-19-96), John had a "chaotic" family life that was characterized by "abuse, mental illness, homelessness, and foster placement." John reported that he has a good relationship with his mother. John reported that his mother is currently living with her boyfriend of 8 months. He also reported that he has a good relationship with his mother's boyfriend. John stated that his mother is currently unemployed, but that his mother's boyfriend provides financial support. John reported that he last saw his mother on June 1 and last spoke with her on June 15. John stated that he has not had any contact with his mother for about 6 weeks because "she never got in touch with me." When John was asked about his relationship with his father, he reported that they were "always tight . . . I love my father and my father loves me." According to the Social History, John's father was incarcerated on several occasions while John was growing up. John reported that his father was in prison for 3 years and 8 months, "because they said he was selling drugs." According to the Social History, there are "[s]ome indications that both mother and father have had drug use history." John reported that his father "did drugs when I was 9 or

10 . . . but never did drugs since." John reported that his father was released from prison about 5 months ago. John also reported that his father is currently living in a halfway house and "might be on parole." The Social History indicates that John's father has been out on parole for 4 months and lives in a halfway house. John reported that his father has been involved with his current girlfriend since being released from incarceration. He also reported that his father has been employed as a caterer for about 5 months. The Social History indicates that John's father works 40–70 hours per week as a caterer. Although the Juvenile History Inquiry indicates that the maternal aunt is John's guardian, the Social History indicates that John's father has sole custody of John. John also indicated that his father has custody of him. According to the Social History, John's mother voluntarily gave custody to John's father.

John reported that he recently completed eighth grade at Thomas Jefferson Middle School. John also said, however, that he is not sure if he will be promoted to ninth grade, because he has not received his report card. According to the Wilderness Challenge Psychological Evaluation, John has been enrolled in special education classes "in the category of Mild Mental Retardation" since second grade. The Court Review from Oakbrook (9-11-97) also indicates that John has been found to be functioning within the "mild range of mental retardation." John was reportedly placed in Learning Support classes as a result of his poor academic performance in first grade at Isaac Newton Elementary School. The Wilderness Challenge Psychological Evaluation and the Psychological Report from the School District of Pittsburgh both indicate that John's program was subsequently changed to full-time "Emotional Support" at John Brown Elementary School and Grover Cleveland Elementary School. The Attendance History Profile from Thomas Jefferson Middle School (7-3-98) indicates that John is currently classified as SED—Full-Time. According to the Social History, John has been classified as SED—Full-Time since November of 1992, when he was in second grade. When John was asked about his educational background, he was unable to provide much information. John did say, however, that he attended "Lincoln, Washington, and Jefferson," but he was unable to re-

member the grades that he attended at each school. The Attendance History Profile from Thomas Jefferson Middle School indicates that John attended the following schools: Isaac Newton Elementary School, Abraham Lincoln Elementary School, John Welsh School, John Brown Elementary School, Grover Cleveland Elementary School, William Allen School, Eliza Dolittle School, Thomas Jefferson Middle School, and George Shannon School. John was also unable to provide any information regarding his grades or attendance. According to the Attendance History Profile from Thomas Jefferson Middle School, John has the following attendance history profile: 43 unexcused absences, 1 excused absence, and 39 lates during the 1991–1992 academic year; 36 unexcused absences, 4 excused absences, and 5 lates during 1992–1993; 55 unexcused absences, 6 excused absences, and 13 lates during 1993–1994; 8 unexcused absences and 20 lates in 1994–1995; 60 unexcused absences, 2 excused absences, and 82 lates during 1995–1996; 23 unexcused absences, 59 excused absences, and 33 lates during 1996–1997; and 35 unexcused absences and 13 lates during the 1997–1998 academic year. The Academic History Profile from Thomas Jefferson Middle School indicates that John's grades have ranged from Bs to Fs.

When John was asked about his behavior in school, he reported that he often got into trouble. John said that he has been suspended "about 30 times." When John was asked about the reasons for the suspensions, he responded that he has been suspended for fighting, "people saying I did things," and bringing a "toy" dart gun to school. According to the Attendance History Profile from Thomas Jefferson Middle School, John has been suspended seven times since the 1993–1994 academic year began. Specifically, John was suspended on the following occasions: 2 days on 12-14-93 (disruption of school), 1 day on 2-8-94 (disruption of school and repeated school violations), 2 days on 4-8-94 (disruption of school), 3 days on 1-26-95 (disruption of school), 2 days on 2-26-96 (assault on student), 2 days on 3-21-96 (disruption of school), and 2 days on 11-7-96 (repeated school violations). John reported that he has never been expelled from school.

John also reported that he has been enrolled in various educational and placement programs.

He indicated that he attended the Sylvan Learning Center for about 1 month, and said that his experience at Sylvan was helpful because it improved his reading ability. John also reported that he attended Franciscan (Aftercare Program) for about 3 months and Oakbrook (a residential facility) for about 1 year (from January 1997 to January 1998). According to the Wilderness Challenge Psychological Evaluation, John was committed to Oakbrook on January 13, 1997. According to the Discharge Summary from Oakbrook (1-12-98), John was ordered to Oakbrook by the Pittsburgh Family Court (Juvenile Division) on January 6, 1997. The Discharge Summary indicates that John was previously "diagnosed in the mild range of mental retardation." The Discharge Summary also indicates that John's "overall behavior since admission has been positive." According to the Discharge Summary, John was scheduled to be discharged from Oakbrook on January 13, 1998. After this discharge, John was placed in the Franciscan Aftercare Program. According to the Wilderness Challenge Psychological Evaluation, John did not adhere to the rules of the Franciscan Aftercare Program.

John reported that he does not currently suffer from any serious medical problems. He also said that he has never been hospitalized or suffered any serious illnesses or injuries. According to the Discharge Summary from Oakbrook, John was taken to Wilson Community Hospital on July 30, 1997, after he accidentally fell in his cottage. The Discharge Summary indicates that John underwent an electroencephalogram (EEG) to assess possible neurological dysfunction on August 21, 1997. The reported results were within normal limits. According to both the Wilderness Challenge Psychological Evaluation and the Social History, however, John's fall may have been the result of a mild seizure. The Wilderness Challenge Psychological Evaluation indicates that John "became dizzy and fell, biting through his tongue." As a result, John reportedly received sutures in his tongue, chin, and lower jaw. The Wilderness Challenge Psychological Evaluation also indicates that the EEG conducted on August 21, 1997, was negative. John reported that he has never been prescribed medication for mental, emotional, or behavioral problems. Later in the evaluation, however, he reported that he was pre-scribed Ritalin but that he refused to take it. According to the Social History, John was prescribed Ritalin on February 29, 1996, but his mother "never picked up the medication." In addition, according to the Social History, John's mother "failed to follow through" with medical appointments and "medical recommendations for medication administration." The Social History also indicates that John "scored high on lead levels in his blood."

A review of John's medical and psychiatric records indicates that he has been evaluated by mental health professionals on several occasions. According to the Psychological Report from the School District of Pittsburgh, John was evaluated at the Pittsburgh Child Guidance Center in May of 1994. The Psychological Report indicates that John was diagnosed with Adjustment Disorder with Depression. On May 10, 1994, John was diagnosed with Major Depressive Disorder and possible lead poisoning. In addition, the psychiatrist recommended that John be hospitalized in a children's psychiatric hospital. John was also evaluated by a court psychologist on January 30, 1996. As part of the evaluation, John was administered the Slosson Intelligence Test-Revised. The results of the Slosson indicated that John was within the Low Average range of intellectual functioning (score of 83). Two recommendations were made as a result of the evaluation. Specifically, the evaluation stated that an "intensive remedial reading tutoring program is crucial to aid [John's] academic progress." In addition, it was recommended that John receive counseling for "family-related issues."

John was also evaluated on February 19, 1996, by a certified school psychologist with the District of Pittsburgh School System. As part of the evaluation, John was administered the WISC-III. John obtained a Full Scale IQ score of 69 on the WISC-III. It was also noted that John was previously administered the WISC-III in November of 1992. During that administration, John obtained a Full Scale IQ score of 73, which placed him in the Borderline range of intellectual functioning. John was also administered the WRAT-3, which produced the following results: Reading (kindergarten equivalent), Spelling (kindergarten equivalent), and Arithmetic (grade two equivalent). Finally, the results of the Connors Behavior

Rating Scale indicated that John obtained significant scores on the following scales: hyperactivity, conduct problem, emotional indulgence, asocial, and daydreaming-inattentive.

John was subsequently evaluated by a psychologist on July 2, 1998 (Wilderness Challenge Psychological Evaluation). As part of the evaluation, John was administered the WISC-III and the WRAT-3. John obtained a Full-Scale IQ score of 81 on the WISC-III, which placed him in the Low Average range of intellectual functioning. John obtained the following grade equivalence scores on the WRAT-3: Reading (grade 3 equivalent), Spelling (grade 3 equivalent), and Arithmetic (grade 3 equivalent). John was diagnosed with Attention-Deficit/Hyperactivity Disorder (combined type), Learning Disorder (not otherwise specified), and Dysthymia (childhood onset).

John was again evaluated by a psychiatrist on July 3, 1998 (Wilderness Challenge Psychiatric Evaluation). The evaluation was conducted to determine if John would benefit from a residential placement and/or placement in a sex offender's treatment program. John was diagnosed with Impulse Control Disorder (not otherwise specified) and Reading Disorder. The evaluator recommended that John be placed in a treatment program that can "address issues related to his sexual aggressivity."

John reported a limited history of substance abuse. John reported that he does not currently use drugs or alcohol, but that he has used marijuana in the past. John also reported that he smokes cigarettes. According to the Wilderness Challenge Psychological Evaluation, John is "unhappy that he has become addicted to cigarettes," and he expressed a desire to stop smoking. The Discharge Summary from Oakbrook indicates that John attended a Drug and Alcohol Educational Group on a weekly basis.

Due to John's age, there is no official employment history to report. John reported that he has never been officially employed, but that he has earned money by cleaning schools; he reported that the school janitors paid him to clean the school. When John was asked about his vocational goals, he reported that he would like to "build things." He reported that he is interested in construction and "fixing bikes." John also stated that he is interested in receiving job training after the disposition of his current charges.

According to the Juvenile History Inquiry, prior to John's arrest for the current charges on June 23, 1998, he was arrested on one other occasion. Specifically, the Juvenile History Inquiry indicates that John was arrested on October 25, 1995, and charged with Aggravated Assault (two counts), Simple Assault, and Recklessly Endangering Another Person. The Juvenile History Inquiry indicates that John was sent to the Baker House on February 12, 1996. The Wilderness Challenge Psychological Evaluation indicates that John attended Allen Middle School from the Baker House. John reported that he did not perform well at the Baker House because he "stopped going." According to the Wilderness Challenge Psychological Evaluation, John's mother "was not cooperating with Baker House, and John was described as a serious behavior problem at school." As a result, John was reportedly sent to the Oakbrook residential program on January 6, 1997. John reported that he performed much better at Oakbrook, adding that he received As and Bs. The Juvenile History Inquiry indicates that John was discharged from Oakbrook and placed in aftercare (Franciscan) on January 13, 1998. John is currently in the Wilderness Challenge Program. According to the Wilderness Challenge Psychiatric Evaluation, John reported that he was sent to Wilderness Challenge because he violated the terms of his probation.

CURRENT CLINICAL CONDITION

John presented as a short African-American male with a muscular build who appeared his stated age. He was casually dressed and well groomed when seen for the evaluation on 7-27-98, at the Pittsburgh Family Court (Juvenile Division), where he was seen for this evaluation. John was initially cooperative but somewhat reserved. He remained cooperative throughout the entire evaluation. He did, however, repeatedly question the evaluators regarding the length of the evaluation and the amount of time remaining in the evaluation. His speech was relatively clear, coherent, and relevant, although somewhat sparse; he did not respond at length to most questions without encouragement and further questioning. He appeared to give reasonable effort to the tasks involved. His capacity for attention and concentration appeared adequate. John did, however, appear visibly fatigued toward the end of the evaluation. It should also be noted that the evaluation was interrupted during the administration of the WISC-III when a court official requested that the evaluation be moved to another location within the building. Nevertheless, John was able to focus reasonably well on a series of tasks during the 5-hour evaluation without becoming visibly distracted. Therefore, it would appear that this evaluation provides a reasonably good estimate of John's current functioning.

His mood throughout the evaluation was largely neutral, and he showed little emotional variability. John was correctly oriented to time, place, and person. Overall level of intellectual functioning was formally measured with the WISC-III and was found to be in the Borderline range (Verbal IQ = 75, Performance IQ = 83, Full Scale IQ = 77). The results of the WISC-III appear to be generally consistent with the results of previous testing. Since John was administered this test within the last month, these results may reflect a "practice effect," resulting in somewhat higher scores than would otherwise be obtained. In addition, it should also be noted that administration of the WISC-III was interrupted for approximately 10 minutes when court personnel requested that the evaluation be completed in a different location within the building. Therefore, the last three subtests of the WISC-III were completed in a fairly noisy environment, possibly having a negative impact on John's performance on these subtests. John's basic academic skills, as measured by the WRAT-3, showed deficits in all three areas measured: Reading (grade 2 equivalent), Spelling (grade 1 equivalent), and Arithmetic (grade 3 equivalent). Each of these areas should be considered in need of remediation.

John did not report experiencing any perceptual disturbances (auditory or visual hallucinations) during the present evaluation, and his train of thought was clear and logical. John also did not report experiencing delusions (bizarre ideas with no possible basis in reality). On a structured inventory of symptoms of mental and emotional disorders specifically designed for use with adolescents (the MAYSI), John reported the presence of various symptoms. Some of the items endorsed by John involved trouble falling asleep, losing his temper easily, nervous or worried feelings that have kept him from doing what he wants to do, problems concentrating, enjoying fighting, being easily upset, thinking about getting back at someone he is angry at, being hyper, seeing things that other people do not see, having too many bad moods, feeling lonely, other people controlling his thoughts, feeling angry, feeling that he cannot do anything right, getting frustrated easily, difficulty feeling close to people outside of his family, breaking something on purpose because he was mad, people talking about him when he is not there, and giving up hope for his life.

John reported that he has had difficulty falling asleep while at Wilderness Challenge. He reported that he will occasionally "stay up all night . . . and do pushups." John reported that he loses his temper when he thinks about his family. He also reported, however, that he tries to "calm it down" so that he will not "say things I don't want to say." John reported that he is worried about his sisters, which often keeps him from doing what he wants to do. John stated that he has difficulty concentrating and listening to teachers because "I can't read well," adding that he gets "fed up" when he tries to read. John reported that he "sometimes" enjoys fighting. He also reported that he will occasionally "mess with people when I'm bored." John reported that he gets easily upset when people talk about his family. John reported that he will occasionally think about getting back at someone he is angry at, adding that he would like to "holler at them . . . push them." John reported that he gets "hyper" in the morning after he eats sugar. John reported that he occasionally sees things that other people do not see. When questioned further, John reported that he sees "stuff jumping around . . . a flash in my eyes." John reported that he has had too many bad moods during the past month, noting that he gets in a bad mood when he is frustrated. John stated that he feels lonely because "I am by myself . . . I miss my brother." John said that other people have been able to control his thoughts.

When questioned further, John reported that "the Devil makes me say one thing, and God makes me say another." John indicated that he gets angry when "people say things about my sisters [and] brother." He also reported that he often feels as if he cannot do anything right. When questioned further, John stated he sometimes feels that he does not "do things good enough for people, so I don't do it." John stated that he gets easily frustrated when he does not know about the condition of his sisters. He said that he has difficulty feeling close to people outside of his family because he "can't share things with people." John reported that he has occasionally broken things on purpose when he was mad. When questioned further, he replied that he has broken windows and bicycles because "I don't know what else to do." John reported that he believes that his family and friends talk about him when he is not there. He reported that his friends talk about him because he has "never been locked up before." John reported that he has given up hope for his life because he "always had a messed up family." John also stated, however, that he does not think about hurting himself or committing suicide.

As part of this evaluation, John was screened for the presence of Attention-Deficit/Hyperactivity Disorder (ADHD). Based on behavioral observations made by the evaluators, John's self-report, and information contained in various documents, it appears likely that John meets the criteria for ADHD. This is consistent with the results of a previous mental health evaluation in which John was diagnosed with ADHD. Specifically, John was recently diagnosed with ADHD (combined type) on 7-2-98 (Wilderness Challenge Psychological Evaluation). In addition, according to the Social History, John was prescribed Ritalin on February 29, 1996, but his mother "never picked up the medication." Therefore, although further observation and evaluation may be warranted, it appears that John may need medical intervention to treat the symptoms of this disorder.

COMPETENCE TO STAND TRIAL

John was first asked about the nature of his charges. John reported that he has been charged with "rape." This is consistent with the information contained in the Juvenile History Inquiry, which indicates that John is currently charged with rape and related offenses. When John was asked if he was charged with any other offenses, he reported that "I asked her [his social worker], but I didn't understand her." John was unable to state whether rape was a felony or a misdemeanor. In addition, John reported that he did not know the difference between a felony and a misdemeanor. At this point in the evaluation, the difference between a felony and a misdemeanor was explained to John. When John was questioned about the difference between a felony and a misdemeanor later in the evaluation (about 25 minutes after first being asked about the difference), he reported that a "felony is worse than a misdemeanor."

John was then asked about the possible penalties that could result from a conviction for his charges. John reported that he is not sure of the possible penalties, but that he could be sentenced to "about 3 years . . . in a juvenile facility." John reported that the longest sentence that he could receive if convicted is "juvenile life . . . up to 8 years." John also said that he could only be held in the juvenile system until he was 21 years old. John reported that he would probably receive a maximum sentence of 5 years if convicted because "I'm a juvenile." It would appear, therefore, that John understands that he has been charged with an offense and could be incarcerated if he is convicted. Moreover, John appears to understand the distinction between juvenile commitment (up to age 21) and adult incarceration.

Following this, John was asked to describe the respective roles of the judge, prosecutor, and defense attorney in the adversarial context. John responded that the judge's job is to "find me guilty and put me away." He also reported that the judge will "find out if I'm a good person or a bad person, and if I'm telling the truth." John reported that the defense attorney's job is to "get rid of the case as much as he can." Finally, John said that the role of the prosecutor is "to put me away," but he was not sure how the prosecutor would accomplish this task. On further questioning, John reported that the prosecutor "would be happy if they find me guilty." Therefore, John's overall understanding and description of the respective roles of the judge, prosecutor, and defense attorney in the adversarial context appears to be limited but reasonably accurate.

John was also questioned about appropriate courtroom demeanor. When John was asked how he would behave in court, he reported that he would "respond to the questions . . . explain myself." He also stated, however, that he is "tired of talking about" his current charges. When John was asked about how he would respond to the judge, he responded that he would answer any questions asked by the judge. He also reported, however, that he "won't answer if the judge asks mean." When John was asked what he would do if a witness made a mistake or lied while testifying, he stated that "there is nothing I can do . . . I'm already locked up." On further questioning, John reported that if a witness lied while testifying he would "speak up for myself . . . say it's a lie." John reported that he would tell the judge if a witness lied. When John was asked to explain the meaning of "testify," he replied that it means to "speak up for myself." He reported, however, that he does not want to testify because "no one believes me." John reported that he is not sure if he would be able to testify on his own behalf, but he was unable to provide any reasons for that belief.

John had difficulty identifying any possible pleas. When first questioned, John was unable to identify any pleas. After further questioning, however, John identified one possible plea: guilty. When John was asked to explain the meaning of a guilty plea, he reported that a guilty plea means that "I did the crime." John was unable to state what rights are waived by entering a guilty plea. At this point in the evaluation, it was explained to John that pleading guilty results in the waiver of the following rights: right to remain silent, right to an appeal, and right to be represented by an attorney. When John was subsequently asked about the consequences of pleading guilty later in the evaluation, he was able to recall two of the three rights that are waived by pleading guilty.

When John was asked about the meaning of a not guilty plea, he reported that it means "I didn't do it . . . what they're saying about me is not true." Two other possible pleas, "not guilty by reason of insanity" and "no contest," were described to John. John was unable to explain the meaning of those pleas when first questioned about them. John was also unable to explain the meaning of a "plea bargain." He did, however, discuss various "deals" that have reportedly been mentioned to him.

Finally, John was asked about his plea preference. When first questioned about his plea preference, John reported that he "won't plead guilty, won't plead not guilty." John also indicated that he is not interested in "deals." When questioned further, John expressed apprehension about the possibility of being sent to an out-of-state program that has reportedly been discussed with him. In addition, John was very clear on what he does and does not want. Specifically, he reported that he does not want a long sentence and does not want to be out of state. He also stated that he would rather perform community service than be incarcerated. Finally, John reported that he would like to be in a program where he could learn how to read because "that's my main problem."

It would appear, therefore, that John's overall capacity to assist counsel in his own defense is somewhat limited. Although it appears that John has a basic understanding of the relevant aspects of the adjudicatory process, he also has some specific deficits that may interfere with his capacity to assist counsel in his own defense. These deficits include intellectual deficits (with particularly relevant deficits in vocabulary and short-term memory), difficulty with attention/concentration, and limited frustration tolerance. It also appears that John becomes easily confused by written material and long questions, with the latter area being particularly relevant if John is asked to testify on his own behalf. It is possible, however, that these deficits would not prevent John from assisting counsel in his own defense if relevant information could be provided to him in simple language and at different times, thereby helping him to understand and process the information.

CONCLUSIONS

In the opinion of the undersigned, based on all of the above, John appears to have a basic understanding of his current legal situation and a more limited ability to assist counsel in his own defense.

Thank you for the opportunity to evaluate John Doe.

David DeMatteo
MCP Hahnemann Graduate Student

Kirk Heilbrun, Ph.D.
Consulting Psychologist

Geff Marczyk, M.S., M.A.
MCP Hahnemann Graduate Student

Teaching Point: What constitutes "good enough" testing conditions?

It is unlikely that an evaluator will consistently encounter quiet, private, and distraction-free evaluation environments in conducting FMHA. The question then becomes whether conditions should be considered marginal but acceptable, or unacceptable. In the present case, the evaluation began in an ideal setting: a private area that virtually eliminated distractions. In criminal and juvenile forensic evaluations, these are nearly ideal conditions. Fortunately, the evaluators were able to complete the clinical interview and other sensitive information gathering in this environment. After the evaluation was moved to the holding area, the conditions became marginal; there was limited privacy and a significant amount of distraction. These conditions might have been unacceptable if the clinical interview and historical information collection had not been completed earlier in the evaluation when there was privacy and few distractions. Given that partitioned space was available, and only three subtests of the WISC-III remained, these marginal conditions did not, in our judgment, become unacceptable. Marginal conditions generally offer some privacy and limits on distraction; a significant compromising of either area would make conditions unacceptable. It should be noted that we are considering "freedom from distraction" broadly to encompass factors such as lighting, temperature, comfort of the chair, and other influences that could adversely affect concentration and performance when they are not minimally adequate. If partitioned space had not been available, even completion of the WISC-III would have been impossible, as this adolescent was tired and showing problems consistent with ADHD.

Note

1. The GCCT and the MacCAT-CA were unmodified because any juvenile over age 7 charged with first-degree criminal sexual conduct is eligible for waiver to adult court in South Carolina.

Chapter 10

Juvenile Waiver and Reverse Waiver

FMHA on juvenile offenders charged in the adult criminal justice system is the focus of the two reports in this chapter. The principle applied to the first case concerns assessing legally relevant behavior, and how this information can be used to aid the court in accurate decision making. The teaching point in the first case highlights the importance of translating legal criteria into forensic capacities, and the value of providing data and reasoning that are directly relevant to forensic capacities and the corresponding legal question. The principle associated with the second case in this chapter—using third-party information to assess response style—discusses how a variety of collateral sources of information can be used to assess the accuracy of self-report information provided in an evaluation. The teaching point in the second case includes a discussion of how to balance the results of psychological testing, self-report, and third-party collateral information as it relates to response style.

Case 1

Principle: Assess legally relevant behavior

This principle addresses the importance of gathering information that is directly related to the forensic issue(s), and more generally, relevant to the legal question being addressed by the court. A forensic assessment must obtain information that clearly describes capacities relevant to the forensic issue(s) being assessed. Depending on the nature of the forensic issues and the functioning of the individual being evaluated, information regarding the capacities in question can be obtained from a variety of sources, including clinical interview, behavioral observation, self-report, collateral interviews, collateral document review, and psychological testing.

Data from these sources can be particularly applicable to relevant legal behavior under certain conditions. First, when such data are gathered while considering the relevant legal capacities, they are more applicable than broader diagnostic or treatment-planning data. Relevant legal behavior in a case involving the defendant's competence to stand trial, for example, would be considerably different from relevant legal behavior when the legal question is guardianship. Second, this kind of approach has the additional advantage of excluding data that would be clearly irrelevant to the legal capacities being assessed. Third, a focus on the relevant legal issue(s) allows the evaluator to use both observable behavior and inferred capacities, and to relate each to the forensic issues through reasoning that is explicitly described in the report. Finally, gathering data on legally relevant behavior and capacities contributes to the accuracy and credibility of the evaluation by providing information to the legal decision maker in a manner that is more readily understandable and more easily applied to the legal question(s).

FMHA should provide data and reasoning that are directly relevant to forensic capacities and to the legal question. However, the evaluator should keep in mind the distinction between the decision-making role of the court and the "providing information and making recommendations" function of the forensic clinician, so that the communication in the report or testimony is not intrusive. Sufficient data should also be gathered, in a way that promotes confidence in its accuracy, to yield conclusions that seem reasonable and well supported.

In the present case, the legal question is *decertification* (reverse waiver) of a juvenile who has been initially charged in criminal court. Under applicable Pennsylvania law (42 Pa. C.S.A. §6355), a juvenile who is between the ages of 14 and 17 (inclusive) can be automatically charged in the adult criminal system if arrested for a certain (very serious) kind of offense. Section 6355 allows the court to consider the following factors in deciding whether a juvenile initially charged as an adult should be decertified:

1. the impact of the offense on the victim or victims,
2. the impact of the offense on the community,
3. the threat to safety of the public or any individual posed by the child,
4. the nature and circumstances of the offense allegedly committed by the child,
5. the degree of the child's culpability,
6. the adequacy and duration of dispositional alternatives available under Pennsylvania law applicable to juveniles in the adult criminal justice system, and
7. whether the child is amenable to treatment, supervision, or rehabilitation as a juvenile.

In weighing the last factor, the court may further consider the following: the individual's (1) age, (2) mental capacity, and (3) maturity; (4) the degree of criminal sophistication exhibited by the child; (5) previous records, if any; (6) the nature and extent of any prior delinquent history, including the success or failure of any previous attempts by the juvenile court to rehabilitate the child; (7) whether the child can be rehabilitated prior to the expiration of the juvenile court jurisdiction; (8) probation or institutional reports, if any, (9) any other relevant factors; and (10) whether there are reasonable grounds to believe that the child is not committable to an institution for the mentally retarded or mentally ill.

The forensic evaluation in such cases is conducted to provide the court with information and guidance on the factors that are not issues of fact or judgments beyond the scope of clinical forensic expertise. Many of the factors just described are, indeed, issues of fact (e.g., age) or questions beyond the scope of clinical forensic expertise (e.g., the impact of the offense on the community), and therefore not an appropriate part of a decertification FMHA. Although these factors are not "assessed" in a decertification FMHA, information in these areas is important for the assessment of legally relevant capacities and behavior that are addressed by the evaluation.

In this case, the relevant legal behaviors and capacities can be identified in part from the statute: the threat to public safety or any individual posed by the child, the adequacy and duration of dispositional alternatives, whether the child is amenable to treatment or rehabilitation, mental capacity, maturity, criminal sophistication, and any other relevant factors. The evaluator then faces the challenge of operationalizing these legally relevant domains into criteria that can be assessed. In this report, the evaluators do this by framing the referral question as follows: "A request for a mental health evaluation to provide the defense with information relevant to John's treatment needs and amenability in the context of public safety, pursuant to Pennsylvania Code, was made by John's attorney." More specifically, the legally relevant forensic issues were identified as risk assessment for reoffending, treatment/rehabilitation needs, and amenability to treatment/rehabilitation. The next step was to identify the legally relevant behaviors and capacities for these areas.

There are a variety of risk factors for reoffending that can be assessed when in a juvenile population. The evaluation considered risk factors in the following domains: family, school, medical, mental health, substance abuse, employment, and peers. The circumstances of the current alleged offenses, as well as history of arrests and previous rehabilitation attempts, were also important to consider.

In the current evaluation, historical information collected across these domains suggested the presence of a number of active risk factors. These included impulsive aggression, poor judgment and decision-making skills, special education involvement and academic difficulties (including truancy), emotional disturbance and Attention-Deficit/Hyperactivity Disorder (ADHD), substance abuse, limited vocational goals, involvement with negative peers, a prior arrest on drug charges, and a history of only partially successful placements in the juvenile system.

The clinical interview and psychological testing allowed the evaluators to assess John's current level of functioning related to each of these capacities. For example, John's scores on the Wide Range Achievement Test, 3rd edition (WRAT-3), showed significant deficits in reading, spelling, and arithmetic. On the Massachusetts Youth Screening Inventory (MAYSI), John reported the presence of auditory hallucinations, suicidal ideation, substance abuse, and anger problems. The Minnesota Multiphasic Personality Inventory-Adolescent version (MMPI-A) suggested interpersonal difficulties, anxiety, personality characteristics associated with substance abuse, and the presence of strange thoughts, experiences, and behaviors. Finally, a structured screening for ADHD, based on DSM-IV diagnostic criteria and including input from collateral sources, self-report, and behavioral observations, indicated that John met criteria for ADHD at the time of the evaluation.

The statutory language in this case also calls for the assessment of treatment needs and amenability. John appeared to have five areas of treatment/rehabilitation needs that, if addressed, should result in reducing his risk for antisocial behavior. These areas included the following: (1) treatment for substance abuse; (2) continued education and training in educational and vocational areas; (3) training in anger control, impulse control, and decision-making/problem-solving skills; (4) the development of more positive peer relationships; and (5) ongoing monitoring and periodic evaluation of his mental health needs, including further evaluation for the possible presence of ADHD. These treatment needs were identified as particularly important in reducing the risk factors documented in the FMHA.

Finally, the statute cites the issue of amenability to treatment in such cases. Amenability to future interventions can itself be considered as the capacity to respond favorably to risk-reducing interventions. In this case, John's reoffense risk (relative to that of other juveniles of his age) was estimated as moderate to high because of his history and the number of active risk factors that he was experiencing at the time of the evaluation. His amenability to treatment, or capacity to respond to treatment, was described as "mixed," based primarily on information obtained from past interventions and placements, as well as his risk factors and the results of the clinical interview and psychological testing. By using multiple sources of historical and diagnostic information, the evaluators were able to assess relevant capacities related to risk and provide an estimate of the level of risk that the individual presented for future antisocial behavior leading to rearrest. Finally, after evaluating these capacities in the context of risk and treatment needs and amenability, the evaluators made a recommendation regarding the general parameters of a placement that would be needed to deliver such interventions, and presented a conclusion about whether (in light of his estimated risk, rehabilitation needs and amenability, and the nature and availability of placements in the juvenile system) John's needs could be addressed in the juvenile system.

FORENSIC EVALUATION

March 2, 1999
Re: John D
P.P. # 123456

REFERRAL

John D is an 18-year-old Hispanic male (DOB: 2-18-81) who is currently charged with Robbery, Aggravated Assault, Carrying Firearms Without a License, Carrying Firearms in a Public Street/Place, Theft (unlawful taking/disposition), Theft (receiving stolen property), Possession of an Instrument of Crime, Terroristic Threats, Simple Assault, and Recklessly Endangering Another Person. He was 17 years old at the time of these offenses, which allegedly occurred on 12-15-98. He has been charged directly in adult court. A request for a mental health evaluation to provide the defense with information relevant to John's treatment needs and amenability in the context of public safety, pursuant to Pennsylvania Code, was made by John's attorney.

PROCEDURES

John was evaluated for approximately 3 hours on 2-23-99. In addition to a clinical interview, John was administered a structured screening instrument for adolescent symptoms of mental and emotional disorder (the Massachusetts Youth Screening Inventory, or MAYSI), a standard test of current functioning in relevant academic areas (the Wide Range Achievement Test, 3rd edition, or WRAT-3), and a standard objective test of mental and emotional functioning in adolescents (the Minnesota Multiphasic Personality Inventory, Adolescent version, or MMPI-A). The following documents, obtained from John's attorney, were reviewed as part of this evaluation:

1. Social Summary (2-18-99),
2. Criminal Complaint (10-24-98),
3. First Judicial District of Pennsylvania Pretrial Services Investigation Report,
4. Juvenile History Inquiry (2-18-99),
5. Closing Statement from the Center for Early Childhood Services (8-87),
6. Psychological Summary (1-6-97),
7. Psychological Summary (8-25-98),
8. Psychological Evaluation (9-25-89),
9. Mountain Valley School Initial Psychiatric Evaluation (9-25-89),
10. Academic and Attendance History Profile (11-3-98),
11. Various documents from the Center for Early Childhood Services,
12. Department of Human Services Case Record,
13. Various documents from the Children's Center,
14. Mountain Valley School Social Service Summary (12-19-89),
15. Various documents from Latino Community Services, and
16. Transcript from the Municipal Court of Philadelphia (dated 11-2-98).

Prior to the evaluation, John was notified about the purpose of the evaluation and the associated limits on confidentiality. He appeared to understand the basic purpose of the evaluation, reporting back his understanding that he would be evaluated and that a written report would be submitted to his attorney. He understood that the report could be used in a decertification hearing, and if it were, copies would be provided to the prosecution and the court.

RELEVANT HISTORY

Historical information was obtained from the collateral sources described above, as well as from John himself. We attempted to assess the consistency of factual information across multiple sources. If additional collateral information is obtained prior to John's court date, a supplemental report will be filed.

John D was born to Mr. and Mrs. D. John reported that his parents are "not married by law," but that they have a common-law marriage. According to the Social Summary, John has one sister and two brothers. John reported that he and his siblings were born in Philadelphia, but that his parents were born in Puerto Rico. John stated that he was primarily raised by his parents. He also reported, however, that he lived in five foster homes and one residential facility between the ages of 6 and 9. When John was questioned further about the reason for his placements, he reported that he was placed in foster homes because "I went crazy . . . insane." According to the Social Summary, the D family was initially referred to the Department of Human Services (DHS) in December of 1986. The Social Summary indicates that on April 24, 1997, DHS filed a dependent petition regarding John and his siblings, requesting that they be adjudicated dependent and placed under DHS supervision due to their living conditions. As a result, the children were placed in a foster home on November 5, 1987, and they remained in the foster home until March 1988, when DHS was notified that the foster parent was relocating to California. According to the Social Summary, John was placed in another foster home on January 9, 1989. The Social Summary indicates that John was subsequently transferred to another foster home on January 13, 1989, because there was limited space in the previous foster home. According to the Social Summary, John's foster mother requested his removal in early 1989 because of his "behavioral difficulties." The Social Summary indicates that John was eventually placed at the Mountain Valley Diagnostic and Evaluation Center on September 25, 1989. John reported that he spent about a year at Mountain Valley.

John reported that he has a "great" relationship with all of the members of his immediate family, and he reported that his mother and father are supportive and helpful. According to the Social Summary, John's mother cannot read or write (English or Spanish), and she reportedly suffers from various medical problems, including diabetes. The Social Summary indicates that John's father is unable to work because of "problems with his legs," and, as a result, the primary financial support for the family comes from the Supplemental Security Income checks that both parents receive. John denied being physically, sexually, or emotionally abused while growing up. John reported that he is currently living with his fiancée and her family. John stated that he does so because he is "trying to stay away from North Philly." The Social Summary indicates that the D family lives in a "drug-infested, crime-ridden neighborhood in North Philadelphia." According to John, he and his fiancée have been together for about 3 years. John stated that his fiancée is about 9 months pregnant. John noted that he sees his family about three times a week.

When John was asked about his educational background, he reported that he completed eighth grade at the Jose Valdez Bilingual School. The Academic History Profile indicates that John completed eighth grade in 1994. John reported that he stopped attending school during ninth grade at Thomas Jefferson High School because "I didn't like it." According to John, he is currently working toward obtaining his General Equivalency Diploma (GED). John reported that he attended the following schools: George Washington Elementary School, Anson Hill School, Jonathan Goldman Institute, Mountain Valley, Thomas A. Jefferson High School, and the Jose Valdez Bilingual School. John was unable to remember which grades he attended at each school. According to the Social Summary, John was also enrolled in the Center for Early Childhood Services when he was 5 years old. The Attendance History Profile indicates that John's current enrollment status with the school district is listed as "withdrawn." John reported that his attendance was "great" but that he missed school during ninth grade at Jefferson High School. An examination of the Attendance History Profile, however, reveals the following. During the 1991–1992 academic year, John had 20 unexcused absences and was late on 1 occasion. In the next (1992–1993) academic year, John had 42 unexcused absences and was late on 12 occasions. During the 1993–1994 academic year, John had 4 unexcused absences, 23 excused absences, and was late on 9 occasions. In the 1994–1995 academic year, John had 164 unexcused absences and was late on 2 occasions. During the 1995–1996 academic year, John had 83 unexcused absences and was late on 1 occasion. Severe problems with attendance continued in the 1996–1997 academic year, as John had 175 unexcused absences. Finally, during the 1997–1998 academic year, John had 78 unexcused absences. When John was asked about his academic performance, he reported that his grades were "good until eighth grade." According to the Academic History Profile, John received all Fs during ninth grade (1995–1996 academic year). The Academic History Profile indicates that John has earned one credit (out of a total of 21.5 credits in required subject areas) toward his high school diploma. According to John, he often experienced difficulty concentrating and paying attention while in school. John reported that he was prescribed Ritalin "to calm me down," but that he stopped taking it because it was not having any positive effects. John also noted that he was enrolled in special education classes (at the Jonathan Goldman Institute) during part of his education. John reported that he occasionally got in trouble for behavioral problems while in school. Specifically, John reported that he had been suspended many times for reasons such as cutting classes, disrupting class, and getting "smart" with the teachers. John stated that he was never suspended for fighting, however. According to the Attendance History Profile, John was suspended six times between 1992 and 1998, three times during the 1992–1993 academic year, twice during the 1993–1994 academic year, and once during the 1994–1995 academic year. The Attendance History Profile indicates that John was suspended for disruption of school, repeated school violations, and damage/destruction/theft of school property. John reported that he was never expelled from school.

John reported that he does not currently suffer from any serious medical problems and that he has never had any serious illnesses. When John was asked about serious injuries, he reported that he was "knocked out for about 5 seconds" when he was 10 years old, and he noted that he never received medical attention for his injury. John stated that he has never been hospitalized for any reason. John also reported that he has had three seizures, two at age 10 and one at age 17. John stated that he does not know the precise cause of the seizures, but he suggested that the first seizure may have been related to his head injury and that the last seizure may have been related to his drug use. John reported that he has never received medical attention for the seizures.

According to John and the Social Summary, John has had contact with mental health professionals on various occasions. John reported that he has participated in therapy and court-ordered evaluations at various times throughout his life. He attributed the initiation of contact with mental health professionals to his "nerves." John noted that he was prescribed Ritalin when he was about 10 years old, but that he stopped taking it after 6 months because it "wasn't working." John denied ever receiving a diagnosis of any type. John's first formal evaluation occurred at the Center for Early Childhood Services. The report indicates that John was referred for evaluation because his parents complained that he is "overly active, does not listen, is uncontrollable, and is excessively aggressive toward family members." The report concluded that "John is a boy of at least average intelligence who has attention problems and mild visual-motor impairment, in addition to problems regulating his emotional responses to overwhelming family problems and school demands." John's next evaluation occurred at the Children's Center on July 16, 1989. The evaluator noted that "John has a history of traumatic experiences" and that "he has suffered physical as well as sexual abuse." It should be noted that John denied being physically or sexually abused. The evaluator offered a diagnostic impression of Adjustment Disorder (with mixed disturbance of emotions and conduct). John was

also evaluated on September 25, 1989, at the Mountain Valley School. According to the Mountain Valley School Initial Psychiatric Evaluation ("Psychiatric Evaluation"), John was referred for evaluation because of behavior problems, including fighting and suspensions from school. The Psychiatric Evaluation indicates that during one of John's foster home placements, he began "hallucinating, hearing voices, stating he was superman, [and] jumping out of windows." The Psychiatric Evaluation also indicates that John was once "found in the corner with no clothes on, cutting sheets into pieces." John also reportedly refused to eat for 3 weeks after being called "fat" by another child. The evaluator diagnosed John with Adjustment Disorder with Disturbance of Conduct. John was also evaluated on December 18, 1989, at the Mountain Valley School's Diagnostic and Evaluation Program due to "neglect, longstanding behavioral problems, unsuccessful foster placements, and school maladjustment." The report indicates that John obtained a Full Scale IQ score of 88 on the Wechsler Intelligence Scale for Children-Revised (WISC-R). The report concluded that "John is experiencing difficulty in several areas of his life" and that the "presence of a learning disability as well as environmental deprivation and behavioral difficulties have hindered [him] from achieving his full potential."

As a result of John's entry into the juvenile court system in 1996, he was ordered to undergo a psychological evaluation on January 6, 1997. The report indicates that John had been previously diagnosed "as being hyperactive with emotional and behavioral problems" and that he was "given medication to control the hyperactivity when it was diagnosed." According to the report, John admitted to a history of suicidal ideation at the age of six. The report indicates that John obtained a third-grade reading score on the WRAT-3. John's most recent evaluation was conducted on August 25, 1998. The evaluator concluded that John "tends to act impulsively, aggressively, and even explosively" when he is angry or under stress.

John reported a significant history of substance abuse. According to John, he has tried marijuana, Xanax, PCP, and alcohol. John reported that he first tried marijuana when he was

13 years old and that he used it "every day" from age 13 until the day he was arrested for the current charges. John stated that he normally smoked "about 12 blunts" on a daily basis with his friends. John also reported that he used Xanax from age 14 or 15 until age 17. He stated that he used Xanax about three times a week, adding that he took about five pills each time. John reported that he stopped using Xanax because he had a seizure, which he attributed to his use of Xanax. John also reported that he tried PCP on one occasion. When John was asked about his use of alcohol, he reported that he used alcohol two or three times a week from age 13 until age 17. In addition, John admitted to involvement in selling drugs, generally "weed" but also "crack" (cocaine) on two occasions. He said that he spent the money he made from selling drugs on clothes and drugs for his own use. John stated that he received treatment for his substance abuse problem on one occasion. Specifically, he reported that he received substance abuse treatment at Latino Community Services, a community-based day treatment program. John stated that he attended Latino for about 5 months until he was removed from the program for violating the rules. John reported that the treatment was helpful because "you can't go with dirty urines." Although John denied having a substance abuse problem at the present time, he reported that he is interested in receiving substance abuse treatment because he wants to "prove to the judge that I changed my life."

Despite his young age, John reported a fairly significant employment history. Specifically, John noted that he has had about six jobs since he began working, including landscaping, working at a sneaker store, and working at a Value Plus store. John reported that he is currently employed as a dishwasher at a luncheonette, where he has worked about 20 hours a week for the past 2 months. When John was asked about his vocational goals, he reported that he would like to obtain a "biological job" at a hospital. He also expressed a strong desire to attend college and receive job training for employment opportunities "related to hospitals."

According to John and the Juvenile History Inquiry, prior to John's arrest for the current charges on October 20, 1998, he had been arrested on one other occasion. The Juvenile His-

tory Inquiry indicates that John was arrested on December 18, 1996, and charged with delivery of a controlled substance, possession with intent to deliver a controlled substance, knowledge and possession of a controlled substance, and criminal conspiracy. When John was asked about this incident, he reported that he was arrested for "selling drugs to an undercover cop." The Social Summary indicates that John was placed on electronic monitoring prior to being adjudicated. According to the Social Summary, John remained on electronic monitoring until March 6, 1997, when he was adjudicated delinquent on the charge of possession with intent to deliver. John reported that he was placed on probation for 2 years. According to John and the Juvenile History Inquiry, John violated his probation on two occasions, resulting in the issuance of two bench warrants. The Social Summary indicates that John was mandated to attend Latino Community Services, where he reportedly adjusted well initially. John reported that he attended Latino for about 5 months, until being removed from the program. According to the Social Summary, it was also ordered that John be referred to the De La Salle Vocational School, which is a component of the Saint Gabriel's System. According to the Social Summary, John's probation officer ordered John to undergo periodic drug testing beginning in September of 1997. The Social Summary indicates that John tested positive for drugs on a number of occasions between September of 1997 and January of 1998, and as a result, John's probation officer began to refer John to residential treatment programs. The Social Summary indicates that John was rejected from several residential treatment programs until finally being accepted at the Summit Academy on September 11, 1998. John was rejected from one residential treatment facility (VisionQuest) because he had too many "psychological issues" and a "history of assaulting staff and aggressive behavior." According to the Social Summary, on October 13, 1998, John was discharged from the December 1996 petition without further jurisdictional restraint.

CURRENT CLINICAL CONDITION

John presented as a Hispanic male of average height and muscular build who appeared his stated age. He was casually dressed and well-groomed when seen for the evaluation on 2-23-99 at MCP Hahnemann University. Initially, he was cooperative and polite, although somewhat reserved. He remained cooperative and polite throughout the entire evaluation. His speech was relatively clear, coherent, and relevant. He appeared to give reasonable effort to the tasks involved. His capacity for attention and concentration appeared adequate, and he was able to focus reasonably well on a series of tasks during the 3-hour evaluation without becoming visibly distracted. Therefore, it would appear that this evaluation provides a reasonably good estimate of John's current functioning.

His mood throughout the evaluation was largely subdued and neutral, and he showed little emotional variability. John was correctly oriented to time, place, and person. Overall level of intellectual functioning was not formally measured, but appeared to be in the Borderline to Low Average range. John's basic academic skills, as measured by the WRAT-3, showed significant deficits in all three areas measured: Reading (grade 4 equivalent), Spelling (grade 2 equivalent), and Arithmetic (grade 4 equivalent). Each of these areas should be considered in need of remediation.

During the present evaluation, John did not report experiencing any perceptual disturbances (auditory or visual hallucinations), and his train of thought was clear and logical. John reported, however, that he occasionally "hear[s] things." When questioned further, John reported that he has heard "voices calling my name" on about three occasions, but he added that this has not happened for about 2 years. John did not report experiencing delusions (bizarre ideas with no possible basis in reality). On a structured inventory of symptoms of mental and emotional disorders specifically designed for use with adolescents (the MAYSI), John reported the presence of various symptoms. Some of the items endorsed by John involved difficulty falling asleep, wishing he was dead, feeling like life was not worth living, hearing voices, having some part of his body always hurt him, feeling like killing himself, substance abuse, feeling like he does not have fun with his friends anymore, feeling that he cannot do anything right, being mad, people talking about him when he is not there, having something bad or

terrifying happen to him, being in danger of getting badly hurt or killed, and seeing someone get severely injured.

John reported that he has had difficulty falling asleep since he was a child. John stated that he was prescribed medication for his sleep difficulties when he was younger, but he was unable to provide additional information concerning the medication. John reported that he thought about committing suicide when he was 9 years old. Although he was unable to describe the reasons for thinking about suicide, he reported that he occasionally felt life was not worth living. When questioned further, John stated that he attempted suicide by choking himself at the age of 9. He reported, however, that he does not currently think about suicide. John reported that he previously "heard voices calling my name" on three separate occasions. John stated that he suffers from migraine headaches "almost everyday." John endorsed various items dealing with substance abuse. Specifically, John reported that he was high both times he was arrested. He also reported that he has occasionally used alcohol and drugs at the same time. John stated that he only spends time with his fiancée because his friends "sell drugs" and he does not have fun with them anymore. John reported that he occasionally feels like he cannot do anything right when he is at work because "my boss is tough." John reported that he when he gets mad, he usually stays mad for a long time, and he added that he usually gets mad "over stupid stuff." When John was asked about terrifying things that have happened to him, he reported that he has been "stuck up" six or seven times, and that someone shot at him when he was 13 years old. Finally, John reported that he saw about four people get severely injured during a "shootout."

John responded to the items on the MMPI-A in a cooperative manner that produced a valid profile and probably a reasonably good basis for describing his current functioning. Individuals with such profiles (Welsh Code: 0-182/467 93:5# LFK/) are often described as being somewhat shy, with some social anxiety and inhibitions. These individuals are often described as being hypersensitive about what other people think of them, and they are occasionally concerned about their relationships with other people. Additionally, these individuals are often inhibited in personal relationships and social situations, and they may try to avoid crowds, parties, and other social activities. Individuals with such profiles may experience difficulty expressing their feelings toward other people. John endorsed various items suggesting that he finds it difficult to be around other people, preferring to be alone. He also reported that he frequently avoids situations where there are likely to be a lot of people. In addition, John reported that he has difficulty making friends and does not like to meet new people. John reported several strange thoughts, experiences, and behaviors, which may include hallucinations, persecutory ideas, or feelings of being controlled by other people. John also endorsed items suggesting that he may be worried that something is wrong with his mind. John's score on one of the MMPI-A special scales (the MAC-R) suggests that he has some personality or behavioral characteristics associated with substance abuse, including risk-taking behaviors and the desire to be the center of attention. Finally, John endorsed items suggesting that he has a desire to succeed in life, which may be an asset to build on in any subsequent treatment/rehabilitation program.

As part of this evaluation, John was screened for the presence of Attention-Deficit/Hyperactivity Disorder (ADHD). Based on behavioral observations made by the evaluators and John's self-report, it appears likely that John meets the criteria for ADHD. Nevertheless, further observation and evaluation is warranted. Although John was not sure if he was ever formally diagnosed with ADHD, he reported that he was prescribed Ritalin when he was younger. Accordingly, after the disposition of his current charges, John should be formally evaluated for the presence of ADHD, and it should be determined whether he needs medical intervention to treat the symptoms of this disorder.

TREATMENT NEEDS AND AMENABILITY

There are five areas in which John has treatment/rehabilitation needs that, if addressed, should serve to reduce his risk for future antisocial behavior. These areas include treatment for substance abuse; continued education and training in educational and vocational areas; training in anger control, impulse control, and decision-making/problem-solving skills; the development of more positive peer relationships; and ongoing monitoring and periodic evaluation of his mental health needs, including further evaluation for the possible presence of ADHD.

First, John has treatment/rehabilitation needs in the area of substance abuse. John reported a significant history of substance abuse beginning when he was about 13 years old. In addition, John endorsed several items on the MAYSI linking the use of drugs to interpersonal and behavioral problems. Furthermore, John reported that he was high both times he was arrested. In addition, according to the Juvenile History Inquiry, John was arrested on drug-related charges in 1996. Moreover, John's MMPI-A profile suggests that he may have personality or behavioral characteristics that are associated with substance abuse. John also reported that he engaged in the sale of drugs for about 4 years. Therefore, treatment for substance abuse would probably have significant risk reduction value for John's risk of engaging in future antisocial behavior. This area may be especially important because John denied having a substance abuse problem at present. This is a fairly common attitude among individuals who have problems in this area, but it can be modified once the individual becomes involved in rehabilitative activities. Although John denied having a substance abuse problem, he reported that he is interested in receiving substance abuse treatment "to prove . . . that I changed my life." Given the length and severity of John's substance abuse problem, he would particularly benefit from a treatment plan that includes relapse prevention strategies, such as the use of periodic monitoring of his abstinence from substance use through blood or urine testing. In addition, because John reported that he has engaged in the sale of drugs, an intervention that addresses the patterns of thinking and behavior associated with drug dealing would be particularly helpful for John.

Second, John would benefit from continued education and vocational training. Although John may be limited in the extent to which he can improve his basic academic skills, an effort should be made in these areas. Due to John's current situation, he would particularly benefit from training in both specific job skills and functional academic areas related to his areas of interest. Training in this area may be especially important because John displayed significant deficits on all three areas measured by the WRAT-3, and he has not attended school on a regular basis for some time. As previously noted, John expressed a desire to continue his education and receive job training in a hospital-related job. Regardless of the career that John eventually chooses, it is important that he further his education and training. When John was asked about continued education and job training, he reported that obtaining his GED, receiving job training, and obtaining a job would be particularly helpful in keeping him from committing future antisocial acts. This area is indirectly relevant to public safety and John's risk for future antisocial behavior to the extent that it enhances John's ability to obtain and keep a job, thereby providing him with an income from a legitimate source that may serve to lessen any financial incentive he might have for committing future criminal acts. This is an important consideration in light of John's self-reported history of engaging in antisocial behavior to obtain money and other items. In addition to providing John with necessary work skills, continued education, and vocational training would also serve to take up free time, thereby lessening the likelihood that John will collaborate with peers in criminal offending.

Third, John is in need of training in the areas of anger control, impulse control, and decision-making/problem-solving skills. John presents as a youth who can be polite, cooperative, and non-aggressive. Although John reported that he is not impulsive and that his temper is "not bad," he stated that he has been involved in about five fights. Furthermore, when John was asked about the circumstances that led to the fights, he reported that he occasionally fought after "bumping someone" or just because he did not like the person. Additionally, John was rejected from one residential treatment facility due to his history of assaulting staff and aggressive behavior. In addition to training in the areas of anger control and impulse control, John would benefit from training in the area of decision-making/problem-solving skills. Although John reported that his decision-making skills are "good," he also reported

that he occasionally exercises bad judgment. Therefore, John may need skills training to help him control his anger, improve his decision-making/problem-solving skills, and recognize and avoid "high-risk" situations that may make it more likely that he will become involved in criminal offending. Training in this area is directly relevant to John's risk for future antisocial behavior. If he responds favorably to such an intervention, it should serve to reduce his risk for future criminal offending.

Fourth, John would benefit from the development of more positive peer relationships. Although John denied participating in the current alleged offense, he reported that he was with his friends on the day the incident took place. In addition, John reported that his friends "sell drugs, hang out, and smoke weed," which may serve to increase his risk for continued substance abuse and antisocial behavior. John stated that he no longer associates with his friends because they "sell drugs." In addition, when John was asked about the influence that his friends have had on him, he reported that his friends are "not good for me." Therefore, if John develops more positive peer relationships, his risk for future antisocial behavior should be reduced.

Finally, John needs ongoing monitoring and periodic evaluation of his mental health needs, including further observation and evaluation for the possible presence of ADHD. As previously noted, John has had contact with mental health professionals on various occasions, and he has occasionally been given a diagnosis and prescribed medication (Ritalin). Furthermore, John reported a history of hearing voices on several occasions. Therefore, following the disposition of his current charges, John's condition should be continuously monitored and periodically evaluated. In addition, based on John's self-report and behavioral observations made by the evaluators, it appears likely that John meets the criteria for ADHD. Therefore, following the disposition of his current charges, John should be evaluated again and, if indicated, treated for the symptoms of ADHD.

CONCLUSION

In the opinion of the undersigned, based on all of the above, John has treatment/rehabilitation needs in the following areas:

1. substance abuse, including an intervention for those involved in selling drugs;
2. continued education/training;
3. anger control, impulse control, and decision-making/problem-solving skills;
4. development of positive peer relationships; and
5. ongoing monitoring and periodic evaluation of his mental health needs, including further observation and evaluation for the possible presence of ADHD.

Considering his arrest history and the number of active risk factors that John is currently experiencing (e.g., recent history of substance abuse, not being enrolled in school, poor decision-making/problem-solving skills, negative peers), John presents as a moderate to high risk for future offending. His amenability to the interventions described in the previous section, based on his self-reported experience at Latino, appears mixed. If these interventions can be made successfully, however, with intensive monitoring to ensure compliance, John's risk of further offending should be reduced. John may respond favorably to skills-based training delivered in a specialized, structured, residential setting. A secure residential facility that has an intervention specifically designed and structured for adolescent males involved with the sale of drugs may be particularly appropriate for John.

It is our opinion that these needs can be met in the juvenile system if the court were to retain jurisdiction over John for the time remaining until his 21st birthday.

Thank you for the opportunity to evaluate John D.

Kirk Heilbrun, Ph.D.
Consulting Psychologist

David DeMatteo
MCP Hahnemann University
Graduate Student

Geff Marczyk, M.S., M.A.
MCP Hahnemann University
Graduate Student

Teaching Point: How does a forensic clinician translate legal criteria into forensic capacities?

Forensic mental health assessments differ from other forms of mental health assessment in the importance of gathering information that is directly related to a forensic issue(s). Even the most thorough and well-reasoned FMHA is lacking unless it is relevant to the legal question being addressed by the court or other legal decision maker. Of particular importance in addressing any legal question is translating legal criteria into relevant forensic capacities; FMHA should provide data and reasoning that are directly relevant to forensic capacities and to the legal question. Generally, the translation of legal criteria into forensic capacities can be accomplished by adopting a three-step approach that initially identifies the broad legal question, operationalizes the question, and then gathers information in specific domains to address it. In addition to providing the overall structure of the evaluation, the translation of the legal standard into forensic capacities guides the methods and sources used in data collection.

The first step in translating legal criteria into forensic capacities is to identify the legal question and forensic issue(s). Forensic issues and legal questions are generally identified and driven by legal standards (e.g., the *Dusky* test for competence to stand trial, the *M'Naghten* standard for insanity, and the "best interests of the child" standard in custody cases), which vary by jurisdiction and are based in statutory and/or common law. Once the forensic issue has been identified, the forensic clinician can then undertake the second step, which involves identifying forensic capacities relevant to the legal question.

There are a number of approaches that a forensic practitioner can take in attempting to translate legal criteria into forensic capacities. One is to look for specialized tools (e.g., the MacArthur Competence Assessment Tool for Criminal Adjudication; Poythress, Monahan et al., 1999; Poythress, Nicholson et al., 1999; and the MacArthur Competence Assessment Tool for Treatment; Grisso & Appelbaum, 1998b) that have been designed to integrate specific forensic capacities and legal criteria into a structured assessment format. Even if such tools are available, guidance should also be sought from applicable statutes, administrative code, rules of procedure, and case law in the relevant jurisdiction. Guidance of this type is generally useful for defining the contours (broad or narrow) of the evaluation, identifying factors that a court will consider as relevant to the legal question, and excluding criteria that do not call for forensic or mental health expertise (e.g., was the offense particularly cruel).

Next, the forensic practitioner should review standards of practice and empirical literature on a national level to ascertain what forensic capacities are most relevant to the forensic issue under consideration, and whether the evaluation should proceed from a broad or narrow focus (e.g., capital sentencing mitigation vs. mental state at the time of the offense). When it is unclear from this review whether courts in a given jurisdiction want an evaluation with a broader or narrower focus, the forensic clinician should proceed with a broad approach. After adopting this broad approach, the forensic clinician—through reasoning and conclusions—should describe the results of the evaluation so that if the court preferred a broad focus (e.g., psychopathology, intellectual deficits, or developmental immaturity as a cause of potential functional deficits in juvenile competence to stand trial) or a narrow focus (psychopathology and intellectual deficits but not developmental immaturity in juvenile competence to stand trial), the evaluation would provide pertinent information. By adopting this sequential approach, it is possible to translate even the vaguest legal criteria into relevant forensic capacities and respond to the relevant legal question on both broad and narrow levels.

Identifying forensic capacities as they relate to a particular legal question or forensic issue can be difficult. Although legal standards are designed to provide guidance for legal decision makers, they are sometimes overly broad, lacking in detail, and do not provide adequate guidance related to the forensic competencies that should be considered in the FMHA. Accordingly, the evaluator then faces the challenge of operationalizing the legal standard into relevant domains and criteria that can be assessed. Whenever possible, the operationalizing of a legal standard into forensic capacities should be grounded in empirically based literature.

For example, in the present case, the legal question was decertification under applicable Pennsylvania law. Based on the requirements of the statutory language, the evaluators operationalized the referral question as "treatment needs and amenability in the context of public safety." The legally relevant forensic issues—risk assessment for reoffending, treatment/rehabilitation needs, and amenability to treatment/rehabilitation—were identified and operationalized by consulting the relevant literature on the subject. Since the empirical literature suggests that substance abuse, poor academic achievement, past criminal activity, a chaotic family environment, and mental illness are significant risk factors for juvenile recidivism, these were among the domains assessed. With the legal issue identified and translated into forensic capacities, the evaluator can then move to the collection of data to address the operationalized forensic capacities.

As with operationalizing the relevant legal standard into forensic capacities, data collection should be guided by empirically based literature and conducted in a reliable and valid way. Reliability and validity can be improved regarding the capacities in question by using a variety of sources of non-empirical data (e.g., clinical interview, behavioral observation, self-report, collateral interviews, collateral document review) and, wherever possible and appropriate, through the use of psychological testing. This final step provides the raw data to address the relevant forensic capacities, which, in turn, are then used to address the broader legal question or forensic issue.

By following this three-step process—identify the broad legal question, operationalize the question into forensic capacities, gather information in specific domains as they relate to the operationalized forensic capacities—the forensic clinician can address legal standards and referral questions that in and of themselves do not provide sufficient guidance. In addition to providing structure for the evaluation, this approach, in conjunction with appropriate methods of data collection, improves the reliability and validity of the FMHA and aids the legal decision maker in making an accurate determination.

Case 2

Principle: Use third-party information in assessing response style

This principle addresses the importance of using third-party information in assessing response style. Third-party information is important in FMHA for a number of reasons. First, the use of third-party information to assess response style is an integral part of a comprehensive approach to FMHA and provides valuable collateral information. Second, some measures relevant to FMHA (e.g., the Hare Psychopathy Checklist-Revised; Hare, 1991) require the forensic clinician to incorporate third-party information as part of the assessment and scoring process. Third, the use of collateral and corroborative information increases accuracy in detecting deception (e.g., Ekman & O'Sullivan, 1991; Rogers, 1997). Fourth, third-party information can increase the face validity of FMHA and enhance the credibility of the evaluation. Finally, third-party information may be helpful in allowing the forensic clinician to clarify a constellation of symptoms and to identify, confirm, and/or disconfirm the presence of various forms of psychopathology. For example, collateral information may help the forensic clinician to distinguish between deliberate distortion and genuine memory loss by providing prompts or cues that can facilitate recall in cases of genuine amnesia (Schacter, 1986).

The *Ethical Principles of Psychologists and Code of Conduct* (APA, 1992) provides the following caution regarding considerations that may reduce the accuracy of assessment:

> When interpreting assessment results, including automated interpretations, psychologists take into account the various test factors and characteristics of the person being assessed that might affect psychologists' judgments or reduce the accuracy of their interpretations. They indicate any significant reservations they have about the accuracy or limitations of their interpretations. (p. 1603)

This underscores the importance of identifying influences that might reduce the accuracy of observations and the resulting conclusions. The use of third-party information to assess response style can help gauge the accuracy of testing results and observations.

The *Specialty Guidelines for Forensic Psychologists* (Committee on Ethical Guidelines for Forensic Psychologists, 1991) describes the role of third-party information in FMHA by noting that the forensic clinician conducting an evaluation actively seeks information "that will differentially test rival hypotheses" (p. 661). Common "rival hypotheses" relevant to response style in FMHA involve the possibilities that an individual (1) experiences a genuine mental disorder and presents these symptoms accurately, (2) experiences a genuine mental disorder but exaggerates or otherwise distorts the experience of symptoms, or (3) presents but does not actually experience the symptoms of a mental disorder.

Further, the *Specialty Guidelines* notes: "When the forensic psychologist relies upon data or information gathered by others, the origins of those data are clarified in any professional product. In addition, the forensic psychologist bears a special responsibility to ensure that such data, if relied upon, were gathered in a manner standard for the profession" (p. 662).

The *Ethical Guidelines for the Practice of Forensic Psychiatry* (AAPL, 1995) considers the potential contribution of third-party information to both enhancing accuracy and facilitating reasoning:

> Practicing forensic psychiatrists enhance the honesty and objectivity of their work by basing their forensic opinions, forensic reports and forensic testimony on all the

data available to them. They communicate the honesty of their work and efforts to attain objectivity, and the soundness of their clinical opinion by distinguishing, to the extent possible, between verified and unverified information as well as between clinical "facts," "inferences," and "impressions." (p. 3)

These sources of ethics authority vary in the specificity with which they support this principle. While the *Ethics Code* reflects the general importance of accuracy, both of the forensic specialty guidelines stress the need for hypothesis testing and distinguishing between facts and inferences. In this regard, they directly support the need to assess response style to improve the overall accuracy of the FMHA, eliminate rival hypotheses, distinguish facts and inferences, and gauge the accuracy of self-reported symptoms and experience—all of which can be done better with the inclusion of third-party information.

There are competing considerations in the law regarding the use of third-party information to assess response style in FMHA. One consideration is the value of providing reliable and relevant information to the decision maker. Where third-party information relevant to response style facilitates this, then its use in legal contexts is desirable. However, the law can also impose limits on the use of third-party information in FMHA. For example, third-party information might be challenged as hearsay on the grounds that it constitutes out-of-court statements being presented to prove the truth of an in-court statement. Under Rule 703 of the *Federal Rules of Evidence*, facts or underlying data need not be admissible if they are of a type "reasonably relied on by experts . . . in forming opinions or inferences upon the subject." Some states have evidentiary rules similar to Rule 703, while others require that expert testimony be based on sources of information that would be independently admissible. In the latter jurisdictions, an entire FMHA could be ruled inadmissible if it relied significantly on the use of such third-party information in supporting its conclusions.

The following report demonstrates the application of this principle in a juvenile waiver case. The forensic clinician identified the relevant sources of third-party information as follows: (1) available records pertaining to the juvenile (Isaiah), including the South Carolina Department of Juvenile Justice (SCDJJ) Preadjudicatory Transfer Evaluation, SCDJJ Behavior Reports, Isaiah's Family Court record, Isaiah's public school records, and Isaiah's police records; and (2) collateral interviews with Isaiah's mother, Isaiah's treating psychiatrist, and a lieutenant from the SCDJJ Detention Center. By identifying and using a number of third-party sources, the clinician provided a more detailed and accurate description of Isaiah and his needs and capacities.

These collateral sources of information were used throughout the evaluation to assess the consistency and accuracy of the information obtained from Isaiah. For example, the clinician obtained information from both Isaiah and his mother regarding several relevant domains, such as Isaiah's family history, educational background, medical history, history of substance abuse, and criminal history. By obtaining information from multiple sources, including several third-party sources of information, the clinician avoided having to rely on self-report and thereby enhanced the credibility of the evaluation. Moreover, using these third-party sources of information increased the "convergent validity" of the clinician's conclusions. By comparing the results of Isaiah's testing during the evaluation with the results of prior testing conducted with Isaiah, for example, the clinician could better assess whether the present testing results were an accurate reflection of Isaiah's functioning. Using collateral sources of information in this manner can also be helpful in detecting deception, particularly when current evaluation results differ from a consistent pattern of previous findings.

May 1, 1999
Re: Evaluation of Isaiah N
Dear Mr. H:

Pursuant to your request and the Family Court's order for independent evaluation, I saw this 14-year-old African American male for a forensic psychological examination of his current mental state, diagnosis, sophistication and maturity, and likelihood of rehabilitation in response to waiver to adult court. At the time of evaluation, Isaiah was detained at the SC Department of Juvenile Justice (DJJ) Detention Center where he had been placed following his arrest on charges of attempted murder, armed robbery, possession of a firearm during commission of a violent crime, and unlawful possession of a pistol by a person under 21 occurring on May 28, 1998. In addition to clinical interviews on April 23, 1999, and April 29, 1999, I administered the Millon Adolescent Clinical Inventory (MACI), the Jesness Inventory (JI), and the Neurobehavioral Cognitive Status Examination (NCSE). I interviewed Donna S-W, MD, Isaiah's treating psychiatrist, Lt. G of the SCDJJ Detention Center, and Isaiah's mother. Prior to the examination on April 23, I had reviewed numerous documents supplied by your office, including the SCDJJ Preadjudicatory Transfer (Waiver) Evaluation of 12/22/98 [which included the Wechsler Intelligence Scale for Children-Third Edition (WISC-III), the Peabody Individual Achievement Test-Revised (PIAT-R), the Benton Visual Retention Test (BVRT), the Vineland Adaptive Behavior Scales (VABS), and

the Reynold's Adolescent Depression Inventory (RADI)]. I also reviewed Isaiah's SCDJJ Behavior Reports from 6/17/98 to 4/20/99, Isaiah's Family Court record, and public school records from Pxxx, PA and Axxxx County, SC.

RELEVANT HISTORY

Family Isaiah's mother reported he was born in Philadelphia, the third of four children; she stated that each of his siblings has a different father. She said that he was born 3 months prematurely and weighed only 3 pounds, 6 ounces, at birth. She indicated that he stayed in the hospital for approximately 3 months while he was treated for underdeveloped lungs and jaundice. She also noted that he did not walk unaided until he was over 2 years old, had difficulty learning to talk or recognize colors and numbers, and resisted toilet training until age 5. Isaiah lived with her after her divorce when he was very young, she said, and they moved from Philadelphia to Atlanta, Delaware, North Carolina, Atlanta, Philadelphia, and finally to South Carolina approximately 2 years ago. She said they moved so often because she had difficulty staying employed, and her relatives in each location were unwilling to keep supporting them. She stated that Isaiah lived with his biological father "off and on" when he would get in trouble with her, then return home when he had conflicts with his father. Isaiah's mother stated that his father has been married "about 5 times," and she believed that none of Isaiah's stepmothers wanted him around because they were raising his father's younger children. She reported that she gave birth to her fourth child last year, and Isaiah has rarely gotten along with her boyfriends or his two stepfathers, whom she divorced before he was 9 years old. She stated that his half-brother, age 23, did not finish high school because he was sent to juvenile detention for theft, and that his other half-brother "did time" as an adult for auto theft and burglary. She stated that his half-sister, age 18, has two children and gets Food Stamps as a single mother in Philadelphia. She reported that her own father was an abusive alcoholic and that Isaiah's paternal grandfather died from complications from alcohol. Isaiah's mother stated that she and his father have had difficulty with alcohol, and Isaiah has seen each intoxicated many times. She stated that when either is drunk they would become verbally and physically abusive, occasionally resulting in brief incarcerations for alcohol-related disturbances. She stated that their divorce resulted from their repeated domestic violence and mutual charges of infidelity. Although she indicated that Isaiah has never been placed in foster care, he has often had to live with other relatives while she was in jail overnight or on weekends. She reported that he has seen his parents smoking marijuana, but that neither has used other illegal drugs. Isaiah's mother stated that she has been sober for approximately 2 years, adding that she entered substance abuse treatment when she discovered that she was pregnant with her fourth child and now maintains her sobriety through attendance at Alcoholics Anonymous meetings and renewed spiritual faith.

Educational Isaiah's mother stated that her son has always been a "slow learner" and has experienced difficulty keeping up with his classmates in reading, arithmetic, and other subjects. She reported that he was retained in kindergarten because his teachers did not believe he was ready for school. She stated that he received special help in all his subjects and was placed in special education classes, with her consent, following the third grade. She also noted that he has often had altercations with other students on the playground and occasionally in the classroom. She indicated that as he became older, his difficulties resulted in periodic suspensions from school for

talking back to teachers or fighting with other children. She stated that because he had been expelled from bus transportation after frequent disruptions with the driver, his tardiness and poor attendance increased when she was required to take him to school. She felt that he was "socially promoted" many years because the school did not know how to control his behavior. She corroborated Isaiah's report that in the months prior to the current offenses he had been expelled from sixth grade for absenteeism and frequent class disruptions, including destruction of schoolbooks and other materials.

Medical/Sexual Isaiah's mother stated that he has been involved in three motor vehicle accidents: with his father at age 5 and twice with her when he was 11 and 12. She stated that in the first accident Isaiah hit his head on the car's dashboard without a loss of consciousness; he was treated and released from medical care the same day. She reported that Isaiah was unharmed in the other two accidents. She stated that he fell and hit his head on concrete at school when in the fourth grade. She reported that she was told by the school nurse that his loss of consciousness was less than 1 minute and that he did not need to be sent to the hospital. Isaiah's mother stated that he has never been diagnosed with Fetal Alcohol Syndrome, but acknowledged that she has always previously denied substance abuse when questioned by physicians or school personnel. She stated that she has often taken Isaiah to counselors and community mental health centers because of his disruptive behavior in school or his previous juvenile arrests. She stated, however, that she would resist attending recommended family counseling sessions and would not push Isaiah to stay in therapy if he did not want to see his therapist. She reported that Isaiah has never been prescribed medication until his current detention at SCDJJ. She stated that an elementary school nurse suggested that he should be put on Ritalin, but she did not follow-up with doctor's appointments for her son. She did not know whether Isaiah was sexually active. She stated that there had never been allegations that he had been sexually abused, nor did he appear to display any inappropriate sexual behavior or personal immodesty. Isaiah has never indicated that he had a girlfriend, nor has he played in the neighborhood with children of the opposite sex, she said, adding that she cannot afford cable TV and only rents videos that have G or PG-13 ratings. She stated that she has not found any pornographic materials in his room. Isaiah denied that he had ever been molested or coerced into any sexual activity. He stated that he began masturbating at age 12, after seeing pornographic magazines at a neighbor's house. He denied any sexual interest or contact with boys or men. Isaiah stated that his first sexual intercourse occurred when he was 12 with a 16-year-old girl who was a friend of his half-sister. He claimed that he has had sex with five girls: "the oldest was 17, and the youngest was 15." He stated that he has not fathered any children, nor have any of his sexual partners reported that they were pregnant. There is no medical evidence that Isaiah suffers from a sexually transmitted disease. He stated that he hoped one day to get married and have children.

Substance Abuse   Isaiah's mother stated she did not know whether her son had begun using alcohol or illegal drugs. She stated that she has never found drugs in his room or noticed that her beer or liquor bottles were missing. His school has never reported that he has been caught smoking or drinking, nor has he entered the school grounds in an intoxicated state, she said, reporting that Isaiah has always denied that he has started to use alcohol or drugs when she has asked him. Isaiah stated that he began drinking beer at age 6 or 7 at his brother's encouragement and began smoking marijuana at age 11. Prior to his arrest and detention on the present charges, Isaiah reported that he was drinking liquor (tequila, rum) frequently during the day, smoking many marijuana "blunts" almost every day, and ingesting Xanax "about once or twice a month." He stated that these were the only drugs he used.

Juvenile Record   Isaiah's mother confirmed his report that he has been detained twice before for altercations occurring during school hours. She stated that he was charged with aggravated assault, unlawful possession of a weapon (knife) on school grounds, and resisting arrest at age 11, when Isaiah attacked a same-age boy who was calling him names. She said that Isaiah was re-

leased to her custody after the charges were dismissed in Family Court. She stated that Isaiah was arrested at age 12 for aggravated assault, possession of a weapon (a knife) on school grounds, and making terrorist threats when he attacked a school janitor/hall monitor as he attempted to leave school following an in-class argument with his teacher. These charges resulted in Isaiah being placed on 1 year's probation, which he completed without incident just prior to his arrest on his current charges of attempted murder, armed robbery, possession of a firearm during commission of a violent crime, and unlawful possession of a pistol by a person under 21.

Description of the Current Offenses   Police records indicate that Isaiah is charged with entering a dry cleaning store before noon, pointing a pistol at the clerk, and demanding that she place the cash register's money into a paper bag he held. Records indicate he fired once, hitting the wall next to the employee, then ran down the street. As he left the store, the clerk began yelling. He was arrested 3 hours later while playing video games at an arcade four blocks away. He was carrying just over $50.

Clinical Impressions   At each examination session, Isaiah was alert, oriented, cooperative, and coherent. Consistent with his SCDJJ Transfer evaluation, he gave his best effort on all interview questions and assessment tasks without malingering, exaggeration, or denial of his emotional and psychological problems. His answers to questions were relevant, well-associated, and goal-directed; there was no evidence of psychosis, delusions, hallucinations, or a formal thought disorder. On the NCSE, he displayed adequate orientation, attention, language comprehension and repetition, naming, abstract reasoning, and calculations. There were, however, indications of neuropsychological deficits: he failed the screening items on visual-constructional memory (consistent with his low scores on the Benton Visual Retention Test in the SCDJJ evaluation), short-term memory (consistent with his failure to recall three of three objects after 5 minutes in the SCDJJ evaluation), and social judgment (consistent with his very low WISC-III Comprehension and Picture Arrangement scores in the SCDJJ evaluation). His affect was constricted and rather flat, consistent with anxiety and depression. His mood was depressed, reflecting his two suicide attempts when first detained at SCDJJ: his attempts led to placement on suicide watch twice and a referral for evaluation by Dr. S-W. His judgment was impulsive and unrealistic, and his decision making was often colored by immaturity, impatience, and low frustration tolerance: He stated that he was tired of being incarcerated, wanted the charges "to be over," and stated the judge would let him "go home like when I was in trouble before."

On the MACI, Isaiah produced a valid, unbiased profile neither exaggerating nor minimizing conflicts or problems. Adolescents with similar test results are likely described as socially awkward, shy, distrustful, anxious persons who are ill at ease with others and who fear rejection despite wanting peers' approval. Such adolescents are sad, brooding, dejected, and gloomy and have likely had a pessimistic outlook on life since childhood. Juveniles with Isaiah's MACI results are often seen as their own worst enemies: They sabotage their best efforts to achieve success by engaging in self-defeating behaviors that undermine others' attempts to help them. His MACI scores were strongly indicative of recurrent suicidal thoughts and plans and a belief that others would be better off without him. On the Jesness Inventory, Isaiah also produced a valid profile with results similar to the MACI. Adolescents with his JI profile, the Introspective (Neurotic, Anxious) type, are described as likely withdrawn, anxious, depressed juveniles with an internalized "bad me" self-image. Their family lives were typically unhappy and conflicted. They often saw their parents as somewhat withholding and unsupportive; adolescents with Isaiah's JI profile tended to have poor rapport with their fathers. Interpersonally with peers, adolescents with Isaiah's JI profile were seen as shy, nervous, lacking in self-confidence, and as not well-liked by others.

In the opinion of Dr. S-W, Isaiah suffers from Fetal Alcohol Syndrome (FAS), a congenital illness and disability caused by prenatal alcohol exposure from the birth mother. FAS produces characteristic facial abnormalities, growth problems, brain and heart malformations, and significant chronic deficits in intellectual functioning and impulse control. FAS occurs in approxi-

mately 1–2 children per 1,000 (with higher prevalence in African-American and Native American families) and is one of the most common causes of mental retardation and behavior disorders, particularly hyperactivity and diminished abilities to understand cause and effect relationships. Undetected and untreated FAS children are typically described as impulsive, unpredictable, learning disabled, verbally and physically aggressive, demanding with expectations of immediate gratification, excessively vulnerable to peer influence, and as having diminished responsiveness to authority at home, school, and other settings.

Isaiah's personal history and physical appearance is consistent with a diagnosis of Fetal Alcohol Syndrome. According to his mother and the SCDJJ Transfer Report, he was born 3 months prematurely with a birth weight under 4 lbs. Because of his low birth weight, underdeveloped lungs, and jaundice, Isaiah remained in hospital for 3 months undergoing medical treatment and observation. Infants who remain hospitalized for prolonged periods after birth do not have normal opportunities to bond emotionally with their mothers; the result is often significant attachment disorders to parents, which may subsequently produce deficits in social and interpersonal relationships. The negative effects of Isaiah's FAS were likely significantly amplified and further complicated by his parents' alcoholism, violence, and divorce and his father's erratic acceptance and nurturance. The SCDJJ report also validated his very low, uneven intellectual functioning with a Full Scale WISC-III IQ of 71. School reports corroborate Isaiah's mother's recollection that he was retained in kindergarten suggesting that, from a very early age, he was developmentally delayed relative to his classmates. His available school records from second grade onward reflect problems with following rules, peer relationships, controlling his classroom behavior, and completing tasks. As he entered the later elementary grades, Isaiah had numerous writeups for fighting and threatening peers, disrespectful behavior toward school personnel, and absenteeism. The SCDJJ report indicated that Isaiah appears to be an "individual with very low self-esteem who has experienced little success in major areas of his life, including school functioning, peer relationships, social activities, and relationships with authority." The very early onset, chronicity, and pervasiveness of Isaiah's social, behavioral, and cognitive deficits are much more consistent with an organically based disorder such as FAS, than a nonorganic oppositional-defiant or conduct disorder.

The remainder of this report focuses on those areas relevant to waiver to adult court: sophistication and maturity, and likelihood of rehabilitation in the juvenile justice system.

SOPHISTICATION AND MATURITY

Isaiah's history, presentation, and psychological testing in this examination and by SCDJJ do not suggest that his sophistication and maturity is equivalent to his own age group or to adult defendants. SCDJJ's report of Isaiah's score on the WISC-III subtest of Comprehension was below the second percentile, meaning that 98 of 100 adolescents his age likely have more fully developed (e.g., more knowledgeable and mature) social, interpersonal judgment. The SCDJJ examiners indicated that this deficit in understanding social situations was "his most pronounced weakness." Additionally, SCDJJ reported that Isaiah's score on the WISC-III subtest of Picture Arrangement, which measures abilities to infer cause and effect in social situations, was also below the second percentile when compared against his same-aged peers. These results further validate the cognitive deficits associated with Fetal Alcohol Syndrome and would be the WISC-III subtests that would be expected to be lowest in FAS adolescents. His performances on the PIAT-R Reading Comprehension and Mathematics subtests were two grade levels below his current educational placement. His Composite score on the Vineland Adaptive Behavior Scales (as completed by his mother) fell within the fifth percentile when compared to his age mates. Lastly, the SCDJJ examiners concluded that (relative to adolescents of similar age) Isaiah "is functioning at a borderline level of sophistication and maturity" and described him as engaging in "pseudomature or 'adult-like' behaviors of truancy, staying out late, marijuana use, and possessing a handgun." The SCDJJ report indicated that Isaiah is aware of the wrongfulness of armed robbery, attempted murder, and possession of a pistol. This, however, is not a sufficient

test of an adolescent's sophistication and maturity: Elementary school children know it is wrong to steal, fire a pistol at someone, and possess handguns.

A more relevant test of sophistication and maturity is whether this adolescent could meet an adult standard of competency to stand trial, as trial in General Sessions Court is the consequence of juvenile transfer. Isaiah's capacity to understand the legal proceedings against him and to meaningfully assist his attorney in his defense is beyond the scope of this report and was not requested by the Family Court. However, Isaiah's significantly low global intelligence (Borderline Intellectual Functioning) and relatively young age are consistent with research suggesting that such adolescents, due to developmental deficits in reasoning and decision making, are much less likely than average-IQ juveniles to be judged as competent to stand trial (CST). In one recent study of 108 South Carolina juveniles undergoing Family Court-ordered pre-trial CST evaluations, only 22.5% of adolescents with Borderline Intellectual Functioning or Mental Retardation were considered to be competent to stand trial by their psychiatric examiners.

LIKELIHOOD OF REASONABLE REHABILITATION

Isaiah has a long history of behavior problems in school, difficulty in responding to authority, and numerous judicial adjudications, as indicated in the records from Pennsylvania and South Carolina. Given that Isaiah has suffered from an apparently undiagnosed and untreated Fetal Alcohol Syndrome, his history of conduct problems is not surprising and is consistent with descriptions of the behavioral and attitudinal effects of the disorder. There are indications that he has the capacity to respond very positively to treatment, given sufficient structure, duration, medication, and supervision. Judging from detention records, Isaiah has apparently received more regular, consistent, and predictable supervision by positive adult male role models during the 11 months of his current detention than at any time during his life. Detention at SCDJJ has allowed Isaiah to completely detoxify from his marijuana dependence and alcohol abuse. His oppositional behavior early in his detention was, in part, likely due to cannabis withdrawal, in addition to immature resistence to limit setting. Dr. S-W, who has diagnosed him with FAS and depression, has been psychiatrically treating Isaiah for a number of months with antidepressant medication. She stated that Isaiah is "a joy to treat" and stated that she had observed a remarkable change in his attitude, behavior, and demeanor in response to her psychiatric care. She reported that with appropriate medications, consistent structure, and close supervision, his prognosis for continued improvement is very positive.

It is notable that since early January 1999, Isaiah's rate of disciplinaries has dropped significantly. Lt. G described him as "one of our best kids in here now with no problems in the last few months; he is like a different kid." Lt. G indicated that Isaiah is more attentive in his classes and is no longer confrontational with his teachers. When asked why he thought Isaiah had changed so significantly, Lt. G stated: "I think he is finally tuning in to us and knows that he does not need to be raising sand in here to be a man, he now helps us watch for contraband." Lt. G also felt that Isaiah's participation in certain work projects had been a very positive contribution to his improved attitude and behavior. Isaiah's SCDJJ Transfer Report of 12/22/98 indicated that he "has not been involved in any long-term residential rehabilitative efforts so there is no record to suggest that he will or will not benefit from long-term residential rehabilitation." The opinions of Dr. S-W and Lt. G, validated by disciplinary records of the past several months, suggest that he has demonstrated the capacity for improvement, is seeking the approval of authority figures, and is responding positively to SCDJJ residential treatment.

In addition to these positive appraisals by SCDJJ personnel, Isaiah's test data on the MACI and the Jesness Inventory are associated with positive treatment prognosis. His average score on the MACI Desirability scale suggests that he is not attempting to "fake good" or give a false impression of his amenability for treatment. On the MACI, his very low scores on the Unruly, Egotistic, Forceful, and Delinquency Predisposition scales suggest that he is likely more responsive to treatment and direction than at the time of his detention in May 1998. Further, his high scores on the Doleful and Depressive Affect scales of the MACI are associated with feelings of guilt and remorse, attitudes that are fundamental for behavior change following delinquent acts. His average to low average scores on the JI Repression and Denial scales indicate Isaiah's willingness for self-disclosure, the most basic requirement of therapeutic treatment. His high score on the JI Withdrawal scale and average scores on Alienation and Manifest Aggression scales suggest an individual who is not manipulative and is no longer oppositional to authority. Research with the JI indicates that adolescents with Isaiah's profile type are quite willing to relate to counselors, seek the approval of authority and staff, and prefer a structured, orderly environment with clear limits and predictable consequences, such as long-term residential treatment.

It is my opinion, therefore, to a reasonable degree of scientific certainty, that (1) Isaiah's sophistication and maturity is not equivalent to an adult's development and is significantly below that of his same-age peers; and (2) Isaiah's likelihood of successful rehabilitation within the structure and treatment available through the SC Department of Juvenile Justice is very high.

RECOMMENDATIONS

1. It is crucial that Isaiah's psychiatric and medication treatment for Fetal Alcohol Syndrome be maintained, regardless of the judge's decision regarding waiver to General Sessions Court, to reduce the likelihood of future altercations and conflicts secondary to his disorder.
2. Isaiah should be enrolled in DJJ's psychoeducational program of Anger Management classes to learn how to avoid conflict and altercations through changes in thinking, perception of situations, and use of verbal assertiveness, rather than physical aggression, to resolve disputes.
3. Isaiah needs individual and group process therapy to manage the significant rage he carries against his mother's history of abandonment, secondary to substance abuse and his father's rejection of him and preference for his other children.
4. Following the Court's waiver hearing, Isaiah's placement into DJJ's general popula-

tion of other juvenile residents will have to be carefully monitored and closely supervised. Isaiah has developed close relationships with the pre-trial detention staff's adult male officers; his leaving that environment will likely reactivate many of the fears and anxieties he had when bounced back and forth from his mother to father. Given his limited cognitive skills, Isaiah does not tolerate change easily; close supervision and continued therapeutic contact with Dr. S-W will reduce the likelihood that he will act out his separation anxiety with new aggressive behavior.

5. If Isaiah remains under the jurisdiction of the Family Court, such that he might be released at age 18, it is recommended that he be referred again for a risk management evaluation to structure post-release continuity of care so that institutional treatment gains are maintained and criminal recidivism is minimized.

Please contact me if you have any questions regarding this report or would like further information about Isaiah.

Sincerely,
Geoffrey R. McKee, PhD, ABPP
Diplomate in Forensic Psychology
Clinical Professor of Neuropsychiatry & Behavioral
  Science
University of South Carolina School of Medicine

Teaching Point: How can results from the interview, testing, and third-party sources be balanced?

The weighting of results from the interview, testing, and third-party sources varies from each source according to relevance and quality. If the response style of the individual being evaluated is not reliable due to malingering, defensiveness, irrelevance, or a lack of cooperation, for example, then self-report and psychological testing results may need to be deemphasized and third-party information weighted more heavily. Accordingly, psychological testing with integrated validity scales are particularly valuable for determining the emphasis that should be placed on the results of these instruments. If third-party sources of information are unavailable or unreliable, then results of psychological testing and the clinical interview, with attention to the limitations of such information, must be weighted more strongly.

Quality and relevance are judged differently across these sources of information. The quality and relevance of a psychological test may depend on the extent to which it has been validated for the purpose at hand, while the quality and relevance of third-party information may vary according to the familiarity of the source with the individual being evaluated and the impartiality of that source. When it is difficult to determine the relevance and quality of certain information, the forensic clinician should be particularly careful to attribute consistently by source (e.g., "according to self-report," "as reflected by psychiatric records," or "the results of the MMPI-2 suggest"). Further, the communication of results should stress consistency across sources, rather than describing input from one source as being "confirmed" or "verified" by another. Rather than stating that "psychiatric records and the results of the MMPI-2 verify Mr. X's self-report of symptoms," for instance, it would be more appropriate to state that "psychiatric records and the results of the MMPI-2 are consistent with Mr. X's self-report of symptoms." By using quality and relevance as guides, the forensic clinician can better weight the value of each of these sources of information, and communicate the relevant data in a fashion that does not compromise the accuracy or integrity of the evaluation.

Chapter 11

Sanity at the Time of the Offense

The mental state of adult defendants at the time of the offense—and the related impact on criminal responsibility—is the focus of the two reports in this chapter. The principle discussed in the first case addresses the importance of determining whether the individual being assessed understands the purpose of the evaluation and the associated limits on confidentiality or, in legal terms, obtaining informed consent. The accompanying teaching point discusses oral and written methods of obtaining informed consent and provides guidance on when each method should be used. Next, the much-debated principle associated with the second case in this chapter—do not answer the ultimate issue directly—discusses the importance of not answering the legal question that is before the court, such as sanity at the time of the offense. The teaching point for the second case provides a framework on how to avoid answering ultimate issue questions while still providing the court with valuable guidance and accurate information.

Case 1

Principle: **Determine whether the individual understands the purpose of the evaluation and associated limits on confidentiality**

This principle discusses the importance of determining whether the individual being assessed understands the purpose of the evaluation and the associated limits on confidentiality. Accurately conveying the purpose of the evaluation and the associated limits on confidentiality is the responsibility of the forensic clinician. Among other things, it helps to identify the clinician's role in the process, and it is an important component of providing notification of purpose and obtaining informed consent for the FMHA. The legal doctrine of informed consent contains three distinct and related elements: disclosure, competency, and voluntariness (Melton et al., 1997). In application, informed consent refers to a person's agreement to allow something to happen that is based on a full disclosure of facts needed to make the decision intelligently and with knowledge of the risks and alternatives involved (see *Black's Law Dictionary*, 1990, p. 779). Informed consent and notification of purpose are particularly important in the FMHA context where serious legal consequences could result from participation in the evaluation. Accordingly, the forensic clinician must be certain that the individual being assessed has an accurate understanding of the nature of the evaluation, its purpose(s), associated limits on confidentiality, and the possible uses of the evaluation.

The *Ethical Principles of Psychologists and Code of Conduct* (APA, 1992) addresses this principle directly: "When psychologists provide assessment . . . or other psychological services to an individual, a group, or an organization, they provide, using language that is reasonably understandable to the recipient of those services, appropriate information beforehand about the nature of such services" (p. 1600).

Similarly, the *Specialty Guidelines for Forensic Psychologists* (Committee on Ethical Guidelines for Forensic Psychologists, 1991) notes that:

> In situations where the client or party may not have the capacity to provide informed consent to services or the evaluation is pursuant to court order, the forensic psychologist provides reasonable notice to the clients's legal representative of the nature of the anticipated forensic service before proceeding. If the client's legal representative objects to the evaluation, the forensic psychologist notifies the court issuing the order and responds as directed. (p. 659)

Both the *Specialty Guidelines* and the *Ethics Code* stress the importance of providing an "understandable statement" of rights, privileges, and limitations on confidentiality applicable to FMHA (Committee on Ethical Guidelines for Forensic Psychologists, 1991, p. 660).

The *Principles of Medical Ethics with Annotations Especially Applicable to Psychiatry* (American Psychiatric Association, 1995) addresses the need for understandable notification indirectly. It focuses on the contractual nature of the relationship and asserts that it is important to determine whether the "explicitly established" provisions of the contractual relationship are understood (p. 3).

The *Ethical Guidelines for the Practice of Forensic Psychiatry* (AAPL, 1995) addresses this principle indirectly. The focus is on the nature of the relationship when determining whether the initial notification or request for consent was understood: "There is a continuing obligation to be sensitive to the fact that although a warning has been given, there may be slippage and a treatment relationship may develop in the mind of the examinee" (p. 2). This guideline stresses the importance of clarifying the nature of the relationship and the need for ongoing assessment of understanding throughout the FMHA.

Although not a source of ethical authority, the *Criminal Justice Mental Health Standards* (ABA, 1989) also emphasizes the importance of providing notification of purpose and obtaining informed consent. Standard 7-3.6 notes that in any evaluation, the mental health professional conducting the evaluation has an independent duty to provide notification of purpose and obtain informed consent. The nature of this notification should include: (1) the purpose of the evaluation, (2) the potential uses of any disclosures made during the evaluation, (3) the conditions under which the prosecutor will have access to information obtained and reports prepared, and (4) the consequences of the defendant's refusal to cooperate in the evaluation (ABA, 1989).

The present report provides a good illustration of the application of this principle in the context of an insanity evaluation. The evaluation was court ordered to help determine whether the defendant, Mr. C, was legally insane, as defined by Ohio statutory law, at the time he committed the alleged offenses (two counts of aggravated attempted murder with a firearm).

In this report, the forensic clinician included a separate paragraph that detailed her discussion with the defendant regarding the purpose of the evaluation and the associated limits on confidentiality, as well as his understanding of this information. In the section of the report entitled "Procedures," the forensic clinician indicated that she first contacted Mr. C's attorney to ensure that he was aware that an evaluation had been ordered and scheduled by the court. Next, the report indicates that the forensic clinician verbally informed Mr. C of the purpose of the evaluation and the associated limits on confidentiality. Specifically, she informed Mr. C that the evaluation was court ordered to determine his sanity at the time of the offense and that, under the controlling statute, the subsequent written report must be provided to the court, the defense attorney, and the prosecutor. In addition to presenting this information to Mr. C in verbal form, the forensic clinician also presented this information to Mr. C in written form (read aloud to Mr. C because of his reading deficit).

Consistent with this principle, the report indicates that Mr. C "appeared to understand" the information presented to him. Specifically, the forensic clinician indicated that Mr. C understood the following: (1) the purpose of the evaluation, (2) the reason his participation was necessary if he wished to pursue the insanity defense, (3) the possible ramifications of being found not guilty by reason of insanity, and (4) the possible ramifications of being found guilty. Finally, the report indicates that the forensic clinician reminded Mr. C of the purpose of the evaluation and the associated limits on confidentiality at the beginning of each evaluation session.

Sanity At The Time Of The Act: Mr. C
Contributed by Kathleen P. Stafford, Ph.D.
Psycho-Diagnostic Clinic
Akron, Ohio
Synopsis

The defendant is a 45-year-old African American man who has pleaded not guilty by reason of insanity to two counts of attempted aggravated murder with firearm specification for allegedly shooting two police officers. He was referred by the Court for an evaluation under the Ohio insanity standard: "whether the defendant, at the time of these offense charged, did not know, as a result of a severe mental disease or defect, the wrongfulness of the defendant's acts charged."

Initially, the defendant had been found incompetent to stand trial and committed to a state mental hospital. After 3 years, the court has now found him competent to stand trial.

REPORT

FORENSIC EVALUATION

Referral Jeffrey C is a 45-year-old African American man who has pleaded not guilty and not guilty by reason of insanity to two counts of attempted aggravated murder with firearm specification for allegedly shooting two police officers 3 years ago. He has been ordered by the Court to undergo an evaluation of his mental state at the time of these acts.

Procedures Mr. C was interviewed in a quiet office at the jail on October 21 for nearly 3 hours and on November 15 for 2 hours. He was also administered the Wechsler Adult Intelligence Scale-Revised Edition (WAIS-R) and the Reading subtest of the Wide Range Achievement Test-Third Edition (WRAT-3) on October 30. His attorney and his mental case manager were interviewed to obtain relevant information. The following documents were reviewed in the course of the evaluation:

1. The journal entry ordering the evaluation
2. The indictment in the case
3. Police reports of the investigation of the alleged offenses
4. Medical and mental health records from the jail
5. Treatment records from the local community mental health center
6. Treatment records from Ohio Department of Mental Health hospitals
7. Prior competency evaluations submitted to the Court in this matter
8. Competency evaluation completed in a misdemeanor case 10 years earlier
9. School record

Prior to the evaluation, Mr. C's attorney was contacted to ensure that he was aware the evaluation had been ordered and scheduled. At the beginning of the evaluation, Mr. C was verbally informed of the purpose of the evaluation and of the fact that, under the statute, the report of the evaluation must be provided to the Court, the defense attorney, and the prosecutor. This information was also provided on a written form to the defendant, which was read to him because he cannot read. He appeared to understand this information, and he readily agreed to participate in the evaluation. He understood that participation in the evaluation was necessary if his attorney was to pursue the insanity defense. He knew that a finding of not guilty by reason of insanity would most likely result in further court-ordered treatment in a hospital or in a community-based residential placement on conditional release. He knew he would otherwise face a potential prison sentence. Mr. C also indicated that he had abandoned his prior beliefs that the case could be resolved by claiming self-defense or by suing the Police Department for $100,000,000. He was reminded of the purpose of the evaluation and the limited confidentiality of the results at the start of each evaluation session.

Relevant History Mr. C is not a good historian, and this history is based on the records reviewed for this evaluation as well as information provided by the defendant.

Mr. C and his five siblings were raised by their parents in an intact, working-class home. His father is a retired railroad worker now residing in a nursing home due to dementia. His mother died 8 years ago of cancer. The defendant has some contact with one brother. Another brother receives treatment for schizophrenia. Prior to his arrest in this matter, the defendant always lived with his family. Mr. C attended special education classes in public school until he withdrew as "overage" in the 11th grade. He reportedly worked for a dry cleaning establishment until it went out of business over 20 years ago. He received Supplemental Security Income most of his adult life. He has never married and has no children.

Mental health records indicate that Mr. C was first seen at a local community mental health center at the age of 32. He was prescribed antipsychotic medication but did not take it. He had appointments about once a month. Mr. C was described as pleasant but delusional. He never displayed hostile, threatening, or aggressive behavior, and therefore he was not considered for civil commitment. The family reported to mental health professionals that the defendant had no history of substance abuse. He was diagnosed with Schizophrenia, Undifferentiated Type, Chronic, and Mild Mental Retardation. Three years after beginning treatment, at the age of 35, Mr. C was arrested for menacing, a misdemeanor. He had been driving a motorcycle and began to tailgate a police officer. The police officer pulled over and put on his blue lights. Mr. C stopped his motorcycle and, as the officer exited his cruiser, Mr. C pointed his finger at the officer and said, "Go for your gun. I've got one too." The police officer approached the defendant in a calm manner, and the defendant became passive and apologetic. Mr. C reportedly told the police officer that the devil had made him behave in a mean way.

During the course of the competency evaluation ordered in the menacing case, Mr. C reportedly was not well-oriented to time, and he reported an inaccurate age. He scored at the kindergarten level on the Reading sub-test of the WRAT-3. His performance on the WAIS-R produced scores in the low borderline range, with considerable intratest scatter attributed to his idiosyncratic thinking. He talked at length in a melodramatic fashion about two different spirits and some kind of psychic force against his family as the result of a curse. He had a rudimentary understanding of the roles of the judge and the prosecutor based on television shows, but he did not understand why he had been arrested and that he could be sentenced to jail if convicted. At one point, he asked, "If I plead guilty, will they throw it out?" The Court found the defendant incompetent to stand trial and unlikely to become competent in the 10 days provided by law for fourth degree misdemeanors. The judge dismissed the charge and urged the defendant to comply with outpatient mental health treatment.

Two years later, at the age of 37, Mr. C was hospitalized in a state psychiatric hospital for 6 months after police were called to his home because he had broken down a door. He had not complied with outpatient treatment and had become preoccupied with the notion that his father was practicing voodoo. At the age of 40, Mr. C was again hospitalized, and he required restraints during this admission. Prior to admission, he had been taking antipsychotic medication and had engaged in threatening and abusive behavior toward his father.

At the time of the alleged offenses of attempted aggravated murder, Mr. C was receiving little mental health treatment. The Court found him incompetent to stand trial and ordered him to be hospitalized. After nearly 3 years of court-ordered hospitalization, the Court has found him competent to stand trial. He is being treated in the jail with intramuscular injections of Haldol Decanoate, and he is described by the consulting psychiatrist at the jail as stable and cooperative, without apparent signs of delusions or disordered thinking.

With exception of obesity, Mr. C has no chronic medical problems. He was shot by the police at the time of the alleged offenses, and he underwent surgery to have the bullet removed from his abdomen.

Current Clinical Condition Mr. C is a short, overweight man who was adequately groomed in jail attire for each evaluation session. He displayed what he described as scars from gunshot wounds on his left arm and stomach. He was alert and friendly during the evaluation. His manner was childlike and rather silly, but he maintained good behavioral control and was cooperative and attentive throughout the evaluation. He did not appear to be hallucinating, and he denied that he is currently experiencing hallucinations. He reported that he had heard voices in his head prior to first receiving mental health treatment over 10 years ago. He displayed some delusional thinking regarding past mental health treatment, stating, "One place I went to they put electricity in my mind," and speculating that injections of psychotropic medication "made me lose my mind." He expressed no current delusional thinking about his treatment or any other topic. He denied any suicidal, aggressive, persecutory, or homicidal ideation. He was oriented to person and place. He provided approximate, but generally accurate, answers to questions regarding present time and timeframes of significant events, such as length of time he has been in jail and the date of the alleged offenses.

Results of psychological testing administered for his evaluation are consistent with those obtained at the time of the competency evaluation in the menacing case 10 years earlier. On the WAIS-R, Mr. C produced scores in the borderline range of intelligence (VIQ = 73, PIQ = 79, FSIQ = 75). There are no significant differences between subtests in his performance. His reading skills remain at the kindergarten level, as measured by the WRAT-3. Mr. C can identify letters of the alphabet, but he could read only two simple words.

Collateral Information Regarding Mental State at Time of Alleged Offense   Records from the mental health center where Mr. C was being treated at the time of the alleged offenses indicate that he had been prescribed a low dose of antipsychotic medication. He was not being followed closely, and there is no documentation that he was actually taking the prescribed medication. One month prior to the offenses, a social worker asked the treating psychiatrist to see the defendant because Mr. C appeared "rather manicky." The treating psychiatrist believed Mr. C was "status quo" and suggested no change in his treatment. Mr. C did not return for subsequent appointments.

Police Department reports indicate that officers were called out to the defendant's home because of a report that a suspect was sitting in a black Chevrolet in front of the home, shooting at passing cars. When the officers arrived, the defendant was sitting in the car and pointed his gun at the officers. The officers reported that, throughout the confrontation with the suspect, he kept waving the gun and saying that he was going to shoot. The police reports document that the defendant "kept talking like he was crazy and ignored numerous loud commands by all three officers to drop his weapon." At some point, the defendant exited the car, and his elderly father held onto the defendant and attempted to hold the gun down. Suddenly, the defendant ran toward the house; once he reached the side door, he turned and shot an officer twice, in the leg and the foot. The wounded officer and a second officer returned the fire. Mr. C was struck in the shoulder with buckshot from a shotgun and was hit by two 9 mm bullets in his stomach and chest.

The paramedic called to treat the defendant at the scene reported that Mr. C "seemed to be somewhat of a mental case." Mr. C reportedly kept saying, "Why did they shoot me? They never gave me a chance." After the defendant was apprehended, evidence was collected from his father's home, which included a .22 caliber revolver, 134 live rounds, and 11 spent rounds.

Mental health records at the jail, where Mr. C was taken after hospital treatment for gunshot wounds, indicate that he rolled around on the floor and removed surgical staples from his abdomen. He refused to take psychotropic medication, referring to it as "poison." He was described as delusional and paranoid, with disjointed thinking. He threatened to kill corrections officers and other inmates and denied that he had shot a police officer.

Mr. C was found incompetent to stand trial and treated for nearly 3 years in a state psychiatric hospital before the Court found him competent to proceed with the case.

The Defendant's Account of the Alleged Offenses   Mr. C stated that he had owned the gun used in the alleged offenses for 9 years. It was common in his neighborhood to discharge firearms on New Year's Eve. He stated that at the time of the offenses he was "trying my gun out early" by "shooting it into the air" in preparation for discharging the weapon on New Year's Eve.

Regarding the offenses, Mr. C said, "The police shot me and I think I shot the police. I don't know. I think it might be a delusion." Mr. C stated that he had believed at the time of the offenses that the police shot him first and that he needed to shoot in self-defense because he thought he was going to die. He reported that he initially wanted his lawyer to "sue the police department for $100,000,000." Mr. C reported that he does not remember the police telling him to drop his gun. When asked if he was shooting the weapon at any cars, he responded, "I don't think so." He thought that he might have been mistaken for someone else who shot at cars. He also does not believe that he attempted to murder the police, because if he had wanted to kill the police he would have shot them in the head, which he referred to as "the killing part." He believes that the police wore bullet-proof shields and that his gun contained "weak bullets" rather than "strong bullets."

Mr. C now believes that "the police were just doing their job." He thinks that it is wrong to shoot at houses, cars, or other people, but he is confused about events at the time of the alleged offenses. He also expressed shock at the effect of being shot, exclaiming with some incredulity, "That hurt!"

Opinion It is the opinion of the examiner, based on reasonable scientific certainty, that the defendant was suffering from the active phase of a severe mental illness, schizophrenia, at the time of the alleged offenses. This opinion is supported by the following factors: (1) the defendant's prior history of experiencing symptoms of this disorder, (2) treatment records that reflect he was symptomatic and not fully involved in treatment at the time of the offenses, (3) observations of abnormal behavior at the time of the offenses and following his arrest, (4) hospitalization records that reflect the need for treatment over several years after the offense until the defendant recovered sufficiently to be found competent to stand trial, and (5) current residual symptoms of schizophrenia, even with treatment. In addition, the defendant's educational history, borderline level of intelligence, and adaptive deficits such as illiteracy and inability to live independently or work in a competitive setting, indicate that he functions in the borderline to mild mental retardation range of intelligence.

It is also this examiner's opinion, based on reasonable scientific certainty, that as a result of Mr. C's severe mental illness and intellectual deficits, he did not know the wrongfulness of the acts charged at the time. The opinion is based on Mr. C's confusion about events at the time of the offenses, his distorted perception that the police shot him first, his lack of attempt to conceal his identity or take other measures to avoid detection, and the lack of a rational or conventional motive for the alleged offenses. Moreover, Mr. C's shock that being shot is so painful, taken in the context of the earlier menacing offense in which the defendant pretended he had a gun by playfully pointing his finger at an officer during a traffic stop, suggests that he did not know the wrongfulness of shooting at a police officer.

Kathleen Stafford, Ph.D.
Diplomate in Forensic Psychology, ABPP

Teaching Point: What are the advantages of using written versus oral notification in determining whether the notification was understood?

The *Specialty Guidelines for Forensic Psychologists* (Committee on Ethical Guidelines for Forensic Psychologists, 1991) articulates the obligation of the forensic psychologist "to ensure that prospective clients are informed of their legal rights with respect to the anticipated forensic service, of the purposes of any evaluation, of the nature of procedures to be employed, of the intended uses of any product of their services, and of the party who has employed the forensic psychologist" (Section IV. E., p. 659). Although the guidelines appear to exempt court-ordered evaluations from the requirement of obtaining the informed consent of the client, party, or legal representative before proceeding with the evaluation, in the case of court-ordered sanity evaluations, it may be important to obtain informed consent for a different reason. The insanity defense is an affirmative defense, with the burden of production and the burden of proof on the defense. A sanity evaluation requires the reconstruction of the defendant's mental state at the time of the offense through the defendant's own account of the offense and through collateral information about the defendant's state of mind and the offense. Case law is not generally supportive of imposing the insanity defense on an unwilling defendant, as long as he or she is competent to make the decision to reject the insanity plea option (*United States v. Marble*, 1991; *Frendak v. United States*, 1979). In proceeding with a sanity evaluation, the defendant is making the decision to communicate potentially incriminating information about the offense that would otherwise be protected under the Fifth Amendment and under attorney–client privilege.

Even when a sanity evaluation is conducted by a psychologist retained by the defense attorney, as part of attorney work product, the prosecution may ultimately obtain access to the expert's report, as provided by *United States ex. rel. Edney v. Smith* (1977) and similar case law. In the case of Mr. C, the examiner is required by statute to provide the report of the evaluation to the prosecutor and the court, as well as to the defense attorney who requested the court order. It is therefore imperative that Mr. C understand that he is essentially waiving his Fifth Amendment rights in agreeing to participate in the evaluation.

In their discussion of assessing criminal responsibility, Stafford and Ben-Porath (1995) recommended that the examiner tell the defendant, verbally and in writing, of the examiner's relationship to the defendant and the limitations to confidentiality that apply to the relationship. They also recommended that the examiner assess whether the defendant understands his or her legal situation and the purpose of the evaluation, and agrees with the defense strategy. If not, the examiner should notify defense counsel so that the defendant has the opportunity to consult further with counsel before proceeding with the evaluation. Even if the defendant agrees to participate in the evaluation, the examiner needs to gauge the defendant's capacity to make an informed decision to proceed with the evaluation.

There are clear advantages to the use of oral notification in determining whether defendants understand and consider the relevant information in consenting to participate in a sanity evaluation. In the case of Mr. C, who cannot read, understand complex vocabulary, or reason abstractly due to his mental illness and limited intellect, an oral discussion of the context of the evaluation and its implications for him was the only option in obtaining informed consent. An informed consent document written in simple language was read to him, using repetition, rephrasing, and examples. As the vignette illustrates, other steps were taken to consider his competence to consent to the evaluation. Mr. C's attorney was contacted to clarify that the attorney was aware that the evaluation had been ordered and scheduled. The history of the case was reviewed, establishing that Mr. C's competency had been evaluated, that he had been provided treatment for competency restoration, that he had subsequently been found competent to stand trial, and that he continued to receive treatment in the jail. The examiner talked with Mr. C about his understanding of the consequences of an insanity acquittal versus conviction and about his previously preferred option of self-defense and suing the police department for

"$100,000,000." Through this discussion and collateral information, it was possible to determine that Mr. C was making an informed, logical decision to participate in the evaluation, despite his limitations.

However, even with higher functioning defendants, oral notification is important. Merely presenting a written document and having the defendant "sign on the dotted line" does not ensure that the notification was understood and that the defendant made an informed decision to participate in the evaluation. Obtaining informed consent for participation in a forensic evaluation is a process that requires the oral presentation of essential information and at least a brief discussion of how the defendant has reached the decision to participate in the evaluation. A signature on a written form has the advantage of documenting the defendant's consent to participate. But a signature is not a substitute for the oral process of determining that the notification was understood and that the defendant consented in an informed manner.

Case 2

Principle: Do not answer the ultimate legal question directly

This principle discusses the importance of conveying information about the "ultimate legal issue" in FMHA. The ultimate legal issue is the legal question that the court must answer—for example, sanity at the time of the offense. Whether a forensic clinician should directly answer the ultimate legal question has been the subject of considerable debate. It has been observed that attempts to avoid answering this question can cause confusion and reduce the credibility of the forensic clinician from the court's perspective (Poythress, 1982). Similarly, proponents also point out that a ban on addressing the ultimate issue is not supported by empirical evidence (Rogers & Ewing, 1989). There is little empirical evidence available on the frequency with which verbal or written ultimate opinions are expressed, and the impact of such communications. Other commentators assert that answering the ultimate legal question will inevitably confound relevant clinical and scientific evidence with unrelated and inappropriate societal values (Melton et al., 1997; Morse, 1978a, 1978b, 1982a, 1982b). It is unlikely that debate in this area will diminish in the near future.

There is little ethical guidance in this area. The APA *Ethical Principles of Psychologists and Code of Conduct* (1992) provides no explicit guidance on this issue. The *Specialty Guidelines for Forensic Psychologists* (Committee on Ethical Guidelines for Forensic Psychologists, 1991) distinguishes mental health and scientific material from legal facts, opinions, and conclusions, and suggests that forensic psychologists should be prepared to explain this distinction but de-scribe the relationship between the two areas:

> Forensic psychologists are aware that their essential role as expert to the court is to assist the trier of fact to understand the evidence or to determine a fact in issue. In offering expert evidence, they are aware that their own professional observations, inferences, and conclusions must be distinguished from legal facts, opinions, and conclusions. Forensic psychologists are prepared to explain the relationship between their expert testimony and the legal issues and facts of an instant case. (p. 665)

Additional guidance can be found in legal precedent and evidentiary stan-dards. Generally, under the common law, conclusions regarding the ultimate legal question were to be made by the trier of fact and not by the forensic clinician. The *Federal Rules of Evidence* (FRE) addresses this principle in the context of mental status at the time of the offense evaluations. Under FRE 704 (a): "Except as provided in subdivision (b), testimony in the form of an opinion or inference otherwise admissible is not objectionable because it embraces an ultimate issue to be decided by the trier of fact."

However, under FRE 704(b): "No expert witness testifying with respect to the mental state or condition of a defendant in a criminal case may state an opinion or inference as to whether the defendant did or did not have the men-tal state or condition constituting an element of the crime charged or of a defense thereto. Such ultimate issues are matters for the trier of fact alone."

Although FRE 704(b) or state law equivalent in some jurisdictions specifi-cally bars ultimate issue testimony in mental state at the time of the offense evaluations, ultimate issue conclusions are not necessarily inadmissible in crim-inal cases involving other types of legal questions and forensic issues. In any event, legal authority suggests that an expert opinion may be used in an advi-sory fashion but should never substitute for the court's consideration of the ultimate legal issue (Melton et al., 1997).

Legal guidelines for standards of practice provide some additional guid-ance. The ABA *Criminal Justice Mental Health Standards* (1989) describes the contents of written reports of mental evaluations relevant to ultimate issue communication as follows: "The evaluator should express an opinion on a spe-cific legal criterion or standard only if the opinion is within the scope of the evaluator's specialized knowledge" (p. 109). On the admissibility of expert testimony concerning a person's mental condition or behavior:

> Expert testimony, in the form of an opinion or otherwise, concerning a person's present mental competency or mental condition at some time in the past should be admissible whenever the testimony is based on and is within the specialized knowl-edge of the witness and will assist the trier of fact. However, the expert witness should not express, or be permitted to express, an opinion on any question requiring a conclusion of law or a moral or social value judgment properly reserved to the court or the jury. (p. 117)

The *Guidelines for Child Custody Evaluations in Divorce Proceedings* (APA, 1994) summarizes the issue as follows:

> Recommendations, if any, are based on what is in the best psychological interests of the child. Although the profession has not reached consensus about whether psychologists ought to make recommendations about the final custody determination to the courts, psychologists are obligated to be aware of the arguments on both sides of this issue and to be able to explain the logic of their position concerning their own practice.
>
>   If the psychologist does choose to make custody recommendations, these recommendations should be derived from sound psychological data and must be based on the best interests of the child in the particular case. Recommendations are based on articulated assumptions, data, interpretations, and inferences based upon professional and scientific standards. Psychologists guard against relying on their own biases or unsupported beliefs in rendering opinions in particular cases. (p. 679)

Although much has been written about this debate, it does not appear resolved. Forensic clinicians are well-advised to consider both the advantages and disadvantages of communicating FMHA results in terms of ultimate legal issue language, and weigh the impact of each alternative on the FMHA process.

The present report provides a good illustration of the application of this principle to an insanity evaluation. As the report indicates, the forensic clinician was retained by the prosecution (an Assistant United States Attorney) in an effort to determine whether the defendant, Mr. Jones, was legally insane at the time he committed the alleged offense. In this case, therefore, the ultimate legal question was whether Mr. Jones was insane at the time he allegedly committed the offense. Consistent with this principle, the forensic clinician did not directly answer the ultimate legal question. Rather, the forensic clinician provided clinical data and conclusions, which are within his area of expertise, that should assist the trier of fact in answering the legal question regarding Mr. Jones's sanity at the time of the alleged offense.

Throughout the report, the forensic clinician provided several types of data regarding Mr. Jones's mental state at the time he committed the alleged offense: relevant historical information, the content of the clinical interview, the content of collateral interviews, and the results of psychological testing. This information was then used in support of the forensic clinician's overall clinical (as opposed to legal) conclusion regarding Mr. Jones's mental state at the time of the alleged offense. At the end of the report, the forensic clinician concluded, based on the results of the interviews and testing, that Mr. Jones suffered from a severe mental disorder at the time he committed the alleged offense, which resulted in his lack of capacity to appreciate the wrongfulness of his behavior.

In this case, the forensic clinician's clinical conclusion, which does not answer the ultimate legal question directly, should assist the trier of fact in reaching the broader legal conclusion regarding Mr. Jones's sanity at the time of the alleged offense. This illustrates the distinction made by some evaluators. By indicating that any conclusion drawn in FMHA is clinical, they distinguish the nature of their conclusion, and their role in drawing it, from the those of the legal decision maker. Other evaluators provide a sentence accompanying their FMHA conclusion that explicitly acknowledges that this conclusion is advisory only, made in recognition of the court's authority to decide the legal question at issue.

An important consideration in this case is the jurisdiction in which the case is being adjudicated. Specifically, because this is a federal criminal case, the forensic clinician should be aware of FRE 704(b) and its limitations on the opinions that may be expressed by experts in a federal insanity case: An expert is not "permitted to state an opinion or inference as to whether the defendant did or did not have the mental state or condition constituting an element of the crime charged or of a defense thereto." Consistent with the principle being discussed, Rule 704(b) concludes that "[s]uch ultimate issues are matters for the trier of fact alone."

The forensic clinician's handling of the ultimate legal question in this case is consistent with the requirements of Rule 704(b). He did not give a conclusion in the report as to whether Mr. Jones was sane or insane at the time he committed the alleged offense, and therefore did not answer the ultimate legal question directly. Rather, he simply provided relevant clinical conclusions regarding the defendant's forensic capacities that will assist the trier of fact in answering that legal question.

David L. Shapiro, Ph.D.
Diplomate in Forensic Psychology
American Board of Professionals Psychology

February 2, 1998
Sally Sanders, Attorney-At-Law
Assistant United States Attorney
Office of the United States Attorney
55 Fourth Street, N.W.
Washington, D.C. 20001

Re: Robert Jones

Dear Ms. Sanders:

Pursuant to your referral, I have completed a psychological evaluation of Mr. Robert Jones, whom I saw at the District of Columbia Detention Center on January 24, 1998. In addition to clinical interview, I administered the Minnesota Multiphasic Personality Inventory. Also, on January 28, 1998, and January 31, 1998, I interviewed by telephone Secret Service Agent Oren Barton, who provided me with his observations of Mr. Jones's behavior at the time that the Secret Service questioned him.

Prior to my seeing Mr. Jones, I also reviewed extensive documents, which not only you had provided but defense counsel, Ms. Ann Jenkins, had provided. Much of the material from Ms. Jenkins represented a series of highly delusional letters that Mr. Jones and his friend, Ms. Dorothy Carter, has sent to various officials, including the President of the United States.

During the course of evaluation, Mr. Jones was very cooperative, subdued but quite willing to discuss the charges against him and what he perceived as the tortures that had been inflicted on him over the course of several years.

Mr. Jones was informed of the fact that had I been retained by the U.S. Attorney's Office, that there was no confidentiality in the interview, and that reports would be sent to the U.S. Attorney and to his defense lawyer. He understood this and consented to the examination.

His opening words were, "They tortured me." He spoke about people who belonged to various fraternity orders having machines that could send sound waves that kept him and his friend, Ms. Carter, in constant pain. He stated that they had been around for "a long time." He spoke about a biblical sect called Midians, who he said were also affiliated with the Masons and currently with the Ku Klux Klan. He spoke about the pain "in my nervous system," describing the pain as being in his spine and brain, and that he would experience vibrations in certain areas of his body, which would also feel "heated up." He stated that these vibrations caused by the machines would make him impotent, and he had "figured out" in 1984 that was due to the machines.

However, he noted that the tortures had really been going on "all the way back to my childhood," in which he described himself as always sickly, suffering from asthma and high fevers and, in his teenage years, migraine headaches. He stated that he now realizes that these people had targeted him all his life. "They were after me ever since I was a child." He stated that they were assigned to him, although he does not know why. He also figured out that the tortures had been assigned to his family because "the machines affected everyone in my family, and I see it now." He related his mother's high blood pressure and kidney problems, as well as his sister's failed marriage, to "the machines." He stated that in 1984, he went to see a Doctor Dalton, a psychologist in St. Louis, Missouri, and noted that Doctor Dalton had an investigator who found eyewitnesses who confessed to the Masons, Midians, and Ku Klux Klan having the secret chamber where the tortures took place. Mr. Jones indicated that the investigator had taken him and Ms. Carter to the eyewitness who told them about the chambers and the machines. He stated that at the point, "we realized what was happening to us." He spoke about Ms. Carter's difficulty with mobility, fatigue, and pains, and his own problems with vibrations, which affect his sexual functioning.

He was able to discuss his charge, "a gun violation," and stated that while he was aware of the fact that as a previously convicted felon he was not possess firearms, "I did not want to come to Washington, D.C. without protection." He stated that he had no intention of harming anyone; he had come to the White House to seek help from President Clinton, who, because of a letter that the White House had sent to him, he was convinced would be able to help him. He stated that he needed the guns in order to protect himself all across the country from the evil forces that were conspiring against him. He stated that he was not going to take chances and that the situation has not been corrected yet. He stated that his pain was so intense that he felt it was worth violating the conditions of his parole in order to protect himself.

He stated that he and Ms. Carter did not know how long they were going to stay in Washington and that they were unaware of rules in Washington, D.C., against the carrying of handguns.

Mr. Jones stated that they came to Washington because "if in any way we could get to Congress" Washington would be the place. He cited the form letter from President Clinton as indicating that "he knew what we were saying because of our letter," referring to the long rambling letter that he and Ms. Carter had sent to the President. He was convinced that, because of this letter, they would have a chance of being heard if they came to Washington, D.C., and that they had actually spoken with a woman in the Justice Department on the telephone every 3 days. Mr. Jones stated that she understood that he and Ms. Carter had nowhere to stay and that they had provided their manuscript to her and "the Justice Department studied it." He indicated that the Justice Department wanted medical statements from both of them to verify what had happen to them. They also indicated that they had gone to the mayor's office to set up an appointment.

When I asked Mr. Jones why they went to the White House, he indicated that Ms. Carter did not feel that their trips to the other places were working and that therefore they needed to "go to the top." He indicated that they had also planned to go to the Black Entertainment Network and set up an appointment with a commentator on the network and that this was reflective of Ms. Carter's sense of frustration.

He stated that since he has been in the jail, he has been treated with the antipsychotic medication Risperdal, and that it does help him to sleep although it does not make the pain engendered by the machines go away.

Mr. Jones indicated that his only adult incarceration was the 20-year-old charge of armed robbery, for which he served a 5-year prison term.

He indicated that he had been hospitalized at the Veterans Administration Hospital in Columbia, Missouri, in 1972 for weeks, having checked himself in "following a bad acid trip." Mr. Jones said that at that time he was experiencing visual hallucinations that he felt were due to drugs, but "I now realize they due to the machines." He stated that he did not tell anyone at the V.A. about the machines, believing that the symptoms were, in fact, caused by the drugs.

He denied any significant history of head trauma, although he did note one period of loss of consciousness in 1992. He stated that this was described as due to his drinking, but he insisted that he was not drinking at the time; rather, it was "due to the machine."

He described a basically unremarkable family history, although there was some obvious dysfunction, with his father leaving the family when Mr. Jones was very young, and his having four stepfathers. He described a close relationship between himself, his mother, and his sister, though he stated that growing up was "tough financially." He stated that he did well in school, graduated from high school, and, in fact, had 1½ years of college courses while in prison in Missouri. He described no major family problems, stated that he had many friends in school, and reported an essentially uneventful period of time in military service between 1968 and 1970.

I interviewed Secret Service Agent Oren Barton on January 28, 1998. Agent Barton stated that he felt that Mr. Jones was delusional, and spoke about the fact Mr. Jones had told him that he was being followed by the Klan and that he wanted protection against them following him. Agent Barton also spoke about the fact that Mr. Jones spoke about other groups, mainly the Masons and the Midians, and he stated that Mr.

Jones told him that the Klan had been writing to them and following them. Agent Barton said that Mr. Jones talked about "the machines being turned up to cause more pain to them." He recalled Mr. Jones telling that they came to Washington so that the President could help them to "stop the pains." Agent Barton's belief was that both Mr. Jones and Ms. Carter were no threat to the President, and, in fact, he described them as "harmless crazy." He stated that he was convinced that they were being truthful when they spoke about the guns and being protected against the Ku Klux Klan.

The Minnesota Multiphasic Personality Inventory reveals a valid profile, though of some significance is the fact that Mr. Jones tended to deny a great deal of material. This is, of course, the total opposite of someone who is attempting to feign or malinger a mental disorder. In fact, despite being extremely guarded and denying, he made a variety of atypical and rarely given responses, and such defensiveness generally covers over psychotic processes.

With these validity constraints in mind, the test profile tends to underestimate the degree of mental illness; the pattern is indicative of a moderate to severe level of emotional instability. While overcontrolled much of the time, Mr. Jones is likely to have transitory episodes in which he would be seen as impatient and narcissistic with a moodiness that would vary from excitable to sullen.

Some of the patients rigidly overcontrol hostility for long periods of time until it erupts in explosive episodes, but of some significance is the fact that theses episodes appear to occur exclusively within a family setting. They do not appear to extend outside of the family, as a general rule, for people with this kind of profile. At the same time, the hostility at times could suddenly be turned inward, such as a dramatic and serious suicide attempt.

The current level of organization of his day-to-day functioning is quite uneven. The profile is suggestive of a frankly paranoid schizophrenic psychosis, characterized by overt projections, chronic suspicions and intense jealousies. Of some note, the patients with such profiles showed relatively little breakdown of reality testing or disorganization of behavior, with the exception of the encapsulated delusional thinking. Patients with such profiles attempt to maintain rigid controls and play strictly correct social roles. The responses also are consistent with Mr. Jones's complaint of physical ailments, which are largely transitory hysterical conversion symptoms. Patients with such profiles strongly overreact to tangible organic illness.

Typical diagnoses with these patterns are of paranoid states and more chronic paranoid psychosis. That is, the profile is highly suggestive of extensive delusional thinking, without the more wide-ranging thought disorganization that would be seen in a schizophrenic disorder. Some of these patients also present depressive trends, along with emotionally explosive (i.e., borderline) personality disorders.

The profile is also suggestive of a mild suicide risk, although the degree of risk is especially hard to evaluate because suicide attempts of these patients are so abrupt, situational, and unplanned. With this pattern, there is also a severe risk of chronic invalidism on the somatic complaints, and this is also consistent with Mr. Jones's history.

In summary, then, I would concur with the diagnosis reached earlier by Doctor Lewis of Mr. Jones, namely of a Delusional Disorder, Persecutory Type. Not only is this diagnosis consistent with the manner in which Mr. Jones presents himself, but it is also consistent with the result of the Minnesota Multiphasic Personality Inventory.

Of course, the fact that Mr. Jones and Ms. Carter share this also leads to the diagnosis of the rare condition called Folie a Deux.

Based on these observations, and the insistence by Mr. Jones on the fact that he had to carry his weapons in order to protect himself against the evil forces that were conspiring against him, as well as the fact that he felt that his need for protection was significant enough to overcome his awareness that as a previously convicted felon he was not supposed to be carrying firearms, it is my opinion that Mr. Jones has established the fact that he did suffer from a severe mental disorder on June 14, 1997, such that he lacked the capacity to appreciate the wrongfulness of his behavior.

I trust the above analysis is of some assistance to you. Please feel free to call on me if you need further information.

Very truly yours,
David L. Shapiro, Ph.D.

Teaching Point: What should be considered in the decision about whether to answer the ultimate legal question?

A forensic practitioner's decision regarding whether to offer an opinion on the ultimate legal issue should be informed by a consideration of several factors. A primary consideration is whether the rules of evidence in a particular jurisdiction address how the "ultimate issue" should be treated by evaluators. Specifically, although a forensic practitioner is required (or permitted) to offer an opinion on the ultimate legal issue in some jurisdictions, other jurisdictions prohibit this. The rules of evidence in most states permit a mental health expert witness to offer an opinion about whether the defendant meets the criteria for insanity (Rogers & Shuman, 2000). By contrast, in the federal system, *Federal Rule of Evidence* 704(b) prohibits an expert witness from offering an opinion "as to whether the defendant did or did not have the mental state or condition constituting an element of the crime charged or of a defense thereto." It should also be noted that evidence law in some jurisdictions does not address this question either way. Additionally, in some jurisdictions the permissibility of offering an opinion on the ultimate legal issue depends on the type of FMHA being conducted.

Another consideration is whether the written report is clear and thorough. A thorough and comprehensive report will provide the reader with well-reasoned and well-supported conclusions regarding relevant forensic capacities (as opposed to opinions regarding the ultimate legal issue). Forensic practitioners should resist the temptation of simply providing an opinion on the ultimate legal issue as an easy "short cut" to writing a thorough, well-reasoned report with conclusions regarding the forensic capacities that are supported by the data.

Several options might be considered in this regard: (1) routinely offering an opinion on the ultimate legal issue in reports, (2) offering an opinion on the ultimate legal issue only when asked to do so while testifying, and (3) trying at all times to avoid offering an opinion on the ultimate legal issue. Forensic practitioners, scholars, and policymakers have been unable to reach consensus with respect to these options. Although viewpoints continue to differ, one particularly strong argument for the second or third option is that forensic practitioners should avoid offering opinions on the ultimate legal issue because such opinions invariably have legal, moral, and community-value components, which are beyond the expertise of forensic clinicians (Heilbrun, 2001; Melton et al., 1997).

Chapter 12

Mens Rea and Diminished Capacity

The implications of mens rea (mental state or, literally, "guilty mind") and diminished mental capacity in the context of sentencing and criminal responsibility are the focus of the single case in this chapter. The principle preceding the case addresses the importance of using information from more than one source to test rival hypotheses and improve the overall accuracy of the evaluation. Related to this principle, the teaching point following the case includes a discussion of the question of when enough information has been collected, using the economic concept of the "point of diminishing returns," in obtaining data across multiple sources. It also provides a framework for maximizing the efficiency of data collection.

Case 1

Principle: Use multiple sources of information for each area being assessed

This principle concerns the sources of information to be used in assessing the forensic issues that are relevant to the legal question(s) in FMHA, and the importance of using information from more than one source. The use of multiple sources of information in FMHA is important for several reasons. First, multiple measures enhance accuracy in measuring a given trait, symptom, or behavior by reducing the error associated with a single source. Second, multiple measures allow the evaluator to test rival hypotheses of behavior that may have been generated, in part, by observations stemming from one or more of the measures. Independently obtained information on a second measure about the same construct can be used to support (or refute) hypotheses that may have been generated by the results of the first measure. Finally, multiple measures allow the forensic clinician to assess the consistency of data across sources and attempt to corroborate particularly important data before reaching conclusions that are being considered in the course of performing a FMHA.

In the present case, the forensic issues are "reduced mental capacity" and the potential contribution of such reduced capacity to the commission of the offense. The applicable federal statute at the time of this evaluation (Section 5K2.13, U.S. Sentencing Guidelines) indicated that:

> If the defendant committed a non-violent offense while suffering from significantly reduced mental capacity not resulting from voluntary use of drugs or other intoxicants, a lower sentence may be warranted to reflect the extent to which reduced mental capacity contributed to the commission of the offense, provided that the defendant's criminal history does not indicate a need for incarceration to protect the public. (U.S.S.G. § 5K2.13, p.s., 18 U.S.C.A)

Interpreting this language, courts have generally agreed that under the Federal Sentencing Guidelines a person may be suffering from a reduced mental capacity for the purposes of section 5K2.13 if the person is either unable to absorb information in the usual way or to exercise the power of reason, or the person knows what he or she is doing and that it is wrong but cannot control his or her behavior or conform it to the law (see, e.g., *United States v. McBroom*, 1997 WL 528657 (3d Cir. N.J.))

The use of multiple sources of information is helpful in gathering information across a variety of domains. Given the forensic issues in this case, the evaluation focused on historical and present-state information from multiple sources that was relevant to the reasoning and volitional capacities of the defendant. Such sources include the self-report of the individual being evaluated (obtained through clinical interview and via psychological testing and structured interview), collateral records, and interviews with third-party informants. In this case, we were able to review information relevant to the offenses for which the defendant pled guilty (the indictment, Guilty Plea Memorandum, and Guilty Plea Agreement), the defendant's diary, and previous mental health assessment material (a psychological evaluation and previous psychological testing), and to interview two collateral observers (his ex-wife and his mother), as well as conduct two detailed clinical interviews. A number of inconsistencies emerged across these sources, suggesting that Mr. W was providing information about his thinking and possible mental health symptoms in a fashion that exaggerated the contribution of psychopathology and minimized the role of other motivations, such as the need for money and his unwillingness to live within his financial means.

Psychological testing was important in this case. To assess the possible presence of symptoms that might be relevant to his present capacities for reasoning or self-control, he was administered the Minnesota Multiphasic Personality Inventory-2. While this instrument can provide good evidence regarding the existence of a present-state disorder, the reconstructive link must be established by other sources. Given that he met the criteria for both Major Depression and Generalized Anxiety Disorder based on structured clinical interview self-report, and that the MMPI-2 profile was consistent with the present experience of these disorders, the next question was whether he experienced these disorders at a comparable level of intensity during the period over which he was convicted of these offenses and what role his symptoms played in his understanding, reasoning, or capacity to behave lawfully. One hypothesis involved the possibility that Mr. W did experience such symptoms around this time, and they had a significant impact on his functioning, particularly related to his understanding, reasoning, and volitional control associated with his offenses.

An alternative hypothesis involved the possibility that he did not experience such symptoms to the same extent, and that these capacities were not impaired by his symptoms. A different alternative hypothesis was that he did experience symptoms of depression and anxiety, but that such symptoms had minimal impact on his understanding, reasoning, or volitional control in committing his offenses. To help distinguish among these hypotheses, Mr. W was administered the Psychopathy Checklist-Revised (PCL-R). The PCL-R focuses on personality characteristics and behavioral history relevant to an alternative explanation for his offending: that Mr. W's criminal behavior was part of a longstanding pattern of antisociality stemming from the kind of personality structure that is measured by the PCL-R. The PCL-R was important for another reason as well. The language of section 5K2.13 of the Federal Sentencing Guidelines is clearly concerned with recidivism: "a lower sentence may be warranted to reflect the extent to which reduced mental capacity contributed to the commission of the offense, *provided that the defendant's criminal history does not indicate a need for incarceration to protect the public*" (italics added).

Severe mental disorder can have a significant impact on reasoning and volitional capacities. Accordingly, Mr. W was given structured clinical interviews for both DSM-IV Axis I and II disorders. In addition to providing a structured approach to diagnosing potentially relevant disorders, the structured clinical interview provides a good way of assessing past and current psychological functioning. Additionally, the Brief Symptom Inventory, a structured screening instrument for currently experienced symptoms of mental and emotional disorder, was administered before other testing as a screening device to allow the evaluators to assess current symptoms and identify potential areas of concern. Although not administered in the present case, a formal measure of intellectual functioning, such as the Wechsler Adult Intelligence Scale, could be used if cognitive impairment appeared to be affecting volitional or reasoning capacities.

In addition to psychological testing and structured clinical interviews, the direct observation of the individual being evaluated is another important source of information. The direct observation of the individual can be considered from two sources: (1) those who frequently observe and interact with the individual (e.g., family members, friends, employers, teachers, nurses, aides), and (2) those who had the opportunity to observe particularly relevant behavior (e.g., victims or witnesses in a criminal offense). We obtained observational data in this case through collateral telephone interviews with Mr. W's mother and ex-wife. In addition to providing general background information and differing perceptions on the capacities of the individual being evaluated, direct observation also allows the evaluator to gauge the consistency of the individual's self-report against collateral reports and possibly make inferences about the accuracy of such self-report, thereby providing one measure of response style. Failure to conduct collateral interviews in this case would have yielded a different and less accurate clinical picture, as Mr. W's self-report frequently conflicted with the reports of the collateral sources.

Finally, records in areas such as mental health, medical, criminal, school, vocational, and military functioning are another source of potentially valuable information in FMHA. The mental health records were particularly helpful in this case, providing information relevant to possible malingering and allowing a better view of Mr. W's clinical condition over a number of years, particularly during the period when the offenses occurred.

Considered separately, each of these sources of information would not have provided a complete or accurate picture of the individual. Given the potential for malingering in this case, self-report alone clearly would have been particularly problematic. Mr. W's ex-wife and mother may have held some of their own biases as well, so collateral interviews also could have yielded distorted information. Similarly, psychological testing and structured interviews in isolation could have yielded clinical impressions unsupported by historical or factual context. Overreliance on one or two measures is a potential source of error in FMHA; only through multiple sources of information can the evaluator create a comprehensive, cross-checked account of the individual's functioning across a range of relevant domains.

FORENSIC ASSESSMENT

Re: Jay W
Criminal Nos. 00-123 & 00-123-1

REFERRAL

Mr. W is a 40-year-old Caucasian male who pled guilty to charges of Forgery of a Judge's Signature, in violation of 18 U.S.C. section 505; Conspiracy, in violation of 18 U.S.C. section 371; Bank Fraud, in violation of 18 U.S.C. section 1344; Mail Fraud, in violation of 18 U.S.C. section 1341; Wire Fraud, in violation of 18 U.S.C. section 1343; Interstate Transportation of Stolen Property, in violation of 18 U.S.C. section 2314; Obstruction of IRS Laws, in violation of 18 U.S.C. section 7212; Preparation of Materially False Income Tax Returns, in violation of 18 U.S.C. section 7206; Forgery and Embezzling of United States Savings Bonds, in violation of 18 U.S.C. sections 510(a)(1) and (2); Money Laundering with Intent to Conceal or Disguise the Location of the Source and Ownership of the Proceeds of a Specified Unlawful Activity, in violation of 18 U.S.C. section 1956(a)(1)(B)(I); Money Laundering Involving Criminally Derived Property of a value greater than $10,000, in violation of 18 U.S.C. section 1957; and Criminal Forfeiture of Criminally Derived Property in violation of 18 U.S.C. section 982. A request for a mental health evaluation to provide the defense with information relevant to sentencing, pursuant to U.S.S.G. section 5K2.13, p.s., 18 U.S.C.A., and Rule 11 of the Federal Rules of Civil Procedure, was made by Mr. W's attorney.

PROCEDURES

Mr. W was evaluated on two separate occasions for a total of approximately 10 hours. In addition to a clinical interview, Mr. W was administered a standard objective test of mental and emotional functioning (the Minnesota Multiphasic Personality Inventory, 2nd edition, or MMPI-2), a clinical interview for primary (Axis I) psychological disorders, a structured clinical interview for Axis II Disorders (the Structured Clinical Interview for DSM-IV Axis II Personality Disorders, or SCID-II), a structured screening instrument for currently experienced symptoms of mental and emotional disorder (the Brief Symptom Inventory, or BSI), and a measure of personality functioning relevant to violence and recidivism risk and rehabilitation potential (the Psychopathy Checklist-Revised, or PCL-R). Two collateral telephone interviews were conducted: a 45-minute interview with Mr. W's ex-wife and a 30-minute interview with Mr. W's mother. The following documents, obtained through Mr. W's attorney, were also reviewed as part of this evaluation:

1. *United States v. McBroom*, 1997 WL 528657 (3rd Cir. N.J.),
2. Indictment, *United States v. Jay W* (undated),
3. *United States v. Jay W*, Guilty Plea Memorandum (Criminal #'s 00-123 & 00-123),
4. *United States v. Jay W*, Guilty Plea Agreement (Criminal #'s 00-123 & 00-123),
5. Personal Notes of Jay W (undated),
6. Confidential Psychological Evaluation (Julian Capp, Ph.D., 2-10-96),
7. MMPI-2 (administered 11-20-95 by Susan Rank, Ph.D),
8. Progress Notes (marital therapy with Susan Rank, Ph.D., 11-22-94 to 5-14-96), and
9. Personality Assessment Inventory (administered by Susan Rank, Ph.D., 12-22-94).

Prior to the evaluation, Mr. W was notified about the purpose of the evaluation and the associated limits on confidentiality. He clearly understood the basic purpose of the evaluation, reporting back his understanding that he would be evaluated and that a written report would be submitted to his attorney. He further understood that the report could be used in his sentencing hearing, and if it were, copies would be provided to the prosecution and the court.

RELEVANT HISTORY

Some of the historical information described in this section was obtained from collateral sources, and some was obtained directly from Mr. W. Whenever possible, we attempted to assess the consistency of factual information through the use of multiple sources. If additional collateral information is obtained prior to Mr. W's court date, a supplemental report will be filed.

Jay W was born in Reading, Pennsylvania. According to self-report, Mr. W is the youngest of three children born to his parents. Mr. W indicated that his brothers have not spoken for the last 25 years. The Progress Notes also indicate that Mr. W is not close to either of his brothers and his brothers are not close to each other. Mr. W's mother described the rift between the three brothers in similar terms. Mr. W also stated that his oldest brother is currently "cooperating" with the prosecution in the present case against him. According to Mr. W, his father worked for a local insurance company until his death approximately 8 years ago. Mr. W indicated that both of his parents worked to support the family while he was growing up.

When asked about his upbringing, Mr. W did not provide significant information or detail. He stated that there was "no involvement, no interaction, no affection . . . I was along for the ride." Mr. W elaborated by indicating that there was little discussion in his family; his family life was very regimented and routine. According to the Progress Notes, Mr. W's parents spent a lot of time apart and did not display affection to each other or the children. By contrast, Mr. W's mother characterized the home environment as "trouble free and supportive." Specifically, she stated that Mr. W was very close to his father, to the point of adoration. Mr. W indicated that as a result of his upbringing he "became a loner and stayed a loner."

Mr. W indicated that he had no close friends or acquaintances as a young child or adolescent. According to Mr. W's mother, however, Mr. W had a number of good friends that lived in the neighborhood. His Personal Notes state that he had a small circle of friends. Similarly, he also indicated that other than his children, he has never had any close friends, relationships, or acquaintances. According to Mr. W's ex-wife, she never saw him spending time with or even mentioning any friends during their marriage. There are indications in the Progress Notes that Mr. W had at least one close friend in high school.

Mr. W's mother indicated that Mr. W had friends throughout childhood and adolescence. According to Mr. W, he never got into trouble as a child because he didn't want to have to face his father afterward. Mr. W's mother characterized Mr. W as a "pleasant and quiet child, who was never any trouble." Mr. W's mother elaborated that this was also true of Mr. W through adolescence. According to the Progress Notes, Mr. W was an "impulsive child." Mr. W denied being impulsive as a child, however. When asked about his current relationships with his family, Mr. W stated "I'm the devil . . . I don't have relationships . . . there's something wrong with me." Mr. W denied experiencing any kind of abuse at the hands of family members.

According to Mr. W, he is recently divorced. The Confidential Psychological Evaluation reports that his ex-wife filed for divorce approximately 5 years ago. According to Mr. W, his ex-wife was the first woman with whom he had ever been involved, either socially or sexually. The Personal Notes state that he never dated in high school or college; however, during the second day of the evaluation, Mr. W stated that he "dated occasionally in high school and college." The Progress Notes suggest that Mr. W dated in high school. According to Mr. W's mother, Mr. W dated infrequently while in high school. Mr. W stated that he dated his future wife for 9 months and was engaged for a year before marrying. Mr. W's ex-wife confirmed the basic facts of their courtship and elaborated that "I was only 21 . . . he swept me off my feet . . . he wined and dined me, and was a real gentleman."

The Personal Notes, self-report, Mr. W's ex-wife, and the Progress Notes all indicate that the marriage started to deteriorate after about 2 years. Mr. W reported that the relationship was based on "control," as his ex-wife dominated the relationship and constantly pressured him to make more money. Mr. W also reported that his ex-wife spent large amounts of money and sent money to her sister without consulting him. The Progress Notes provide similar information. On the second day of the evaluation, Mr. W indicated that at least part of his criminal behavior was motivated by a need to make more money to satisfy his ex-wife. The Progress Notes characterize Mr. W's ex-wife as using "aversive control"

and being "blunt to a strong degree" in the relationship. There is no further explanation of this comment in the Progress Notes.

According to Mr. W's ex-wife, she handled all of the day-to-day financial aspects and general management of the household. She also acknowledged spending large amounts of money on home furnishings. She noted, however, that Mr. W had told her that he was making over $200,000 a year, and that she had "carte blanche" to buy whatever she wanted. When asked why she thought Mr. W began stealing from others, she stated that "he bit off more than he could chew financially . . . I would have gotten a job if he would have told me . . . it just snowballed from there." Mr. W's mother described Mr. W's ex-wife as "one of the nicest people that I have ever met . . . she was very good to me."

Mr. W also indicated that as a result of the divorce and current criminal charges against him, his ex-wife has custody of their children. Mr. W indicated that one of his children currently takes the medication Ritalin for Attention Deficit Disorder (ADD). The Progress Notes and Mr. W's ex-wife also indicate this. Finally, Mr. W stated that his ex-wife is cooperating with the prosecution in the current case against him.

According to self-report, Mr. W graduated from high school in 1972. Mr. W stated that he had perfect attendance in high school and was a below average student. He denied all behavioral problems in high school but described himself as a "nonentity," without friends or outside interests. Mr. W's mother again suggested otherwise, indicating that Mr. W had friends and numerous outside activities such as athletics. She also stated that Mr. W was not afraid to try new things that interested him. Mr. W indicated that he attended college after graduating from high school, majoring in accounting and graduating with honors. In addition, Mr. W indicated that he graduated from law school in 1983. According to self-report, Mr. W's educational career culminated with an advanced degree in Tax Law in 1985. Mr. W's educational history was described in similar terms in both collateral interviews. When asked about his future vocational and educational plans, Mr. W stated that he would "worry about that later . . . because if I don't get a substantial reduction [in sentencing] I'm done."

Mr. W reported that he has held numerous positions in the field of accounting and tax since 1976. He said that from 1976 to 1980 he worked for both of his brothers in their accounting firm. According to Mr. W, "family squabbling" caused his two brothers to split, and Mr. W went to work for another firm as controller from 1980 to 1983, when the company went bankrupt (according to Mr. W, the company was in financial trouble when he accepted the position). Mr. W's ex-wife indicated that Mr. W's brothers "fired him before the firm split." According to self-report and the Personal Notes, Mr. W also worked as a law clerk from 1982 to 1983, until his graduation from law school. Mr. W reported that he held positions in tax and accounting with three different firms between 1983 and 1990. He cited personal differences, as well as inadequate advancement opportunities, as his reasons for changing firms so frequently. In 1990 he started his own firm with a partner. This partnership was dissolved shortly thereafter, and Mr. W became a solo practitioner. Mr. W stated that he dissolved the partnership because his partner was "not a good person." According to Mr. W's ex-wife, the partnership was terminated because Mr. W's partner found that "checks were missing," and improper charges had been made to corporate credit cards. According to self-report, Mr. W remained in private practice until early 1997. The Personal Notes are consistent with Mr. W's self-report of his vocational history.

The following is a general account of Mr. W's criminal activity, as reflected in the Indictment, two Guilty Plea Memoranda, and his self-report. Mr. W engaged in a variety of white-collar crimes over a 2-year period. As a tax professional and an attorney, Mr. W possessed specialized skills and knowledge that frequently put him in positions of power that engendered the trust of others. He utilized this position to perpetrate a number of fraudulent activities. Initially, Mr. W defrauded individual clients through a variety of means, including fictitious settlement agreements, contracts, real estate investment schemes, and lawsuits. These activities led to a brief confinement in a federal correctional facility and a similarly short period of time on home confinement. Eventually, Mr. W's clients became suspicious and started to demand their money back. In order to

meet these obligations, Mr. W began defrauding the IRS, creating fraudulent tax credit schemes, providing fraudulent business loans, forging judicial signatures, and engaging in money laundering schemes with business associates.

When Mr. W was asked about what influenced his behavior in committing such offenses, he stated that he needed the funds to "keep the game going." He clarified that this meant that he was hopeful that the next "deal" would be the "big one" that enabled him to set things right. Mr. W stated that he knew right from wrong and expressed remorse for the acts he committed. When asked about his emotional state during the commission of his offenses, Mr. W indicated that he was generally nervous, excited, and scared. He also indicated that his criminal offending was impulsive, stating that "I never took the time to think about anything . . . I just lied."

According to Mr. W, he does not have any serious medical problems. Mr. W's mental health history is noteworthy. According to self-report, the Personal Notes, and the Progress Notes, Mr. W and his ex-wife attended marital counseling. According to Mr. W, he initiated counseling for the couple. Mr. W's ex-wife reported that she initiated the counseling sessions. The Progress Notes confirm that the couple attended counseling for approximately 18 months.

The Confidential Psychological Evaluation indicated that Mr. W has been in court-mandated therapy for approximately 3 years. According to the Confidential Psychological Evaluation, Mr. W had been taking the antidepressant Prozac for an unspecified period of time. Mr. W denied ever having taken any type of psychotropic medication. Mr. W's ex-wife confirmed the basic facts of the couple's therapy history and added that she was not aware that Mr. W ever took psychotropic medications.

According to Mr. W, he currently takes the medication Synthroid, but was unable to explain the exact nature of his thyroid condition. Synthroid is generally taken for hypothyroidism. According to the Progress Notes, Mr. W was on the medication Synthroid when he began individual therapy approximately 4 years ago. The Progress Notes also indicate that Mr. W was suffering from symptoms of depression when first seen in therapy on an individual basis. Additionally, the

Progress Notes show that Mr. W was experiencing suicidal ideation at this time. Mr. W stated that he attempted to take his own life with a plastic spoon while incarcerated at Fairton Federal Correctional Facility. He also reported that he currently experiences suicidal ideation, but denied that he had any present plan to act on such thoughts.

It should be noted that Mr. W indicated that he had read the *Diagnostic and Statistical Manual of Mental Disorders* (4th edition) in an attempt to determine what was "wrong with me." As part of the Personal Notes, Mr. W identified a number of disorders that he believes describe him. These include Attention Deficit Disorder, Conduct Disorder, Mood Episodes, Major Depressive Episode, Dysthymic Disorder, Generalized Anxiety Disorder, Adjustment Disorder, and Antisocial Personality Disorder. Mr. W denied all familial history of serious mental disorder on either side of his family. Mr. W's mother also reported the absence of a family psychiatric history.

Mr. W was administered the Personality Assessment Inventory (PAI), in 1994 by Dr. Rank. The validity scales suggest that Mr. W responded consistently to the test content but portrayed himself as relatively free of the common shortcomings to which most individuals will admit. She characterized Mr. W's response style as "defensive" and recommended caution in interpreting the profile. Clinically, the PAI did not reflect the experience of significant psychopathology, but this may have been due to a reluctance to admit dysfunction or problems across many areas. Interpersonally, Mr. W's style was described as one of "autonomy and balance . . . his assertiveness, friendliness, and concern for others is typical for that of normal adults." Dr. Rank noted that Mr. W was experiencing suicidal ideation, and indicated that he "experienced his level of social support as being somewhat lower than that of the average adult . . . he may have relatively few close relationships or be dissatisfied with the quality of these relationships . . . however, he reports relatively little stress arising from this or other major life areas." Diagnostically, the PAI suggested the following possibilities based on DSM-III-R criteria: rule out dysthymic disorder and mixed personality disorder with narcissistic features.

Mr. W was administered a MMPI-2 as part of his therapy. The results suggest that he responded by openly endorsing a number of unusual thoughts, feelings, and experiences; although the profile appeared valid, there may have been some exaggeration of symptoms, particularly in the latter part of the test. The results must therefore be interpreted cautiously. Individuals with such profiles are often described as acutely distressed, depressed, and tense. Such profiles are also associated with moodiness, anger, mistrustfulness, and resentment of others, as well as a tendency to blame others for his problems. Interpersonally, poor social skills, disturbance in interpersonal relationships, and marital difficulties were suggested. His profile also suggested that he was overly sensitive and resistant to the demands of others. Similarly, the profile suggests dependency feelings, an exaggerated need for affection, suspicion of others, and rejection of emotional ties. Diagnostically, such profiles have been associated with mental health disorders as well as antisocial features, with the alternative or additional possibility of exaggeration or even fabrication of symptoms.

The Confidential Psychological Evaluation also includes other relevant testing. First, Mr. W was administered a mental status examination. At the time [of the evaluation], he presented in a disheveled manner, with excessive motor activity reportedly driven by emotional feelings of anxiousness, irritability, and depression. His speech was pressured, rapid, and accelerated. His thought processes were circumstantial, as his speech contained numerous trivial details that made the major theme and goals difficult to comprehend. Flight of ideas was also noted. Sensory perception appeared intact and no hallucinations were noted. Memory for past and present events was somewhat hazy, and he also appeared distractable. Suicidal thinking but no thoughts of aggression toward others were present. Second, Mr. W was administered the Beck Depression Inventory, Revised in order to determine the severity of his depression. On the Beck, Mr. W obtained a score of 35. Scores of 30 and higher indicate severe clinical depression.

Mr. W denied all forms of substance abuse. There is no evidence to the contrary contained in any of the collateral sources reviewed as part of this evaluation.

As noted previously, Mr. W was indicted and pled guilty in November 1995 to charges related to his money laundering activities. He apparently has no history of other criminal or juvenile arrests.

CURRENT CLINICAL CONDITION

Mr. W presented as a Caucasian male of average height who appeared his stated age. He was dressed in casual clothing and was well-groomed when seen for the evaluation. Initially, he was co-operative and polite, and remained so throughout the entire evaluation. His speech was clear, co-herent, relevant, and slightly pressured. Mr. W repeatedly sought to clarify the purpose of the evaluation and the intent of the evaluators as it related to his pending sentencing hearing. He was particularly anxious to know if the evaluators were "part of the team." Mr. W responded at length and in great detail to most questions asked of him throughout the evaluation. When asked personal questions of a sensitive nature, Mr. W would frequently either make a self-derogatory or humorous remark. His capacity for attention and concentration appeared adequate, and he was able to focus well on a series of tasks during the 10-hour (over 2 days) evaluation without becom-ing visibly distracted. Therefore, it would appear that this evaluation provides a good estimate of Mr. W's current level of functioning.

Mr. W's mood throughout the evaluation was largely neutral and his affect constricted, although his attempts at humor made him appear glib at times. In addition, Mr. W frequently made com-ments that suggested low self-esteem. He also ac-knowledged that he liked to "kid around" when discussing sensitive topics. This occurred mainly while discussing his family history and the possi-bility of his potential incarceration. Mr. W was correctly oriented to time, person, and place. Overall level of intellectual functioning was not formally measured but appeared to be in the Av-erage to Above Average range.

Mr. W did not report experiencing any per-ceptual disturbances (auditory or visual hallu-cinations), and his train of thought was clear and logical. Mr. W also did not report experiencing delusions (bizarre ideas with no possible basis in reality). On a structured inventory of symptoms of mental and emotional disorders (the BSI), Mr. W reported various symptoms of distress. Some of the symptoms reported by Mr. W include ner-vousness, trouble remembering things and con-centrating, feeling afraid in open spaces or on the street, suicidal ideation, feeling that most people cannot be trusted, poor appetite, being suddenly scared for no reason, feeling generally fearful, feeling lonely, feeling inferior to others, trouble falling asleep, having to check and double check what he does, difficulty making decisions, hope-lessness, urges to beat, injure, or harm someone, urges to break or smash things, never feeling close to another person, spells of terror and panic, feel-ing as though he's not given proper credit for his achievements, restlessness, worthlessness, guilt, and thoughts that something is wrong with his mind. Mr. W reported that he has been experi-encing symptoms of depression and anxiety for a number of years. He also indicated that his recent divorce and current legal situation have exacer-bated these symptoms. According to Mr. W, he is afraid of law enforcement officers and will go out of his way to avoid them if he sees them on the street. Similarly, Mr. W stated that he has been "sold out" by his legal counsel, elaborating that his attorney and opposing counsel "are just too friendly." Mr. W stated that he has to check everything he does just in case he made a mis-take. He elaborated by indicating that this behav-ior doesn't interfere with his day-to-day function-ing and is a result of his perfectionist tendencies. Mr. W also indicated that he would someday kill his older brother, Mike, due to his involvement in his divorce, custody hearing, and the current legal situation. Later in the interview, Mr. W in-dicated that he meant this statement as a joke and would never harm another human being. (Mr. W's defense counsel was notified about this state-ment.) Similarly, Mr. W stated that he has urges to break or smash things, but although it would make him feel better, he was afraid to act on the impulse because the prosecution might find out if he did. According to Mr. W, he has never felt close to another person and has felt that way all of his life. Additionally, Mr. W indicated that he frequently has suicidal ideation, although he de-nied having any plan or intention to act on those thoughts. Finally, Mr. W stated that "there has to be something wrong with my mind." He was un-able to elaborate further.

Mr. W's MMPI-2 profile is likely to be a good indication of his present personality functioning, although his responses to the items that appear near the end of the MMPI-2 reflected an approach that was either careless, random, or deceitful, thereby invalidating that portion of the test (Welsh Code: 2" 7068'4 + 3-1/95: LF-/K:). Individuals with such profiles are often described as experiencing a significant amount of psychological distress, self-doubt, and low morale in the context of a mixed pattern of psychological problems. Particular problems are often seen with anxiety and depression. Additionally, such individuals tend to be high-strung and insecure, and may also be having physical problems that are the result of, or intensified by, stress and the individual's style of coping with it. Disturbances in sleep and appetite, as well as decreased energy, are often associated with such profiles. Individuals with such profiles are often described as shy, emotionally distant, and uneasy in social situations. These characteristics are probably symptomatic of a broader pattern of social withdrawal. Individuals with such profiles frequently receive diagnoses related to depression and anxiety, and may also receive an Axis II diagnosis of some type of personality disorder.

From a treatment standpoint, individuals with this MMPI-2 pattern are usually feeling a great deal of discomfort and usually want help for their psychological problems. Symptomatic relief for depression may be provided by medication. Psychotherapy, particularly cognitive-behavioral treatment, may also be beneficial. Mr. W's passive, unassertive personality style might be a focus of behavior change.

Mr. W was administered the Structured Clinical Interview for DSM-IV Axis II Personality Disorders (SCID-II) as part of this evaluation. The SCID is a structured clinical interview using the diagnostic criteria for DSM-IV. Based on the results of this interview, collateral information, interviews, MMPI-2 results, PCL-R results, and the clinical interview, it was apparent that Mr. W exhibits specific maladaptive personality traits (avoidant, dependent, narcissistic, and asocial), but does not meet the full criteria for any of the personality disorders in DSM-IV.

However, Mr. W does currently meets the criteria for Major Depressive Disorder and Generalized Anxiety Disorder. Based on the information available, it is unclear how long Mr. W has been suffering from these disorders. However, the Progress Notes report symptoms of depression as early as 11-22-94. The results of the 2-96 MMPI-2 report significant symptoms of anxiety.

The results of the PCL-R indicate that Mr. W would not be classified as a psychopath, which would put him at lower risk for reoffending for crime in general and for violent crime. Mr. W's PCL-R score (24), as rated by both of the undersigned, would place him at the 51st percentile relative to male prison inmates. Mr. W's score on Factor 1 (13), which measures features often associated with lack of remorse and interpersonal manipulativeness, would place him at the 86th percentile relative to male prison inmates. His Factor 2 score (10), which measures features often associated with a persistent pattern of antisocial behavior, would place him at the 34th percentile relative to male prison inmates. In general, these results would suggest that, relative to psychopathic inmates, Mr. W's risk for reoffending is lower, and his capacity to respond to treatment or other rehabilitation interventions is higher.

SENTENCING CONSIDERATIONS

U.S.S.G. section 5K2.13, p.s., 18 U.S.C.A. provides: If the defendant committed a non-violent offense while suffering from significantly reduced mental capacity not resulting from voluntary use of drugs or other intoxicants, a lower sentence may be warranted to reflect the extent to which reduced mental capacity contributed to the commission of the offense, provided that the defendant's criminal history does not indicate a need for incarceration to protect the public.

1. Non-violent Offense   According to *United States v. McBroom*, the matter of whether Mr. W's crime was a non-violent offense is a question of law, and therefore cannot be addressed by this forensic assessment.

2. Reduced Mental Capacity Not Resulting from Voluntary Use of Drugs or Other Intoxicants There is nothing to indicate that Mr. W was under the influence of drugs or other intoxicants over the period of time that he has acknowledged committing these offenses. In addition, all sources of information considered in this evaluation indicate that Mr. W does not have a substance abuse problem.

United States v. McBroom states that the "[s]entencing commission intended to include those with cognitive impairments and those with volitional impairments within the definition of 'reduced mental capacity,'" and laid out the following two part test:

A person may be suffering from a "reduced mental capacity" for the purposes of 5K2.13 if either:

1. the person is unable to absorb information in the usual way or to exercise the power of reason; or
2. the person knows what he is doing and that it is wrong but cannot control his behavior or conform it to the law.

There is nothing in Mr. W's history to suggest that he has defects in cognition that would make him unable to absorb information in the usual way or to exercise the power of reason. Further, there is little to indicate that Mr. W did not know what he was doing and that it was wrong; Mr. W himself directly acknowledged that he was aware of the wrongfulness of his behavior. Even though Mr. W currently experiences Major Depression, Generalized Anxiety Disorder, and a number of maladaptive personality traits, it is difficult to describe a relationship between these disorders and their symptoms and any significant impairment of his capacity to control his behavior or conform it to the law. It is possible to describe Mr. W's distress with his marriage and failure to communicate with his ex-wife about their financial affairs as related to his avoidant tendencies and perhaps exacerbating his symptoms of depression. This was a connection that Mr. W talked about in the second evaluative session but not the first, and it would be accurate to describe such a connection (in light of all the information gathered in this evaluation) as somewhat tenuous, and only one of several possible contributors to his thinking and feeling about the acts of which he has been convicted. Mr. W's attempts to obtain a great deal of money (to make himself more "successful" and to satisfy his perceived domestic financial needs), his sense of excitement about "the game," and his caring about consequences less than he might otherwise have (perhaps related in part to his depression) all apparently contributed to this behavior. However, we cannot conclude that his mental health symptoms and personality characteristics, taken together, appeared to influence his behavior so greatly that he could not conform his conduct to the requirements of the law.

CONCLUSIONS

In the opinion of the undersigned, based on all of the above, Mr. W

1. is suffering from Major Depression and Generalized Anxiety Disorder,
2. did not experience symptoms that clearly and significantly impaired his capacity to absorb information in the usual way or to exercise the power of reason or impaired his knowledge of the wrongfulness of these criminal acts or his capacity to conform his conduct to the requirements of the law around the time of the offenses.

Thank you for the opportunity to evaluate Mr. W.

Kirk Heilbrun, Ph.D.
Consulting Psychologist

Geff Marczyk, M.S., M.A.
MCP Hahnemann University
Graduate Student

David DeMatteo
MCP Hahnemann University
Graduate Student

Teaching Point: How much is enough? Diminishing returns from information sources

How much information is enough? How many sources of information should be considered? When is it time to stop collecting information from multiple sources? The collection of data from multiple sources can be time consuming. It is important to recognize that there are diminishing returns in the number of sources of information that might be used in this process. The following suggestions may help to identify this "point of diminishing returns." First, the evaluator should identify an appropriate investigation strategy. As part of this strategy, the evaluator should identify the key domains and constructs that are most relevant to the forensic issues being assessed. In this case, psychological testing, clinical and structured interviews, and collateral documents were used to gather historical information and assess a broad range of domains and constructs. Each source provided valuable information on Mr. W's functioning across a variety of domains and also targeted key areas for follow-up through collateral phone interviews. Second, it is useful to focus on the domains that are the most relevant to the forensic issues, or most unclear, rather than spend time on domains that are only tangentially related or noncontributory to the forensic issues. For example, in this case Mr. W reported an extremely high level of formal education. This self-report was confirmed through collateral interviews. It would probably not have been useful, therefore, to formally assess his intellectual functioning as it might contribute to diminished capacity. Finally, the evaluator should discontinue the investigation of a domain or construct after a number of data sources have yielded comparable information. In this case, for example, Mr. W's self-report of his criminal activities was consistent with collateral documents provided by his attorney. It was therefore unnecessary to confirm the factual aspects of these charges through further collateral interviews. Further investigation in this area would only have been justified if new or different information (e.g., the impressions of clients who had lost money through Mr. W's actions) might result, and that information was particularly relevant to the assessment of a particular forensic capacity.

Chapter 13

Sex Offender Sentencing

This chapter focuses on considerations in the sentencing of adult sexual offenders. The principle preceding the first case addresses the importance of considering both relevance and scientific validity in considering how to seek information and select data sources in forensic assessment. The teaching point in the first case discusses the strengths and weaknesses of classification systems for sex offenders. The principle associated with the second case in this chapter—use scientific reasoning in assessing the causal connection between clinical condition and functional abilities—discusses the importance of hypothesis formulation, testing, falsifiability, parsimony in interpretation, awareness of the limits on accuracy, and the applicability of nomothetic research to forensic mental health assessment. Finally, the teaching point for the second case includes a discussion of the development and empirical underpinnings of taxonomic sex offender typologies and their limitations.

Case 1

Principle: **Use relevance and reliability (validity) as guides for seeking information and selecting data sources**

This principle is discussed in some detail in Chapter 9. Therefore, we move directly to address how the present report illustrates the application of this principle.

The first report in this chapter provides a good example of the application of relevance and reliability to the selection of data sources in a FMHA. The purpose of the evaluation was to determine: (1) whether the individual being assessed could be classified as "repetitive and compulsive," which would place him under the New Jersey Sex Offender Act (making him eligible for specialized treatment services and subject to increased community notification requirements); (2) what risk the individual being assessed presented to the community; and (3) a suitable treatment plan. Generally, statutes such as the New Jersey Sex Offender Act (1997) require that (1) the offense be sexual (usually

259

involving force, aggression, or minors), (2) the conduct be repetitive (actual demonstration of specific past offenses is not always required—repetition may be satisfied by the prediction of future conduct), (3) there is a mental illness (broadly defined), and (4) a treatment plan is needed (Melton et al., 1997). In this case, relevance and reliability served as guides for determining which sources of information should be considered in addressing the requirements of the New Jersey Sex Offender Act.

We noted earlier that relevance in a forensic context can be considered by describing the logical basis for a connection between a mental health construct and the relevant forensic issue(s). In this case, the forensic clinician was asked to provide a risk assessment and to determine if the individual being assessed was "repetitive and compulsive" in his behavior. There are a variety of mental health constructs and historical data that might be relevant to these forensic issues, with some data sources more relevant than others when the forensic issues are considered.

For example, in this report, the forensic clinician chose historical and psychometric data sources that are directly relevant to the forensic issues being considered. Specifically, the New Jersey Sex Offender Act requires repetitive and compulsive behavior and the presence of a mental illness, broadly defined. Relevant historical information was obtained through a collateral document review and a clinical interview. These sources of information revealed a pattern of sexual offending over a period of years, and a history of recurrent behavior in both sexual and nonsexual areas that might be relevant to the forensic issue of repetitive and compulsive. The personality characteristics suggested by history relevant to this forensic characteristic were measured, in part, using psychological testing. Specifically, the Million Clinical Multiaxial Inventory-III (MCMI-III; Millon, 1994)—a measure designed to assess personality style, the presence of specific symptom patterns, and the presence of severe mental disorders—suggested paraphilias focusing on child molestation, sexual coercion, and exhibitionism. In addition to verifying the self-report of the individual, the MCMI-III suggested the presence of a DSM-IV disorder (paraphilia), which is required under the New Jersey Sex Offender Act. The use of the MCMI-III also provided some empirical evidence about the strength of the relationship between such profiles and paraphilia, based on the empirical data used to validate the instrument.

Additional examples of empirically relevant measures can be found in the risk assessment section of the report. The Multiphasic Sex Inventory (Nichols & Molinder, 1984) was used to describe the individual's static and dynamic risk factors for sexual reoffending. This tool was constructed after review of available empirical studies on sex offender characteristics and recidivism rates. It is not supported by empirical research performed specifically with using the MSI and validated against the outcome of sexual reoffending with large samples across multiple studies. However, it does use risk factors that are commonly cited in the literature, allowing a better description of empirically relevant (as opposed to empirically validated) risk factors.

PSYCHOLOGICAL REPORT

Name: John J
Age: 45 years
Date(s) of Examination: 9/8/98
Examiner: Philip Witt, Ph.D.

REASON FOR REFERRAL

Mr. J was referred for a psychological evaluation by his attorney, Robert Singleton, Esq., after having been charged with sexually abusing a 9-year-old girl. Mr. Singleton requested opinions as to:

1. whether Mr. J is repetitive and compulsive, which would place him under the purview of the New Jersey Sex Offender Act, thus making him eligible for the specialized treatment services (and increased community notification requirements) associated with such a finding,
2. what risk Mr. J presents to the community, and
3. what treatment plan would be suitable for Mr. J?

SOURCES OF INFORMATION

1. Individual interview of John J.
2. Review of Discovery materials.
3. Psychological assessment instruments:
   - Millon Clinical Multiaxial Inventory-III (MCMI)
     The MCMI is a 175 true-false objective personality test designed to assess personality style, presence of specific symptom patterns, and the presence of severe mental disorders. The MCMI also has validity scales that evaluate the attitude with which the individual answered the test questions.
   - Multiphasic Sex Inventory (MSI)
     The MSI is a 300-item objective personality test specifically standardized on a sex offender population. Its scales measure qualities of relevance in assessing sex offenders, such as extent of justifications of deviant sexual practices, degree and type of deviant sexual fantasies and deviant sexual behavior, presence of specific fetishes, presence of sexual dysfunctions, and sexual history.
   - Registrant Risk Assessment Scale
     The RRAS is an instrument developed by the New Jersey Attorney General's Office to evaluate and place sex offenders in risk tiers. It evaluates seriousness of the offense, characteristics of the offender, characteristics of the offense, and community support.

REVIEW OF DISCOVERY MATERIALS

The records indicate that Mr. J has been charged with one instance of fondling the vaginal area of a 9-year-old girl; the girl reported digital penetration during this offense. He has two prior sexual charges for exposing himself to teenage girls. These prior charges resulted in probation in municipal court.

INTERVIEW OF JOHN J

Mr. J presented as a tall, thin white male who appeared his stated age. He was oriented to time, place, and person. His thought processes, as assessed through the interview, were relevant and coherent. There were no signs of hallucinations or delusional thinking, or of suicidal thoughts or intent. In summary, there was no evidence of a thought disorder.

Throughout the interview, Mr. J was open, verbal, and cooperative. He answered all questions and provided information spontaneously, of his own accord. In fact, he readily recounted his life history in detail, requiring very little prompting. Included in this life history were a variety of actions that cast him in a non-flattering light, suggesting a high level of candor. He showed pressured speech; it was difficult to get a word in edgewise once he began his account of his life.

In his junior year in high school, he began a romantic relationship with a female high school classmate with whom he had sexual intercourse. By his senior year, however, he was dating four or five different high school girls, and had sexual intercourse with two or three. He hid all of these relationships from his then-girlfriend. During college, Mr. J became, by his own description, even more sexually promiscuous. He had sexual relations with scores of age-appropriate women, on more than one occasion contracting sexually transmitted diseases. Throughout college, he ostensibly had a steady girlfriend, but without her knowledge, he was having sexual relations with a variety of other women. He also began frequenting massage parlors for casual sexual encounters with prostitutes.

During high school, he began to engage in sports betting. By college, he was heavily in debt because of his betting, and his father settled his debts on more than one occasion. His involvement with gambling has continued intermittently to the present. He described times when he would be obsessed with sports betting, on the phone continually with bookies and forever looking for a big win that would recover his losses.

Mr. J reported that since his early teens, he has felt sexually attracted toward younger girls. On one occasion in his teens, he slept at his cousin's home, and he went into a younger cousin's bedroom and masturbated in her presence.

After graduating college, Mr. J attended optometry school; during optometry school, he visited massage parlors approximately every other week. At the same time, he dated age-appropriate women. He eventually married his then-girlfriend. During his marriage, Mr. J increased his gambling and frequented massage parlors more often, sometimes as often as four times per week. He then began masturbating while driving in his car. He would cover his penis with a map or newspaper, pull over, and ask teenage girls directions while sexually aroused. He occasionally exposed himself to adult women as well; once he drove completely naked on the NJ Turnpike, obtaining change for his toll from a startled female tolltaker. He convinced himself that he wasn't harming anyone (other than himself), so he continued this activity throughout his first marriage.

During 1990, his sexual compulsivity led to serious consequences: He was arrested for lewdness. He had masturbated in his car while watching two teenage girls rollerskating. One of the girls felt threatened, and she notified the police. He received probation on the condition that he enter psychotherapy; unfortunately, he did not discuss his pedophilic sexual urges openly while in treatment. Rather, he convinced his therapist that he was guilty only of poor judgment—having been inadvertently seen masturbating in his car.

Through the 1990s, Mr. J frequented streets near local high schools, masturbating in his car while high school girls were walking home from school. In 1993, he was arrested for exposing himself while in his car to teenage girls near a high school. This led to a charge for exhibitionism, eventually pled down to municipal disorderly persons charges.

He then began psychiatric treatment with Martin Clark, M.D., who prescribed Prozac. He also began attending Gamblers Anonymous meetings, but has had a number of gambling relapses.

Unfortunately, Mr. J has had a serious relapse with regard to deviant sexuality. This year he fondled the genitals of a 9-year-old girl under her bathing suit in his swimming pool. He acknowledged digitally penetrating the girl during this incident. At the time he was experiencing strong pedophilic urges, and he impulsively put his hand under the girl's bathing suit.

Mr. J expressed distress regarding his actions. He considers himself to have a serious sickness and appears highly motivated to do whatever necessary to prevent any recurrences.

PSYCHOLOGICAL TEST RESULTS

On the MCMI-III, Mr. J presented himself in a negative manner. His self-esteem is low. He views himself as having done many reprehensible things in his life and berates himself as a result. He is a depressive, pessimistic man who has a bleak, negative view of himself, his life, and the future. These characteristics were evident in his responses of "true" to: "I've had sad thoughts much of my life since I was a child"; "I've always had a hard time stopping myself from feeling blue and unhappy"; "I've never been able to shake the feeling that I'm worthless to others"; and "Even in good times, I've always been afraid that things would soon go bad."

His MCMI results indicate that he has a deep self-defeating streak. He acts impulsively, causing disruptions in his life and the lives of his loved ones. He finds it difficult to control his rash, reckless acts, after which he experiences deep guilt and contrition. His moods can fluctuate wildly depending on whether he has recently experienced some unpleasant consequence of his impulsive actions.

On the MSI, Mr. J displays a high level of sexual drive and interests; he appears preoccupied with sex and acknowledges significant difficulty controlling his sexual urges. He also reports a variety of thoughts and urges regarding serious paraphilias, focusing on child molestation, sexual coercion, and exhibitionism. He reports interest in a variety of lower level paraphilias as well, including voyeurism, obscene phone calls, and bondage and discipline. His MSI in general indicates a high level of paraphilic interest and substantial difficulty managing his urges.

RISK ASSESSMENT

On the RRAS, Mr. J receives a score of 72, placing him at the upper limit of the moderate risk range (37 to 73 points). He receives many points for seriousness of offense, involving digital penetration of a young victim, and the extensiveness and duration of his illegal sexual activity, involving years of gradually escalating exhibitionistic activity focused on teenage girls and culminating in the instant offense with a prepubescent girl.

INTEGRATION OF FINDINGS AND RECOMMENDATIONS

John J is a 45-year-old optometrist presently charged with sexually abusing a 9-year-old girl. Mr. J has a long history of sexual interest in minor females, which has resulted in two prior charges for exposing himself to teenage girls. He has struggled to manage his urges toward young females for many years. Unfortunately, his behavior recently escalated to an offense involving physical contact with a young victim.

Mr. J also has a long history of compulsive gambling. During high school, he began sports betting, and by college, his father had to settle his gambling debts on more than one occasion. He had to take a loan from his father 10 years ago to settle additional gambling debts. He has managed to avoid heavy gambling debts since then, although he still has difficulty with strong impulses to gamble.

I will address the referral questions in turn.

Is Mr. J repetitive and compulsive?

Mr. J's pattern of illegal sexual behavior extends over a period of years and has escalated in his current offense. On the sexual preoccupation factor of one risk assessment scale, he scored quite high. His illegal sexual acts are clearly re-

petitive; these acts have continued despite legal consequences and Mr. J's best efforts to cease. Moreover, he has a history of compulsive sexuality in a variety of areas. Consequently, in my opinion Mr. J is repetitive and compulsive.

What risk does Mr. J present to the community?

On both risk assessment scales, Mr. J scores in the moderate risk range. He receives a score of 72 points on the RRAS, and a score of 9 points on the ASORAS. His risk total is higher than that of the typical probationer, more similar to that of an individual incarcerated at New Jersey's specialized sex offender treatment facility, the Adult Diagnostic and Treatment Center. His illegal sexual acts have escalated from his exposing himself to minor females to his present hands-on offense.

What treatment plan would be suitable for Mr. J?

It is my opinion that Mr. J requires intensive, long-term, sex-offender-specific treatment. I recommend the following treatment plan:

1. Relapse prevention training: Mr. J should complete relapse prevention exercises designed to increase his awareness of the internal (emotional) and external (situational) risk factors that led to his deviant sexual behavior. Presently, he has little awareness of these factors, particularly of the internal factors.
2. Victim empathy: Mr. J should complete victim empathy exercises. Such exercises are designed to raise the awareness of the patient to the negative emotional consequences that his actions have had on the victim.
3. Sexual reconditioning exercises: Conservative treatment would require that he complete sexual reconditioning exercises designed to help him disrupt and moderate any deviant sexual arousal that might be present. Mr. J reports strong pedophilic urges, and he lacks the skills to effectively disrupt such urges.
4. Sex offender treatment group: Involvement in a sex offenders treatment group would have a variety of benefits for Mr. J. First, he would have a support group to whom he could talk openly regarding his offense, a support group that he would feel would not reject him for having committed an illegal sexual act. Second, he would be able to receive feedback from

other offenders regarding his rationalizations and justifications for having committed the deviant sexual acts. Frequently, such feedback has more impact from other offenders than from a treating professional.

5. Individual psychotherapy: Mr. J requires individual treatment focused on broader personality issues, such as his reckless, stimulation-seeking interpersonal style, which may be related to his offenses. His compulsive gambling is one indicator of this problem and would need to be addressed in treatment as well.

6. Medication review: Mr. J is presently being prescribed Prozac, an antidepressant. I suggest that he be psychiatrically evaluated for a mood-stabilizing agent—such as lithium—as well. His pressured speech in the interview and his history of impulsive, excitement-seeking behavior and sexual compulsivity suggest the possibility of hypomania, so a mood-stabilizing agent may be helpful.

7. Continued involvement in Gamblers Anonymous: Mr. J has a longstanding gambling problem. He has been productively involved in Gamblers Anonymous, and he needs to maintain his involvement in a gambling-related support group.

Philip Witt, Ph.D.
Diplomate in Forensic Psychology, ABPP

Teaching Point: Strengths and weaknesses of classification systems

Classification systems for sex offenders were in existence in the 1960s. However, current classification systems owe much of their development to the seminal work of Nicholas Groth (Groth & Birnbaum, 1979), who proposed that child molesters could be considered either fixated or regressed, with fixated offenders having sexual interest patterns focused entirely on children and regressed offenders having adult-oriented sexual interest patterns, but lapsing back under stress to earlier sexual attachment figures. Rapists, in Groth's framework, were motivated by power, anger, or sadism. While intuitively appealing, Groth's child molester and rapist taxonomy systems remained speculative, with no empirical support.

While many sex offender taxonomy systems exist, most lack empirical support, as does Groth's. As a consequence, in the 1980s, Knight and Prentky (Knight, 1988, 1989; Knight & Prentky, 1987) empirically validated a sex offender taxonomy system, perhaps the best validated system to date. Knight and Prentky's child molester typology system involved two decision trees. The first decision tree, or axis, had decisions for level of sexual fixation on children and level of social competence. The second decision tree had decisions for amount of contact with children, extent of physical injury, meaning of the sexual contact (purely exploitive or interpersonal), and sadistic or nonsadistic motivation. Knight and Prentky's rapist taxonomy focused on the motivation of the rapist—opportunistic, pervasively angry, sexual, or vindictive—with high and low social competence decisions within most of these motivational types.

Such taxonomies can serve a number of purposes. First, they can help clinicians and researchers think clearly about sex offenders by carefully examining the characteristics of the individual offender under consideration. Second, taxonomy systems are useful for treatment planning, allowing treatment needs to be clarified. For example, a sex offender with a high degree of pedophilic sexual fixation and drive might be suitable for sexual reconditioning exercises or medication to dampen sex drive. Third, a taxonomy can guide research. Different subgroups might have different recidivism rates or respond differentially to treatment interventions.

Although initially promising, taxonomy systems have generated relatively little discussion or research in recent years. More effort has been devoted to developing sex offender risk assessment scales, such as the Mn-SOST-R (Epperson, Kaul, & Hesselton, 1998), Static-99 (Hanson, 2000), HCR-20 (Webster, Douglas, Eaves, & Hart, 1997), and RRAS (Witt, DelRusso, Oppenheim, & Ferguson, 1996; Ferguson, Eidelson, & Witt, 1998). Such tools are used in different jurisdictions to place sex offenders in risk tiers, which are then used in accord with community notification and civil commitment statutes. Much of the same information can be gathered from a risk assessment instrument, which systematically samples criteria empirically associated with relapse. Not surprisingly, factor analytic studies of these instruments show two stable predictive factors: a psychopathic, antisocial personality or lifestyle, and a paraphilia (Witt et al., 1996).

Case 2

Principle: **Use scientific reasoning in assessing the causal connection between clinical condition and functional abilities**

This principle describes the importance of using scientific reasoning in FMHA. Several aspects of scientific reasoning are particularly relevant to this principle. These include hypothesis formulation and testing, falsifiability, parsimony in interpretation, and awareness of the limits on accuracy. These in turn affect the applicability of nomothetic research to the immediate case.

In any FMHA, there may be several competing explanations for the clinical symptoms or personality characteristics, deficits in relevant legal capacities, and causal relationship between the two. An important goal in FMHA is to test these competing "hypotheses" to determine which is best supported by the available data. For such hypothesis testing to be meaningful, however, the hypotheses must be evaluated in a way that allows them to be fairly tested, and rejected when they are not supported.

Sources of ethics authority in psychology provide direct support for the application of several kinds of scientific reasoning in FMHA, including hypothesis testing, the application (and misapplication) of psychological assessment procedures, and the parsimonious interpretation of psychological test results. The *Ethical Principles of Psychologists and Code of Conduct* (APA, 1992) contains several sections relevant to this principle. Appropriate operationalization depends, to some extent, on selecting procedures that have been developed for a purpose comparable to the purpose of the evaluation: "Psychologists who develop, administer, score, interpret, or use psychological assessment techniques, interviews, tests, or instruments do so in a manner and for purposes that are appropriate in light of the research on or the evidence of the usefulness and proper application of the techniques" (APA, 1992, p. 1603). Selecting inappropriate procedures can adversely affect the successful operationalization of variables. This error would limit the overall accuracy of the findings and the extent to which nomothetic results would be applicable:

> Psychologists refrain from misuse of assessment techniques, interventions, results, and interpretations. . . . Psychologists do not base their assessment of intervention decisions or recommendations on data or test results that are outmoded for the current purpose. . . . Similarly, psychologists do not base such decisions or recommendations on tests and measures that are obsolete and not useful for the current purpose. (p. 1603)

The *Ethics Code* also addresses the importance of personal contact with the individual being evaluated: "Except as noted . . . , psychologists provide written or oral forensic reports or testimony of the psychological characteristics of an individual only after they have conducted an examination of the individual adequate to support their statements or conclusions" (1992, p. 1610). In this context, personal contact is important because it can facilitate hypothesis formulation and testing. When personal contact is not possible, hypothesis testing is considerably more difficult, as the evaluator cannot observe the reaction of the individual to specific questions or procedures.

When, despite reasonable efforts, such an examination is not feasible, psychologists "clarify the impact of their limited information on the reliability and validity of their reports and testimony, and they appropriately limit the nature and extent of their conclusions or recommendations" (APA, 1992, p. 1610). Finally, the *Ethics Code* addresses the interpretation of FMHA results in two ways. The first involves the applicability of validation research for a test or procedure used with an individual:

> Psychologists attempt to identify situations in which particular interventions or assessment techniques may not be applicable or may require adjustment in administration or interpretation because of such factors as individuals' gender, age, race, ethnicity, national origin, religion, sexual orientation, disability, language, or socioeconomic status. (p. 1603)

Second, the *Ethics Code* addresses the interpretation of FMHA test results:

> Psychologists recognize limits to the certainty with which diagnoses, judgments, or predictions can be made about individuals. . . . When interpreting assessment results

. . . psychologists take into account the various test factors and characteristics of the person being assessed that might affect psychologists' judgments or reduce the accuracy of their interpretations. (p. 1603)

Support for the use of scientific reasoning in FMHA, particularly hypothesis testing, can also be found in the ethical guidelines for both forensic psychology and psychiatry. The *Specialty Guidelines for Forensic Psychologists* (Committee on Ethical Guidelines for Forensic Psychologists, 1991) emphasizes the value of hypothesis testing:

In providing forensic psychological services, forensic psychologists take special care to avoid undue influence upon their methods, procedures, and products, such as might emanate from the party to a legal proceeding by financial compensation or other gains. As an expert conducting an evaluation, treatment, consultation, or scholarly/empirical investigation, the forensic psychologist maintains professional integrity by examining the issue at hand from all reasonable perspectives, actively seeking information that will differentially test plausible rival hypotheses. (p. 661)

Similarly, the *Ethical Guidelines for the Practice of Forensic Psychiatry* (AAPL, 1995) indirectly supports hypothesis testing by emphasizing the distinction between "verified" and "unverified" information.

Legal support can also be found for this principle. Both the U.S. Supreme Court's decision in *Daubert* (1993) and the *Federal Rules of Evidence* underscore the importance of reasoning in cases involving scientific evidence.[1] In *Daubert*, the Supreme Court, in dicta, used the phrase "reasoning or methodology" in outlining the criteria that might be used to determine the scientific validity of the evidence. The *Daubert* opinion also suggested that the Supreme Court took a broad view of "science," with both data and reasoning considered as expert evidence.

Rule 703 of the *Federal Rules of Evidence* provides some role for reasoning in FMHA: "The facts or data in the particular case upon which an expert bases an opinion or inference may be those perceived by or made known to the expert at or before the hearing." The nature of this reasoning is elaborated in Rule 702: "If scientific, technical, or other specialized knowledge will the assist the trier of fact to understand the evidence or determine a fact in issue, a witness qualified as an expert by knowledge, skill, experience, training, or education, may testify thereto in the form of an opinion or otherwise."

There is relatively little empirical evidence regarding the role of scientific reasoning in FMHA. However, one recent study involving forensic psychologists and psychiatrists examined the perceived desirability of various elements of FMHA, including elements that are clearly relevant to reasoning (Borum & Grisso, 1996). In rating the value of providing a "mental illness rationale" that describes how the examiner reached an opinion about the presence/absence and degree of mental illness, the majority of responding psychologists and psychiatrists rated this rationale as either essential or recommended. Other elements of FMHA relevant to reasoning were also strongly endorsed, with more than 75% of responding psychiatrists and psychologists rating each as either essential or recommended (Borum & Grisso, 1996).

Heilbrun (1992) stressed the importance of reasoning in FMHA, particularly in the context of hypothesis formulation, testing, and test interpretation. He compared the process of FMHA to a scientific experiment:

> Following the formulation of falsifiable hypotheses, the verification process can proceed much as it would in a scientific experiment. Does the defendant exhibit behavior consistent with the presence of the hypothesized psychological characteristic? (A researcher might call this construct validity.) Does the defendant show the absence of behaviors that are not consistent with the presence of the hypothesized construct? (We could analogize this to discriminant validity.) The remaining task is then to offer conclusions in terms that reflect the consistency of support for the hypothesis that was framed in psychological rather than legal terms (e.g., psychosis, cognitive awareness and volition rather than insanity). (p. 269)

The present report provides a good illustration of this principle. The evaluation was conducted to determine the individual's risk to others and treatment needs and amenability in the context of a specialized sentencing evaluation. The evaluator demonstrates the applicability of scientific reasoning in the operationalization of variables (through the selection of appropriate and relevant testing procedures), hypothesis formulation and testing, parsimonious interpretation, and an awareness of the limits on accuracy.

The evaluator selected psychological tests that were relevant to the purpose of the evaluation. For example, because the individual presented with a history of sadistic sexual fantasies, the evaluator selected tests that would provide information in this area. Hypothesis formulation and testing was facilitated through the evaluator's personal contact with the individual, which allowed the evaluator to observe the reactions of the individual to specific lines of questioning. These observations were subsequently integrated into the "Clinical Impressions" section of the report.

The evaluator also used scientific reasoning in the interpretation of the psychological test results and considered the characteristics of the individual that could potentially affect the accuracy of interpretation of test results. For example, the evaluator considered conflicting data from the clinical interview when interpreting test results. This facilitated a parsimonious, "best" explanation for the existing clinical symptoms and relevant personality characteristics.

The evaluator supported his conclusion about the individual's level of risk by referring to data gathered throughout the evaluation. Specifically, the evaluator indicated that the level of risk for violence toward self or others was based on factors such as the individual's history of violence and violent fantasies, feelings of anger and low threshold for insults, history of alcohol and drug abuse, lack of compliance with medication, and blurring of fantasy and reality.

Finally, the evaluator recognized the limits on the accuracy of his data, reasoning, and conclusions. In making a prediction about the individual's future behavior, the evaluator clearly specified the behavior being predicted. For example, the evaluator stated that the individual "is at very high risk to engage in acts of *extreme interpersonal violence*" (emphasis added). This specification of outcome limits the scope of the prediction being made, and facilitates the communication of a particular conclusion. The information obtained in this evaluation did not allow a conclusion regarding the likelihood of success in therapeutic intervention, however, as the evaluator conveyed the limits on applicability of these FMHA data.

FORENSIC EVALUATION

March 31, 1999
Re: John D.

REASON FOR REFERRAL

John is a 24-year-old Caucasian male who was convicted of Sexual Battery, which occurred on 2-10-98, and is awaiting sentencing. A forensic psychological evaluation was ordered pursuant to 42 Pa. Con. Stat. § 9794, as amended in 1996, to be conducted by a member of the Sexual Offender Assessment Board to provide the sentencing court with the following information:

- age of the offender
- offender's prior criminal record, sexual offenses as well as other offenses
- age of victim
- whether the offense involved multiple victims
- use of illegal drugs by the offender
- whether the offender completed any prior sentence and whether the offender participated in available programs for sexual offenders
- any mental illness or mental disability of the offender
- the nature of the sexual contact with the victim and whether the sexual contact was part of a demonstrated pattern of abuse
- whether the offense included a display of unusual cruelty by the offender during the commission of the crime, and
- any behavioral characteristics that contribute to the offender's conduct.

This information is to be provided to assist the court in determining whether the defendant shall be designated as a sexual predator, defined as "any person convicted of a sexually violent act under Section 9793 (B) and who suffers from a mental abnormality, or personality disorder which makes that person likely to engage in predatory violent offenses."

FOCUS AND CONDUCT OF THE EVALUATION

The evaluation took place over an 8-hour period on March 15–16, 1999. The evaluation included a 5-hour interview with John, 2 hours of psychological testing, and a 1-hour psychiatric consultation regarding medication. He was informed prior to the beginning of the evaluation that it was being conducted to assist the court at sentencing, that a report would be written describing the findings of the evaluation, and that testimony of the undersigned at sentencing was also possible.

The interview with John included inquiry into his family, developmental, victimization, educational, social, sexual, vocational, and psychiatric history. In addition to gathering historical information that might shed light on his current level of functioning, we focused on his understanding of the sadistic fantasies and behavior associated with his recent conviction.

Psychological testing included the administration of the Millon Clinical Multiaxial Inventory-III (MCMI), a widely used standardized personality test that examines distinctive, longstanding features of personality, such as depression, anxiety, social discomfort, passivity, dependence, self-confidence, and aggression, as well as acute symptoms; Briere's Trauma Symptom Inventory (TSI); Putnam's Dissociative Experiences Scale (DES); Speilberger's State Trait Anger Expression Inventory (STAXI); the Beck Depression Inventory (BDI); and Davis's Interpersonal Reactivity Index (IRI), a multidimensional measure of empathy.

Because of his high level of distress after completing the above-mentioned tests, I decided *not* to have him complete the two remaining components of the battery that focus on sexual fantasies and behavior (New England Sexual Compulsive Disorder scale and the Multidimensional Assessment of Sex and Aggression).

FAMILY AND VICTIMIZATION HISTORY

John stated that he was an only child born to unwed parents on February 9, 1975. He reported that his home environment was unstable, and that his father was a drug addict who was not involved with his care. During his childhood, he lived in many places with his mother and her numerous boyfriends. He recalled no memories of his father prior to the age of 8. He stated that his mother told him that his father would visit him, but he has no recollection of these visits. At age 8, he recalled playing with and smelling someone's feet. He recalled that it was dark, he was scared, and that there were other people there. He further recalled that, "Something really bad happened. I don't know why, but it scares me when I think about it." He reported a fragment of another memory in which his father's hands were pulling his knees apart. He stated, "I wanted to be asleep. I remember looking down like I was on the ceiling, sort of floating." He reported being very scared of men and feeling particularly vulnerable at night.

John reported that his father died when John was 9 years old. His mother married after his death, and John attempted to get close to his stepfather. He stated that these attempts always ended in failure, and that he was estranged from his stepfather for many years. At the age of 20, when he was a college student, he initiated contact with his stepfather. He always had "bad feelings" about these meetings. Despite his attempts to gloss over his stepfather's neglect, he could never forgive him. His stepfather could not accept his homosexuality, stating that he (stepfather) told him that he (John) was going to burn in Hell. During one visit to California to see his stepfather, he (stepfather) arranged a surprise religious ceremony that was intended to rid John of homosexuality.

John stated that he loved his mother and hated her at the same time. He described being enmeshed with his mother and that he continues, to this day, to be enmeshed with her. He remarked that he loved her because she could be fun to be with, and she was proud of him. When asked why he hated her, he stated that he was always receiving confusing and disturbing messages from her. At times she could be very fair in her treatment of him, and at other times she would lash out at him in a loud angry voice and smack him in the face. He said that, "this was her rage," commenting that his mother would frequently give him the silent treatment, which would make him feel, "Like I had no ID. I felt like nothing." He also reported that his mother had improper physical boundaries. He stated that, "When she hugged me, it was too close, too hard, long and lingering." He noted that he often felt like a surrogate husband to his mother, because whenever it was time to kiss her goodnight, she would stick her tongue out. He also recalled slow dancing with his mother at parties. Although he has vague memories of sleeping with his mother, he did not recall being sexual with her. He denied, moreover, ever being sexually aroused by his mother. Although John recalled these behaviors when he was as young as 6 years old, it seemed to get worse after his father died. John was 8 years old at the time, and he remembered that his mother started calling him "Daddy." He stated that her inappropriate behavior always made him feel "silly and uncomfortable."

He reported that because of his mother's frequent moves, he spent a considerable time living with his maternal grandparents. He stated that his grandmother was frequently intrusive and had very improper boundaries. He reported that she would walk in on him when he was changing his underwear and would always find an excuse to come into the bathroom and wipe him after he made a bowel movement. He never questioned his grandmother's intrusive behavior, stating that "I felt it was necessary." John added that he didn't realize his grandmother's behavior was inappropriate until later.

PSYCHIATRIC HISTORY

John has an extensive psychiatric history, which is briefly reviewed below.

1992 [age17]: inpatient psychiatric commitment for sexually assaulting a 13-year-old. John strangled the victim and fantasized that he would render him unconscious and play with his feet

1994 [age 19]: inpatient psychiatric stay. He signed himself in because he feared hurting someone.

1995 [age 20]: drug rehabilitation.

1996 [age 21]: suicide attempt (liquor and antidepressants).

1997 [age 22]: inpatient psychiatric commitment for depression and fear of violent fantasies.

1998 [age 23]: inpatient psychiatric commitment for depression and suicidal ideation.

1999 January [age 23]: inpatient psychiatric commitment for suicidal ideation. He stated that, "I was feeling real bad over not feeling anything about strangling my friend's friend. I was still masturbating over the strangulation incident."

When asked about his history of suicidality, John reported that most of his suicide attempts resulted from his "disgust" with his homicidal fantasies and impulses. He reported that his most recent psychiatric hospitalization was because he was despondent over breaking up with his boyfriend and feeling "unworthy."

CURRENT MEDICATION

Provera, 20 mg q A.M.

Fluoxetine, 20 mg, IV tab Q.D.

Trazodone, 100 mg, I tab q hs

Depakote, 250 mg, II caps q A.M., II caps q eve, I cap q noon

SUBSTANCE ABUSE HISTORY

John reported that he started drinking in high school, mostly beer on weekends. He reported that his alcohol consumption escalated during the summer after high school when he began drinking beer more frequently and started drinking hard liquor. He also reported that he began smoking marijuana during the summer after high school. He stated that he drank at least three bottles of beer daily while in college, and that he smoked marijuana four times per week. He began to cut classes in order to get high and often drank until he blacked out. He admitted that he tried cocaine, crack, and amphetamines. He stated that his more recent use of alcohol and drug was to avoid painful memories and to bring back his sex drive, which the Provera dampens.

He reported that he has had several periods of sobriety since he joined AA in 1994. His longest period of sobriety was for 3 years. His last reported use of alcohol was February 7, 1999. His last reported use of marijuana was February 11, 1999.

EDUCATION AND SOCIALIZATION HISTORY

John stated that school was his lifesaver. He attended high school in a suburb of Boston, MA. He stated that he was an A student. He reported that he had several friends, but he would not call them close friends. He had one best male friend in high school, with whom he was infatuated. He stated that his friend was never aware of his infatuation.

He reported that he attended college for a year, then dropped out during the first semester of his sophomore year due to drug and alcohol abuse. He stated that he was "an emotional wreck" during this time period. He told people that he had Huntington's Disease so that people would feel sorry for him and hug him. When questioned further about this, he stated that, "It's a great cop out. If you can't handle somebody feeling angry with you, you try to get them to feel sorry for you." During this time period, his favorite television shows were *Batman* and *The Wild Wild West*, because they played out his fantasy of one male getting hurt while the other male rushes in to comfort him. He stated that, "In movies, the man had to be dying to be held."

He called himself a "chameleon," because while in college he associated with many different types of people such as "jocks, band members, and nerds." He reported that he had a girlfriend in college, but he could only get aroused by her if he fantasized about his male roommate.

He reported having had approximately 10 male sex partners since leaving college in 1995. He described these relationships as "healthy, with lots of touching, kissing, and hugging." John reported that he had no violent fantasies in these relationships. He stated that his last male lover lasted approximately 6 months. The relationship ended in December 1998 because his lover wouldn't commit to him. He said that he felt "unworthy" and began having increasingly intense suicidal and homicidal fantasies. His drug use increased in response to distress from the fantasies. He was hospitalized approximately 1 month later.

SEXUAL AND HOMICIDAL FANTASIES

John recalled that the first time he fantasized about playing with feet was when he was 4 years old, and he wanted to play with his friend's feet. He stated that the first time he acted on this fantasy was when he was about 12 or 13 years old. He stated that he hit a friend over the head with a shovel, knocked him out, and played with his feet. He reported having his first wet dream when he was 16 years old. He dreamed about knocking out his friend and playing with his feet. He stated that in his homicidal fantasies, "I'm drowning them [his victims] in a trash can. I reach a climax when I'm holding their legs and they stop struggling." He also reported fantasizing about putting his victims in a trance or drugging them so that they don't remember anything and then "I can do what I want with their body." He acknowledged frequently masturbating to these violent fantasies. He also indicated that the fantasies and subsequent masturbation were soothing and helped him cope with his anger. He stated that he was preoccupied with these violent fantasies "25 out of 30 days." He reported that his medication decreases the amount and the intensity of the fantasies. John further remarked that, "The line between fantasy and reality has always been a problem for me."

He admitted to acting on his fantasies at least five times. He stated that although he thought he has been able to stop himself short of killing his victims, he hasn't always been sure that his victim was alive when he left. He reported that the last time that he acted on his fantasies was in October 1997, when he attacked and strangled a young man that he picked up in a bar and brought home. He stated that he was about to drown his victim in a trash can when the victim became semiconscious and pleaded for his life. He reported that he remembers thinking at the time, "If I keep going, he will die. If I stop, he will live." He further stated that, "The fantasy was that I could get away with it and hide the body." His fantasized victims are mostly white, slim, emotionally unavailable men.

RESULT OF PSYCHOLOGICAL TESTING

John's score on the Beck Depression Inventory places him in the severe range, indicating the presence of clinical depression. John's responses on the Interpersonal Reactivity Index were in the average range for Empathic Concern, an affective measure of the ability to feel compassion for those in distress, but about 2 standard deviations below average in Perspective Taking, a cognitive measure of the ability to appreciate other people's point of view. The most noteworthy scale score, however, was on Personal Distress, a measure of the extent to which an individual is capable of sharing the distress that other are experiencing. John's score on this scale was 1.5 standard deviations above the mean. Since a low score on this scale often reflects one's inability to tolerate or cope with their own distress, we may infer that Mr. D is aware that he is coping with a very high level of distress.

John's responses on the STAXI reveal frequent, very intense angry feelings. His scores on two scales, reflecting both the suppression of angry feelings and the behavioral expression of anger were well above the 90th percentile. John's anger appears to be chronic, rather than situationally determined. He is highly sensitive to criticism, perceived insults, and negative or devaluing remarks and is likely to experience anger in those situations. John does *not* appear, however, to be quick tempered and impulsive in the expression of anger. He is more likely to brood for some time before expressing his anger.

John's response on the MCMI-III provide no evidence of psychosis (i.e., Thought Disorder or Delusional Disorder). John scored very high on a number of Clinical Syndromes, however, including Anxiety, Dysthymia, Alcohol Dependence, and Drug Dependence. There is evidence, moreover, of longstanding and pervasive character pathology, most notably Borderline Personality Disorder. Consistent with this, John has shown evidence of impulsive and volatile outbursts, markedly labile mood with shifts from normality to extended periods of depression interspersed with anger and anxiety, rapid fluctuations in thoughts and perception about life about events, and a highly confused, wavering sense of identity. In addition to this constellation of traits associated with Borderline Personality Disorder, there also is evidence of egotistic self-involvement, as indicated by his interpersonally exploitative style and features of personality that would be associated with Passive Aggressive (or Negativistic) Personality Disorder. Not surprisingly, John also scored in the "trait range" for Aggressive/Sadistic Personality.

John's scores on all 10 of the Trauma Symptom Inventory scales were above the 90th percentile. His scores on seven of those scales were at 99th percentile. Overall, his responses reflect a very high degree of trauma-related symptomatology. This profile indicates a high level of sexual distress and dysfunctional sexual behavior, chronic depression, and constant, vigilant attempts to avoid extreme internal (often posttraumatic) distress. His high score on Tension Reduction Behavior reflects the frequency with which he engages in behaviors intended to interrupt, discharge, or attenuate negative or aversive feelings. His high score on Dissociation suggests a high frequency of avoidance responses to overwhelming emotional distress. These responses may include cognitive disengagement, depersonalization and derealization, and emotional numbing. Given his high score on the DIS scale, I administered the Dissociative Experience Scale (DES). John endorsed 19 of the DES items, slightly below the median of 22 for people with Post Traumatic Stress Disorder (PTSD). His median score for those 19 items, however, was 18, which is substantially lower than the median score of 39 found among people with PTSD. Thus, the DES

provides an unclear symptom picture with regard to dissociation. Although John endorsed many items, the frequency with which he has these experiences is highly variable (4 of the items less than 10% of the time, and 12 of the items less than 20% of the time).

CLINICAL IMPRESSIONS

John presented as a pleasant, cooperative 24-year-old Caucasian male, who was mildly anxious. He was fully oriented. In the early part of the interview, he made frequent use of humor. Although self-disclosing, his facial expression was tense, and he appeared to choose his words carefully. His speech appeared to be without pressure. He often spoke in great detail, though seemingly without circumstantiality, looseness of association, or flight of ideas. He frequently displayed poor eye contact, particularly when he appeared to be daydreaming with the imagery of these events that he was reporting. His respiration appeared rapid at times, and the interview was stopped on several occasions due to the acute distress that he exhibited (e.g., reaching up and grabbing his hair). He often grew agitated, and on several occasions he became visibly upset about a particular topic, stating, "I don't want to say anything more about that." Short-term memory was instant. Long-term memory was roughly intact. Both insight and judgment were poor.

There was no evidence of auditory or visual hallucinations or delusions. He acknowledged having extremely vivid, intrusive fantasies, which he often finds disturbing as well as arousing. These fantasies have both an obsessive-compulsive quality to them (i.e., he experiences acute distress, if he can't act on them). He has a long history of substance abuse, primarily ETOH and marijuana. He has a long history of both suicidal and homicidal ideation, which he has acted on in the past. He denied any current suicidal or homicidal ideation.

DIAGNOSTIC IMPRESSIONS

Based on historical, clinical, and psychometric data, the following *DSM-IV* classifications would be appropriate:

Axis I: Major Depression in partial remission, severe, recurrent (296.35), Dysthymia (300.4), Alcohol Dependence (303.90), Cannabis Dependence (304.30), and Sexual Sadism (302.84);

Axis II: Borderline Personality Disorder (301.83).

RISK ASSESSMENT

John should be regarded as being at very high risk of violence toward self or others. This conclusion is based on consideration of the following factors:

1. He has a long history of *acting* on his fantasies. He reported having at least five victims of strangulation;
2. He reported clear evidence of planning in these offences, including the use of manipulation and subterfuge. In his October 1997 offense, for example, he brought to his apartment a young man that he picked up in a bar under the pretext of "getting high." Once high, he rendered his victim unconscious;
3. He reported active, intrusive, at time preoccupying fantasies of strangulation and postmortem sexual acts that consume him 80% of the time. When he does *not* act on these fantasies, he feels "intense frustration," as well as "extreme disgust" due to his enjoyment and lack of remorse over his homicidal fantasies. His recent hospitalization in January 1999 for suicidal ideation was precipitated by constant preoccupation with highly arousing sexual fantasies about a prior (October 1997) offense and consequent "self-loathing" because of these fantasies;
4. He lives, on a daily basis, with very intense angry feelings, and he possesses a very low threshold for experiencing what he perceives to be insults and abuse from others. His controls, even in the presence of medication, are fragile. He was unable, for example, to complete the battery of inventories and questionnaires for this evaluation, because he found them to be too upsetting. Indeed, he reported in the beginning of a second session that he had a "bad weekend" because he had been consumed by anger. What prompted all of his anger was several general personality questionnaires that, in reality, were quite benign (i.e., they did *not* inquire about any potentially "high voltage" subjects such as childhood abuse or sexual behavior, thoughts, or fantasies);
5. He has a long history of chronic relapsing to use of alcohol and drugs, undoubtedly for purpose of self-medication. His reliance on substances fulfills the criteria for dependence;
6. He acknowledged intentional lack of compliance with medication in order to intensify his sexual fantasies and sexual drive. He reports that masturbation to these sexual fantasies are "soothing" and attenuate feelings of intense anger;
7. Lastly, it should be noted that he often experiences a blurring of fantasy and reality. As he commented, "The line between fantasy and reality has always been a problem for me."

CONCLUSIONS

Based on all of the above, we would recommend that the court consider the following in determining whether John D should be classified as a sexual predator. He appears to have serious psychiatric difficulties in the form of sexual sadism and borderline personality disorder that would increase his risk of further sexual offending. He also has a substantial history of intrusive and violent sexual fantasies and a tendency to act on these fantasies. The nature of past sexual conduct in this area suggests a consistent pattern of abuse and cruelty to his victims. John also appears to be an individual with a number of other active risk factors associated with interpersonal aggression toward others, namely substance abuse, sporadic medication compliance, poor anger and impulse control, a history of trauma, and poor judgment. Accordingly, his current risk factors would seem to increase the risk for reoffending in both a sexual and nonsexual context.

John should be closely monitored and stabilized on medication, with consideration to further reduction in the intensity of his sexual and violent fantasies. In this regard, I would recommend a combination of an antiandrogen and an SSRI. His lack of compliance with medication must be addressed and appropriate means of monitoring compliance instituted. Following stabilization, he should be treated for symptoms of Post Traumatic Stress Disorder, followed by cognitive-behavioral treatment for his cycle of sexualized violence (including substance abuse) and aversive counterconditioning to decrease arousal associated with his violent fantasies. John's own victimization history, the precise nature of which is unclear at this point, may have to be addressed in trauma therapy before he can effectively work on his own victimization of others.

If I can clarify any aspects of this report or provide any further assistance to you on this matter, please feel free to call.

Yours sincerely,
Robert A. Prentky, Ph.D.

Teaching Point: Sex offender typologies in sentencing

Science has traditionally proceeded by simplifying complex, diverse domains of information. Simplification is typically achieved through a methodical process of assigning members of a large heterogeneous group to subgroups that possess common characteristics, thereby bringing some degree of order to diversity. The process of classification ("taxonomy") is fundamental to all science. The task is to uncover the laws and principles that underlie the optimal differentiation of a domain into subgroups that have theoretically important similarities. The resulting subgroups or subtypes are not simply notational; they connect the content of science to the real world. In fact, one might argue that classification reflects a normal cognitive process of integration and reduction. Through such a process of classification we make sense of our experiences. The process that helps us to apprehend our world at a sensory level is the same process that scientists use to order and simplify their world at an empirical level.

Over the past 40 years, classification systems have been designed, implemented, and tested on virtually every aspect of human behavior. The profusion of these systems during the past several decades resulted from the proliferation of clinical data and the need for an organized approach to complex and diverse behavioral domains. One area that certainly has been the beneficiary of classificatory efforts has been depression. We have witnessed something of a revolution in the treatment of depression and anxiety-related disorders through the identification of increasingly homogeneous subgroups. The clinical literature clearly indicates that valid classification models lead to more informed decisions.

In general, the more heterogeneous the area of inquiry, the more critical is classification. One of the few indisputable conclusions about sexual offenders is that they constitute a markedly heterogeneous group (Knight, Rosenberg, & Schneider, 1985). The childhood and developmental histories, adult competencies, and criminal histories of sexual offenders differ considerably. The motives and patterns that characterize their criminal offenses differ considerably. Sex offenders can, quite literally, come from any walk of life and present with any composite or profile of attributes. As such, reliable and valid classification of sexual offenders is, arguably, more important than for any other group of criminals. Although sexual offenders have been the subject of intense clinical interest and speculation for at least 50 years, it is only within the past 20 years that progress has been made on the development of empirically validated systems for classifying this population (Prentky & Burgess, 2000). Indeed, classification research reveals that rapists and child molesters are each very heterogeneous and that each offender group may include a half dozen to a dozen discrete subtypes (Knight & Prentky, 1990).

Classification systems do not serve all purposes. Classification research typically begins by pinpointing the purpose that the resulting model is intended to serve. For example, a taxonomy may be designed to classify the structural, biochemical, or reproductive characteristics of a particular genus or species of plant or animal. In the case of criminal offenders, the same principle holds. A classification system that is intended to assist with treatment planning and clinical decision making may look quite different from a classification system that is intended to inform forensic decision making (e.g., risk).

In the criminology domain, the clear purpose of most taxonomic efforts has been to inform discretionary decisions about offenders, and to assist with decisions about dangerousness or reoffense risk. However, because sex offenders are often placed in treatment programs, voluntarily as well as involuntarily, the need for assisting with more informed treatment-related decisions has also been a high priority.

A valid classification system can inform and improve the discretionary and dispositional decisions made by the criminal justice system. These decisions include reoffense risk, risk of violence, appropriateness for probation, custody level (i.e., security risk), parole risk, and discharge from community-based treatment or other conditions of parole. This clearly is an area where classification can serve a very useful purpose. Although there has been relatively little research on validating a classification system specifically for this purpose, recent validity studies on several empirically derived taxonomies are promising.

In one 25-year follow-up study of 111 child molesters, for example, the predictive efficacy of several critical dimensions of an empirically derived classification system for child molesters (MTC:CM3; Knight & Prentky, 1990) was examined. It was found that Fixation (degree of sexual preoccupation with children) and number of Prior Sexual Offenses were significantly related to sexual recidivism, while Amount of Contact with Children was significantly related to nonsexual, victim-involved, and violent recidivism (Prentky, Knight, & Lee, 1997). In that study, it was evident that classification as high in Fixation on Axis I and low in amount of Contact with Children on Axis II were associated with increased risk of recidivism.

Similarly, in a 25-year follow-up of 106 rapists released from a maximum-security treatment facility, Prentky, Knight, Lee, and Cerce (1995) examined impulsivity, a dimension critical to the classification of rapists (MTC:R3; Knight & Prentky, 1990). We found that the hazard rate for the high impulsivity rapists was at least twice as great as the hazard rate for the low impulsivity rapists, across all domains of criminal behavior. In fact, the hazard rate for committing a new sexual offense was almost three times greater for the high impulsivity rapists. For nonsexual, victimless offenses, the hazard rate was almost four times greater for the high impulsivity rapists. In other words, the simple construct of lifestyle impulsivity was a powerful predictor of those who reoffended, even in a sample comprised entirely of "hard core" offenders classified as "sexual psychopaths."

A second possible benefit of classification would be to inform treatment planning and clinical decision making. To the extent that rehabilitation within the criminal justice system remains a viable goal and to the extent that limited resources require prudent allocation, classification systems that shed light on optimal interventions for different types of offenders are very important. This is not a novel application of classification. Over 25 years ago, Quay (1975) remarked, "This question of the match between offender characteristics and treatment modalities, i.e., differential classification and treatment, remains perhaps the most important problem for research in applied corrections" (p. 412).

Using the MTC:R3 taxonomic system for rapists, John was easily classified as a Type 4 (Overt Sadism). In John's case, his report of a long history of fantasy and behavior consumed by sexual sadism was ample evidence for this classification. Using the component rating sheet for the MTC:R3, four of the eight Category A criteria for sadism were coded as present. Only one Category A criterion is required for Type 4 classification. The Type 4 offender is characterized by the following: (1) a high level of aggression and gratuitous violence, typically in sexual offenses; (2) a history of pervasive (undifferentiated) anger may be present; (3) sexual offenses evidence a fusion of aggression with sexual arousal; (4) a moderate history of impulsive, antisocial behavior in adolescence and adulthood is often present; (5) a history of other paraphilias is often present; and (6) offense planning and premeditation are evident.

John's treatment needs are numerous, including trauma therapy for a history of victimization, anger dyscontrol, impulse dyscontrol, and highly intrusive and repetitive sexual fantasy that is dominated by sexual sadism. Because of the high potential for dangerous behavior inflicted against self or others, I emphasized that such treatment should be provided in a secure, specialized setting, and that John be stabilized on medication prior to treatment. Although John had been on the anti-androgen Provera for a brief time, he was essentially noncompliant by using alcohol and street drugs to restore his sexual drive. Thus, ensuring compliance should also be a focus in the beginning of treatment. I recommended, in this regard, consideration of a GnRH medication (gonadotrophin releasing hormone) such as Lupron, which can drop testosterone down to castrate levels. I further recommended that trauma therapy precede offender therapy, because of the overwhelming influence of the distal effects of trauma on his life, most notably extreme anger and depression, and intrusive memories.

Because of the very nature of its use by the criminal justice system, classification systems must be applied with utmost care and caution. When applied properly, classification can inform and increase the accuracy of difficult decisions made by the criminal justice system. When applied improperly or misused, classification can lead to erroneous decisions that can adversely affect individual liberty interests. In an article three decades old on the "care and feeding of typologies," Toch (1970) warned that, "Classifying people in life is a grim business which channelizes destinies and determines fate. A man becomes a category, is processed as a category, plays his assigned role, and lives up to the implications. Labeled irrational, he acts crazy. Catalogued dangerous, he becomes dangerous, or he stays behind bars" (p. 15). Hans Toch, who has spent much of his professional life attempting to classify violent people, reminds us that, "Individuals can be jailed as representatives of a probable category" (p. 18).

Toch's message, which is as true today as it was 30 years ago, is a sobering one. Although we should not reject the benefits afforded by classification because of the potential for misuse, we must adhere to scientific rigor in the development and validation of classification systems and employ utmost care in the application of those systems. Casual or careless assignment of individuals to categories is far worse than no assignment at all, and improper use of a classification system is far worse than no use at all.

Note

1. Because the U.S. Supreme Court has also decided (in *Kumho v. Carmichael*, 1999) that expert evidence that is "technical" or "other specialized knowledge" may be scrutinized in the same way as "scientific" evidence under *Daubert*, it is clear that *Daubert* may be applied to FMHA regardless of whether the latter is considered to be scientific, technical, or other specialized knowledge.

Chapter 14

Release Decision Making

The release decision-making process as it relates to the adult criminal justice system is the focus of the three reports in this chapter. The principle to be applied to the first case addresses the process of assessing legally relevant behavior, and how the information can be used to aid the court in accurate decision making. The first teaching point addresses the management of social desirability and defensiveness in forensic mental health assessment. For the second case, the principle concerns the value of nomothetic data, derived from groups and applied through general laws, to forensic assessment. The teaching point in this case concerns the proper application of scientific and empirical data to the reasoning and conclusions generated in forensic decision making. The third case's principle involves both the substance and style relevant in providing effective testimony in an adversarial setting. Finally, the teaching point for the third case provides specific comments on moving from "adequate" to "outstanding" in expert testimony.

Case 1

Principle: Use third-party information in assessing response style

This principle is discussed in some detail in Chapter 10. Therefore, we will move directly to how the present report illustrates its application in FMHA.

This report provides a good example of using third-party information to assess response style in the context of release decision making. The forensic clinician identified the relevant third-party sources of information considered in the evaluation to include (1) review of available records that would (2) allow completion of a PCL-R. The review of collateral documents is a good way to gauge the consistency of self-reported information with that from other sources. A review of available records in this case indicated that the individual being assessed had a history of mental health problems resulting in hospitalization. More specifically, the collateral documents provided historical observations consistent with schizophrenia, and suggested that this disorder played some role in the prior criminal behavior. File review also revealed that this individual had been prescribed anti-psychotic medication (Haldol) for approximately 12 years. In addition, the document review suggested that he had been stable while on this medication over at least the last year. This was generally consistent with the individual's report of symptoms experienced at the time of the evaluation. This apparent pattern in reported symptoms is consistent with information provided in collateral documents, which suggested that his symptoms had been stabilized through medication. The PCL-R was also administered during the evaluation. Scoring this instrument requires the use of third-party information; information gathered as part of the PCL-R administration would therefore provide another source of information with which to assess this individual's response style.

The Parole Board Report
Robert G. Meyer, Ph.D.
Professor of Psychology
University of Louisville
Consultant
Kentucky Dept. of Corrections
and
Kentucky State Reformatory
LaGrange, Kentucky

PSYCHOLOGICAL EVALUATION
CONFIDENTIAL

Name: Mr. I
Age: 35
Number: 000007
Date: January 12, 1999
Examiner: Robert G. Meyer, Ph.D.

Mr. I was evaluated on January 5 and 6, 1999, as he is due to go before the February Parole Board. He was fully apprised of the purpose of this evaluation and the absence of confidentiality therein, and all indications are that he had more than adequate comprehension of these issues.

The present evaluation consisted of a review of available records, an MMPI-2, a PCL-R, and clinical interviews. The reader is also referred to the August 15, 1998, report by Dr. Munsterberg, which evaluated Mr. I's response to the medication, as much of that material is still relevant here.

Mr. I is presently taking Haldol as well as medication for high blood pressure. He states that he has been taking Haldol pretty consistently over the last 12 years, including all of his 5 years in this institution, and he does believe that it has typically been helpful for him. He reports neither psychiatric contact nor any administration of psychotropic medication prior to going on the Haldol. The reports in Mr. I's file from his prescribing psychiatrist, Dr. J, indicate that Mr. I has been quite stable on the Haldol over at least the last year.

Mr. I has been hospitalized on two occasions outside of the institution for mental-emotional problems, the first time at age 23. Mr. I reports that these were a result of his "hearing and seeing things that were not there." His last hospitalization, which was for 2 weeks, occurred 7 years ago. He has carried consistent notations of a schizophrenic diagnosis and average intelligence. He did obtain his GED 2 years ago. As is described in the file, he was likely actively schizophrenic at the time of his offense, and file data and Mr. I's report suggest that his disorder played at least some part in the production of the arson behavior. These latter data sources suggest that Mr. I would have likely earned the diagnosis of Conduct Disorder by age 9, mainly by way of petty thievery, skipping school, mild assaults, and runaway behavior.

Mr. I was initially disinclined to admit any present hallucinations, but then rather quickly did admit to consistent but periodic auditory hallucinations, usually in the several hours before he falls asleep at night. But, he does emphasize that "they don't really bother me . . . I just let 'em go unless I'm real upset for some reason . . . if I am I tell K [the officer on his walk] about it, and he gets me something to sleep." Mr. I does describe an uncle on his mother's side as apparently having manifested a schizophrenic pattern, and an uncle on his father's side as alcoholic. However, Mr. I denies any significant history of substance abuse, and there is nothing in the file data or the present test data to contradict that assertion.

Other than the admission of hearing voices and an ambivalent desire to move to another dorm, Mr. I denies other concerns or any psychological symptoms. He denies ever making a suicide attempt, which is supported by the file data, and he denies any present or recent suicidal ideation or intent.

In the present interview, he related reasonably appropriately. On occasion, affect was a bit flat, although not depressed. However, at other times, affect was appropriate, even in the manifestation of positive affect. The only indication of thought disorder occurred when he was in the midst of discussing the content of his hallucinations, and he was able to provide an appropriate attitude of perspective and distance in this discussion. It is probable that the critical factor in his present adequate adjustment is the continued regimen of psychotropic medication and the structure from his present institutional status.

On the MMPI-2, standard indexes of psychosis were within normal limits, likely reflecting the factors noted in the prior sentence. Mild, subclinical elevations on these scales do point to the residual elements of active schizophrenia. Controlling for these mild elevations, Mr. I's profile is similar to a mild, subclinical form of the Able profile described in the Megargee classification system. The main implications are that absent the active schizophrenia, there is a mild proclivity toward antisocial behavior, and a reduced likelihood of adequate vocational function outside of the institution.

Mr. I scored in the low to moderate range on the PCL-R, relative to most inmates. He was somewhat higher on Factor II than on Factor I. This indicates that classic psychopathy is not a compelling factor in his offense and life history.

Mr. I states that he would be living with his brother in Jamestown. Mr. I's report and the file material suggest that this would be a reasonably supportive environment, and he has a mental health counselor there who has indicated a willingness to counsel Mr. I again. Mr. I does have a few marketable skills. This issue is not as critical as it is in most cases, as he has received SSI support in the past because of mental disability, and it is probable that he will receive it in the future.

Mr. I is adjusting adequately at present, especially considering his mental history. His verbalized attitudes are positive, both in general and in his willingness to continue with his medication, and to return to contacts with his counselor in Jamestown. There are other positives regarding parole prognosis: the lack of sexual acting-out or serious interpersonal aggression in his offense history; a relatively short offense history; absence of data to indicate a substance abuse history; a reportedly positive living environment and probable financial support; and an absence of marked psychopathy. At the same time, I believe that he will at least be a risk for a reversion into active schizophrenia for the foreseeable future. This would in turn heighten the possibility of reoffending in some fashion.

Consistent contact with a mental health agent, preferably his counselor in Jamestown, is essential if parole is granted. Such contact would not only provide counseling and access to a medication provider, but consistent monitoring of his mental status. It would be even better if Mr. I's brother and his family could receive some training in recognizing relevant symptoms of Mr. I's disorder, and advice on behaviors that would facilitate a positive status in Mr. I.

Robert G. Meyer, Ph.D.
Licensed Clinical Psychologist
Board Certified in Clinical and in Forensic Psychology (ABPP)

Teaching Point: How can the influences of social desirability and defensiveness be managed in FMHA?

Social desirability and defensiveness are potential sources of bias that can influence the results and accuracy of a FMHA. Generally, social desirability and defensiveness can result from a variety of sources that may be present in FMHA. These include the desire to avoid or minimize incarceration or other sanctions, the hope of being released from incarceration or secure hospitalization, the goal of obtaining other kinds of privileges in a secure setting, or the hope of convincing treating clinicians that they are making progress in therapy. The influence of such biases can be especially problematic and difficult to manage when the forensic clinician relies solely on clinical judgment, rather than also employing methods and techniques designed to help gauge the influence of such responding. Although it is impossible to eliminate social desirability and defensiveness, there are a number of ways of managing and minimizing its impact on the results of FMHA.

The first approach to minimizing the impact of defensiveness is the use of psychological testing. Some psychological testing, such as the Minnesota Multiphasic Personality Inventory and the Millon instruments, incorporate validity scales that can add to the accuracy of clinical impressions in the areas of diagnosis and clinical characteristics. Such tests are particularly valuable when they can provide information both about global clinical functioning *and* possible defensiveness in responding.

The second method for managing or minimizing social desirability and defensiveness involves the use of third-party collateral information. Such collateral information, including records and interviews, is a valuable source of data that can be used to compensate for the potential inaccuracy in self-report from an individual who is highly defensive on evaluation.

The use of these approaches is helpful in reducing the impact of responding defensively in FMHA. By using these approaches, the forensic clinician cannot only manage and minimize such bias, but increase the accuracy of the overall evaluation and the resulting conclusions in the process.

Case 2

Principle: Use nomothetic evidence in assessing causal connection between clinical condition and functional abilities

This principle is discussed in Chapter 2, so we will not repeat this discussion. Rather, we will move directly to showing how the present report illustrates the application of this principle.

The individual being evaluated in this case, Mr. Nebbish, was sent to Mishegoss State Psychiatric Hospital (MSPH) in February of 1999 after he was found Not Guilty by Reason of Insanity (NGRI) on theft charges. Mr. Nebbish was sent to MSPH to address treatment needs and functional deficits that kept him from living safely and responsibly in the community. In this report, it is noted that Mr. Nebbish's treatment team has concluded that he should be granted conditional release from MSPH; the purpose of the evaluation was to evaluate the appropriateness of the treatment team's recommendation for conditional release.

As part of the evaluation, the forensic clinician interviewed Mr. Nebbish and Mr. Nebbish's attending physician at MSPH. Additionally, he reviewed various records regarding Mr. Nebbish, including the patient's medical and psychiatric records from MSPH.

The medical and psychiatric records from MSPH contained valuable information regarding the results of various medical tests that were conducted during Mr. Nebbish's hospitalization. Specifically, in the section of the report titled "Hospital Course," the forensic clinician notes that from early March to mid-May of 1999, Mr. Nebbish "experienced confusion that was uncharacteristic of his prior illness." To determine why Mr. Nebbish was confused, his physician ordered laboratory tests, an electroencephalogram (EEG), and a magnetic resonance imaging (MRI) scan. According to the forensic clinician, the results of these tests did not reveal the source of Mr. Nebbish's confusion.

The use of such medical testing for this purpose, however, is consistent with the principle of using nomothetic evidence. Because these medical tests have an established empirical base, with demonstrated levels of validity and reliability, the forensic clinician was able to rely on the results of these tests. Specifically, because EEGs and MRIs are accurate diagnostic modalities, the medical forensic clinician can rely on the results of these tests to determine potential contributors to Mr. Nebbish's behavior. Although the specific tests results were not provided in the report, the forensic clinician had access to the test results in Mr. Nebbish's medical records from MSPH. Accordingly, because the forensic clinician is a physician, he was able to consider how the results of the EEG and MRI might determine how they could account for Mr. Nebbish's confusion.

After it was determined that EEG and MRI results did not clarify the source(s) of such confusion, the report notes that Mr. Nebbish's treatment team examined his regimen of psychotropic medication. The team observed that he was taking benztropine, an anticholinergic medication that can cause confusion and delirium, and lithium. Using his medical training, the forensic clinician was able to review Mr. Nebbish's medical records from MSPH to assess whether Mr. Nebbish's medication levels might account for his confusion. In addition, because these medications have undergone extensive clinical trials research, the psychiatrist could confirm his recollections by consulting the relevant research literature to learn whether (1) Mr. Nebbish was receiving the proper doses, and (2) confusion was a documented side effect of these medications. The report indicates that Mr. Nebbish's confusion temporarily remitted after the benztropine was discontinued.

However, Mr. Nebbish's confusion returned several months later. Further medical testing revealed that his lithium level was in the toxic range. Again, the forensic clinician's medical training enabled him to assess whether this documented lithium level could account for Mr. Nebbish's confusion. Part of this assessment involved his knowledge of the relevant literature. Another part was observing his response to a dosage reduction; after his attending psychiatrist controlled Mr. Nebbish's lithium level through a dosage reduction, the patient's confusion dissipated and his clinical condition improved rapidly.

CONFIDENTIAL PSYCHIATRIC REPORT

Identifying Information
Patient's Name: Stephen Nebbish
Date of Birth: February 29, 1963
Date of Admission: June 31, 1998
Legal Status: Not guilty by reason of insanity
Original Charge: Theft
County: Gevalt
Judge: Honorable Oliver Wendell Holmes
Prosecutor: Hamilton Burger, Esq.
Defense Attorney: Clarence Darrow, Esq.
Date of Report: April 31, 2000

COURT REFERRAL QUESTION

Stephen Nebbish, a 37-year-old single Caucasian man, came to the Mishegoss State Psychiatric Hospital (MSPH) in June 1998 for competence restoration. Two months earlier, authorities had charged Mr. Nebbish with theft related to his alleged actions in late April 1998. In January 1999, the Court ruled that he was competent to stand trial, and in February 1999, the Court found Mr. Nebbish not guilty by reason of insanity (NGRI) on the theft charge. Since his insanity acquittal, Mr. Nebbish has resided on Ward C, a locked civil unit at MSPH; his privilege level permits him to go outside locked areas only when accompanied by MSPH staff members. Recently, the staff members on Ward C carefully reviewed his treatment and progress; they concluded that Mr.

Nebbish would not benefit from additional hospitalization and that he was ready for a conditional release from MSPH. This report, prepared pursuant to Ohio Revised Code § 2945.401(D)(1)(a), addresses the appropriateness of the treatment team's recommendation.

SOURCES OF INFORMATION

- A 90-minute interview of Mr. Nebbish on April 27, 2000
- A 30-minute discussion with Mr. Nebbish's attending physician, Sigmund Freud, M.D.
- All records from the present MSPH hospitalization
- Gevalt County Police Records and Witness Statements, April 25–27, 1998
- Discharge Summary, Sigmund Freud, M.D., September 21, 1995 (for Mr. Nebbish's previous MSPH hospitalization)
- Competency Evaluation, Carl Rogers, Ph.D., May 31, 1998

BACKGROUND INFORMATION

Childhood Mr. Nebbish was born to married parents and grew up Chelm, Ohio. He has two brothers and one sister. His parents divorced when he was a fourth grader, and he lived with his mother for the next 4 years. Our records report that Mr. Nebbish's mother drank heavily and often left him alone at home. When Mr. Nebbish was 14 years old, his mother moved to

California, and he spent his high school years living with his father, who still resides in Chelm. His mother died in 1989; his father is still living.

Education Mr. Nebbish graduated from West Chelm High School in the middle third of his class. Over the next 5 years, he attended Shlmiel College and Shlmazzel University; he took primarily business courses and obtained a total of 2 to 3 years of college credits.

Adult Relationships Mr. Nebbish never married and has no children. As a young man, he had two multimonth, live-in heterosexual relationships, but over the last 10 years, he has had few close friends. During previous interviews he said that he could not recall when he last dated. Mr. Nebbish lived in low-income housing for the 2 years preceding his April 1998 arrest. Before this, he lived with family members, principally his brother Phillip.

Employment Mr. Nebbish has held several jobs, which have involved working as a trash collector, a busboy and dishwasher, and a janitor. He worked in early 1996 at a local factory, and he sorted and displayed items at a local consignment shop for approximately 8 months until January 1998, when he quit his job. Asked why, he responded, "I don't know, . . . it just happened. . . . It made no sense at the time, and it doesn't now." He recalled, however, that the store owner, who at first had liked him, got "on my case" about his argumentativeness with customers and his drinking before work and during breaks. Over the next several weeks, Mr. Nebbish did "nothing; I just walked around, had some drinks with people, and watched TV." As his mental illness became more pronounced, he stopped eating and slept less. When visiting his brother Phillip's home, he told family members that he had heard Elijah's voice saying that he was "a prophet."

Psychiatric History Mr. Nebbish underwent his first psychiatric hospitalization in 1983, during his college years. He had experienced a severe depression with psychotic features, and ultimately recovered with the help of desipramine (a tricyclic antidepressant) and perphenazine (an anti-

psychotic medication). He has undergone six psychiatric hospitalizations, including a previous MSPH hospitalization (August–September 1995). Dr. Rogers's 1998 competence report documents an unambiguous history of manic episodes preceding many hospitalizations; Dr. Freud's 1995 discharge summary describes several symptoms (grandiose thinking, pressured speech, and extreme irritability) that are typical of mania. Over the past 10 years, Mr. Nebbish has taken several mood-stabilizing medications (e.g., lithium and divalproex sodium) while hospitalized, but has not taken these consistently after discharge, even when they were prescribed for him.

Substance Use History Mr. Nebbish began drinking as a teen. He reported "spells" of heavy drinking beginning in college, when he sometimes drank daily from the time he left classes until the local bars closed. After he left college, Mr. Nebbish continued to drink to intoxication "once or twice a week" at local bars. Hangovers sometimes compromised his work performance, and when he quit or lost jobs, drinking at bars became too expensive for him. In recent years, he reduced his drinking to "one or two beers a couple of times a week," but he drank more than this in the first part of 1998. He has never had an alcohol-related arrest, though he once drove his car into a barn while drunk. He said that he has had several blackouts, but has never experienced alcohol withdrawal symptoms. As a young man, he could drink up to 12 beers in a few hours without feeling "drunk."

Although Mr. Nebbish said he "experimented" with cocaine (powder), marijuana, and stimulants as a young man, he has used none of these substances for more than a decade. He denied past use of hallucinogens or injectable drugs (e.g., heroin).

Medical History Mr. Nebbish is receiving treatment for lithium-induced hypothyroidism. He has no other known medical problems.

Legal History Before the 1998 theft charge, Mr. Nebbish had been arrested for criminal damaging (1983), criminal trespassing (1988), and domestic violence toward his father (April 1995). He was jailed in July 1995 after failure to comply with bond or probation rules; shortly after that, he came to MSPH for treatment of a manic episode. He also has had seven traffic charges for offenses that include speeding, failure to appear in court, and driving under suspension.

Family History Mr. Nebbish's mother died in January 1989 following a myocardial infarction. His father, now age 68, still works as a landscaper. Mr. Nebbish thought that one of his brothers had received outpatient treatment for depression, and said that his father "enjoys a few drinks every evening."

HOSPITAL COURSE

When Mr. Nebbish first came here for competence restoration, reports from the Gevalt County Jail (where he had spent the previous 2 months) said that he had been confused and had exhibited labile affect immediately after his arrest. His relatives told MSPH staff members that before his arrest, he said "crazy things," had been drinking heavily, and was probably not taking any psychotropic medication. On admission to MSPH, he displayed blunted affect and had trouble thinking clearly; he also seemed irritable, isolated, and withdrawn.

Throughout his current stay at MSPH, Mr. Nebbish has not posed any behavioral problems and has never required seclusion or restraints. Immediately after his arrival, he resumed taking medication as prescribed. By early September 1998, he was clear-headed, although he felt "depressed," was mildly euphoric, and sometimes seemed overly talkative. By late September 1998, staff members noted no evidence of manic symptoms during the many therapeutic groups in which he participated.

From early March to mid-May 1999, Mr. Nebbish experienced confusion that was uncharacteristic of his prior illness. The ward treatment team requested an internal medicine consultation to learn if these problems had a nonpsychiatric medical cause. A thorough work-up—including blood test, an EEG, and an MRI head scan—did not reveal any source for the confusion. The treatment team noted, however, that Mr. Nebbish was taking benztropine, an anticholinergic medication that sometimes causes confusion, delirium, or other syndromes with mental symptoms. When doctors stopped the benztropine in May 1999, Mr. Nebbish's confusion diminished quickly.

Mr. Nebbish remained well for approximately 3 months, until September 1999, when he became confused again. Laboratory tests revealed a lithium level of 1.61 mEq/L, in the toxic range (despite no recent change in his medication doses). His lithium dose was lowered and he improved rapidly. However, in early October 1999, he behaved oddly; he showered with his clothing on, and one night he donned his pajamas and "went to bed" in the dining area of Ward C. The reasons for this behavior remain unclear. Lab tests, however, revealed another high lithium level (1.5 mEq/L) and changes in his thyroid functioning (low thyroid hormone level, low free thyroid index, and an elevated thyroid stimulating hormone), possibly related to lithium therapy. After doctors again reduced the dose of lithium and began prescribing an oral thyroid supplement, Mr. Nebbish gradually improved.

Mr. Nebbish has done very well mentally and physically since December 1999, and has impressed staff members as pleasant, cooperative, and friendly. He has attended several group therapies, including medication education classes, leisure skills group, ceramics, library, the game room club, and the substance abuse group; he also has participated in weekly individual psychotherapy sessions with Jean Piaget, Ph.D., the Ward C psychologist. He has had occasional problems sleeping, but has managed satisfactorily in the crowded, sometimes noisy environment where he lives. His relationships with other patients are cordial, but he has not made close friends with anyone. Progress notes from the last several weeks show that Mr. Nebbish understood why he was arrested, jailed, hospitalized, and ultimately found NGRI. He has told MSPH staff members that he will not repeat "my past errors."

Throughout this calendar year, Mr. Nebbish has tolerated his medications well and taken all doses as prescribed. As of late April 2000, his medications were lithium carbonate 600 mg twice a day (most recent blood level = 0.89 mEq/L, March 2, 2000), olanzapine 5 mg at bedtime, and levothyroxine 150 µg each morning.

PSYCHIATRIC INTERVIEW

Disclosure   I began my meeting with Mr. Nebbish by explaining in simple language that I would be evaluating the appropriateness of the treatment team's recommendation for a conditional release. I also explained that our conversation was not for treatment purposes and was not confidential, that I would prepare a report of my findings for the Court and other parties involved in his case, and that I might have to testify about my findings. To make sure Mr. Nebbish understood this information, I asked him to paraphrase my explanation. He did so accurately, and then agreed to speak with me.

When asked how he was feeling, Mr. Nebbish responded, "I think I'm doing quite well, myself." We next discussed the events that had led to his arrest, his theft charge, and his insanity acquittal. Concerning his behavior in April 1998, he said, "I wasn't, clearly, thinking right, or I wouldn't have taken the clothing from the store," referring to the consignment shop where he had worked a few months before. He described several eschatological ideas that influenced his decisions in spring 1998; as part of his effort to prepare for "the end of days, . . . I thought I had to feed the hungry and clothe the naked." He felt divinely inspired to give the store's clothing to those who needed it. Because he had what he termed a "relationship of obligation" with his former employer, Mr. Nebbish then believed that taking clothing was a fulfillment of his prophetic mission to save his employer from becoming what the hallucinated voice of his grandfather called a "shvir afn tuches." Mr. Nebbish explained that he felt "quite depressed," and that the actions that led to his arrest had left him feeling "spiritually uplifted." These beliefs had felt quite genuine in 1998, but he recognized that they had been "grandiose delusions" that doctors thought were "symptoms of my manic-depression." Although he still espoused a belief in the Almighty and attended on-grounds religious services each week,

he no longer thought he was a prophet and did not believe the end of time was imminent.

If conditionally released, he said, he would live in a group home and might spend his free time visiting family members. Conditions of his post-hospitalization monitoring would include abstinence from intoxicants, taking medication as prescribed, attending AA meetings, and coming to the Gevalt County Mental Health Center for outpatient treatment. He wanted to become gainfully employment again, and described several jobs (e.g., working as a store clerk) that he thought he could do successfully. He also discussed his hope for getting more education, and thought it might be interesting to work with computers. Noting that his medications had made him susceptible to gaining weight, he hoped he could get more exercise than his hospital confinement had allowed.

Mr. Nebbish understood that his clinicians believed he suffered from bipolar disorder, "a new name for what used to be called manic-depression." He also knew that his doctors thought he was "an alcoholic"; he questioned this diagnosis, but recognized that before hospitalization he had "a tendency to drink too much." He thought that medication had helped him, but "my faith has helped me [more] . . . I believe G-d has given people talent and wisdom, and the ability to invent things. . . . It's kind of hard to explain, because Solomon said that there was nothing new under the sun, and he was supposed to be the wisest ruler. He said that all was vanity, but Solomon turned away from G-d in his later years." He listed several individuals (including Ernest Hemingway, G. F. Handel, Abraham Lincoln, and Winston Churchill) who had been creative despite having drinking problems or mood problems.

Mental Status Examination   Mr. Nebbish presented as a well-groomed, nicely dressed, overweight man who appeared his stated age. He made good eye contact, showed no evidence of medication side effects, and displayed no unusual behavior or movements. He looked anxious; although he answered questions honestly, he was obviously concerned about making a good impression.

He was alert and fully oriented. His speech was clear, audible, and normally paced. He displayed a somewhat-reduced amount of spontaneous elaboration, although generally his answers contained adequate detail. Once during our meeting, he gave a complicated and circumferential explanation (quoted above) for his viewpoint concerning the comparative efficacy of medication and spiritual beliefs. All of his other answers were relevant, coherent, and well-concatenated. He denied any recent delusions or hallucinations, and I noted no objective evidence of these during the interview. His affect ranged broadly, but was appropriate to the topics we discussed; he did not seem euphoric, irritable, or depressed. His facial expressions were consistent with his reported mood (which he described as "pretty good") and with the interview-related anxiety that he was experiencing. He denied any recent homicidal or suicidal ideation.

He could repeat three objects ("ball, flag, tree") immediately and after a 5-minute delay. He did serial subtractions from 100 by 7s without error. He did the mental multiplications 2×192 and 2×384 correctly, but said 2×768 equaled "a thousand and something." He could repeat eight numbers forward and could reverse six. He could name the U.S. presidents back through Eisenhower and gave short but accurate summaries of news stories that had received recent television coverage (e.g., the previous day's baseball results and events concerning Elián González in Miami). He gave abstract explanations of easy and difficult similarities, but gave idiosyncratic or concrete explanations of proverbs. He displayed no gross evidence of problems with attention or concentration. Based on his active vocabulary, educational background, and responses to my mental status questions, I estimated that his intelligence was at least average. He showed a fair degree of insight about his mental illness and its connection to his past behavior and legal situation, although he did not recognize the full array of symptoms, disorganization, and drinking problems that he experienced before his 1998 arrest. Nonetheless, he seemed able to assume responsibilities commensurate with the proposed level of movement.

PSYCHIATRIC DIAGNOSIS

Axis I   296.66   Bipolar I Disorder, most recent episode mixed, in full remission

303.90   Alcohol dependence in a controlled environment

Axis II   V71.09   None

Axis III   Obesity

Lithium-related hypothyroidism

Axis IV   Problems related to interaction with the legal system

Axis V   GAF = 63 (current)

SUMMARY AND OPINION

Mr. Nebbish is a 37-year-old man who came to MSPH for competence restoration in June 1998, and whose hospitalization continued under O.R.C. §§ 2945.40 and 5122.15 following his February 1999 NGRI finding. His insanity acquittal on a charge of theft stemmed from actions that occurred in April 1998. From several months before his arrest until September 1998, Mr. Nebbish suffered from symptoms of bipolar disorder, including thought disorganization, delusions with grandiose and religious content, and altered mood; before his arrest, he also drank heavily. The delusional ideas served as motivations for his taking items from his former employer; these ideas also prevented him from recognizing the wrongfulness of his behavior. His mood disturbance, irritability, delusional thinking, and alterations in thought processes were manifestations of a severe mental disorder that had its onset in the early 1980s.

Mr. Nebbish's symptoms diminished several weeks after he began taking antipsychotic and mood-stabilizing drugs here at MSPH. Throughout the hospitalization, he has been a cooperative patient who has followed all staff recommendations regarding treatment. Because of this hospitalization and his experiences over the past 20 months, Mr. Nebbish understands that his mental illness has caused severe interpersonal problems and several run-ins with the law. He knows that, should the Court grant him a conditional release, the Court would expect him to undertake sustained, daily compliance with medication recommendations and to participate in supervised outpatient treatment for years. He is willing to take prescribed medications regularly, to refrain from alcohol and recreational drug use, and to have his compliance with treatment monitored through blood testing and urine screening. He also wishes to participate in structured activities (as these are prescribed or recommended), and to resume gainful employment.

Mr. Nebbish's treatment team members believe that he will not benefit from further hospitalization, that a conditional release would be appropriate, and that if he were monitored properly as an outpatient, he would pose an acceptably low risk of danger to the community. I agree. *It is my opinion, held with a reasonable degree of medical certainty, that Mr. Nebbish is ready for conditional release, that outpatient treatment is the least restrictive setting for his current care, and that outpatient treatment can be accomplished with an acceptably low risk to the community.*

Ohio Revised Code § 2945.401(E) sets out several factors for the Court to consider when granting unsecured status to an insanity acquittee. I address these factors in the following paragraphs.

Safety of the Community The following considerations suggest that, were Mr. Nebbish to receive a conditional release, his risk of acting violently would be acceptably low:

- Past behavior is the best predictor of future behavior. My evaluation and review of Mr. Nebbish's psychiatric history reveal that he has acted violently only during manic episodes. He has not required seclusion or restraint and has not acted aggressively during this hospitalization. He has no thoughts of harming others or himself. Mr. Nebbish appears unlikely to act violently while his symptoms remain in remission.
- Some studies suggest that severe psychotic symptoms increase an individual's risk to act violently. Mr. Nebbish has not experienced the mental symptoms that led to his arrest since summer 1998.
- Substance abuse increases an individual's risk to act violently. Before his arrest, Mr. Nebbish drank heavily, and in past years, heavy drinking may have contributed to his aggressive behavior toward family members. He now realizes that drinking could affect his ability to function and might interfere with his treatment. He is willing to abstain from alcohol and illicit drugs, and to undergo monitoring (e.g., through urine

testing) if this were a requirement of a conditional release. Mr. Nebbish's intent and the availability of post-hospitalization testing will reduce his risk of engaging in drug- or alcohol-related violence.
- When he is not suffering from symptoms of mania, Mr. Nebbish does not have features of antisocial personality disorder or other conditions that increase an individual's risk of acting violently.
- Mr. Nebbish does not want to hurt, or have any contact with, the complainant in his original criminal case. He recognizes that he took items that he should not have, and is sorry he did this.

Mental and Physical Condition of the Individual

- The psychiatric symptoms that led to Mr. Nebbish's arrest have ceased, and appear well-controlled with medications.
- During his stay at MSPH, Nebbish experienced episodes of bizarre behavior that were not like his previous episodes of mental illness. They probably resulted from drug toxicity; hypothyroidism may have been a complicating factor. Mr. Nebbish's hypothyroidism has been treated, his medications have been adjusted, and he has not experienced any confusion or bizarre behavior for several months. Successful treatment of thyroid abnormalities makes it easier to control mood symptoms with medication. Mr. Nebbish's physical health is satisfactory, and he is under no restrictions that would affect his community functioning.

Insight Mr. Nebbish understands his mental illnesses. In the past, he did not take medications regularly and did not recognize episodes of mania when they occurred; he often drank more heavily at these times. Mr. Nebbish knows this, however, and wants mental health care that will help him live responsibly in the community and remain symptom-free.

Grounds for the Commitment Although the symptoms of Mr. Nebbish's mental illness have remitted, his illness is chronic and requires ongoing treatment. Were Mr. Nebbish to be conditionally released, the Court would continue to receive updates on his compliance with the Court's requirements, his long-term response to medications, and his ability to work with outpatient caregivers. If his condition worsened, the Court could revoke his conditional release and order him back to a hospital for treatment.

Degree of Conformity to Laws, Rules, Regulations, and Values The following items support my belief that Mr. Nebbish would abide by rules and conditions of a conditional release:

- Mr. Nebbish has behaved responsibly at MSPH and has not tried to escape while he was outside the locked areas of the hospital.
- Mr. Nebbish knows he needs medication for his mental illness. He has found his current medications to be very tolerable and believes that they have treated his symptoms well.
- Although Mr. Nebbish drank heavily before his arrest, he plans to abstain from alcohol because it could adversely affect his treatment.

Likelihood of Remaining in Remission Mr. Nebbish's current medications will reduce his chances of developing the symptoms he experienced in early 1998. However, bipolar patients who take medications faithfully may nonetheless experience recurrences of their mental illness. Rapid identification and treatment of recurring symptoms will be an important part of Mr. Nebbish's community treatment, should the Court grant him a conditional release. As is the case with many other individuals who suffer from bipolar disorder, Mr. Nebbish sometimes has not recognized recurrences of his illness, but careful monitoring by outpatient mental health professionals can address this problem.

Should the Court order a conditional release, the Court and Mr. Nebbish's caregivers should address the following matters to promote his successful return to the community:

1. *Housing:* Mr. Nebbish should initially live in a group home setting where supervisors can help him adjust to community living, help him to continue taking medications properly, and monitor his progress.
2. *Income:* Mr. Nebbish is eligible for SSDI benefits and could apply for these were he released from the hospital. This would provide a modest source of financial support until he found competitive employment.
3. *Psychiatric Medication:* Compliance with medications often poses a problem for patients after they leave the hospital. However, Mr. Nebbish is tolerating his current medications and knows that they improve his health. He has had no problems complying with medications. His good insight into his illness and recognition that his current medications are working well are factors that make him more likely to continue taking prescribed medications.
4. *Community Treatment:* Mr. Nebbish's family members will be critical sources of emotional sustenance once he leaves the hospital. However, he also will need professional support in the form of assertive community treatment. Local agencies that monitor forensic outpatients now offer an intensive program in which community support specialists visit or contact patients up to twice a day. Such frequent professional contact would provide a level of individual support that is close to what Mr. Nebbish has had at MSPH. Outpatient caregivers would assess medication compliance, anxiety reduction, and time management, and could help Mr. Nebbish navigate benefits and entitlement systems until he can become economically self-sufficient. They also would share information on Mr. Nebbish's condition with his psychiatrist, other members of the treatment team, and the Court. This process would help promptly identify recurrences of problem drinking or manic symptoms and make early intervention possible.

Jonathan Narishkeit, M.D.
Staff Psychiatrist, Mishegoss State Psychiatric Hospital

Teaching Point: How can forensic clinicians use nomothetic evidence to apply science to practice?

Besides discussing the results of standard medical tests and diagnostic techniques, Dr. Narishkeit's report contains two other illustrations of "nomothetic" reasoning. The first relates to the original and literal meaning of "nomothetic," from the Greek νομοθεκός (*nomothetikos*), meaning "law-giving" or "legislative." The report addresses the statutory (that is, legislatively prescribed) criteria that an Ohio trial court should use when deciding whether an insanity acquittee should receive an "unsecured status" (that is, be allowed to travel or live in the community without being constantly supervised by mental health professionals). By preparing his report this way, Dr. Narishkeit obviously hoped to persuade the Court that Mr. Nebbish satisfies statutory criteria for a conditional release. But he also showed that he had systematically considered a set of prescribed factors that Ohio legislators deem important when a court grants more freedom to an insanity acquittee.

A second illustration of nomothetic reasoning is found in how Dr. Narishkeit's report addresses Ohio's statutory criteria. Because the report concerns a specific individual's circumstances, many of Dr. Narishkeit's comments are "idiographic," and refer to specific developments that are unique to Mr. Nebbish's situation and course of treatment. Examples of this include Dr. Narishkeit's statements that Mr. Nebbish did not want to hurt the original complainant and had previously lacked contemporaneous recognition of his manic episodes.

However, Dr. Narishkeit does not rely merely on individualized, "clinical judgment" to support his opinion. He also mentions several factors concerning Mr. Nebbish's condition and situation that reflect current scientific knowledge about what raises or lowers a person's risk of acting violently. One finds several examples in the report's "Safety of the Community" subsection.

Dr. Narishkeit notes, "Past behavior is the best predictor of future behavior," and connects Mr. Nebbish's history of violent actions to his manic episodes. Dr. Narishkeit cites "studies suggest[ing] that severe psychotic symptoms increase an individual's risk to act violently," and points to the absence of psychotic symptoms as a factor that reduced Mr. Nebbish's current risk of violence.

After stating that "[s]ubstance abuse increases an individual's risk to act violently," the report describes how this well-documented risk factor has applied to Mr. Nebbish, and how it can be addressed. Mr. Nebbish's lack of a personality disorder is another scientifically supported finding favoring lower risk of violence. There is no rule for translating the presence or absence of these and other factors into a decision about conditional release. However, Dr. Narishkeit's discussion of these factors reflects a growing and well-grounded trend away from using unguided, individualized clinical intuition to make forensic determinations, and toward ruled-based, data-supported, actuarial aids to decision making.

Case 3

Principle: Testify in an effective manner

This principle addresses the importance of both substance and style in effective FMHA testimony. Substantive strength involves the extent to which testimony is thorough, accurate, impartial, relevant, and supported by scientific reasoning, as well as data. For the sake of convenience, we will define substantive strength as the overall degree to which the testimony is consistent with the 28 principles of FMHA described by Heilbrun (2001) and elaborated on in this book. Stylistic strength involves a combination of professional dress and demeanor, courtroom familiarity, speech that is clear, largely free of technical jargon, fluid and variable in pace, directed toward the judge or jury as well as the attorney, and the capacity to handle the challenge of cross-examination well (Heilbrun, 2001). The effectiveness of expert testimony can be considered in terms of both substantive and stylistic strength, with the most effective (accurate, ethical, persuasive) testimony high in both.

There is substantial ethical guidance for this principle. The APA *Ethical Principles of Psychologists and Code of Conduct* (1992) suggests that the ethical standards contained therein are broadly applicable to expert testimony: "Psychologists who perform forensic functions, such as assessments, interviews, consultations, reports, or expert testimony, must comply with all other provisions of the Ethics Code to the extent that they apply to such activities" (p. 1610). In addition, the *Ethics Code* specifically addresses the topic of FMHA testimony and reports: "In forensic testimony and reports, psychologists testify truthfully, honestly and candidly, and consistent with applicable legal procedures, describe fairly the bases for their testimony and conclusions" (p. 1610).

The *Specialty Guidelines for Forensic Psychologists* (Committee on Ethical Guidelines for Forensic Psychologists, 1991) makes it reasonably clear that stylistically strong testimony is not precluded by other parts of the *Specialty Guidelines*:

> When testifying, forensic psychologists have an obligation to all parties to a legal proceeding to present their findings, conclusions, evidence, or other professional products in a fair manner. *This principle does not preclude forceful representation of the data and reasoning upon which a conclusion or professional product is based.* It does, however, preclude an attempt, whether active or passive, to engage in partisan distortion or misrepresentation. Forensic psychologists do not, by either commission or omission, participate in a misrepresentation of their evidence, nor do they participate in partisan attempts to avoid, deny, or subvert the presentation of evidence contrary to their own position. (p. 664; emphasis added)

The substantive aspects of testifying effectively are addressed at length, and in detail, through the other principles described by Heilbrun (2001) and in this book. The key to applying these principles to the substantive aspects of expert testimony involves considering FMHA as a process composed of distinct steps. These steps culminate in the communication of FMHA results in a detailed, thorough report describing data, reasoning, and conclusions. When these principles are followed, the communication of results (whether in the form of the report or the testimony based on this report) is guided by the cumulative application of these substantive principles.

The application of this principle that has not been discussed at length in this book—the stylistic aspects of effective testimony—can be considered by reference to empirical research on impression management and standards of practice for expert testimony. Empirical research on the social psychology of persuasive communication has suggested stylistic factors that may enhance credibility and persuasiveness. Some of these factors include expertise (training and experience, such as degrees and positions), trustworthiness (perceptions by the judge and jurors of trustworthiness), and dynamism (style, charisma, and nonverbal aspects of credibility) (Brodsky, 1991; Champagne, Shuman, & Whitaker, 1991; Melton et al., 1997; Rosenthal, 1983; Shuman, Champagne, & Whitaker, 1994).

Other specific factors relevant to stylistic effectiveness have been described as style of dress, familiarity with courtroom protocol, speaking to the jury, and style of speech (Brodsky, 1991; Melton et al., 1997). Generally, style of dress should be conservative, professional, and neat; flashy and bright clothing should be avoided. The expert should also display familiarity and comfort with the courtroom. Specific examples include pausing before answering each question, using a clear and even tone of voice, not volunteering information, and knowing how to react when an objection is made. The expert should also speak to the jury, particularly during cross-examination, using understandable language, and making ample eye contact. Speech should be fluid, conversational in tone, clear, and confident.

Brodsky (1991) has elaborated on a number of ways in which to enhance the effectiveness of testimony. Some of his guidelines that are relevant to style include: (1) handling loaded and half-truth questions by first admitting the true part in a dependent clause and then strongly denying the untrue part in an independent clause; (2) meeting with the attorney prior to the direct examination and helping to prepare the questions; (3) after a "disaster" during testimony, either correcting the error as soon as possible, or letting it go; (4) neither fraternizing nor discussing any aspect of the case with opposing counsel, other witnesses, clients, or jurors; (5) speaking slowly, stressing syllables, and varying the loudness of speech during testimony; and (6) when the time is right to disagree with cross-examination questions, doing so with strength, clarity, and conviction.

Effective testimony is an important part of the FMHA process. The mastery of both substantive and stylistic aspects of testimony contributes substantially to making the forensic clinician a more effective practitioner of FMHA.

FORENSIC PSYCHOLOGICAL REPORT

Emily A. Johnson

PURPOSE OF THE EVALUATION

Emily Johnson was adjudicated Not Guilty by Reason of Insanity in February 1997 and committed to the Department of Mental Health and Mental Retardation. The purpose of this evaluation was to conduct an independent assessment of Ms. Johnson's psychological functioning, presence or absence of a psychological disorder, risk to self or others, and suitability for graduated release from the State Hospital.

Tests and Questionnaires

> Greenberg Forensic History Questionnaire
>
> Millon Clinical Multiaxial Inventory-III (MCMI-III)
>
> Rotter Incomplete Sentences Blank (ISB)
>
> Thematic Apperception Test (TAT)
>
> Peabody Picture Vocabulary Test-III (PPVT)
>
> Child Abuse Potential Inventory, Form VII (CAPI)

Evaluation Contacts

> 1/25/99   Meeting with Mr. S, Ms. G, and Dr. H, all from Ms. Johnson's Unit at State Hospital
>
> 1/27/99   Review of records
>
> 1/28/99   Clinical Interview and beginning of testing of Ms. Johnson
>
> 1/29/99   Continued clinical interview and testing of Ms. Johnson
>
> 2/1/99   Completion of Testing

Collateral Reports   As part of seeking independent verification of clinical judgments, I spoke to the key people at her State Hospital unit about their observations of Ms. Johnson. Mr. S is Ms. Johnson's caseworker. He reported that she has been compliant with the program in the unit. He noted that she has been "largely sweet and nice," but that her insight and judgment are suspect. She sometimes makes poor decisions, a product in part of her limited intelligence. Similar observations were made by Dr. H. He reported that this patient has decent social skills and is one of the most prominent and attractive of the patients; indeed, she is sometimes mistaken to be a staff member by visitors. She was described as often manipulative, and her social skills and poise were observed to diminish markedly when one goes into depth with her. She also was reported to have no remorse, and to tend toward being manipulative and accusatory.

Ms. Johnson's Presentation of Self   Three primary features appeared in Ms. Johnson's ways of relating to me during the interview and testing. To begin with, she questioned much of what was happening and the purpose of the examination. She asked demanding questions, such as: "What is this for?" "Who gets the reports?" "Why didn't they get someone from Bryce?" "Are you trying to figure out if I can spell?" and "What kind of report are you going to give me?"

The second feature of this patient's presentation was her effort to figure out the purpose of each of the tests. When she had an idea of what the purpose of the test would be, she then answered in ways she thought would serve her best.

The third feature of her presentation was her persistent and obvious effort to deny problems and describe herself as well-adjusted. Thus, she described herself as an emotionally normal person. She denied most areas of problems, although she does acknowledge that she is dyslexic and not intelligent. She stated: "God gives some people the talent to be smart. Not me. But I know how to read, do math, work, get up, and go to bed on time."

All of the results of the assessment were considered in light of Ms. Johnson's efforts at positive impression management. The first issue to be discussed is her intelligence.

INTELLECTUAL FUNCTIONING AND COMPREHENSION

A considerable background of intellectual assessments was present for this patient. When her hospital records were abstracted, the following test results were identified:

Previous Intelligence Testing Results

Year	Test	Results
1978	WISC: Full Scale IQ (FSIQ)	53
1981	WISC-R: FSIQ	47
1992	WISC-R: FSIQ	47
1995	WAIS-R: FSIQ	61
	Verbal IQ (VIQ)	54
	Performance IQ (PIQ)	71
1997	WAIS-R: FSIQ	69
	VIQ	63
	PIQ	78

Despite statements by Ms. Johnson that she was able to read, she was unable to read sufficiently well to understand any of the tests administered to her. Psychologists on the Admissions Unit had been unsuccessful in using tape-recorded administration and read-aloud administration of the MMPI-2. I chose tests at a lower level of comprehension than the MMPI-2 and read them slowly, seeking to ensure that she understood before she answered. Ms. Johnson had a tendency to give quick responses, whether or not she actually understood. This pattern was particularly true in the instances of double negatives or sentences with complex structure or words outside her comprehension.

In order to assess how well she did understand the questions and test items, this patient was administered the Peabody Picture Vocabulary Test (Form III-A). In this test, subjects are shown pages with drawings of four objects or scenes and are asked to point to or identify the one that matches the word read aloud. Ms. Johnson was 30 years and 7 months of age at the time of the testing. She achieved an age-equivalent score in listening comprehension of 7 years and 4 months. That is, she understood a little above the level expected of an average 7-year-old child.

Ms. Johnson gives an initial impression of functioning at a higher level than her actual abilities. She was unable to understand the meanings of words such as garment, fragile, cooperating, solo, and rodent. Her efforts to conceal her lack of understanding of words and ideas appears to be part of a pattern to pass as intellectually normal, which has persisted throughout her adulthood. For the purposes of this evaluation, the implications are that even with my efforts to ensure that she understood questions, she often responded when she did not comprehend in a manner designed to make me believe that she did comprehend.

Assessment of Psychopathology and Hallucinations
Ms. Johnson had been diagnosed as having mild mental retardation and schizophrenia, paranoid type, by Dr. F in his December 1995 assessment and in his 1996 report. In her initial hospital evaluation, the diagnostic impression was that Psychotic Disorder, not otherwise specified, should be ruled out, and that mild mental retardation was present. In the later reports and treatment team notes, the psychotic disorder question had indeed been ruled out, and the only remaining diagnosis was mild mental retardation.

Using the clinical interview, psychological testing, and specific probes into patterns of symptoms she had reported in earlier assessments, I assessed the degree to which Ms. Johnson might be psychologically disturbed. None of the psychological tests revealed patterns of severe disturbance. On the MCMI-III, she answered none of the items in the scored directions associated with a thought disorder or major depression. The delusional disorder score was also very low, as were the scales measuring other clinical syndromes. In other words, no signs of significant psychological disorder appeared on this test, or any other tests. On the Rotter Incomplete Sentences Blank, a test in which patients complete sentences from given stems, Ms. Johnson gave conventional and normal responses that fit closely with her level of intellectual functioning.

The TAT is a test in which subjects are shown 20 standard drawings of people in different situations, and then asked to make up stories in which they describe what the characters are thinking and feeling. Her responses drew a fairly detailed presentation of how Ms. Johnson sees and understands the world in which she lives. Her responses were conventional. No bizarre features that would support a serious clinical disorder were present. Although she did not show any depth of understanding of social conflict between men and women, her level of comprehension was higher than would be expected of an individual of her mildly retarded intellectual level. Ms. Johnson often avoided describing interpersonal conflicts, but some of her responses indicated that she identifies and experiences moderate amounts of sadness and anger. Overall, the results of this test were consistent with her other indications of adequate functioning without significant psychopathology.

The clinical interview similarly yielded no indications of serious disorder. I paid particular attention to the issues of command hallucinations—voices instructing her to do something—and visual hallucinations. She denied any command hallucinations. When I inquired in depth about her seeing people or things that were not there, the following information was elicited:

SLB: Have you seen things that weren't there?

EJ: White ghosts.

SLB: Tell me about them.

EJ: When I see them, I see them, but when I reach out to touch them, they are never there.

SLB: When do you see them?

EJ: Off and on.

SLB: When?

EJ: I ain't seen them since I've been here.
(I asked her to draw them for me, so I could see what they looked like. She drew two connected ovals, within an inverted u design. There were two circles representing eyes and one circle representing a nose in the top oval.)

EJ: I ain't seen them for a long time.

SLB: Tell me more about them.

EJ: Hard to remember what they look like.

SLB: Did they say anything?

EJ: I think I told the doctor they said something, but I can't remember. I think I said the ghosts said, "Don't sit up, don't stand up," but never anything bad.

SLB: Did they move?

EJ: I think they did. When I reached out to touch them, they disappear.

SLB: Did they walk or float?

EJ: Disappear when I tried to touch them.

SLB: They come back?

EJ: No. I would see them just off and on.

SLB: Colors?

EJ: White.

SLB: Eyes?

EJ: I don't know. It's been so long.

SLB: When did it start?

EJ: I don't know whether when all this stuff happened, or before, but I never told Steve or nobody, because I was afraid they would take my kids away.

SLB: Were you scared by them?

EJ: Yeah.

SLB: Tell me about it.

EJ: When I first saw them, I was scared, because I never saw them before.

SLB: Did they threaten you?

EJ: No, sir.

SLB: Were their voices in your head?

EJ: I don't think so. It's been so long. I've been through so much. So much happened. It's hard to remember for one person.

SLB: Thought you were crazy?

EJ: No.

SLB: Were you sure they were there?

EJ: I don't know. It's been so long.

SLB: They never spoke?

EJ: Said, don't sit down.

SLB: Did they order you to eat?

EJ: No, sir. I don't know if I was crazy or not crazy.

SLB: Do you believe in ghosts?

EJ: No, sir. I don't believe in ghosts. I don't guess.

SLB: Were the voices telling you to hurt somebody or yourself?

EJ: No, sir.

This long excerpt from my questioning about hallucinations is presented to illustrate the minimal presence or, indeed, absence of hallucinations. Ms. Johnson reported a vague, ill-formed report of ghosts. When I inquired into various aspects of these ghosts, she seemed to struggle to maintain a credible story. Although it is difficult to assess what her functioning may have been at the time of her competency to stand trial assessment, the present behaviors indicate that hallucinations are not part of her current personal experience, and that they probably have been absent for a matter of years. Given this individual's efforts at impression management, it is not an unreasonable hypothesis that her earlier reports may have been a product of the legal situation she faced.

Parenting and Potential for Child Abuse Ms. Johnson was consistent in responding to all of the interview and test inquiries about past or possible future abuse of her children. She consistently and strongly denied any hint of abuse. Her denials included refusing to admit even ordinary ways in which parents are upset or distressed by their children's problem behaviors.

On the CAPI (Child Abuse Potential Inventory), she engaged in such a high level of denial of most problems and selective reporting of other problems that the cutoff score for validity of responses was exceeded. Her total "abuse" (potential) score on the CAPI itself was 78; scores of 210 or over are interpreted as highly indicative of potential for abuse. Six separate scores make up the overall Abuse Scale. Ms. Johnson scored at very low levels on five of these scales and very high on "rigidity." Rigidity with one's children is indicated by answering the following items (and others like them) affirmatively:

Children should always be neat

A good child keeps his toys and clothes neat and orderly

Children should never cause trouble

Children should never disobey

Children should be quiet and listen

A child should never talk back

When parents endorse these items, they often believe that children should be forced into strict molds of behavior, and the parent becomes the enforcer. In combination with Ms. Johnson's low scores on distress, unhappiness, and problems with children, self, family, and others, the high rigidity score does not point with any clarity toward likelihood of abuse. Instead, her response set was one of selling herself to me as a good parent and as psychologically healthy. The questions about validity of this test suggest that while future abuse is not obviously predicted, it is not clearly ruled out.

When I inquired about her relationships with her children, Ms. Johnson offered elementary explanations. She told how DHR took her children and that made her unhappy. She asserted that she loved her children. In response to the question of what about them she loved, she stated that she gave birth to them, and when you give birth to a child, you love them. I then asked just what was it about the children she loved. Ms. Johnson replied: "They mind me. The little boy mind me. The little girl help me out. The little boy help with the babies. The only time they cry is when they are hurt. You can hold them. They is good babies."

In her characteristic challenging style, she then asked me, "Why you want to know that?" I explained I was trying to learn more about what she was like as a parent.

CONCLUSIONS

No indications were present that Emily Johnson is manifesting a diagnosable clinical disorder. She shows good reality contact, intact thought processes, and emotional functioning that is not discrepant for her intellectual level. Her listening comprehension was at the 7-year, 4-month mental age. Despite her initial ability to actively engage people, and her assertive and challenging style with others, she has a limited depth of understanding. Nevertheless, there is nothing about her psychological test results, clinical interview, or interaction style to lead me to believe that she suffers from a mental disorder, or that she is dangerous to herself.

Ms. Johnson has a simplistic and rigid understanding of relationships with her children. There is no indication of unhappiness and dysfunctional relationships with the children (or with other persons) that would lead to harmful acts with her children. However, she has inflexible and constricted ideas of what parenting and children's behaviors are and should be. Although she does not score in the high-risk range in potential for child abuse, her rigidity, combined with her history with her children, suggests caution and graduated and supervised steps in her contacts with them.

Throughout the tests, Ms. Johnson worked unceasingly to present herself as healthy, well-adjusted, and without risk. These efforts were highly transparent. The results of this evaluation have taken into account these efforts at positive impression management.

Stanley L. Brodsky, Ph.D., Licensed Psychologist
February 17, 1999

Teaching Point: How can the forensic clinician move from "adequate" to "outstanding" in presenting expert testimony?

Forensic clinicians should anticipate the possibility of providing expert testimony in every forensic assessment case in which they are involved, even though such testimony actually occurs in a minority of cases. Given this, it is important that forensic clinicians master the skills that make a good expert witness. There are several ways to do this.

Two books on this topic by Brodsky (1991, 1999) address expert testimony in terms of substance and style. These books can be particularly useful if the clinician already has a good familiarity with the empirical and practice literatures that are relevant to the population from which the individual being evaluated was drawn. Interestingly, the theme of Brodsky's second book (which presents maxims for expert witnesses in the same way the first book did) is similar to the question posed in this teaching point: How can an expert improve skills in this area to the level that might be described as mastery?

Another potentially useful strategy for improving skills as an expert witness is observing the expert testimony of other forensic clinicians. Several highly publicized trials featuring experienced forensic clinicians providing expert testimony are available on videotape. For example, Court TV filmed the Jeffrey Dahmer trial, which featured expert testimony provided by a total of seven psychiatrists and psychologists. Observing the strengths and weaknesses of testimony given by such individuals, particularly in the context of Brodsky's maxims, is an effective way to refine skills as an expert witness.

Finally, the importance of preparation and posttestimony critique in a given case cannot be overemphasized. Forensic clinicians should meet with the attorney who will present their testimony prior to the deposition, hearing, or trial. A review of the direct examination and anticipation of cross-examination material are both useful. After providing testimony, forensic clinicians should critique their own performances. This can be accomplished by reviewing the transcript, if available, or obtaining feedback from the attorney.

Chapter 15

Child Custody

The four reports in this chapter are assessments in the area of child custody. Requests for child custody evaluations typically come from the court or from attorneys representing one of the divorcing parties. In the first case, the principle being applied addresses the importance of obtaining appropriate authorization from these referral sources before conducting the evaluation. The teaching point in the first case elaborates on how the nature of the required authorization can vary according to the forensic issues being evaluated and the role assumed by the forensic clinician. The principle associated with the second case—avoid dual relationships—focuses on the implications of assuming simultaneous professional roles, such as therapist and evaluator, in the context of FMHA. How to avoid dual-role relationships is the particular focus of the teaching point in the second case; it is recommended that the evaluator ensure that there is no relationship or conflict of interest between the examiner and any of the parties or their attorneys, clarify their role as an evaluator, standardize assessment procedures, and reserve opinions and recommendations for the final report. The principle applied to the third case stresses the importance of basing testimony on the results of the forensic evaluation. The teaching point for case three establishes a framework for a properly prepared report that focuses on the most relevant issues as they relate to the legal question. The principle to be applied to the final case in this chapter concerns the fundamentals of effective testimony in an adversarial setting. The related teaching point highlights errors that can reduce the credibility of expert testimony.

Case 1

Principle: Obtain appropriate authorization

This principle concerns the importance of obtaining appropriate authorization prior to conducting a forensic evaluation. The nature of the required authorization, however, can vary according to the forensic issues being addressed and the role assumed by the forensic clinician. In some cases, the initial authorization is obtained through a signed order from the court that provides the forensic clinician with the legal authority to conduct the evaluation. In other cases, however, when the evaluation is performed at the request of the attorney for one of the parties involved in the litigation, the evaluation may be privileged under attorney work product. In such cases, authorization from the court is not required to conduct FMHA.

There is strong support for this principle among ethical, legal, and practice sources of authority. The *Ethical Principles of Psychologists and Code of Conduct* (APA, 1992) indirectly addresses the importance of authorization in FMHA: "In performing forensic roles, psychologists are reasonably familiar with the rules governing their roles" (p. 1610).

There is more direct support for such authorization in the *Specialty Guidelines for Forensic Psychologists* (Committee on Ethical Guidelines for Forensic Psychologists, 1991). The *Speciality Guidelines* describes various ways in which a forensic evaluation may be authorized. First, a forensic evaluation may be authorized "via contract with the 'legal representative of the party seeking services'" (1991, p. 658). Second, the authorization may be obtained as follows:

> [I]n situations where the client or party may not have the capacity to provide informed consent to services or the evaluation is pursuant to court order, the forensic psychologist provides reasonable notice to the client's legal representative of the nature of the anticipated forensic service before proceeding. If the client's legal representative objects to the evaluation, the forensic psychologist notifies the court issuing the order and responds as directed. (p. 659)

Finally, the *Speciality Guidelines* indicates that authorization may be obtained in a third manner: "[A]fter a psychologist has advised the subject of a clinical forensic evaluation of the intended uses of the evaluation and its work product, the psychologist may not use the evaluation work product for other purposes without explicit waiver to do so by the client or the client's legal representative" (pp. 659–660).

The *Ethical Guidelines for the Practice of Forensic Psychiatry* (AAPL, 1995) describes several forms of authorization:

> The informed consent of the subject of a forensic evaluation is obtained when possible. When consent is not required, notice is given to the evaluee of the nature of the evaluation. . . . In particular situations, such as court-ordered evaluations for competency to stand trial or involuntary commitment, consent is not required. In such a case, the psychiatrist should so inform the subject and explain that the evaluation is legally required and that if the subject refuses to participate in the evaluation, this fact will be included in any report or testimony. If the evaluee is not competent to give consent, substituted consent is obtained in accordance with the laws of the jurisdiction. (p. 2)

The *Ethical Guidelines for the Practice of Forensic Psychiatry* also notes that, in criminal cases, ethical considerations preclude conducting a forensic evaluation until legal counsel has been obtained.

The nature of the authorization to be obtained from the individual being evaluated depends on the role assumed by the forensic evaluator. For example, in a court-ordered forensic evaluation in a capital sentencing case, the individual being evaluated may have a Fifth Amendment right to refuse to answer certain questions, or to participate at all (see *Estelle v. Smith*, 1981; Slobogin, 1982, 1984). In these cases, the defendant should receive a warning that incorporates the elements of *Miranda v. Arizona* (1966) prior to beginning the evaluation.

In many jurisdictions, however, there are explicit statutory protections in criminal cases against the use of material obtained in a forensic evaluation for any purpose other than deciding the legal issue that triggered the evaluation. If such protection exists, then the individual being evaluated typically does not have a legal right to refuse to participate in a court-ordered evaluation. In such cases, the individual should be informed about the nature and possible uses of the evaluation, and the associated limits on confidentiality. However, the individual does not need to consent to FMHA under these circumstances.

There are other circumstances in which the individual's consent is needed, and the individual can refuse to participate in the evaluation. For example, if the forensic clinician is performing a criminal evaluation that has been ordered by the court on a "defense expert" basis, the individual is not legally compelled to proceed and can thus refuse to participate in the evaluation. Similarly, if a forensic evaluation is being conducted at the request of one of the attorneys in the litigation, rather than under court order, the individual is not legally compelled to proceed and may legally refuse to participate in the evaluation.

When a forensic clinician is seeking to obtain records or other documented third-party information, authorization for their release can be obtained in two ways. First, the individual being evaluated can provide signed written consent for the release of the records/documents. Second, authorization to obtain the records/documents may be obtained through a court order for their release.

There are several sources in the practice literature that address this principle. The *Criminal Justice Mental Health Standards* (ABA, 1989) notes that the authority for initiating a pretrial mental health evaluation in a criminal case should reside with the court or the defense attorney, except in cases in which the sole purpose of the evaluation involves diverting the defendant from the criminal process or determining whether emergency mental health treatment or habilitation is warranted. According to the *Criminal Justice Mental Health Standards*, evaluations at other stages in the criminal process (e.g., sentencing, commitment of insanity acquittees, transfer of mentally ill inmates) should also be controlled by the court or the defense attorney.

This approach to obtaining authorization is consistent with the recommendations offered in standard texts on FMHA (e.g., Melton et al., 1997; Roesch & Golding, 1980; Shapiro, 1991). It is also consistent with recommendations made by the American Psychological Association's Task Force on the Role of Psychology in the Criminal Justice System (Monahan, 1980). The APA Task

Force concluded that because there may be multiple clients for the different services delivered within the criminal justice system, it is important to specify the client(s) for any particular service.

The present report provides a good example of obtaining appropriate authorization. In this case, the child custody evaluation was authorized by court order. The evaluation was ordered by the court when the mother of two children decided to move to another state; the mother sought joint legal and sole physical custody of both minor children, while the father was seeking joint legal and shared physical custody. As part of the evaluation, the evaluator met with both parents and both children. Because the evaluation was court ordered, the evaluator was legally authorized to proceed regardless of whether the parties consented to participate.

In addition to evaluating both parents and their children, the evaluator reviewed various documents and interviewed several collateral parties. The evaluator noted in the introductory paragraph that the documents were provided by the parties. Therefore, in this case, the parties themselves provided the evaluator with the required authorization to review the documents. With respect to collateral interviews, the introductory paragraph notes that the evaluator obtained specific authorization from both parents to interview the collateral parties.

RE: Marriage of AZ & LZ
Dear Judge:

In response to your order appointing me to conduct a child custody evaluation (pursuant to E.C.) in this matter, I met with the adult parties and the minor children (Child A, a 2-year-old boy, and Child B, a 4-year-old boy) individually and conjointly (in relevant combinations) for observation, case and clinical interviews, and psychological testing (see Schedule and Procedures). Mr. Z is represented by Esq. 1, while Ms. Z is represented by Esq. 2. In addition to the diagnostic sessions, I also reviewed multiple sets of records (see List) provided by the parties and their attorneys, and contacted multiple collateral parties (see List) with specific authorizations by the parties to do so.

SCHEDULE OF APPOINTMENTS AND CLINICAL PROCEDURES

Mother (age 33)
DATE (4 hours). Individual case/clinical interviewing, Minnesota Multiphasic Personality Inventory-2, Child Behavior Checklist

DATE (2 hours). Conjointly with Child B and Child A; and individual assessment of Child B; Millon Clinical Multiaxial Inventory-II

DATE (3 hours). Individual case/clinical interviewing; Rorschach Psychodiagnostic

Father (age 40)
DATE (4 hours). Individual clinical/case interview; Minnesota Multiphasic Personality Inventory-2; Millon Clinical Multiaxial Inventory-II; Child Behavior Checklist

DATE (2 hours). Conjointly with Child B and Child A; individual assessment of Child B; Individual interview with Mr. Z

DATE (1.5 hours). Individual clinical/case interviewing; Rorschach Psychodiagnostic

CENTRAL ISSUES

This is a move-away case in which the mother plans to move with the two children to a distant city in State-Two, while the father remains in the family residence in State-One.

The record reflects a number of conflicts and disagreements between the parties. Psychological findings can enlighten only a portion of the confusion and ambiguity involved. They can address issues of credibility and deception, as well as psychopathology and parental competencies in the context of the best interests of the children. The issue of whether the mother sought to conceal the children from their father and prevent his access to them is an example of an issue that obviously has both legal and psychological implications, but which psychological findings can only indirectly address. The mother has moved to a distant state with the children. The mother reports that the father is angry, hostile, impulsive, uses illegal guns, has dealt and used illicit drugs, acts aggressively to dogs, walls, and so on in uncontrolled fashion, and is socially isolated. The father denies these reports, just as the mother denies the father's allegations regarding concealment. Psychological findings are useful here.

Mother (age 33)   Ms. Z was born 33 years ago. Her childhood family moved multiple times as a result of her own mother's career, then later because of her own academic and career involvements. She worked outside the home until childbirth, but has not since, in order to be a full-time mother to her sons.

Her own parents separated when she was in middle childhood. After their separation, she lived primarily with her mother. She has positive childhood memories of both parents and her siblings. Abuse history (as either victim or prepetrator) is denied. She also indicated that she has never been arrested, either as a juvenile or as an adult. Neurological history is denied. Medical history is unremarkable. Family psychiatric history is denied. She reported using alcohol, at times heavily, until age 25, but not since. She was involved in therapy when she quit alcohol several years before childbirth. Currently, she is involved in therapy with a social worker for stress associated with marital dissolution and child custody issues.

Her marriage to Mr. Z was her first. They separated after 6 years of marriage, when she asked him to leave the home following an argument. He returned home a week later, after she and the children had departed. She had relocated to State-Two with the boys, first to her mother's home, then to her father's home, where she and the boys remain. Mr. Z visited soon thereafter, she says, but then filed charges against her for child concealment and kidnapping. He had traveled to State-Two to see his boys, she explained, but "he didn't (see them) . . . because there was no plan for pick-up, drop-off. . . . I was afraid he'd take them away . . . to Mexico," the mother adding that he has antisocial tendencies. A hearing followed, resulting in a court order that permitted visits by the father alternating between the two states.

The impetus for this child custody evaluation was the failure of mediation. Ms. Z explained that she had originally agreed to negotiate and to sign the proposed mediated parenting plan in order to avoid arrest ("pressured to sign because of arrest warrant"), but withdrew because she felt it was "totally unrealistic" due to disruptions to the boys' daily routine and because of the financial problems associated with it. The plan had the father spending 1 week each month in State-Two, while the mother would spend 3 nights each month in State-One. The children would reside with her at all other times.

Best Interests   In her view, it would be joint legal and sole physical custody (to herself) because she had stayed home full time to raise them and had been their primary caregiver, while their father had not been involved in this way. Ms. Z has indicated that the father is a very volatile, angry person who can be calm one moment, in a rage the next, then calm again. Asked about whether Mr. Z had ever abused her in any way, she recalled that once he had squeezed the wind out of her, and otherwise he was verbally critical, demeaning, and blaming. However, she also reported that Mr. Z had never abused the children. She feels that if Mr. Z moves also to State-Two, it would be suitable for him to see the boys on alternate weekends plus a midweek visit.

Regarding Parental Strengths and Competencies   Mr. Z's strengths as a parent in her view are that he takes his boys for walks, hugs them when things are calm, and is good with medical emergencies. His limitations, she feels, include low self-control, anger, short temper, perfectionism, guns, and "he's also a pathological liar." Her own strengths, according to her, involve being warm and caring, building self-esteem/worth/emotional well-being, and attending to nutrition, health, education, and recreation. She described her own limitations as "just the normal patience and temper problems dealing with the stressors." Ms. Z plans to return to her career and after that move into a place of her own. She wishes to remain with her children near her own childhood family in State-Two.

Regarding her children, she describes her older son as very sociable, friendly, and outgoing and with no problems. The younger son is described as very demanding, outspoken, persistent, extremely active.

Test Findings: Mother On the Minnesota Multiphasic Personality Inventory-2 she produced an accurate and credible set of test results. Elevations were only on Scale 9 (Hypomania, T65) and a (secondary) elevation on Scale 3 (Hysteria, T63; Welsh Code: 9+3-6518/2740: F-/LK:). High energy in a sociable person with dramatic and outgoing flair is evident. Scale 9 at T65 is clinically significant (approximately 95th percentile), although moderate in elevation, and would predict a tendency toward overactivity and unrealistic self-appraisal. Limited self-awareness would also be likely.

On the Millon Clinical Multiaxial Inventory-II, she showed a markedly defensive response set. Elevations are on Axis II personal maladjustments rather than Axis I clinical disorders. She is elevated on histrionic and obsessive compulsive and narcissistic personality traits (Personality Code: -** 4 * 7 5 3 + 1 6A " 6B 2 8B 8A ' ' //-**-* //). Emotional intensity and exaggeration of complaints certainly would be consistent with this profile. She tends to get lost in emotional complexity, finding it overwhelming and personally disorganizing. Yet she cannot disengage from it, or does so but only with great ambivalence. Underlying insecurity, anger, perfectionisitic strivings, and an anxious conformity to perceived expectations of others are characteristics also associated with her profile.

Rorschach Psychodiagnostic findings are consistent with those from both the MMPI-2 and the MCMI-II, and all test data are consistent with interview findings. Although Ms. Z gave an unusually high number of responses (51) to the 10 ink blot cards, she frequently asked if she was providing enough responses, giving elaborate and lengthy explanations of her responses and requiring twice the average administration time. There was a markedly obsessional, hypervigilant, and paranoid approach applied to ambiguous (unstructured) material. She applies this coping style also in non-test situations. Other significant findings were high levels of anger, tension, and intense emotional experience, which she has difficulty modulating. She uses psychological defense mechanisms of repression and intellectualization to conceal or deny her feelings. These defenses appear to be mostly ineffective during times of heightened stress and intense emotional turmoil, and inappropriate emotional displays and impulsive behavior result. Although there were no findings of a thought disorder, her thinking is marked by peculiar and inaccurate perceptions and mediational distortions.

Father (age 40) Mr. Z moved a number of times in his childhood as a result of his own father's career changes. His parents are still married to each other, and he continues to work with his father in the family business. He described his childhood relationship with his father as "stormy" and his father's authoritarian control as "borderline abusive," adding that he got along with his father by "staying out of his way." Their relationship is described as "pretty good" at present. He indicated that his relationship with his mother and his siblings has always been good. According to Mr. Z, there is no history of family psychiatric disorder, no abuse history, no alcohol/drug history (as either victim or perpetrator), and no medical/neurological history of any significance. He also denied any history of arrests. He completed high school when he was 18 and has been regularly employed since then. He described one previous marriage; he and his former wife have a teenage daughter. There is joint legal custody, and his daughter lives with her mother. He reported that he is currently in mental health treatment, focusing on divorce and child custody issues. Prior treatment was denied.

He described the current evaluation as a consequence of Ms. Z's refusal to accept mediated resolution to child custody and parenting issues. Three separate efforts to mediate disputed issues were necessary, he said, because she "backed out" each time. He felt that she behaved in similarly frustrating ways in the marriage, providing examples of her disproportionate refusal to problem-solve or consider his needs. He said he would cope with this by splitting wood ("that's my therapy"), or punching his truck occasionally. He denied abuse of persons, and Ms. Z's report that he had hit his head on the bedroom door and knocked himself out. His version is that out of a sense of abject frustration (the day they separated), he hit his head on the bedroom door and in despair fell to the floor crying. He denied ever hitting anyone in anger, and also indicated credibly that Ms. Z had not been accurate about his aggressive behavior.

He also credibly described his efforts to see the children in State-Two and being denied access. He describes the visits he has had with his boys in positive terms, adding that he was very attached to them.

Best Interests   Mr. Z felt that it would be best for the boys if there were joint legal and shared physical custody. He indicated that he would move to the State/City-Two to be near them, but was also concerned about the hostility from Ms. Z and her family there. If he does not move there he does not know what else is feasible, as he cannot afford to work only 2 weeks per month in order to accommodate Ms. Z's move. If he does move there, he added, he wants a substantial and meaningful amount of parenting time and wants to do whatever is needed to be meaningfully involved in his sons' lives. He would like 50/50 shared physical custody. Regarding the boys, he reflected a sensitive appreciation of each of them and the stressors associated with this transition in their lives. He acknowledged that he had never been the primary parent; this is how he and Ms. Z agreed to divide the work during their marriage. He does need to learn more about children in his sons' age groups, but expresses interest and motivation in doing so.

Test Findings: Father   On the Minnesota Multiphasic Personality Inventory-2, he produced an accurate and credible set of test findings. Clinical scales were within normal limits (Welsh Code: 6-7845/0291: KL/F:). There is a subclinical elevation (T64, on Paranoia) reflecting hypersensitivity to slights and rejection. On the Millon Clinical Multiaxial Inventory-II there is no evidence of deceit. There is also a tendency toward angry aggression or antisocial tendencies (Personality

Code: -** 3 7 * 4 8B + 1 6B 2 b " 6A 8A ' ' //-**-* //). There is evidence for personal sensitivity (within normal limits) and for being emotionally hurt by personal rejection. Results from MCMI-II are consistent with those from the MMPI-2 and also from interview findings. There is no evidence of mental or emotional disorder. The only elevations are on personality patterns of dependency and compulsivity, suggesting conventionality and desire/need for others on whom to rely.

Rorschach Psychodiagnostic findings suggest that Mr. Z is currently experiencing high levels of distress and situationally related stress, coping with angry feelings and negative emotions generally by trying to avoid situations that could provoke emotional displays and aggravate underlying difficulties with the expression of his feelings. Feelings and emotional displays are generally maintained under tight control. Negative self-rumination may lead to episodes of depression. Interpersonally, findings indicate strong needs for closeness and for harmony in interactions with others. Thinking tends to be influenced unduly by his feelings and at times may result in flawed logic and perceptual inaccuracy.

The Children   Seen individually, they each present as pleasant and well-socialized. The older child presents as bright and verbal. He drew a picture of himself, then of himself and his father, and chose not to draw one with his mother. Both children related warmly and well to their father, who was appropriate with them at both verbal and nonverbal levels. Both children related warmly and well with their mother as well, and their interaction was characterized by good verbal and nonverbal communication. The boys appeared to trust both parents, are afraid of neither, and are appropriately attached to both.

Collaterals   The mother's collaterals support her position; the father's collaterals support his position. It is the father against whom there are more problematic reports, given Ms. Z's descriptions, so it is useful to review collateral information to see if it substantiates her concerns about his misbehavior and integrity. Collateral information does not substantiate her accusations. Treating therapists of respective parties view them as adequate persons and competent parents.

RECOMMENDATIONS

Both parents are adequate on indicia of personal rectitude, psychological maturity, and parental competency. The mother has moved to State-2 and plans to remain there. The father will move there as well in order to be actively involved in his sons' lives. There is little to suggest that he cannot provide for them as well as the mother. The boys love their mother and are psychologically attached to her, and she is emotionally bonded to them. The same is true for the father. Both parties expressed knowledge, interest, and experience in providing a safe, secure, and healthy environment for the children, and in promoting their welfare, education, and opportunities for positive psychosocial development consistent with their best interests.

Mr. Z is willing to relocate to State/City-Two, where Ms. Z plans to settle. If she does not plan to settle there, this is a problem, because he would move there only for the purpose of being close to his sons. Of course, if she seeks to relocate with the boys after the father has himself relocated in order to be close to them, then suspicions of concealment/alienation would be confirmed.

If they reside in the same community, there is nothing to suggest other than 50/50 shared physical parenting and joint legal custody. To make it work, co-parenting counseling would be essential. Weighing against a 50/50 parenting arrangement, in addition to ongoing parental discord, is the fact that the children are so young—ages 4 and 2— and frequent visits are necessary for stability, continuity, and security. Because of this, it would probably be better for the boys to have primary residence with the mother, with their father having generous visitation and extra time during summers and holidays. Thursday P.M. to Monday A.M. on alternate weeks, plus midweek, overnight visitation, is one possible schedule; another plan would be week on/week off, with midweek visitations to the other parent. This could be implemented in 2 years, when the boys are ages 4 and 6, as there is no reason for other than a 50/50 parenting plan except developmental considerations. If the father remains in State-One, then he could also be considered for primary parent status. Alternatively, a plan worked out in mediation should be adopted. If the mother continues to resist and impede visitation/attachment of the children with their father, then the father becomes the more suitable primary parent. The boys need and benefit from close attachments to both parents. The parent interfering with such attachment is not functioning in the children's best interests. Whatever parenting plan is adopted should be well-structured in both form and content and should be adhered to rigorously. Given the parties' level of pre- and post-dissolution discord, coupled with personal tendencies to misperceive and misinterpret events/circumstances, decision making and problem solving will likely remain difficult and fraught with conflict. A professional mediator or special master would play a relevant role in addressing issues the parties cannot resolve on their own. The parties are addressing some of these issues with respective counselors. This should continue so that the children are safeguarded from parental conflict as much as possible, and receive the benefits of their parents' enhanced personal boundaries and co-parenting skills.

Thank you for the opportunity to examine the parties and the minor children. Should there be any questions or need for elaboration or clarification, please feel free to contact me.

Respectfully submitted,
Herbert N. Weissman, Ph.D., A.B.P.P.
Clinical Professor of Psychiatry,
School of Medicine, University of California, Davis

Teaching Point: Who must authorize FMHA—and how?

The nature of the necessary authorization can vary according to the forensic issues being evaluated and the role assumed by the forensic clinician. The nature of the specific authorization differs according to whether a request for consent is included. For example, a child custody evaluation can be ordered by the court or agreed to by the parties. Evaluators who deliver an inaccurate notification can create a number of difficulties. An individual being evaluated who is incorrectly told that consent is required for a court-ordered evaluation, and subsequently informed that a report will be sent to the court regardless of whether he or she consents, may understandably become confused, frustrated, and angry. A parent involved in child custody litigation, who is mistakenly notified that her consent is not required for the evaluation that has been requested by her husband's attorney, might become defensive and suspicious as well as angry when the mistake is corrected. The importance of obtaining appropriate authorization, linked with providing accurate initial notification, cannot be overemphasized.

Case 2

Principle: Avoid dual roles of therapist and forensic evaluator

Forensic evaluators are often confronted with the dual-role relationship issue in practice. A dual-role relationship in the FMHA context is one in which two roles are assumed by a mental health professional in a single case. This might arise under a variety of circumstances, and the dual-role relationship can be the result of a combination of various roles played by a mental health professional. For example, a dual role could result when a professional role is combined with a personal or vocational role, or when two professional roles are combined (e.g., treating therapist and forensic evaluator). This discussion will focus on simultaneous professional roles from different contexts, such as therapist and evaluator, in FMHA.

The assumption of dual roles is frequently a source of complaints to ethics committees and licensure boards for both psychiatrists and psychologists (Bersoff, 1995; Glassman, 1998). Various sources of ethics guidance and authority discourage dual-role relationships. Generally, it is the responsibility of the professional to avoid relationships that would "interfere with the psychologist's effectively performing his or her functions as a psychologist, or might harm or exploit the other party" (APA, 1992, p. 393), or to take "reasonable steps to minimize the potential reactive effects of these circumstances on the rights of the party, confidentiality, and the process of treatment and evaluation" (Committee on Ethical Guidelines for Forensic Psychologists, 1991, p. 659).

The potential for dual-role relationship problems is particularly salient in the emotionally charged area of child custody evaluations. Generally, psychologists avoid conducting a child custody evaluation when their impartiality might be compromised; a common example is when the psychologist has previously served as a therapist for the child or his or her immediate family (APA, 1994). This caveat also applies to mental health professionals who find themselves in the role of a fact witness for the courts. Under some circumstances, a court of law may require a psychologist to testify as a fact witness regarding information to which the psychologist was privy in the course of a professional relationship with a client. Preferably, however, the psychologist should decline the role of expert witness and avoid giving a professional opinion regarding custody and visitation when that psychologist has previously served as a therapist (APA, 1994). This also applies to treating psychiatrists, who "should avoid agreeing to be an expert witness or to perform an evaluation of their patients for legal purposes because a forensic evaluation usually requires that other people be interviewed and testimony may adversely affect the therapeutic relationship" (AAPL, 1995, p. 3).

In addition to ethical considerations, standards of practice also discourage dual-role relationships. Some commentators have advocated a strict separation of roles (Greenburg & Shuman, 1997; Heilbrun, 1995), even to the extent of barring treating mental health professionals from the courtroom in cases in which they have treated one of the litigants (Shuman, Greenberg, Heilbrun, & Foote, 1998). Similarly, other commentators emphasize the importance of functioning within a single role from the outset of a custody evaluation (Emery & Rogers, 1990) and support the view that custody evaluators should be unknown to the respective parties to avoid ethics complaints in custody cases (Glassman, 1998). Despite the limited legal and empirical support against the dual-role relationship, current ethics guidelines and professional standards of practice strongly discourage the dual-role relationship (Heilbrun, 2001).

There are also a number of practical reasons for avoiding dual-role relationships. First, the selection and maintenance of a single role makes the clinician's participation safer, in the sense that this role becomes the only basis for participation in the evaluation. Focusing only on a single role also encourages forensic clinicians to think clearly about which role they will choose, and to avoid being drawn into forensic participation with clients for whom the role was not initially selected. Multiple roles can potentially create complications and make matters more complex. There is also an associated enhanced risk of client dissatisfaction, in some cases leading to ethics complaints and litigation against clinicians involved in dual roles. Clinicians should be exceedingly cautious under circumstances that might result in dual-role participation, and avoid assuming more than one role in a single case whenever possible.

Evaluation for Child Custody and Parenting
  Time
File No. 96-5582-DM
Mother: Mary J

Date of Birth: June 30, 1958
Age: 39
Dates of Evaluation: May 18, May 30, 1997
Father: James J

Date of Birth: January 15, 1962
Age: 35
Dates of Evaluation: May 6, June 1, 1997
Child: Kenneth J
Date of Birth: April 12, 1995
Age: 2 years, 3 months
Dates of Evaluation: May 30, June 6, 1997

Date of Report: June 15, 1997

This evaluation was conducted pursuant to the order of the Honorable Jesse T and stipulated to by Harold M and Sarah P, attorneys for the father and mother, respectively. It consisted of a clinical interview of both parents and the child, observation of the child with each parent, and psychological testing of both parents. The test battery consisted of the Rorschach (Exner Comprehensive Method) and the Minnesota Multiphasic Personality Inventory-2 (MMPI-2). Each parent also completed two psychological inventories regarding their child, the Child Behavior Checklist (CBCL), and the Parent–Child Relationship Inventory (PCRI).

A number of documents were reviewed, including a "summary of abuse" prepared by Ms. J, a list of her reasons for seeking sole custody, a written note dated 4/7/97, an affidavit of a friend, a certificate of completion for attendance at a parenting class, a Mothers of Preschoolers newsletter, a calendar from 3/12/97, noting Mr. J's visits and missed visits, a 1/30/97, police report of a complaint that Mr. J's father was disorderly, and an undated letter from Ms. J to attorney Judith J. Also reviewed were Mr. J's complaint for divorce, plaintiff's referee hearing brief, an agreed order regarding personal property and discipline of the child, Kenny's medical records and/or reports of Arthur E, MD, Peter C. N, MD, Katherine C, MD, and affidavits of Kenneth and Patricia J, Jeff S, and Patsy J. Also reviewed was a police report of 1/12/91, the 5/2/95 Friend of the Court recommendation, and a number of commendatory letters about Mr. J. In addition, Mr. J requested that I review several letters written to and by Ms. J that he found after she moved out, and tape-recordings he made without her knowledge. I declined to review these as it was unclear whether they had been obtained legally or could be introduced as evidence. Rita D, MSW, was contacted

by telephone, and a letter from her was reviewed. An attempt was made to contact Dr. Marie B, without success.

Both Mr. and Ms. J were informed that because of the court-ordered nature of the evaluation, it would not be confidential and results could be shared with the court and attorneys in the form of testimony or report. Both indicated that they understood and agreed to proceed.

PRESENTING PROBLEM

Mr. and Ms. J both reported that they are still in the process of completing a divorce. They each described the marriage as difficult from the beginning, reporting a brief separation within a few months of the marriage and a decision to reconcile. Ms. J reported that Mr. J has been emotionally abusive to her throughout the marriage, and that she often felt isolated from others because they spent so much time with his family. She also reported a history of physical abuse by Mr. J, including being pushed up against walls and having her hair pulled. She described Mr. J as also abusing her sexually. Ms. J had prepared a summary of her experiences, which was reviewed by the evaluator. She denied any physical actions on her part. While admitting that he and Ms. J had had many heated arguments with swearing, Mr. J completely denied ever having physically or sexually abused her, saying he was willing to take a polygraph test. He indicated that he felt Ms. J was saying this to try to influence the court and get attention from others. Mr. J described two instances in which he said he had been physically attacked by Ms. J—once when he accidentally scared her, and once during their first separation when she threw a glass object at him, hitting his leg. Both indicated that the police were called (apparently on the advice of Mr. J's father) during this incident because she would not come out of the bedroom. Mr. J said that the police had to break down the door to the room. Ms. J reported that she had not thrown anything, adding that the police did not break down the door. However, the police report indicates they had to kick the door open. She said she had never locked herself in but did not come out because she was frightened of her father-in-law, who she said is an alcoholic. She indicated that another time she called the police because her father-in-law was drunk and trying to break down her door.

Mr. J indicated that he was quite concerned about Ms. J's mental stability, saying that she had rarely gone out of their house after the marriage and had experienced frequent rages. He described one in which he said she had threatened to smother Kenny, and said that Ms. J often threatened to kill him, herself, or his family. Ms. J denied ever having done this.

Both said that money and finances had been a major problem area in the marriage. Mr. J said that he wanted all of their assets to be held jointly because this is what his family always did. Ms. J said that she felt that he was trying to control her and that he used her money to buy expensive items like cars and stereo equipment. She felt he was using the custody situation to manipulate the financial settlement in the divorce.

Ms. J became pregnant early in marriage but had an elective abortion after discovering that the child was deformed and had Down's Syndrome. Both denied having affairs, although Ms. J said she thinks Mr. J has been having one for a number of years.

Mr. J and Ms. J described difficulties with each other's families. Ms. J said that she was rejected by Mr. J's family after Kenny was born. She said this was partly because she became upset at her brother-in-law after he convinced Ms. J to give away her dog and then reported the dog was lost. She indicated that both Mr. J and his family have painted her as disturbed and unstable and that she is not at all this way. Mr. J said that he felt both of them had been too involved with their respective families, often telling their parents inappropriate things about the marriage and seeking support of their parents against their spouse.

Mr. J expressed concern about Ms. J's history of mental illness. He said he felt that she could be unstable and angry. However, he indicated that he had not seen her behave this way with Kenny. He preferred to refer me to medical records, which will be described later in this report. He did express worry about several injuries that Kenny has experienced, wondering whether they reflected lack of supervision on Ms. J's part.

The parents' reports are at odds with each other about Kenny's care. Ms. J maintained that she did the great bulk of the child care and that Mr. J was unhelpful and unsupportive, even though she was disabled by a back problem caused by her pregnancy. However, review of the pediatrician's records show several notations regarding the father being helpful and indicating he attended many appointments. She said that one of the reasons she left was that Mr. J called Kenny names and lost his temper with him. Mr. J denied having done this. He said that he had been actively involved in Kenny's care at all times he was at home, saying Ms. J would often sleep until noon.

Ms. J said that she finally decided to move out from the home in July 1995. She moved to her cousin's home and then several months later into her own apartment. Mr. J and Ms. J both said they had tried to reconcile during 1997, going to marriage counseling with Rita D. However this apparently was unsuccessful. Both, however, continue to report mixed feelings about the end of the marriage.

Ms. J indicated that from the beginning she had felt it important that Mr. J see as much of Kenny as possible. They had an informal parenting time schedule, where Mr. J saw Kenny twice a week for short periods of time until the Friend of the Court recommended that she have temporary custody. A parenting time schedule for Mr. J of Monday, Wednesday, and Friday from 9–3:30 and every other weekend from 9 A.M. Saturday until 3:30 P.M. Sunday was established. Ms. J maintained that Mr. J did not follow that schedule and often called and made excuses for not taking Kenny. Mr. J said that he had missed only two visits with Kenny in the 2 years since the separation and that he called to tell her both times. He said that Ms. J at times is not home when he comes to get Kenny.

Both parents express concern about how the other parents Kenny. Mr. J noticed that Kenny knows how to get his own food and worried that this is because Ms. J is not caring for his needs. Ms. J said that Kenny now swears and that she believes he has learned this from his father. She also said that Kenny has told her that he sleeps with his father and a name that she thinks may be Mr. J's girlfriend. Both said the transitions between their homes have been hard for Kenny and that he often is cranky at these times.

CURRENT SITUATION

Ms. J said she currently has temporary physical and legal custody of Kenny; Mr. J said that they have temporary joint custody. The Friend of the Court order indicates a recommendation for joint legal custody and sole physical custody for Ms. J. Ms. J lives in an apartment where Kenny has his own bedroom. She reported that Kenny is currently experiencing some new problems with separation anxiety and persistently asks to sleep in her bed, which she allows him to do. She said she is not happy with this and wants to change it, but feels sorry for him because of all the stress of the divorce and visiting schedule. Ms. J supports herself through a retirement pension from her former place of employment, Social Security Disability because of physical problems, and child support. She is currently unemployed. She said she is not involved in any relationship at this time nor has she been since the separation. A typical day with Kenny was described as getting up, going out somewhere (often with her parents or to her older sister's home, or with friends), then returning home for dinner and bedtime. Kenny is in a monthly mother-child playgroup and Ms. J said she is joining a mothers of preschoolers group, where he will be able to play with other children. He also plays with children in the apartment complex.

Mr. J resides in his own home where Kenny has his own bedroom. Mr. J also reported some separation problems at transition times, saying Kenny will cling to him and not want to go to his mother. He was not sure whether this was normal behavior. He said that for a time Kenny was sleeping with him, but on the advice of his pediatrician, Mr. J has stopped this. Mr. J said he has been employed for many years, most recently as an assembler on the night shift. Kenny's parenting time schedule is coordinated with his work schedule. He said he has no current "significant other," but does have a number of male and female friends. A typical day with Kenny was described as making sure Kenny has eaten, then either playing at home or going out to the community or to visit family, all of whom live in close proximity.

The current parenting time scheduled for Mr. J is Monday and Wednesday from 2 to 8:30 P.M. and Friday 2 P.M. to Saturday 2 P.M. This is supposed to increase to another overnight visit when Kenny turns 3. However, Ms. J expressed concerns about this. She indicated that currently the communication between her and Mr. J is almost nonexistent, and she must rely on what Kenny tells her to find out what is happening at Mr. J's home. She indicated that she would rather wait until he can talk better to increase overnights. She felt that the current schedule was not good for Kenny; she feels he needs more of a routine and that he is stressed by the number of transitions, citing continuing separation anxiety problems. She also expressed some concerns about the consistency of Mr. J's parenting and whether his interest really is in Kenny or in using him to pressure her regarding the divorce's financial settlement. She stated that it would be better for Kenny if she had sole custody, with parenting time for Mr. J set at 1 day per week and every other weekend.

Mr. J said that he thought the schedule was going well at present, although he would like to have Kenny longer on Saturdays, as a 2 P.M. return disrupts their time together. He indicated that he would like to share in all decision making about Kenny and said that he believed that he and Ms. J would be able to agree on most issues. Ms. J, however, said that she thought that they might disagree, because Mr. J wanted Kenny to go to a private school and she thought public school would be better. When asked about this, Mr. J said that he thought some public schools were good but that he was concerned about the quality of the local school system. Regarding actual parenting time, Mr. J said that he wanted as much time as possible with Kenny so that he could fully parent him.

Both parents said that communication about Kenny has broken down in the last year. They described minimal information being exchanged at transitions or at other times. Mr. J said that he has sometimes not been notified regarding doctor's appointments. Ms. J stated that she has just taken Kenny to a dermatologist and not told Mr. J because she thought he did not need to know as it was a preliminary appointment.

EVALUATION OF MARY J

Relevant History Ms. J reported that she had what she thought was a normal and "perfect" childhood. She got along well with her parents and sister and completed high school with no significant problems. She described herself as being rather naïve and sheltered. Ms. J reported no history of legal problems, mental or emotional disorder, or substance abuse in her family.

Ms. J said she began working at age 18 and retired last year. She held a number of jobs and was off work several times for educational leaves, during which she completed an associate's degree in medicine and most of the credits for a certified x-ray technician. She was off work for about 4 years on a medical leave due to what she described as stress from sexual harassment at work, in addition to family illness. The medical leave is described in the next section. She returned to work and was employed until receiving a medical leave during her pregnancy with Kenny, when she gained a great deal of weight and developed pelvic torsion, which she said rendered her unable to lift or walk without assistance.

Mental Status and Test Results   Ms. J presented as a well-dressed, well-groomed 39-year-old woman who cooperated with the evaluation. She did not appear to be unusually anxious or guarded during the interview, although her manner was rather ingratiating. She occasionally referred to a number of documents that she had brought with her, including calendars, journals, and notes. She did not appear to be in any significant pain, although she said her back was stiff after sitting for a long period. She said she did not take any prescribed medicine for her back, nor was she taking any other prescribed medication.

Ms. J's speech was clear and articulate, though a bit pressured—that is, she spoke quickly and for long periods of time without interruption. She spent much of the time speaking of the history of her marriage and her difficult relationship with Mr. J. She seemed somewhat preoccupied with relating issues about her health problems. She was able to divert from this material to speak about Kenny. At times, she had some difficulty staying with the topic at hand, relating tangential material. However, she appeared to be reasonably well-organized in her thinking. Recent and remote memory were essentially intact, although she had trouble doing math problems. She appeared to be of at least average intelligence. Her

emotions during the evaluation ranged from friendly and happy to tearful when she spoke of the end of her marriage. There was no indication of current serious depression or anxiety. She complained of sleep problems related to a back injury and having a small child, but said she has gotten used to it. She denied any problems with appetite or eating disorders. Ms. J reported no history of serious problems in thinking, such as hallucinations or delusions, and there was no indication of the presence of these in the interview. She denied ever abusing alcohol or drugs.

Ms. J reported a history of a single episode of depression and anxiety beginning in 1985, which coincided with a stressful time at work and several other life stressors. She said that a friend suggested that one way to get away from all the stress was to have herself hospitalized. She said she was hospitalized for 2 weeks and given medication and then attended a partial hospitalization program where she received therapy and medication. She said she went off the medication on her own in the early 1990s, mostly because she had to change doctors and the psychiatrist she was sent to prescribed too much and too many different kinds, causing side effects. (Document review is consistent with this.) She reported that sometime during this period she had taken several Xanax at once and slept for a long time. She claimed she was not really suicidal, but that this was a cry for help. She denied any other suicide attempts or gestures or any other period of serious depression.

Document review showed a mental health history somewhat more involved than Ms. J had reported. There was evidence of a reported first depression as early as 1981. She told an evaluating psychiatrist that she had, indeed, overdosed on Xanax and was unconscious for 2 days before being found. Records also note problems with ulcers dating to the age of 15. The psychiatrist's records also reflect a history dating back to her difficulties at work of panic attacks and agoraphobia, to the point where she sometimes had trouble leaving the house. She was accompanied to the interview with the psychiatrist by Mr. J. Dr. S diagnosed a general anxiety disorder, with a history of possible previous major depressive episodes or bipolar disorder. He also noted a number of maladaptive personality traits and considered the possibility of borderline personality disorder. In an evaluation dated January 12, 1991, Dr. D diagnosed her as major depression/panic disorder due to harassment at work. Dr. C diagnosed her similarly. His records indicate that Ms. J was concerned about her explosive temper and that she might hurt someone at work if they tried to harass her. They also show that she reported problems with anxiety when having to leave her home (this was after her marriage).

Ms. J reported no other history of therapy. She said that Mr. J began marital treatment with Ms. D in May 1996, and that she has continued in individual treatment with Ms. D to the present to work on the stresses surrounding the divorce. Contact with Ms. D revealed that Ms. J has indeed continued in therapy. Ms. D also indicated that she felt that Ms. J has made progress in acknowledging her own problems and is dealing quite well with the stresses of the divorce. She did not see Ms. J as seriously depressed or anxious at present.

Ms. J's MMPI-2 was highly defensive, to the point of being of questionable validity. While some guardedness is to be expected in an evaluation of this type, this profile was even more so. It was indicative of someone who is trying to present themselves as a person of unquestionable moral stature, with none of the faults even to be expected of most people. People with this profile are typically immature and tend to lack self-awareness and to deny problems. They are often quite dependent on others and may become frustrated and angry when their needs are not met. They will deny having these feelings, though others may clearly be able to see them. Ms. J gave too few responses on the Rorschach, invalidating the test. This was likely due to the same guardedness she displayed on the MMPI-2.

Description of and Observation with Child   Ms. J was able to describe Kenny extensively and in great detail. She showed me several albums of pictures of him. She had a good grasp of what the typical needs of a young child are and could clearly relate how she applied this knowledge to Kenny.

Her pregnancy was complicated by her back problem and weight gain, and Ms. J described herself as quite tearful and exhausted from lack of sleep. Birth was difficult but with no problems for the child. She reported that Kenny has not been an easy child; he has never had a regular sleeping schedule and has always been fussy. He walked at 13 months, which she described as a bit late, and also talked late, "blossoming" at around 2. His physical health has been good. Ms. J described him as a child who loves to sing and who enjoys and plays well with other children, sharing well and showing affection. She said he has good relationships with her family members. Kenny has never had serious tantrums. She reported that she has disciplined him by talking to him but that now he is getting older, this is less effective. She said she now has him sit in a chair, as she does not believe in spanking. She expressed some concerns that Mr. J is using timeout, worrying that he shuts him in a room and this might cause problems with his separation anxiety.

Ms. J described herself as a loving and attentive parent who has provided most of the care for Kenny. She was able to report the age at which he has reached developmental steps, his particular interests and talents, and his temperamental style. She said that she had attended several parenting classes, belongs to a "mothers of preschoolers" group, and reads extensively about good parenting. She has him play with other children in her apartment complex and is thinking of having him go to a preschool program when he gets older. While indicating that she did not want to give the impression that he is the only thing in her life, she described herself as wanting a child more than anything and talked of how much she loves and is proud of her son. She said she felt quite able to parent him, and strongly denied any inattentiveness. When asked what she thought was the worst thing about herself as a parent, Ms. J said she felt she spoiled Kenny and was concerned about him sleeping in her bed. She said at this time she was not sure how to deal with this issue.

During the observation session, Ms. J seemed quite anxious and concerned about what the evaluator would think and depended on her for direction. She asked me a number of times whether she could do a certain activity or if what she was doing was all right, despite having been told that whatever she and Kenny chose to do was fine. Ms. J appeared, understandably, to want to show

Kenny's skills of counting, colors, and singing, asking him numerous times to do these things. However, her wishes seemed to run contrary to Kenny's, who for the most part refused to do them. Kenny was appropriately interested in playing with small trucks and cars and some dominoes he called "blocks." Ms. J kept trying to move him into other areas of play and direct the process, rather than go with his stream of play. When she did this, he for the most part ignored her. However, at times he accommodated her briefly in a very sophisticated way—by going along with what she wanted briefly and then shifting back into his own play. When she was able to engage him in play, or to follow his own play, Ms. J did so well. There was easy and appropriate physical closeness between them, and she used the play both to help Kenny enjoy himself and to learn new things. Kenny frequently spoke to her in long sentences.

Ms. J was concerned when Kenny picked up a toy gun and said "Daddy's gun." Later in the session she asked me if I would talk to Kenny to try to find out more information about the gun. When I said that any information I could get would not be reliable, Ms. J asked if she could ask him. She asked Kenny a number of questions, from which it sounded like Kenny had played with his father with a squirt gun. Ms. J again talked about her concern about the things she was hearing from Kenny and pointed out how much better it would be if she could talk to Mr. J directly about any concerns.

At the end of the session, Kenny began to display typical 2-year-old resistance to leaving. Ms. J had a difficult time setting limits with him, asking him to help clean up, then telling him, and then just cleaning up herself. Kenny responded by ignoring her or fussing and loudly refusing, at one point hitting her. There were a couple of times when Ms. J physically attempted to get Kenny to begin cleaning up. The observation ended with Ms. J not able to set limits for Kenny, and him running out of the office and into the hall with her following. While it is understandable that many parents hesitate to set strong limits in observation sessions of this type, the interaction between her and Kenny was of note.

Ms. J's responses about Kenny on the CBCL did not reveal any clinically significant problems.

She did list a number of problems regarding his sleeping, consistent with what she had reported about Kenny wanting to sleep with her. Ms. J answered the PCRI in a valid manner. Her scores on all parenting dimensions were within normal limits and indicated that her attitudes and practices regarding parenting were consistent with people who parent well. People with similar profiles enjoy their role and feel comfortable with their parenting, can communicate adequately with their child, are attempting to appropriately discipline the child, and are not likely to be too controlling.

EVALUATION OF JAMES J

Relevant History Mr. J said that he was raised locally and still lives in the home in which he grew up. His parents and two sisters and their husbands live nearby. He described his family life as excellent, saying that his father ran a tight ship so no one misbehaved. He denied any family history of emotional problems or drug abuse. In some contrast to the rosy picture he painted of this family, he reported that his mother is an alcoholic who has been to rehabilitation three times without success. He described her as a binge drinker who becomes a different person when she is drinking. He said that at one time his father drank a lot, but that he would not consider him an alcoholic.

Mr. J is a high school graduate with no reported school problems. He indicated that he has never been arrested or had any other legal problems. He spent 3 years in the army, which he very much enjoyed, and was honorably discharged. He denied ever having any history of drug or alcohol abuse or mental or emotional problems. He reported no history of being physically or sexually abused.

Mental Status and Test Results James J presented as a carefully groomed and dressed 35-year-old man. He was cooperative with the evaluation, though his manner was somewhat ingratiating. He brought a number of documents with him for me to review. He appeared to be of average to high average intelligence. Mr. J approached the evaluation in an intense and emotional manner. He cried a number of times, especially when talking about or showing me photographs of Kenny. He had difficulty explaining why he was crying, except that he loved his son so much. He also became tearful several times when asked about some of the allegations Ms. J has made about him. At these times, he would deny the allegations and say that he could not understand how she could be saying and doing these things to him now. He described how hurt he was that he was being accused of not loving or properly caring for his son. At times he appeared anxious, but not out of proportion to what is expected in this type of evaluation. He did not display inappropriate anger or frustration, though there was a somewhat immature quality to his presentation.

Speech was coherent, relevant and well-organized. Recent and remote memory appeared intact. He denied ever having experienced any problems such as depression, anxiety, or psychotic symptoms. He denied problems with physical fighting or anger. Judgment appeared to be adequate, although there were some indications that he might not always think things through before acting. For example, when asked what he would do if he saw smoke and fire in a theater, he said he would yell fire, even though he has worked as a volunteer fireman. Another example of questionable judgment was his decision to taperecord his wife without her knowledge. Other than the marriage counseling, he reported no history of any type of psychotherapy. Physical health was described as good. He said he has a recurring back problem that occasionally requires time off from work and that he was currently on medical leave for a few days.

Mr. J's MMPI-2 was invalid because of his unusually high level of defensiveness and guardedness, even in the child custody evaluation context. Like Ms. J., he tried to present himself as moral beyond reproach, and as a person with no problems or concerns. Feelings, especially those of anger and hostility, were strongly denied. The Rorschach was valid. It was indicative of someone who is under a great deal of stress and not coping very well with it, probably misperceiving situations and vacillating about what to do. However, people with this profile are able to introspect and have some insight. They typically have problems dealing with feelings, and may have a stubborn or negative streak that can cause problems in their relationships with others. They frequently are uncomfortable around others and tend to keep their distance. They are often immature in their thinking and social actions. People with this profile are usually dependent on others and may feel lonely and abandoned when a relationship is lost.

Description of and Observation with Child   Mr. J was able to speak at length and in great detail about all aspects of his son's life. He said that he went to childbirth classes and participated in his birth. He was able to tell me Kenny's birth weight and length, his early sleeping patterns, developmental milestones and the kind of formula that he drank. He described dealing with childhood issues such as discipline and toilet training quite appropriately and said that he has several books to which he refers. One of these books is about dealing with children after a divorce. Mr. J was able to describe a number of things he has learned from this book.

He was able to describe Kenny's temperament and likes and dislikes and his usual schedule. While concerned about his behavior during transition times, Mr. J described Kenny as quite attached to him and did not indicate any serious behavior or emotional problems. He cited a number of times when he has asked the advice of Kenny's pediatrician. He said that he feels that Kenny may be quite bright and that he has subscribed to several children's book clubs. He reads to Kenny frequently. Mr. J said that Kenny also enjoys music, and he looks forward to nurturing this mutual interest. While he said he himself was never very interested in sports, he would encourage Kenny to pursue sports if he were so inclined. He said he is interested in having Kenny attend preschool. He maintained that he did not think there would be a problem around religious training because he did not object to any particular religion that he thought Ms. J might propose.

When asked what the best thing about himself as a parent was, Mr. J said that it was that he put Kenny first and that he loved him more than anything. When asked what the worst thing was, he said it was that he had to work and that kept him away from his son.

Mr. J's responses on the CBCL were similar to those of Ms. J, and were not indicative of any problems outside of what would be expected developmentally for a 2½-year-old. He reported fewer sleep problems than did Ms. J. The PCRI was valid, indicating he was not trying to present his parenting in an overly positive manner. The profile generally reflected good parenting attitudes and practices. His score was low on a scale reflecting how controlling of the child a parent is, possibly reflecting some difficulty with overprotectiveness. Most other scales were in the high range, showing that he feels he is being supported in his parenting by others, and is responding similarly to people who are comfortable in their roles as parents, who spend a large amount of time with their children and are interested in them, who believe in communicating directly with their children, and who feel in control of the disciplinary role.

Mr. J and Kenny arrived early for the observation session and were already playing when I arrived. Kenny showed no fear when I came into the room and was not anxious when his father briefly left the room. Father and son related easily and comfortably. There was appropriate physical contact. During the first part of the session Mr. J was somewhat anxious and spent much time trying to control Kenny's play, suggesting things to do. At times this was distracting to Kenny, as his father would try to pull him away from something he was absorbed in. As the session went on, Mr. J let Kenny lead the play more. At one point, Kenny became quite insistent that his father go out to his truck to get a screwdriver. When Mr. J explained this was not possible, Kenny became angry, insisting that his father go and pushed him once. Mr. J handled this reasonably appropriately—he indicated there would be a timeout if Kenny continued. Although he did not follow through on the timeout, Mr. J was able to successfully distract Kenny and defuse the impending tantrum. Mr. J did a good job allowing Kenny to use both quiet and more active play and was not too strict or too lenient. He spoke with him appropriately, repeating his statements to him and adding more information where needed.

EVALUATION OF KENNY J

Kenny presented as a blond 2½-year-old boy who was tall for his age. He was well-dressed and well-groomed both times he was evaluated. His gross motor coordination was very good, and his fine motor skills were excellent—he was able to stack small dominoes into a tall tower. Kenny's speech was within normal limits for a child his age: He was talking in sentences and most of his words were understandable. It was obvious that his parents have worked with him on his verbal skills, as he was able to name a large number of colors and objects in the playroom. He did not show separation anxiety toward the evaluator or any other anxiety during the sessions. Kenny displayed willfulness typical of a 2-year-old. The level of anger and frustration did not appear out of the ordinary, and he was able to be distracted relatively easily. He did not seem to be unusually active or hyperactive. He appeared to be attached to and comfortable with both parents. However, by parental report, he does appear to be mildly stressed by the communication difficulties his parents are having, which appear to make transitions somewhat difficult for him.

FORMULATION

This divorce has been marked by serious charges and countercharges by each parent. There is no reasonable way for the evaluator to ascertain the truth of the allegations, as there is little corroboration, other than by interested parties, in the materials provided. If they were true as reported, then neither parent would be very fit to parent a child. What appears to have happened is that Mr. and Ms. J, who both have strengths and weaknesses, have focused on and likely reported out of context some of the less seemly events of their marriage. Both appear to be somewhat immature people who are more likely to place blame on the other at this point than to be able to look at themselves and acknowledge problems with their own behavior, especially problems with anger. There also appears to be some continued ambivalence about ending the marriage, which interferes with their communication. Unfortunately, this has served to focus their attention away from the needs of Kenny, who they both clearly love. Test and interview data reveal that both parents seem to have at least adequate parenting skills and are knowledgeable about parenting in general and Kenny's needs in particular. However, their communication has broken down to the point where they are not sharing essential information about Kenny. As a result, they are probably misinterpreting what is happening by inappropriately trying to get information from Kenny rather than from each other, or by withdrawing and withholding information. There is a great deal of mistrust between the two, especially around financial issues, which are clearly a major focus of their litigation. Unfortunately this mistrust has interfered with their parenting.

Ms. J has a history of difficulty with depression and anxiety symptoms and possibly problems with anger. However, document review, the report of her therapist, and the current evaluation have satisfied me that she does not currently suffer from a serious mental illness and that much of her reported previous difficulty was work-related. She is knowledgeable about parenting and able to focus on Kenny's needs. She does not appear to place him in any unusual physical danger and is able to negotiate community contacts without difficulty. However, there are some issues, in addition to the communication problems with Mr. J, which are of concern. First, she in particular appears to be making assumptions about what is happening during Mr. J's parenting time on the basis of what Kenny says to her. It is important that she realize that this not only puts Kenny in the middle, but yields information that is not reliable because of Kenny's age and the current circumstances. Second, though knowledgeable about discipline, she may not be able to apply it consistently.

Mr. J is also quite clearly attached to Kenny, is an involved and attentive parent, and has demonstrated responsible behavior in his work life. However, he appears to be immature, has trouble with his emotions, especially anger, and is dependent on others. Though he strongly denied ever physically abusing his wife, he did admit to mutual verbal abuse that, if it continues, will create difficulties for Kenny. He indicated that he is highly dependent on his extended family, who obviously have taken sides in the divorce and join him in vilifying Ms. J. This "family feud" is not in his child's best interest.

CONCLUSIONS AND RECOMMENDATIONS

According to the Michigan Child Custody Act of 1970, as amended, there appear to be emotional ties existing between Kenny and both of his parents. Though adversely affected by the acrimony of the divorce, both parents seem to have the capacity to give the child love, affection, and guidance. Both will need support in appropriately setting limits for Kenny as he goes through toddlerhood and beyond. Both are committed to good schooling and a religious life for Kenny, but the particulars of this are likely to be a source of disagreement between them as Kenny gets older. Both parents are able to provide adequately for Kenny's material needs.

Kenny has primarily lived with his mother. There is a dispute about whether Mr. J has always consistently kept his parenting time responsibilities. He does have ample parenting time now, with which he apparently has been consistent. Both parents have established adequate custodial homes. Each parent has accused the other of problems with morality that are difficult to substantiate. Mental health was discussed earlier. Both parents are in adequate physical health to care for a child. Kenny is too young to have a community or school record or to express a preference.

Because of their poor communication, both parents are currently impaired in their ability to encourage a close relationship with the other parent. I think there will be problems with this regardless of the custody arrangement. On the basis of each parent's past behavior, I would predict that Ms. J would be in danger of continuing to make allegations about Mr. J on the basis of Kenny's reports, without checking with Mr. J. I would also predict that Mr. J will continue to denigrate Ms. J, possibly to Kenny, when he is upset with her, and to involve his parents in this process. There are unsubstantiated allegations of domestic violence; Ms. J indeed appears to be frightened at times by Mr. J. She may well also "lose it" emotionally at times. Both parents admit to verbal altercations that have occurred in Kenny's presence. Research is clear that children exposed to serious and prolonged levels of parental fighting are harmed by this and in danger of being on the receiving end of inappropriate parental anger; both parents will do well to avoid these things at all costs.

As mentioned earlier, I do not think there is any custody and parenting time arrangement that will serve to completely eliminate the difficulties between these parents. However, I recommend joint legal custody so that both parents can have appropriate input into important decisions about Kenny's life. Given that (1) Kenny is very young and has spent the bulk of his life with his mother, (2) I do not see substantial evidence to see her as an inadequate parent, (3) the current parenting time arrangement is going reasonably well, and (4) there is a high level of conflict between the parents, I recommend primary parenting time/physical custody be with Ms. J. Given that Kenny appears to be a sturdy, normally developing child who is attached to both parents and appears to be able tolerate transitions reasonably well, I recommend liberal parenting time for Mr. J and would follow the plan that was established in October 1996.

Research shows that no matter what the custody and parenting time arrangement, children do better when parental conflict is reduced. In order to improve parental communication and avoid future pitfalls, I recommend the following: Ms. J and Mr. J should meet with a parenting coordinator, who must be a therapist skilled in divorce and child custody issues, with the specific and limited purpose of establishing appropriate communication about Kenny. I would predict that this would take at least four to six weekly sessions, with monthly follow-up sessions and "troubleshooting sessions" as needed. The purpose of these sessions would be to focus on Kenny, how best to communicate about him and how best to discipline him; the purpose would not be to focus on the problems they have with each other. Planning for Kenny's schooling and religion should happen soon, and may be best settled with the parenting coordinator after the heat of the divorce itself subsides. Resolving these issues now will serve to help avoid such conflicts in the future. I also recommend that Ms. J continue her therapy with Ms. D to prevent the possibility of her redeveloping an anxiety disorder or depression and for parent guidance around discipline.

Kenny is a lively, smart, and normally developing little boy. If his parents can set aside their own issues, work on how they discipline him, and focus on what is best for him, he can have a bright future.

Respectfully submitted,
Beth K. Clark, Ph.D., ABPP
Clinical & Forensic Psychologist
Diplomate in Forensic Psychology,
American Board of Professional Psychology

Teaching Point: What strategies do you use in trying to remain impartial in the course of forensic assessment?

Although evaluator impartiality is important in all forensic assessments, there are few areas in which impartiality is as vital (or difficult to maintain) as child custody. In the family law arena, cases such as that of Kenny J are often evaluated at a time of high family conflict and distrust. Divorcing parents are very concerned that they be treated fairly and impartially by the forensic clinician. Thus, when a case is referred, the examiner should first ensure that there is no prior relationship or conflict of interest between the examiner and any of the parties or their attorneys. If such a relationship is discovered, then immediate contact with the attorneys to inform them of the issue, and possibly declining involvement with the case, is advisable.

The examiner should also ensure that his or her role is clear from the beginning, and remains so. In custody matters, parents will often ask for advice or seek hints about the outcome of the evaluation. The examiner should be clear with the parties that the relationship is evaluative, not therapeutic, and should not give advice during the course of the evaluation. Opinions and recommendations are best left to the final report, which is distributed upon completion of the evaluation. Giving this information to a party during the evaluation could give the appearance of bias toward one party or the other, even if it did not reflect genuine bias. Similarly, attorneys may want to speak at length with the examiner about their clients, or may request a "preliminary opinion." Lengthy *ex parte* contact with only one attorney during a custody evaluation may well seem improper to the other attorney and parent, and therefore should be avoided. Attorneys can be told in the beginning that they will be notified by the examiner of any contacts made with the examiner by other attorneys.

The examiner should use the same procedures with one party in a custody matter that have been used with the other. Interview length should be comparable. In the case example, if one parent had been interviewed for 1 hour and the other for 5, the first parent might have felt that there had not been sufficient opportunity for a fair hearing of her concerns. Similarly, the same tests should be given to each party.

Finally, it is important to note that child custody is inextricably intertwined with social values and beliefs. The evaluator should constantly examine his or her perspectives that may interfere with impartiality. Attention to relevant and current research is helpful in reducing bias. However, if an examiner has a strong opinion about a social issue involved in a case and this opinion would interfere with his or her impartiality, then it is better to decline the referral. If an evaluator held a religious belief that homosexuality is immoral, for example, it would be preferable to avoid involvement in cases involving gay and lesbian parents.

Case 3

Principle: Base testimony on the results of the properly performed forensic mental health assessment

A properly performed FMHA creates a solid foundation for expert testimony. Conversely, a poorly performed FMHA is detrimental to expert testimony, often because of problems with validity or relevance. This principle addresses the relationship between the evaluation and the expert testimony, and underscores the need to base testimony clearly and directly on the results of the

FMHA. In this context, a properly performed FMHA should be consistent with the principles discussed in detail elsewhere (Heilbrun, 2000) and illustrated in this book. When these principles are followed, it is likely that the quality of the FMHA will be good, and will provide a substantive basis for expert testimony in that case.

The APA *Ethical Principles of Psychologists and Code of Conduct* (1992) notes that expert testimony is an activity that is regulated by the *Ethics Code*: "Psychologists who perform forensic functions, such as assessments, interviews, consultations, reports, or expert testimony, must comply with all other provisions of the Ethics Code to the extent that they apply to such activities" (p. 1610). The *Ethics Code* particularly emphasizes the importance of considering the behavior and performance of the individual being assessed. Accordingly, personal contact with the subject of the evaluation is stressed. When this is not possible, the impact of this absence should be noted:

> Except as noted in (c) below, psychologists provide written or oral forensic reports or testimony of the psychological characteristics of an individual only after they have conducted an examination of the individual adequate to support their statements or conclusions. When, despite reasonable efforts, such an examination is not feasible, psychologists clarify the impact of their limited information on the reliability and validity of their reports and testimony, and they appropriately limit the nature and extent of their conclusions or recommendations. (p. 1610)

The *Specialty Guidelines for Forensic Psychologists* (1991) also emphasizes the importance of personal contact:

> Forensic psychologists avoid giving written or oral evidence about the psychological characteristics of particular individuals when they have not had an opportunity to conduct an examination of the individual adequate to the scope of the statements, opinions, or conclusions to be issued. Forensic psychologists make every reasonable effort to conduct such examinations. When it is not possible or feasible to do so, they make clear the impact of such limitations on the reliability and validity of their professional products, evidence, or testimony. (p. 663)

The *Ethical Guidelines for the Practice of Forensic Psychiatry* (AAPL, 1995) provides similar guidance on both report writing and testimony:

> Forensic psychiatrists . . . adhere to the principles of honesty and they strive for objectivity. [The] clinical evaluation and the application of the data obtained to the legal criteria are performed in the spirit of such honesty and efforts to attain objectivity. Their opinion reflects this honesty and efforts to attain objectivity. . . . Practicing forensic psychiatrists enhance the honesty and objectivity of their work by basing their forensic opinions, forensic reports and . . . forensic testimony on all the data available to them. They communicate the honesty of their work, efforts to attain objectivity, and the soundness of their clinical opinion by distinguishing, to the extent possible, between verified and unverified information as well as between clinical "facts," "inferences," and "impressions." (p. 3)

Legal authority also supports the importance of this principle. Specifically, evidentiary standards under both *Frye v. United States* (1923) and *Daubert v. Merrell Dow Pharmaceuticals* (1993) address the admissibility of evidence based on the quality of the data available. Under *Frye*, the admissibility of evidence depends on whether the proposed evidence is of a kind "sufficiently established" to have gained "general acceptance in the particular field to which it belongs." In the forensic context, the question of admissibility under *Frye* would be whether the testimony was based on data and techniques that were "generally accepted" in the particular field of psychology or psychiatry.

The *Daubert* decision suggested several factors that might be considered in weighing the admissibility of scientific evidence that are consistent with this principle. These factors include whether the scientific method was applied to yield the inference forming the basis for the opinion, whether the reasoning or methodology underlying the testimony is scientifically valid, and whether it can be applied to the facts of the given case.[1]

These sources of ethical and legal authority provide support for basing testimony on the results of a properly performed FMHA. Sources of ethics authority stress the importance of describing the basis for expert testimony, whiles sources of legal authority emphasize relevance and reliability for admissibility of expert testimony. Taken together, these sources of authority underscore the importance of relevance and reliability in FMHA, for both the report and the expert testimony.

The current report provides a good example of how a properly performed FMHA enhances both relevance and reliability and lays a solid foundation for expert testimony. Guided by Section 20-124.3 of the Virginia Code, this relocation custody evaluation considered both parents and the needs of the child. Section 20-124.3 requires the forensic clinician to address nine elements related to the "best interests of the child" standard: (1) age and physical and mental condition of the child, (2) age and physical and mental condition of the parents, (3) relationship between the parents and child, (4) needs of the child, (5) role of the parents in the upbringing of the child, (6) propensity to support the relationship with the other parent, (7) reasonable preference of the child, (8) history of abuse, and (9) other relevant elements.

In Virginia, there are two questions considered by the court in relocation custody cases: (1) Is there a meaningful change in circumstances? and (2) Is the change in the best interests of the child? Expert testimony in such cases, to be admissible, must not be "speculative or founded under assumptions that have an insufficient factual base" (*Tittsworth v. Robinson*, 1996). The forensic clinician's role in this case was that of court-ordered evaluator.

Some of the elements of a properly performed FMHA can be seen clearly in this report. Among these are the consideration of forensic issues relevant to the legal question, the use of collateral sources, and the use of psychometrically sound instruments and clear reasoning to yield more accurate results. First, the report clearly identifies the relevant forensic issues and the sources of information used to obtain relevant information. The report is organized around the nine elements established by Virginia statutory law. Not only does this make it easier for the reader to understand, it is also helpful in testimony, allowing the forensic clinician to go directly to a specific section to answer questions posed during testimony.

Second, the forensic clinician provides detailed information from each parent in the nine areas involved in the custody decision. The report also makes it clear that the forensic clinician had personal contact with each of the parents. Self-reported information was supplemented with collateral information, as the forensic clinician used collateral interviews and documents to assess the consistency of the self-reported information provided by the parents.

Relevant psychological testing was also used. For example, the forensic clinician administered the Minnesota Multiphasic Personality Inventory-2nd edition (MMPI-2; Butcher, Dahlstrom, Graham, Tellegen, & Kaemmer, 1989) to assess the personality and personal adjustment of both parents, areas that are particularly relevant in child custody litigation.

Accordingly, this report is good example of a properly performed FMHA that would serve as a solid basis for effective testimony. The forensic clinician clearly addressed the forensic issues through the use of personal contact and self-reported information, collateral documentation and interviews, and psychological testing. This combination enhances the reliability and validity of the evaluation, and provides an adequate factual and scientific basis for the report's conclusions.

PSYCHOLOGICAL CUSTODY EVALUATION

Joan Smith v. Bill Black
In Re John Wilson, DOB 2/12/92
Style & Identification Data
Springfield County Juvenile and Domestic
   Relations District Court
The Honorable Harold W. Edwards, Jr.
Case No.: A23057–01-01
Hearing Date: December 30, 1998, 2 P.M.
Petitioner: Joan Smith
Respondent: Bill Black
Attorney: Patricia Jones
Attorney: Katherine Young
Father: Bill Black
Age: 33
Birth Date: 8/31/65
Mother: Joan Smith
Age: 28

Birth Date: 10/10/69
Minor Child: John Wilson
Age: 6
Birth Date: 2/12/92
Stepfather: Tom Smith
Age: 25
Birth Date: 4/23/73

REFERRAL AND PROCEDURAL HISTORY

On 7/22/98 the court heard several motions from the parties, including mother's petition to modify custody and to appoint a neutral evaluator and father's motion for custody and child support. The parties agreed that this examiner would serve as a neutral evaluator and that the matter would be continued until 12/30/98, with interim arrangements for visitation set forth. The evaluation was conducted in accordance with the controlling standards of the psychology profession, Forensic Specialty Guidelines, Guidelines for Conducting Custody Evaluations, as well as Dr. Hagan's *Provisions*.

The parties were cooperative in producing volumes of information. Everyone made themselves available for interviews and home visits. The mother and the father presented third-party informants who commented on the respective parenting styles. This examiner believes there is sufficient information on which to form an opinion in light of the referral question.

Procedural History

Date	Event
2/12/92	John Wilson was born as the sole issue of the unmarried relationship between the parties.
1/7/93	Father's petition to Dillard County J&DR regarding visitation.
1/14/93	Dillard County J&DR entered Order for child support.
2/11/93	Dillard County J&DR set visitation.
3/17/93	Father petitioned Dillard County J&DR for reduction in child support.
4/16/93	Father asked Dillard County J&DR for a show cause summons against mother for failure to obey visitation order (Easter holiday).
2/24/94	Dillard County J&DR heard the evidence regarding visitation and modified its previous Order of 2/11/93, set forth a specific visitation schedule, and ordered that pick up and drop off occur midway between the parental residences.
8/11/94	Mother petitioned Dillard County J&DR for an increase in child support and continuance of health care insurance due to childcare cost increase.
(undated)	Mother petitioned Dillard County J&DR to modify visitation and support and to transfer venue to Franklin County; Franklin County never took jurisdiction.
6/13/96	Mother brought motion to Dillard County J&DR to transfer all matters to Springfield County courts.
6/13/96	Father brought a motion to Springfield County J&DR to amend child support because mother had married.
4/29/98	Mother gave notice to Springfield County J&DR regarding intent to relocate from Springfield County to Newtown, VA on 6/16/98.
5/19/98	Mother brought show cause summons against father for failure to provide support as ordered.
6/25/98	Father brought motion and order to amend physical custody and support citing mother's relocation as the change of circumstances.
7/8/98	Mother brought motion to continue Springfield County J&DR so that neutral evaluation, home studies, transportation and temporary visitation could be investigated.
8/27/98	Springfield County J&DR Order for neutral evaluation with interim visitation schedule and neutral evaluator's reports to go to counsel and parties and the matter is set for the contested docket on 12/30/98, 2 P.M.

Procedures

Date	Item	Source	Regarding
8/1/98	Best Interest Questionnaires	Joan Smith	Dr. Hagan's questionnaires
8/2/98	Best Interest Questionnaires	Bill Black	Dr. Hagan's questionnaires
7/30/98	Confirmation of informed consent	Joan Smith & Bill Black	Informed consent to proceed with evaluation
6/98	Consent Order (draft)	Bill Black	Father's proposal to mother
2/4/97–3/25/97	Counseling records: John Wilson	Cawson, Ph.D.	John's treatment for anxiety—resolved; 4 visits

Date	Item	Source	Regarding
8/6/98	Home visit: Father	Hagan, Ph.D.	Father's home situation
8/30/98	Home visit: Mother	Hagan, Ph.D.	Mother's home situation
8/30/98	Interview & social history: Tom Smith (stepfather)	Hagan, Ph.D.	Stepfather's history and current role with child
7/30/98	Interview: both parties jointly	Hagan, Ph.D.	Initial evaluation conference
9/16/98	Interview: Peggy Anderson	Hagan, Ph.D.	Family history & parenting
9/22/98	Interview: Pat Wyatt	Hagan, Ph.D.	Family history & parenting
9/21/98	Interview: Christina Wells	Hagan, Ph.D.	Family history & parenting
8/30/98	Interview: Joan Smith	Hagan, Ph.D.	Personal history
9/21/98	Interview: Lynn Johnson	Hagan, Ph.D.	Family history & parenting
8/27/98	Interview: Agnes Peterman	Hagan, Ph.D.	Family history & parenting
1997/98	Kindergarten Progress Report	Crestview Elementary	John consistently demonstrating grade-level expectations
4/29/98	Letter: to whom it may concern	Joan Smith	Notice of relocation
7/30/98	Medical opinion letter: John Wilson	Stollen, M.D.	Child's unremarkable health status
7/30/98	Medical opinion letter: Joan Smith	Brody, M.D.	No medical problems
6/25/98	Motion & Order to Amend	Bill Black	Change of circumstance due to mother's relocation
2/24/94	Order	Dillard County J&DR	Modification of 2/11/93 Order; revised visitation schedule; transfer of child halfway between parents' residences
undated	Order (consent)	Dillard County J&DR	Transfer all matters to Springfield County J&DR
8/27/98	Order: Custody Evaluation	Springfield County J&DR	Custody Evaluation
1/7/93	Petition to Dillard County J&DR	Bill Black	Visitation
7/30/98	Provisions for custody evaluation endorsed by each parent	Hagan, Ph.D.	Parameters for custody evaluation
7/31/98	Psychological Testing: Joan Smith	Hagan, Ph.D.	Personality & personal adjustment
8/5/98	Psychological Testing: Bill Black	Hagan, Ph.D.	Personality & personal adjustment
9/18/98	School information: John	Kingston Elementary School, Newtown	Calendar & policy
5/19/98	Show cause summons	Springfield County J&DR	Father's failure to pay child support
4/16/93	Show cause summons	Dillard County J&DR	Mother's failure to obey Order re: Easter visitation

COMPARATIVE ANALYSIS OF BEST INTEREST

Age, Physical and Mental Condition of Child
John Wilson (DOB 2/12/92) is the only child of the unmarried relationship of Bill Black and Joan Smith. John is now 6 years old and has no chronic or acute medical problems that pose special demands of parenting. According to the medical opinion letter from G. Thomas Stollen, M.D., John's immunizations are current, he is on no medication presently and all developmental

milestones have been achieved within normal limits.

The child was seen by a psychologist (Ted Cawson, Ph.D.) beginning 2/4/97 for treatment of an anxiety disorder. The presenting problems included excessive anxiety and fear of burglaries at night. Insomnia and some difficulties separating from his mother were seen as well, as were frequent tantrums and complaints of illness without a physical basis. The child was 4 years, 11 months old at the time. The counseling concluded when John's aggressive behavior decreased, the night anxiety was resolved, and the child was playing out of doors with no difficulty. There have been no mental health services for the child for any reason since that time.

Educational history shows that John attended Crestview Elementary for Kindergarten (1997–1998). He consistently demonstrated grade-level expectations for language arts, math, science, social studies, physical education, and social/emotional skills. There were no attendance problems and he was promoted to the first grade.

Now living in Newtown, John attends Kingston Elementary School. Kingston Elementary is on a different system from Springfield County schools. Rather than interim grades, the child is tested for skills in math and reading, the parents are called in for a conference, and the teacher reviews the child's progress level based on those test scores. The school does not give the traditional letter grades, but indicates "Improving, Needs Improvement, or Successful."

The mother describes John as self-assured, loving, independent, affectionate and forgiving. He sometimes has difficulty controlling himself and, like many his age, does not have a great deal of patience. The matters for which he saw Dr. Cawson are now well-resolved and John is a happy, healthy 6-year-old.

According to his father, John is independent and very sociable and has a great deal of commonsense. The father indicated that John is fairly well-adjusted. He has chores to do in the father's home and understands the rules and expectations of both households. The father is aware of the child's special food interests and play activities. The father is concerned that John has been made aware of some of the negative feelings between the parents, and the father feels that the child does not need that information. Otherwise, the father feels that the child is doing well.

Age, Physical and Mental Condition of Each Parent

Joan Smith. Ms. Smith is the 28-year-old mother of John. Medical opinion letter from Dr. Brody indicates that the mother has no medical problems that pose a limitation to safe parenting, nor is she under treatment for any acute illness that might compromise her capacity to provide safe oversight for the child. Other than oral contraception, Joan does not take any medication.

Joan was born in Lakeland, MN, and grew up in Sacramento. The family moved to Virginia during Joan's junior high school years. She grew up in an intact home until her parents separated when Joan was 8 years old. She is the older of two biological siblings and has a half-brother by her mother's second marriage. The mother remarried when Joan was 10 years old. Joan denies any abuse, neglect, Child Protective Services involvement, or police intervention in her childhood home. The mother's second marriage ended in divorce because of the new husband's alcoholism.

Joan left home at age 19 and took an apartment with a roommate. She moved back home but left again to take a job as a live-in nanny for a year at age 20. She then moved back home again with her mother after becoming pregnant by Bill Black at age 21. John was born on 2/12/92, and Joan moved out and took an apartment when John was 19 months old (12/26/93).

Joan met Tom Smith in August 1995, and they married on 4/5/96. This union produced a daughter, Jenny, who is John's half-sister. In August 1996 they moved to Springfield and built a house on Wooddale Drive off of Main Street. Tom was accepted into the master's program in Environmental Engineering at the university in Newtown, VA. In April 1997 Joan gave written notice of her intention to relocate to Newtown. They moved to Newtown on 6/16/98 and took an apartment at 13600 Bull Run, Newtown, VA 24888. She advised this examiner that the move is temporary until Tom finishes his degree. At this point they plan to return to Springfield.

Self-reported mental health history from Joan includes an episode of counseling during her teenage years because of some problems with a boyfriend. Those issues resolved quickly. Her alcohol use is not significant, as she described only occasional and moderate drinking. Use of drugs was denied.

Her educational history includes a high school diploma from Springfield after repeating 11th grade due to relocation and abuse by her boyfriend. She said that he beat her up if she went to school.

Self-reported legal history includes a previously suspended driver's license for failure to pay a speeding ticket at age 22. Presently, her driver's license is fully restored. She was fined for contempt regarding visitation. There are no criminal matters.

In order to assess personality and personal adjustment, both parents completed the Minnesota Multiphasic Personality Inventory, 2nd edition (MMPI-2). There is scientific evidence to indicate that litigants in custody disputes tend to be more defensive when answering MMPI questions. Moderate efforts to "look good" are considered average or normal under these test conditions. Joan's responses to the MMPI-2 were well within normal limits on all indicators. There was no intentional effort to "look good" through this instrument. There were no concerns raised with respect to mood, conduct, or interpersonal relations as measured by this instrument. The scores were consistent with others who are emotionally stable and not likely to evidence aberrant behavior.

The Insight Inventory is a 64-item rating scale through which respondents describe their usual style of managing tasks and dealing with people. This instrument has sound statistical and psychometric properties. The respondent's self-ratings are compared with a reference group of 2,000 persons between 18 and 75 years of age. According to this instrument, Joan has a fairly indirect style of dealing with people. She is more likely to use hints or suggestions rather than commands in her efforts to influence others. At the same time, she is an outgoing individual who likes being involved in the give and take of relationships. She is comfortable in expressing thoughts and feelings and taking care of relationship maintenance issues.

In her personal life, she responds to tasks with a degree of urgency. She does not like to leave issues unresolved. She usually takes care of the details and moves on to the next task. She is likely to feel uncomfortable with matters left unfinished.

Bill Black. Bill Black is the 33-year-old single father of John. He does not report any particular health problems that would interfere with parenting responsibilities. He is not taking any medication and rarely sees a physician. He was born and raised in Smithfield in an intact family. His parents separated when Bill was 10 years old. He and his mother then moved to Wildwood 4 years later when his mother remarried. Bill is the older of two children. His mother is a factory worker. The biological father was a carpenter who, according to Bill, had problems with alcohol. The stepfather and Bill lived in the same home from age 14 to 18. The stepfather was a mechanic at Simpson, Inc. There was one episode of police intervention at the home due to parental discord, but there was no Child Protective Services intervention. There was no physical or emotional abuse, but the biological parents' divorce was stressful for Bill.

He moved out on his own at age 18 and met Joan at Foodland where he was an assistant manager and she was a customer. About a year into the relationship they lived together for a week. The relationship ended in July 1991 when she told him of the unplanned pregnancy. Bill felt cornered and was not interested in marrying at that point in his life.

Bill indicated that he was in individual counseling at Springfield County Mental Health in 1995 and those issues were resolved quickly. He estimates his current alcohol use at three beers per week. He said that he wants to avoid the problems with alcohol that he saw in his biological father.

Bill graduated from Wildwood High School without any repeats or special education services. There were no suspensions.

Work history indicates that he has been self-employed as a route salesman since February 1995. Previously, he was with Small's Distributing Company (9/89–2/95) as a Mountain Beer route salesman. Prior to that he was an assistant manager at Foodland (1983–1989). He has not served in the military.

Self-reported legal history is unremarkable. His driver's license is intact.

Bill took the same two psychological measures (MMPI-2 and Insight Inventory) as Joan. Like Joan, Bill's responses were straightforward without special effort at positive impression management. Bill's MMPI-2 had two clinical elevations, which were consistent with persons who have some tension, restlessness, and worry. He tends to mull things over and may build mild resentment over perceived violations in a relationship. He is a fairly reserved and private individual who tends to work things out to his own satisfaction before taking action. He certainly prefers to be his own boss and is much happier in his current work arrangement.

Like Joan, Bill is somewhat indirect in his way of influencing others. Although he comes across as quiet and perhaps shy, Bill is certainly not detached or disinterested. He thinks things through in considerable detail but is not always public about his deliberations. His quiet indirect approach should not be interpreted as indifference.

In summary, Bill is the 33-year-old never-married father of John. Bill has no special medical or mental health difficulties that interfere with parenting. He has a quiet, reserved style of thinking through issues on his own without relying on a support network. As with Joan, Bill does not have any psychological impediment to parenting.

Relationship Existing Between Each Parent and the Child

Joan Smith. John has always lived with his mother except during periods of visitation with the father. She concedes that she was not always patient in John's younger years when she was a single parent and the child tested limits. She also concedes that learning to discipline effectively was difficult when she was a single parent. She feels that she now has more maturity and experience and is at a much more stable place in her life. John is older and can respond to reasoning. Joan also has more of a built-in support system in her marriage.

This examiner observed Joan together with John, John's sister, and stepfather at a home visit in Newtown. Joan was appropriate and attentive to the child's emotional considerations and needs for limit setting. Although Bill feels that Joan intrudes into the father-son relationship and makes negative comments about the father in front of the child, this examiner did not see any evidence

of this from Joan, nor did the child report any such concerns. This examiner also interviewed collateral informants who had firsthand observation of Joan in her role as a parent to John. Those sources were consistently favorable and uncontradicted with respect to the loving, nurturing, and affectionate bond between Joan and John.

Bill Black. Bill indicated that the relationship with Joan had been troubled for some time. She was 17 and he was 20 when they met, and they had several breakups in the relationship. They had split up for 4 months and then were back together for a month when she announced her pregnancy. He was in disbelief and asked for a paternity test. He was also somewhat incredulous because she had told him that she was taking birth control pills. He conceded that he simply was not ready to marry or to be a father at that time in his life.

Bill indicated that he and John never lived under the same roof except during visitation. The first 3 years of John's life were somewhat difficult because Bill perceived Joan to be "bossy and I didn't need a momma." He also conceded that the last 3 years have been somewhat better. He attributed this to the fact that they have both grown up a bit and have become allies for the child. Joan is married and has focused on her marriage and has let go of a lot of anger.

When asked about any fault he finds in his own parenting, Bill offered some insights from his own developmental years. His parents divorced, and he raised his sister without much parenting himself. He indicated that he goes by instinct and noted "I got a long way to go." This candid self-assessment is rather refreshing in a parent under these circumstances.

When John is with his dad, they spend time together and in the company of John's cousins. They enjoy putting things together and going out on the boat, or visiting with extended family about 20 miles away.

Like Joan, Bill brought forward collateral informants who offered firsthand observations of Bill in his role as a parent to John. Those reports were also favorable and uncontradicted by other sources. This examiner appreciated that Bill's informants acknowledged their bias on his behalf and were able to distinguish between firsthand observations and their natural advocacy for Bill.

Needs of Child: Relationships, Siblings, Peers and Extended Family

Joan Smith. When in his home in Newtown, John lives with his mother, stepfather, and half-sister, Jenny. In his early years, the maternal grandmother was John's main daycare provider while Joan was single and working. The child has developed a relationship with his stepfather, but Tom is not trying to take Bill's place. John may occasionally call Tom "Daddy," but Joan has told John about the distinction between the stepfather and biological father.

John does have a special relationship with his half-sister. By virtue of her presence, John enjoys a degree of seniority and seems to enjoy the teaching and protective role that comes with being an older brother. His sister's presence also gives John the chance to learn important life lessons, such as sharing resources including Mom's time and attention.

Bill Black. Bill does not have plans for marriage or children in the foreseeable future. The paternal grandmother has not played a major role in John's life, because she lived in North Carolina for a period of time and then moved to Merryville. The child does have cousins and other extended family with whom he has enjoyed some recreation during visitation.

Although Bill holds Tom in some regard, stating "I think Tom is a nice guy," he also said that "I think he is a puppet for Joan." Bill simply does not want the relocation to result in any diminishment in the child's connection with family in Springfield and Franklin counties. "John needs to know that he has two families and that he's loved by all family members."

Role of Each Parent in Upbringing and Care of Child

Chronology of Custody

Biological parents' union: 9/88

Parents' separation: 7/91

Custody: sole to mother

Paternity established: Bill Black

Contempt: Mother fined by Dillard County J&DR 4/16/93

Visitation revised: Dillard County J&DR 2/24/94

Petition: Mother's motion to amend visitation and support

Petition: Father's motion to change custody, visitation and support 6/98

Joan Smith. The child has always lived with his mother. Bill does not contest that Joan is the primary caregiver. His visitation was set forth in some detail by Dillard County J&DR Court, allowing for every other weekend and alternating holidays, with a week and two long weekends in the summer with the parents to share the transportation. Joan conceded that Bill brings a positive contribution, stating, "I feel that Bill is an OK father. He has been involved with John's sports and pays his child support."

She did not report any special problems with the previous visitation. The mother viewed the relocation as temporary. "Our previous visitation has, in my opinion, worked well. The changes we are seeking are temporary due to the fact that my husband and I will be returning to the Springfield area once he has completed his schooling." She noted temporary negative consequences from the relocation. "This move will impact midweek visits with his father. I plan to give Bill every opportunity to see and visit John while in Springfield on weekends, holidays, etc."

Joan is a stay-at-home mother. "My career is my children and my family." She conceded a prior contempt of court for failing to comply with the visitation schedule.

From the earliest days she took John to doctors' appointments, took care of feeding, got him ready in the morning, and drove him to her mother's house for daycare. By age 1, John had learned to talk and was proceeding with other developmental milestones on time. This pattern continued until John reached age 4, at which time Joan quit her job shortly after marrying Tom. She has stayed at home since that time. She has volunteered at PTA and has been involved in school activities on a regular basis. In Newtown, she is at home every day when John comes home from school. They take their meals together and engage in the normal activities of daily living appropriate to John's age group. She was the team mom for John's soccer team.

During the period in which she lives in Newtown, Joan proposed the following access time between father and son: every other weekend, shared holidays, one full week each month of the summer and one weekend each summer month. She also proposed special plans for extra visitation with reasonable notice.

Bill Black. At the father's home visit on 8/6/98, this examiner found a single-story home in a residential area off Chowan Road not far from Route 6. The father has lived there for 9 years. This is where the visitation has always taken place.

John has his own room and all the things a boy his age would need. He clearly understands the rules of the house and is able to describe some of his age-appropriate chores. There are no children his age nearby. There was a spontaneous and genuine display of affection between father and son. It was also clear that the father provides discipline. The child appeared comfortable in the setting. He described boating and sport activities in which he and his father routinely engage.

Bill asserted that he was not allowed much of a parenting role until the child was 8½ months old. He was then given day-long visitation, but was not allowed to have an overnight with his child. At age 1 or 2, John and his father had more time together, and the father believes there is now a better connection between the two of them. Bill felt that he has been much more involved in the child's life, including school activities and sports, adding that he assisted the teeball coach in the spring of 1998. In the winter and spring, Bill said, he attended nearly all of the games and practices. He said that he did not understand why the mother and Tom were listed as the parents on the teeball registration forms. He did not miss a single visitation.

Until the Springfield County J&DR proceedings in the summer of 1998, the parenting access plan was set by the Dillard County J&DR Order of 2/24/94. In the summer of 1998 visitation was reset by Springfield County J&DR at alternating weekends from Friday, 6 P.M. until Sunday, 4 P.M. beginning 8/28/98, and continuing to alternate thereafter until 12/30/98, when the matter will be heard again. The parents have been meeting in Middleburg. The mother will deliver and pick up the child for the Thanksgiving weekend. Pending the hearing of 12/30/98, it is anticipated that the parties will alternate Thanksgiving each year.

In his draft of a Consent Order, the father proposed that during the school year there will be visitation of one 3-day weekend each month, coordinated with the school calendar in conjunction with early release days or holidays. For Christmas, the father proposed visitation with the child from December 26, 2 P.M. until January 3, 4 P.M. In 1999, he proposed that the child be with the father in the first half of the Christmas with that interval ending 12/26/99, 2 P.M. He asked for the entire spring break and for the mother to take care of the delivery and pick up of the child, and that the visitation scheme run no greater than 18 months based on the mother's proffer of a temporary relocation.

Propensity to Support Relationship with Other Parent: Parental Cooperation in Matters Affecting Child In this examiner's experience, parents who enter into a contested custody dispute often assume the posture of litigants first and parents second. This is often a result of the problems between the two parents. It is also this examiner's experience that while some parents treat each other with great contempt and hostility, such animosity is not necessarily indicative of their relationship with their children. Some parents are able to compartmentalize the conflict with their former partner as separate and distinct from their relationship with the children.

It is also this examiner's experience that the end of litigation often brings a significant reduction in the adversarial relationship between the parents. When they no longer have the judicial forum for their dispute, they return to their priorities as parents. It is reasonable to anticipate that the emotional environment that the parents create during litigation will change, and perhaps for the better, but not always soon enough.

Joan Smith. Joan asserted that both parents are able to communicate and cooperate in making decisions about the major issues in the child's life. She felt that the track record so far is favorable on that point. She conceded that there is much more conflict, tension, and mistrust between the parties, partly because of the custody dispute, but added that matters have improved over the last few years.

Bill Black. Bill was somewhat skeptical about the communication and cooperation between the parties. He felt that Joan has been strategic in withholding the child and information. He saw the move to Newtown as her unilateral effort to advance her own interests without consideration of the relationship between father and son. He did not like the fact that the stepfather is sometimes called "Daddy." He thought that the stepfather should be called "Tom." The father felt that the relocation has diminished his role because he cannot sign John up for teeball and is not there to be called Daddy very often. He wanted his child to have the same last name as one of his parents. Right now John has his mother's maiden name. Although the father did not like what he perceives to be the mother's controlling style, he did not want to argue with Joan about this. He advised Joan, in my presence, "I want to be an ally about our son."

Reasonable Preference of Child: Intelligence, Understanding, Age, and Experience   The mother felt that the child can offer a reasoned and intelligent preference regarding the living arrangement. She believed the child will say that he wants to stay with her in Newtown.

The father did not believe that child has the experience and wisdom to offer a controlling preference regarding the living arrangement. The father believed that John would say that he wants to stay with his mother. However, Bill also asserted that the child has not been with the father for an extended period of time, noting, "When John and I were beginning to have a bond as father and son, she moved to Newtown. I want John to be comfortable living with me as he does with his mother. I feel that the 2 weeks that he has stayed with me he did not say that he missed his mom."

History of Family Abuse   Neither parent accuses the other of a history of family abuse as defined by Virginia law. They both considered the issue and found it to be of no concern.

Other Relevant Elements

Joan Smith. The mother asserted that John is close to his stepfather and half-sister, Jenny. She said that the child is attending a very good school in a low crime area and has more social activities and exposure to broader world issues in a university setting than in Springfield County. In support of her argument, she cited the fact that she is a stay-at-home mother so that the child needs no daycare.

The mother cited the following benefits to the child from relocation: growing up in a university environment, more community and school-based resources for the child's education, better elementary school that is fully wired for information access, university resource support, 3-minute bike ride to university campus, presence of role model and expectation for the child's higher education, low crime rate in the town and university communities, child's exposure to peers with broader ethnic diversity and world cultures, and the child's immediate access to friends within his cul-de-sac.

Bill Black. Bill countered that Joan has put John in the middle of this situation and caused very awkward circumstances by bringing the child to the courthouse. Bill conceded that give and take is needed by both parties. However, he felt that he has made more concessions than she over the last 6 years. He was concerned that his relationship may suffer as a result of the relocation.

Summary of Comparative Analysis

	Factors Favoring Child Development	Factors Impeding Child Development
Joan Smith's Parenting	Lifelong primary caregiver	Relocation impedes midweek visitation
	Temporarily resides in stimulating educational environment	Relocation diminishes father's role in extracurriculars
	Child has younger sister at mother's	
	Mother is aware and attentive to child's interests	
	Diminished conflict between parents in recent years	
	Wants father to have a presence in child's life	

	Factors Favoring Child Development	*Factors Impeding Child Development*
Bill Black's Parenting	Awareness and sensitivity to child's needs	Necessity for daycare
	Commitment to the child's interest Increasing bond with child over recent years	No playmates in father's neighborhood
	Diminished conflict with child's mother	

SUMMARY

Element	Finding	Change Since 2/24/94
1. Age, physical, mental condition of child	Six-year-old first grader, physically and mentally healthy	No substantial change
2. Age, physical, mental condition of each parent	Mother: 28-year-old homemaker, physically and emotionally healthy. Father: 33-year-old unmarried self-employed route salesman, physically and emotionally healthy	No substantial change
3. Relationship between each parent and child	Mother: Remains primary caregiver Father: Increasing visitation and bond with child	Mother: No change Father: Enhancement in father-son relationship
4. Needs of child (extended family)	Mother: Stepfather and half-sister Father: Paternal grandmother moved from NC to VA	Mother: Enhanced relationships Father: No substantial change
5. Role of each parent	Mother: Primary caregiver Father: Increased visitation and involvement in extracurriculars. Relocation diminishes certain enhancements	Mother: No substantial change Father: Certain enhancements diminished by relocation
6. Uphold other parent in child's eyes	Both parents are able to communicate and cooperate on major decisions affecting the child	No change
7. Child's preference	Child now 6 years old in first grade and has certain limited insights	Some maturation but not of sufficient experience to voice controlling preference
8. History of abuse	Neither parent alleges abuse	No change
9. Other relevant factors	Mother: Richer educational and cultural opportunities with role model for higher education Father: Concerned about diminishment in frequency and quality of father-son contact	Mother: Meaningful enhancement Father: Potential detriment depending on interim visitation plan

PROPOSED PARENTING PLAN

This examiner proposes the following parenting plan in light of all sources available at this time. The parties independently concurred that the examiner has been given all of the essential information with which to formulate a proposal. At the end of this report this examiner lists some conditions under which the proposal should be reconsidered.

OPINIONS

Change of Circumstance This examiner offers the following opinions with a reasonable degree of psychological certainty:

1. The relocation constitutes a change in clinical circumstances relative to the benchmark Order from Dillard County J&DR of 2/24/94.
2. The changes in circumstances are negative in part and positive in part.
3. Although the original motivation for the relocation arose from the interest of the stepfather and mother, the child benefits substantially with respect to resources and opportunities.
4. The detrimental factors caused by the relocation can be at least partially corrected by revising the visitation schedule and with the understanding that the relocation is temporary.

Decision Making (Legal Custody)   The parents have sufficient capacity for communication and cooperation regarding the major decisions in the child's life, and they have been more successful in this regard in the last 3 years than they were in the first 3 years of the child's life.

Residential Arrangement (Physical Custody)   There is not sufficient clinical evidence to recommend a change in the child's primary residence.

Recommendations: Father-Son Access
1. Midweek and Weekends:
   a. Midweeks: Although a logistical impracticality, there should be a provision for midweek access between the father and son as the father's schedule permits, with 24-hour notice from the father to the mother.
   b. Weekends: The weekend is defined as the earliest opportunity after the last day of the school week until 6 P.M. the night before school reopens.
      i. There will be visitation on 2 weekends per month with the mother being responsible for delivery and pick up of the child to the father's home in Springfield County on one of those weekends.
      ii. The father can exercise visitation rights on the other weekend each month in Newtown. Mother will reimburse the father for up to 2 nights' lodging, not to exceed $70 per night. The mother will also reimburse the father $47 for mileage (24 cents per mile for 194 miles, Springfield to Newtown) when the father exercises his scheduled visitation in Newtown one time per month. The reimbursement for lodging and mileage does not apply for midweek or other additional visits.
      iii. In October 1999 there is a fifth weekend. The parents agreed to meet each other halfway on that weekend.
      iv. This plan does not obligate either parent to drive any greater distance per month than currently required under the present visitation Order. It reduces the child's travel by 50 percent. This recommendation allows the child to maintain his relationship with his father through activities in Newtown without any appreciable increase in out-of-pocket expense.
2. Birthdays and Holidays:
   a. Birthdays: No special arrangements need be made for birthdays, Mother's Day, and Father's Day.
   b. Holidays:
      i. Thanksgiving is defined as the end of the school day preceding the holiday until 6 P.M. the evening before school reopens. The parents will alternate Thanksgiving each year.
      ii. Spring break and other extended school holidays are defined from the close of school until 6 P.M. the evening before school reopens. Those holidays will be shared equally with the father being with his son on the first half of such holidays.
      iii. Christmas is defined as the close of school prior to the holiday until 6 p.m. 2 days before school reopens. The child will be with his father December 26 until 2 days before school reopens.
3. Summer: Summer is defined as 2 days after school closes until 2 days before school reopens. Father and son will have three consecutive weeks in the summer of 1999 to begin immediately after mother's Fourth of July holiday. Mother will deliver the child to father. Father and

mother will meet halfway at the end of the 3-week visit. The parties will finalize details about weekend visitation for June and August of 1999 before the December hearing date.

Other Recommendations

1. Telephone Contacts: Limited only by civility.
2. Medical, Psychological, and Educational Information Sharing: Notwithstanding any other provision of law, neither parent shall be denied access to the academic, medical, or other records of that parent's minor child unless otherwise ordered by the court for good cause shown. The mother will provide the father, in writing, sufficient contact information for the child's school, physician, coaches, and other points of contact for extracurricular activities. The father is responsible for keeping abreast for the child's development by contacting the sources directly. Each parent will notify the other of conditions relating to the child.
3. Communication Between Parents: The parents can communicate by phone, mail, e-mail, and other means from time to time as necessary to address the needs of the child.
4. Other Periods of Parenting Responsibility: Each parent will give the other parent right of first refusal for any other parenting opportunity if the person having parenting responsibility is not available to the child for periods of 3 days or more.
5. Noninterference Clause: Absent a finding by the court that a parent has acted without concern for the child's well-being or best interest, has demonstrated irresponsi-

ble conduct, or has interfered with basic decisions in areas that are the basic responsibility of the other parent, or finding that the activity that is questioned presents a danger to the child's safety or well-being, neither parent nor the court may intervene to restrict activities of parent and child.

Factors Warranting Reconsideration of This Opinion

1. The opinions and recommendations above are predicated on the mother's indication that the relocation is for approximately 18 months (6/16/98–12/16/99). It is reasonable that the relocation could extend until the end of the child's third grading period, which is approximately January 22, 2000. This has an advantage over relocating the child in the middle of a grading period.
2. This examiner would want to reconsider his opinions if presented with new, relevant information that departs substantially from the source material listed herein.
3. This examiner would want to reconsider his opinions if the information provided thus far was shown to be flawed, substantially incomplete, or fraudulent.
4. This examiner would want to reconsider his opinion if there is an aberration in parenting or other compelling change in clinical circumstances before the court hears the evidence on 12/30/98.

Leigh D. Hagan, Ph.D.
Clinical Psychologist
Diplomate, American Board of Forensic Psychology
Affiliate Assistant Clinical Professor of Psychology, VCU

Teaching Point: How does the forensic clinician use the report to facilitate effective testimony?

What is the connection between the FMHA report written in the examiner's office and effective oral testimony in the courtroom? A well-constructed report provides a clear framework for testimony, explains honestly, is legally relevant, and focuses on priorities. It does not waste time. It serves several audiences. A properly prepared report helps the litigant understand what the examiner did. It helps the attorney understand the most significant factors among the many considerations. It focuses the court on the most relevant behavioral science findings in the context of the immediate legal question. It becomes the script for the examiner's testimony. The report should also anticipate the legal objections and scientific attacks likely to arise during cross-examination. It provides a framework for rebuttal testimony for subsequent ethics complaints, which are more likely to arise in custody cases than in any other area of forensic practice.

Where does the report begin? As with any FMHA, the report begins with the law. The legal question is the referral question; it initiates the evaluation and concludes the report. Although the report does not give a legal opinion or a conclusion of law, it must take a position with reasonable scientific certainty if it is to be admissible.

Is the examiner qualified to give an opinion in court? The first issue of any testimony is the qualification of the expert. In this custody case, the examiner served as the neutral evaluator by consent of the parties and secured informed consent at three times in the FMHA. By doing so, the examiner reduced the likelihood of troublesome voir dire in court. When the report clearly documents this framework, the examiner can focus on the relevant findings and opinions rather than responding to extensive questions regarding experience, role, and methods.

Will the report be admitted into evidence? Once the court qualifies the examiner as an expert, the next question is whether the report is relevant and helpful. Lacking either, the court could find the report inadmissible. Relevant means that the report must bear on the legal issue. Because a custody case requires a comparative analysis of the parties, the report and proposed testimony must reflect a FMHA of both parties and must apply those findings to the pertinent legal framework (that varies somewhat across jurisdictions) for considering the child's best interest.

Is the report helpful to the court? A well-constructed report clearly demonstrates that the proposed testimony and its underlying methodology were of a type relied on by others in the same field when performing an evaluation for the same purpose. The information in the report must be of a type not usually within the understanding of ordinary lay people. The report must set forth the scientific merit of the examiner's methodology because, without that foundation, the examiner could be stuck on the witness stand trying to rehabilitate a report that does not bring helpful scientific understanding to the court. Reports that fail to show scientific merit are sometimes referred to as "Cousin Fannie" reports, and they can result in a very awkward moment on the witness stand for the "expert."

Was the FMHA appropriately scientific? A good report demonstrates the fundamentals of scientific methods. By listing in the report the reasons for the referral and providing a thorough iteration of source materials, the expert's testimony is more likely to focus on substantive matters rather than deflecting attacks on bias and prejudice. A well-developed report also alleviates concerns about other potential methodological flaws, such as selective attention to evidence and premature closure of the opinion. Toward that end, the report can facilitate effective testimony by anticipating competing theories of the case, recognizing opposing points of view, and then responding to them in a thoughtful fashion without waving the flag of advocacy when rendering an opinion on custody.

Does the report communicate effectively with the audience? The report that flows from a FMHA should teach, explain, and focus the audience. It is not a vehicle to enhance the ego of its author. Many attorneys and judges are not entirely conversant in the vocabulary of behavioral science. A good report draws on the appropriate body of peer-reviewed scientific subject matters (e.g., psychological testing, parental alienation, attachment theory, separation anxiety, predictions of future behavior) and presents the material in an interesting and instructive style that enlightens the audience. The examiner invites a host of problems on cross-examination by submitting a report that is overly pedantic, excessively technical, internally inconsistent, or whose opinions and recommendations depart substantially from the findings.

What do the FMHA procedures have to do with the legal question? The report should set forth a clear connection between the behavioral science findings and the legal issue before the court. In Virginia, at the time of this custody report, there were nine statutory factors to consider regarding the best interest of the child. The examiner adopted those nine factors as headings throughout the report. This report format greatly facilitated effective testimony. Because the reference points corresponded to the law and the legal questions, it was easier for the attorney, the court, and the expert to stay on the same page, literally and figuratively. The expert did not have to waste time searching through the report when answering questions from the witness stand. This resulted in greater poise and confidence, further enhancing the quality and effectiveness of testimony.

Where should the report end? The report will facilitate effective testimony by stopping at the boundary determined by the examiner's role and the limits of scientific certainty. The testifying expert is a guest in the court. The expert does not take liberties or overstay this welcome. An effective report reflects these principles. In a custody FMHA, the report does not try to "win the day." It concludes with opinions held to a reasonable degree of scientific certainty. If the report is solid in its scientific underpinnings and respectful in its presentation, the expert will not have to fend off attacks about overreaching. This will make for more effective testimony and help to build a solid reputation for future evaluations for the courts.

Case 4

Principle: Testify in an effective manner

This principle is discussed in Chapter 14. It stresses the importance of both substantive and stylistic aspects of testifying effectively. For a more detailed discussion of the substantive aspects of expert testimony, the reader is directed to related guidelines offered by Brodsky (1991, 1999) and principles described by Heilbrun (2001). Empirical research has suggested that several stylistic aspects of expert testimony may be particularly important, including perceived expertise, trustworthiness, and dynamism, each of which may enhance credibility and persuasiveness (see, e.g., Bodsky, 1991; Champagne et al., 1991; Melton et al., 1997; Rosenthal, 1983; Shuman et al., 1994). Others have discussed specific influences such as style of dress, familiarity with courtroom protocol, speaking to the jury, and style of speech (see, e.g., Brodsky, 1991, 1999; Melton et al., 1997).

The present report does not provide an indication of how the forensic clinician would testify more effectively by using such influences as perceived expertise, trustworthiness, style of dress, and approach to communication. However, it is a long and complex evaluation report. The amount of information provided could make it difficult for a decision maker to attend to the entire testimony. It is likely that stylistic influences in expert testimony affect a kind of "cognitive shortcut" for decision makers, whereby forensic clinicians who are seen as more expert and trustworthy are accorded greater credibility and influence, even when all the information is not absorbed by the decision maker (see Heilbrun, 2001, for a more extensive discussion of this point).

Gerald Cooke, Ph.D.
Margaret Cooke, Ph.D., P.C.
Clinical and Forensic Psychology

CUSTODY EVALUATION REFERRAL AND PROCEDURES

This evaluation was agreed on by the parties and their attorneys. The evaluation consisted of the following: Mrs. Z and Mr. Z were seen in the office on separate occasions. The procedure was the same with both adults. In addition to a clinical interview and history, each was administered the following tests:

1. Minnesota Multiphasic Personality Inventory-2: an objective personality test indicating test-taking attitude and the nature and degree of psychopathology;
2. Rotter Incomplete Sentences Blank: a projective test providing information on needs, attitudes, values, and the quality of interpersonal relationships;
3. Rorschach Inkblot Technique: a projective test revealing unconscious fears, wishes,

conflicts, and the degree to which reality is accurately perceived;

4. Parents Questionnaire: a form on which the parent provides information about the child's developmental landmarks, medical history, interests, and emotional and behavioral characteristics. There is also a section on parenting style, and one asking the parent to estimate the percent of caretaking done during the last year prior to the separation.

The home visit was made to Mr. Z when the children were with him and to Mrs. Z when the children were with her. The children were seen together in the office. Subsequent to the formal interviews, I had follow-up phone calls from each of the parents regarding subsequent incidents. The children, T and K, were each administered the following tests:

1. Kinetic Family Drawing: a projective test indicating the child's perception of himself/herself and his/her family constellation;
2. Children's Incomplete Sentences Blank: a projective test revealing the child's perception of himself/herself and the people and environment around him/her.

No tests were administered to B (the third sibling) because of his age. Each of the children was also interviewed separately.

In addition, I had the opportunity to review the following records and make the following telephone consultations:

1. Petition for Emergency Hearing
2. Temporary Court Order
3. Bank records showing that Mrs. Z cashed the children's bonds on aa/bb/cccc (the issue here is that Mrs. Z says that she cashed them after the separation because Mr. Z wasn't giving her any money, and Mr. Z says that she cashed them before the separation for her own use. The discrepancy may have to do with the date one considers as the separation. They both agree that Mrs. Z left for the shore with the children and that they were never physically together again. However, Mr. Z found that instead of return-

ing she moved with the children to her mother's house);

4. Paperwork from Aetna Insurance Company that led Mr. Z to believe that when Mrs. Z saw Dr. X for treatment, part of that treatment was because of a drug problem. While the coding on the Aetna form includes something that means "drug management," a review of the form submitted by Dr. X (which Dr. supplied to me) indicates that the treatment was only for therapy. A telephone consultation with Dr. X confirmed that there was no drug problem or drug management. He indicated that Mrs. Z consulted him because she was upset when Mr. Z did not return T and was seeking advice. She was very concerned about all three children, because apparently the boys had worried that the same thing might happen to them, as well as worrying about whether they would see their sister again;

5. Forms filed with Dawson County by Mr. Z regarding two incidents: One reported incident (admitted to by Mrs. Z and documented by the children, as will be discussed later in this report) when he was returning the children, his wife reached in the car window and smacked him hard across the face. In that complaint for harassment he also referred to a prior incident in which Mrs. Z was reported to have struck him in the head with a duffel bag, also in front of the children. (That incident, too, was documented by the interview with the children);

6. School records on T accompanied by a letter from her fourth grade teacher, indicating that during the period T was back at school (during the 3 weeks she was with her father) she was happy and doing well academically;

7. Records on T from the School District through the third marking period showing that, despite being absent for the 3-week period, she is doing very well. There are also records for K for the first grade that show that he is working for the most part at a "satisfactory" level, but does show some difficulties. He has problems with attention and concentration, and other problems (somewhat less significant) in the following areas: listening

when others speak and read, understanding and following oral directions, exercising self-control, staying on task, organizing time and material, and showing effort. Despite these problems, the report card does show improvement, particularly in completing his homework on time, from the second to the third grading period;

8. Pictures from Mr. Z supporting his contention that Mrs. Z smoked in the car and in the home with the children;

9. Telephone consultation with the staff of the Nursery School where T, K, and B attended. They indicate that most of their contact was with their mother, though occasionally their father picked up. They observed that she is a very good and concerned mother and came to all the nursery school functions. She would talk about the children's problems. She was much more involved than the father;

10. Telephone consultation with the head of B, T, and K's daycare. B had told her about the incident in which his mother hit his father. She said all three have a good relationship with both parents. B is doing very well behaviorally and academically; although she describes him as a normal 5-year-old who plays rough sometimes, she does not observe anything out of the ordinary. K and T's behavior is also fine;

11. Telephone consultation with Mrs. Z's individual therapist, who indicated that for insurance purposes he diagnosed her as an Adjustment Disorder reactive to the marital situation and the conflict over the children, but otherwise observed no emotional problems or pathology. He indicated that she feels her husband provokes her and that she has reacted to that in the past, but has been working on taking responsibility for her behavior in reaction to his provocation. She is timely in her appointments and responsible about cancellations;

12. Telephone consultation with Ms. A, who worked with the family for several months. She indicated that all three of the children told her that they want to live with their mother. They did say that Dad sometimes says negative things about Mom. They also report that Mom

had screamed at Dad in the past but not at them. They feel they get better care from their mom. They said that they go all weekend with Dad without brushing their teeth or taking a bath, while they bathe on alternate nights at Mom's. They are among the more active children that Ms. A has seen but can be obedient and focused. For example, they do pick up toys when their mother says to do so. B is more active. Ms. A sees both boys as somewhat immature. At the time Ms. A saw her, she believed T was depressed. Ms. A has had more contact with Mrs. Z. She sees no emotional problems or pathology in Mrs. Z. She indicated that Mrs. Z has been able to acknowledge when she "screwed up and shouldn't have handled it that way" and has shown the ability to change in response to that perception. Ms. A obtained information that both parents have smacked the children at times but have stopped in the course of the custody evaluation. However, Ms. A does not believe that the smacking was very frequent or severe by either parent;

13. Telephone consultation with Mr. Z's therapist. She indicated that she saw him six times and the last session was 12/10/96. He was distressed over the situation and also had financial concerns about his wife having custody, but did not raise issues regarding parenting;

14. Telephone consultation with Dr. B, who worked with Mr. Z two or three times and saw the children twice. She indicated Mr. Z seemed pretty tuned in and sensitive to the children. She said the children did not seem very stressed. Mr. Z felt that both he and Mrs. Z had spoken inappropriately to the children at the time. Both times Dr. B saw the children it was in Mr. Z's presence and she did not see them separately;

15. Telephone consultations with a good friend of both parents. She confirmed Mr. Z's statement that he spent quality time with the children on the weekends. Her observations were primarily based during the summer period down at the shore, since she has a shore house near them. She said that her observations of Mrs. Z indicates she is a good mother

and the children are clean and always well-cared for. She saw nothing deficient the parenting skills of either.

Both parents should be aware that this report does not contain all of the allegations and counterallegations made. Though I realize they may be important to the parties, I have omitted those that, in my opinion, are trivial and/or irrelevant to custody issues. Where "he said-she said" material is presented, it is to advise the court regarding the particular issue. This examiner assumes neither the truth nor falsity of any allegations or counterallegations by either party unless it is confirmed by my testing and clinical observations or independent external corroboration.

RELEVANT HISTORY

While they agreed on the date of separation, they disagreed on how this came about. Mr. Z said that on that date Mrs. Z told him that she wanted him out of the house, though at the time she was at the shore with the children. He came home and found that she had moved the children to her mother's, and near the end of the month she moved to the two-bedroom apartment where she still lives. Mrs. Z said that during the summer, when he came down the shore on the weekends she would leave and go back to the home. She added that he had agreed to leave the home, but 3 days before they were to return he said he wouldn't, and that is why she took the children and went to her mother's.

Each parent was asked about problems in the marriage. Mr. Z indicated that they were both headstrong, neither bent to the other's view enough and therefore communication was not that good. He said finances were also a problem because he didn't like to spend, and she liked to spend everything. He also indicated that Mrs. Z used drugs and alcohol socially, including beer, marijuana, and crack and powder cocaine. He also felt that how the children are being raised is a problem. He wanted them to go to church every Sunday and then Catholic School, but she felt public school was good enough and didn't care whether they went to church every Sunday. He indicated they did go to Catholic School until she left, and then she placed them in public school. He indi-

cated that he took the kids to church about every other Sunday, and she never went except for a christening. He also reported that he never liked smacking and hitting except on the rear, but they would fight over it because she would hit the children, even on the face. (As will be discussed further, it seems apparent that both parents hit the children and that there is not as much difference in how this is done as Mr. Z would represent.) He also indicated that Mrs. Z seemed to resent that she was no longer the major focus after T was born.

Mrs. Z perceived the problems differently. She said that Mr. Z was very controlling; for example, she was not allowed to be on the phone with friends for more than 10 minutes and had to explain the money she spent. She said that money and sex were also intertwined, and she was not allowed spending money unless she subjected herself to his sexual desires. Mrs. Z also said that Mr. Z is a slob and recalled the first summer at the shore when she came home with the children; it appeared the toilet had never been cleaned and the sheets were never changed all summer. She said that he would come home from softball and want to have sex and would get angry if she asked him to shower first. She also reported that they never really got along and never did anything together. She said sports was important for him, but he never did anything with her. This examiner discussed with Mrs. Z some of the issues Mr. Z had raised, and she indicated that she went along with Catholic School though she thought public school was fine. She felt there was no disagreement on childrearing because he was never around. She said he would smack the children because they bothered him when he was reading the newspaper or watching TV. She also said that he hit the children on the average of once a weekend, and has also kicked or punched them and thrown things at them when they have angered him. She said he would smack them wherever his reach landed the blow. When she was asked if she hit the children, she indicated that after trying to reason with them and giving them time out she would. She said she has not done it often or in a long time; rather, she said, she had started to discipline them by taking away something, separating them, or sending them to their rooms. She said he never had a problem with her smacking the kids, was never really around to know, and that it really seldom happened. She indicated that she has smacked them for saying "F you," but they don't talk like that often because they know they will get a smack in the mouth from her. While she said that she knows Mr. Z does have a problem with smacking them in the mouth, he will hit wherever he reaches and that includes the head. She indicated that he never played games with them. She reported that on weekends at the shore he would go crabbing or to the beach with them, while she went shopping for groceries. She said that he would then complain about it because she had gone shopping for an hour and a half and be angry at her, asking where she had been and calling her names such as "wacko" and "loser," often in front of the children.

Each parent was asked about child care in the marriage. Mrs. Z indicated, and Mr. Z agreed, that when T was about 6 to 8 months old, Mrs. Z went back to work, at first part-time and then full-time, though Mrs. Z said full-time was during a 3-month separation and for a period after that. They agreed that she stopped working when she was pregnant with K. She said that other than one year at Christmas, she did not work again until after the separation. She reported that Mr. Z would leave at 7:30 in the morning and would almost never return home until 8:00 P.M. Mr. Z disagreed, indicating that in the non-summer months he would be home at 7:00 P.M. and then in the summer months at 6:00 P.M. Both acknowledged that Mrs. Z was the primary caretaker from the time she stopped working. Mr. Z said that he wanted her to be at home and worked hard to make a good enough living so that she could do that. Mrs. Z indicated that he got home so late that he never had a meal with them during the week in the non-summer months. She said that the reason he left earlier in the summer was to make a 6:45 softball game. Therefore, while he would occasionally stop home and eat, he would then go to the game. She said he also played hockey Sunday afternoon. She was resentful that he could leave work early for softball but not for his family, and that the Sunday afternoon hockey also interfered with family outings. She said as the children got older their bedtime moved from 7:30 to 8:00, and presently to 8:30.

She reported that sometimes he would get home at 8:00, and they would still be awake; after 5 minutes, he would ask when they were going to bed. She described him as basically never around and never doing very much with the children. She also pointed out that she has been at home with the children for 8 years and he never had any complaints, and that if she was unfit or unbalanced, as he is now claiming, he should have complained before. She believed that his reason is anger over her following through with the divorce. She felt that he has no idea how to care for the children.

Mr. Z said that in the non-summer months he would be involved with them on the weekends, either in the house or by taking them somewhere. He reported that in recent years when he took the kids, she didn't go. In the summer at the shore, he said, he would come down Friday night and described the kids as "mine" from Friday night until he left for work Monday morning. (As mentioned earlier, there is some support for his statement that he spent a good deal of quality time with the children on the weekends at the shore.) In the non-summer months, he said, he would see T off to the bus in the morning and might or might not see B or K, depending on whether they were awake. He acknowledged that in the evenings he would miss dinner a lot, but said when he got home the children would be with him while he ate dinner, and then after dinner until bedtime.

Though there are some discrepancies in the parents' account of child care, it does appear clear, and is acknowledged by both, that Mrs. Z was the primary caretaker.

Each parent was asked about events since the separation. Mr. Z said he saw B and K the next day at Mrs. Z mother's house (T was in school). He added that it was agreed that he could take them overnight, and shortly thereafter he began having them alternate weekends, picking them up between 5:00 and 7:00 P.M. Friday and returning them Sunday at 7:00 P.M. In addition, he has them Wednesday night from around 5:00 or 6:00 until 8:00 for dinner. They live 45 minutes apart, so transportation is an issue. Each parent was asked how this arrangement has worked. Mr. Z indicated that it is not enough time for him, but in the weeks prior to the evaluation, Mrs. Z had given him extra time with the children when they were off school. He also indicated that three or four of her weekends she has given the children to him, and he said that whenever she lets him have extra time he will take the children. He felt that her partying is more important to her, indicating that she drinks and uses drugs. He also said that on occasions she has been volatile, and he thinks that may be associated with drug and alcohol use. He said that the children want to be with him, and T said once that she wants to be able to see him every day. He said B and K ask why can't they stay with him for 10 days and Mom for 10 days. The children have witnessed a lot of conflict, he reported, and that is not good for them. However, he felt that such conflict is diminishing. He was pleasantly surprised with their adjustment. He said Catholic School was more challenging for T, but she is a tremendous student and is doing well. He reported that K is interested in his first grade. Mr. Z acknowledged that on their weekend of 9/27/96, he took the three children and returned only the boys, keeping T. He did so because she seemed to be the most upset and wanted to be with him, he said; he subsequently kept her for 3 weeks and reregistered her at school. There was an emergency hearing in which she was returned to her mother. He showed me a letter that T wrote when she was returned to her mother; it basically said that her mother is being unfair, and she is better off with Daddy.

When asked about how things have gone since the separation, Mrs. Z focused primarily on Mr. Z taking T and not letting her see T for those 3 weeks. Mrs. Z believed that during that time T was going to Mr. Z's sister's house after school and he wasn't arriving to pick her up until 8:00 P.M., so he was not getting homework done with her. Mrs. Z said it had to be close to 9:00 P.M. before T got to bed, and her usual bedtime was 8:30. Mrs. Z was curious about why he took T and not the other two, and speculated that it was because they are younger and need more attention. She also said that things have not gone well because he has filled the children's heads with "nasty things." She reported that he gave her no support, and she had to cash in the children's savings bonds (the timing of which was discussed earlier), and he told the children that their

mommy spent their money, though he didn't tell them that he wasn't giving her any money to take care of them. She said that she did tell the children about why she cashed their bonds. She said he has stated in front of the kids that she is happy when she is not with the children on the weekends, and it made the children feel that she doesn't want to be with them and that is the reason they have to go with their father. She said that he has also told them that she was going to come and break his door down, adding that she knows this because the children came to her and asked her if she was going to do that, and told her that their father said she was. They also asked if she threatened his life with a knife, and that their father had showed them a suit that had been cut with a knife. Mrs. Z traced this to an argument a couple of years ago over a DUI that Mr. Z had received, and that he was still coming home late and drinking. Mrs. Z also indicated that T stopped wanting to go with him for the last several weekends before this evaluation. Mrs. Z said that T told her that her father never spent time with her, and they constantly had cousins over who were boys. Mrs. Z indicated that Mr. Z has always idolized the boys and never paid much attention to T. She also said there are problems with the visitation because he doesn't bathe the children. She said they have only bathed at his house twice; both times, she added, were after she said he could keep them longer if he bathed them before he brought them home. She also reported that the children tell her they never brush their teeth at his house. In addition, she is concerned that the children watch violent R-rated movies, such as *The Crow* and *Dangerous Minds* while they are at his house. She said that after seeing *Copy Cat*, B had a nightmare. At her house, she indicated, they see only Disney and family movies.

Mrs. Z acknowledged the incident in which she smacked Mr. Z across the face in front of the children. She said that he was always late dropping off and picking up the children, often as late as a half-hour to an hour. She added that on the date of the incident, she had run an errand and was 5 minutes late returning. His response was to call her a "wacko," "simpleton," and "loser" in front of the children, she reported. She went on to say that she asked him to stop, and he started to roll up the window on her arm, which is when she hit him. She said that she was found guilty, but that Mr. Z lied on the stand and said he never said anything like that to her.

PARENTAL WISHES REGARDING CUSTODY

Each parent was asked what they want at this time. Mr. Z wanted primary physical custody and shared legal custody. However, Mr. Z indicated that if this evaluator determined that Mrs. Z was a stable and good parent and did not have a drug problem, he would accept shared custody. Under those circumstances, he continued, he would want Mrs. Z to move back to the area, even into the marital home, and he would move out if he had to. He felt it would be better for the children to be back in their neighborhood and school. Mrs. Z wanted to retain primary custody and have the children see their father as they do now, but she wants the Wednesday night time to be earlier (at 7:30), partly because he is always late. She said that he had them more over the Christmas holidays than she did, and tried to take them when they are off school—and that is okay with her. She gave examples of other times when she has let him have the children. She generally wanted major holidays to be split and alternated. She said that he can have them for 2 weeks in the summer. She was aware that he wanted them all summer but felt that he can't take care of three children.

Each parent was asked why they felt the children would be better off under the arrangement they proposed. Mr. Z went through a list of five areas based on literature he has read, including spiritual, physical, intellectual, educational, and social. He indicated that he has been their connection to church all along. He acknowledged that perhaps she is better in the physical, indicating that she was the one who used to take them to the doctor and dentist, though he has taken T to the dentist twice since. He also acknowledged that she is a neater person. He thought he was better in his educational background and job. He has always been concerned about saving money for their college and said that Mrs. Z has seen no need for that, as no one in her family went to college. He reported that he was always the one

who went to parent-teacher conferences, while Mrs. Z stayed home with the children. Socially, he indicated that he has an extended family and takes the children to see their uncles and cousins. In addition to these reasons, he also felt that he is more stable, citing the incident in which she slapped him and his report that she threatened him with a knife. He said that she gets so angry that she is out of control; this includes hitting the children as well as hitting him.

Mrs. Z felt that the children are better off in her care because she is emotionally expressive and Mr. Z is not—he does not cuddle them, hold them when they are sick, and so on. She indicated that the children feel safe when they are with her because she has always been there for them and they know that she takes care of them well. She felt that she knows them better than anybody and that taking care of the children is something she has done extremely well. She said that they feel happy with her and can laugh and be silly and goofy, but at the same time they know she has rules. They know Mom can holler and scream but that she loves them, she indicated, adding that they are comfortable coming to her for hugs and kisses and don't feel that way with their father, though they do know that he loves them. She indicated that in her care they have done well in school. She said K had a bedwetting problem, but it has been getting better since the separation.

EVALUATION OF MR. Z

Psychological evaluation was conducted with each parent. Psychological evaluation of Mr. Z reveals the following: During the evaluation he was slightly hypomanic and appeared to be both anxious and somewhat flustered. However, he was enthusiastic, pleasant, cooperative, and spontaneous. He was also psychologically minded and introspective. Mr. Z approached the testing in a candid and straightforward manner, showing less defensiveness than most parents in a custody evaluation. Despite his appearance on interview, the testing shows that he has a very low level of subjective anxiety. Stress is more likely to be experienced through somatic channels. His low level of anxiety, along with scales indicating a tendency to be outgoing and spontaneous, may lead him at times to fail to inhibit statements and behaviors that are impulsive or inappropriate. Yet he showed some awareness of this and later was able to recognize and attempt to modify such behaviors. Mr. Z is a very competitive individual who is motivated to succeed and transfers those same values to his children. Independence and self-sufficiency are important to him. However, social relationships are also important to him, and he feels he gets along well with people. He was deeply concerned about the time he will have with his children, and this examiner gets the sense that since the separation he has begun to see what he has missed by not being as available to them in the past and wants to change that in the future. He seemed very proud of his children; however, this did not keep him from being aware of their behavioral and emotional characteristics and problems. On the Parents Questionnaire he showed a good knowledge of each of their emotional and behavioral characteristics. Projective testing of Mr. Z indicated that at times he has some difficulty responding to ambiguous situations. His response initially may be somewhat vague and disorganized, but after awhile he is able to respond appropriately. His response to the Rorschach card that is usually identified with perception of the females is interesting because it is consistent with Mrs. Z's view that in their relationship she felt like a trophy—usually kept up on a shelf but sometimes taken down, dusted, and shown off. He does tend to see women in this manner rather than in a deeper interpersonal way, as well as to be overly evaluative, which includes being very critical of them sometimes. On the Parents Questionnaire he showed an average knowledge for fathers of his children's developmental landmarks. He knew the names of their friends. On the parenting part of the Questionnaire he emphasized verbal expression of love and, particularly with the boys, a kind of masculine interaction such as high-fives. However, he also indicated that he is physically expressive of his love for his children. In terms of discipline, he acknowledged that he can yell loudly and that when other methods fail he will smack his children on the butt. He was able to review his parenting behavior and recognized that at times he has become too angry, adding that he is making an effort to control that. He was aware of his chil-

dren's individual needs, strengths, and abilities, and has appropriate ways of meeting and responding to these. He was able to describe each child as an individual in this regard, and was able to tailor his responses to their individual characteristics.

To summarize regarding Mr. Z's psychological functioning, he has strengths and weaknesses and specific personality dynamics, but there is no evidence of psychopathology and he is seen as a loving parent. As will be discussed below, he does lack some parenting capacities and will need to work on these, but the nature of his personality is such that I believe he will be able to take this feedback and work diligently at improving weaknesses.

EVALUATION OF MRS. Z

Psychological evaluation of Mrs. Z reveals the following: During the evaluation she was very friendly and cooperative. However, she was also very emotionally responsive, both verbally and in terms of facial expressions. At times she became very loud and angry; at other times she was close to tears or crying. Despite this, and her admission that she can scream a lot at her children, this appears to be more a style based on attitude and background than an indication of personality pathology, as the testing does not give any indication that anger or emotional control is a significant problem. As part of her history she denies any use of illicit drugs, inconsistent with what Mr. Z had represented. This examiner is not able to independently corroborate whether drug use has occurred and, if so, whether it has affected her care of the children.

Mrs. Z approached the testing in a candid and straightforward manner showing less defensiveness than most people in a custody evaluation. The testing indicates good self-esteem, an average tension level, and no difficulty with anger or emotional control. Her perception was that it takes a lot to get her angry. However, there appear to be certain types of situations in which she is quick to anger and then has difficulty controlling it. Part of this may relate to her own childhood, with an alcoholic father who beat her mother and occasionally the children. Part of her emotionality in dealing with Mr. Z may be a reaction to the residual feelings from her own childhood. She felt the best part of her life has to do with her role with her children, and she was very concerned about their emotional well-being. She is struggling with the way she has allowed herself to be treated over the years of her marriage. She does appear to be a highly emotional person. She acknowledged that her feelings are easily hurt, and she cries when this happens. The testing is also consistent with this emotionality, which also contributes to the positive type of emotionality in the relationship with her children. She also prizes her ability to be funny and goofy with her children. On the Parents Questionnaires she showed an excellent knowledge of all three children's developmental landmarks and a much more precise knowledge than Mr. Z. She knew the names of her children's friends. She was very aware of her children's emotional and behavioral characteristics. In addition to verbally expressing her love for her children, she was oriented toward physical contact, including cuddling, rolling around on the floor, dancing, and so on. Her reasons for disciplining are appropriate, and her preferred method is timeout, though she acknowledged that at times, she has spanked. She believed that she became more angry than she should once with T, but denied that this ever happened with either of the boys. This is not consistent with what this examiner has observed. It also is somewhat inconsistent with her other acknowledgments that the children know that Mom can scream and yell; perhaps she is not as aware as she should be of the degree to which she may do this. She, like Mr. Z, was aware of the children as individuals and knowledgeable about their needs, activities, and abilities, and has appropriate involvement and ways of meeting these needs. She stressed the importance of praising the children for their accomplishments. To summarize the psychological evaluation of Mrs. Z, she has her individual personality characteristics and strengths and weaknesses, but is seen as a competent and loving parent. There is no question that she is an emotional person and that in certain instances she has lost control over her emotions, particularly in dealing with Mr. Z, and that this is something that she has been working on (according to her therapist) and continues to need to work on.

HOME VISIT: MR. Z

The first contact with the children was the home visit to the father's, which was the marital home. The boys share a room and a bunk bed. K is on the top bunk, and Mr. Z mentioned that he has fallen out a couple of times but did not appear to be aware that he could put a rail on to prevent that. T has her own room. Mr. Z. served them dinner of spaghetti and meatballs and salad, although it appeared that preparing meals is not something he is accustomed to. For example, he forgot to provide them with napkins until about two thirds of the way through the meal. There was a frantic and disorganized sense around the meal time. While Mr. Z was upbeat and joking with the children, they all tended to be somewhat defiant. This was particularly true of K, after there was conflict between him and B over a pool game. B swung a pool stick at K, and K threw a pool ball at him in what was a dangerous interaction. Mr. Z created the situation by being insensitive to the needs of the children. He let them play the pool game, but instead of having the children play a game together taking turns, he allowed K to play a whole game while the others just watched. This took about 15 minutes, and it was clear that the others were bored. Though T should have gone next, he let B go instead, and it was when B started his game that K began to act up and Mr. Z had to intervene. He was right to intervene and said that K had to go upstairs and they would talk, but the way K ignored this direction suggested that this is not Mr. Z's usual approach. He then asked the children about homework and wanted T to go out to the van and get her book bag. She refused repeatedly. He took her off and talked to her and then she went out; this examiner could not hear what he said to her. By that point, it was too late for her to have her turn in the pool game. This appeared to be consistent with a general impression of this examiner and with Mrs. Z's comment that Mr. Z tends to favor the boys over T. When this examiner first arrived, Mr. Z said that T had been upset and was crying. Mr. Z indicated that she was upset because of some of the things that were reportedly said about her mother in the course of this evaluation. I gave T the opportunity to talk to me separately, and we discussed this. It became clear to me, based on other evidence as well, that both parents talk to the children about the present situation in highly inappropriate ways; this has been extremely difficult for T. T then asked me who I was going to say they should live with, and I indicated that I was not ready to make a recommendation like that until I completed the evaluation. She then spontaneously and forcefully stated that she wanted to live with her mother. Overall, the home visit to Mr. Z raised serious concerns about his parenting practices.

HOME VISIT: MRS. Z

The home visit to Mrs. Z's was to her two-bedroom apartment. They have a dog and a cat. Mrs. Z and T share a room, and the boys share a room. The home is neat, clean, and child-oriented. Mrs. Z does continue to be somewhat loud and emotionally labile, but she is much better with the children than Mr. Z had been, and they respond better to her. She made some effort during dinner to reinforce table manners, saying please, asking that the children not use their fingers, and the like—none of which were observed with Mr. Z. Nevertheless, the boys are not particularly well socialized. Mrs. Z sets limits, and unlike with Mr. Z, the children tend to respond to them and do what she asks, rather than being defiant as they were with him. For example, she insisted that the boys wash their hands before dinner. B got angry and sulked, and she ignored him for a few minutes, appropriately, and then distracted him well. All the children scraped their dishes after dinner and put them in the sink. Mrs. Z displayed a good combination of limits, a sense of humor, and drawing the children out. When B kicked her and she said it hurt, he began crying. I observed that the apartment is on a cul-de-sac and there are lots of other kids so that it provides a safe and good area for the children to play outside and still be within sight of Mrs. Z from the window.

EVALUATION OF THE CHILDREN

For the children's office visit, Mr. Z arrived first and then Mrs. Z arrived with the children. B was loud and Mr. Z made some attempt to quiet him.

When they were all leaving after the evaluation, it was Mrs. Z who took the primary responsibility for cleaning up and having the children clean up. Mr. Z's interactions seemed to be more with the boys than with T, consistent with other observations.

Evaluation of T   The evaluation of T revealed the following: On interview she was quiet and seemed sad. She is very upset and sensitive to the conflict between her parents and the mean things they say to each other in front of the children. She confirmed that they never take baths while with Dad, while she showers every other day at her mother's. They also do not brush their teeth at Dad's, while their mother reminds them to every night. She said that her parents "yell about the same." She said her mother usually doesn't hit them, and they would have to do something really bad to be hit by her. She indicated that her father smacks them when they hit each other, but added that this was on the butt. She stated that her mother does not question what her father does, but her father does ask them questions about where their mother goes over the weekend and similar questions. This makes T uncomfortable, and she would like him to stop doing this. She also acknowledged that their father is usually late returning them to their mother because he leaves late. She, as the boys, indicated that their father doesn't usually serve them salad, and it became apparent to this examiner that it was something done only for my benefit. Both parents helped with homework equally. T indicated there have been times she didn't want to go with her father, but she described it as a long time ago and said that she forgot why. She indicated that she liked the school better, saying that the math is easier but the spelling is harder, but that is good because she is good in spelling. She has never seen her father hit her mother, but she has seen her mother hit her father two times, once was the slapping incident in the car and once with a duffel bag. However, with the slapping incident, she indicated that though Dad was really late, their mother wasn't at the apartment so her dad began yelling at her mother. She said that her father curses her mother and calls her "wacko," "psycho," and "loser." However, she added that her mother also curses her father. When asked what this examiner could recommend to make things better, she reiterated her desire that her parents not fight.

T's testing shows that she is embarrassed and upset about the divorce situation. She is a sensitive and psychologically minded child, and while in many ways this is a very positive quality, it makes her exquisitely sensitive to the family conflict. She is also sensitive in her relationship with her peers. When this was explored with her, she indicated that for the 3 weeks that she stayed with her dad and returned to school, she was happy to be there because of her friends and her school, but still didn't want to live with her dad. She indicated that she would rather live with her mom and added this is because she is more caring, is really neat, and doesn't let the home get really dirty, whereas he does. She indicated that her father cleaned up before this evaluator's visit to impress me but that at mom's house it is always clean. Despite her preference, the testing indicates that she does have a positive view of both parents. She perceived both parents as very caring and her mother also as very sensitive. She perceived both parents as thinking that she is very smart. Consistent with the importance of independence and self-sufficiency for Mr. Z, she perceived her father as expecting her to think for herself and saw her mother as expecting her to be good. She tended to see her mother as the more nurturing parent, as revealed both by the Kinetic Family Drawing and the Incomplete Sentence Blank.

To summarize regarding T, there is no question that she is upset and sad over the current situation and wishes that her parents would stop fighting. She does seem to have a consistent preference to live with her mother, and this appears to be a well-reasoned preference in terms of both parenting and hygiene types of issues.

Evaluation of K   On interview with K he was calm. On test tasks he worked attentively. He indicated that both parents do fun things with them and both help with homework. He said that he gets upset over yelling by his father. He acknowledged that his mother also yells, but it seems to upset him less. When asked about hitting, he indicated that once his mother hit him in the face, and once his dad hit him on the shoulder. He indicated that all of the children have been smacked by both parents, and they hit about the same. He then indicated that for 3 weeks they got no smacks. This examiner offered that perhaps they had been really good, and he spontaneously stated "That's when you came over." I asked him if there was anything else different when I came over, and he indicated that he couldn't believe it when his dad served salad. He indicated that Mom doesn't usually make salad either, but she does so more than dad. Certain questions asked of K suggested that he was not a good informant because he has difficulty with frequencies and time duration. He tended to make general statements when, upon exploration, he was really responding to single or infrequent incidents. This was true regarding questions about baths and teeth brushing. When asked about videos, he indicated that the ones Dad gets are cool but the ones Mom gets are boring. However, he then went on to describe what are basically violent movies at his father's and appropriate movies at his mother's, corroborating Mrs. Z's concern. When K was asked if he wanted to change the current arrangement, he indicated that he did not and wanted to keep it the way it is. However, he did not have a well-reasoned preference. When asked why he didn't want to change it, he responded "Because they might want to get along with each other again and they might not." When asked if he wanted more or less time with Dad, he indicated one more day, and his reason was because almost every day they get to go to the video store with him. When asked if his dad gets him back to his mother on time, he replied not usually. In response to several questions, it became clear that K has been told of various incidents by both parents.

Testing of K indicates that he wants to perceive the whole family as intact, but he tends to feel somewhat isolated and distant from the rest of the family. Despite this, he perceived both parents positively and believed that both parents perceive him positively. However, he did express some concern over his father's anger and cannot understand why he gets as angry as he does. He seemed to perceive his mother's anger as more appropriate to their behavior. He felt things would be better if his parents got together again.

He has a good self-image and views himself as smart and good looking.

Evaluation of B   On interview with B, he indicated that he has fun with both parents and is also upset when his parents fight. He indicated that he wants to change the current arrangement and would like it if Dad and Mom had the same number of days, and insisted that this was his own idea. It is obvious that he, too, has seen movies with violence in them at his father's, but it was his mother who told them they were R-rated. Because of his age and immaturity, minimal interviewing was conducted with B.

SUMMARY AND RECOMMENDATIONS

Several factors emerge that are relevant to the custody recommendation. First, it is clear that Mrs. Z has always been the primary caretaker, but also (with the possible exceptions of weekends at the shore) that Mr. Z has had relatively little involvement with the children. It also seems clear that despite his concern that Mrs. Z has emotional problems, Mrs. Z is correct in stating that this apparently was never a sufficient enough issue for him to get involved during the marriage and has only become an issue since the separation. I find her to be an emotional woman who certainly has a temper and can get loud, but I see this as part of a general emotionality that includes many positive characteristics as well and can lead to great warmth, humor, and very positive interaction with her children as well. However, she certainly needs to work on controlling her anger in dealing with Mr. Z even if he is provocative.

Similarly, Mr. Z needs to work on refraining from those kinds of provocative statements, particularly in front of the children. Both need to cease making negative statements about the other to or in front of the children. Thus, it is my opinion that we can dispense with Mr. Z's allegation that the children should not be in their mother's custody because she has serious emotional problems. Whether she has used drugs and, if so, in a manner that would affect her care of the children is something that I was unable to determine. Another relevant issue is T's and K's preference to have the arrangement stay essentially the way it

is now; it is my opinion that K's preference is not well-reasoned, but T's is. B is too young to have a consistent and well-reasoned preference. I believe that hitting is a non-issue in the sense that both parents are guilty of doing this. I would advise both parents to rely more heavily on other means of disciplining the children. This is particularly true because I find both boys to be somewhat immature and undersocialized. Both parents, but particularly Mr. Z, need to put more emphasis on manners, limits on behavior, and having an environment, such as mealtimes, that is more organized and calmer. Both parents, but particularly Mr. Z, seem to contribute to a somewhat frantic and disorganized situation that, rather than helping the children to exercise control over their behavior, exacerbates the situation. Mr. Z needs to learn more about parenting. The situation in which he let one child play a game while the other two became bored and waited, certainly was insensitive to the needs and tolerances of children of that age. The resulting conflict between the boys was quite dangerous. These children need even more than most to learn to take turns, follow rules, and so on, and this is the responsibility of the parents. In that regard, Mrs. Z was better able to consistently set limits, and the children responded better to those limits. Finally, there is the issue of hygiene and health. It appears quite clear that Mr. Z does not make the children bathe or brush their teeth regularly, and that his house is frequently dirty. This is not the case with Mrs. Z. This is part of the more general finding that Mrs. Z seems more accustomed to parenting the children than is Mr. Z.

These considerations lead me to a recommendation that there should be shared legal custody but that Mrs. Z have primary physical custody of the children. I would recommend that Mr. Z continue to have alternate weekends with the children from Friday evening. I recognize that it is a considerable distance from his home to where the children live with their mother, but if he could arrange his work schedule so he could take them to school Monday morning, then I see no reason why he should not also have them overnight Sunday night to Monday morning. This would give him more time with the children, which, though not for particularly good reasons, is something the boys want. However, if this is done, he must implement consistent bathing, tooth brushing, and house cleaning, as well as following some of the other recommendations as far as table manners and other aspects of socialization. He should continue to have the children on Wednesday evening, and I see no problem with him taking them to his sister's (who lives closer to Mrs. Z) rather than making the long trip back. However, either the time should be changed or Mr. Z should adhere to the schedule in returning the children on time, particularly since it is a school night. The same is true if he is going to be returning them on Sunday night so they can be in bed in time to be properly rested for school on Monday. I would certainly recommend that any time Monday is a school holiday the children should remain with Mr. Z until either Monday night or when he takes them to school Tuesday morning, if he can arrange that. Mrs. Z indicated that she has already let Mr. Z have extra time when the children are off school, and I would recommend that that be written in to the Court Order so that on days off from school the children can be with their father if he can arrange it. To some extent, this should also apply to holidays and school vacations. While I feel that the holidays themselves should be alternated and split in the usual manner, I would recommend that at times such as the Christmas holidays, Mr. Z get a little extra time. Similarly, depending on how much time Mr. Z could take off in the summer, I would recommend that he have as much time with the children as his time off allows, rather than being limited to the two 1-week periods.

Regarding treatment, it is my opinion that the first priority is that the conflict between Mr. Z and Mrs. Z be reduced. Therefore, the focus of treatment should be on the two of them in the short run. Perhaps once the custody issue is resolved, that will take place. If not, I would say that they need the intervention. It is likely that the children will adjust quickly if the conflict ceases between the parents. If not, then continued treatment for the children, particularly T (who has a sensitivity and sadness that is greater than that of the boys), would be recommended.

Thank you for the opportunity to evaluate the family. Please contact me if you have any further questions.

Very truly yours,
Gerald Cooke, PhD

Teaching Point: What kind of errors do you avoid to make your testimony more effective?

First, it is important to understand that the context in which testimony is presented in a custody case differs in some ways from that in other types of legal proceedings. In most custody cases, we appear as "court-appointed" and/or a "mutually agreed upon" neutral evaluator. As neutral evaluators, in most jurisdictions, we are not allowed to meet with the attorneys to prepare the testimony. Testimony is before a judge, not a jury, and often the judge has had the opportunity to read the report before testimony is presented. When the judge has read the report, the direct examination is often a brief summary of the procedures utilized and the main points leading to the recommendation. When the judge has not read the report, direct examination is more lengthy. Often, the judge as well as the attorneys will question the evaluator. However, the "meat" of the testimony is cross-examination, with the cross-examining attorney being in the unenviable position of questioning the findings of an expert to whose appointment he or she has previously agreed. Because of this unusual circumstance, the issue of effective testimony really focuses on the cross-examination.

In custody cases, I always remind myself that the issue is what is in the best interest of the child(ren). This is more important than defending any specific recommendation I have made. With few exceptions, the research indicates that there is no one custodial arrangement that is the best predictor of the children's adjustment. Adjustment is often a function of other factors, such as the level of parental conflict. Therefore, reaching a custodial arrangement that is acceptable to both parents, which will reduce conflict, is important. Also, it is often difficult to predict the short- and long-term effects of a particular arrangement. One should be familiar with relevant guidelines such as the *Specialty Guidelines for Forensic Psychologists* (Committee on Ethical Guidelines for Forensic Psychologists, 1991) and the *Guidelines for Child Custody Evaluations in Divorce Proceedings* (APA, 1994), when conducting child custody evaluations.

Effective testimony involves presenting the strengths and weaknesses of both parents. The parenting ability of each parent must then be related to the specific characteristics and needs of the children. The recommendation must also reflect pragmatic considerations, such as the parents' work schedules, distance to schools, and distance between homes. The part that each of these play in contributing to the recommendation should be presented clearly. Testimony should also elucidate why, in a particular case, one factor carries more weight than another.

Finally, testimony in custody cases does share some characteristics of effective expert testimony in other kinds of forensic assessment. One should be able to defend the tests and procedures used and describe why others were not. One should clearly acknowledge where data are insufficient or where we do not know the answer. Finally, one should recognize that effective cross-examination is important to ensure that the recommendation follows from the data.

Note

1. Some jurisdictions have adopted *Daubert*, others have rejected it and retained the *Frye* standard, and still others have yet to rule on the issue (Melton et al., 1997). Forensic clinicians should be attentive to the applicable standard in their jurisdiction.

Chapter 16

Termination of Parental Rights

The termination of parental rights is the focus of the report in this chapter. Requests for termination of parental rights usually originate with the court, and the principle being applied addresses the importance of obtaining appropriate authorization from this referral source before conducting the evaluation. The teaching point discusses how the forensic clinician can manage and reduce the impact of reluctance and refusal in court-ordered evaluations of this kind.

Case 1

Principle: Obtain appropriate authorization

This principle is discussed in Chapter 15, so we will not repeat this discussion. The present report provides a good example of obtaining appropriate authorization. In this case, the evaluation was conducted to assess the mother's mental health functioning, her abilities related to parenting competence, and whether she posed a risk of harm to her son. The evaluation was authorized by the Department of Social Services through a court order in response to allegations of neglect, sexual abuse, and maternal substance abuse. Because the evaluation was ordered through the Department of Social Services via court order in response to allegations of abuse of a minor, the evaluator was legally authorized to proceed regardless of whether the relevant parties consented to participate.

PSYCHOLOGICAL EVALUATION

Name: Troubled Monroe
Date of birth: July 8, 1964
Age: 34

Re: Parenting of Latency Howard
DOB: February 12, 1989
Age: 9 yrs 7 mo.
Dates of evaluation: June 12, 1998; August 23, 1998; August 28, 1998

Location of evaluation: University of Massachusetts Medical Center Department of Psychiatry

Examiner: Lois B. Oberlander, Ph.D., ABPP

Date of report: November 14, 1998

IDENTIFYING DATA AND REASON FOR REFERRAL

Ms. Troubled Monroe was referred for an evaluation by the Center City Office of the Department of Social Services in order to assess her mental health functioning and her abilities related to parenting competence.

STRUCTURE OF THE EVALUATION

Prior to my evaluation, I informed all parties I interviewed that I am a psychologist and that I was ordered to evaluate Ms. Monroe to gather information that the Court could use in considering her mental health status and her risk of harm to her son. I informed them that the content of the interview, assessment results, and my observations would be shared with the court in the form of an evaluation report, and that I might be asked to testify in court concerning the report contents.

I reviewed the Department of Social Services (DSS) record concerning Ms. Monroe and Latency Howard and a psychological evaluation by Dr. Psychologist Abbott and Dr. Psychologist Costello. I had contact with Ms. S W Ball (DSS worker), Ms. S W Arnold (former DSS worker), Ms. S W Middler (former DSS supervisor), Ms. S W Streisand and Ms. S W Harlow (of Kid foster placement service), Ms. Fosmom Ross (Latency Howard's foster mother), Ms. Therapist Field (Latency Howard's therapist), Dr. Primary Care Murray (Ms. Monroe's physician), Dr. Coverage Aykroyd (who provides coverage for Dr. Murray), Dr. Orthopedic Kostner (Ms. Monroe's physician), Ms. Substance-abuse McLean (of ScreenNow), Mr. Labrat Crystal (of AnalyzeNow Laboratories), Ms. Nurse Streep (nurse practitioner in the orthopedic department of the West City Hospital), Dr. Pharmacist Nicholson (pharmacist at the West City Hospital), and Mr. Counselor Bridges (Ms. Monroe's therapist).

EVALUATION TECHNIQUES ADMINISTERED

Clinical Interview (1½ hours) Mental Status Examination

Minnesota Multiphasic Personality Inventory, 2nd edition (MMPI-2), Millon Clinical Multiaxial Inventory, 2nd edition (MCMI-II), ADHD Rating Scale (retrospective self-rating), Disassociative Experiences Scale

RELEVANT BACKGROUND INFORMATION

Ms. Monroe said she was raised by her mother. She has two brothers and one sister. She has a "not so good" relationship with her mother, about whom she said, "She was a drug addict, and it was really hard to have a relationship with her." She described her mother as verbally and physically abusive. She said the abuse occurred "all the time." Her mother "was in prison for 10 years," at which time she finally stopped drugging (she has been clean for 14 years). Her mother was imprisoned for "dealing drugs." Ms. Monroe was about age 19 when her mother was imprisoned.

The previous evaluation report stated that Ms. Monroe's mother also earned money under the table as a topless dancer and as a numbers runner for a bookie. Ms. Monroe described domestic abuse by her mother and her mother's boyfriends, including witnessing sexual behavior between her mother and the boyfriends, watching her mother play strip poker with groups of people, and having to leave her bedroom in the night so that her mother's guests could use it for sexual activity. Ms. Monroe said her sister was raped by one of her mother's guests. Ms. Monroe said recently that her relationship with her mother "improved somewhat, it's just a good casual relationship . . . I don't go out of my way to go spend weekends with her." She said, "She has to be very distant, it's only a 10-minute conversation . . . by telephone or in person . . . it's not really a loving relationship."

Ms. Monroe said she has occasional contact with her father, with whom she has a "great" relationship. She did not see him until age 20 because "He had to do what he had to do, he had a life." She said that her father knew her whereabouts but did not contact her until her adulthood. The previous evaluation report stated Ms. Monroe's father was "on the run because of a number of armed robberies." After they established contact, "She watched her own father overdose in front of her and had to call 911 to take him to the hospital where he remained in a coma for 2 months."

Ms. Monroe said that her mother was involved with the DSS. Her mother "had a nervous breakdown" when Ms. Monroe was in fifth grade. As a result, Ms. Monroe and her siblings were placed in foster care for 3 years. She was placed in "13 foster homes." She said she and her siblings were moved around "because they couldn't keep us in places long enough." She said, "We never even went to school in fifth grade because they couldn't keep us in a home long enough." When asked to explain why she was placed in 13 different homes, she said, "I really don't know. I really don't want to go back there." She said it probably was due to her behavior, the behavior of her siblings, and the behavior of the foster parents. She said some of the foster parents "used to beat us."

Ms. Monroe said her relationship with her siblings is "okay." The previous evaluation report states that Ms. Monroe described her siblings by indicating that her older sister lived on the streets and lost six children to DSS custody due to drug abuse, prostitution, car theft, and drug dealing. Her oldest brother, she went on, had substance abuse problems but developed control over this abuse and has led a relatively stable life. Ms. Monroe has had little contact with her younger sister, who is "clean and sober and critical of me."

With respect to her educational background, Ms. Monroe said that she is a high school graduate. She nearly dropped out of school in ninth grade, but she decided to complete school due mainly to the intervention of the school principal who met with her on a regular basis. She obtained "good grades" in high school. She repeated 11th grade because she was behind in her credit hours due to an accident at age 14 that caused her to miss class. She described her school conduct as rebellious because, "I wasn't the happiest kid, coming from a drugging home, always being verbally and physically abused." When asked about her high school friendships, Ms. Monroe was evasive and then said, "I had friends in every category." Ms. Monroe was she was suspended from 10th grade 16 times. She was suspended for "being late, not being attentive in school, having arguments with my teachers, smoking in the bathroom." In the previous evaluation report, Ms. Monroe said she had a reputation for hitting high school classmates if they challenged her or criticized her.

Ms. Monroe said she hoped to attend college, but she did not get a student loan (the previous evaluation said her mother refused to sign the loan papers). She did not respond to questions concerning her occupational history. She currently supports herself with SSI disability income and child support payments from her infant son's father.

Ms. Monroe said she currently lives in South City with her infant son Junior (age 10 months). She and Junior's father, Mr. Drinker Presley, separated after cohabiting for 1 year. They separated so that they could each work on their problems. She said she asked Mr. Presley to leave because "he relapsed and was drinking." She said, "He had a drinking problem. He is working on his sobriety, counseling, medication," adding, "He's doing really well." She said that Mr. Presley lives with his mother in Lake City and plans to rent an apartment. He does well-drilling and water irrigation for a living. He is paying child support for Junior. Ms. Monroe said she met Mr. Presley at an AA meeting. She said they are considering a reconciliation but, "My concern is to have my son back and to have Junior and Latency be together." She described her children as her main priority.

Ms. Monroe refused to discuss her relationship with Mr. LatencySenior Howard (Latency's father) and Mr. Abusive Monroe. She refused to provide other information about her dating history. She also refused to provide information about past friendships. In the previous evaluation report, she said she married Mr. Abusive Monroe when she was 19. He was her best friend in high school. She indicated that she married him in order to get away from her mother. Mr. Monroe was stationed in Belgium, where they relocated for 2 months. Ms. Monroe returned to the United States because of "money troubles, I was homesick, and it wasn't working." She became pregnant with her first son while Mr. Monroe was home on leave. Mr. Monroe denied paternity of their son until their son was 2½ years old. After their son's birth, Ms. Monroe resided with her mother for a short time. She left because, "My mom didn't want me there. She was big into drug dealing with the Central Americans then." Shortly thereafter, her mother was sentenced to 10 years in jail at Center City.

According to the previous evaluation report, Ms. Monroe met Mr. LatencySenior Howard, who she knew from high school. She had a crush on him in high school. In 1986 they began a relationship. The previous evaluation report described the relationship as "a volatile, explosive relationship that included binge drinking, doing lines of cocaine, and severe domestic violence." The report said, "Numerous restraining orders were followed by coming back together and then more violence." The report indicated, "The relationship ended after Ms. Monroe hit Mr. Howard with a glass that caused him to require 80 stitches in his face, and a prison sentence of 24 months for Mr. Howard's violation of a restraining order. It also ended with Ms. Monroe 6 months pregnant with Latency."

The previous evaluation report stated, "Ms. Monroe stayed in Chelsea, living off welfare and child support until 1993. These years were characterized by serious heroin abuse. She met More-Abusive Grant in 1991 while he was working in Boston on prerelease from prison where he had been incarcerated for Manslaughter. She thought he was there for drug dealing. Ms. Monroe wrote and visited him in prison until his release. They moved to South City together in November 1994." The report said, "Ms. Monroe described Mr. Grant as a possessive and controlling man. She states that she went along with his control because he took care of her."

When asked who is in her current support network, Ms. Monroe named her sponsor and others in her Alcoholics Anonymous (AA) group. She estimated that she could rely on anyone in her Get Up Early morning AA meeting. She also relies on people at Recovery Place and her counselor for support.

When asked about her medical history, Ms. Monroe said she has no history of serious injuries. At age 6, she had one seizure. She was diagnosed

with epilepsy, for which she took Dilantin and Phenobarbital. At age 12, she stopped taking medication. She had no subsequent seizures. Ms. Monroe said when she was age 7, she was evaluated by a pediatric specialist at East City Hospital. She said he thought she might have Attention Deficit Hyperactivity Disorder (ADHD); however, he did not prescribe medication for her. To her recollection, she never took medication for ADHD. Currently, she has a slipped, perforated disk and a herniated disk. She said, "They're on top of one another in the lower back." She added, "I have pain from that a lot." She said carrying and holding her infant son has been a strain on her back. She finds it painful to go up and down the stairs in her townhouse when she is tired and her back is sore. She reported that she takes Talwin for back pain. Ms. Monroe declined to provide information about her substance use history and her history of mental health treatment. She complained that she already had provided this information to DSS and to previous evaluators.

In the previous evaluation, Ms. Monroe described her substance use history. The report said

Ms. Monroe reports an extensive history of substance abuse and involvement with drug dealing. She has had numerous detoxifications, participated in numerous short-term rehabilitation programs, and has currently (as of 5/1/97) maintained her sobriety for approximately 10 months while living in sober housing in Center City, Massachusetts, attending day treatment at Recovery Place in Near City, attending vocational training, and numerous other ancillary treatments. Her ambivalence and improvement have been reflected in her record of sobriety: clean 3 months followed by a relapse, clean 9 months followed by a relapse, and now clean approximately 10 months.

The report continued, "Ms. Monroe reports that she first tasted alcohol when she was 7 years old. She states that it was always around the house. Next, she reports snorting a line of cocaine between 9 and 10 years old. After returning from foster care at 12 years old, Ms. Monroe remembers drinking alcohol with other teenagers at the Hangout Lake on weekends to the point of being "out of control" and beginning to experiment with illegal drugs such as mescaline, THC, acid, valium, cocaine, quaaludes, and MM714." The report also indicated that Ms. Monroe's sister sold marijuana and Ms. Monroe was caught "with a shoe box full of paraphernalia for rolling and selling pot, as well as the money from her sales." When her mother confiscated the money and paraphernalia she began to sell marijuana with her daughters. Ms. Monroe recalled rolling marijuana cigarettes "like it was a production line." The report said, "Ms. Monroe also began to sell mescaline with her friends, with enough left over for herself." Ms. Monroe indicated that she and her friends stole money and alcohol from the Bigg Auditorium commissary where she worked between ages 13 and 15.

The report next indicated that "Ms. Monroe began bringing bottles of wine to school almost daily by the ninth grade and drinking them with her friends in the morning." The report said that in 10th grade, "She recalls drinking and using Valium almost daily. . . . Her attendance and grades improved, despite almost daily cocaine use and alcohol most evenings and weekends. Ms. Monroe reports that she experienced her first blackouts during this period. . . . Her sister, Ms. Monroe, and their mother began to deal drugs at a much higher volume. . . . She reports that she and her sister used to remove taped bundles of heroin from the bodies of Colombians who were in the drug business with their mother."

The report said, "While married to Abusive Monroe, she reports binge drinking and snorting lines of cocaine on the weekend. She maintains that she remained clean during her pregnancy with her first son." After she moved back in with her mother, "She became quickly reengaged in her mother's business. . . . Ms. Monroe made 'drug calls' for her mother, brought in bundles of drugs under her baby's blanket, and made deliveries for her . . . she snorted cocaine on weekends and drank Pabst to get a buzz. Over the next 1½ years, Ms. Monroe built back up to smoking one-half gram of crack cocaine over a 2-week period."

After her relationship with Mr. Howard, according to the report, "She entered the most serious phase of her drug dependence. She began by doing angel dust and Valium . . . 'scamming' doctors for clonopin and Valium and selling these drugs to buy bread and milk. She was introduced to heroin by this friend of her sister and 'couldn't

wait to do it again.' She began to sell drugs again in order to supply her own need. Ms. Monroe was shooting heroin at least once a week by age 24. By age 26, in 1994, Ms. Monroe was fully trapped by a lifestyle completely focused on heroin. She was 'scamming' on the street and selling bundles of heroin to supply her own habit." The report continued, "Ms. Monroe moved into a home with MoreAbusive Grant after 10 months' being clean. He was also a recovering addict. She reports that she was smoking crack cocaine twice a week during their 4 months together. She reports that she did this during the day so that she would have come down by the time Mr. Grant returned home from work. She used again immediately after her children were taken away in February 1995 and again 10 months ago when she felt hopeless about getting her boys back after losing visitation."

When asked about her legal history, Ms. Monroe reported that she was never the subject of a CHINS petition and had no involvement with the Department of Youth Services. She said she was 17 or 18 the first time she was arrested, for Assault and Battery related to an incident in a bar. She described this arrest by saying, "Somebody grabbed my butt and I started swinging." The charges were dropped. She was arrested for Shoplifting at age 21 and for not paying a fine at age 28. She said, "Friends of mine were in the store shoplifting. I was in the car waiting. I did know they were shoplifting, and I wanted no part of it. They charged me because I was in the car waiting." She said the charges were dropped, but she had to pay a court fee. She also indicated that she had been in trouble for not paying a fine for cashing a check that belonged to her boyfriend. She said that she had permission to cash the check, but he later accused her of forging the check. She refused to pay the fine because she did not think she was guilty. She later paid it after she was caught running a red light and incarcerated for a brief period of time until she agreed to pay the fine.

Ms. Monroe said her sister-in-law once attempted to file a restraining order against her when she tried to see her son (Latency's older brother). The judge vacated the order. Ms. Monroe said she once filed a restraining order against Latency Howard's father, adding, "He was eventually put in jail for 18 months for violating the restraining order."

Relevant Information from DSS Records   DSS records indicate that Ms. Monroe first became involved with DSS in 1994. A 51A report was filed on <date>, 1994, alleging Ms. Monroe neglected Latency's brother. Another 51A report was filed on <date>, 1995, and third 51A report was filed on <date>, 1995. The latter reports alleged the neglect of Latency Howard (and his brother) by Ms. Monroe, indicating that "due to mother's crack cocaine use, children were left unsupervised at times." On <date>, 1995, it was alleged that Ms. Monroe was smoking crack cocaine and she did not meet her children at the school bus. On <date>, 1995, the children were found home alone with no supervision. The report described this as "children left alone by mother with no appropriate caretaker."

The 1995 reports were supported for neglect and maternal substance abuse. On <date>, 1995, a Care and Protection Petition was filed on behalf of Latency and his older brother. Both boys were placed in the custody of DSS. Latency and his brother were placed in foster care on <date>, 1995, returned home 3 days later, and then returned to foster care 2 days later after Ms. Monroe had a positive drug screen for cocaine. The children have been in foster care since then. (Latency turned 6 one day before entering foster care.)

DSS investigation records indicate that on <date>, 1995, the foster parent said Latency "pulled his pants down and 'urinated all over the car.' He did this as he was upset that ongoing worker was not going to take him to see his mother. Foster parent stated he also urinated under his bed." When the foster parent asked him what was bothering or upsetting him, Latency said,

> He did not like being called MoreAbusive's "little white slave." Latency stated as MoreAbusive's "little white slave boy he had to do the slave thing." Latency reported to the foster parent that he would have to "run MoreAbusive's pee pee." Latency stated that there were bumps on MoreAbusive's penis. Latency stated MoreAbusive told Latency that a raccoon bit him on his penis when he was hunting. Latency was told he would have to rub it to make it feel better. Latency stated he also had to rub cream or baby oil all over his mother's body. Latency stated that he

would have to rub cream on all parts of her body. Latency stated he had to "kiss his mother's butt." Latency stated to foster parents that MoreAbusive would show Latency where to kiss mother and how to kiss mother. Latency stated that MoreAbusive would go first then Latency would "kiss mother on her privates and her butt."

A note from <date>, 1995, stated, "Mother completely denied all allegations made against her. Mother denied any knowledge of any sexual abuse her children may have suffered. Mother stated that MoreAbusive had never been left alone to care for children. Mother stated the only cream children may have applied to her body is suntan lotion on her back. Mother presented as completely overwhelmed and distraught. Mother stated she may need psychiatric hospitalization after hearing children's disclosures. Mother stated MoreAbusive has moved out of the home . . . as a result of DSS removing the children. Mother stated she has used cocaine twice since her last dirty urine, 3 weeks ago."

On <date>, 1995, a 51A petition was filed and supported for sexual abuse of Latency (and his brother) by Ms. Monroe and her boyfriend, Mr. MoreAbusive Grant. On March 11, 1995, a SAIN team interviewed Latency at Psychiatric Center Place. He "refused to talk and hid under the table." On <date>, 1995, Latency was discharged from Psychiatric Center Place and placed in a Kid foster home with Ms. Fosmom Ross. (DSS records state that on <date>, 1995, Ms. Monroe "admits she and MoreAbusive had sex in front of the children.") On <date>, 1995, the allegation was "supported for the sexual abuse of <brother> and Latency Howard by their mother Troubled Monroe and mother's live-in boyfriend MoreAbusive Grant. Latency disclosed being sexually abused in detail . . . Latency drew pictures of the abuse and verbalized the events that took place."

About a year later, on <date>, 1996, a 51A report was filed. The report was "screened in based on alleged sexual abuse of two boys, ages 8 and 6, by mother and mother's boyfriend. Both boys are in foster care. They are disclosing that mother's boyfriend has made 6-year-old fondle his penis and perform oral sex on him. Same child has also touched mother in a sexual way. His 8-year-old brother has disclosed that mother has rubbed his private parts and has had him rub cream on her chest." In <date> 1996, Latency began weekly therapy with Ms. Therapist Field. On <date>, 1996, Ms. Field wrote a letter of concern that the DSS plan to reunify Latency with his mother "beginning with unsupervised visits in <date> 1996" was, in her opinion, "premature and clinically inappropriate at this time." She said, "Latency has been significantly traumatized by the abuse and neglect he experienced while in his mother's care. Without significant therapeutic work by his mother to address her role in his abuse and neglect, acknowledgement and validation by her of his experiences, and repair work between she and her son, it is highly likely that Latency will experience his return home as significantly retraumatizing."

Investigation records from <date>, 1996, state that while in foster care, Latency exhibited bizarre behavior. He

jumped in front of the school bus and has gotten under excessively hot water in the shower. He has also urinated in the foster family's van . . . This weekend, 6-year-old Latency urinated under his bed at the foster home. . . . Latency said that he hated himself because he's white and his father is black. He refers to mother's boyfriend MoreAbusive as his father. He said that MoreAbusive calls him his "little white slave." As a slave, More-Abusive makes Latency rub him on his penis. Child also said that MoreAbusive made him put a band aid on his hurt penis. Child said that mother told him this was a "family secret." . . . He said that MoreAbusive likes him to kiss him on the buttocks, the legs, and the pee pee. MoreAbusive told Latency to do the same things to mommy. He has done the same things to mommy. He also said that his mother burned him behind the ear with a cigarette. . . . The children have told foster mother that their mother "grilled" them during the unsupervised visit and told them not to tell anyone what has happened.

On <date>, 1996, two 51A reports were filed for the sexual abuse of Latency by the mother and an unknown male. The allegations were supported. According to investigations records concerning the <date>, 1996, 51A reports,

Latency had soiled his pants while out in the community . . . child had a rash which was red and sore. Child has rashes about once a week. Ms. Ross put vaseline on the child's rash. Latency <said>, "My mother used to put vaseline on my bum and then More-Abusive would put stuff in there . . . child has never before put his mother at the same place when the alleged abuse took place. . . . Latency asked Fosmom Ross why <brother> was not seeing mother any longer . . . Latency said, "Because my mother touched his private parts?" Later in the day Tuesday, Latency was still very angry. Fosmom Ross asked Latency why he was angry and child reported, "My mother touched my private parts, OK." Yesterday, child met with a representative from Kid services and told her that his mother "touched my private parts." That night Latency told reporter "my mom would stretch my penis and pull it." He described putting his penis on her "boobies." Latency said his mother would lie on the bed with no clothes. He ended by saying she would then put her mouth on it and suck it and make funny noises.

According to investigation records concerning the <date>, 1996, 51A reports

During therapy, child was doing an activity around his anger at MoreAbusive. Child had drawn a bullseye and placed MoreAbusive in the middle. Reporter asked if anyone else belonged there. Child disclosed another one of mother's boyfriends touched and hurt him. He got "highly anxious" and did not describe the touching. It came up in the context of discussing the sexual abuse by MoreAbusive. Reporter's sense is that the child was talking about being sexually abused by this other boyfriend of mother's. Child described this person as dressing up in his mother's clothes and sleeping in mother's bed, which made child angry. Child did not say if mother was there or not. Child called this other person "Bull" as he did not know the person's name. Child became so anxious, child left the office. Reporter attempted to address it with child the next session, but child wouldn't engage in the conversation.

During the investigation of the <date>, 1996, 51A petition, the investigator, Ms. SloppyWork Hunt, interviewed Latency in the presence of his foster mother, Fosmom Ross. The interview took place on <date>, 1996. Latency refused to disclose the same information to the investigator that he allegedly had previously disclosed to the foster mother. The interview consisted of questions by the foster mother with the investigator recording notes. For reasons that I discuss later in this report, I do not believe the <date>, 1996, investigation interview yielded valid information. However, on <date>, 1996, Ms. Hunt concluded, "This investigation is being supported on sexual abuse of Latency Howard, by his mother Troubled Monroe and unknown male adult nicknamed 'Bull.' Child has a known history of sexual abuse by mother's ex-boyfriend (MoreAbusive). He is recently disclosing to his therapist and Kid foster mother. Stating his mother's boyfriend 'Bull' dresses in women's clothes and is touched in his private parts. He states that his mother was naked and she would stretch his penis and pull it. He stated his mother would sit in a chair naked telling him to touch her 'boobies' with his hand. Specific timeframes, and places of events were not disclosed. Latency did mention he was 5 years old, and living in Upstate City. Unsupervised visits with mother were supposed to start this month (April)."

Records suggest Ms. Monroe's compliance with her service plans typically was good, but there were some problems. In <date> 1996, Ms. Monroe did not meet her service plan. She tested positive for opiates and was terminated from South City Sober Housing. Her recent DSS Service Plans contain the following goals: (1) weekly meetings with her therapist (Mr. Counselor Bridges), (2) intensive involvement in substance abuse treatment, (3) continue in AA meetings (including commitments, 12-step, discussion and women's groups), (4) random drug and alcohol screens, (5) address parenting issues in individual treatment (including an adequate ability to respond to Latency's emotional needs surrounding his sexual abuse), (6) a working knowledge of how Latency's development has been affected by his sexual abuse, (7) consistent employment as an indicator of increased stability in Patty's life, (8) maintain abstinence from drugs and consistent participation in all portions of her drug rehabilitation program, (9) appropriate releases for all collaterals, and (10) monthly meetings with the DSS worker.

More recent goals include (1) strengthening parenting skills, (2) improving parent/child relationship, (3) recovery from alcohol/drug abuse/misuse, (4) safety/protection of child from sexual abuse, (5) assist child in recovery from past abuse, (6) resolve child's need for temporary placement, (7) continue with individual therapy, (8) work with an aide or attend parenting classes (if deemed appropriate by DSS worker), (9) engage in therapy sessions with her Latency (once Latency's therapist deems it appropriate), (10) refrain from use of any drugs or alcohol, (11) participate in substance abuse treatment (weekly AA meetings including commitments, 12-step, discussion, and women's groups), (12) provide documentation to DSS to obtain random drug screens within 24 hours of request from DSS worker, (13) continue collecting SSI and notify of any change in income, (14) provide DSS with current address, (15) adhere to parent/child visitation, (16) sign and update releases for collateral contact, and (17) maintain monthly meetings with DSS.

Based on a Foster Care Review report (dated <date>, 1998) in <date> of 1996, the DSS set a goal of adoption for Latency. At a later meeting in <date> of 1997, the DSS resumed the goal of reunification. The plan was to give Ms. Monroe 1 year to determine if reunification was possible because

> Ms. Monroe had fully cooperated with the Department for the previous year. She had visited regularly with Latency and was appropriate during visits. Mother does not acknowledge or recall sexually abusing her children; however, she reportedly does not believe they are lying. Mother has continued in therapy to address her own sexual abuse history and the sexual abuse history of her children. . . . Mother has participated in visits with Latency consistently. Latency is reportedly very anxious before and after visits, but does not display anxiety during visits. Visits are supervised. . . . Mother has reportedly continued to attend AA weekly. Several collaterals expressed serious concern for Latency at this time. Latency has reportedly regressed substantially since around <date> 1997, when he learned that reunification is a possibility. Latency's therapist stated that Latency has stated that he does not want to go home and that he is afraid of reunification with mother.

In <date> 1997, the Department learned that Latency had engaged in coercive sexual activity with a 9-year-old boy and a 6-year-old girl. Latency's school noted that Latency's behavior changed in <date> 1997 from compliance to belligerence and resistance.

DSS notes indicate that after <date>, 1998, maternal visits with Latency were increased to 2 hours at a time per month. Some effort was made to have Ms. Monroe's therapist and Latency's therapist consult with each other "to help with the transition home." Because they saw the case differently, and because of managed care restraints, they had only one telephone conversation concerning Ms. Monroe and Latency.

Records state Ms. Monroe took six drug screens beginning in January of 1998. The results were negative "except for prescribed pain medication for her back." Her physician, Dr. Orthopedic Kostner, wrote a letter to DSS stating she had back pain and confirming that she was prescribed pain medication. The plan was to conduct an MRI to gauge the consistency of medical data with her complaints of the severity of her pain. (However, see collateral information below for further information concerning the pain medication.)

Ms. Monroe's Account of the Neglect and Sexual Abuse Allegations Ms. Monroe said that she regained custody of Latency and his older brother in <date> of 1994 or 1995. She, Latency, and MoreAbusive moved to South City so she could enter a drug rehabilitation program. A 51A was filed and supported for abuse by Mr. Monroe on Latency's older brother. DSS conducted a home visit while Ms. Monroe was out paying bills. The children were under the care of a child care worker. While she was away, DSS took her children. She said that she called DSS and yelled and swore at them. She reported that DSS thought she was attempting to hide from them and had abandoned her children. She went to court and explained that she had child care for the children and she had not abandoned them. The judge asked when she last used drugs. Although she had used over the weekend (February of 1995), she told the judge she had not used since September. DSS asked her to give a urine sample. When the urine screen produced a positive result, DSS resumed custody of the children.

Ms. Monroe complained that she had been asked to do "anything and everything" by DSS. She complained about all of the evaluations and urine screens she completed. She said, "I can't believe it's been all this time and I still don't have him back." Ms. Monroe said she "could not keep up with the 51As because they were so silly and stupid." She went to detoxification after the birth of her child, Junior, in order to come off narcotics. She said DSS threatened to take Junior. She said, "He was safe. He was home with his father."

Ms. Monroe stated that, "On <date>, 1995, Latency said he was sexually molested by More-Abusive." She said she was implicated as well. She asserted, "I swore then, and I'll tell it to you now, I never sexually molested those children." She said she may have unknowingly bathed them after an incident in which Mr. Grant sexually abused them. She said the circumstances probably became confused in her son's mind, adding, "I can't stress to you how frustrating it was. I was evaluated and they said I don't fit the profile of an offender." She said, "That never even registered in my head that I'm gonna sexually abuse my children." She explained that one must first have thoughts of sexual abuse in order to act on those thoughts. She insisted she never had any such thoughts.

Ms. Monroe explained that she is willing to apologize to Latency for anything she did that might have caused direct or inadvertent harm to him. She said, "I admit to total neglect of my children, but the physical abuse, sexual abuse—no way shape or form." She said, "I couldn't meet their needs when I was using. That's a selfish thing. I'd say, 'I'll do this tomorrow,' 'I don't have time.'" She said, "Why they have me labeled as a perpetrator—I keep saying to my counselor over and over, 'How can this happen.'" She again wondered if, "just after something happened to Latency—whether Latency became confused and mistook a bath or some other type of maternal care, because he had just been sexually abused and thought his mother was doing the same thing."

Ms. Monroe said, "I don't believe for one second my son is lying. I believe he was molested. The only thing is I have never been able to work with him and tell him no harm will come to him anymore. I'll keep him safe. I would never allow this to happen to him. I would protect him." She said, "MoreAbusive never smoked, never drank, never drugged, went to work in the early morning, came home late at night, and went to bed. I left those kids alone with him only two times." She said, "I read the reports, I re-read the reports, I heard the audiotapes, I thought to myself, 'I can't believe how all this could happen to him and I left him alone for all of 20 minutes.' " She said, "I can't believe people think I'm a sex offender. A year ago I almost gave this child up in order to give him stability and routine. It's not fair to him no more." She said, "DSS turned it around and said the goal was reunification. They gave me 80 percent of the hope I have." Crying, she added, "I don't want my child to end up in foster care or residential care." She said, "I own the responsibility for neglecting them. But that's not the type of person I am today. It took a lot of recovery, a halfway house, a three-quarter house, counseling, to get me the help I need . . . I could have said, 'Let them stay in foster care,' but I can't. I love them children too much."

Ms. Monroe said, "I've been given five-page Service Plans, and I've met all of the conditions." She said she recently was given "partial compliance," because she missed two urine screens. She added that she obtained psychological evaluations, substance abuse evaluations, educational evaluations, and offender evaluations. She also said she attended weekly counseling, met with DSS once per month, attended scheduled supervised visits with Latency, completed urine screens, entered a halfway house (Recovery Place), attended parenting classes, entered sober housing (three-quarter living) for 1 year, and obtained her own apartment. "The Service Plans have been extremely full, and I've complied with all of them," she reported.

Ms. Monroe said she found the parenting classes particularly helpful: "I was always the one talking." She "asked how to deal with a child who was molested, how to deal with a child who thinks I sexually abused him, how to deal with a child who is traumatized, how you help him break a bond with a foster parent when he's emotionally connected to her, biologically connected to me, and psychologically connected to both of us." She said the parenting teacher suggested she work with counselors and that they all work to-

gether. "That's when we decided maybe Latency's counselor and my counselor should meet and decide what to do next," she said, adding "Ms. Field feels very strongly Latency should not return home. She's not impartial. But I can't say I blame her because she's been working with Latency for 2 years. She's attached to him." Ms. Monroe stated that she was in favor of the joint meetings, but they never took place.

The treatment she received "taught me how to stay clean and sober, taught me how to talk about things, taught me how to get honest, to stop living my life a big lie," Ms. Monroe offered, and "It taught me how to be a better person, a better friend, a better mother. It taught me how to be a part of life instead of not be there at all. Be part of something other than myself. When I was using I was very selfish, I didn't care. All I wanted was to get high and numb."

When asked to describe her relapse prevention plan, Ms. Monroe said, "Anything can set me off. If I gained weight, I wanted to lose weight by getting high. It all comes down to being honest, having someone to go to, knowing when the red light's there." She described other triggers of use, including having a bad day, missing the children, feeling angry, having difficulty expressing her anger, feeling guilty, feeling embarrassed, feeling ashamed, anything that has to do with making her feel insecure, fear, and doubt. She said, "Those are the things I have to watch out for. They can vary anywhere from going to get an apple and the last one is gone, and just not liking the weather one day." Ms. Monroe said when she feels the urge to use, "I get on the phone with my sponsor. I have a group with plenty of people I can call and talk to. I'm still in touch with people from the halfway house and the three-quarter house group. I go to speaker meetings at AA." She noted that she also attends Al-Anon to talk about how she was affected by the substance abuse of others, including her parents.

Ms. Monroe said her counselor is "very helpful . . . I go in there and I tell him the truth, and I tell him how I feel. It's always good for me to get out of my feelings. For the longest time, I lived my life a big lie. I couldn't tell anybody anything." Overall, she reported, "Everything has been helpful. None of it has been negative. I can't even tell you how much better my life is. I feel better about who I am and what I am. There's no shame in it. I try to live life a day at a time, staying away from drugs and alcohol. I learned that not everyone gets their family back." She expressed frustration, however, that "it's taking so long."

At AA, Ms. Monroe said she attends open-speaker meetings, discussion, closed meetings, women's step, traditions, regular step meetings, and the Get Up Early meetings. She said she has been through the fourth and fifth step with her sponsor. She described steps one and two: "I stopped using." She described step three as follows: "I get on my knees and I humble myself in the morning and at night. I thank God I'm sober and I have food and a place to live." She said, "Step four is a tough one. It took me some time to write down all the things I've done. There's three parts to it. One is sexual, one is about relationships, and one is about people I've hurt." The fifth step, she said, is "talking about the fourth step. You say a prayer and admit it to God, and then to another human being why you did what you did. And then you go to step six, which is the shortcomings. And then step seven is about having all your shortcomings removed. It's about humbling yourself. Step eight is making a list of people you harmed and then making amends without injuring them and others. Nine is making that approach to those people you have on the list. Ten is taking the inventory at the end of a day, like a journal or something. Eleven is about your conscious contact with God. Twelve is about helping another addict get through detox. If you can't help them, don't hurt them."

When asked to describe her idea for a plan to reunify with Latency, Ms. Monroe said, "It would have to be a slow process because it takes Latency a long time to separate. It would have to be in a slow way so he could handle it. It could be a day visit, to an overnight visit, to weekend visits, then eventually he would come home." She added, "Then getting him home is a whole totally different ball game. It consists of constant safety precautions for Latency, protecting Junior if there are concerns for Junior being touched by Latency—there are concerns about perpetrating—being ready for family counseling, I would want DSS still involved with Latency's counseling, work in the school that Latency goes to, to make sure that Latency's doing okay—even if it's a vol-

unteer to sweep the corridor. Setting up his room, getting him ready for the house, the neighborhood, an the area—it would slowly happen on weekend visits. To see how well he adjusts, to see how he likes it."

When asked about Latency's supervisory needs, she said, "Constant supervision. I need to make sure that it's gonna be a lot of supervision. I'm going to have to constantly watch them. That's not going to be a problem for me knowing what's happened in the past. There's a lot of work involved." When asked how she will remain active in AA and counseling, she said she would take her children with her to the meetings and counseling. She explained the children sit at the back of the room and color, and in the morning meeting, they are in a separate room (with a supervisor). She said, "Everybody in my home group knows what's going on with Latency—that he's been sexually molested." She said she told her group members that DSS fears Latency is at risk of offending. Ms. Monroe added it would be necessary to involve Latency in the transition, giving him choices and explaining things as much as possible.

Ms. Monroe stated that if her parental rights were terminated she would want an open adoption, with an exchange of pictures and information, and with visits as often as possible without causing emotional distress for Latency. She said. "I want him to know I fought for him, that Mummy never never stopped fighting."

COLLATERAL CONTACTS

Ms. Fosmom Ross said Latency has been with her for 3½ years. In the first couple of months of foster care, Latency was "off the wall, tantruming constantly, he just couldn't contain himself for more than an hour." She said at night after bedtime stories he would talk about his life with his mother and stepfather, and he sometimes screamed in the nighttime and ran into her bedroom. She described him as "overwhelmed" and unable to say what woke him up or what was in his dreams. It took one-half hour to calm him and rock him to sleep. He was wet with sweat. She said at other times he came in at night and stood over their bed. When she spoke to him, he did not answer. He seemed to be walking in his sleep. He did not recall the night terrors or the sleepwalking in the morning. Ms. Ross said they had to place limits on their activities because Latency had a tendency to wander off. When she attempted to use a wrist band connecting them together, he "totally went berserk at the mall." During periods of anxiety he "told things that were done to him when he lived with his mother and mother's boyfriend."

Ms. Ross said Latency sometimes had good days, but when visits, counseling appointments, or evaluation appointments drew near, he had more frequent "outbursts or tantrums." Over time, however, his "outbursts and tantrums" lessened. She said Latency fears she will leave him at appointments and never return. She said he had episodes of behavior that seemed like flashbacks. For example, they were preparing for a camping trip and used some tape. Latency reacted to the tape and reported a memory of having tape on his eyes that, when removed, took off some of his eyebrow and eyelash hairs. She said, "You never know what's going to trigger him." Latency once thought he saw his stepfather in a store and stood frozen; he reacts to men whose appearance reminds him of his stepfather.

Ms. Ross said when Latency first came to live with them, he attempted to play with the private parts of their dog. She corrected his behavior a number of times before it abated somewhat. He sometimes threw toys, tipped a chair, or knocked things off of his bureau when his behavior was corrected. When his behavior improved she allowed him playtime with the dog. At other times, she had to prevent any contact between Latency and the dog. She still remains vigilant about his behavior with the dog.

When asked to describe the incident with the neighbors, Ms. Ross said she and her husband purchased property in Onset. Their friends helped them paint and work on the house. A family with two children (ages 10 and 7) joined them one weekend. They were children that Latency knew from their neighborhood. Latency played with them on the weekends and saw them at church. Ms. Ross had not noticed any inappropriate behavior up to that time. During the weekend at Onset, the children went outside to play in the afternoon. They were outside alone for 10 minutes. The parents called and the children came

running. They all walked to the beach. She said, "No one's behavior changed at that point. I wouldn't have suspected anything." The children continued to play together in the neighborhood. However, the neighbor began to report her children's behavior had changed. The day before New Year's Day the children were playing in a closet. The neighbor children began to cry. They called their parents. The children told their parents what happened, and Ms. Ross "got a phone call from the parents telling me they needed to get together with me and something had happened at Onset that included Latency and their two children."

Ms. Ross said she explained to Latency that the neighbor called about an incident involving him. She asked him what might have happened, and "He began telling me in detail what had happened." She said, "He told me that during the day when they were down in Onset he had been asking the children if they would show him their private parts. They kept saying no. They were playing tag. They were waiting for us to go get ice cream. He kept asking them. Latency pulled the boy's pants down. Latency put his mouth on the boy's private parts. Then the boy put his mouth on Latency's private parts. The girl watched. Then Latency heard us calling them in the front of the house. They just stopped what they were doing and came to the front of the house." She said Latency told her about this "with no fear or remorse."

When asked to describe Latency's behavior around maternal visits, Ms. Ross said at first Latency was excited about seeing his mother. He asked to see her. She said, "He would become very excited. If I told him the day before, he would tell everyone at school, 'I'm going to see my mother.'" She said, "During the visits he was also seeing his brothers. Leaving his mother and brother would be awful. He would cry. He would either fall asleep on the ride home or else argue with me all the way home." She said, however, "As time went on he stopped asking to see his mother. He began to refuse visits." His behavior prior to visits became "out of control, crying, arguing, running back into the house, yelling at me, 'I'm not going, I don't want to see her.'" She said his attempts at visitation refusal corresponded to his disclosures of abuse in counseling, and he told

Ms. Ross that his mother was lying because his mother did not acknowledge the abuse.

Ms. Ross said Ms. Monroe began to purchase gifts for Latency each month. Latency began to look forward to the visits because of the gifts. However, he said he did not want his mother to hug him during visits. She encouraged Latency to tell the DSS worker so that the DSS worker would "stop his mom doing that." Recently his behavior after visits has varied: Latency sometimes "moped" or "was out of control, didn't want us to talk to him." At other times, his behavior seemed like "no big deal."

Ms. Ross said in this academic school year, Latency's teacher has given him less homework than the other children because of concern that he cannot keep up with the other students. She said Latency's teacher called last Friday and reported that Latency has been argumentative and talking back in school. Ms. Ross said Latency recently began to say he wanted to return to the custody of his mother. Ms. Ross said she believes Latency now is aware that he cannot remain in her home indefinitely as a foster child. Although the Ross home initially was identified as a preadoptive home for Latency Howard, the goal changed after Mr. and Ms. Ross opted not to adopt Latency. Ms. Ross said she was afraid she might not be able to handle Latency as he enters his teenage years. She said, "He's getting harder and harder to control." She said two of her adult daughters refuse to provide child care for Latency because, "He won't listen to them." However, she said she cares for Latency and expressed a strong interest in helping Latency transition slowly to his next placement.

Ms. Therapist Field, therapist for Latency Howard, reported that 18 months ago in treatment, "Latency disclosed his mother being sexually inappropriate with him." She said, "After the disclosure he was anxious. He said he was afraid she would be mad that he told, she might hit him." She said, "Latency has more disclosures about his mother when he sees his (older) brother . . . Latency wanted rules around visits, no hugs or kisses unless he wanted to." Ms. Field said she has observed only one visit between Latency and Ms. Monroe: "Latency ran around the parking lot. Mother was in the parking lot, too. After all the rules, which were made clear by DSS to mother,

she came in and swooped him up in her arms." She said, "Since that visit, he gets anxious, oppositional, more aggressive, more impulsive before visits."

Ms. Field said she spoke with Ms. Monroe and her therapist in April of 1998: "In April, Troubled said it was possible MoreAbusive sexually abused and physically abused Latency, but she did not witness any of it and she never left them alone. She wasn't able to say she was a perpetrator at all. She minimized her substance abuse and how that impacted the situation. She took responsibility for having allowed MoreAbusive in her life." Ms. Field said Ms. Monroe's admission of responsibility was "further than she has been but not consistent with what Latency said." Ms. Field explained that April 1998 was her last contact with Ms. Monroe and her therapist.

Ms. Field expressed concern about the impact of the sexual abuse on Latency's functioning. She said he is shy when he meets new people. For example, "He hides under the table and runs from the room with most investigators." She said Latency showed a pattern of disclosing the information to Ms. Ross and then to Ms. Field: "They appeared credible though because he added details he hadn't told the foster mother." She said, "Most of his disclosures have to do with MoreAbusive." Ms. Field commented, "In general most was about MoreAbusive physically and sexually abusing him. He said MoreAbusive tied him up with tape and performed anal sex. He said MoreAbusive made him perform oral sex. He thought MoreAbusive snorted salt through a straw until his nose bled. He talked about a man who wore a dress and slept in his mother's bed." She added, "He said MoreAbusive put stuff on his butt. He said MoreAbusive put a needle in their arms and made them woozy. He said he saw MoreAbusive humping his mother."

Ms. Field said, based on her understanding of Latency's disclosures, "Mother left him for long periods of time in MoreAbusive's care. He said his mother participated in the physical abuse. He described the belt MoreAbusive hit them with. He said his mother held him down while MoreAbusive hit him. We had one conversation about mother being a perpetrator. . . . He has not spoken about it again." She said, "He said his mother touched his privates and she pulled on his penis and stretched it. He said his mother had him kiss her on her breast and on her genitals. He said his mother lay on the bed naked and put his penis on her breast. He said he watched scary movies at her house."

Ms. Field observed that "Latency has a very intense relationship with his foster mother." She said when the issue of leaving the foster home comes up in conversation, "He is not happy. Since Latency realized last fall that he's not staying in the foster home, he talks less." She said, "Latency has worries about whether Junior (younger brother) would be safe. He was worried because DSS can't be there all the time."

Ms. Field called several months after our initial conversation and expressed frustration that the issue of permanency planning for Latency was not settled. She noted that "Latency's behavior is escalating. He's clinging to his foster mother. He won't let her leave the room." She said Latency saw another boy run into her office and proudly ask if she wanted to meet his new parents. After the incident, Latency asked why the boy took up his session time, and why he did not have new parents.

Mr. Counselor Bridges, Ms. Monroe's therapist, said Ms. Monroe has attended sessions regularly. Exceptions occurred when she was busy after the birth of her child and with this evaluation. He said she missed sessions "in May and June" because Junior was an infant and because Dr. Oberlander was evaluating her. She missed sessions "in July and August" because she moved. She missed sessions "in August and September" because both of them were taking vacations. However, from his perspective, she canceled sessions for appropriate reasons and always maintained telephone contact when she had a period of absence from treatment. He sometimes has difficulty reaching her because she has no answering machine, but "We have a good treatment relationship."

Mr. Bridges said Ms. Monroe has used individual therapy to "deal with recovery" and "to deal with the effect of being accused of being a sexual offender with Latency." He reported that they have discussed how she will parent Latency and handle his acting out should he be returned to her physical custody: "She knows Latency will be a handful. She assures me she'll use help." He said he counseled Ms. Monroe to "be prepared to apologize, not deny or cry," should Latency accuse her of sexual molestation.

Mr. Bridges said he confronted Ms. Monroe about her neglect and unavailability to Latency due to her drug use. At first she denied she was unavailable to him, but, "Over time she has been able to say that's a problem." Mr. Bridges said he is willing to continue working as Ms. Monroe's therapist, regardless of the outcome of the hearing concerning physical custody of Latency. From Mr. Bridges's perspective, Ms. Monroe spent a great deal of time with me in May and June, resulting in the need for her to miss sessions with him. It is noteworthy that Ms. Monroe attended only one appointment with me in June. Mr. Bridges said, "Enough's enough. She should have been evaluated a long time ago, or they should have used the evaluation from Boston."

Ms. Arnold (former DSS worker) reported that the parent-child visits typically went smoothly between Ms. Monroe and Latency. However, she described several exceptions. She said that Ms. Monroe sometimes wanted physical contact with Latency though there was a rule against such contact. She also said she found Ms. Monroe's behavior during the July 1, 1998, parent-child supervised visit to be out of character; Ms. Monroe "slurred her words," and was "overly happy and excited to see me." She did not observe any other behavioral signs suggestive of substance use, so she continued with the supervised visit. However, she had a coworker join her in the supervision. Ms. Arnold said Ms. Monroe sometimes was noncompliant with her requests to get a drug screen. She said, for example, that Ms. Monroe did not complete any drug screens between May 18, 1998, and July 1, 1998.

Ms. S W Ball (current DSS worker) said her initial interactions with Ms. Monroe were positive. She found Ms. Monroe to be cooperative with DSS meetings. When she attempted an unannounced visit and found Ms. Monroe was away, she left a note, and Ms. Monroe promptly called the next day. She said that on September 9, 1998, and on September 14, 1998, Ms. Monroe had negative drug screens at South City Hospital. On September 23, 1998, the drug screen at ScreenNow was positive for opiates. Three days later, Ms. Monroe received a negative drug screen at ScreenNow.

Ms. Substanceabuse McLean of ScreenNow initially said she expected Ms. Monroe's urine screen to be positive because Talwin, the prescription drug that Ms. Monroe takes for back pain, contains an opiate. When the September 23, 1998, drug screen was positive for opiates, she interpreted the positive screen to be a result of Ms. Monroe's Talwin use. However, I told her about my conversation with Ms. Monroe's physician (see paragraph below), in which he said Talwin should not produce a positive opiate screen. After I provided Ms. McLean with the information from Dr. Murray, she called AnalyzeNow Laboratories, the drug screening company. She said she was advised that Talwin should not appear as a positive opiate on a urine screen. Ms. McLean explained the urine test they use is the same as that used by the Massachusetts Parole Board.

When I consulted Dr. Primarycare Murray, Ms. Monroe's physician, he said Talwin should not show up as a positive opiate result on a urine drug screen. He explained that he last prescribed Talwin for Ms. Monroe on September 9, 1998, (at which time he prescribed 12 tablets) because, "She complains of a back problem." He explained that Ms. Monroe does not follow up on other treatment recommendations. Dr. Murray was surprised when I asked him if Ms. Monroe informed him of her substance abuse history, responding that she did not, although he "was suspicious the way she was asking about medication. She kept on asking for more pain medication." Dr. Coverage Aykroyd, who provides coverage for Dr. Murray, described Ms. Monroe as "heavy on the narcotics. She has real back pain." He said her request for Talwin was "a little of each" (both pain management and getting high).

Dr. Orthopedic Kostner, who wrote a letter to DSS in the past explaining Ms. Monroe's need for Talwin, declined to respond to telephone interview questions out of concern for the gravity of the interview questions. He requested time to put his concerns in writing. At the time of the preparation of this report, I had not received any written response from him. Dr. Kostner carefully chose his words when we spoke by telephone. He declined to describe Ms. Monroe's use of Talwin as either appropriate or inappropriate. He said, "It could be interpreted both ways."

I consulted with Ms. Nurse Streep (a nurse practitioner in the orthopedic department) and Dr. Pharmacist Nicholson (a pharmacist) of the West City, and they both said Talwin should not show up as a positive opiate on a urine screen. Dr. Nicholson explained that Talwin contains a synthetic opiate that does not register on urine screens. He said urine screens do not select for Talwin. Dr. Brukim explained, "The test has no cross reactivity with Talwin. Talwin does not come up positive as an opiate." I called Mr. Labrat Crystal, technical support specialist for AnalyzeNow Laboratories (the company that ScreenNow uses for urine screen analyses). He said ScreenNow uses the Ontrack test cup, which tests for opiates of the type that would appear with morphine use. The cup also tests for amphetamines, cocaine, and marijuana. He said Talwin should not show up as positive for opiates in a urine screen using the Ontrak test kit for morphine. He added that Talwin has not specifically been tested for cross-reactivity, but because of its chemical structure, it is "not a cross-reactive drug." He said, "Based on the chemical structure, it is not expected to show up positive for opiates." He explained that the screening test has 97 to 98 percent accuracy in both sensitivity (avoiding false positives) and specificity (avoiding false negatives).

ASSESSMENT RESULTS, TROUBLED MONROE

Mental Status Examination Ms. Monroe was easily irritated when asked about her childhood and adolescent conduct. She became emotionally overwhelmed and asked to leave the first appointment after only one half hour. She said she would return in the afternoon when another appointment was finished. She did not return, however. Ms. Monroe did not show up for her second appointment, and canceled the third appointment because of a family emergency involving her niece. She apologized frequently for missing the meeting, but she would not disclose the details of the emergency.

During the second interview, Ms. Monroe became belligerent when I asked her about her relationship with Mr. Latency Howard. She yelled about being judged for past actions. I ended the interview for a break; after the break, she refused to discuss this information. It was necessary to rely on the records and a previous evaluation for information about her past relationships, dating history, substance use history, and mental health history. In general, her cooperation with the interview was limited, her attendance for evaluation appointments was poor, and her affect during evaluation appointments was labile. Her emotional expression was more controlled during the parent-child visit. Ms. Monroe's mood was anxious, angry, and overwhelmed. She remained calm during the parent-child visit, but she became tearful at the end of the visit.

Ms. Monroe showed no problems with self-care. She demonstrated no abnormalities in her motor behavior. Her speech showed normal rate. She described no problems with her appetite, sleep patterns, or weight. She said she has had no recent thoughts of harm to herself or others. She endorsed no symptoms consistent with distorted perceptions, disorganized thinking, or delusional thinking. Complaints about DSS were made frequently, some of which had the quality of delusions of reference (people being out to get her). Her complaints contained frequent attribution of blame to others.

Neuropsychological and Cognitive Functioning During the interview, Ms. Monroe had difficulty discussing issues from her history, but her problems were unrelated to organic deficits or memory impairment. She was oriented to person, place, time, and situation. Her assessment results are inconsistent with memory impairment of the type associated with brain trauma or neurological deterioration. She did not report functional memory impairment on the Dissociative Experiences Scale (see below).

On the WAIS-III Ms. Monroe obtained scores that fell in the Average range of functioning on the Working Memory Index and the Processing Speed Index. She did not demonstrate difficulty on tasks requiring attention and concentration; however, she showed some difficulty sustaining attention during mental manipulations compared with attention required for less intense tasks. She demonstrated no difficulty with rote memorization. Although her weakness was not pervasive, she showed some weakness on tasks requiring abstract reasoning skills.

Because the history revealed possible Attention Deficit Hyperactivity Disorder (ADHD) in her childhood, Ms. Monroe was asked to complete the ADHD Rating Scale based on her recollection of her functioning in junior high school. She endorsed all 14 items, giving the most severe rating to 13 of the 14 items. She endorsed items associated with inattention and hyperactivity. Results suggest she retrospectively viewed herself as having persistent and severe symptoms associated with ADHD.

On the WAIS-III, Ms. Monroe obtained a Full Scale IQ of 89, which falls in the Low Average range of intellectual functioning. She obtained a Verbal IQ score of 93 and a Performance IQ score of 84, a nonsignificant difference. Relative to her other subscale scores, she demonstrated weakness (at a statistically significant level) on the Matrix Reasoning subscale (associated with abstract reasoning and conceptual reasoning skills). Although the differences were not significant, she also showed a trend toward weakness on the Picture Arrangement subscale (associated with social reasoning and sequencing abilities) and strength on the Comprehension subscale (associated with common sense reasoning).

Affective and Personality Functioning On the MMPI-2, Ms. Monroe obtained a profile on the validity scales associated with an unusually high rate of endorsing problems, symptoms, and unusual experiences. This type of validity configuration is unusual in parents involved in custody proceedings (in fact, being more defensive and underendorsing problems is more common). She obtained an elevation on Scale F, which is associated with four possible types of behavior: (a) malingering; (b) exaggeration of symptoms and problems as a plea for help; (c) uncooperativeness, lack of concentration, or difficulty understanding items; and (d) psychosis. She did not obtain elevations in TRIN or VRIN (associated with inconsistent responding); however, her Fb Scale was elevated (reflecting the elevated F Scale and also suggestive of fatigue toward the end of the assessment). The F-K ratio was nonsignificant, suggesting an interpretable profile (for the Clinical Scales) indicative of a plea for help.

On the clinical scales of the MMPI-2, Ms. Monroe obtained elevations on scales 4, 7, 8, and

9. This configuration of elevations is seen in individuals who show patterns of problem behavior (e.g., in areas such as substance abuse and sexual behavior) and who are insensitive to the consequences of such behavior. Individuals with this configuration of elevations might feel transitory remorse but typically have difficulty using remorse to inhibit further conduct problems. They often report somatic symptoms associated with distress, and tend to be seen as nonconforming, resentful of authority, unpredictable, angry, irritable, distrustful, and manipulative. Difficulty delaying gratification and a tendency to project blame for their problems onto others are often seen, as well. Overall adjustment is typically marginal. This configuration of elevations is common in individuals with florid symptoms of Posttraumatic Stress Disorder; however, it also reflects comorbid problems with the integrity of thinking.

On the MCMI-II, however, Ms. Monroe responded in a different manner. Her approach was more defensive, and she tended to endorse items with greater social desirability. Despite her attempts to minimize problems and pathology, however, the profile was suggestive of interpersonal problems associated with histrionic behavior, narcissistic behavior, antisocial behavior, paranoid thinking patterns, a history of drug dependence, and delusional thinking. The results suggest a moderate level of character pathology of the type associated with attention-seeking behavior, denial of interpersonal problems, difficulty viewing problems or issues from the perspective of another individual, chronic anger and anxiety, hostility, authority problems, and difficulty delaying gratification. The MCMI-II profile suggests that Ms. Monroe is likely to project blame for her problems onto other individuals. It is likely she has difficulty with intimacy, and feels more comfortable in superficial relationships. She likely responds better to supportive individuals than to those who might confront her about her interpersonal difficulties. The profile is consistent with that seen in individuals who are at risk of temper outbursts and possibly assaultive behavior. The results suggest that she would respond better to behavioral treatment and skill building than insight-oriented treatment. Like the MMPI-2, the MCMI-ll does not distinguish between individuals who have history of substance abuse problems and those who currently are abusing substances. She obtained an elevation consistent with an addictive orientation, endorsing items suggestive of both alcohol and drug problems.

On the Dissociative Experiences Scale, Ms. Monroe obtained a nonsignificant score. This suggests that she presently does not experience severe symptoms of dissociation, escape into fantasy, amnestic episodes, feelings of derealization or depersonalization, or functional memory impairment.

Abilities Related to Parenting Competence Ms. Monroe described Latency as a boy with a "very short attention span . . . a very unsettled child right now. He's going through a lot where he's very easily disturbed meeting new people. He's afraid of change. His environment, things like that, he's afraid of stuff that's new—environment, people, change." She said, "He's hard to handle as far as sitting him down and bringing him back down when he is abruptly out of control. Latency needs a lot of attention and he needs to be always praised, always told he's safe, he's gonna be safe, no more harm's gonna come to him. He's a very loving child. He's proud of himself when he does well. He needs encouragement when he does not do well. He can get really out of control at times. He's adorable—totally cute kid." Ms. Monroe said her son has special academic needs, including a need for assistance in reading and math. She said his attention span is a problem for him in school. She believes his reading problem is related to his attention problems: "He doesn't like to sit still for a long period of time."

When asked about her methods of discipline, Ms. Monroe said, "I know you don't hit children, I know you don't yell and swear. You have to be consistent with children. You have to be totally patient and tolerant, having to constantly tell them things. Time-out if necessary." She described time-out as "putting them in a chair and having them sit, explaining why you're making them sit." She said time-out consists of one minute per the age of the child. When asked how to manage a child having a temper tantrum, she said, "Holding them until they're calm enough to ask what's the matter, what's going on? Telling them when they're ready to talk, you're right there."

When asked to whom she turns for parenting advice and support, Ms. Monroe named her sponsor, her sister, her counselor, and the member's of the women's group and the women's step group (both M groups). She said she manages the stress of parenting by "talking to people, walking away from the situation long enough to calm down and go back to it and deal with appropriately, not to instantly react but to sit and think." She said, "Most parents fail because they react without thinking. I don't do that no more." When asked about her difficulty with impatience, she attributed her impatience to her situation (i.e., "having to go through so much in order to please DSS"). She added, "At home, it's not like that. It doesn't affect Junior in any way. I come here, I get stressed out." She said, "Whenever I leave DSS meetings, I call my sponsor. I run short of patience because I'm tired of going through this." She relies on two adult child care workers, both of whom DSS checked, who she said live nearby and are typically available when she needs them.

Ms. Monroe described her home as a three-bedroom dwelling with a kitchenette and living room, a washer and dryer. Her bedroom and Junior's room are "all set up." She purchased furniture for Latency's room, but she has not purchased sheets and bedding. She said Junior has difficulty sleeping through the night in his own room because of his age. Were Latency to return home, she would keep Junior in her room in order to provide close supervision at night. She said she would explain to Latency that Junior is young, and would not want Latency to feel accused or mistrusted. When asked what type of activities she would plan for the children if she had both of them, Ms. Monroe said she would take them to Near City State Park, to the park up the street, to the Kids Club in South City, to karate and gymnastics, and on walks. She would plan water painting, crayons, finger painting, drawing, coloring, videos, and video games.

When asked to describe the routine on a typical weekday during the school year (if she had both children), Ms. Monroe said the day would start with breakfast, then the Get Up Early meeting (and perhaps breakfast afterward if the children were not hungry before the meeting), playing outside, putting on a movie if it is a rainy day, talking about the movie, lunch at 11:00 or 12:00,

rest time, play outdoors or indoors depending on the weather, games, dinner, baths, story time, talking about the day, and then bedtime. She described a nutritional and balanced diet for them. She said she enjoys cooking. Since Latency's school would be several miles away and it would be necessary for him to ride the bus, Ms. Monroe said she would be candid with the school system about what Latency has been through (his history of sexual molestation, his attention problems). She said she would try to volunteer in the school in order to help them out.

Observed Parent-Child Visit When Latency saw his mother in the DSS parking lot, he hugged her. He did not seem fearful of physical touch between them. Ms. Monroe chose a movie called "Little Troopers." Prior to the movie, she gave Latency some quarters. Latency played a video game involving shooting people with guns. (The movie theater had nothing less violent to offer in their selection of video games. However, a pinball game without violent themes was available.) The movie was rated PG-13, and it contained a significant amount of violence. Ms. Monroe expressed no concern about the movie content.

Latency pouted when his mother ended his video game play, but he did not have a tantrum. During the movie, he offered part of his candy bar to his mother. They shared some questions and answers during the movie. After the movie, Latency and Ms. Monroe sat in a booth at a fast food restaurant. She did not have enough money to purchase food for both of them, so she bought food for Latency. Latency made spontaneous statements in his conversation with her. He was talkative, and he told his mother about camp, swimming, and other water activities. He shared the details of a wiffle ball game, and he told his mother that he is a fast runner. They talked about his new school clothes and planned his next visit. Ms. Monroe gave Latency a picture of Junior. Latency played outside the restaurant with spitballs; Ms. Monroe set appropriate limits concerning the placement of the spitballs.

I asked Ms. Monroe to explain to Latency the rules of safety during visits with Junior. She appeared resentful of my request, but complied. She explained that there should be no rough play between them and then she asked Latency to explain what roughhousing meant. She said nothing about refraining from sexual touch. Ms. Monroe then noticed that Latency's teeth needed to be cleaned. She gave him a mini lecture about dental hygiene. Latency did not show any discomfort when she touched his mouth and peered in at his teeth. At the end of the visit, they shared hugs, and Ms. Monroe gave Latency an appropriate kiss. He was unafraid when she hugged and kissed him, but he also watched for Ms. Ross's van. Ms. Monroe cried at the end of the visit, but she attempted to shield her tears from Latency.

ASSESSMENT RESULTS, LATENCY HOWARD

Latency identified himself as a fourth grade student. When I asked if he knew the reason for my visit, he glared at me and said he would not answer any questions. When I changed the subject to child activities, he said he enjoys swimming, playing with his friends, playing outdoors, and going on activities with his foster family. I told him he would not be the one to decide where he might live in the future, but the judge might like to know what he thinks. He said he wanted to stay where he was. He refused to answer any further questions without his foster mother's presence. In the presence of his foster mother, he said his first, second, and third choice of where he wanted to live was "here" with his foster parents.

After a visit with Ms. Monroe, I asked Latency the same interview questions. In general, he was more talkative about himself. He said he enjoyed visits with his mother, and he especially liked going to movies with her. He expressed a preference for living with her. He said he would miss his foster parents, and he hoped he could see them regardless of where he might live. He said it would not bother him to change schools if he went to live with her. When asked to describe three things he liked about his mother, he said he liked "everything" about her. When asked if there was something he wished was different about her, he could think of nothing. He said he enjoys talking with her and going to the park with her. He said he feels "happy" during visits with his mother, and was sick of waiting for a family. He said he wanted to see his brother Junior more often, and told me about his older brother.

Mental Status Examination   Latency showed no unusual appearance or hygiene problems for a boy his age. His facial expression was sullen, but he showed some variations in his facial expressions when he interacted with his foster mother and his mother. His refused to participate in a full clinical interview. He was withdrawn, with episodes of irritability. During the first interview, he ran out of the room and slammed the door. He said he did not want to answer questions about himself. He initially responded to the limits set by his foster mother, but then his behavior worsened. He attempted to bang his head on the doorpost. He then responded to limits set by me, but he stared defiantly, apparently wondering if I would set further limits. He also refrained from head banging when his foster mother told him to stop.

Latency's motor behavior was restless, and his mood was apprehensive and suspicious. He reported fear that he would be taken away from his foster home. His speech was sparse, with long pauses. However, in his interaction with his foster mother and his mother, he sometimes demonstrated a normal rate and prosody of speech. His affect was easily disorganized with episodes of irritability. He sometimes complied with directives and other times did not. He was oriented to person, place, time, and situation. He showed a short attention span and difficulty with concentration due to high distractibility. Thought content was remarkable for magical thinking and extreme fear of being removed from foster care.

During my final visit with him, Latency refused to answer any questions. He had difficulty remaining in the same room with me. He ran back and forth, outside and inside of the house. He had an episode of disruptive tantrum behavior with a near assault. (He had been promised Fast Food Joint's French fries as an incentive for answering interview questions. When he was told there would be no Fast Food Joint's trip due to his behavior, he ran after me and nearly jumped on or hit my back.) His foster mother had difficulty containing his threats of runaway behavior. At several points, Latency nearly ran out into the street. He finally refrained from running away. Ms. Ross was nearly in tears as I left the interview. She expressed exasperation over how difficult it sometimes was to manage Latency's behavior. She later said Latency continued to tantrum for 2½ hours after I discontinued the interview.

Special Needs Based on information from the DSS record and from treatment providers, Latency is enrolled in individual therapy and group therapy. His psychiatrist, Dr. Abusive Shrand, has prescribed medication for Latency since February of 1998. Latency currently takes 0.25 mg of clonidine (an anxiolytic) per day. He currently is receiving special attention from his teachers (i.e., less homework than other students, more disciplinary concerns than other students), but he is not identified as a special needs student. He reportedly has symptoms consistent with inattention, hyperactivity, hyperarousal, anxiety, night terrors, sleepwalking, and conduct problems.

INTERPRETATION OF PSYCHOLOGICAL ASSESSMENT RESULTS

Ms. Monroe reportedly has a history of significant and chronic childhood and adult trauma. This history includes reported instances of paternal abandonment, paternal substance abuse, paternal substance abuse overdose in her presence, maternal substance abuse, maternal physical abuse, maternal verbal abuse, maternal sexual behavior in her presence, maternal illegal behavior, victimization by and witnessing abuse by her mother's boyfriends, maternal mental illness, maternal abandonment and imprisonment, out-of-home placement (reportedly in 17 different foster homes), foster parent abuse, victimization by domestic violence, and the need to use violence in self-defense. She currently has only distant relationships with the members of her family of origin. Based on her description of her history, it is likely that her distant relationships with them reflects good judgment on her part. Affiliating with the non-substance abusing members of her family likely would serve as a trigger for traumatic recollections; affiliating with the substance abusing members of her family would place her at risk of relapse.

Ms. Monroe is a high school educated woman with no significant occupational history. She supports herself with SSI disability income and child support payments from her infant son's father.

She functions in the Low Average to Average range of intelligence, with weaknesses in abstract reasoning skills and strength in common sense reasoning skills. She has the intellectual capacity to benefit from vocational training and from verbal psychotherapies. However, assessment results suggest it is unlikely that she would would benefit from insight-oriented approaches to treatment because of emotional overwhelm and character problems.

Ms. Monroe developed conduct problems in high school. She was suspended from school, engaged in drug dealing, was introduced to alcohol at age 7 and cocaine at age 9, abused alcohol and drugs, stole from her place of employment, and fought with high school peers. Her alcohol and drug use continued into adulthood. Records suggest she developed a severe substance abuse problem. Assessment results suggest she continues to show problems with character, such as temper outbursts, projection of blame, difficulty delaying gratification, risk of acting out, insensitivity to behavioral consequences, resentment of authority, manipulative behavior, suspicious or persecutory thinking patterns, difficulty tolerating intimacy, and chronic negative emotions (anger, anxiety, hostility).

In addition, Ms. Monroe recently had a urine screen that was positive for opiates. Results of consultation suggest the positive drug screen is not a result of taking prescription medication (Talwin) for back pain. Because of her history of heroin use, it seems reasonable to conclude that a likely explanation of the positive urine screen is heroin use. It is noteworthy that she refused to discuss her substance abuse history in this evaluation. However, her extensive description of her AA involvement suggests she has a high degree of familiarity with the AA approach to recovery. Based on the detailed nature of her description of the 12-step program, for example, it is likely she attempts to use this approach in her recovery. She has some understanding of relapse prevention planning, but her description of her plan was incomplete, suggesting this particular approach may not be a strength for her.

Ms. Monroe has a history of detoxifications, short-term rehabilitation programs, sober housing, day treatment at Recovery Place in Near City. She has used alcohol, cocaine, mescaline, THC, acid, Valium, cocaine (powder and crack), marijuana, Quaaludes, MM714, and heroin. Her most recent drugs of choice included heroin and crack cocaine. In 1995 she was using crack cocaine. In 1996, she was terminated from South City Sober Housing because of heroin use. Ms. Monroe obtained some positive urine screens in January of 1998, and she recently had a positive opiate screen in September of 1998. If she currently is using heroin, then she is not meeting her service plan with respect to the need to remain drug free.

At the present time, Ms. Monroe has income from her disability payments, and she qualified for Section Eight housing; she maintains an apartment in South City. She is separated from her infant son's father so that they both can prioritize sobriety and so that she can prioritize parenting. She has a support network that consists of AA peers and her counselors.

In addition to her substance abuse, it is likely that Ms. Monroe's diagnostic history includes Attention Deficit Hyperactivity Disorder, Posttraumatic Stress Disorder, conduct problems, and problems of character. To my knowledge, she is not seeing a psychiatrist for consultation or medication concerning any of these problems. Her psychotherapist described their therapy relationship as good, but his description of her therapy attendance suggested that since May of 1998 she has frequently canceled appointments. Although Mr. Bridges thought that she canceled for good reason, it appears he misunderstood the amount of time she spent attending evaluation appointments with me. Based on this misconception, it seems likely he might sometimes believe her reasons when she attempts to mislead him. Nonetheless, he described frequent telephone contact and appropriate treatment content, with one possible exception. That is, if Ms. Monroe sexually abused or participated in sexual abuse of Latency, then her lack of attention to this issue in treatment is of concern.

Mr. Bridges is a good advocate for Ms. Monroe and should remain involved in her treatment as her individual therapist. However, any court-ordered treatment for sexual offending (if applicable) should be provided by a different mental health professional. In addition, it should be noted that Mr. Bridges and Ms. Field have a conflicted understanding of the case that prevents them from working together with Ms. Monroe and Latency. For example, Mr. Bridges believes it is unlikely Ms. Monroe is a sex offender, whereas Ms. Field believes it is quite likely Ms. Monroe is a sex offender. Ms. Field strongly stated her concern that Latency has problems before and after maternal visitation, but at the same time she observed only one visit. Because of the polarization on these issues, the court may wish to consider their sentiments about the case in plans for the custody of Latency. Should the court order any conjoint sessions with Ms. Monroe and Latency, they should be conducted by someone other than Mr. Bridges or Ms. Field. (Even if their sentiments were more objective, the ethics of the profession suggests this role should be assumed by a third party.)

With due respect to the difficulty of the task of conducting child sexual abuse investigations, the DSS record of the final 51A investigation (in 1996) raises serious concern about the validity of that interview. It should be noted that concern about the possibility that Ms. Monroe committed sexual abuse of Latency arose prior to this particular 51A investigation. However, the final 51A investigation lacks validity because the interview method, as documented by the DSS investigator, was full of problems. First, the DSS investigator allowed the foster parent to conduct the investigation interview. Second, the foster mother used leading and suggestive questions when she conducted the interview. For example, in the investigation, the foster parent said to Latency, "You told me your mom took off her clothes . . . you told me MoreAbusive was there. . . . You told me someone put your penis in their mouth." Latency responded by saying "Ya" to these questions. Third, the DSS investigator allowed the interview to continue despite the inappropriate structure of the foster mother's interview questions. (It is doubtful the foster mother recognized the structure of her questions was inappropriate, nor should she have been placed in this awkward role.) Accordingly, I find it difficult to evaluate Ms. Monroe's response to treatment relevant to sexual offending. Because of the suggestive nature of the investigation questions, any further information from Latency likely was tainted by the interview. Again, however, it should be noted that concern about the possibility that Ms. Monroe sexually abused Latency arose prior to the final DSS 51A investigation.

The DSS records indicate the 1995 51A were supported for maternal neglect, maternal substance abuse, sexual abuse by Mr. MoreAbusive Grant, and sexual abuse by Ms. Monroe. Although the 1995 51A was supported for maternal sexual abuse, the DSS did not specifically recommend sex offender treatment for Ms. Monroe. They recommended she should "address issues regarding her own sexual abuse history and sexual abuse history of the children." The previous evaluation (and her therapist) concluded she did not meet the profile of a sex offender; however, it should be noted there is no "profile" of a sex offender. Little is known about the characteristics of female sex offenders. There are known factors associated with risk of violence and sexual offending. In my clinical opinion, Ms. Monroe's history contains risk factors (see below).

Based on the lack of specific recommendations concerning sex offender treatment, it seems Ms. Monroe technically cannot be held accountable for a failure to address her alleged sexual abuse of Latency Howard. This technicality, the passage of 3½ years, and her therapist's belief that it is unlikely that she is a sex offender, suggest that it is unlikely Ms. Monroe would take this issue seriously were the court to order sex offender treatment. In addition, because of Ms. Monroe's sense of being very overwhelmed by her own history of abuse, it seems unlikely she would respond well to the phase of sex offender treatment that requires an analysis of the events that contributed to the offending behavior.

With respect to her understanding of basic parenting information, Ms. Monroe has a good knowledge base concerning discipline methods. She had difficulty describing a daily routine for Latency because she misunderstood the need to think about his school attendance, and she provided an incomplete description of how she might use methods of distraction, reward, and discipline to keep the children safe and free from conflict with each other. Her difficulty talking to Latency about his risk of sexual offending suggests the possibility that Junior is at risk of sexual play or sexual offending in the absence of close supervision of the interaction between Latency and Junior. However, it should be noted that La-

tency's tender age (and the lack of literature concerning the offending risk of young children) prevents any reasonable prediction of his likelihood of sexual offending.

It is clear that Latency's temper is difficult to manage. Because Ms. Ross, who has close supervision from Kid and who appears to have a great deal of skill in managing Latency's behavior, reported feeling overwhelmed in her parenting of him, I am concerned that Ms. Monroe will have a similar reaction in her parenting of Latency. Her assessment results suggest she does not manage anxiety and overwhelming feelings very well. She is at risk of temper outbursts, hostility, and anger when she experiences such anxiety and overwhelming emotion. She has difficulty with emotional regulation. Sometimes she continues to turn to avoidance and fabrication as coping mechanisms. She may have problems with the integrity of her thoughts. In addition, in the past she sometimes turned to substance abuse during periods when she was frustrated and overwhelmed. Were she to be awarded custody of Latency, she would continue to need intensive skill-building treatment and parenting support.

Ms. Monroe continues to minimize the significance of her past neglect of Latency, which is relevant to her future risk of attending to him sufficiently. She initially said she was away paying bills when DSS took custody of her children. She did not acknowledge that she had a positive cocaine screen shortly thereafter. Although she has a significant substance abuse history, she thought DSS was intrusive and excessive in their request for frequent drug screens. However, she complied with most of the requests for drug screens. She apparently used drugs during her pregnancy with Junior because of her need to go to detoxification after he was born. She minimized the DSS concern about her substance abuse, stating that Junior was safe because he was with his father.

Ms. Monroe acknowledged that Latency might have been sexually abused by Mr. Grant in her absence, but continued to maintain that she left her sons with Mr. Grant only twice, for no more than 20 minutes. To her credit, Ms. Monroe admitted that her drug use was selfish. She expressed a willingness to apologize to Latency for things he believes she might have done. She believes that he was sexually abused by Mr. Grant. She spoke highly of the parenting classes, and she said she found them helpful. She may need some additional tutoring concerning shielding traumatized children from movies and toys with violent themes, and the bond between Ms. Ross and Latency (it would be important not to break this bond, but to acknowledge it and allow it to gradually but never fully dissipate). She acknowledged the need for a slow transition for Latency should she regain custody of him.

Latency is a boy whose parenting needs consist of close supervisory attention, help with homework, steady discipline, management of temper outbursts, comfort for periods of anxiety and feeling overwhelmed, attention to his school schedule and his medical appointments (including individual therapy, medication appointments, and group therapy), management of sleep disruption, sensitivity to triggers of traumatic recollections, monitoring his use of prescribed anxiolytic medication, consultation with his schoolteacher concerning classroom conduct and academic progress, preventing inappropriate touching of pets, and monitoring what may be a risk of sexual play or sexual acting out. He will have a long period of mourning at the loss of his foster family. Latency's primary attachment is to his foster mother. It is likely that he will act out his anger during one phase of his mourning. Regardless of where he is placed, the transition should occur slowly, with a provision for foster parent visitation of Latency for as long as DSS deems practical. Because of Latency's volatile behavior, a transitional residential placement may be necessary. Although he is not inclined to run beyond the local neighborhood, he may be at risk of property damage to his room, head banging, or runaway behavior should he disapprove of a new foster placement, placement with his mother, or placement with a preadoptive family.

Latency has a secondary attachment to his mother; however, it is unclear whether his expressed wish to live with his mother is due to an attachment to her or an inability to imagine living anywhere other than with his foster family or with his mother. He showed no discomfort in the presence of his mother; however, his foster mother reported occasional deterioration before and after visits. It is noteworthy that Latency's deterioration did not occur until he received the news last fall that his foster family would not be a permanent placement. It is likely his acting out around maternal visits was his way of protesting his impending removal from foster care. However, another possibility involves the recollection of trauma triggered by his mother's presence: Latency was overwhelmed by any mention of his preference of where to live. His sense of being overwhelmed is primarily due to his attachment to his foster parents.

CONCLUSIONS

Risk Factors   Ms. Monroe has a significant history of childhood and adult trauma that continues to overwhelm her to a significant degree. She suffers from periods of hyperarousal, which place her at risk of avoidant behavior, fabrication in order to rationalize her avoidance, and difficulty with emotional regulation. Her cognitive resources are compromised by significant deficits in coping resources specific to emotional dysregulation and intrusive or compromised thoughts. She sometimes has florid symptoms of Post Traumatic Stress Disorder, which make it difficult to focus beyond her immediate concerns. She has no history of successful employment. Because of the intractable nature of some of her character problems, she is unlikely to benefit from insight-oriented treatment. Her response to other methods of treatment designed to address character problems likely will be slow. Her recent attendance in therapy has been poor due to frequent cancellations.

Ms. Monroe has a history of adolescent-onset conduct problems, including school suspensions, school fighting, stealing, drug dealing, alcohol abuse, and drug abuse. In adulthood, she developed a severe substance abuse problem. Her most recent drugs of choice included crack cocaine and heroin. Her recent positive drug screen raises suspicion about the likelihood of recent heroin use. Ms. Monroe minimized her neglect of Latency. She refused to discuss her substance abuse history. She did not acknowledge any maternal sexual abuse of Latency. It is likely that she minimized the amount of time she left Latency alone with Mr. Grant. Should the court conclude that Ms. Monroe sexually abused Latency, then her risk of further sexual abuse remains high because she denies that she behaved in this way and because she obtained no treatment specific to sexual offending. (However, it should be noted that no such treatment was specifically requested of her.) It is unlikely she would take sex offender treatment seriously in the future because of the mixed messages she received concerning the need for sex offender treatment, and because of her individual therapist's support of her view that she did not sexually abuse her child. Although there were allegations and a supported 51A in 1995, the problematic approach to the most recent 1996 DSS 51A investigation obfuscated any possibility of clarifying the allegations of possible sexual abuse by Ms. Monroe. In addition, the passage of time suggests a decision about custody should be made for the sake of parenting continuity for Latency. Ms. Monroe understands basic parenting information, but she likely will still require intensive monitoring in order to provide for the special needs of Latency, and for the safety needs of both of her sons. Should the court decide to return physical custody of Latency to her, it is recommended that DSS remain involved in order to provide intensive monitoring and treatment services for both Ms. Monroe and Latency. She should be advised not to take Latency to treatment or AA meetings with her.

Factors Associated with the Ability to Refrain from Child Maltreatment During calmer periods, Ms. Monroe described the capacity to turn to her support network for help. She described detailed knowledge of the AA method of substance abuse recovery, suggesting she sometimes takes this treatment method quite seriously. She reportedly avoids close relationships or close affiliation with individuals who might influence her to relapse. She is a high school graduate with the cognitive capacity to benefit from a variety of helping interventions. She has a strong relationship with her individual therapist.

Ms. Monroe acknowledged that Latency might have been sexually abused by Mr. Grant in her absence. She admitted her drug use was selfish. She expressed a willingness to apologize to Latency for what he believes she might have done. She believes he was sexually abused by Mr. Grant. She expressed a positive attitude about the helpfulness of parenting classes. She acknowledged the close bond between Latency and Ms. Ross and the need to make a slow transition to a different parenting plan for Latency.

RECOMMENDATIONS

1. In my clinical opinion, Ms. Monroe has significant parenting deficits and character problems that would make it difficult for her to provide proper parenting of Latency. Her deficits include florid symptoms of mental illness that interfere with her capacity to use productive coping resources, and a relative lack of patience and specialized knowledge to address the special needs of Latency. Her character problems include the likelihood of recent substance abuse, difficulty refraining from hostility and temper outbursts, and avoidance of important appointments with helping resources.

2. In my clinical opinion, should the court terminate Ms. Monroe's parental rights, she should be afforded the opportunity to meet with Latency to tell him goodbye. The court may wish to provide for open adoption exchanges of information. Open adoption visits are contraindicated if the court deems that she is abusing substances or that she sexually abused Latency.

3. In my clinical opinion, should the court terminate Ms. Monroe's parental rights, Latency may need a transitional placement in order to manage the behavioral disruption that can be expected when he reaches the angry phase of mourning of the loss of his foster parents. The court may wish to provide for indefinite visitation between Latency and his foster family. Because of the high level of intensity in the relationship between Ms. Ross and Latency, DSS may wish to monitor foster care support of Latency as he transitions to a new home.

4. In my clinical opinion, should the court terminate Ms. Monroe's parental rights, Latency will need a specialized adoptive placement in order to provide for his special needs as described earlier.

5. In my clinical opinion, should the court retain Ms. Monroe's parental rights, Ms. Monroe should be required to remain involved in parenting classes, Alcoholics Anonymous, and individual treatment. The court may wish to add Nar-

cotics Anonymous and continually updated written substance abuse relapse prevention plans to her Service Plan. The court may wish to require that Ms. Monroe prove that she recently maintained her sobriety. The court may wish to order sex offender treatment, with the caveat that it is unlikely Ms. Monroe would take such treatment seriously.

6. In my clinical opinion, should the court retain Ms. Monroe's parental rights, Latency should be transitioned slowly back to her physical custody with the provision of temporary residential placement should Latency's behavior become unmanageable. The guardian ad litem and the DSS should remain involved. Latency will need to be transitioned to a new individual therapist who is

supportive of reunification with Ms. Monroe. The DSS should continue to provide close monitoring and intensive treatment services for Ms. Monroe.

7. In my clinical opinion, Latency has suffered significant emotional distress due to the long length of his foster placement and due to his awareness of the lack of a permanent plan. He would benefit from a permanent plan with significant helping resources to minimize the risk of a failed parental or adoptive placement.

Lois B. Oberlander, Ph.D., ABPP
Assistant Professor of Psychiatry
Board Certified in Forensic Psychology
American Board of Professional Psychology

Teaching Point: How can the forensic clinician handle reluctance and refusal to participate in court-ordered evaluations?

There are a number of approaches that a forensic clinician can use to address reluctance and refusal in court-ordered evaluations. Reluctance refers to an unwillingness or active resistance to participating in the FMHA process. When faced with reluctance, it is useful for the forensic clinician to first ask the participant about the reasons for their unwillingness to participate. In many instances, this line of questioning will reveal that the participant does not fully understand some aspect of the evaluation, and therefore requires more information. Similarly, questioning may reveal that the participant has some misconception about the evaluation process and its consequences. In either case, the forensic clinician should make every effort to provide missing information and clarify any misconceptions that arise from this line of questioning.

Misconceptions and limited information about the evaluation are not the only sources of reluctance in court-ordered evaluations. Anxiety regarding the evaluation process itself, and related testing procedures, can also contribute. In such instances, the forensic clinician should explain the evaluation process and the techniques to be used in as much detail as possible to ease the participant's apprehension. This approach not only reduces reluctance, but can also be used to help establish rapport with the individual being evaluated.

Certain legal questions require extensive and lengthy evaluations, and some participants might initially be unwilling to engage in such an activity for an extended period of time. It is usually helpful to explain that breaks will be given as needed, including time for meals and refreshment. The forensic clinician must also be aware that certain populations, such as children with ADHD or adults with cognitive limitations, might demonstrate ongoing reluctance because it is difficult to sit quietly, concentrate, and engage in question-and-answer for a long period of time. Special needs can be accommodated by scheduling shorter periods for evaluation over different sessions.

Refusal is an outright decision against participating in the evaluation. The response to refusal in court-ordered evaluations varies depending on the context and referral question of the case. If the individual does not have a legal right to refuse, as in most court-ordered evaluations, then the forensic clinician should explain the consequences for not participating. For example, in an insanity case, failure to participate could result in counsel not being able to mount an adequate defense; failure to participate in a court-ordered insanity evaluation could also prevent the defense from introducing the results of an evaluation performed by a defense-retained forensic clinician. In the civil context, refusal to participate in a court-ordered child custody evaluation could result in charges for contempt of court, and could also have a negative outcome on visitation or other parental rights. Joint custody can pose special problems in the context of refusal. If a parent with joint custody does not give permission to have the child evaluated, even when the other parent has given permission, it is advisable for the clinician to defer the evaluation until it has been expressly authorized, either through court order or through the authorization of both parents.

If the individual does have the legal right to refuse, as in an attorney-requested evaluation, then the prudent response to an initial refusal is to reschedule or delay the evaluation to allow the person to contact their attorney or receive advice from anyone else with whom they need to speak. Similarly, it may be possible to reschedule the evaluation for a later date if the person's refusal stems from a particular problem (e.g., with jail staff) that is unrelated to the case. Regardless of the basis for the reluctance or refusal, the forensic clinician should treat all individuals being evaluated with courtesy, dignity, and respect, which may have the related benefit of reducing reluctance in some cases.

Chapter 17

Civil Commitment

The impact of forensic assessment on civil commitment decisions is the focus of the report in this chapter. Civil commitment questions can, in some cases, involve committed individuals exercising legitimate legal rights to secure their release, sometimes against medical advice. As a result, the results of a FMHA in this context can be subject to adversarial scrutiny in the same way it could with other kinds of FMHA. Accordingly, the principle applied to this case emphasizes the need to describe evaluation findings in terms of strengths and weaknesses, and communicating in terms of the consistency for their support. Results communicated in this fashion will need to change little under cross-examination. The teaching point for this case provides a discussion and model for the communication of risk of violence to self or others by addressing the relationship between risk factors, risk level, nature of harm, imminence of harm, and protective factors.

Case 1

Principle: Describe findings so that they need change little under cross-examination

This principle focuses on how the results of FMHA reports and testimony are communicated. Because many forensic issues involve complex questions, it can be useful to describe data in terms of their strengths and weaknesses. Accordingly, this discussion focuses on communicating the limitations and accuracy of the data and reasoning used in FMHA. There are numerous factors that can influence the accuracy of FMHA, including the unavailability of relevant information, the use of psychological tests with limited reliability or validity, and the response style of the individual being evaluated. When there are questions that do not have clear and consistently supported answers, the forensic clinician must clarify the limits of knowledge in a report or during testimony.

The presentation of FMHA findings is always subject to challenge, typically in cross-examination. One effective way to cope with such challenge involves anticipating the weak or inconsistent aspects of data and reasoning—and incorporating this characterization into the communication of findings. By challenging his or her own findings, appropriately characterizing their strength and consistency, and giving fair consideration to alternative explanations, the forensic clinician can contribute to a fairer consideration of both sides in an adversarial context. Results that are communicated in this way will need to change little under cross-examination, as the important data and reasoning consistent with an "alternative hypothesis" have been identified and considered. Some (e.g., Greenberg & Brodsky, in press) have even advocated writing a section of the FMHA report citing data and reasoning for different conclusions than were actually reached, and in this way demonstrating the existence and "fair testing" of alternative findings. Communicating results in this fashion accomplishes two purposes. First, as we will discuss shortly, it satisfies ethical obligations and is consistent with legal evidentiary standards relevant to FMHA. Second, it places the forensic clinician in a stronger position to withstand the rigors of cross-examination. Explicitly communicating the "alternative explanation," as Greenberg and Brodsky suggest, is a useful option to consider. Incorporating such alternatives into the FMHA communication of data and reasoning, however, is essential.

Ethical guidance suggests that the forensic clinician should clarify the limits of knowledge in an evaluation or testimony (Heilbrun, 2001). The *Ethical Principles of Psychologists and Code of Conduct* (APA, 1992) documents that

> Psychologists recognize limits to the certainty with which diagnoses, judgments, or predictions can be made about individuals. Psychologists attempt to identify situations in which particular interventions or assessment techniques or norms may not be applicable or may require adjustment in administration or interpretation because of factors such as individuals' gender, age, race, ethnicity, national origin, religion, sexual orientation, disability, language, or socioeconomic status. (p. 1603)

There is additional guidance in the *Ethics Code* regarding accuracy and limitations when the results of such assessments are being interpreted and such interpretations are communicated to others: "When interpreting assessment results, including automated interpretations, psychologists take into account the various test factors and characteristics of the person being assessed that might affect psychologists' judgments or reduce the accuracy of their interpretations. They indicate any significant reservations they have about the accuracy or limitations of their interpretations" (p. 1603).

Next, the *Ethics Code* addresses the circumstance in which a personal examination cannot be conducted: "When, despite reasonable efforts, such an examination is not feasible, psychologists clarify the impact of their limited information on the reliability and validity of their reports and testimony, and they appropriately limit the nature and extent of their conclusions or recommendations" (p. 1610).

Finally, the *Ethics Code* directly underscores the importance of accuracy: "Whenever necessary to avoid misleading, psychologists acknowledge the limits of their data or conclusions" (p. 1610).

The *Specialty Guidelines for Forensic Psychologists* (Committee on Ethical Guidelines for Forensic Psychologists, 1991) provides additional guidance on the importance of clarifying limits. The first consideration is the need to test "plausible rival hypotheses":

> As an expert conducting an evaluation, treatment, consultation, or scholarly/empirical investigation, the forensic psychologist maintains professional integrity by examining the issue at hand from all reasonable perspectives, actively seeking information that will differentially test plausible rival hypotheses. (p. 661)

The *Specialty Guidelines* specifically addresses the use of third-party information that cannot be corroborated:

> While many forms of data used by forensic psychologists are hearsay, forensic psychologists attempt to corroborate critical data that form the basis for their professional product. When using hearsay data that have not been corroborated, but are nevertheless utilized, forensic psychologists have an affirmative responsibility to acknowledge the uncorroborated status of those data and the reasons for relying upon such data. (p. 662)

Similarly, the *Specialty Guidelines* addresses the use of third-party mental health information in the form of notes, reports, depositions, and interviews that have been gathered by other mental health professionals. There must be appropriate observation about the possible limitation on accuracy that may result if the data are not gathered in conformity with professional standards:

> When a forensic psychologist relies upon data or information gathered by others, the origins of those data are clarified in any professional product. In addition, the forensic psychologist bears a special responsibility to ensure that such data, if relied upon, were gathered in a manner standard for the profession. (p. 662)

Finally, there is language in the *Specialty Guidelines* about clarifying limitations on findings when, despite reasonable efforts, it has not been possible to examine the individual personally or for an adequate period of time:

> Forensic psychologists avoid giving written or oral evidence about the psychological characteristics of particular individuals when they have not had an opportunity to conduct an examination of the individual adequate to the scope of the statements, opinions, or conclusions to be issued. Forensic psychologists make every reasonable effort to conduct such examinations. When it is not possible or feasible to do so, they make clear the impact of such limitations on the reliability and validity of their professional products, evidence, or testimony. (p. 663)

The *Ethical Guidelines for the Practice of Forensic Psychiatry* (AAPL, 1995) provides similar guidance on this issue. Generally, there is a broad emphasis on the importance of honesty and striving for objectivity and the need to clarify limits when personal contact with the individual is not possible:

The adversarial nature of our Anglo-American legal process presents special hazards for the practicing forensic psychiatrist. Being retained by one side in a civil or criminal matter exposes forensic psychiatrists to the potential for unintended bias and the danger of distortion of their opinion. It is the responsibility of forensic psychiatrists to minimize such hazards by carrying out their responsibilities in an honest manner striving to reach an objective opinion. Practicing forensic psychiatrists enhance the honesty and objectivity of their work by basing their forensic opinions, forensic reports, and forensic testimony on all the data available to them. They communicate the honesty of their work, efforts to attain objectivity, and the soundness of their clinical opinion by distinguishing, to the extent possible, between verified and unverified information as well as between clinical "facts," "inferences," and "impressions." (p. 3)

While there are authorities who would bar an expert opinion in regard to an individual who has not been personally examined, it is the position of the Academy that if, after earnest effort, it is not possible to conduct a personal examination, an opinion may be rendered on the basis of other information. However, under such circumstances, it is the responsibility of forensic psychiatrists to assure that the statement of their opinion and any reports of testimony based on this opinion clearly indicate that there was no personal examination and the opinion expressed is thereby limited. (p. 3)

Legal evidentiary standards under both *Frye* (1923) and *Daubert* (1993) also provide guidance on this issue. Under *Frye*, the court considers whether the technique in question is generally accepted in the field to which it belongs. The issue of whether a technique is generally accepted would depend in part on empirical questions, such as the degree of recognition and use by mental health professionals. Because the answers to such questions are usually not known, we may use criteria that should apply to the question of general acceptance: the technique's purpose; availability; the population for which it is used; and its available documentation on administration, scoring, and reliability, and validity. Each of these is relevant to the limits of the technique, which should be clarified in communicating FMHA findings. Using this reasoning, the *Frye* standard supports the principle that the forensic clinician must clarify the limits of their data, reasoning, and conclusions.

The support for this principle under *Daubert* is even clearer. When the court may consider questions such as whether the technique is testable, whether it has been tested, and the "error rate," there is the explicit expectation that available scientific studies will be applied toward evaluating the admissibility of the technique—and that the absence of such research will be regarded as limiting. This is consistent with the clarification of limits on data and reasoning in FMHA.

The present report provides an example of how the results of FMHA reports and testimony should be communicated in a civil commitment evaluation. The first step in effective communication that would change little upon cross-examination is an understanding of the forensic issues and relevant legal questions. In this case, the legal question was whether Mr. W should be subject to involuntary emergency examination and treatment for suicidal behavior pursuant to § 7301 of the Pennsylvania Mental Health Procedures Act.

Section 7301 allows for involuntary intervention when an individual is severely mentally disabled and poses a clear and present danger of harm to others or to him or her self. Under § 7301, an individual is severely mentally disabled when, *as a result of mental illness*, his or her capacity to exercise self-control, judgment, and discretion in the conduct of their affairs and social relations or to care for their own personal needs is so lessened that the individual poses a *clear and present danger* of harm to self or others. In this case, clear and present danger is established when the individual "has acted in such a manner as to evidence that they would be unable, without care, supervision, and the continued assistance of others to satisfy their need for . . . protection and safety, and there is a reasonable probability that death, serious bodily injury or serious physical debilitation would ensue within 30 days unless adequate treatment" is provided. Accordingly, the forensic issues in this case were (1) whether Mr. W had a mental illness, and (2) whether the symptoms of such an illness (if present) diminished his capacities to exercise self-control, judgment, and discretion and thereby created a clear and present danger of harm to self or others. The focus of the evaluation, therefore, was on whether Mr. W was suffering from a mental illness that affected his judgment to a point where he was likely to engage in self-injurious behavior within the next 30 days.

The effective communication of FMHA reasoning and conclusions is directly related to the quality and accuracy of the data gathered for the evaluation, and the reliability and validity of results can be strengthened through the use of multiple sources of information. In this case, the forensic clinicians used a number of data sources that included self-report, collateral interviews, collateral documents, and structured assessment instruments to address whether Mr. W was suffering from a mental illness that made him a clear and present danger to himself or others.

Self-report, structured assessment instruments, collateral documents, and collateral interviews were used to gather historical and current information on whether Mr. W was suffering from a mental illness that had impaired his judgment to the point that he was at risk for self-injurious behavior. For example, self-report, collateral documents, and collateral interviews provided risk-relevant information regarding Mr. W's past and current functioning, mental status, and behavior on the night in question. These sources provided other valuable risk-related information, such as mental health history, level of perceived social support, access to weapons, precipitating factors, and the presence of suicidal ideation, intent, and planning. The synthesis of this information suggested that Mr. W's judgment was impaired to the point that he was a serious risk for self-injurious behavior and a "clear and present danger" to himself under § 7301.

The evaluators also administered a standard screening instrument for currently experienced symptoms of mental and emotional disorder (the Brief Symptom Inventory) and a structured clinical interview for Axis I Disorders

(Structured Clinical Interview for DSM-IV-I) to strengthen the validity and reliability of their conclusions in this area. The results of the BSI and SCID-I produced diagnoses of Major Depression and Generalized Anxiety Disorder, disorders that can impair judgment across a variety of domains. In conjunction with information from multiple sources indicating clear, serious suicidal intent, this suggested that both the mentally disabled and the danger to self or others criteria of § 7301 were satisfied.

The evaluators clarified the limits on data and reasoning, and presented them in a way that should withstand adversarial challenge, by (1) offering diagnoses based on data from multiple sources, including self-report, collateral interviews, relevant records, and testing; (2) including direct quotations from these sources when relevant and illustrative; (3) attributing factual information to its respective source, with limiting language (e.g., "to her knowledge") used as needed; and (4) describing Mr. W as a "high" and "imminent" risk for suicide, addressing both level and imminence of risk, rather than using the term "danger," which confounds these considerations.

FORENSIC EVALUATION: CIVIL COMMITMENT

February 9, 1999
Re: Mr. W

REFERRAL

Mr. W is a 38-year-old African American male who was brought to the admissions unit of the Pleasantville Psychiatric Hospital by local police after threatening to commit suicide. A request for a mental health evaluation was made by the Pleasantville Police Department to determine whether Mr. W should be subject to involuntary emergency examination and treatment pursuant to § 7301 of the Pennsylvania Mental Health Procedures Act.

PROCEDURES

Mr. W was evaluated for approximately 3 hours in the admissions unit of Pleasantville Psychiatric Hospital. In addition to a clinical interview, Mr. W was administered a standard screening instrument for currently experienced symptoms of mental and emotional disorder (the Brief Symptom Inventory, or BSI), and a structured clinical interview for Axis I Disorders (the Structured Clinical Interview for DSM-IV Axis I Disorders, or SCID-I). Mr. W's mother, Jane W, and his wife, Sally W, were interviewed regarding Mr. W's past and current functioning. The Pleasantville Police Department Incident Report was reviewed as part of this evaluation.

Prior to the evaluation, Mr. W was notified about the purpose of the evaluation and the associated limits on confidentiality. He appeared to understand the basic purpose of the evaluation and reported back his understanding that he would be evaluated and, based on the results of the evaluation, could be subject to involuntary treatment at Pleasantville Psychiatric Hospital.

Historical information was obtained from the collateral sources described above, as well as from Mr. W himself. Whenever possible, the consistency of the factual information provided by Mr. W was assessed through the use of multiple sources.

RELEVANT HISTORY

Mr. W was born in Philadelphia to Jane W and Bradley W Sr. Mr. W reported that his father was incarcerated before he was born and that they first met before Mr. W was old enough to enter elementary school. According to Jane W and self-report, Mr. W lived with his parents in Philadelphia until he enlisted in the Army in December 1987.

According to Mr. W, both of his parents had difficulty controlling their tempers. He stated that his father's temper was far worse than his mother's, and characterized it as "spontaneous and volatile." In addition, Mr. W indicated that his father was an alcoholic who also abused marijuana. According to self-report, Mr. W was introduced to drug use at age 13 by his father. Mr. W elaborated that his father encouraged him to use marijuana because he thought marijuana was "the lesser of evils" and would prevent him from abusing more dangerous drugs like heroin and cocaine.

Mr. W described a strict household where physical punishment was used as the primary means of discipline. Mr. W characterized his home environment as "emotionally abusive at times." He also indicated that his mother and father argued constantly and divorced in 1993. Mr. W indicated that he still maintains contact with his father.

Mr. W reported that he has been married for 14 years to Sally W. Mr. W also reported that he has an 11-year-old autistic daughter and a 9-year-old son as a result of this marriage. Mr. W identified chronic interpersonal problems in his marital relationship and described his current domestic situation as "unsupportive and unstable."

Mr. W reported that he attended LaSalle University through December of 1978 before enlisting in the U.S. Army. According to self-report, Mr. W attended Central Texas College from August 1985 to May 1991 and obtained his associate's degree in science. Mr. W reported that he attended the Philadelphia Computer Learning Center from September 1994 to January 1996. He indicated that he completed an associate's degree in specialized technologies and graduated at the top of his class.

Mr. W reported a stable and accomplished employment history. According to Jane W and self-report, Mr. W worked various odd jobs throughout middle and high school. According to self-report, Mr. W enlisted in the U.S. Army in December 1978. Mr. W reported a consistent pattern of advancement and achievement in the Army that led to his promotion to Staff Sergeant, before a severe back injury sustained during field maneuvers in December 1985 led to his honorable medical discharge in March 1987.

According to Mr. W, he went to work as a computer instructor after his discharge from the Army. He was next employed as a firefighter and emergency medical technician until his back injury forced him to resign in February 1993. Mr. W reported that he left this position for a better opportunity with a large consulting firm, where he worked until his back deteriorated to the point where he had to take sick leave. According to Mr. W, he further aggravated his back injury in January 1998 and was placed on disability from January 1998 to early March 1998. Mr. W unsuccessfully attempted to return to work in April of 1998 and began collecting disability benefits through the Veterans Administration. Mr. W has a history of back pain dating back to the injury he sustained while in the Army. He underwent surgery (a lumbar laminectomy) in 1986 in an attempt to correct the damage. Mr. W added that he currently does not experience any significant physical impairment from the injury except for slight discomfort after exercise. Mr. W currently takes the hypertension medication Nifedipine (60 mg once per day).

Mr. W reported a limited mental health history. He denied any prior involvement in treatment, either prescription medication or psychotherapy, on either an inpatient or an outpatient basis; this was consistent with the account of Sally W. According to the Pleasantville Police Department Incident Report, the police arrived at the W's residence after a 911 call was made by Sally W. According to the responding officers and Sally W, Mr. W was actively suicidal when the police arrived. The Pleasantville Police Department Incident Report elaborates that Mr. W "threatened to shoot himself and begged on-scene police to kill him because he could no longer take care of his children."

According to Mr. W, he started to feel depressed shortly after he stopped working in late April 1998. Mr. W reported weight loss, poor appetite, difficulty concentrating, feelings of hopelessness, and a general apathy toward most activities beginning in early May 1998. On numerous occasions during the current evaluation, Mr. W emphasized that a large portion of his self-esteem and self-worth revolves around his ability to provide emotionally and financially for his family. He elaborated that his family began to experience severe financial difficulties during this period because his disability benefits were insufficient. His mood continued to deteriorate and he became increasingly irritable and angry as the months progressed. Mr. W stated that from early August until the day of the current incident, he was so preoccupied with his family's increasingly desperate financial situation that he was averaging only one hour of sleep per night.

Sally W stated that she noticed a change in Mr. W's mood in early May 1998. She attributed this change in mood to Mr. W's inability to work and mounting financial difficulties. Sally W indicated that in April 1998 Mr. W was extremely afraid that he would never be able to return to work because doctors told him that his back might not get any better. Sally W also noted that Mr. W's mood would always deteriorate whenever he was unemployed, even for a short period of time. She described Mr. W as withdrawn and very irritable beginning in early May 1998. Sally W noted that she hid Mr. W's handgun because she was afraid "he might hurt himself."

According to Sally W, Mr. W's symptoms escalated in August, and he continued to deteriorate through January. She elaborated that beginning in early August, Mr. W began to experience chronic insomnia that did not respond to non-prescription medication.

Mr. W denied ever making a previous suicide attempt. Sally W reported that, to her knowledge, this was accurate. Mr. W also reported, however, that he had "off and on" considered killing himself during the last 5 years, particularly as his back problems and employment difficulties intensified. He said that "the thought of my family" had always stopped him from killing himself. Very recently, however, he said that he had come to see himself as a burden to his family, and the idea of "ending . . . stopping it all" would "stop my torment . . . and help my family."

Mr. W reported a consistent history of marijuana use, stating that he started using marijuana at his father's insistence when he was approximately 13 years old. Mr. W indicated that his marijuana use averaged between two to three joints per day. He elaborated that marijuana was his way of "self-medicating" because it "calmed me down" and let him escape from his problems. He denied all other forms of drug and alcohol abuse.

CURRENT CLINICAL CONDITION

Mr. W presented as an African-American male of average height and muscular build, who appeared his stated age. He was casually dressed and well-groomed when seen for the evaluation on 2–9–99 in the admissions unit of Pleasantville Psychiatric Hospital. Initially, he was cooperative, polite, and slightly apprehensive. He remained cooperative and polite throughout the evaluation, and his initial apprehension subsided somewhat as the evaluation progressed. His speech was clear, coherent, and relevant; he responded at length to most questions without encouragement and further questioning. He appeared to give significant effort to the tasks involved. His capacity for attention and concentration appeared adequate, and he was able to focus well on a series of tasks during the 3-hour evaluation without becoming visibly distracted. Therefore, it would appear that this evaluation provides a reasonably good estimate of Mr. W's current functioning.

Mr. W's mood throughout the evaluation was variable. On a number of occasions during the evaluation he became noticeably agitated, and broke into tears while discussing his immediate family and his inability to provide for them financially or emotionally. Mr. W was correctly oriented to time, place, and person.

Mr. W did not report experiencing any perceptual disturbances (auditory or visual hallucinations), and his train of thought was clear and logical. Mr. W did not report experiencing delusions (bizarre ideas with no possible basis in reality). On a structured inventory of symptoms of mental and emotional disorders (the BSI), Mr. W reported the presence of various symptoms. The symptoms endorsed by Mr. W suggest significant symptoms of depression and anxiety and included thoughts of ending his life. Mr. W indicated that he noticed these symptoms in early May 1998 and elaborated that the severity of the symptoms continued to increase throughout September and into February. He denied past suicide attempts.

Mr. W confirmed the police's account of his behavior this evening and acknowledged suicidal intent, plans, and means. Mr. W stated, without equivocation, that he intended to take his own life this evening. He elaborated that he planned to shoot himself in the head in the upstairs bathroom. He was unaware that his wife had hidden his gun, and he became "enraged and despondent" when he couldn't find it. He began to "tear apart" the house searching for it, which prompted his wife to call the police. Mr. W stated that he "would be dead right now" if his wife hadn't hidden his gun, and insisted that he deserved to die because he couldn't provide for his family and, as a result, had placed his marriage in jeopardy. He elaborated that he believes that his marriage is "over" because of his inability to provide for his family. Mr. W was unable to generate alternative solutions to his current situation, and was unwilling to entertain alternatives proposed by the evaluators (including voluntary treatment) and his wife. Mr. W stated that he "deserved to die," and suggested that he would eventually find a way to take his own life "for the benefit of his family." He could not be dissuaded from this line of thinking and became increasingly agitated and despondent with further questioning.

Mr. W was administered the Structured Clinical Interview for *DSM-IV* Axis I Disorders (SCID-I) as part of this evaluation. The SCID-I is a structured clinical interview using the diagnostic criteria for *DSM-IV* disorders in a flow-chart method where the patient responds to the direct questions of a trained interviewer. Based on the results of this interview, behavioral observations made by the evaluators, Mr. W's self-report, collateral documents, and collateral interviews, it appears that Mr. W meets criteria for Generalized Anxiety Disorder and Major Depression.

INVOLUNTARY EMERGENCY TREATMENT

Section 7301 of the Mental Health Procedures Act provides in relevant part:

Whenever a person is severely mentally disabled and in need of immediate treatment, he may be subject to involuntary emergency examination and treatment. *A person is severely mentally disabled when, as a result of mental illness, his capacity to exercise self-control, judgment and discretion in the conduct of his affairs and social relations or to care for his own personal needs is so lessened that he poses a clear and present danger of harm to others or to himself* (emphasis added).

Clear and present danger to himself shall be shown by establishing that within the past 30 days: (i) the person has acted in such manner as to evidence that he would be unable, without care, supervision and the continued assistance of others, to satisfy his need for nourishment, personal or medical care, shelter, or self-protection and safety, and there is reasonable probability that death, serious bodily injury or serious physical debilitation would ensue within 30 days unless adequate treatment were afforded under this act. . . .

Mr. W currently meets *DSM-IV* criteria for Major Depression and Generalized Anxiety Disorder. Collateral interviews and self-report indicate that Mr. W began to experience symptoms of depression beginning in early May 1998, and also note an escalation in symptoms leading up to the events of this evening. The presence of Major Depression, severe insomnia, and an increasing level of anxiety-provoking environmental stressors appears to have had a significant impact on Mr. W's judgment and ability to generate alternative solutions to his current situation. Negative mood can affect judgment, and many individuals with Major Depression report an impaired ability to effectively think, concentrate, or make decisions. Of particular note is the severe insomnia that Mr. W began experiencing in early August. Sleep deprivation can have a significant negative impact on all aspects of cognitive and intellectual functioning, including judgment and decision making. Further exacerbating Mr. W's condition was the presence of immediate and severe environmental stressors created by his inability to work and perceived marital discord. In addition, Mr. W described clear suicidal intent during the present evaluation, noting that he would eventually be successful in taking his own life.

CONCLUSION

In the opinion of the undersigned, based on all of the above:

1. Mr. W is "severely mentally disabled" under § 7301 of the Mental Health Procedures Act. Specifically, Mr. W is currently suffering from Major Depression and Generalized Anxiety Disorder.

2. Mr. W appears to present as a high risk for self-injurious behavior and is, therefore, a "clear and present danger" to himself under § 7301 of the Mental Health Procedures Act. The presence of Major Depression, Generalized Anxiety Disorder, sleep deprivation, and severe environmental stressors has clearly and significantly impaired his judgment. This, in conjunction with active suicidal ideation, intent, planning, and a perceived lack of social support in his marriage, creates a reasonable probability that death, serious bodily injury, or serious physical debilitation might ensue unless adequate treatment is provided.

3. Mr. W is in need of immediate treatment for his current symptoms. Every effort should be made to gain Mr. W's consent for voluntary treatment. If he does not consent to voluntary treatment, Mr. W should receive immediate treatment under § 7301 of the Mental Health Procedures Act.

Kirk Heilbrun, Ph.D.
Consulting Psychologist

Geff Marczyk, MS, MA
David DeMatteo, M.A.
MCP Hahnemann University Graduate Students

Teaching Point: How should the forensic clinician communicate violence risk?

The communication of the risk of violence, whether to self or others, has been the subject of considerable debate. However, there have been significant conceptual advances during the last decade that facilitated writing a clearer report in this case. It has been observed that "dangerousness" can be described more clearly in terms of its component parts: risk factors, risk level, and nature of harm (National Research Council, 1989). It is also important to consider imminence of harm and protective factors (Heilbrun, Dvoskin, Hart, & McNiel, 1999; Rogers, 2000). The report was specific as to risk factors (depression, serious suicidal intent, presence of a specific plan with highly lethal means, possession of that means—a gun), risk level (high, in our judgment, at the time of the evaluation), and nature of harm (suicide). The report also addressed imminence (highly imminent, based on his recent attempt and no significant changes in risk factors since that attempt) and protective factors (family and employment, both of which had recently stopped functioning effectively as protective factors for Mr. W). As a consequence, Mr. W's "danger to self" could be considered in more specific terms, and a more informed decision made, than if the report had described him as "dangerous to self based on depression and suicidal thinking."

The legal question concerning dangerousness to self in this case calls primarily for a prediction: How likely is it that Mr. W, if not civilly committed, would try again to kill himself in the near future? Predictive accuracy is generally better when using a well-validated actuarial tool than clinical judgment.

However, such an actuarial tool should be applied for the purpose for which it was developed and validated if we are to be confident about such improved accuracy. In a case like Mr. W's, however, in which risk factors are clear and imminence is high, it is not likely that any actuarial tool would be preferred as a primary assessment measure. This partly reflects the enormous difficulty in developing a short-term predictive tool for suicide; for obvious ethical and clinical reasons, there will not be a study in which we assess the potency of risk factors such as weapon possession and plan seriousness by monitoring but not intervening in some cases when such factors are present.

Finally, there is growing evidence that clinicians most prefer to communicate risk by describing risk factors and specifying relevant interventions for each risk factor (Heilbrun, Philipson, Berman, & Warren, 1999; Heilbrun, O'Neill, Strohman, Bowman, & Philipson, 2000; Heilbrun et al., under review), although that form of risk communication would have been less appropriate in this case than a prediction. Further, clinicians who provide estimates of risk on a probability scale tend to assign a higher risk when the scale is of greater magnitude (e.g., 1–100 rather than 1–40; Slovic & Monahan, 1995), a response bias that is not eliminated by having judgments made in frequencies rather than probabilities or instructing clinicians how to make such judgments (Slovic, Monahan, & MacGregor, 2000). Such emerging evidence on risk communication should serve to caution forensic evaluators: FMHA is less effective when the results are understood differently by the decision-maker than they were intended by the evaluator. Slovic et al. cite a particular example in risk communication. Frequency scales (e.g., 10 out of 100) are associated with lower mean likelihood judgments than probability scales (e.g., 10%), but with higher perceived risk. Thus, an identical probability is regarded differently depending on the form of its communication, which they suggest may result from the frightening image invoked by the numerator in a frequency scale.

Chapter 18

Civil Psychological Injury

The two reports in this chapter focus on forensic assessment in the context of civil psychological injury. The principle to be applied to the first case explains why it is usually inappropriate and undesirable to assume multiple roles in a case of this nature, and highlights the importance of identifying the specific role that the forensic evaluator assumes. The teaching point associated with the first case provides guidance on how to recognize and resist pressure to assume multiple roles in civil psychological injury evaluations. The principle associated with the second case—write report in sections, according to model and procedures—emphasizes the organizational aspects of a forensic mental health report. Proper organization facilitates the effective communication of findings and can also be useful when testimony is needed. The teaching point for the second case elaborates on the organizational theme by discussing the sequential communication of forensic mental health results.

Case 1

Principle: Determine the role to be played if the referral is accepted

This principle concerns the identification of the specific role that an evaluator will assume in a forensic case. For many reasons, it is undesirable to assume the roles of both therapist and forensic evaluator in the same case (Greenberg & Shuman, 1997; Heilbrun, 1995; Heilbrun, 2001; Melton et al., 1997). This can cause particular difficulties in child custody evaluations, for example, when a clinician who has provided therapy assumes the role of forensic evaluator. Having a previous or ongoing therapy relationship with any of the parties involved might (1) reduce the evaluator's impartiality because of existing preconceptions, (2) interfere with subsequent therapeutic effectiveness, (3) require a change in the mental health professional's stance from supportive and empathetic to impartial and skeptical, (4) require a revision of the understanding of the nature of the service and limits of confidentiality, and (5) result in one of the parties feeling angry and betrayed by an unfavorable recommendation.

Ethical guidance addresses the issue of role selection. The first ethical consideration addressing role selection is competence. The *Ethical Principles of Psychologists and Code of Conduct* (APA, 1992) indicates that psychologists "provide services . . . only within the boundaries of their competence, based on their education, training, supervised experience, or practice" (p. 1600). This ethical consideration also encompasses services involving "new areas" or "new techniques." Under the *Ethics Code*, a psychologist provides services in new areas or with new or unfamiliar techniques "only after undertaking appropriate study, training, supervision, and/or consultation from persons who are competent in those areas or techniques" (p. 1600). Expanding on this, the *Ethics Code* also notes that in "emerging areas in which generally recognized standards for preparatory training do not yet exist, psychologists nevertheless take reasonable steps to ensure the competence of their work and to protect patients, clients, students, research participants, and others from harm" (p. 1600).

Consistent with this, the *Specialty Guidelines for Forensic Psychologists* (Committee on Ethical Guidelines for Forensic Psychologists, 1991) indicates that psychologists should provide services in areas that represent specialized knowledge, skill, experience, and education, and that this expertise must be made known to the court if the clinician testifies.

The first step in FMHA role determination involves consultation between the forensic psychologist and the legal representative of the party seeking services. The *Specialty Guidelines* provides that:

> During initial consultation with the legal representative of the party seeking services, forensic psychologists have an obligation to inform the party of factors that might reasonably affect the decision to contract with the forensic psychologist. These factors include . . . prior and current personal or professional activities, obligations, and relationships that might produce a conflict of interest. (p. 658)

The *Specialty Guidelines* delineates another consideration after this notification has been provided:

> forensic psychologists recognize potential conflicts of interest in dual relationships with parties to a legal proceeding, and they seek to minimize their effects. . . . When it is necessary to provide both evaluation and treatment services to a party in a legal proceeding (as may be the case in small forensic hospital settings or small communities), the forensic psychologist takes reasonable steps to minimize the potential negative effects of these circumstances on the rights of the party, confidentiality, and the process of treatment and evaluation. (p. 659)

Notification of purpose is the most reasonable way to minimize potential negative effects and ensure that clients are informed of their legal rights when the forensic clinician will be providing both evaluation and treatment services. According to the *Specialty Guidelines*, the information in the notification of purpose can change depending on the clinician's role and the legal issues being evaluated, however:

> Forensic psychologists have an obligation to ensure that prospective clients are informed of their legal rights with respect to the anticipated forensic service, of the purpose of any evaluation, of the nature of procedures to be employed, of the intended use of any product of their services, and of the party who has employed the forensic psychologist. (p. 659)

The *Principles of Medical Ethics with Annotation Especially Applicable to Psychiatry* (American Psychiatric Association, 1995) addresses this principle by indicating that psychiatric services are dispensed in the context of a contractual relationship. Because the parameters of such a relationship should be "explicitly established," the initial agreement between attorney and psychiatrist should include the roles that are to be played later, with any changes to these roles explicitly discussed and agreed on.

The *Ethical Guidelines for the Practice of Forensic Psychiatry* (AAPL, 1995) alludes to one particular aspect of this principle: "Psychiatrists should clarify with a potentially retaining attorney whether an initial screening conversation prior to a formal agreement will interdict consultation with the opposing side if the psychiatrist decides not to accept the consultation" (p. 2). A small but important part of the role distinction, this suggests that any involvement as an evaluator on behalf of one litigant's attorney may bar participation in the same case on behalf of the opposing attorney.

The ABA *Criminal Justice Mental Health Standards* (1989) offers guidance on the approach to determining the appropriate role to be played in FMHA in the criminal context. The roles of scientist, consultant, evaluator, and therapist are described. The *Standards* indicate further that the nature and limitations of each respective role should be clarified at the onset with all appropriate parties when a role may involve obligations and functions that may conflict.

Consider the determination of role in the following case report. Ms. S, the plaintiff, brought suit against her former employer, alleging that she had been subjected to a hostile work environment. Specifically, Ms. S alleged that a male supervisor harassed, discriminated, and then retaliated against her, and that this harassment caused her significant mental injury. Proof of injury is an essential element in a successful hostile work environment claim. Accordingly, the specific forensic question was whether Ms. S had suffered mental injury from the alleged harassment.

The forensic clinician in this case was retained by counsel for the plaintiff. He assumed the role of impartial evaluator acting on behalf of a particular attorney rather than at the request of the court itself. Consistent with the principle discussed in this chapter, the clinician agreed to assume this role when contacted by the attorney; the clinician had no prior relationship with Ms. S. Next, the clinician obtained Ms. S's informed consent, clarifying for Ms. S the clinician's role, the purpose of the evaluation, the limits of confidentiality, and the evaluation's potential applicability to her case and legal rights.

Ethics authorities stress the importance of the clinician's competence to play a given role, with competence defined by education, training, and experience. In this case, the forensic clinician should be familiar with the legal standard for hostile work environment claims, and have experience evaluating adult populations generally and workplace populations specifically. The forensic clinician should also be familiar with general considerations related to the evaluation of mental injury in civil litigation; both the nature of the mental injury and the relationship between the act in question and the mental injury must be evaluated. Further, the forensic clinician must be aware of potential motivations and their possible impact on the clinical presentation of the individual, manifested in their response style (particularly the exaggeration or fabrication of symptoms).

The forensic clinician discussed his understanding of the circumstances surrounding the case and clarified his role and the purpose of the evaluation in the report:

> The goal of this evaluation was to assess genuineness and substantiality of claimed impairments, and to ascertain whether (and if so the extent to which) whatever mental and emotional impairments are present, are associated proximately/substantially with her complaints. Other contributing factors are also examined in this context, including preexisting and coexisting influences, the dynamics of deception and convenient focus, and the role of protracted litigation. Proximate as well as alternative sources of stress are addressed by examining historic and current levels of personal functioning and the potential contribution of these factors in the causal nexus of impairment. Ms. S was minimally forthcoming about any aspects of her life other than events described in her cause of action (and the problems she believes resulted from these events) around which she appears to have consolidated.

The forensic clinician has not only clarified the role to be played within the evaluation, but also displayed a clear awareness of important issues such as malingering, preexisting conditions, and proximate cause in civil psychological injury assessments. Through the use of collateral documents, clinical interview, and psychological testing, the forensic clinician then addresses each of the domains established in the discussion of purpose section of the report.

November 1998
RE: Ms. S v. Agency
Date of Birth: DATE (age 30)
Date of Injury: 4/96
Date of Evaluation: 10/98
Last Day Worked: 4/96 (Complaint)
Agency Employment: 3/95–5/96

Allegation Period: 7/95–12/97 ("Damages" after 4/96)

Dear Attorney:

In response to your September 1998 referral, I met with Ms. S in October 1998 in comprehensive clinical examination and psychodiagnostic evaluation, involving a full day of clinical and case-oriented interviewing and psychological testing of cognitive/intellectual functioning and personality/emotional functioning. The interviews were audiotape-recorded with Ms. S's consent. I also reviewed multiple sets of records your office forwarded to me, consisting of mental health and medical records, deposition testimony, and other legal documents including the complaint. Prior psychological test data from psychiatric evaluations conducted in the Workers' Compensation context by Dr. PD in 2/97 and 5/98 also were available for my review and analysis.

I understand that Ms. S had been employed as an administrator in a state agency. Hired there in 3/95, she was placed on medical leave in 4/96, according to the Complaint, after a 14-month period of employment. In her interviews here, Ms. S asserted that the allegation period for her legal claims spanned from 7/95 to 12/97, during which time her male supervisor harassed, discriminated, and then retaliated against her. Hostile environment is alleged, with special and general damages resulting.

The goal of this evaluation was to assess genuineness and substantiality of claimed impairments, and to ascertain whether (and if so the extent to which) whatever mental and emotional impairments are present are associated proximately/substantially with her complaints. Other contributing factors are also examined in this context, including preexisting and coexisting influences, the dynamics of deception and convenient focus, and the role of protracted litigation. Proximate as well as alternative sources of stress are addressed by examining historic and current levels of personal functioning and the potential contribution of these factors in the causal nexus of impairment. Ms. S was minimally forthcoming about any aspects of her life other than events described in her cause of action (and the problems she believes resulted from these events) around which she appears to have consolidated.

LIST OF RECORDS (DESCRIBED WITHOUT SPECIFICS FOR PURPOSE OF SANITIZING REPORT)

Mental Health Records
Medical Records

Deposition Testimony
Complaint
Other Legal Documents

LIST OF CLINICAL PROCEDURES

Clinical/Case-Oriented Interview
Wechsler Memory Scale-Form I
Halstead Trail Making, Forms A and B
Wechsler Adult Intelligence Scale-Revised
Wahler Physical Symptoms Inventory
Personality Assessment Inventory
Millon Clinical Multiaxial Inventory-II
Life Change Index
Minnesota Multiphasic Personality Inventory-2

CENTRAL ISSUES

Ms. S has a pattern of perceiving herself to be abused and persecuted by supervisors at several jobs since graduating college in 1990. In her first full-time job following college, she accused a supervisor of endangering her health. In her next job she accused her supervisors of requiring her to hide documents in her car. In her subsequent job there was a problem pertaining to suspicious timesheets, and feeling abused by a supervisor who refused to support her promotion. Then, following promotion to the present job in 3/95, problems began by 7/95. Her goal was to become director of the department by age 40, and she thus feels particularly abused by the "state" on the belief that it snatched this career goal from her. Because of events that she attributes to her boss and to the state, she claimed to be frightened, saying, "I'm terrified of the state—anyone affiliated with the state—other than my husband—unfortunately he works for the state. . . . I don't trust anyone else. . . . I feel *they* have an agenda to destroy me." On the positive side, the symptoms reportedly relax when physically outside the boundaries of the State, such as when she is on vacation in other states.

The allegation period for her legal claims spans the period 7/95 to 12/97, even though she had left her state job in 5/96. While events in the allegation period reportedly began in 7/95, psychological impact of such events did not occur until 4/17/96. On that date, Irritable Bowel Syndrome was reportedly diagnosed. She added that on or by 5/22/96 she had become "very anxious and very suicidal." She has not worked since. Psychotherapy with Dr. O commenced in 5/96 and with Drs. M and K thereafter.

CURRENT MEDICAL AND MENTAL HEALTH TREATMENT

Medications currently include Serzone (for depression), Klonopin (for anxiety), Clonidine (for hypervigilance), Zyprexa (for auditory hallucinations) and Prosom (for sleep), prescribed by psychiatrist Dr. K. She began treatment in mid-1996 with both Dr. K and the psychologist with whom he shares the suite, Dr. M. Prior history of mental health treatment reflects four to six sessions around 1991 with a social worker for relationship problems, and meeting with another therapist in 1994 in a hospital emergency setting secondary to an anxiety reaction. Her responding with an anxiety reaction severe enough to require emergency care is noteworthy, because it apparently followed her receiving a notice of an investigative interview regarding discrepancies in her travel claims. Also in 1994, she felt abused by a woman supervisor who had refused to support her promotion.

MENTAL STATUS

Ms. S arrived on time for her scheduled appointment on 10/98. She presented as oriented to time, place, person, and situation. She was dressed casually and appropriately. At first tense and quiet, she relaxed somewhat and became more verbally fluid in a relatively brief time. There were very few breaks that she took, which seems odd given her IBS complaints. Affective expression was limited. Verbal expression was focused when describing complaints, but otherwise limited and vague.

Relevant to her credibility and response style, she was very focused on her complaints and on the lawsuit. There was exaggeration in terms of content, range, and magnitude of symptoms. She became upset when asked for ordinary details of her symptoms/complaints, such as onset, frequency, intensity, duration. She got upset in an angry way, rather than in an emotionally distressed way, as a defensive means of avoiding the questions and/or the answers, preferring that the examiner accept a global picture of symptoms based on the labels and diagnostic categories she used to describe herself. When the examiner did not readily accept her categories and her assumptions (instead asking for additional information), she got impatient and annoyed. There is no question that she is very angry, although she may not be aware of the magnitude of her anger. Such anger has the effect of emotionally disorganizing her and contributing to her symptoms. Anger also raises credibility questions; she repeatedly asserted that her goal was to become director of the department and *he/they/it* stopped her. She is angry and her anger is being internalized (i.e., Irritable Bowel Syndrome, Depression) and externalized (i.e., into litigation toward the state) through active as well as passive-aggressive expressions of hostility.

Inconsistent with the extreme and pervasive clinical picture she presents are numerous findings: (1) Her demeanor is tense, but she is oriented and clear, and there is no formal thought disorder. Neither is there intrusion of affective states on cognitive functioning. She speaks clearly and remembers dates, events, and circumstances; (2) She is overstated in her expression of symptoms. This was also true of both sets of test findings from Dr. D's psychological evaluations in 1997 and 1998, and from Dr. S's 1997 psychological test findings; (3) She externalizes her symptoms by attributing the validity of their existence to others (e.g., "Dr. O said" or "Dr. M said" that she has X, Y, or Z symptoms and that she is very distressed and impaired); (4) The content of her symptoms are extreme, but the form of her thought and presentation is not, based on cognitive, affective and behavioral findings, and observations; (5) Test results are extreme, elevated to an improbable degree; (6) Wechsler Memory Scale-Form I and Halstead Trail Making, Forms A and B are within normal limits. She could not have produced normal findings on indicia of attention, concentration, recent recall, and the like if she were impaired to the degree she represents herself to be; and (7) She took paper and pencil tests rapidly, thereby exhibiting good information-processing and efficiency.

INTERVIEW FINDINGS

Current Symptoms, Conditions, Disorders, and Complaints Ms. S described experiencing complaints in the following areas:

Physical Irritable Bowel Syndrome (IBS) for which she says the state retired her in 9/98 "because it is so severe," involving diarrhea "12–20 times a day," urgency, loss of bowel control, and "no normal stool in more than 2 years, except when out of the state." She also described migraine headaches, which had been weekly, but now occur once every 3 weeks, and fatigue and lack of motivation.

Psychological Ms. S recited the names of a number of diagnostic disorders that she said she experiences. These included Depression, Obsessive Compulsive Disorder, Insomnia, Panic Attacks, and Agoraphobia. She said, "These are the main ones (conditions) I grapple with daily." Persecutory ideas were pervasive. She dated the onset of most problems to 4/96 and of paranoid-like symptoms to 5/96; she described the latter as being watched and stalked. Her description of her symptoms and of their manifestations was extreme and dramatic. She reported the daily experience of headaches, dizziness, shoulder and chest pain, IBS, hypervigilence, and paranoia. She described her depressive symptoms as hiding in the closet, lying in bed for days at a time, not eating, crying all the time, lacking energy or motivation, and previously suicidal thoughts and urges. Panic attacks reportedly began in mid- to late-1996 "a few times a week" and involved hiding in her closet with a knife, frightened, desperate, and hyperventilating.

Preexisting mental health history Denied other than "anxiety attack" 2 years earlier in 4/94.

Course She reported that her doctors tell her that medications help. Thus, she has not hidden in closet since early 1998 and there were no suicide attempts since 11/97 (and 5/96 before that). Auditory hallucinations still occur at times, she indicated, with a voice saying something like, "You hold her down and I'll slit her throat."

Rational versus Irrational Asked if she experiences her symptoms as irrational or as real, she responded, "I believe people out there are trying to destroy my life." Asked if she believes it is true that everyone in the State wants to destroy her, she responded "I believe that's completely true." She added that her logical side attributes such thoughts to "an overactive imagination" but that her "illogical side is very much in control of (my) life."

She reported that she is limited in her activities of daily living, and spends many hours each day cleaning her house. She added that it is because she has Obsessive-Compulsive Disorder, caused by the Defendants, that she cleans her house like this (not because, for example, she may be healthy or adaptive enough to clean a house that has seven animals, herself, and her husband in it). However, by her own account, she also regularly takes care of her animals and prepares meals, tends to her family, and is involved in some church activities. She takes occasional boat rides and exercises. She plays games with her husband, does chores, runs errands, visits her mother, father, brother, and grandfather and has good friends whom she and her husband both visit and entertain. Her activity level seems about average for her, that is to say, it appears to be within normal limits. It is very different from what her alleged "damages" would imply.

The Event(s) The incidents that gave rise to her allegations involve a male medical supervisor who she feels harassed, degraded, and demeaned her rather than supported her. She said that "he called me incompetent, stupid, a passive-aggressive bitch." These incidents also involved a female coworker who called her "a filthy, dirty, repulsive person" in 4/96 at a class that Ms. S was conducting. The reported problems began in 7/95 with her supervisor refusing to sign timesheets and angrily throwing her proposals in the trash. When asked why, she replied that she "just wanted to move up the ladder and be the director one day . . . . Maybe I was too good." She felt that she may have psychologically threatened her boss by her superior competencies. (Intellectual assessment indicates average functioning in a rigid, concrete person. It is unlikely that she would have intellectually threatened her superiors.) Further inquiry revealed that her therapist told her that she is a black and white, concrete person who would go to administration to report her supervisor whenever she felt he violated policy and procedure. She would also go to administration with her ideas "to streamline costs and make things more efficient." Her interpersonal operational style was evidently competitive and combative. Such a style, with limited accommodation or negotiation, often generates tension and interpersonal conflicts in the work setting. She had this interpersonal style before she took this job.

Psychosocial History   She speaks positively of relationships with her parents, who remained married. She described her father (when she was a child) as strict, strongwilled, authoritarian, and loving. Her mother has a history of experiencing depressive disorder. She denied personal mental health history prior to 1994 and described an unremarkable medical history, including an absence of alcohol/drug dependency or abuse. Absence of traumatic childhood experiences or need (reportedly) for psychiatric treatment would predict adequate ability to cope with stressful events in life and positive prognosis for recovery from the impact of such events. Offsetting formative factors predictive of resiliency are those associated with risk and vulnerability. In this regard, maternal depressive illness is significant. She stated that after the 4/96 incident with the coworker she felt "a complete failure because this is what was told to me over and over again." Interestingly, the 4/96 incident was with a woman coworker who challenged her with questions she evidently did not like in the context of a class she had been conducting. She is sensitive and overreactive to perceived criticism.

PSYCHOLOGICAL TEST FINDINGS

Cognitive Screening   On objective standardized measures of attention, concentration, recent recall, visual-motor speed and accuracy, she scored entirely within normal limits and in the High Average range. Her Wechsler Memory Scale-Form I Memory Quotient score was 112 (79th percentile, high-average range). Halstead Trail Making, Forms A (16 seconds) and B (49 seconds) place her at the 90th percentile (Superior range) on these tasks measuring visual-motor ability and re-

action time. Her strengths appear to be greater on visual-motor performance tasks than on verbal ability and abstract thinking. Prior psychological testing by Dr. S found her in the average range on verbal tasks, as I did. She presents and tests on all measures as rigid and concretistic, but overall in the average range (approximately 50th percentile) and within normal limits. At her level of intellectual functioning, successful attainment in her field would most likely be limited to "journeyman-level" work. Her expectations for rapid and successful ascension up the career ladder are/were unrealistic, due both to intellectual limitations and to personal maladjustments that would result in conflicted interpersonal relationships.

Personality Functioning   On the Wahler Physical Symptoms Inventory, she endorsed an unrealistically large number and variety of physical symptoms on this self-report measure of perceived frequency of physical symptoms. It measures the differential contribution of somatic versus functional factors in physical complaints. Noteworthy is that Ms. S exhibits a somatoform disorder involving the cause or exacerbation of physical symptoms by psychological factors. It is also important to observe her extreme symptom magnification, consistent with malingering, as well as her overattribution and misattribution (false imputation) of symptoms to the job in 1995–1996. For example, she said "the State" caused the following symptoms: nausea, neck aches or pains, shakiness, stuttering or stammering, difficulty sleeping, losing weight, backaches, intestinal or stomach trouble, feeling tired, muscular weakness, twitching, and tension, difficulty breathing, excessive gas, weight gain, poor appetite, bowel trouble (constipation or loose bowels), chest pains, and generally poor health. All or virtually all of these physical complaints were apparently present before she began working for her recent employer (the subject of this lawsuit).

On objective, standardized measures of emotional states, personality traits, overall mental health functioning and of deception (the Minnesota Multiphasic Personality Inventory-2, the Millon Clinical Multiaxial Inventory-II, and the Personality Assessment Inventory), Ms. S tests (as she presents) as deceptive. These sets of test findings indicate that she is exaggerating and "faking-bad," just as she did on Dr. D's MMPI-2 and MCMI-II in 1997 and 1998 and on Dr. S's tests in 1997. Because of her efforts to present a picture of herself different and worse than it truly is, differential diagnosis is also more difficult. Her deceptive response set goes both to malingering (exaggeration and false statement of symptoms) and falsification (misattributing the source of her symptoms). She evidently took the tests accurately and understood the items (TRIN and VRIN, two MMPI-2 special scales that measure whether the individual paid attention to the item content, are within normal limits), but answered items to present herself as extremely emotionally disturbed. Seven of the nine clinical scales are elevated above the 99th percentile, F-K is +8, and her Welsh Code 26***078"14'+53-/9: F*'"L-/:K#. In descending order of magnitude (as well above the 99th percentile), these scales are Depression (T109), Paranoia (T103), Social Introversion (T84), Psychasthenia (T83), Schizophrenia (T82), Hypochondriasis (T71), and Psychopathic Deviate (T71).

Paranoid-level persecutory ideas dominate her clinical picture (Persecutory Ideas, Pa1 = T117). A person entering a job situation with such distorted beliefs would have great difficulties getting along with others due to underlying hypersensitivities, anger, resentment, and tendencies to personalize and distort communications. Such perceptual distortions result in conflictual interactions, blaming others for personal problems, and misunderstanding circumstances and events due to misperceiving and thus misinterpreting them.

FINDINGS FROM RECORDS

Dr. O treated her briefly from 5/96 to 6/96. She complained that her "boss will not listen to my policy recommendations regarding change." He diagnosed Adjustment Disorder/Mixed, the symptoms of which should remit upon cessation of stressor giving rise to them. Dr. O's entries are noteworthy because they occur at a time when she would have been most distressed, and therefore at her worst clinically. People typically improve with the passage of time, especially when psychotherapy and psychoactive medications are available to them. For reasons such as these, early clinical observations and findings can be important and revealing. Dr. O said Ms. S was frus-

trated by her supervisor, with whom she had been arguing (since taking the job there) "as to what are the appropriate policies and procedures that should be taken in treating employees as well as inmates." Dr. O qualified her for Workers' Compensation stress disability, on 5/19/96, and opined there was no loss of pre-injury capacity.

In 3/94, more than a year before her State job, she complained of anxiety, panic, headaches, and multiple other symptoms—including somatic complaints secondary to alleged work stress. She refused EKG, refused psychiatric medications, and was viewed by staff as contradicting herself and her symptoms and as noncompliant. She told staff that the purpose of her visit was to document stress at work. Staff saw her as in No Apparent Distress. In 3/94 her reported job-related problems were described as "wants promotion" (p. 16). Somatic/anxious symptoms continued through 4/94 (Acute Situational Reaction). She was reportedly accused of falsification of travel vouchers during this period. Symptoms continued with complaints of abdominal and chest pains and migraines. Medical records in 7/95 reflect migraines, pain in neck, and double vision. These same somatic symptoms were noted again in 11/95.

Noteworthy is that in 4/94 (and on other medical visits prior to her job), there is documentation of symptoms similar to those complained of postallegation period, including anxiety, tears, fear of job retribution and fear of the unknown. In 4/94 she was said to have been anxious over 4 months because of her work situation, with symptoms of anxiety, chest pain, vomiting, bad dreams, and visual and auditory hallucinations. She also complained of nightmares and sleep problems and depression and headaches, as well as IBS symptoms in 4/94.

Several psychological evaluations occurred in the Workers' Compensation context involving the administration of objective, standardized psychological tests. Noteworthy is Dr. S's Wechsler Adult Intelligence Scale-R (WAIS-R) of 8/97 in which he tested her verbal IQ as 102 (55th percentile). She tested on the WAIS-R verbal subtests in 10/98 with a verbal IQ of 91. These scores fall in the Average to Low Average range of adult intellectual functioning. It is unlikely that the recommendations to her supervisor about which she regularly argued and felt frustrated would have been uniformly meritorious of acceptance and influence. Further, an inflated sense of self-worth is probably responsible for both the aforementioned arguments and for her belief that but for job discrimination, harassment, and retaliation, she would have become director by age 40.

On objective personality tests that Dr. S and I both independently reviewed (administered in 1997 and 1998 by Dr. D), Ms. S tests as exaggerated and inconsistent. She tests similarly exaggerated (malingering) on other objective tests that Dr. S administered. On the Rorschach that Dr. S administered in 8/97, she tests as possessing a longstanding (preexisting) and underlying depressive disorder and as exaggerated. Dr. K's 8/97 psychiatric examination, in which he incorporated Dr. S's findings, found inconsistency and marked exaggeration of symptoms, and at least partial malingering.

I concur mostly with Dr. K's and Dr. S's findings. My findings are firmer, perhaps because there has been more time (and treatment) for her condition to improve and/or for her to present her condition less inconsistently, and because there are more objective test findings.

Diagnostically, there is Depression and Somatoform Disorders and Malingering on Axis I. There is also Delusional Disorder (Persecutory Type) on Axis I. On Axis II there is Personality Disorder NOS with Narcissistic, Histrionic, Paranoia, Borderline, and Avoidant Traits. On Axis III there is IBS and Migraine Headache.

Diagnoses provided by her therapists are noteworthy. Dr. O (her first therapist) diagnosed Adjustment Disorder with Mixed Emotional Features in 6/96. Dr. J K, her current psychiatrist, diagnosed also Adjustment Disorder with Mixed Emotional Features a month later in 7/96. He also diagnosed Psychophysiological reactions secondary to stress, as did Dr. N, Dr. K, and others. Adjustment Disorders are the mildest and briefest of the DSM-IV disorders and are expected to resolve as the stressors that gave rise to them cease.

FORMULATIONS

Ms. S is immature and compensating with an overinflated sense of self-worth driven psychologically by personal conflicts and maladjustments (chronic, longstanding, preexisting) and by over-driven needs for career status and irrationally based demands that these needs be met on her own terms and on her own timetable. Because of this neurotic dynamic, she is extremely concerned with getting ahead and getting ahead quickly. Any threats to this self-defined pacing, and to her own narcissistic self-driven definition of reality, are externalized, and are viewed by her as harassment—then persecution. When stressed, paranoid ideation results in persecutory beliefs. Thus, she feels picked on when criticized or otherwise not getting what she feels entitled to. Secondary to these irrational perceptions, she feels anxiety, fear, anger, moodiness, and stress-related psychophysiological reactions. She is markedly histrionic, so exaggerates, dramatizes, and generalizes both the sources of perceived threat (the whole state) and the reactions she has to such threat. Unable to face her own personal limitations, she externalizes blame and responsibility and criticizes others for holding her back. Markedly avoidant, she would in any case be extremely sensitive to criticism. But avoidance, combined with paranoid and histrionic traits, creates a litigious person in this medicolegal context.

Regarding Ms. S, prior examiners (e.g., Dr. D, Dr. S, Dr. K) found her condition and situation very complex. This was because they all found inconsistencies, sometimes gross inconsistencies, marked exaggeration, and at least partial malingering, especially Drs. S and K. The objective standardized tests support Drs. S's and K's opinions, exhibiting fake-bad response sets and patterns of psychological test findings consistent with spurious claims of trauma. Drs. M and K did not comment on this problem, which is commonly the case with clinicians who are the treating versus examining doctors. Treating clinicians usually have few records, do not otherwise do an independent case study, and are their patient's advocates. Hence, they do not have the opportunity to objectively examine the full range of issues and do not raise alternative hypotheses. Psychological testing was done by Dr. D, and by Dr. S for Dr. K. I also did psychological testing. All test results, based on objective indicia of credibility and deception, indicate the latter, that Ms. S is being deceptive as regards her symptoms. This broad response set to deceive about frequency, intensity, range of symptoms, probably also generalizes to whether her veracity is strong as regards her legal complaints, and suggests it is not. Clinical observations and other (investigative) findings correlate with test findings to exhibit a pattern of symptom magnification and distortion.

The reason why examiners have found her condition complex and confusing is that, at clinical levels, it is both. Her condition is complex because she is exaggerating *and* inconsistent to a markedly elevated degree (on all data sets), and she is *also* emotionally disturbed *and* personality disordered. But there is a difference between clinical formulations versus forensic formulations. The latter address issues of causation (i.e., proximate factors versus alternate factors of causation). At forensic levels, there is virtually nothing about Ms. S's symptom presentation or the disabilities she is claiming that correlate with the alleged events that ostensibly had given rise to such symptoms and disabilities. In other words, it is complex and confusing because it is entirely unclear what could possibly be proximately responsible for the grossly disturbed clinical posture she is effecting. Job stress (with or without harassment) is not a known risk factor for dementia, personality disorder, or psychotic symptoms. Hence, at forensic levels there is no nexus to her legal claims, even though at clinical levels there is a degree of psychological disturbance. Whatever present degree of psychological disturbance appears nondisabling, and in any case, was not caused by the events in question; it is based instead on preexisting factors.

Thus, at clinical levels, there is some degree of both Axis I and Axis II disturbance. At forensic levels, where causation is the primary issue, there is no current nexus to the allegation period. Nor should there be, given passage of time and extensive psychotherapy. There is evidence for non-legally relevant clinical impairments. There is evidence for job stress having operated on underlying psychoneurotic processes and preexisting personality maladjustments and insecurities to have resulted in episodes of gastrointestinal distress and probably brief adjustment reactions. Her physician diagnosed *functionally/psychologically based IBS*, thus *Somatoform Disorder*. *Dr. O* was the initial examiner and diagnosed *Adjustment Disorder/Mixed in 5/96*. He was probably correct. *Dr. K* also *diagnosed Adjustment Disorder*

in 7/96. The rest is based on partial or full malingering. Her underlying paranoid disorder would (in forensic formulation) contribute or cause projections and distortions, particularly when feeling stress in her life from whatever sources. She would be predisposed to be hypervigilant. Angry and resentful of others, especially those in authority, she would be afraid they would wish to hurt her, given her paranoid mentation, and she would misinterpret events and their meaning by assuming others wish to harm or to otherwise disadvantage her.

In sum, the clinical disorders she currently has, both medically and psychologically, she also had prior to working for Defendants. She is exaggerating complaints and magnifying symptoms to a markedly deceptive degree, reflecting malingering. She is misattributing and falsely imputing symptoms to the State job that either do not exist at all, may have existed at some time in the past (i.e., 1994), or that derive from influences other than proximate ones.

Temporally proximate (albeit perhaps not legally proximate) factors associated with her employment include job stress, for which she was awarded compensation and treatment under Workers' Compensation for stress-related physiological (i.e., IBS) and emotional reactions (i.e., Adjustment Disorder with Mixed Emotional Features). She claims that job stress emanated from a woman coworker's criticism of her performance while teaching a class, and from a male supervisor who would not accept her proposals for policy and procedural changes. It is unclear where or how disparate treatment, based on gender or other protected classes or behaviors, was involved.

Preexisting factors are significant and noteworthy. Believing that she would/could/should become director of the State agency within the decade, required in her mind that she be on the fast track for promotions. It also required an overinflated estimate of her own performance and worth on the job. Criticism by a supervisor or a coworker would have been very upsetting to this pride-sensitive person for whom praise and approbation (not criticism) would have been the route to promotions into leadership positions. It was previous threats to her career and refusals to support bids for promotion (in 1994) that also resulted in similar stress-related disorders. Preexisting maladjustments and conflicts at personal levels and limitations at intellectual levels are most likely responsible for her stress-related reactions. Coworkers have a right to give feedback to instructors, and supervisors have a right to set standards for their employees. Delusional/persecutory, angry, resentful, and competitive dynamics within herself would have rendered her relatively unamenable to feedback—even legitimate feedback. Underlying (preexisting) maladjustments and conflicts would cause her to distort their meaning into personal attacks.

While deception is clearly present (both in terms of magnitude and attribution), Ms. S also believes that she is disturbed and that her disturbance was caused by her job. Resolution of the lawsuit, then, would be important for enabling her to return to gainful employment. She can return to her usual job but not under her former supervisor because of the way she has come to hold him responsible for her problems. Her first therapist basically said this back in 5/96 and 6/96. Along with resolution of the lawsuit, competent psychotherapy that directs itself optimistically to positive functioning and gainful reemployment would be helpful. A combination of cognitive-behavioral psychotherapy and psychotropic medications for 4 to 6 months should enable Ms. S to get on with her life once the lawsuit is resolved.

Thank you for the opportunity to examine Ms. S. Should there be any questions or need for elaboration or clarification, please feel free to contact me.

Respectfully submitted,
Herbert N. Weissman, Ph.D., A.B.P.P.
Clinical Professor of Psychiatry,
School of Medicine, University of California, Davis

Teaching Point: What are strategies for resisting pressure to play multiple roles in FMHA?

In the context of FMHA, forensic clinicians may frequently be confronted with the pressure to assume several different roles. However, because most sources of ethical guidance and authority discourage forensic clinicians from assuming more than one role in any given FMHA, forensic clinicians should resist this pressure. Therefore, it is essential that forensic clinicians have well-developed strategies for resisting the pressure to play multiple roles in a given case. In the first case report, the forensic clinician conducted an impartial evaluation and presented his findings in written form; he could also have presented them in expert testimony. However, the defendant's attorney could also have asked him (in the course of their preparation for testimony) to play an expanded role, perhaps offering detailed criticism of the reports of opposing experts and even sitting with the attorney during the trial and helping during the cross-examination of such opposing experts. It is this kind of expansion from the single role of impartial expert into the dual role of both expert and consultant that this teaching point addresses.

One particularly important strategy for avoiding the pressure to play multiple roles is entering into a clear agreement with the hiring attorney prior to accepting the case. The agreement should delineate what services the forensic practitioner will and will not provide, and it should also indicate whether (and under what circumstances) the agreement can be amended to include additional services or roles. If the pressure to play more than one role arises after the forensic practitioner has already accepted the case, the forensic practitioner should explain to the attorney the ethical and standard of practice problems that may result if more than one role is assumed.

Forensic clinicians should also avoid inviting requests to expand their role in a given case. For example, if a forensic practitioner is serving as a consultant in a case, he or she should avoid making representations about the testimony they would provide if they were serving as an evaluator and testifying as an expert in the case. Such representations may encourage the attorney to pressure the forensic clinician into playing more than one role.

A related strategy involves exercising caution in accepting cases in which dual role problems are more likely to arise. For example, forensic clinicians are frequently confronted with the pressure to play multiple roles (usually therapist and evaluator) in child custody cases. Therefore, if a forensic practitioner decides to accept a child custody case, it is particularly important that he or she be aware of the potential dual role problems that may arise and decline forensic involvement in the case if there has ever been a treatment relationship with any member of the family.

Finally, if the services provided by a clinician in an additional role are needed, forensic clinicians should be aware of other professionals who might be willing to provide those additional services and make a referral for their services. Having different clinicians perform separate roles is an effective strategy for avoiding dual role problems.

Case 2

Principle: Write report in sections, according to model and procedures

This principle addresses the importance of the organization of a FMHA report. Such organization is important for two main reasons. First, it facilitates the effective communication of findings, and the relationship between the data, reasoning, and conclusions in the report (particularly important because the FMHA report is often the only formal mechanism for communicating FMHA results). Second, a well-organized report can also be useful when testimony is needed. The effective communication of FMHA results in testimony can be enhanced by presenting the data and reasoning that have already been documented in the report.

There is little ethical guidance that is directly relevant to this principle. The *Ethical Principles of Psychologists and Code of Conduct* (APA, 1992) notes that the explanation of assessment results should be done "using language that is reasonably understandable" (p. 1604). Interpreted broadly, this could support the use of a structure (like the sections of a FMHA report) that facilitates communication. Similarly, the *Specialty Guidelines for Forensic Psychologists* (Committee on Ethical Guidelines for Forensic Psychologists, 1991) addresses report organization and structure only indirectly: "Forensic psychologists make reasonable efforts to ensure that the products of their services, as well as their own public statements and professional testimony, are communicated in ways that will promote understanding and avoid deception, given the particular characteristics, roles, and abilities of various recipients of the communications" (p. 663).

It is also useful to consider the impact of a poorly organized report. FMHA reports are provided as part of litigation, in a context that is adversarial. A report that is well-written and organized can be used to describe data and reasoning clearly, and deliver effective and persuasive testimony. By contrast, a poorly organized report can be used to discredit the forensic clinician (Melton et al., 1997). One effective approach to challenging a poorly organized FMHA report involves asking a number of detailed questions, each of which calls for a very specific answer. Without access to an effectively condensed description of the evaluation, the forensic clinician is left to rely on memory, search through notes, or offer an "approximate" answer. Contrast this to testimony in which the forensic clinician can refer to a well-organized report that provides a great deal of information that can be located quickly.

Some flexibility in choosing a report's overall organization is indicated, depending on the nature of the evaluation and the clinician's purpose. At a minimum, however, the following areas should be addressed in the FMHA report: (1) circumstances of the referral, (2) date and nature of clinical contacts, (3) collateral data sources, (4) relevant personal background information, (5) clinical findings, and (6) psycholegal formulation (Melton et al., 1997; Rogers & Shuman, 2000). This approach to report writing allows the forensic clinician to describe relevant symptoms or characteristics, functional legal capacities, and the relationship between these two areas. In addition, this kind of structure reveals inconsistencies in findings and facilitates preparation for testimony.

The current case report provides an example of a FMHA report written in sections, using the kind of structure that is consistent with this principle. Conducted in a medical malpractice case, the evaluation addressed the psychological effects of a newborn's death on the mother. The organization of the report facilitates clear communication of the results, and would be useful if testimony were required.

In the report's "Referral" section, the forensic clinician provides the dates of clinical contact and clearly delineates the legal question guiding the evaluation. Next, the report lists the collateral sources of information used in the evaluation. The following sections include relevant background information, corroborative sources, information collected from the clinical interview conducted with the mother, and the results of psychological testing. Finally, the report integrates the data reported in the previous sections of the report, and then addresses the forensic issue. These steps are consistent with the six broad areas, noted earlier, that should be included in some form in any FMHA report.

The model used for this report prompts the forensic clinician to describe relevant symptoms or characteristics, functional legal capacities, and the relationship between these two areas. The report clearly and logically leads the reader toward the final conclusion by providing increasingly specific information. For example, the "Background" section gives information about the mother's history, including the absence of any history of receiving mental health services. The latter is clearly relevant to her functioning prior to the event in question. Interviews with the mother and with collateral sources provide more specific information on her functioning and current clinical condition. The consistency of the mother's account with collateral accounts provides a kind of "convergent validity" to the report of agreed-on symptoms. Such validity is strengthened by psychological test results, which are consistent with self- and collateral reports. Finally, the "Integration of Findings" section incorporates the data already reported, and addresses the forensic issue by describing a well-reasoned relationship between the death of the infant and the current psychological functioning of the mother.

PSYCHOLOGICAL REPORT

September 5, 1998
Name: June F
Age: 30 years
Date(s) of Examination: 8/8/98, 8/12/98.
Examiner: Philip Witt, Ph.D.

REASON FOR REFERRAL

Mrs. F was referred for a psychological evaluation by her attorney, Fred Adams, Esq. In 1994, Mrs. F gave birth to a son, William; in the process of a difficult delivery, requiring suction to assist the birth, the baby sustained brain injury. William lived for 2 weeks, and after various procedures, died of complications secondary to the brain injury. Mr. Adams requested an evaluation as to the psychological effect of William's death on Mrs. F.

SOURCES OF INFORMATION

1. Individual interview of June F (8/8/98).
2. Review of materials provided by Fred Adams, Esq., including depositions of June F and John F (husband); work performance evaluations of June F; pediatric and hospital records regarding William F; reports of Alan Michelson, M.D. (medical expert for plaintiff).
3. Telephone interview of Christine James (friend of Mrs. F) (8/12/98).
4. Telephone interview of Wendy Willows (Mrs. F's sister) (8/12/98).
5. Telephone interview of John F (husband) (8/12/98).
6. Psychological testing:
   - Millon Clinical Multiaxial Inventory-III (MCMI)
     The MCMI is a 175 true-false objective personality test designed to assess personality style, presence of specific symptom patterns, and the presence of severe mental disorders. The MCMI also has validity scales that evaluate the attitude with which the individual answered the test questions.
   - Personality Assessment Inventory (PAI)
     The PAI is a 344-item objective personality test designed to assess four validity indicators, 11 clinical scales, five treatment consideration scales, and two interpersonal style scales, as well as a number of more specific subscales.

BACKGROUND

William F's delivery was difficult by all accounts. The obstetric reports of the birth indicate the baby was in an improper position for delivery, and the birth canal was small. Suction was applied to the baby's head, resulting in brain trauma. He died in the hospital 2 weeks later. Mrs. F, in her lawsuit, contends that the physician who delivered the baby was negligent by not performing a cesarian section. The expert reports by Dr. Michelson indicate that the birth canal was too small, and the attempt at a normal delivery assisted by suction was inconsistent with accepted medical practice.

In his deposition, Mr. F (Mrs. F's husband) reported that he is a tax attorney and associate professor at the local law school. He and Mrs. F married in 1985. William, the infant who died in 1994, was their only child. In her deposition, Mrs. F reported that since March 1995, she has worked as a marketing director in a telecommunications company. She reported obtaining a bachelor's degree in history and a master's degree in business administration.

In her deposition, Mrs. F indicated that after William's death she saw a social worker, Laura Handy, M.S.W., for counseling from spring 1994 until 1996, with her regular contact ceasing in 1995. She reported no prior history of mental health services.

INTERVIEW OF CORROBORATIVE SOURCES

Christine James, Mrs. F's friend, and Wendy Willows, Mrs. F's sister, gave similar accounts of Mrs. F. Both parties indicated that prior to William's death, Mrs. F was an optimistic, cheerful, outgoing woman. They both indicated that Mrs. F was devastated by the death of her infant son and still—to this day—holds herself somewhat responsible, blaming herself for somehow having failed to protect her newborn son. They indicated that she no longer appears as happy or outgoing as she was prior to her son's death. Additionally, both reported that since her son's death, she has difficulty being around young children, who apparently remind her of her son's death.

John F, Mrs. F's husband, reported that since William's death, Mrs. F has had persistently low mood, severe at first. He indicated that she still shows many signs of chronically low mood, such as irritability. To this day, she also shows a high level of preoccupation with William, for example, sitting for hours holding William's hospital bracelet.

INTERVIEW OF JUNE F

Mrs. F presented as a tall, thin, attractive woman who appeared her stated age. She was oriented to time, place, and person. Her thought processes, as assessed through the interview, were relevant and coherent. There were no signs of hallucinations or delusional thinking, or any other evidence of a thought disorder.

Mrs. F did show some signs of suicidal ideation. Although she denied any current suicidal intent, she acknowledged that since her son William's death, she has experienced such chronic unhappiness and that she sees death as a relief. She has gone as far as to imagine herself staging a fatal auto accident, although she has not made specific plans or made any such attempt.

Mrs. F was a reluctant interviewee. She acknowledged at the outset of the interview that she did not wish to talk to me. She found her baby's death too painful a subject to discuss. At first, when I was taking general background, she gave one-word answers and required considerable encouragement to elaborate at all on her answers.

From virtually the first minute of the interview to the end, a span of 2 hours, Mrs. F cried almost continuously. During the initial section of the interview, when discussing general background, her expression was unhappy and she occasionally wiped away tears. As the interview progressed to discussing her son's death and her life since then, her crying became profuse, and her speech volume decreased. In fact, by the end of the interview, I had to move my chair closer to her simply to hear her through her sobbing. Toward the end of the interview, she was in so much distress that she requested that the interview be terminated, although with some encouragement she allowed completion of the interview.

Mrs. F reported a normal childhood and adolescence. She reported no history of depression, anxiety, or behavioral problems. She indicated no history of delinquent behavior, substance abuse, or unusual eating habits as an adolescent. She obtained a B average in college and later obtained a master's degree in business administration.

Mrs. F reported that she focused a lot of interest and energy on her work and friends. She stated, "We had a lot of friends. He [her husband] was busy with his work . . . I spent a lot of time working or with friends. I bicycled. Went to school. For the most part I was happy."

Mrs. F was candid in acknowledging that there had been some difficulties in the marriage prior to William's death. She and her husband had had conflicts regarding children, since he wished to have no children and she wanted a large family. She indicated, however, that despite whatever difficulties she and her husband may have had in their marriage, she was satisfied with her life and had not experienced significant depression or anxiety prior to William's death: "I wasn't depressed about the marriage. I just brushed the problems aside and didn't think too much about it. I wasn't completely happy, but it wasn't something I dwelled on. The depression I have now is different. When my husband did have time, we went out together. We spent time together . . . and it was gratifying to set goals as to where we wanted to be in 3 or 5 years, and have accomplishments. I read and bicycled a lot for recreation."

Mrs. F described William's death as an emotionally shattering experience. She reported intense feelings of anger, depression, and anxiety throughout the experience: "It was my worst nightmare. I always feared that if I had children, they would get sick and they wouldn't be able to tell me what was wrong and I wouldn't be able to help them. . . . It was very severe. I can't describe how horrible it was to see it, to live through this. I wanted it to be me, not him. I felt as if I had failed my son, even though I don't know how. I know it's not rational. [After my son's death] I thought I'd lose my mind. I tried to keep busy. I just couldn't stand being in the house by myself. . . . I started to see a social worker for a while. . . . In some ways my counselor was helpful. My husband and I have no other children, so this was shattering for us."

She indicated that she has never recovered fully from the emotional ordeal of William's death. She described numerous areas of emotional and cognitive impairment: "I used to be very focused and could do things, but I don't feel the same. Now I build up anxieties about things that relate to my litigation. I feel I used to be a much stronger person. I cry easier than I used to . . . I'm still pretty depressed. I don't expect this grief to ever go away. I can only manage it, I can't make it go away."

Prior to her baby's death, Mrs. F rarely missed a day at work. She spoke with obvious pride about her dependability. Since her baby's death, she has had numerous work absences. Many days she simply lacks the motivation and energy to go to work. Although she has not lost her job, she has received lower performance evaluations since her son's death.

I reviewed the specific diagnostic criteria for major depressive episode with Mrs. F. She reported that, particularly during the first year after William's death, she met virtually all of the diagnostic criteria—constant dysphoric mood, loss of pleasure in virtually all activities, loss of 10 to 15 pounds, sleep disturbance, loss of energy, intense guilt regarding her son's death, and suicidal thoughts, among other symptoms. Many of these symptoms are still present today, although in lesser intensity or frequency. I also reviewed the criteria for a Post Traumatic Stress Disorder. Mrs. F reports still experiencing more than enough post-traumatic stress disorder criteria to reach a diagnosis. She shows numerous signs of intrusion of the events, such as nightmares, flashbacks, and intense psychological reaction to stimuli that remind her of her son's death. She vacillates between preoccupation with and immersion in reminders of her son's death and attempts to avoid thinking about or exposing herself to stimuli that would remind her of her son's death. Finally, she shows many signs of intense physiological overarousal, such as irritability, sleep disturbance, and concentration difficulties.

PSYCHOLOGICAL TEST RESULTS

On the MCMI-III, Mrs. F's profile indicates that she is an unhappy, despondent woman. She sees her life as affording her little pleasure and, in fact, does not believe that she deserves to experience pleasure. For example, she responded true to: "I often feel sad or tense right after something good has happened to me"; "Few things in life give me pleasure"; and "I can't experience much pleasure because I don't feel I deserve it." Her self-esteem is low, and she tends to blame herself for any difficulties she experiences in life. For instance, she responded true to: "I began to feel like a failure some years ago"; and "I tend to always blame myself when things go wrong." She broods on past failures and pessimistically expects similar failures in the future. Her mood is chronically dysphoric with strong aspects of apprehension, melancholy, and moroseness. She is likely to be seen by others as struggling to keep her spirits up. There is some indication of at least fleeting suicidal ideation, as evidenced by her response of true to: "I have given serious thought recently to doing away with myself."

On the PAI, examination of her validity scale pattern indicates that her test results are valid. On the clinical scales, she showed strong evidence of anxiety and depression, consistent with her MCMI-III results. Regarding anxiety-related symptoms, she particularly endorsed items indicating that she has experienced traumatic stress. For example, she responded either very true or mainly true to: "I keep reliving something horrible that happened to me"; "I've been troubled by memories of a bad experience for a long time"; "I have had some horrible experiences that make me feel guilty"; and "Since I had a very bad experience, I am no longer interested in some things I used to enjoy."

Additionally, on her PAI she reports significant dysphoria, again consistent with her MCMI-III results. She characterizes herself as an unhappy woman who, unfortunately, experiences a significant amount of suicidal ideation. For example, she responded slightly true to: "I have made plans about how to kill myself"; "I have no interest in life"; "Death would be a relief"; and "I'm considering suicide."

INTEGRATION OF FINDINGS

June F is a 30-year-old woman whose newborn son, William, died in February 1994 because of complications secondary to brain trauma associated with birth. Mrs. F contends—with supporting medical reports—that medical negligence caused her son's death. She reports, understand-

ably, that the entire experience was "a nightmare."

Prior to her son's death, there are no indications that Mrs. F experienced psychological problems during her life. She shows no history of psychological or psychiatric treatment prior to her son's death. She was a productive, sociable, happy woman who enjoyed her life and her family. She has a history of achievement, having obtained both a bachelor's degree in history and a master's in business administration, and having risen to a middle-level management position in a telecommunications company. Her marriage, although there were some disagreements between her and her husband, was not causing her undue distress prior to her infant son's death.

Since William's death in 1994, Mrs. F's life has changed dramatically. She takes little pleasure in her life and finds herself no longer enjoying activities and relationships she once enjoyed. Although she gets some feeling of accomplishment from work, she sees little purpose in her work since her infant son's death, and her work performance is impaired. Her mood is consistently dysphoric.

Regarding diagnosis, during the first year after her son's death, she suffered a major depressive episode. Although these symptoms are in partial remission, she still experiences many depressive symptoms and, at the least, now qualifies for a diagnosis of dysthymic disorder.

Mrs. F, even 4 years after her son's death, experiences more than sufficient diagnostic criteria to make a diagnosis of Post Traumatic Stress Disorder secondary to her son's death. She shows many signs of intrusive thoughts and recollections, avoidance behaviors, and hyperarousal.

In conclusion, it is my opinion with a reasonable degree of professional certainty that Mrs. F's major depressive disorder and PTSD were proximally caused by the death of her infant son, William, in 1994. There are no signs of preexisting depressive or anxiety disorders, and I can find no plausible alternative hypotheses to account for the presence of these disorders. Although it is possible that time and treatment (which Mrs. F greatly needs) may cause some moderation of her symptoms, it is likely that some degree of anxiety and depression are permanent features of Mrs. F's life as a result of William's death.

DSM-IV diagnoses

Axis I: 1. Major depressive disorder, single episode without full recovery, severity Moderate, secondary to death of son (298.22)

2. Post traumatic stress disorder (309.81), secondary to death of son

Axis II: no diagnosis

Philip H. Witt, Ph.D.
Diplomate in Forensic Psychology, ABPP

Teaching Point: Why is sequential communication of FMHA results important?

The results of FMHA can be communicated in several different ways (e.g., oral report to retaining attorney, testimony), but the primary method of communicating the results is the written report. Therefore, such reports should be "stand alone" (avoid references such as "See Source A for a fuller description"; if the material from Source A is sufficiently important to the report, it should be included at the appropriate level of detail) and effectively communicate the information—data, reasoning, and conclusions—contained within. One particularly important aspect of effective communication is the organization of the FMHA report—specifically, the order in which the information is provided.

A primary goal of any FMHA report is to address the particular forensic issues in the case. For the effective communication of data and reasoning relevant to those forensic issues, it is often helpful for the FMHA report to convey the information in the order in which questions arise. For example, the report should begin by presenting general information (e.g., identifying information, referral question being addressed, procedures used), followed by increasingly specific information (e.g., personal history across several psychosocial domains, current clinical condition, case-specific psychological-legal formulation, conclusions).

Beginning the FMHA report with the referral section, which provides general information about the individual being evaluated and specifies the legal question(s), provides the reader with the relevant context for the evaluation. The context is further clarified by providing history. Although the depth of the history should depend on several factors, including the nature and complexity of the forensic issues being addressed (e.g., present state vs. reconstructive vs. predictive FMHA), the historical information always provides the reader with the relevant context for the current observations. In addition, presenting an in-depth history of the individual being evaluated makes deception or misinterpretation of the current results less likely, as a detailed history provides the forensic clinician with a basis for identifying inconsistencies that may arise later in the FMHA.

The section of the report addressing current clinical functioning has clear relevance for most types of forensic issues encountered in FMHA. For example, information regarding the individual's current clinical functioning is obviously important to present-state forensic issues such as competence to stand trial.

In addition, however, information regarding the individual's current clinical functioning has some relevance for both reconstructive and predictive forensic issues. In mental state at the time of the offense, for example, which requires a reconstructive evaluation of the individual, information regarding the individual's current clinical functioning may help to establish a diagnosis that is relevant to previous functioning, particularly for diagnoses that have stable symptoms. Similarly, in a risk assessment calling for a prediction, information regarding the individual's current risk factors will enable the forensic clinician to make a better informed assessment of the likelihood that the individual will engage in future antisocial behavior.

If the forensic clinician obtains an appropriate amount of good information, and if the information contained in the report is conveyed in a logical, orderly, and sequential format, the forensic clinician will be better able to communicate the reasoning and conclusions clearly. The reasoning section of the report should pull together all the relevant information that has been described previously. If the report is structured sequentially, the reader should not be surprised by any of information cited in the sections describing reasoning and conclusions.

Chapter 19

Competence to Consent to Treatment

The single case report in this chapter is on the competence of adults to consent to treatment in a civil context. The principle to be applied to this case concerns the importance of assessing clinical characteristics—symptoms of disorders of mental, emotional, or cognitive functioning that are recognized in an authoritative source such as the *DSM-IV*—in ways that are reliable and valid. The teaching point addresses how structured assessment instruments can be used to increase the validity and accuracy of conclusions in competence to consent to treatment evaluations.

Case 1

Principle: Assess relevant clinical characteristics in reliable and valid ways

This principle describes the importance of assessing clinical characteristics in ways that are both reliable and valid. Clinical characteristics are symptoms of disorders of mental, emotional, or cognitive functioning relevant to a specified forensic issue or legal question. Generally, the assessment of clinical characteristics in FMHA is performed through the use of properly validated assessment measures, clinical interviews, and various sources of collateral information. Although empirical research regarding actuarial and clinical approaches does not provide a compelling consistent advantage for either approach in FMHA, these studies do underscore the advisability of using actuarial approaches whenever possible.

The assessment of clinical characteristics in ways that are both reliable and valid is important to FMHA on both a broad and narrow level, depending on the context of the evaluation and the forensic issues under consideration. For example, a wide variety of clinical characteristics might be relevant when the forensic issue or the legal standard in question is broad, such as in a capital sentencing mitigation evaluation. Conversely, other forensic issues might lend themselves to a narrow evaluation of clinical characteristics. For example, a competence to stand trial evaluation typically focuses on severe mental illness, neurological dysfunction, and cognitive limitations as they bear on an individual's ability to understand the nature of the charges and assist counsel in mounting an effective defense. Regardless of the approach used, the assessment of clinical characteristics must ultimately be relevant to the forensic issue(s) and legal question(s) being addressed by the evaluation. This is consistent with legal guidance that stresses the importance of the relationship between clinical characteristics and functional capacities under Rule 401 of the *Federal Rules of Evidence*. Specifically, Rule 401 defines relevant evidence as "evidence having any tendency to make the existence of any fact that is of consequence to the determination of the action more probable or less probable than it would be without the evidence." Further, Rule 402 mandates that evidence not relevant under the definition in Rule 401 is not admissible. Accordingly, the assessment of clinical characteristics in a reliable and valid way is very important for accurate and effective FMHA.

There is substantial ethics support for this principle. The *Ethical Principles of Psychologists and Code of Conduct* (APA, 1992) indicates that:

> Psychologists who perform interventions or administer, score, interpret, or use assessment techniques are familiar with the reliability, validation, and related standardization or outcome studies of, and proper applications and uses of, the techniques they use . . . recognize limits to the certainty with which diagnoses, judgments, or predictions can be made about individuals . . . attempt to identify situations in which particular interventions or assessment techniques or norms may not be applicable or may require adjustment in administration or interpretation because of factors such as individuals' gender, age, race, ethnicity, national origin, religion, sexual orientation, disability, language, or socioeconomic status. (p. 1603)

This clearly refers to the most valid possible assessment of clinical characteristics, noting that it is important to determine not only what areas will be assessed but the measures used to assess them and the psychometric properties of these measures. The *Ethics Code* also indicates that: "Psychologists' assessments, recommendations, reports, and psychological diagnostic or evaluative statements are based on information and techniques (including personal interviews of the individual when appropriate) sufficient to provide appropriate substantiation for their findings" (p. 1603). This statement applies as well to "forensic assessments" (p. 1610). Closer to the question of actuarial interpretation, it is noted that:

> When interpreting assessment results, including automated interpretations, psychologists take into account the various test factors and characteristics of the person being assessed that might affect psychologists' judgments or reduce the accuracy of their interpretations. They indicate any significant reservations they have about the accuracy or limitations of their interpretations. (p. 1603)

The *Specialty Guidelines for Forensic Psychologists* (Committee on Ethical Guidelines for Forensic Psychologists, 1991) addresses the assessment of clinical characteristics by noting the importance of personal contact with the individual being evaluated:

> Forensic psychologists avoid giving written or oral evidence about the psychological characteristics of particular individuals when they have not had an opportunity to conduct an examination of the individual adequate to the scope of the statements, opinions, or conclusions to be issued. Forensic psychologists make every reasonable effort to conduct such examinations. When it is not possible or feasible to do so, they make clear the impact of such limitations on the reliability and validity of their professional products, evidence, or testimony. (p. 663)

Without such contact, there is no opportunity to observe the individual's presentation, behavior, form of communication, capacity for attention and concentration, response to stress, and reaction to the evaluator—all of which are important to the accurate assessment of clinical characteristics. There is also no opportunity for direct questions that would yield responses about relevant clinical characteristics that cannot be observed (e.g., thoughts, fantasies) and are therefore difficult or impossible to infer through the behavioral observations offered by others. Accordingly, without personal contact, there is less face validity to the evaluation.

The *Specialty Guidelines* also makes the following point that is relevant to objective measures and actuarial judgment:

> Because of their special status as persons qualified as experts to the court, forensic psychologists have an obligation to maintain current knowledge of scientific, professional and legal developments within their area of claimed competence. They are obligated also to use that knowledge, consistent with accepted clinical and scientific standards, in selecting data collection methods and procedures for an evaluation, treatment, consultation or scholarly/empirical investigation. (p. 661)

The *Principles of Medical Ethics with Annotation Especially Applicable to Psychiatry* (American Psychiatric Association, 1998) does not provide material that is relevant to this issue. The *Ethical Guidelines for the Practice of Forensic Psychiatry* (AAPL, 1995) refers to the "clinical evaluation and the application of the data obtained to the legal criteria" (p. 3) and "the soundness of his clinical opinion" (p. 3). It is also observed that forensic psychiatrists "communicate the honesty of their work, efforts to attain objectivity, and the soundness of their clinical opinion by distinguishing, to the extent possible, between verified and unverified information as well as between clinical 'facts,' 'inferences' and 'impressions'" (p. 3). It should be noted that there is some explicit contrast between the approach to achieving reliability that is advocated by the AAPL *Ethical Guidelines*, which appears to be more of the "hypothesis testing" than the "actuarial measures" approach that is apparent in the APA *Ethics Code*. The *Specialty Guidelines* explicitly endorses both as approaches to improving the validity of evaluations.

The present report provides an example of assessing clinical characteristics in ways that are both reliable and valid in the context of competence to consent to treatment. An evaluation of this type involves an assessment of functional and decisional capacities. Each of these capacities can be negatively affected by severe mental illness, neurological dysfunction, and cognitive limitations. Gathering data on the impact of such clinical characteristics on these functional capacities is best accomplished through the use of well-validated objective assessment measures, clinical interviews, and various sources of collateral information. Although collateral sources of information were unavailable (as is sometimes the case in evaluations that must be done relatively quickly), this report provides examples of the use of a clinical interview, psychological testing, and structured interview instruments to address the mental and cognitive functioning as it related to the issue of competence to consent to treatment in a 52-year-old, homeless, Caucasian male who presented for treatment at a local psychiatric facility.

Initially, a clinical interview was conducted, which identified an array of possible mental health issues and symptoms that should be the focus of a more structured and reliable assessment. The clinical interview was guided by the Brief Symptom Inventory (BSI), which is a structured screening instrument for currently experienced symptoms of mental and emotional disorders. This broad screening identified an array of presenting complaints and escalating symptoms that suggested the presence of depression, anxiety, and a chronic thought disorder.

With broad areas of concern in mental and emotional functioning identified by the BSI, the evaluators then administered the Structured Clinical Interview for *DSM-IV* Axis I Disorders, Clinical Version (SCID-I), a structured interview for primary psychological disorders. The SCID-I was administered to gain a more accurate diagnostic picture than the BSI could provide. The results of the SCID-I confirmed the general information obtained through the BSI, and suggested more precise diagnoses of severe, recurrent, major depressive disorder with mood incongruent psychotic features and generalized anxiety disorder.

Further assessment of Mr. S's mental and emotional functioning was obtained through the use of the Minnesota Multiphasic Personality Inventory, 2nd edition (MMPI-2), a standardized measure of personality functioning. Mr. S responded to the items on the MMPI-2 in an extremely exaggerated manner by endorsing a wide variety of rare symptoms and attitudes; as a result, the profile was invalid. Mr. S's invalid profile may have stemmed from a number of factors that include an actively psychotic condition, falsely claiming psychological problems, a plea for help, confusion, or otherwise having difficulty in understanding or concentrating on the items. Although his profile was invalid, the results, taken in context with the results of the BSI and SCID-I, suggested that a plea for help or a confused emotional state might best account for Mr. S's MMPI-2 profile. Taken as a whole, the results of the BSI, SCID-I, and MMPI-2 suggested the presence of serious psychiatric difficulties.

In addition to mental and emotional functioning, cognitive functioning can also have a significant impact on an individual's decision-making capacities. Cognitive functioning is especially important in cases of this type, because the individual must possess sufficient intellectual ability to understand the information presented to him in the process of obtaining informed consent to treatment. Overall level of intellectual functioning in this case was formally measured with the Wechsler Adult Intelligence Scale, Revised edition (WAIS-R), a standardized test of intellectual functioning. The results of the WAIS-R indicated intellectual functioning in the Average range, suggesting that Mr. S possessed sufficient intellectual ability to understand the information presented to him in the process of obtaining informed consent. Mr. S's performance on the Wide Range Achievement Test, 3rd edition (WRAT-3), a standard test of current functioning in relevant academic areas, suggested reading skills at the post high school level. Assessment of Mr. S's reading ability was conducted to determine whether he had a deficit in this area that would preclude him from reading and understanding written material presented to him during the informed consent process.

The final step in the evaluation was to establish the impact of Mr. S's mental and cognitive functioning on his capacity to consent to inpatient psychiatric treatment. A structured assessment instrument for competence to consent to treatment, the MacArthur Competence Assessment Tool for Treatment (MacCAT-T), was used to establish the nexus between Mr. S's clinical characteristics, both cognitive and emotional, and his capacity to consent to treatment. The results of the MacCAT-T structured interview suggested that Mr. S had sufficient decisional abilities to support a judgment of competence to consent to treatment. Specifically, the MacCAT-T suggested that Mr. S possessed an understanding of treatment related information, could apply the treatment information to his own disorder and current situation, was able to consider treatment alternatives, and expressed a choice about treatment despite the presence of serious psychiatric difficulties.

Through the use of these structured instruments and a clinical interview, the evaluators were able to assess clinical characteristics as they pertained to Mr. S's competence to consent to treatment in a reliable and valid way and establish a nexus between those characteristics and the decisional competencies at issue in this case.

FORENSIC EVALUATION

Re: Mr. S

REFERRAL

Mr. S is a 52-year-old homeless Caucasian male who was brought to the Admissions Unit of the Pleasantville Psychiatric Hospital by an unidentified bystander. A request for a mental health evaluation to determine Mr. S's competence to consent to inpatient treatment, under § 7203 of the Pennsylvania Mental Health Procedures Act (50 P.S. § 7203), was requested by legal counsel for Pleasantville Psychiatric Hospital.

PROCEDURES

Mr. S was evaluated for approximately 4 hours on October 3, 1997, in the Admissions Unit of

Pleasantville Psychiatric Hospital. In addition to a clinical interview, Mr. S was administered a structured interview for primary psychological disorders (the Structured Clinical Interview for DSM-IV Axis I Disorders, Clinical Version, or SCID-I), a structured screening instrument for currently experienced symptoms of mental and emotional disorder (the Brief Symptom Inventory, or BSI), a structured assessment instrument for competence to consent to treatment (the MacArthur Competence Assessment Tool for Treatment, or MacCAT-T), a test of intellectual functioning (Wechsler Adult Intelligence Scale-Revised edition, or WAIS-R), a standard test of current functioning in relevant academic areas (the Wide Range Achievement Test, 3rd edition, or WRAT-3), and a standardized measure of personality functioning (the Minnesota Multiphasic Personality Inventory, 2nd edition, or MMPI-2).

Prior to the evaluation, Mr. S was notified about the purpose of the evaluation and the associated limits on confidentiality. He appeared to understand the basic purpose of the evaluation, reporting back his understanding that he would be evaluated to determine his competence to consent to inpatient treatment.

Historical information was obtained solely from Mr. S. Although Mr. S volunteered information readily, there were numerous inconsistencies and gaps. Collateral information was not available at the writing of this report. Attempts to identify family members or a legal guardian were unsuccessful.

CURRENT CLINICAL CONDITION

Mr. S presented as a 52-year-old Caucasian male of above average height and medium build. He appeared younger than his stated age. Mr. S wore dark sunglasses and a baseball cap that was pulled down to the top of his sunglasses. Mr. S stated that "he needed the glasses for protection." He wore the baseball cap pulled down low throughout the evaluation, and did remove his sunglasses to use his reading glasses during certain parts of the evaluation. Dark circles were present under his eyes. He was dressed in casual clothing and was slightly disheveled. Although he did not present as hostile, he was extremely suspicious of the evaluators and asked numerous questions regarding the evaluators' identities and purpose. Despite this, he was cooperative with the interview and testing procedures.

Overall mood was depressed, and he did not exhibit appropriate emotional variability. His attention and concentration appeared adequate for testing and interview purposes. Mr. S spent a significant amount of time considering his answers on the MMPI-2 and the BSI. The response forms indicate that Mr. S made numerous changes. When asked about this, he replied that he was not sure of himself. There were times when questions asked by the evaluators were initially met by a blank stare (when his sunglasses were off). However, Mr. S would eventually answer the question, usually without the evaluator having to repeat it.

Mr. S was alert and correctly oriented to person, place, time, and setting. He remained oriented throughout the evaluation. His speech was clear, coherent, and relevant at all times. Even though he appeared to remain suspicious throughout the interview, he did volunteer some information; it was not always necessary to elicit such information through direct questioning. He acknowledged a history of auditory hallucinations and a diagnosis of paranoid schizophrenia dating back to 1978.

He did not deny the presence of strange or unusual thoughts or ideas. Mr. S clearly expressed paranoid and possibly psychotic symptoms. He reported that he can read the minds of others and that others can read his mind. He also stated that it is possible for others to remove thoughts from his mind without him knowing it. In addition, Mr. S repeatedly stated that he is unsure whether the thoughts he experiences are his own, someone else's, or the result of a mystical force that is manipulating his life for his own benefit. He admitted to at least three past suicide attempts and said he occasionally experiences suicidal ideation. He denied current suicidal and homicidal ideation.

Mr. S described his current sleep patterns as very poor, waking numerous times each night and having difficulty falling back asleep. He also reported sleeping until late in the day at times. He stated that his sleeping has been consistently poor since 1978 and is frequently interrupted by nightmares. When asked how he is currently feeling, Mr. S stated that he feels "depressed and anxious most of the time." This is consistent with his BSI and structured interview results. In addition to frequently feeling depressed, Mr. S also reported feelings of hopelessness.

During the clinical interview, Mr. S discussed his recent and current emotional condition. He stated that he is experiencing a period of increased symptoms that he attributed to his current situation and being homeless. He is particularly concerned with a reported conspiracy that has been put in place by a mystical force whose goal is to improve his life. Mr. S also consistently reported a decrease in his ability to handle frustration. Accordingly, he indicated that his temper is becoming worse. He characterized his temper as becoming "explosive." He also indicated ongoing interpersonal conflicts with others.

On a structured inventory of symptoms of mental and emotional disorders (the BSI), Mr. S reported a significant amount of current distress. Mr. S indicated that he was experiencing moderate distress with the following: nervousness or shakiness inside; feeling others are to blame for his troubles; difficulty remembering things; feeling afraid in open spaces or on the streets; feeling lonely even in the presence of others; having his feelings easily hurt; feeling inferior to others; having to check and double check what he does; feeling afraid to travel; feeling nervous when left alone; feeling restless; and feelings of guilt. Similarly, Mr. S indicated that he was experiencing significant difficulty with the following: feeling easily annoyed or irritated; feeling that most people cannot be trusted; being suddenly scared for no reason; feeling blocked in getting things done; feeling lonely and blue; feeling fearful; feeling that people are unfriendly or dislike him; feeling that he is watched and talked about by others; trouble falling asleep; having to avoid certain things, places or activities because they frighten him; feeling hopeless about the future; trouble concentrating; feeling tense or keyed up; feeling self-conscious around others; feeling uneasy in crowds; never feeling close to another person; and feeling that people will take advantage of him. Finally, Mr. S indicated that he was experiencing extreme distress from the following: feeling no interest in things; difficulty making decisions; feelings of worthlessness; and the idea that something is wrong with his mind.

Mr. S's responses indicate that anxiety is a constant presence in his life, and has been since 1978. He reported that he constantly feels nervous and indicated that he has been especially anxious during the previous week. Mr. S also indicated that every morning he wakes up with a "feeling of doom" that makes him extremely anxious. He interprets this feeling as a sign that "he is not doing the right thing according to the force that controls his life . . . the force that controls his skin." Associated with this "feeling of doom," he also described symptoms consistent with panic attacks. Finally, Mr. S indicated that most forms of interpersonal contact make him anxious—to the point where he shuns contact with others except for a few people that he is comfortable with and trusts.

Mr. S's responses are also suggestive of depressive symptoms. He indicated that his memory is poor at best. He also reported being unable to make decisions in every aspect of his life and difficulty concentrating on the simplest of tasks, such as reading a book. Mr. S related general feelings of worthlessness and felt that he had absolutely no future at all. He also reported feeling lonely, and said these symptoms have been ongoing since 1978. Mr. S also reported nightly sleep disturbance, specifically, frequent awakening. Finally, he indicated that he had attempted suicide on three separate occasions and that he frequently thought about ending his life. He again denied any current suicidal ideation or plans. When asked if his depression ever improves, Mr. S indicated that the only thing that can lift his depression for even a short period of time is the belief that the mystical force exists and has a grand plan to improve his life.

Mr. S also reported symptoms consistent with social alienation, paranoia, and psychosis. He indicated that he frequently did not know whether the thoughts he experiences are his own or someone else's. He also reported that he can read the minds of others at times, and that sometimes other people can read his mind or place thoughts in his mind. He is not sure if others can remove thoughts from his mind, but he thinks that it is likely because "if they could, I wouldn't be aware of it." For this reason, he is never sure if what he is thinking are his own thoughts. He also stated that this situation sometimes makes him feel like he is "losing [his] personality." When asked about this, Mr. S stated that sometimes he "just doesn't feel real." He also stated that there is "a force" that sometimes places thoughts in his mind. When asked about this "force," Mr. S indicated that there is a mystical force that is guiding his life. He frequently looks for hidden or cryptic meaning in his interactions with others and will impulsively act on the suggestions or comments of others because he believes that "the force" is trying to get him to do certain things. He also related that there is a massive conspiracy against him. This conspiracy includes family members and other individuals. Mr. S indicated that he does not have contact with his family anymore because they are an integral part of the conspiracy. In general, Mr. S believes that he cannot trust anyone, and that practically everyone is watching him and/or talking about him. Finally, Mr. S reported that he has been having increasing difficulty with his temper. He reported feeling extreme frustration over his current situation and indicated that he frequently has the urge to break things, and often thinks of harming and torturing the people who are persecuting him. He elaborated that he would not act on these urges.

Mr. S was administered the SCID-I/Clinical Version as part of this evaluation. The SCID is a structured clinical interview using the diagnostic criteria for *DSM-IV* disorders in a decision-tree method in which the client/patient responds to the direct questions of the trained interviewer. According to Mr. S's responses to the SCID-I/ Clinical Version, which pertains to *DSM-IV* Axis I Disorders, Mr. S is presently experiencing Major Depressive Disorder, Severe, with Mood Incongruent Psychotic Features. In addition, Mr. S meets criteria for Generalized Anxiety Disorder.

Mr. S responded to the items on the MMPI-2 in an extremely exaggerated manner, endorsing a wide variety of rare symptoms and attitudes. These results may stem from a number of factors, but in this case the most likely explanation is a combination of a psychotic condition with a tendency to acknowledge symptoms and unusual experiences in a kind of "cry for help." Accordingly, Mr. S's MMPI-2 clinical profile is not a valid indication of his personality and symptoms (Welsh Code: 76**8*2"4013'+ 5-/9: F***""+-/K:L#).

Overall level of intellectual functioning was formally measured with the WAIS-R and found to be within the Average range (Verbal IQ = 95, Performance IQ = 105, Full Scale IQ = 100). Relative strengths and weaknesses were not observed; Mr. S appears to function fairly consistently across subtests at the level measured by the overall Verbal and Performance areas. Mr. S's Verbal and Performance IQ scores suggest average skills in both areas. Mr. S's performance on the WRAT-3 suggests basic academic skills (Reading, Spelling, and Arithmetic) at the post high school level.

DIAGNOSTIC IMPRESSION

Axis I: 296.34 Major Depressive Disorder, Recurrent, Severe With Mood Incongruent Psychotic Features (Principal Diagnosis)
300.02 Generalized Anxiety Disorder

Axis II: V71.09 No Diagnosis

Axis III: No Diagnosis

COMPETENCE TO CONSENT TO TREATMENT

Section 7203 of the Pennsylvania Mental Health Procedures Act provides in relevant part:

Before a person is accepted for voluntary inpatient treatment, an explanation shall be made to him of such treatment, including the types of treatment in which he may be involved, and any restraints or restrictions to which he may be subject, together with a statement of his rights under this act. . . . The Consent shall include the following representations: that the person understands his treatment will involve inpatient status; that he is willing to be admitted to a designated facility for the purpose of such examination and treatment; and that he consents to such admission voluntarily, without coercion or duress; and, if applicable, that he has voluntarily agreed to remain in treatment for a specified period of no longer than 72 hours after having given written notice of his intent to withdraw from treatment.

Mr. S has significant mental health problems for which treatment is indicated. The results of the SCID-I, clinical interview, and MMPI-2 suggest diagnoses of major depression with psychotic features and generalized anxiety disorder. Although Mr. S is currently reporting active symptoms of a thought disorder, these symptoms do not appear to substantially impair his ability to provide informed consent to treatment.

Mr. S was administered the MacArthur Competence Assessment Tool for Treatment (the MacCAT-T) to evaluate his decision-making capacities in the context of informed consent to treatment. The MacCAT-T assesses four areas of decision-making capability: (1) understanding of treatment-related information that must be disclosed as required by the law of informed consent; (2) appreciation of the significance of the information for the patient's situation, focusing on the nature of the disorder and the possibility that treatment could be beneficial; (3) reasoning in the process of deciding on treatment, focusing on the ability to compare alternatives in light of their consequences, including the ability to draw inferences about the impact of the alternatives on the patient's everyday life; and (4) expressing a choice about treatment. Mr. S obtained the following scores: Understanding = 5 (maximum score of 6); Appreciation = 3 (maximum score of 4); Reasoning = 6 (maximum score of 8); Expressing a Choice = 2 (maximum score of 2). Mr. S's summary ratings in each of the four areas were in the average range based on appropriate norms.

The results of the MacCAT-T support Mr. S's ability to provide informed consent, even in the presence of his current symptoms. First, Mr. S demonstrated a clear understanding of treatment-related information that must be disclosed as required by the law of informed consent. Specifically, Mr. S articulated his understanding that he would be admitted to inpatient examination and treatment at Pleasantville Psychiatric Hospital. Mr. S also acknowledged that the interventions required to treat his condition would most likely involve antipsychotic medication in conjunction with verbal and skills-based therapies, and described the risks associated with those interventions. He was also able to distinguish between inpatient and outpatient treatment. Second, Mr. S was able to articulate an appreciation of the significance of the information given to him, the nature of his disorder, and the possibility that treatment could be beneficial. Specifically, Mr. S indicated that his current functioning was "not normal" and possibly dangerous to himself and/or others if left untreated. Third, Mr. S's reasoning in the process of deciding on treatment focused on the possible consequences of not receiving treatment, and the possible impact on his everyday life. Specifically, Mr. S indicated that treatment would not only reduce his distress, but might also enable him to find appropriate housing and possibly vocational training. Finally, Mr. S expressed a clear choice about treatment and indicated that he was willing to undergo pharmacological intervention despite the possibility of unpleasant side effects. The results of the WRAT-3 suggest reading skills at a post high school level, and Mr. S was able to read the informed consent and admissions material without help from the evaluators. He therefore does not possess a reading deficit that would keep him from providing informed consent. The results of the WAIS-R suggest that Mr. S possesses sufficient intellectual ability to understand the information presented to him in the process of obtaining informed consent to treatment.

Thank you for the opportunity to evaluate Mr. S.

Kirk Heilbrun, Ph.D.
Consulting Forensic Psychologist

Geff Marczyk, M.S., M.A.
David DeMatteo, M.A.
MCP Hahnemann University Graduate Students

Teaching Point: How do structured instruments such as the MacCAT-T increase the relevance and reliability of FMHA?

Generally, the assessment of clinical characteristics and functional capacities related to competence to consent to treatment can be obtained through the use of properly validated objective assessment measures, clinical interviews, and various sources of collateral information. Although each of these data sources is valuable, empirically validated tools should be integrated into FMHA whenever possible. The MacArthur Competence Assessment Tool for Treatment (MacCAT-T; Grisso & Appelbaum, 1998b) allows forensic clinicians to integrate such a tool into the assessment of the capacities relevant to competence to consent to treatment.

The MacCAT-T is the first structured interview schedule for assessing decision-making abilities in the context of competence to consent to treatment. During the interview, the clinician gathers information relevant to the legal construct of informed consent, such as the patient's understanding of their disorder, their understanding of treatment options, and their understanding of the risks and benefits of such treatment options. Using a rating scale system, this information is used to assess decision-making capacities in four distinct areas (Grisso & Appelbaum, 1998b).

The four capacities—understanding, appreciation, reasoning, and expressing a choice—are closely linked to legal definitions of informed consent and competence to consent to treatment (Appelbaum & Grisso, 1988, 1995). The first area involves the patient's understanding of treatment-related information, and focuses on categories of information that must be disclosed under the legal doctrine of informed consent. The second area involves appreciation of the significance of the information for the patient's situation, and addresses the nature of the disorder and the possibility that treatment will have a beneficial effect. The third area, reasoning, involves the process of deciding on treatment, and focuses on the patient's ability to compare alternatives in light of their current consequences. The final area explores the patient's ability to express a choice regarding treatment. Ratings in the average range or better for all four capacities suggest sufficient decisional abilities to support a judgment of competence to consent to treatment (Grisso & Appelbaum, 1998b). Normative data for the MacCAT-T are limited, and the instrument was not designed to provide scores that translate directly into a determination of competence. The MacCAT-T should therefore be used in conjunction with other sources of information such as psychological testing and collateral interviews in the FMHA of competence to consent to treatment.

Chapter 20

Guardianship

The case report in this chapter is on the competence of adults to manage their own affairs. Evaluations of this type help the court decide whether a guardian should be appointed to handle the day-to-day affairs of the individual deemed incompetent to do so. The principle applied to the case explains why it is inappropriate and undesirable to assume multiple roles in a case of this nature, and highlights the importance of identifying the specific role that the forensic evaluator will assume. Further clarifying this principle, the teaching point distinguishes the roles of scientist, consultant, evaluator, and therapist, and it offers a brief comment regarding when the forensic clinician could fulfill the dual roles of expert and consultant.

Case 1

Principle: Determine the role to be played if the referral is accepted

This principle is discussed in some detail in Chapter 18, so we move directly to its application to the case. This case provides an example of determining the role to be played in FMHA. The forensic evaluation was ordered in anticipation of guardianship proceedings for a 95-year-old man. A legal petition brought by a concerned relative initiated the guardianship proceeding, and alleged that the subject of the evaluation was not oriented to time, place, or person, impaired in his hearing, and required assistance to perform all activities of daily living. The petition further raised questions regarding the financial motivations of his wife, suggesting that she might be exercising undue influence over the subject's financial affairs. Accordingly, the relevant forensic issue concerned his capacity to manage his own personal, medical, legal, and financial affairs.

The forensic clinician in this case was one of three members of a guardianship committee appointed by the court. The forensic clinician thus assumed the role of impartial evaluator acting on behalf of the court. Consistent with the present principle, the clinician clarified this role with the subject through a formal notification. Without such notification, the subject might not have been aware of the clinician's role, the purpose of the evaluation, and the way in which the findings would be reported and could be used.

GUARDIANSHIP EVALUATION

Name: Adam S
Date of evaluation: 1/17/99
Case no: P-98-0001817
Date of report: 1/21/99
Date of birth: 6/11/03
Age: 95
Marital status: Married
Education: BS, Electrical Engineering

IDENTIFYING INFORMATION/REASON FOR REFERRAL/NOTIFICATION

Adam S is a 95-year-old, married, white male who this evaluator was ordered to assess in anticipation of guardianship proceedings. This evaluator was one of three examiners directed to evaluate Mr. S with respect to his ability to manage personal, medical, legal, and financial affairs. Accordingly, Mr. S was evaluated in his home on January 17, 1999. Mr. S was interviewed, his wife (Jean S) was also interviewed, and Mr. S was administered the Independent Living Scales, a structured evaluation instrument. The entire evaluation process was completed in 3.5 hours. Additionally, the materials identified below were also reviewed in preparing this evaluation.

In the petition that initiated the guardianship proceedings, Louisa A, a cousin of Mr. S's deceased wife, alleged that Mr. S was not oriented to time, place, or person, his hearing was impaired, and he required assistance to perform all activities of daily living. The petition further raised questions regarding Mrs. S's motivation with respect to Mr. S's finances, and it was alleged that Mr. S lacked capacity to make decisions related to his financial affairs. The petitioner alleged that Mr. S lacked capacity to exercise any of his personal, legal, medical, or financial rights, and a plenary guardianship was requested.

In a letter to this evaluator, Marla G, the attorney representing the petitioner, reported that in December 1998 Mr. S married his caregiver of 7 years. She alleged that Mrs. S executed a power of attorney to borrow against her new husband's insurance policies, and Mr. S had executed a document "purported to revoke all wills, trusts, and advance directives." Ms. G, on behalf of her client, alleged that Mrs. S was exercising undue influence over Mr. S, and that the result of these concerns was the guardianship petition.

Prior to initiating the evaluation, its nature and purpose was explained to Mr. S while in the presence of his wife. Mr. S demonstrated only the most basic understanding of the evaluation process, but it was conducted since it had been court ordered and his attorney had been informed that the evaluation would take place.

SOURCES OF INFORMATION

In conducting this evaluation, the following sources of information were relied on:

1. Clinical interview and evaluation of Adam S (January 17, 1999, 1.25 hours).
2. Administration of Independent Living Scales (January 17, 1999, 1.33 hours).
3. Interview with Jean S, examinee's wife (January 17, 1999, 1.25 hours).
4. Review of petition to determine incapacity (January 16, 1999).
5. Review of handwritten notes on letterhead of Michael G. R, M.D. and phone interview with Dr. R (January 16 & 21, 1999).
6. Review of evaluation of Mr. S completed by Ronald A, M.D. (January 16, 1999).
7. Review of letter to this evaluator completed by Charlotte G, dated January 13, 1999 (January 16, 1999).
8. Review of psychological testing administered by Geoffrey C, Ph.D. (January 21, 1999).

CURRENT CLINICAL PRESENTATION AND BEHAVIORAL OBSERVATIONS

Adam S is a short, frail, 95-year-old man who appears somewhat younger than his stated age. When this evaluator arrived at his home, Mr. S was finishing breakfast at the kitchen table. Mr. S was wearing a suit coat and matching pants along with a button-down shirt. He was well-dressed and well-groomed. He was seated in a wheelchair, and his wife explained that scoliosis limited his walking.

Despite use of hearing aids, Mr. S's hearing is quite limited. Accordingly, this evaluator had to speak loudly and slowly so that Mr. S could hear and read lips. At times, words had to be written when Mr. S had difficulty understanding them. Overall, Mr. S was quite cooperative during the evaluation process, and he did not display any indications of agitation or discomfort.

When interviewed, Mr. S was able to identify himself by name. While he correctly reported that he was living in Bradenton, he was unable to provide his address or phone number. He also believed, when asked a number of times, that he was living in either Pennsylvania or Ohio, rather than Florida. Mr. S correctly identified the month (January), the day of the week (Sunday), and the year (1999). He incorrectly reported the date to be the 7th, however.

Mr. S volunteered little information, and his responses to questions were brief and minimal. He was unable to provide a fair amount of information regarding his past, and at times became confused. For example, Mr. S demonstrated considerable confusion regarding the number of times he was married and when he married. He also demonstrated some confusion with respect to his wives' names. As noted earlier, he also demonstrated confusion regarding his current location, as noted in the preceding paragraph.

According to his wife, Mr. S has cataracts and is scheduled for cataract surgery. As a result, in addition to wearing glasses, Mr. S typically had to use a magnifying glass in order to read materials that were presented to him. In order to be certain that his reading abilities did not affect assessment of his overall abilities, items were read to him when necessary to ensure understanding and comprehension.

Mr. S demonstrated significant limitations with respect to short-term and long-term memory. As indicated earlier, he demonstrated considerable confusion regarding the number of times he married, the length of these marriages, and his wives' names. He also demonstrated some confusion regarding how long he had been in his current residence, and how long he had been married to his current wife.

As will be described in more detail below, Mr. S demonstrated considerably limited insight into his limitations and level of functioning. For example, despite his limited mobility, limited vision, and hearing difficulties Mr. S, in response to repeated questioning, stated that he was fully capable of driving, although he indicated that he chose not to. Similarly, despite his many physical limitations and need for supervision, Mr. S maintained that he was fully able to live independently, although he once again indicated that he chose not to do so.

Mr. S did not evidence any signs of emotional difficulties or psychopathology. There were no indications that the content of his thought process was impaired. That is, he evidenced no indications of delusional thinking. Mr. S did not appear to be responding to internal stimuli (i.e., he did not appear to be experiencing auditory or visual hallucinations). Finally, Mr. S did not evidence any signs or symptoms of depression or unusual mood. His responses to items on the Independent Living Scales suggested a positive mood and outlook, and there were no indications of depression or other affective disorders. Mr. S displayed a range of emotion during the course of the evaluation, and his expressed emotion was always appropriate to the content of his speech. Indeed, Mr. S occasionally teased his wife and laughed appropriately at these times.

RELEVANT HISTORY

The information in this section was provided by Mr. S and his wife. Other sources of input are as noted earlier under Sources of Information.

Mr. S stated that he was born and raised in southern Ohio. He indicated that he had a younger sister who died at birth. Mr. S reported being raised by his mother and father, his father was a carpenter and his mother stayed at home.

He reported that he lived with his parents until the age of 18, when he left to attend college.

Mr. S reported a history of good academic achievement and denied any history of grade retention, learning disabilities, or behavioral problems in school. He reported obtaining a bachelor's degree in electrical engineering from Ohio State University. Dr. C, a second member of the guardianship examining committee, administered a number of psychological tests to Mr. S and made some of the results available to this evaluator. Mr. S's full scale score on the WAIS-III, a standard measure of intelligence, places him in the low average range of intelligence when compared with same-age peers. A significant difference between his obtained verbal and performance scores suggests some diminishment of nonverbal, visual-motor abilities relative to verbal abilities.

Mr. S denied any history of military service. He reported working for most of his life as an electrical engineer for a utility company in Indiana. Mr. S displayed some confusion with respect to this issue, however, as he indicated that he worked for this company for 50 years but retired from the company at the age of 50. Despite repeated questioning about this issue, Mr. S continued to make this claim and did not appreciate the obvious inconsistency. Mr. S reported that after retiring and ending his career as an electrical engineer, he managed a opened and managed a hardware store in Pennsylvania for approximately 10 years. He stated that he ceased this activity as a result of failing health.

Mr. S was confused about his current state of residence. He was also unable to provide information regarding when he retired and moved to Florida. Information provided by Mrs. S, however, indicated that Mr. S retired and then moved to Lido Key, where he and his first wife lived for a period of time prior to her death a number of years ago. Records provided by Dr. A indicate that Mr. S was placed in an adult living facility (ALF) after his wife's death. A trust was established at some point subsequent to the death of Mr. S's wife, and the trustees have managed Mr. S's financial affairs since.

According to Mrs. S, while Mr. S was living in the ALF she was hired by his trustees to care for him, initially for 12 hours per week and increasing to 40. Approximately 7 years ago Mr. S began living with Mrs. S as a boarder. They continued this relationship until December 1998, when they married. Mr. and Mrs. S claimed that this was a mutual decision but that the proposal was initiated by Mr. S. Mrs. S described her husband as affectionate, caring, and witty, and she noted that he was the best husband she had ever married.

This apparently is Mr. S's second marriage, although he claimed, at times, to have married three times. There was clearly some confusion around this issue, as Mr. S claimed that his first two wives died when he was relatively young. This obviously conflicts with reports that he retired and moved to Florida with his deceased wife, Delilah. Mr. S has no children from his marriages.

Mr. S described himself as being in overall good health. His only complaint was that he needed to use a wheelchair because of weakness in his legs. Contrary to Mrs. S's report and indications in medical records, Mr. S reported that he was not taking any medication. He was unable to identify his family physician, but claimed that he practiced in Pittsburgh, rather than Bradenton. A review of the evaluation completed by Dr. A indicates that Mr. S has a medical history remarkable for appendectomy and hypothyroidism. According to Dr. A's evaluation, his current medications include Hydergine and Synthroid. Dr. R reported Mr. S's diagnoses to be arteriosclerosis, nerve deafness, diverticulitis, and scoliosis, which is responsible for his limited mobility.

Mr. S denied any history of emotional problems or contact with the mental health system. This was corroborated by his wife. Mr. S also denied any history of alcohol problems, describing himself as a minimal drinker. This, too, was corroborated by his wife. Mr. S denied any history of use or experimentation with illegal drugs, and he denied any history of contact with the criminal justice system.

A handwritten note dated December 18, 1998, on the letterhead of Mr. S's family physician, Dr. R, described him as "of sound mind and able to handle his financial and personal affairs." In an evaluation completed on December 17, 1998, in anticipation of issues of competency,

Dr. A concluded about Mr. S, "he is no (sic) incompetent from my examination."

Mrs. S described her husband as showing limited abilities with respect to activities of daily living. According to Mrs. S, her husband's abilities are largely affected by his limited physical mobility. Mr. S, according to his wife, is able to complete many basic activities such as washing himself, brushing his teeth, feeding himself, and preparing basic food. Indeed, Mr. S was eating breakfast when this evaluator arrived. Mr. S requires some assistance with, and supervision of, other activities of daily living, however. For example, he needs assistance with dressing and transportation. With the exception of making decisions about driving, Mrs. S believed that her husband was able to exercise all rights that the petitioner sought to restrict in the petition for guardianship.

Ms. S reported that her husband was well-adjusted emotionally and enjoyed activities they engaged in together. The S's live in a large home outside of Bradenton where Ms. S also cares for two elderly boarders.

Mrs. S became emotional as she discussed the guardianship petition, noting that the petitioner spent little time with her husband (visiting him once or twice per year) and had never previously expressed much interest in his affairs. She also offered complaints about the trustees, noting that they had failed to provide her husband with information about his financial affairs in the past, and they had raised no concerns about his capacity to manage his finances until the S's jointly made inquiries about his trust.

CLINICAL INQUIRY AND TEST RESULTS

Mr. S was administered the Independent Living Scales (ILS). The ILS items target situations relevant to independent living and require the examinee to problem solve, demonstrate knowledge, and perform various tasks required of persons living independently.

The ILS has five scales: Memory/Orientation, which assesses general awareness of surroundings and short-term memory; Managing Money, which assesses the examinee's ability to count money, complete monetary calculations, pay bills, and protect money; Managing Home and Transportation, which assesses the individual's ability to use the telephone and utilize public transportation; Health and Safety, which assesses awareness of personal health status and ability to evaluate health problems, handle medical emergencies, and take safety precautions; and Social Adjustment, which assesses the individual's mood, adjustment, and attitudes about social relations.

In addition to the five scales, two ILS factors are derived from a number of the items. The Problem-Solving Factor is comprised primarily of items that require knowledge of relevant facts, as well as those that assess abstract reasoning and problem-solving abilities. The Performance/Information Factor consists of items that require general knowledge, short-term memory, and the ability to perform simple, common tasks.

Mr. S's performance on the ILS reveals significant and pervasive deficits with respect to essentially all activities of daily living. More specifically, Mr. S's performance on the Memory/Orientation items indicate that his memory is quite limited, and he is unable to remember very basic information such as his phone number, address, and appointment times. Obviously, this has significant implications with respect to his ability to make and keep appointments, remember commitments, take medicine, manage his financial affairs and household, and travel independently and safely.

Similarly, Mr. S's responses to items on the Managing Money scale suggest significant limitations with respect to handling finances. For example, he is unable to balance a checkbook, write a check, account for money, count change, pay bills, or demonstrate awareness of assets to which he is entitled (e.g., Social Security, Medicare).

His responses to items on the Managing Home and Transportation scale also suggest significant limitations. Although he is likely able to use the phone, his hearing impairment will limit the utility of this device. Although Mr. S may be able to utilize public transportation, ensuring the safety of his home and living independently in a safe way will likely prove problematic for Mr. S given his responses to items on this scale. Mr. S's responses to items on the Health and Safety scale also suggest significant limitations in his ability to respond safely and appropriately in emergency situations.

Mr. S's performance on the Performance/Information and Problem Solving items indicates that he is unable to perform many of the basic tasks required of a person living independently. He also lacks adequate knowledge about various issues important to living independently. He is unlikely to be able to solve problems and apply relevant information in a reasonable way so as to live independently across essentially all domains. Problems with judgment are likely to place him at risk with respect to safety, managing a household, or protecting himself from others who may not have his interests at heart.

Social adjustment, by contrast, appears to be reasonably good. As reflected by Mr. S's responses on the Independent Living Scales, clinical observations, and the report of his wife, Mr. S appears to show good social and emotional adjustment, and he appears to be happy and content in his current living situation.

In addition to administration of the Independent Living Scales, an inquiry was made with respect to specific abilities and rights addressed in the Florida guardianship law. Consistent with results of structured testing, the clinical inquiry revealed significant limitations in terms of judgment, memory, and understanding on Mr. S's part. Mr. S does not believe that he has any physical or mental limitations that affect his ability to drive. This is clearly not the case, and Mr. S's judgment and decision-making capacity with respect to holding a driver's license and driving are quite limited. Similarly, Mr. S did not believe that he had any physical or cognitive limitations that affected his ability to live independently. Mr. S believes that he is capable of living alone, although he pointed out that he chooses not to do so. This lack of self-awareness and judgment is significant insofar as it could place Mr. S at risk if he is allowed to make decisions on his own behalf in these areas.

With respect to financial matters, Mr. S also showed significant limitations. For example, he reported that he did not receive Social Security benefits, nor was he entitled to them. He could not describe what Medicare benefits were, he re-

ported not being a Medicare recipient, and he believed that he was not entitled to these benefits. Additionally, Mr. S has essentially no awareness of his financial status, assets, or holdings. When presented with this information, Mrs. S replied that Mr. S's trustees failed to provide him with information about his finances. Assuming this to be true, Mr. S nonetheless failed to exercise his rights to this information or even try to obtain it, at least until recently. This suggests that Mr. S's ability to manage his financial affairs and apply for government and other benefits is significantly compromised.

These limitations also have implications for other individual rights. For example, Mr. S's capacity to make decisions regarding disposing of property or making gifts is quite limited insofar as he is unaware of his assets, unable to complete even the most basic monetary calculations or transactions, and shows poor judgment generally regarding important life decisions. Similarly, his abilities with respect to contracting, seeking employment, and making purchases is significantly limited by his difficulty in managing money and his limited insight and judgment more generally. His general lack of awareness and poor judgment further suggest that his ability to make decisions related to initiating and responding to litigation is impaired. For example, according to Mrs. S, her husband has failed to protect his rights and respond to what she describes as inappropriate behavior on the part of the trustees.

Mr. S's testamentary capacity is likely impaired insofar as he has no understanding of the nature and extent of his assets. Although he understands the purpose of a will (as indicated in his responses to questions), his lack of knowledge regarding his financial assets (and his inability to understand and appreciate their significance once such information is provided to him) likely impairs his testamentary capacity. Furthermore, Mr. S showed only a limited knowledge of distant relatives (including the petitioner) who may be his "natural" heirs.

Such deficits also have other implications with respect to Mr. S's ability to care for himself and manage his affairs. For example, physical, cognitive, and sensory limitations clearly impair Mr. S's ability to travel independently and make those decisions on his own behalf. It is interesting to note that Mr. S has no insight with respect to these issues and believes that he is fully capable of traveling independently.

With respect to entering into a marriage contract, Mr. S showed some capacity, as well as certain limitations. For example, he was aware that on one's death, assets are inherited by one's spouse. He was unable, however, to identify how a marriage was legal or contractual in nature other than the above. More specifically, he was unable to indicate that marriage entailed assumption of a spouse's assets and debts.

Mr. S's ability to make decisions regarding medical care is also compromised. This was particularly evidenced by his failure to note that he was taking medication, his inability to identify his family physician, his beliefs that his physician's office is in Pittsburgh, and general limitations with respect to judgment that are described in more detail above.

Mr. S showed some capacity with respect to voting. Although he incorrectly reported voting in the last election and identified the current president as a Republican, he correctly reported his party affiliation (as corroborated by his wife), noted that he would partly rely on the opinions of friends when deciding for whom to vote, indicated that it was illegal to sell one's vote, and was aware of the absentee ballot process.

DIAGNOSTIC IMPRESSION

Axis I: Dementia, Vascular or Alzheimer's Type
Axis II: No Diagnosis
Axis III: Arteriosclerosis, Impaired Hearing, Scoliosis
Axis IV: Problems Related to Interactions with the Legal System (the guardianship petition process)
Axis V: GAF = 65 (current)

SUMMARY AND GENERAL IMPRESSION

Adam S is a married, 95-year-old, white male who was referred for evaluation in the context of guardianship proceedings. Review of his medical record and structured psychological testing indicates that Mr. S demonstrates significant cognitive, physical, and sensory limitations at the current time, which significantly impair his ability to manage his personal, legal, medical, and financial affairs. Mr. S shows no awareness of the nature and extent of his limitations. Information provided by the court, Mr. S, and Mrs. S indicates that Mr. S has essentially not made any important decisions over the past few years with respect to personal, medical, legal, or financial matters; rather, they have been made on his behalf, either by Mrs. S or his trustees.

A review of the medical record and test results suggest that Mr. S had shown a gradual and progressive decline in cognitive functioning due to dementia, most likely of a vascular or Alzheimer's etiology. Given the present findings, it is the recommendation of this evaluator that a limited guardianship be considered by the court, with the restriction or transfer of all rights with the exception of voting. Of course, such a decision is ultimately a legal one to be made by the court.

Placement in a supportive, structured, and supervised living arrangement (similar to the one in which Mr. S currently resides) is appropriate. Despite the limitations described in this report, Mr. S shows a good social and emotional adjustment—he appears quite content and happy in his current living situation and environment. Continuation in this environment may be most beneficial for Mr. S, if this is possible once the guardianship issue is addressed. He has apparently functioned well during his stay with his caregiver-turned wife, and he appears happy and content at the current time.

Thank you for this opportunity to serve the court. If you have any questions about my evaluation, please do not hesitate to contact me.

Respectfully submitted,
Randy K. Otto, Ph.D.
Licensed Psychologist
Diplomate in Forensic Psychology
American Board of Professional Psychology

Teaching Point: Can one ever play more than one role in a single FMHA case?

Elsewhere in this book and in Heilbrun (2001) is a more detailed discussion of the only circumstance in which it is appropriate to play more than one role in a given case. Specifically, the previous discussion suggests that a forensic clinician may be able to assume multiple roles in a case if he or she initially serves as an impartial expert and, then, if the report or testimony will definitely not be needed because the findings were not favorable, moves into the role of consultant. It should be noted, however, that this is only appropriate if all parties—forensic clinician, attorney, and litigant—agree. Once the forensic clinician makes the transition from impartial expert to consultant, it would be inappropriate to return to the role of impartial expert in that case. Other than this one circumstance, other role combinations and role transitions are not recommended.

Since this case was authorized by court order, and the forensic clinician was working with the court as the primary client, this kind of role shift would not arise. Imagine, however, that the clinician had performed this evaluation at the request of the attorney for Mr. S. Given the present results, it is likely that the attorney would decide against using this evaluation as evidence in a guardianship hearing. Under these circumstances, if both the attorney and the forensic clinician agreed that the clinician would then become a consultant and that *under no circumstances would testimony regarding the results be used*, then the shift into the role of consultant (in which the clinician would provide the attorney with feedback on strategies for challenging the results of other evaluations, if they were not helpful, presenting the results of those that were, and offering relevant conceptual and empirical information from the literature) would be possible.

Chapter 21

Malpractice

The single case in this chapter is in the area of malpractice of mental health professionals and resulting psychological injury. The principle preceding the case discusses the importance of using information from more than one source to test rival hypotheses for behavior and to improve the overall accuracy of the evaluation. This approach is very important in malpractice cases, with the associated possibility of malingering for secondary financial gain that must be considered. The teaching point clarifies the role of the forensic evaluator in collecting collateral information from multiple sources, and identifies possible pitfalls and legal issues revolving around third-party disclosures.

Case 1

Principle: Use multiple sources of information for each area being assessed

This principle is discussed in chapter 12, so we begin the present chapter by showing how the present report illustrates the application of this principle.

The purpose of this evaluation was to provide information relevant to the legal decision of whether Ms. A's therapist, Dr. W, committed malpractice by acting in a manner contrary to the standard of care for psychologists in their community. Consistent with this principle, the forensic clinician obtained a good deal of information from multiple sources as part of the evaluation. For example, the forensic clinician in this case obtained information from the following sources: (1) clinical interviews with Ms. A; (2) psychological testing with Ms. A, including the MMPI-2, MCMI-III, Rorschach, WAIS-R, Rey-Osterrieth Figure, Trails A & B, 15-item Memory Test, Paced Auditory Serial Addition Task, and Draw-A-Person; (3) collateral interviews with Ms. A's ex-husband, Ms. A's sister, and Ms. A's psychotherapist; and (4) an examination of Ms. A's medical and psychiatric records.

This report illustrates the importance of using information obtained from multiple and diverse sources. The value of using multiple sources of information can be seen in three particular aspects of this report. First, the use of multiple sources of information helped the forensic clinician to obtain a more accurate picture of Ms. A's clinical functioning in a number of relevant domains. For example, using multiple sources of information strengthened the conclusion that Ms. A "has been prone to depression for most of her adult life." The forensic clinician reached this conclusion by using information from clinical interviews and psychological testing. The forensic clinician also used clinical interviewing, as well as objective and projective testing to conclude that Ms. A was presently experiencing a great deal of emotional distress. Using multiple sources of information, the forensic clinician was able to increase the "convergent validity" of his conclusions regarding Ms. A's clinical functioning.

Second, using multiple sources of information allowed the forensic clinician to test rival hypotheses regarding Ms. A's clinical condition that may have been generated from information obtained from other sources. For example, an important question in the evaluation was whether Ms. A's clinical condition was caused (or exacerbated) by her contact with Dr. W. Accordingly, the forensic clinician had to determine which of the following hypotheses was supported (or not supported) by the information obtained in the course of the evaluation: (1) Ms. A's clinical condition was preexisting, and her contact with Dr. W did not cause or exacerbate her clinical condition; (2) Ms. A's clinical condition was preexisting, but its severity was exacerbated by her contact with Dr. W; or (3) Ms. A's clinical condition was the result of her contact with Dr. W. The forensic clinician's use of multiple sources of information enabled him to consider and weigh these different hypotheses. On the basis of information obtained from several different sources (clinical interviews, psychological testing, and a review of medical and psychiatric records), the forensic clinician concluded that although Ms. A "has been prone to depression for most of her adult life," her contact with Dr. W exacerbated her condition, which resulted in her hospitalization on three occasions. In addition, on the basis of his clinical interview and psychological testing, the forensic clinician concluded that Ms. A's contact with Dr. W resulted in her developing "new trauma-related symptoms." Third-party information can also be very useful in distinguishing between such hypotheses and reaching conclusions like this.

Finally, by using multiple sources of information, the forensic clinician was able to corroborate important data that formed the basis for his conclusions. For example, another important question in this case was whether Dr. W's treatment of Ms. A was consistent with the standard of care for psychologists in their community. On the basis of information obtained from several different sources, such as Ms. A's self-report and the interviews conducted with her ex-husband and her sister, the forensic clinician concluded that Dr. W's treatment of Ms. A was problematic in certain important respects. Consistent with this principle, the forensic clinician's use of multiple sources of information had allowed him to corroborate important data that formed the basis for his conclusions regarding Ms. A's clinical condition.

April 29, 1996
Denise York, Esq.
Re: Bernadette A
Dear Ms. York:

As you requested, I have a conducted an evaluation of Bernadette A. I met with her initially on 12/27/95 and conducted a 3-hour clinical review. At that time, she was administered the MMPI-2 and MCMI-III. She returned to my office on 1/5/96, and I conducted a 2.5 hour clinical review and administered the Rorschach technique. She returned to my office on 1/15/96, at which time I conducted an initial 2.5 hour clinical interview. She was also seen on that day by my testing assistant, Jane Evans, who administered an additional battery of cognitive testing, including the Wechsler Adult Intelligence Scale-Revised, Rey-Osterrieth Figure, Trails A & B, 15-Item Memory Test, Paced Auditory Serial Addition Task, and Draw-A-Person. In addition, we readministered the MMPI-2 and MCMI-III to her at that time. On 2-20-96, I conducted a 1.5 hour clinical review with Roy Smith, Ms. A's ex-husband. Bernadette A returned to my office on 2-23-96 for an additional 2.5 hour clinical interview. On 4-1-96 I conducted a .75 hour clinical review with Becky Price, Ms. A's sister. On 4-4-96 I conducted my final interview with Ms. A, and on 4-10-96 I conducted a 1.5 hour consultation with Ms. A's psychotherapist Dr. Swanson.

I have spent a total of approximately 13 hours conducting interviews with Ms. A. In addition, I had an opportunity to review a full packet of her medical records. These include the records of her hospitalizations at General Hospital, Dr. Kirk's records, Dr. Swanson's records, and Dr. Jones's records. I have also reviewed Dr. W's records.

The purpose of this preliminary evaluation is to review two main issues of the case of Bernadette A. The first is whether, in his 5-year treatment of Ms. A, Dr. W acted in a manner contrary to the standard of care for psychologists in this community. The second major issue is the extent to which Ms. A was damaged by Dr. W's conduct. I will begin by reviewing Ms. A's complex history. This will be followed by a review of her psychological testing. The report will then address the standard of care issues in this case. The report will conclude with a discussion of damages and future treatment needs.

HISTORY

Bernadette A was born on September 12, 1952, in Los Angeles, California. Her father was Arturo A, who died in 1970. Her mother, Eloisa A, is still living and is currently 74 years old. She has a brother, Ricardo, who is 4 years older. Her sister, Becky, is 5 years older. Her father worked as a book salesman, and her mother worked for a local school district.

Throughout her childhood, she said, she suffered from a series of ear problems and frequent nose bleeds. She developed a serious lisp is the third grade and saw a speech therapist. It was also in the third grade that she began playing the viola. She had very few friends in her neighborhood, in part because her family never allowed her friends to come over and stay for the night. Her father was an alcoholic and highly unpredictable in his behavior. Her mother did not drink, but was apparently a codependent spouse who facilitated her husband's substance abuse, according to both Ms. A and her sister, Ms. Price.

When she was 8 years old, she said, her brother Ricardo began sexually abusing her. It should be noted that Ms. A apparently began to recall this abuse for the first time in the course of her psychotherapy with Dr. W. There is currently a significant professional controversy about the accuracy of memories that are "recovered" in this fashion, particularly when it is unclear whether questionable therapeutic techniques may have resulted in altering a genuine recollection or even in creating the recollection of events that did not occur. When such a report is made in a forensic context, therefore, it is important to (1) seek collateral verification of the reported events, and (2) exercise caution concerning whether such memories are accurate pending a careful analysis of internal consistency, plausibility, and external verification through third-party information. In this case, many of the recollections of childhood sexual abuse of Ms. A. were discussed with her sister, Ms. Price, who indicated that she herself had been sexually abused by the father in their family. Although she did not report directly observing abuse of Ms. A by either her brother or her father, she confirmed that there were many occasions on which Ms. A was alone with each of them, and (in retrospect, and tearfully) thought it quite possible that such sexual abuse was ongoing when Ms. A. was a child.

Ms. A reported that the sexual abuse by Ricardo continued until she was 15, and included almost every conceivable form of sexual activity, including fellatio and intercourse. He intimidated her physically, she said, and threatened to kill her if she told. He also told her that no one would believe her if she did tell her parents. Ricardo left for the army in 1967, and attempts to locate him to interview him for this evaluation were unsuccessful.

Her mother was physically and verbally abusive to Ms. A. According to both Ms. A and Ms. Price, she would hit Ms. A with objects such as a broom or a spoon. Ms. Price went on to say that she had experienced similar kinds of treatment from her mother and that was one of the reasons she never told anyone (particularly her mother) about the ongoing abuse that she experienced from the father. Ms. A reported that was also sexually abused by her father on "maybe five" occasions between the ages of 13 and 15. She and Ms. Price both reported that Ms. A was not allowed to date until she was 18 years old. She graduated from high school in 1970 and married Ralph Brown, but the marriage lasted only from June 1971 through October 1972.

After her graduation, she went to Lewis and Clark College, although she reported that she became ill in the middle of her first semester and had to drop out. Eventually, she and her husband moved to New Mexico. The marriage was annulled, she said, when she and her husband discovered they had very different ideas about having children together and after they both realized that they were too young to get married.

After Ms. A started school in New Mexico, she worked various jobs, sometimes working two jobs at a time. She then met Jack Vaughn, whom she married in March 1974. She reported that she and Mr. Vaughn moved to Portland, where their son Jack was born. This marriage lasted less than 5 years; Ms. A described Mr. Vaughn as an alcoholic and very passive.

She met Roy Smith in December 1978 and started going out with him in January 1979. He moved in with her and her children, Jack (then 5 years old) and Amber (then 4 years old), after several months; they lived together until November 1980, when they were married. According to Ms. A, it was not until after they were married that Mr. Smith became drunk and abusive. Mr. Smith acknowledged that he had a "drinking problem" during their marriage and would sometimes get very angry at Ms. A when he was drunk, but he denied that he had ever physically abused her. Ms. A said that they lived in Utah for about 4 years, where he worked for a manufacturing company and she worked for an oil company. She added that she also worked as a purchasing clerk for ABC, then for VISA. They returned to New Mexico in 1986, where she worked for a bank. She began working with the Workers' Compensation Division in 1985 and has worked there since.

She described her marriage to Mr. Smith was no great improvement and, in some ways, a distinct lack of improvement over her previous relationships. She stated that he was sometimes physically abusive to her and would continually put her down and humiliate her. He acknowledged that drinking could sometimes make him "mean" but he repeated several times that he had not been physically abusive toward Ms. A. In retrospect, she indicated, she had a long history of depression and feeling lonely and empty, and relied on him to provide her with an identity and with attention.

Since then she began working with Workers' Compensation Administration. She has been promoted on several occasions and now is supervisor of the local office. She has also since divorced Roy Smith and married Roger Richardson.

COURSE OF TREATMENT WITH DR. W

Ms. A had her first session with Dr. W in February 1990. Her last session was almost exactly 5 years later. This history of her treatment with Dr. W is taken from three primary sources: Ms. A's self-report, Dr. W's notes, and the interview with Ms. A's current therapist, Dr. Swanson. Ms. A said that she began seeing Dr. W to help her deal with her marital problems with Roy Smith. Several of the initial sessions were joint sessions, but Dr. W decided to refer their marital therapy to Dr. Timothy Stewart, while Dr. W continued to work with Ms. A. Dr. Stewart saw them as a couple for 2 years with occasional single sessions with Roy Smith.

Ms. A reported that early in the course of her treatment with Dr. W, she began to become aware that she may have been sexually abused as a child. According to Dr. W's notes, their weekly sessions between July and September 1990 contained frequent discussion of her childhood, and the notes from the sessions in August and September document her emerging memories of being sexually abused by her brother Ricardo and her father. According to both the notes and Ms. A, these memories were recounted with strong emotion, including anger and a sense of betrayal.

Over the subsequent course of the treatment, Ms. A reported, she dealt with many ongoing issues, including problems with her daughter, Amber, and continuing marital problems with her husband. Dr. W's notes allude to her growing unhappiness with her marriage, her sense that she was with her husband primarily because "I have to be with somebody" and "he at least makes me feel like I'm needed." As the treatment progressed, however, she became increasingly convinced that she must sever the relationship with Roy Smith. She also "gave up" other relationships, including those with friends. Dr. W's notes are fairly clear about her unhappiness with her husband, but rarely allude to other relationships, such as friendships, which Ms. A said she felt she no longer needed.

In September 1994, Ms. A reported, she had her first "romantic" experience with Dr. W when they kissed on the way back from a trip to northern New Mexico. Subsequently, she said, they had four separate instances in which they had overt sexual contact, including intercourse and oral-genital contact. These occurred over the fall and winter of 1994 and early 1995. Dr. W's notes around this time describe how Ms. A seems "happier," but also refer to her as "needy." The notes also indicate that Ms. A reported that she was "trying new things" in her attempt to become "a different person." Ms. Price, Ms. A's sister, re-

called that Ms. A seemed happier than she had ever seen her—"almost giddy sometimes"—but also indicated that she had less contact with her sister than usual around that time. She described Ms. A as calling less and often not returning phone calls when Ms. Price called her.

According to Ms. A, following some of these experiences there was an abrupt change in her mood. She became very depressed and actively suicidal. She was hospitalized in General Hospital in December 1994 and treated for depression and suicidal ideation. She was hospitalized again in early February 1995. Dr. W's notes during this time refer to her feeling "empty," "very down," and "worthless," although the treatment plan for addressing these problems was not described (typically it would be "continue next week"). Shortly after her hospitalization in February, when she revealed to her attending psychiatrist that she and Dr. W had a sexual relationship, Dr. W terminated their therapy and she began working with Dr. Swanson. Dr. W's termination rationale, as reflected in his note of 2-8-95, was only "patient unwilling to work in therapy."

Not surprisingly, Dr. W's notes do not reflect any indication of either an extratherapeutic friendship or a sexual relationship with Ms. A. However, in his May 30, 1995, letter to the New Mexico Board of Psychology Examiners, he wrote, "With mixed thoughts and feelings of both humility and the greatest of fervor, I acknowledge . . . friendship with Bernadette A and that it evolved innocuously in natural ways at the end point of her treatment and separation from my practice" (May 3, 1995, NMBPC letter, p. 2). In this letter, he basically acknowledges that he and Ms. A developed a relationship that went beyond their therapeutic work together, although the letter does not describe that friendship as sexual, nor does it indicate that the friendship had developed during the period of their therapy.

PSYCHOLOGICAL TESTING

Psychological testing done with Bernadette A indicates that she is a woman of about Average intelligence with a Full Scale IQ of 104, a Verbal IQ of 106 and a Performance IQ of 101. The testing indicates some deficit in social judgment, but excellent verbal and clerical skills.

Personality testing done with Ms. A indicates that she is in a great degree of distress at present. On most of her self-report testing (administered on two separate occasions because of profile invalidity of the initial tests), she produced very extreme profiles reflecting high degrees of emotional distress. The second group of profiles were more valid but still indicated significant elevations on a number of scales reflecting confusion and depression, along with a high degree of suspiciousness.

Other self-report testing indicated strong paranoid thinking along with a tendency to avoid being around other people. All of the profiles indicated a propensity toward unusual thought processes and personality disintegration. Projective testing done with Ms. A indicated a complex pattern showing a combination of fundamental emotional strengths and personality deficits, including severely impaired judgment and a tendency toward disorganized thinking. Her condition is currently stable but could disintegrate rather rapidly given the uncertain basis for her decision making and her related tendency to enter into destructive relationships.

STANDARD OF CARE AND PROFESSIONAL EFFECTIVENESS

Bernadette A was under the care of Dr. W over the course of 5 years. She began this treatment as a person with multiple life problems and prone to recurrent anxiety and depression. At the time that they first began working together, Bernadette A had just made a very serious suicide attempt and was psychiatrically hospitalized. She was also being treated at that time by a psychiatrist, Dr. Kirk, who was prescribing antidepressant medication. According to Ms. A, Ms. Price, and Mr. Smith, Ms. A made a serious suicide attempt in 1989 prior to entering therapy with Dr. W. At that time, Ms. A recalled, her marriage was in disarray and highly unstable, and her children were emotionally troubled. She added that she was just beginning to grapple with recurrent nightmares, which she thought in retrospect were the beginning of reported memories of an extensive and serious history of childhood sexual abuse. Ms. A thus came into therapy as a highly vulnerable and emotionally unstable individual who required ef-

fective psychotherapy in order to show improvement.

In that context, Dr. W bore a fiduciary responsibility in relation to her. That is, he was required by ethics applicable to psychological practice to place his patient's interests ahead of his own personal interests. He repeatedly failed to do this. Most of these failures fall into a general category of therapeutic boundaries. There were a number of problems in this area, which will be described. In addition to general boundary problems, there was the serious and more specific dual role problem resulting from the apparent development of a "friendship" and, subsequently, a sexual relationship with her. Finally, he terminated the therapy on her report of, and the apparent end to, their sexual relationship. Each of these will be discussed.

Boundary Violations

General　In most psychotherapeutic relationships, maintenance of proper therapeutic boundaries is critical for effective therapy. In part, this is because the organization of the therapy and the barriers maintained in that context provide a safe environment for the client to deal with very intimate and difficult details of her life. Thus, boundaries define a safe environment in which the patient and psychotherapist can work toward improving emotional conflict and interpersonal dysfunction. In Ms. A's case, therapeutic boundaries were especially important. Because she apparently had experienced repeated and protracted incestuous experiences by her brother, and because other individuals in her life (e.g., her father) had also seriously violated her personal boundaries, development and maintenance of therapeutic boundaries were especially important for her. This was something she couldn't do well for herself, because her own boundaries were so distorted by her prior experiences. Also, because of the many emotional and nurturance deprivations in her life, Bernadette A. had strong dependency needs that were rarely met because of her fundamental distrust of others. Dr. W, in his fiduciary duty to Bernadette A, was required to develop and maintain therapeutic boundaries with her. He failed to do this in a number of respects.

Therapeutic Structure　There are two main aspects of the structure of psychotherapy that assist in boundary formation and maintenance: dealing with fees and dealing with the time of the psychotherapy. These are two aspects of psychotherapy that may become distorted by a patient's unrealistic demands on the psychotherapist. Dr. W failed in both respects.

First, he made special fee arrangement for her, according to both Ms. A and the notes of therapy. At one point in his treatment with her, Dr. W had raised his hourly rate to $150, having charged her (and other patients) $120/hour prior to that time. In this case, he gave her special treatment by leaving her hourly rate at $120 rather than increasing it to $150.

In addition, he also arranged the periods of their appointments with her in a nonstandard way. First, the sessions would sometimes go as long as 2 hours, according to both Ms. A and the notes, but he would only bill her for 1 hour. He would set the appointments for the end of the day and possibly provided her with unscheduled emergency sessions. Ms. A described having at least four unscheduled sessions in late 1994, although the notes do not reflect any of these. As treatments progressed, she said that she became irritated that she could only reach him through his answering service, so he gave her his direct pager number. (Ms. A was able to provide this number to me, and I confirmed that it was Dr. W's number.)

In one sense, Dr. W's accommodations on scheduling and fees might be seen as kindness and flexibility. However, this special way of dealing with fees, time allocation, and other aspects of therapy indicated that he would violate the most fundamental and simple of boundaries with her. She reported that this gave her the expectation that more important boundaries would be violated were she to make those demands as well.

Compliments In psychotherapeutic relationships it is common for the topic of conversation to stay on the "business" of psychotherapy: that is, the person and her problems. Compliments, like most things therapists say to patients, should further the goal of treatment. In Dr. W's treatment of Ms. A, he violated this role by frequently complimenting her clothing or perfume. He also commented that Ms. A looked like "dynamite" when she lost weight. These were Ms. A.'s recollections; they are not documented in therapy notes. If they occurred as Ms. A described, however, they would have been personal comments without apparent therapeutic justification, therefore having limited utility in her psychotherapeutic relationship and probably reflecting a boundary problem in Dr. W's behavior.

Personal Revelations It is not unusual for psychotherapists to engage in "self-disclosure" as a means of therapeutic intervention with their clients. Such disclosures should be rare, brief, and carefully chosen to reflect past, not current problems. They should be used with sensitivity to their impact on other boundaries in psychotherapy. Dr. W apparently engaged in excessive self-disclosure and personal revelations, talking about his own family life, his own history of abuse, and also his history of self-mutilation. Each of these are separate recollections of Ms. A's; however, the notes do indicate that during several different sessions, Dr. W made comments about his personal life and history (e.g., "11-2-90, shared that sexual abuse in childhood is common & that I was victim," "10-5-94, addressed importance of deciding on making a change when very unhappy, used my marriage as example"). However, those were very personal disclosures, and more intimate disclosures about his own current family life indicated a lack of proper therapeutic boundary maintenance on the part of Dr. W.

Extratherapeutic Contacts In Dr. W's work with Ms. A, he apparently developed a series of extratherapeutic contacts when he began a dual relationship. These extratherapeutic contacts happened on a number of occasions. For example, they would "run into" each other fairly often at a local restaurant. On these occasions, they would often talk about their respective families.

On one occasion, as part of a seemingly therapeutic endeavor, he took her and her sister out to lunch at a hotel and paid for the lunch, an event that was recalled by both Ms. Price and Ms. A. The lunch included consumption of alcohol and discussion of quite personal matters in that relatively public setting. He allowed her to take him to lunch for his birthday, because she wanted to thank him for letting her talk to him whenever she needed to. Early in the psychotherapy, Ms. A invited Dr. W and his spouse to her home for a Christmas party, and they attended it. They once spent the day shopping together, which both Ms.

Price and Ms. A described. They traveled to Chimayo to visit the Santuario, a local religious shrine, where, according to Ms. A, they had their first sexual encounter. Those extratherapeutic contacts were so extensive and occurred over such a long period that they constituted a "dual relationship" with Bernadette A, as the contacts reflected would have been described as a social relationship even if it were not sexual.

Personal Space Violations Psychotherapists recognize that it is important to respect the personal space of their patients. This is especially true in patients who have been physically or sexually abused, as violations of personal space can quite often prove overly threatening or overly gratifying. In either case, the psychotherapist must deal with personal space violations very carefully. Dr. W reportedly began personal space violations very early in psychotherapy when he hugged her, usually with her permission. According to her recollection, he also hugged her after a particularly stressful session and sat next to her on the couch at that time. Although these were minor space violations when compared to his later sexual contact with her, they set they set the stage for that sexual contact by indicating his willingness to gratify her nurturance needs.

Confidentiality It is clear that Dr. W's wife knew that Ms. A was his patient. In fact, Dr. W's wife (who worked for Technical Vocational Institute [T-VI]) arranged for Ms. A to play viola at the T-VI graduation. In short, Ms. W (through the actions of her husband) violated Bernadette A's right to maintain confidentiality of her relationship with him.

Sexual Misconduct Beginning in November 1994, Dr. W had repeated intimate contact with Ms. A, according to her account to me and also according to her description to her current therapist, Dr. Swanson. The contact began when they spent the day together in Chimayo visiting the Santuario and shopping. At one point outside the therapy session, Ms. A said that Dr. W admitted to her that he had "very deep feelings" for her. On the trip back from Chimayo, they "made out" (Ms. A's words) in the car on several occasions, which included some sexual fondling. Over subsequent contacts they began having intercourse, and had intercourse on four occasions. According to Ms. A, their sexual contact once began in Dr.

W's office after a session. On another occasion, she said, there was some sexual contact during the session. Sexual contacts between psychologist and their patients is specifically prohibited by psychological ethics (APA *Ethical Principles and Code of Conduct*, 4.04).

THERAPEUTIC FAILURES

Failure to Recognize Dynamics of Incest Survivors It is not unusual for incest survivors to have serious problems in their ongoing interpersonal relationships. These problems tend to center around issues of trust and control. It is also not uncommon for memories of childhood sexual abuse to become clarified through the therapeutic process, which often occasions an increase in both distrust and concerns about control. These both occurred with Ms. A, according to her, around the time she began to deal in therapy with her incest experience. By her report, Dr. W failed to warn her concerning the degree of alienation that can occur at this time, or about the impact such realizations could have on her ongoing relationship with her husband. As noted earlier, this marital relationship was already tenuous as a result of a number of previously experienced problems.

Bernadette A also experienced an increase in confusion and disorientation as a result of the emerging incest memories. This is not an unusual reaction because revelation of the abuse often disrupts preexisting ways of viewing the world and brings up serious questions concerning parental love, family stability, and one's own worth as an individual. Dr. W failed to help her deal effectively with this increase in confusion and disorientation and did not advise her to warn members of her family about those reactions. Ms. A described her therapy in these terms, and there was no indication in the therapy notes that Dr. W had communicated these matters to her (or even that they were discussed in therapy) when the incest was being addressed.

Erosion of Support System Psychotherapists recognize that effective interpersonal and familial support is often critical in the recovery process. However, the impact of Dr. W's treatment of Bernadette A had the result of seriously eroding her relationship with her husband, and caused her to be somewhat alienated from her family and her friends. Mr. Smith reported that their relationship became increasingly tense during the first 9 months of Ms. A's therapy with Dr. W; following that, he said, she became more distant and withdrawn. As a result, he said, their relationship worsened, and she seemed to blame him increasingly for problems at home and with the children. At the same time, Ms. A indicated, she was becoming more dependent on Dr. W. Because he was so indulgent of her dependency, she did not need to rely on other people and became progressively more detached from her social support system.

Failure to Encourage Independence It is apparent that Dr. W caused Bernadette A to become extremely dependent on him over the course of his treatment with her. This meant that by the end of her treatment with Dr. W, she was no more capable of independently dealing with her problems than she was at the initiation of that work, a characterization made by both Ms. Price and Dr. Swanson, as well as Ms. A. Rather, she had all of her emotional investment in Dr. W. He was her psychotherapist and her "best friend." Toward the end of the treatment, he was also her lover. Such total investment of emotional energy and dependence on one person not only made it more probable that such boundary violations, including sexual relationships, would occur, but also interfered with a fundamental goal of psychotherapy.

Failure to Deal with Transference Dr. W failed to deal effectively with the constellations of thoughts and feelings that Bernadette A had toward him. It is recognized that the psychotherapist comes to symbolize and to serve as a repository for many idealized thoughts and feelings of the patient. This constitutes a transference of feelings associated with other people in the person's life (e.g., a parent, teacher, or other authority figure) to the psychotherapist. Therapists recognize that this transference is an important basis for forming a therapeutic relationship, but must be dealt with in the context of therapy in order to progress in treatment. There is no evidence that Dr. W dealt effectively with Bernadette A, in part, because her idealization of him continued until he terminated their therapeutic relationships.

Failure to Deal with Countertransference Over the course of insight-oriented long-term treatment, it is not unusual for the psychotherapist to develop strong feelings of various sorts for the patient. Properly trained psychotherapists recognize these feelings and use them as a means of effectively intervening with a patient. In part because of the dual relationship with Ms. A (e.g., as both a patient and as "friend"), Dr. W was unable to effectively use his feelings for her to advance the therapeutic process. His failure to monitor his own countertransference led to the many boundary violations, including apparently sexual contact with her.

Failure to Obtain Consultation When psychotherapists encounter difficulty in dealing with a patient or therapeutic situation, it is appropriate to obtain consultation with another psychotherapist. It is also the case that had Dr. W consulted with another psychotherapist or psychologist concerning the development of his "friendship" with Bernadette A, this consultant would have immediately recognized the inappropriateness of such an extratherapeutic relationship and would have counseled against it. Further, consultation could have helped Dr. W avoid the "slippery slope" of boundary violations, which led him to have a sexual relationship with his client. There are no indications in the therapy notes that Dr. W sought such consultation; indeed, there are no indications that he recognized the development of an inappropriate relationship or acknowledged that his own feelings for her created a risk of his acting in a countertherapeutic fashion.

Failure to Monitor and Refer Dr. W worked with Ms. A for 5 years. He failed to properly monitor her treatment to determine why it was not progressing. Her condition, as seen by her husband and sister, was fluctuating, and it seriously deteriorated in late 1994. Because he was failing in his role as psychotherapist for Ms. A, Dr. W had a duty to refer her to another psychotherapist. While he did discuss referring her for medication evaluation on one occasion, which was documented in the notes, he failed to refer anyone who could have provided psychotherapy for Ms. A.

Improper Termination   Following the initiation of her sexual relationship with Dr. W, Ms. A was hospitalized in late December 1994. Their sexual relationship continued, and she again became suicidal in early February 1995. It was during this hospitalization that she revealed her sexual relationship with Dr. W to her treating psychiatrist. Shortly after that, Dr. W terminated their therapy relationship.

This did not constitute a proper termination of psychotherapy. First, this had been a very long therapeutic relationship, as it had lasted 5 years. A therapeutic relationship of such duration requires a relatively lengthy and gradual period in which termination is discussed and accomplished. Her termination was, in fact, rather abrupt and done without preparation.

Because the treatment was terminated so abruptly, and because of the ongoing dual sexual and social relationships that he had with her, the termination did not occur because she had reached any point of adequacy in functioning. She still had limited self-support skills, and her social support, as noted earlier, had decreased over the course of her treatment. In addition, Ms. A said that she felt confused, disoriented, and guilty about the sexual relationship with Dr. W. It was, therefore, an inopportune time to terminate treatment, especially as she had been discharged from the hospital against medical advice.

Because of this abrupt termination, there was no effective referral by Dr. W to another psychotherapist. Dr. Jacobs, her psychiatrist, referred her to Dr. Swanson, who is her current psychotherapist. Moreover, because Dr. W did not facilitate the referral of Ms. A, there was no effective communication concerning her condition. In fact, according to Dr. Swanson and Ms. A, she did not reveal the sexual nature of her relationship with Dr. W until the 12th session with Dr. Swanson.

PSYCHOLOGICAL DAMAGES

Through the multiple failures described in this report, Dr. W left Bernadette A in worse shape than he found her. I refer to these in sequence, beginning with Dr. W's below standard care of her, along with his sexual contact with her, both of which caused her preexisting condition to worsen. I then discuss a number of other ways in which she was damaged by these actions.

EXACERBATION OF PREEXISTING CONDITIONS

Depression   Ms. A has been prone to depression for most of her adult life. While her depression has rarely interfered with her occupational functioning, it has interfered with her interpersonal functioning and has contributed to her overall sense of ineffectiveness and malaise. As a result of Dr. W's treatment failures and sexual abuse of her, Bernadette A's depression has deepened to the extent that she required three psychiatric hospitalizations in a year and experienced acute suicidal thinking.

Cognitive Disarray   She is prone to impaired thinking when she is anxious or depressed. The confusion caused by her multiple dual relationships with Dr. W has, in my view, caused her to be more cognitively disturbed than she was prior to her treatment with him. This confusion is evident in her psychological testing.

Alienation   Bernadette A has always had difficulty in effectively relating to other people, especially those who should be closest to her. This alienation has been exacerbated by the abuse of trust created by Dr. W's actions, an abuse that apparently repeated previous betrayals by her brother and her father in the context of sexual behavior.

Dissociation   Bernadette A has a tendency to dissociate following distress, especially in some interpersonal relationships. This dissociation has been exacerbated by the sexual contact she had with Dr. W, so that dissociative experiences are now a more frequent part of her life. While Ms. A describe this in detail, it is consistent with the accounts provided by Ms. Price and Dr. Swanson.

CREATIONS OF A NEW DISORDER

Bernadette A had a preexisting trauma-related disorder caused by her sexual abuse by her brother, her father, and others. This was the main focus of her initial treatment. However, because of Dr. W's behavior during this treatment, she has developed a new Post Traumatic Stress Disorder. He essentially recapitulated her childhood abuse experience, and thus created new trauma-related symptoms.

New Trauma-Related Symptoms   Ms. A has experienced nightmares concerning her sexual contact with Dr. W. In these dreams, she reports feeling trapped and helpless. Quite often she cites having sleep disturbance as a result of these dreams. She experiences increased distress when she goes to places that she used to visit with Dr. W, and even avoids visiting in parts of town where she used to meet him. She reports becoming anxious when entering the building in which Dr. W's office was located. In addition, she has difficulty recalling important aspects of the traumatic incident; for example, reconstruction of the chronology of the sexual misconduct has been difficult for her.

In addition, she has diminished interest in life activities, especially going to church and playing the viola, which is consistent with accounts of both Ms. Price and Dr. Swanson. She relates both of these to her contacts with Dr. W. She has experienced increased detachment or estrangement from other people as a result of her abuse by Dr. W. She does not want to spend time with friends, and generally attempts to limit her life to spending time only with her family. She also has experienced changes in the ability to experience emotion, and says she has been "mostly angry" during the last year.

In addition, she has concerns about her future and experiences difficulty concentrating and hypervigilance. Overall, she has many symptoms of an ongoing Post Traumatic Stress Disorder that has been created as a result of the ineffective treatment and sexual misconduct of Dr. W.

Increased Suicide Risk   At the onset of her treatment with Dr. W in 1990, she was hospitalized for medication management and depression. Over the course of her treatment with him, her suicide risk was under control. However, she began to "slide downhill" following the initiation of her sexual relationship with Dr. W in November 1994. She became suicidal again in February 1995, just prior to the termination of her treatment. Following that termination, she was hospitalized in November 1995, again for suicidal ideation. Finally, the confusion, disorientation, and guilt engendered by Dr. W's ineffectiveness as a therapist,

and his sexual misconduct with her, actually increased her suicide risk, in my opinion.

Increased Need for Hospitalization   Ms. A's three hospitalizations since November 1994 represent her lowest level of functioning as an adult. As described earlier, they appear directly related to her reactions to the therapy process and related events in her relationship with Dr. W.

OTHER PERSONAL AND INTERPERSONAL PROBLEMS CAUSED BY DR. W'S FAILURES AND CARE

Difficulty in Trusting   Bernadette A placed a great deal of trust in Dr. W. Toward the end of her treatment with him, she said, he was the only one who she really trusted. Having this trust so egregiously violated by his sexual misconduct, she has experienced difficulty trusting other people, especially her new psychotherapist, Dr. Swanson. Dealing with this trust has been a major focus of her treatment with Dr. Swanson and has carried over to her other relationships as well. This is in one sense an exacerbation of a preexisting problem, in that her prior abuse by those who should have loved and taken care of her was very similar to Dr. W's abuse of her.

Reduction of Self-Esteem   Bernadette A now describes herself as being "lower than dirt." While she had always had self-esteem problems, the embarrassment, humiliation, and guilt that she experienced as a result of her sexual relationship with Dr. W have been very difficult for her to bear. She feels as though what happened was her fault, even though the relationship occurred in the context of greatly disparate power levels between her and Dr. W.

Distrust in Own Judgment   In relation to her sense that the sexual relationship between her and Dr. W was her own fault, she has grown to distrust her own judgment about many things. It is almost as though she believes that if she made this kind of mistake then she should be prone to experiencing similar mistakes in other situations. Secondguessing herself has become a way of life and this has caused her to ruminate excessively about decisions.

Disruption of Marital and Friend Relationships
As noted in the Standard of Care Section of the report, over the course of treatment with Dr. W, her relationship with Roy Smith disintegrated. The extent to which Dr. W may have contributed to the disruption of that relationship is not entirely clear. It is clearer, however, that by the fall of 1994, Ms. A believed that Dr. W was the only one who cared about her, and she had cut herself off emotionally, not only from her relationship with Roy Smith but also from her family (particularly her sister, Ms. Price) and many of her friends. This isolation has been difficult for her to reverse, and she has still not reestablished effective relationships with many of those from whom she was alienated over the course of her treatment with Dr. W. In part, this is because she is still socially withdrawn as an element of the Post Traumatic Stress Disorder caused by her treatment with Dr. W.

Loss of Spiritual Faith Bernadette A is a person who has had strong religious faith. Her involvement in the monastic retreats and her extensive involvement with her church have been an important part of her life. The therapeutic relationship in which she was involved with Dr. W has caused her to doubt her faith, she said, and it is only very recently that she has returned to church (which both she and Ms. Price reported).

TREATMENT NEEDS

Ms. A is in need of continued treatment with Dr. Swanson or another similarly qualified psychotherapist. Her relationship with Dr. Swanson appears to be good, well-controlled in boundaries, and effective. Because of the delay in effective treatment and because of the damages caused by Dr. W's treatment of her, Ms. A will require at least 3 to 6 years of additional treatment. This should occur on a twice weekly basis and will cost about $12,000 a year at today's psychotherapy rate. It is also the case that Ms A may need future hospitalizations. I would recommend provision for at least 30 days for such treatment, at a cost of $1,000 a day.

SUMMARY AND CONCLUSIONS

Bernadette A was involved in psychotherapy with Dr. W for 5 years. In the course of that treatment, she was able to recall an extensive history of childhood physical and sexual abuse. Treatment with Dr. W incorporated that issue, but because of severe distortions of power, control, and boundaries, the relationship was ineffective in treating that problem. In fact, she has developed new emotional problems that did not exist prior to her treatment by Dr. W. She is currently involved in a positive therapeutic relationship with Dr. Swanson. This relationship should continue for 3 to 5 years. With effective treatment, I believe Ms. A's many strengths may be utilized to allow her to have a more effective personal and family life.

Thank you for the referral of this most interesting and complex case. If I may provide any further information, please feel free to call or write.

Yours truly,
William E. Foote, PhD

Teaching Point: What is the role of the forensic clinician in collecting third-party information?

Third-party information is a valuable and important data source in FMHA. Given its value and importance, the forensic clinician should not rely solely on the referral source to identify all sources of relevant third-party information. Requests to the referral source for such information should be kept as broad as possible, and, whenever possible, made to both sides of the civil or criminal matter under consideration.

On a related topic, it is also important to avoid relying on an attorney's description of the record without obtaining that record and personally inspecting it. If the record cannot be obtained, then the forensic clinician should either exclude the information from the FMHA or attribute it to a source that has been reviewed. An attributed statement such as "Ms. Jones's attorney stated that collateral sources reflect that she is suffering from severe depression" would look odd, to say the least, in a report documenting a presumably impartial evaluation, and could be providing information that is inaccurate. Therefore, it is recommended that the forensic clinician not accept information from the record without personally inspecting it.

Collateral interviews are an excellent way of collecting third-party information, and such interviews are almost always conducted by the forensic clinician. Occasionally there might be a witness statement, deposition, or preliminary testimony that is sufficiently thorough and relevant so there is no need to interview that individual. In most cases, however, a direct interview is preferable to obtaining such information through records.

Ideally, collateral interviews should be conducted in person. This may not be possible when numerous interviews have to be conducted in a short period of time. Under those circumstances, it is more practical to conduct the collateral interviews in the evening by telephone. Whatever is lost in not being able to observe the collateral source directly is probably gained in the ability to conduct more interviews; because multiple data sources provide more information, such additional information can be used to assess the consistency of information across sources and thereby substantially increase the accuracy of FMHA.

The forensic clinician must also be aware of the possible legal ramifications of conducting collateral interviews because direct contact with some third parties who are involved in the litigation could be problematic from the standpoint of evidentiary considerations. In cases where contact of this type is necessary, the forensic clinician is advised to consult with one or both attorneys and, if there is remaining doubt, obtain a court order authorizing collateral interviews of relevant third parties as part of the FMHA.

In the case in this chapter, important collateral interviews were conducted with Ms. A's ex-husband, sister, and current treating therapist. All three were very important, as many of the events described by Ms. A as occurring in her therapy with Dr. W could have been denied by the therapist, and therefore needed to be checked through collateral observers. As reflected in the report, there were occasions in which the treatment notes seemed consistent with Ms. A's recollections, and other times when the notes were either silent or actively inconsistent. In cases like this, it is likely that notes would sometimes be even less supportive of a patient's claim of sexual misconduct or other boundary violations by a therapist. There is also an intense professional controversy about the accuracy of "recovered memories" of sexual abuse, so the forensic clinician should make every effort to obtain third-party information relevant to the accuracy of such memories. Given the frequent consistency of the reports of Ms. A and collateral observers, her account of the therapy with Dr. W appears more credible, and the report more accurate.

Chapter 22

Worker's Compensation

This chapter focuses on the role of FMHA in the context of worker's compensation claims. Two reports are included. The principle preceding the first case discusses the use of specialized structured interviews and instruments to assess response style in forensic mental health assessment. This principle distinguishes between tests that have empirical support for measuring response style and tests without such empirical support. Elaborating on this principle, the teaching point associated with the first case provides a framework for the effective integration of all types of response style data, with a particular emphasis on the integration of data obtained through structured interviews and instruments. The principle relating to the second case addresses the process of assessing legally relevant behavior, and discusses how the information can be used to assist the court in accurate decision making. Building on this principle, the teaching point in the second case discusses the importance of establishing a causal nexus between clinical characteristics and symptoms and work capacity disability.

Case 1

Principle: Use testing when indicated in assessing response style

This principle is discussed in chapter 5, so we turn to the question of how the present report illustrates this principle.

The report is an independent medical evaluation conducted to determine whether Mr. S has a mental or emotional disorder that might justify the continued payment of disability benefits. Mr. S was claiming that symptoms of depression and anxiety had debilitated him to the point that he could no longer run his business. Because the primary issues being assessed were the nature of his clinical condition and its impact on his capacity to work, the evaluators wanted to obtain as much accurate information as possible that was relevant to each of these issues. A related issue in this case involved the possibility of secondary financial gain by Mr. S. Specifically, there was the possibility that

438

Mr. S exaggerated or malingered his symptoms and associated impairment in his work capacities to ensure the continuation of his disability benefits. Therefore, because an accurate assessment of Mr. S's response style was necessary, the evaluators addressed the possibility of malingering by Mr. S. The assessment of possible malingering incorporated the use of interview strategies, collateral document review, and psychological testing. Collateral document review was used to assess the accuracy of his self-reported historical information and symptoms during the current evaluation. Interview questions were rephrased and repeated throughout the evaluation to further assess the consistency of Mr. S's self-report. His self-report was consistent throughout the evaluation, and was supported by the collateral sources considered for the evaluation.

Next, Mr. S was administered several psychological tests, such as the MMPI-2 and the Wechsler Adult Intelligence Scale, 3rd edition (WAIS-III). The MMPI-2 has demonstrated empirical support in the detection of malingering. Mr. S appeared visibly fatigued throughout administration of the MMPI-2, and responded by endorsing a large number of unusual thoughts and experiences. Actuarial interpretation of the MMPI-2 validity scales suggested that this pattern of responding is typically seen in individuals who are either openly acknowledging a high level of distress or deliberately exaggerating their account of such difficulties. Accordingly, Mr. S's MMPI-2 profile was interpreted with caution and considered in relation to its consistency with collateral information from other sources. The MMPI-2 clinical profile was consistent with depressed mood, significant anxiety, difficulty making decisions, and an overall reduced level of efficiency.

The WAIS-III does not have demonstrated empirical support in the detection of malingering, but it provided valuable information regarding Mr. S's cognitive functioning at the time of the evaluation. Mr. S's overall level of intellectual functioning was measured as within the Borderline range, which did not appear consistent with his intellectual functioning and vocational achievement suggested by relevant history. This result suggested low motivation and/or fatigue, and Mr. S did appear to be visibly fatigued throughout the test. Reduced cognitive functioning, consistent with the presence of a mood disorder, was also consistent with Mr. S's self-report. Given these findings, it might have been useful to administer a measure of cognitive malingering such as the Validity Indicator Profile (Frederick, 1997; Frederick & Crosby, 2000). This would have allowed the direct consideration of the possibility that Mr. S was exaggerating his cognitive deficits.

The possibility of symptom exaggeration was addressed in the clinical interview and the MMPI-2. The evaluators concluded that secondary financial gain was not a significant factor contributing to the findings. Symptom exaggeration was considered, and there was some evidence from his MMPI-2 profile that Mr. S may have been exaggerating his current symptoms. Nevertheless, given Mr. S's psychiatric history and the available collateral information, it appeared more likely that he was experiencing a significant amount of psychological distress.

FORENSIC PSYCHOLOGICAL
ASSESSMENT
INDEPENDENT MEDICAL
EXAMINATION

November 2, 1999
Re: Mr. S

REFERRAL

Mr. S is a 36-year-old Caucasian male who was employed as President, Owner, and Chief Operating Officer of ABC, Inc. Mr. S has been unable to work since May 22, 1997, when his attending physician placed him on medical disability. This independent medical examination was requested by Mr. S's insurance carrier for the following purposes:

1. To determine if there is a psychological condition that prevents the policyholder from engaging in *the substantial and material duties of [their] regular job.*
2. To determine, specifically, what impairments exist as they apply to the insured's occupation.

PROCEDURES

Mr. S was evaluated for approximately 7 hours on September 20, 1999. The evaluation was conducted at the Department of Clinical and Health Psychology at MCP Hahnemann University in Philadelphia. In addition to a clinical interview, Mr. S was administered a structured screening instrument for currently experienced symptoms of mental and emotional disorder (the Brief Symptom Inventory, or BSI), a test of current intellectual functioning (the Wechsler Adult Intelligence Scale, 3rd edition, or WAIS-III), and a standardized measure of personality variables (the Minnesota Multiphasic Personality Inventory, 2nd edition, or MMPI-2). The following documents, obtained through the referral source, were reviewed as part of this evaluation:

1. Correspondence from Insurance Company (dated 8-17-99),
2. Correspondence from Disability Consultants (dated 9-9-99),
3. Memoranda from Ms. E, Director of Claims for Insurance Company, to Dr. B (dates 2-20-98 and 7-1-98),
4. Insurance Company Proof of Claim (dated 6-25-97),
5. Attending Physician's Statements (dates 6-25-97, 8-18-97, 12-10-97, 1-26-98, 3-30-98, 5-6-98, and 5-27-99),
6. Claimant's Statements (dates 10-14-97, 12-15-97, 1-26-98, 3-30-98, 5-6-98, and 5-17-99),
7. Insured's Supplemental Application for Disability Benefits (dated 7-23-99),
8. Medical Provider's Statement Progress Report (dated 7-99),
9. Evaluation Form I from Insurance Company (completed by Dr. R, dated 8-17-99),
10. Psychological Evaluation (completed by Dr. R, dated 8-14-98),
11. Progress Notes from Dr. R,
12. Description of Occupation Form (dated 10-14-97),
13. Investigative Reports (dated 7-24-97, 7-9-98, 10-21-98, 5-27-99, and 8-12-99),
14. Evaluation Form I from Insurance Company (completed by Dr. L, dated 12-28-97),
15. Initial Psychiatric Evaluation (completed by Dr. L, dated 9-22-97),
16. Correspondence from Dr. L to Dr. S (dates 10-7-97 and 11-6-97),
17. Correspondence from Ms. E, Director of Claims for Insurance Company, to Dr. L (dated 6-29-99),
18. Correspondence from Dr. L to Dr. R (dated 9-11-98 and 11-23-98),
19. Evaluation Form I from Insurance Company (completed by Dr. S, dated 9-18-97),
20. Correspondence from Ms. E, Director of Claims for Insurance Company, to Dr. S (dated 9-26-97 and 12-18-97),
21. Correspondence from Dr. S to Ms. E, Director of Claims for Insurance Company (dated 10-15-97),
22. Correspondence from Dr. B to Dr. L (dated 4-3-98), and
23. Various medical records from Dr. C.

Prior to the evaluation, Mr. S was notified about the purpose of the evaluation and the associated limits on confidentiality. Initially, Mr. S had some difficulty reporting back his understanding of the purpose of the evaluation. After further explanations were provided to Mr. S, however, he indicated that he understood that the information and findings from the evaluation would be reported to his insurance company in relation to his disability status. He further understood that, under the conditions specified by Insurance Company, no information regarding the results of this evaluation would be provided directly to him by the undersigned.

RELEVANT HISTORY

Historical information was obtained from the collateral sources described above, as well as from Mr. S himself. Whenever possible, the consistency of the factual information provided by Mr. S was assessed through the use of multiple sources.

Family and Social History   Mr. S was born in Philadelphia, Pennsylvania. Mr. S reported that he is the oldest of three children, adding that he has a younger sister and a younger brother. Mr. S described his childhood as "normal." He also stated that his parents were "strict and old-fashioned." According to Mr. S, his parents were "very affectionate." Mr. S stated that his parents emphasized the importance of honesty, respect, hard work, and love. Mr. S reported that he was raised as a Catholic, and he described religion as being "moderately helpful" in his life. Mr. S denied being physically, sexually, or emotionally abused while growing up. According to the Investigative Report, Mr. S currently is married and has three children.

Educational and Vocational History   Mr. S reported that he graduated from City College in Philadelphia, earning a Bachelor of Science degree in management. Mr. S reported that he attended school regularly and was an "average C" student. Mr. S described being involved in various activities while in school, such as soccer, football, and baseball.

Mr. S reported that he has held three jobs since he graduated from college. According to Mr. S, he worked in the sales and marketing department of an engineering company for 1 or 2 years after college. Mr. S stated that after he ended his employment with the engineering firm he established his own printing company. Mr. S reported that he and his partner ran the printing company for a few years before he started his current business, ABC, Inc. According to Mr. S, a disagreement with his partner was the impetus for starting ABC. He described ABC as an environmental consulting firm. The Investigative Report notes that ABC is involved in various environmental matters such as soil and groundwater testing, the regulation and compliance of soil and groundwater permits during construction, and the management of soil and groundwater in residential and business-type areas. Mr. S was President, Owner, and Chief Operating Officer of ABC for about 10 years before he stopped working in May of 1997 due to a claimed mental disability.

Medical and Psychiatric History   There is no indication that Mr. S has a remarkable medical history. According to the Investigative Report, Mr. S denied being hospitalized in the past 10 years. Mr. S has had contact with mental health professionals on several occasions. According to the Investigative Report, Mr. S reported that he has been totally disabled due to stress and anxiety since May 22, 1997. The Investigative Report indicates that Mr. S was first treated for his symptoms on April 22, 1997. According to correspondence from Dr. L to Dr. S, Mr. S stated that he experienced insomnia, mind racing, decreased concentration, and irritability since April of 1997. On May 22, 1997, Mr. S filed the present disability claim, alleging that he cannot function as Chief Operating Officer of ABC due to stress and anxiety. According to the memorandum from Ms. E, Director of Claims for Insurance Company, to Dr. B ("Memorandum"), Mr. S was seen by Dr. S on June 9, 1997. The Memorandum indicates that Dr. S stated that Mr. S was "unable to make decisions as CEO of his company" at that time. As a result, Dr. S prescribed Buspar and Zoloft. On September 18, 1997, Dr. S completed Evaluation Form I for Insurance Company. Dr. S diagnosed Mr. S with General Anxiety Disorder and Depression. Dr. S refused, however, to complete a Psychiatric Limitation Form and a Hamilton Depression Scale, which are required by Insurance Company. Instead, Dr. S referred Mr. S to Dr. L.

Dr. L completed Evaluation Form I on December 28, 1997. According to Evaluation Form I, Dr. L diagnosed Mr. S with Bipolar Disorder. In addition, Dr. L recommended a treatment plan of medication management one to two times per month. Evaluation Form I indicates that Dr. L prescribed Serzone on September 22, 1997, and discontinued it on November 3, 1997. On November 3, 1997, Dr. L prescribed Wellbutrin, which he subsequently discontinued on December 31, 1997. In correspondence from Dr. L to Dr. S, Dr. L indicates that Mr. S has also been prescribed Prozac, Zoloft, and Buspar. The correspondence also indicates that an examination of Mr. S's family history does not reveal any evidence of psychiatric illness. Finally, on December 31, 1997, Dr. L prescribed Paxil. Dr. L noted that Mr. S's response to treatment has been "poor." Dr. L stated that Mr. S should be able to return to work within 1 to 3 months, adding that the nature of Mr. S's condition would not prevent a resumption of his usual work. Correspondence from Dr. B to Dr. L indicates that Dr. L also prescribed Depakote (mood-stabilizing medication) in April 1998 to treat Mr. S's symptoms of anxiety and irritability. A progress note from Dr. R indicates that Dr. L prescribed Lithium and Parnate to treat Mr. S's depression. A subsequent progress note indicates, however, that Dr. L considered discontinuing Mr. S's lithium prescription because it was ineffective in reducing his symptoms.

On August 14, 1998, Dr. R evaluated Mr. S, who reportedly sought help for "the treatment of intractable depression." Mr. S reported suffering from tightness in the back of his neck, heightened frequency of headaches, weight loss of 20 pounds, and memory difficulties. Dr. R concluded that Mr. S was suffering from a "Major Depressive Episode and a Bipolar Disorder." The psychological mevaluation indicates that Mr. S could not "recall any member of his extended family who has suffered from a mood disorder."

Dr. R completed Evaluation Form I on August 17, 1999, for the insurance company. Dr. R diagnosed Mr. S with Bipolar Disorder. Dr. R noted that Mr. S suffered from "symptoms of depression" for 2½ years. According to Evaluation Form

I, Dr. R evaluated Mr. S on August 16, 1999. Dr. R noted that Mr. S presented with "symptoms of severe depression, including reports of sleep impairment, difficulty concentrating, anger outbursts, crying spells, sadness, poor judgment, [and] hopelessness." Dr. R also noted that Mr. S "has been compliant [with his medication] but without significant improvement or relief from his symptomatic complaints." Similarly, during the present evaluation, Mr. S reported that he took his medication consistently but that he did not experience a significant reduction in symptoms. Mr. S also reported that he often experienced unpleasant side effects from the medication. Specifically, Mr. S reported that he occasionally vomited and lost or gained weight.

As previously noted, there are no indications of a familial mental health history in any of the collateral documents reviewed for this evaluation. During the present evaluation, Mr. S reported that he is not aware of a familial history of mental health problems either in his immediate or extended family.

Substance Abuse History There are no indications of a history of substance abuse in any of the collateral documents reviewed for this evaluation. Evaluation Form I completed by Dr. S indicates that Mr. S denied any history of drug use. Evaluation Form I indicates that Mr. S admitted to social drinking in the amount of two bottles of wine per week. The Psychological Evaluation completed by Dr. R indicates that although Mr. S reported that his consumption of alcohol had increased, Mr. S reported that it was not problematic for him. During the present evaluation, Mr. S denied all drug use and admitted to drinking moderate amounts of alcohol. Although Mr. S denied that his consumption of alcohol is problematic, he stated that he currently drinks on "different occasions" than he used to. When questioned further, Mr. S reported that he is currently more likely to drink alcohol by himself and at home as opposed to in a social situation.

CURRENT CLINICAL CONDITION

Mr. S presented as a 36-year-old Caucasian male of average height and weight who appeared his stated age. He was casually dressed (jeans, base-ball cap) and well-groomed when seen for the evaluation on 10-20-99 at MCP Hahnemann University in Philadelphia. Initially, Mr. S was subdued and reserved, and he remained relatively reserved throughout the entire evaluation. His speech was relatively clear, coherent, and relevant, although somewhat sparse; he did not respond at length to most questions without encouragement and further questioning. Mr. S provided very little detail to questions without persistent questioning and prompting from the evaluators. At times during the evaluation, Mr. S's speech was barely audible due to the low volume of his speech. Mr. S appeared visibly tired and fatigued throughout the entire evaluation, and he occasionally asked about the amount of time remaining in the evaluation. Specifically, Mr. S often expressed concern over the length of the evaluation, particularly with respect to his ability to concentrate throughout a lengthy evaluation. Mr. S appeared to have some difficulty focusing on some of the tasks presented to him during the 7-hour evaluation, and he requested several breaks throughout the evaluation. Nevertheless, it would appear that this evaluation provides a reasonably good estimate of Mr. S's current functioning.

Mr. S arrived for the evaluation about 15 minutes late accompanied by his attorney and a court stenographer. His mood throughout the evaluation was largely subdued, neutral, and depressed, and he showed little emotional variability. Mr. S reported that he is currently experiencing significant problems with sleep, concentration, memory, appetite, loss of interest in usual activities, decision making, fatigue, interpersonal irritation, and anger management. Mr. S appeared to be correctly oriented to time, place, and person. Overall level of intellectual functioning was formally measured with the WAIS-III and was found to be within the Borderline range (Verbal IQ = 88, Performance IQ = 72, Full Scale IQ = 78). These results do not appear to be consistent with Mr. S's intellectual capacity, and they may be attributable to low motivation and/or fatigue during the administration of the WAIS-III. The WAIS-III was administered toward the end of the evaluation, and Mr. S was visibly fatigued throughout the test. He requested, and was

granted, several breaks throughout the administration of the WAIS-III.

Mr. S did not report experiencing any perceptual disturbances (auditory or visual hallucinations), and his train of thought was clear and logical. Mr. S also did not report experiencing delusions (bizarre ideas with no possible basis in reality). On a structured inventory of symptoms of mental and emotional disorders (the BSI), Mr. S reported a significant amount of current distress. Specifically, he reported being "quite a bit" or "extremely" bothered by various symptoms, including trouble remembering things, feeling easily annoyed or irritated, poor appetite, suddenly being scared for no reason, temper outbursts that he cannot control, feeling lonely even when he is with people, feeling blue, feeling no interest in things, feeling inferior to other people, trouble falling asleep, difficulty making decisions, trouble getting his breath, hot or cold spells, his mind going blank, feeling hopeless about the future, trouble concentrating, having urges to break or smash things, never feeling close to another person, getting into frequent arguments, feelings of worthlessness, feelings of guilt, and the idea that something is wrong with his mind.

Mr. S reported that he has trouble remembering things that people say to him, and he reported that he will occasionally forget things quickly. Mr. S stated that he occasionally becomes annoyed or irritated if he cannot follow a conversation, adding that he will occasionally "flip out" and become angry and argumentative. According to Mr. S, he has been eating fewer meals and smaller amounts of food for quite some time, which has resulted in unintended weight loss. Mr. S stated that he occasionally experiences temper outbursts that cause him to "go off . . . verbally . . . and throw something." He added that his mind goes blank when he loses his temper. Mr. S reported that he often feels lonely, adding that his "desire to talk to or be with people is not what it used to be." He also reported that despite feeling lonely, he has no desire to engage in social activities. Mr. S reported that he has lost interest in things that he used to enjoy. Mr. S reported that he feels inferior to other people because he feels as if "there's not a situation I can handle." Mr. S reported that he has difficulty falling asleep. When questioned further, he reported that he will sleep for a few hours, get up several times, and then not be able to fall back to sleep. Mr. S stated that he has difficulty making decisions because it is "hard to concentrate on things." According to Mr. S, his mind will occasionally go blank when someone asks him a question. He added that although he knows the answer to the question, he feels as if he has "no recollection." Mr. S reported that he has urges "to punch something" when he gets angry. Mr. S described getting into frequent arguments with his wife and children, but he was unable to articulate the reasons for the arguments. Mr. S reported being extremely bothered by feelings of guilt over "not being able to be there like I was before for my family." Finally, Mr. S reported that he is bothered by the idea that there is something wrong with his mind, but he was unable to elaborate any further.

Mr. S completed the MMPI-2 in about 75 minutes, and he appeared visibly fatigued throughout the administration of the MMPI-2. He responded to the items on the MMPI-2 by endorsing a large number of psychological problems. Individuals with such profiles (Welsh Code: 2**8*37"601'+4-5/9: F*'"L+-/K:) are typically seen as either responding in an open fashion to a high level of distress or deliberately exaggerating their account of such difficulties. In Mr. S's case, it appears likely, based on the available collateral information, that he is responding in an open fashion to a high level of distress. Nevertheless, Mr. S's MMPI-2 profile should be interpreted with caution, and it should be considered in relation to its consistency with collateral information from other sources.

Individuals with such profiles are often described as being quite depressed. These individuals may exhibit a chronic pattern of alienation and isolation, and they may be intense, anxious, and withdrawn. Individuals with such profiles often experience a great deal of difficulty concentrating. This is consistent with Mr. S's self-reported difficulties with concentration and attention. Due to a depressed mood, these individuals often function at a reduced level of efficiency. In addition, they may present as lethargic, apathetic, and not interested in life. Emotionally, these individuals are often described as flat and blunted.

Mr. S endorsed several items suggesting that he is experiencing a depressed mood. He reported a preoccupation with feeling guilty and unworthy. He also reported that he feels regretful and unhappy about life, and he appears to be plagued by anxiety and worry about the future. In addition, Mr. S endorsed items suggesting that he occasionally feels hopeless about the future. He also endorsed items that reflect low self-esteem and longstanding feelings of inadequacy. Mr. S reported experiencing difficulty managing routine affairs, and he endorsed items suggesting that he has a poor memory, concentration difficulties, and an inability to make decisions. Mr. S also endorsed items suggesting that he experiences some inability to control his anger.

Individuals with such profiles often experience many interpersonal problems. These individuals may experience alienation in social relationships, and they may feel vulnerable to being hurt interpersonally. In addition, these individuals often lack trust, which may prevent them from forming close interpersonal relationships. These individuals may also present as shy and emotionally distant. Mr. S endorsed items suggesting that he is introverted and has difficulty interacting with other people.

CONCLUSIONS

According to the information provided, Mr. S's Policy Type and Definition defines disability in the following manner: "The Insured cannot do the substantial and material duties of his or her regular job. The cause of the disability must be an injury or sickness."

There are two specific questions that the referral source would like answered as a result of this evaluation.

1. To determine if there is a psychological condition that prevents the Insured from engaging in the "substantial and material duties of his regular job."

There is conflicting information regarding Mr. S's current clinical diagnosis. Based on Mr. S's self-reported symptoms during the clinical interview and his MMPI-2 profile, it appears that Mr. S is currently suffering from a DSM-

IV diagnosis of Major Depressive Disorder, Single Episode, Severe Without Psychotic Features. There is conflicting information, however, regarding whether Mr. S has ever experienced a manic or hypomanic episode. Accordingly, DSM-IV diagnoses of Bipolar I Disorder and Bipolar II Disorder should be ruled out after further evaluation. Mr. S exhibits apparently genuine symptoms that are consistent with the above diagnosis. The severity of the symptoms of this disorder is currently preventing Mr. S from engaging in the substantial and material duties of his occupation.

2. Specifically, what impairments exist as they apply to the Insured's occupation?

As part of Mr. S's most recent employment, he was required to perform the day-to-day activities of President, Owner, and Chief Operating Officer of ABC. Mr. S reported that he is "ultimately responsible for everything" related to the operation of the company. Mr. S's responsibilities require extensive interpersonal contact in a highly stressful environment. Given his current level of functioning, it is quite apparent that Mr. S would be unable to handle the inherent interpersonal difficulties and stress because of his impaired concentration, memory difficulties, interpersonal irritation, fatigue, impaired decision-making abilities, and lack of motivation secondary to clinical depression. If such symptoms remain at their current level of intensity, it also seems apparent that Mr. S would be unable to function in any job that required interpersonal contact, regular hours, concentration, and productivity.

The possibility of secondary gain and symptom magnification was addressed in the clinical interview and the MMPI-2. It would appear that financial secondary gain is not a significant factor contributing to the results described in this evaluation. Mr. S has been financially weakened by not working. In addition, Mr. S has given up a highly successful and lucrative career in consulting since being placed on disability. Furthermore, Mr. S's current symptoms have placed some interpersonal strain on his family relations. Specifically, Mr. S reported that he frequently argues with his wife and children and does not participate in as many family activities as he used to. There may be an issue of secondary gain, however, in that by not having to return to work, Mr. S does not have to face the stress that is inherent in operating a successful environmental consulting business. Mr. S stated, however, that he would like to return to work in his former capacity if he experienced significant symptom reduction.

Symptom exaggeration was considered during the interview, and there was some evidence that Mr. S may be exaggerating (or at least being very open about acknowledging) his current symptoms. Specifically, Mr. S's MMPI-2 profile suggests that he may be exaggerating his current symptoms. Nevertheless, given Mr. S's psychiatric history, the results of the BSI, and the available collateral information, it is more likely that he is currently experiencing a significant amount of psychological distress. Mr. S's presentation during the clinical interview was consistent with his self-report of symptom severity and the collateral information reviewed for this evaluation.

Given the definition of total disability provided by the referral source, it would appear that Mr. S is presently totally disabled. If the recommendations provided in this report are implemented, however, Mr. S may be able to return to work. Although Mr. S may not be able to resume his duties as President, Owner, and Chief Operating Officer of ABC, it is possible that he may be able to function in other capacities that involve less stress, less interpersonal contact, and shorter hours. It is difficult to establish a timeframe for treatment because Mr. S has been treated for over 2 years with virtually no significant symptom reduction. Specifically, Mr. S has not responded favorably to a variety of antidepressant medications despite apparent compliance with treatment specifications.

RECOMMENDATIONS

Based on all of the information described in this report, it is our recommendation that the Insured, Mr. S, would benefit from the following therapeutic interventions.

1. *Continued attempts at appropriate psycho-*

pharmacological intervention. Currently, Mr. S is taking antidepressant medication, as prescribed by his psychiatrist (Dr. L). Despite apparent compliance with his medication requirements, this medication has been ineffective in significantly reducing Mr. S's symptoms of depression. In addition, as previously noted, Mr. S has not responded favorably to a variety of other prescribed antidepressant medications. Although Mr. S is frustrated with his lack of improvement through the use of medication, he expressed a strong desire to achieve symptom reduction. Accordingly, it is recommended that Mr. S continue working with Dr. L on the type and titration of medication that would be most helpful to him. This is an important consideration because Mr. S's clinical depression will significantly interfere with the effectiveness of psychologically based interventions in general. In addition, although Mr. S reported that he is generally compliant with his medication requirements, it may be helpful to monitor his future compliance with his prescribed medications.

2. Even if Mr. S's depressive symptomatology does not respond favorably to psychopharmacological intervention, *increased cognitive-behavioral psychotherapy is recommended.* Mr. S reported that he currently sees Dr. R for therapy once or twice per month. The Evaluation Form I completed by Dr. R indicates that Mr. S currently sees Dr. R for about one hour "1–2 times per month or on an emergency basis if needed." Cognitive-behavioral therapy is an empirically validated treatment for depression that will provide Mr. S with the opportunity to address certain psychological issues. In addition, cognitive-behavioral therapy may provide Mr. S with the tools necessary to become more comfortable in environments that have triggered his depression in the past. Because Mr. S's MMPI-2 profile suggests that relationship-based psychotherapy may be ineffective, any intervention in this area should be highly focused and structured.

3. When Mr. S's symptoms of depression have been significantly managed pharmacologically and psychotherapeutically, *referral to a competent vocational counselor is recommended.* Mr. S expressed a desire to resume working in his for-

mer capacity as President, Owner, and Chief Operating Officer of ABC if his depressive symptoms can be significantly reduced or eliminated. Mr. S did not identify any alternative vocational interests or options. This inability to generate alternatives may be due to his depression and impaired decision-making ability. If Mr. S were to receive assistance from someone who could evaluate his vocational and educational strengths and weaknesses at a time when he is regaining his self-confidence through a decrease in his psychological symptoms, it might ease his re-entry into a vocational context. This is an important consideration because Mr. S's MMPI-2 profile suggests that he currently has a number of negative work attitudes and feelings that could interfere with work adjustment. Due to events that Mr. S has experienced in the past, consideration to low-stress workplace environments in which he has minimal management responsibilities may be crucial in obtaining Mr. S's cooperation in finding a new vocation.

4. Mr. S would benefit from *training in the areas of anger control and interpersonal problem solving.* During the clinical interview, Mr. S reported that he is extremely bothered by temper outbursts that he cannot control. He also reported that he would occasionally "yell" at employees and "punch something" when he got angry. In addition, Mr. S endorsed items on the MMPI-2 suggesting that he has some inability to control his anger. Accordingly, based on Mr. S's self-report, his responses on the BSI, and his MMPI-2 profile, Mr. S may need skills training to help him control his temper and improve his interpersonal problem-solving skills.

DIAGNOSTIC IMPRESSION

Axis I: 296.23—Major Depressive Disorder, Single Episode, Severe Without Psychotic Features
Rule Out 296.53—Bipolar I Disorder, Most Recent Episode Depressed, Severe Without Psychotic Features
Rule Out 296.89—Bipolar II Disorder

Axis II: V71.09—No Axis II diagnosis

Axis III: None
Axis IV: Unemployment
Axis V: GAF = 30 (current)

Thank you for the opportunity to evaluate Mr. S.

Kirk Heilbrun, Ph.D.
Consulting Psychologist

David DeMatteo, M.A.
Geff Marczyk, M.S., M.A.
MCP Hahnemann University Graduate Students

Teaching Point: How does the forensic clinician integrate response style data?

The use of multiple measures, such as psychological tests, structured interviews, and collateral interviews, is a useful approach to assess an individual's response style. Once obtained, the results of these measures must be integrated into the FMHA report. Integration of response style data in FMHA is important for several reasons. Ruling out malingering, or managing its impact, increases the accuracy of the measurement of relevant capacities. The integration of response style data also adds credibility to the overall report, and facilitates accurate and effective communication in both the report and testimony. Finally, such integration facilitates better informed legal decision making.

All testing results relevant to malingering should be included in the report, accompanied by reasoning, limits, and conclusions. In addition, the report should include a detailed account of the individual's self-report, and the information obtained from collateral sources. Inconsistencies in the data should be noted and potential explanations for such inconsistencies discussed. The integration of data from multiple sources facilitates the consideration of different hypotheses, eliminating those that are less consistent with the overall pattern of results observed.

This report reflects the integration of psychological testing results, self-report data, and collateral information relevant to response style. The History section interweaves Mr. S's self-report with available collateral information. This integration provides a basis for comparing the consistency of Mr. S's self-reported history in various domains with information from other sources regarding these domains. The Clinical Condition section includes data directly relevant to Mr. S's presentation during the evaluation. Incorporated in this section are the results of psychological testing, including the MMPI-2. Response style is discussed by offering two rival hypotheses. Specifically, the validity scales of the MMPI-2 suggested that Mr. S was either responding openly to a high level of distress or deliberately exaggerating his account of such difficulties. These hypotheses were evaluated against self-report and collateral information, and the evaluators concluded that it was more likely that Mr. S was openly acknowledging a high level of distress. The reasoning for this conclusion can be found in the final section of the report, where the evaluators directly addressed the issue of secondary financial gain. This section provides an example of the integration of psychological testing, self-report, and collateral information in considering competing hypotheses, and reaching conclusions that have been drawn only after response style was carefully considered.

Case 2

Principle: Assess legally relevant behavior

This principle is discussed in chapter 10, so we turn directly to an application of this principle to the present case.

The present case provides an example of assessing legally relevant behavior in the context of a worker's compensation/disability claim. Specifically, Mrs. T is claiming various emotional difficulties related to traumatic experiences she suffered at work, and that these difficulties prevent her from returning to work. Therefore, the relevant behaviors and capacities to be assessed are those that have a direct impact on Mrs. T's ability to return to work. Accordingly, the evaluators gathered data from multiple sources across these domains.

There are a variety of domains related to occupational functioning that can be assessed when conducting an evaluation of this type. The evaluators gathered relevant data in the domains of employment history, medical history, mental health history, and social history. In addition, particular attention was paid to the circumstances surrounding the events that precipitated Mrs. T's current symptoms of depression, anxiety, and Post Traumatic Stress Disorder (PTSD).

In the current evaluation, historical information collected across these domains suggested the presence of a number of factors that could affect Mrs. T's ability to return to her previous occupation as a liquor store employee. These included the presence of symptoms of PTSD and depression, other emotional disturbance, and an inadequate treatment regimen for her symptoms. Historical information also suggested that exposure to certain high-risk environments, such as those where robbery was a likely possibility, could exacerbate her symptoms.

The clinical interview and psychological testing allowed the evaluators to assess Mrs. T's current level of functioning as it related to her ability to work. For example, the results of the Minnesota Multiphasic Personality Inventory, 2nd edition (MMPI-2) suggested that Mrs. T had seriously contemplated suicide and had been experiencing a depressed mood, with anxiety and worry. A clinical interview—including input from collateral sources, self-report, and behavioral observations—suggested that Mrs. T met criteria for PTSD, chronic, and Major Depressive Disorder, in partial remission, at the time of the evaluation. Both of these disorders can have a serious impact on an individual's ability to work.

Worker's compensation evaluations also call for the assessment of treatment needs and amenability as they relate to improvement in occupational functioning. Mrs. T appeared to have treatment needs that, if addressed, should result in an increase in her ability to return to work, even if in a less stressful environment. These treatment needs included medication and psychotherapy for symptoms of depression and PTSD. In addition, the evaluators defined the approximate duration of interventions needed in each of these areas.

By using multiple sources of historical and diagnostic information, the evaluators were able to assess relevant capacities related to occupational functioning and provide an estimate of the level of impairment that Mrs. T was experiencing at the time of the evaluation. After evaluating these capacities in the context of occupational functioning and treatment needs and amenability, the evaluators made a recommendation regarding the general parameters of a placement that would be needed for Mrs. T to return to work. In this way, the evaluators linked Mrs. T's current level of functioning and relevant behavior with her present occupational capabilities.

FORENSIC EVALUATION

Re: Mrs. T

REFERRAL

Mrs. T is a 63-year-old African American female who was examined for 3 hours at the request of her employer after she had been a victim of armed robbery four times while working in a liquor store, after which her physician placed her on medical disability. She has been out of work for approximately 8 years. This examination was requested by Mrs. T's employer to determine what impairments exist as they apply to her capacity to return to work.

RELEVANT HISTORY

Mrs. T's first experience of being robbed was while she worked as a manager of a liquor store when she was in her early 30s. She indicated that soon after opening the store, she was accosted by a man who seemed to be "high" on drugs. She said that the robber had a .45 caliber revolver and left the store immediately after taking the money.

Mrs. T reported that she did not recall having nightmares or flashbacks and did not take any time off work.

The second robbery occurred 6 years later, when Mrs. T was in her late 30s. She indicated that she was working at the liquor store and five armed men came into the store and held it up. She reported that another manager was there, as well as a number of employees. Mrs. T described that one female employee became "so hysterical I thought they would shoot her." Mrs. T then found herself taking charge of the situation by telling the gunmen that she would give them any money they wanted if they would leave the hysterical employee alone. Again, Mrs. T did not recall having nightmares or flashbacks after this robbery. She also reported that she did not recall having severe anxiety or difficulty returning to work after the second robbery.

The third robbery occurred in November 1991. Mrs. T said she was working as a manager at the liquor store and men "waving guns" came into the store late in the afternoon. Mrs. T reported that the security guard was told to lie down on the floor, and Mrs. T began experiencing chest pains. She reported that the men left quickly with the money and she went home. Soon after arriving home, she decided to go to the hospital when the chest pain did not resolve. Mrs. T was in the hospital for 4 days and then released.

Mrs. T said that on her return home, and in the several weeks after the robbery, she experienced flashbacks, nightmares, and was very anxious. She reported that she became somewhat irritable and had problems sleeping. She said that she had no interest in sexual relations with her husband and felt more distant from here husband and children because she did not wish to talk about the incident. Her son and daughter were in college at the time and stayed at home with her only on the weekends. Mrs. T saw a psychologist for the first time just after the Christmas holiday in 1991, after she could not get over her anxiety. She was treated for several months and returned to work in March 1992. Mrs. T reported that her psychologist did not recommend that she return to work at that time, but Mrs. T insisted. Even though the recommendation by the psychologist was to have her transferred to another store, in a safer neighborhood that was less likely to be robbed, this request was refused. She returned to work at the same store where the robbery had occurred. She said she worked there approximately 3 weeks and then was transferred to a new location.

Mrs. T said that although she had returned to work, she had continued to experience anxiety and had problems sleeping. She reported an exaggerated startle response. She also reported that she continued to have nightmares that involved different aspects of the robbery. She said, for example, that during the robbery she saw that one of the gunmen had a beeper. She began having nightmares about being accosted in a department store by the man who had a beeper. She reported that her nightmares were variations of details that occurred during the actual robbery itself, but not instant replays of the robbery. Mrs. T reported that she did not recall feeling dread driving to work and returning to work after her third robbery.

Mrs. T reported that the fourth robbery occurred in July 1992, just 8 months after the third robbery. She stated this robbery was different from the others because she could immediately tell that the gunmen were "amateurs." She reported that they stayed in the store long after they had obtained the money and the alcohol that they had come for, and she did not understand this. Mrs. T reported that she was told to open the safe, and a gun was held to her head, with the robber saying "You're a dead woman." The robber repeated it several times. Mrs. T reported that she felt helpless because she could not open the safe as the robber had requested because she needed the second key that was held by the district manager. Mrs. T reported that she recalled that one man, the one who held the gun to her head, had a "9 millimeter Glock," and another man had a sawed off shotgun.

After the robbery, Mrs. T waited for the police to arrive, and reported what had occurred. She then returned home. She reported that she had chest pain and took numerous nitroglycerin tablets, but the chest pain did not resolve. She said that she sat at home for several hours alone after the robbery until her husband arrived. Mrs. T reported that her husband said she looked "ashen" and took her to the hospital. When asked why Mrs. T waited for her husband instead of going to the hospital immediately, she said, "I just couldn't face going out of the house. I felt like the gunmen would be looking for me." Mrs. T spent several days in the hospital for her chest pain until a heart attack was ruled out. Mrs. T reported that soon after returning home, she developed chest pain again, returned to the hospital, and was hospitalized for another 7 days, during which time she was diagnosed with a "mild heart attack."

Mrs. T reported that after the fourth robbery things changed for her. She said she was not sleeping and was very anxious. She had become exceedingly irritable and was beginning to have outbursts of anger, especially at her husband. She reported that she became very depressed and her personal hygiene declined. She said that she stopped bathing, wore the same clothes for several days in a row, and stopped wearing makeup. She reported, "I was so depressed, I just spent 18 hours a day in bed. The other 6 hours I dragged myself around feeling exhausted." Mrs. T reported that she lost 40 pounds over 6 months, lost her appetite, had poor concentration, and had diminished interest in her usual activities. She reported having recurring nightmares about three young men robbing and beating her. This was not the same as the actual robbery itself, but the perpetrators were the same. She reported that those nightmares occurred on an average of two times per week. She also said she was having flashbacks that occurred frequently, but she could not recall exactly how frequently. Mrs. T reported that she had not returned to the liquor store since the robbery and was unable to return to work due to her excessive anxiety about being robbed again at work. Mrs. T also admitted to hypervigilance and an exaggerated startle response.

Mrs. T stated that since the time of 1992 robbery, she had been treated by her psychologist and continued in psychotherapy. She was referred to a psychiatrist at one point who prescribed Paxil for her. However, she reported that she did not like the psychiatrist, nor did the psychiatrist like her. Therefore, it was decided that she would not return to see the psychiatrist; the family doctor would prescribe the Paxil. She reported that at times she wanted to kill herself. She recalled gathering several bottles of Tylenol with which she planned to take to kill herself in 1995. However, when she actually started to open the bottles, she envisioned her husband's face finding her dead when he returned from work. She thought it would ruin his life and her children would be left to deal with his "devastation," which she felt was cruel. She then flushed each bottle of Tylenol down the toilet "so it wouldn't tempt me." Mrs. T reported that this was the closest she had come to a suicide attempt. She denied ever being hospitalized in a psychiatric hospital and reported that she recalled being on one antidepressant other than Paxil. She stated that she had been on Tranxene for anxiety for a long time, but was unable to remember exactly how long. She stated she had not been on any other antidepressants.

Mrs. T reported that at the time of examination, she was "just existing." She reported that her nightmares occur every 6 or 8 weeks. She said her concentration was not as good as it had been, but was somewhat improved compared to the months after the fourth robbery. She noted low energy, but still enjoyed certain activities, such as knitting and babysitting her niece's 18-month-old baby.

Mrs. T reported during the examination that she feels somewhat depressed, but noted that her depression gets worse when her health problems worsen. She reported that she had been on Paxil since 1993 (about 6 years). She reported that she no longer has anxiety when she is alone; however, she avoids crowds and often gets anxious in public places. She reported two panic attacks in the last year, one of which occurred when a rack of clothing fell over in a department store, causing a loud noise. Mrs. T noted that she avoids liquor stores and fast food restaurants. She noted difficulty falling asleep, and stated that she sleeps approximately 8 hours a night, and then takes a 3- or 4-hour nap in the afternoon. She reported that her appetite is good.

Mrs. T has a history of insulin-dependent diabetes, heart problems, diabetic neuropathy in her feet, and diabetic retinitis, which has necessitated five operations. She also has a number of other chronic medical problems such as arthritis and hearing difficulties.

CURRENT CLINICAL CONDITION

Mental status examination revealed a woman who was cooperative with the interview and neatly dressed. She had good eye contact. Her mood was "anxious," and her affect was anxious. Her speech was fluent and of regular rate and volume, and her thought process was goal directed. She showed no evidence of suicidal ideation, homicidal ideation, paranoid ideation, or delusions, and denied auditory or visual hallucinations.

Mrs. T was oriented to the exact day, date, and time of the interview. However, she initially reported the date that she graduated from high school as 20 years later than it actually was. She had difficulty recalling past presidents of the United States and was only able to identify three out of the last four. The rest of her mental status was within normal limits. She was given the Minnesota Multiphasic Personality Inventory-2, and the test indicated that she had seriously contemplated suicide and had been experiencing a depressed mood with anxiety and worry. It also suggested that she had serious problems with alienation and social relationships.

A number of medical records were reviewed, including the treatment records of her physicians, her psychiatrist, and her psychologist. She was given a diagnosis of Post Traumatic Stress Disorder, chronic, and Major Depressive Disorder in partial remission.

CONCLUSIONS

It is the opinion of these examiners, within reasonable medical certainty, that Mrs. T has a diagnosis of PTSD chronic, and Major Depressive Disorder in partial remission. Further, it is our opinion that Mrs. T's Post Traumatic Stress Disorder was initially caused by the third robbery, since this was when her symptoms began. The most resent and fourth robbery triggered an exacerbated severity of her PTSD. She has stopped working since the fourth robbery 8 years ago, and her symptoms of PTSD have improved in the last 8 years. She has residuals of fear of liquor stores and ongoing intermittent anxiety, with frequent nightmares. It is unlikely that Mrs. T will ever be able to return to working in a liquor store. She may also have a relapse if she were ever subjected to a robbery again. Her symptoms of PTSD, however, do not prohibit her from working in another setting with less exposure to the public.

It appears that Mrs. T's medical problems have been most instrumental in continuing her depression over the years since the robbery in 1992. Mrs. T has not received the appropriate treatment by a psychiatrist over the past 8 years. With her diagnosis of Major Depression and her ongoing symptoms, she should be seen regularly (at least every 2 to 4 weeks) by a psychiatrist, and her medications should be monitored regularly by a psychiatrist.

In conclusion, it is our opinion, with reasonable medical certainty, that Mrs. T can return to part-time employment immediately, as long as it is not at a liquor store in which she could again get robbed. She should be placed in a low risk of violence job position that has low contact with the public. Further, it is our opinion that she is in need of further treatment for at least the next 6 months to 1 year. However, her treatment should be administered by a psychiatrist and focus on medication management. Further, Mrs. T should continue to see psychologist several times a month for psychotherapy for the next 6 months to 1 year.

Lauren Wylonis, M.D.

Robert L. Sadoff, M.D.

Teaching Point: What is the relationship between symptoms and disability in capacity to work?

The relationship between symptoms and a corresponding disability in capacity to work is complex. In conducting this type of evaluation, the forensic clinician should address four distinct questions. First, what symptoms does the individual currently experience, in what intensity, and as part of what larger diagnostic category? Second, what are the requirements (e.g., knowledge, skills, abilities, energy, and judgment) required in the person's most recent job, and what are the requirements for other jobs that the person might be able to perform? Third, what is the relationship between the symptoms or disorder and the requirements for the previous job, and, hypothetically, for other jobs? Finally, if the person experiences significantly impairing symptoms of psychopathology, what is the nature of the treatment currently received, and could such treatment be delivered differently to promote improvement more quickly? These four questions provide a valuable framework for addressing workplace disability issues, and help identify relevant domains for assessment and data collection.

Each of these questions should be addressed in detail, and the forensic clinician should not assume that genuine symptoms of psychopathology automatically preclude all types of occupational duties and responsibilities. The fact that a person cannot work at certain kinds of jobs or combinations of jobs due to currently experienced psychiatric symptoms does not mean that he or she is incapable of working in a position involving fewer hours or less intense demands. In other words, modifications can be made to the individual's responsibilities and schedule to accommodate the current level of symptoms or other functional impairments.

When making such recommendations to modify work responsibilities and/or schedules, the forensic clinician should stress the importance of assessing the impact of such an intervention over a period of time. Similarly, the forensic clinician should be sensitive to treatment considerations and how they can affect the individual's ability to return to work or assume new or less taxing responsibilities. Treatment of some common forms of psychopathology (e.g., depression and anxiety) is often less intense than it could be, resulting in a slower recovery for the individual being treated. In addition, course of treatment can also be affected by the motivation of the client. An individual who does not exhibit significant symptom relief in response to effective treatments might be malingering or overreporting symptoms. Therefore, the delivery of more intensive and effective treatment can also be used to gauge the potential impact of secondary financial gain, which should always be considered in an evaluation of this type.

Chapter 23

Threat/Risk Assessment

In this chapter, we present three cases on risk assessment. The principle applied to the first case addresses the importance of identifying forensic issues as they apply to both the broad and specific aspects of the legal question in a given case. The teaching point associated with the first case describes the distinction between prediction and risk reduction in risk assessment, and discusses some strategies for each task. The second case principle concerns explicit role clarification in the beginning of FMHA, and the teaching point considers strategies for avoiding dual roles. The third case principle discusses the use of nomothetic data, which is derived from groups and applied through general laws to forensic assessment; the discussion highlights the distinction between idiographic data and nomothetic data. This distinction will be expanded in the teaching point, in which the use of structured assessment instruments in risk assessment is addressed.

Case 1

Principle: Identify relevant forensic issues

This principle discusses the importance of identifying the relevant forensic issue(s) in a case. Forensic issues can encompass functional abilities, capacities, and skills that are relevant to a broader legal question. Forensic evaluations can address a wide variety of legal questions. Some of these questions, such as sanity at the time of the offense, are well-defined by statute or case law, making it reasonably straightforward to identify relevant forensic issues. Unfortunately, this is not always the case. Some legal questions are poorly defined by statute and case law, making it difficult for the forensic clinician to identify the relevant forensic issues. When the forensic issues are unclear or vaguely defined, the forensic clinician must clarify them to the extent possible. Some potential sources of guidance for the forensic clinician include legal and behavioral sciences literature and consultation with the referring attorney or legal decision maker in the event of a court ordered evaluation.

There is little direct ethical guidance on this issue, and none of the sources describing ethics for forensic assessments directly addresses the need to identify relevant forensic issues. However, the *Specialty Guidelines for Forensic Psychologists* describes the importance of the forensic clinician having "a fundamental and reasonable level of knowledge and understanding of the legal . . . standards that govern their participation as experts in legal proceedings" (Committee on Ethical Guidelines for Forensic Psychologists, 1991, p. 658). Similarly, the *Specialty Guidelines* indicates that forensic psychologists "have an obligation to ensure that prospective clients are informed of . . . the purposes of any evaluation" (p. 659), which presumably would include a notification of the forensic issue(s) being evaluated.

Legal sources of authority indirectly support the importance of identifying relevant forensic issue(s). Relevant case law suggests that the evidentiary principle of relevance is consistent with identifying the forensic issue(s) of a given case. For example, in *United States v. Green* (1977), the U.S. Court of Appeals for the Sixth Circuit adopted four criteria for reviewing trial court decisions involving expert testimony. One of these factors was that the expert testimony had to concern the "proper subject" of the issue at hand. This appears to be consistent with the principle that the proper identification of forensic issue(s) might directly impact on the admissibility of expert testimony. The U.S. Supreme Court's holding in *Dusky v. United States* (1960) is also indirectly relevant to this principle. In *Dusky*, the Court addressed the issue of competence to stand trial and adopted a functional standard that requires that an individual have sufficient present ability to consult with counsel with a reasonable degree of rational understanding, and a rational as well as factual understanding of the proceedings against him. This case underscores the importance of identifying relevant forensic issues by offering a specific legal test with functional criteria ("forensic issues") identified as part of the test.

Identification of the relevant legal question and related forensic issues is an essential first step in a properly performed FMHA. Although this seems obvious, past criticisms of forensic assessment have noted that insufficiency and irrelevance are common problems (Grisso, 1986). Accordingly, it is critical that the forensic clinician identify relevant forensic issues and capacities, because the failure to do so can directly compromise the accuracy, relevance, credibility, and effectiveness of the FMHA.

In this report, the forensic clinicians were asked to evaluate Mr. S for the purpose of determining his risk for workplace violence. Consistent with this principle, the evaluators began the report by explicitly identifying the relevant forensic issue. Specifically, in the "Referral" section of the report, the evaluators stated that the "forensic evaluation was requested by Mr. S's employer to determine Mr. S's risk for workplace violence and to provide treatment recommendations."

Explicitly identifying the relevant forensic issue in this manner provides several benefits. First, by identifying the relevant forensic issue, the evaluators effectively avoided any confusion regarding the purpose of the evaluation. Second, identifying the relevant forensic issue enabled forensic clinicians to conduct an evaluation that was focused and relevant (Grisso, 1986). Specifically, by identifying and focusing on the relevant forensic issue, the evaluators in this case avoided gathering information that would be irrelevant to the issue being addressed. Finally, identifying the relevant forensic issue helped the evaluators to structure the content of the evaluation; the evaluators only selected psychological tests and techniques that would provide information relevant to workplace violence. For example, one test the evaluators used was the Psychopathy Checklist-Revised (PCL-R), which has been empirically shown to be effective in evaluating an individual's risk for engaging in future acts of violent and aggressive behavior. In addition, when interviewing Mr. S, the evaluators focused on risk-relevant information within the individual's family, educational, psychiatric, substance abuse, and aggression histories.

FORENSIC EVALUATION

10-30-99
Re: Mr. S

REFERRAL

Mr. S is a 42-year-old African American male who was placed on unpaid suspension after reportedly making threatening statements at his place of employment. Specifically, according to Mr. S's employer, Mr. S suggested that he "sometimes felt like coming in and blowing people away with a gun." This forensic evaluation was requested by Mr. S's employer to determine Mr. S's risk for workplace violence and to provide treatment recommendations.

PROCEDURES

Mr. S was evaluated for approximately 7 hours on October 21, 1999, at the Department of Clinical and Health Psychology of MCP Hahnemann University. In addition to a clinical interview, Mr. S was administered a structured screening instrument for currently experienced symptoms of mental and emotional disorder (the Brief Symptom Inventory, or BSI), a standardized measure of personality variables (the Minnesota Multiphasic Personality Inventory-2, or MMPI-2), and a measure

of personality functioning relevant to recidivism risk and rehabilitation potential (the Psychopathy Checklist-Revised, or PCL-R). In addition, Mr. S's friend of 15 years, Mr. B was interviewed (collateral phone interview on 10-22-99) regarding Mr. S's past and current functioning. Repeated attempts to contact Mr. S's wife were unsuccessful. Mr. S indicated that his family was in the process of moving, and that he wasn't sure when telephone service would be installed.

Prior to the evaluation, Mr. S was notified about the purpose of the evaluation and the associated limits on confidentiality. He appeared to understand the basic purpose of the evaluation, reporting back his understanding that he would be evaluated and that a written report would be submitted to his employer.

RELEVANT HISTORY

Historical information was obtained from the collateral sources described above, as well as from Mr. S. Whenever possible, the consistency of the factual information provided by Mr. S was assessed through the use of collateral sources. If additional collateral information is obtained, a supplemental report will be filed.

Family History Mr. S reported that he was born in a semirural part of New Jersey, where he lived with his parents until he entered the U.S. Marine Corps in 1975. According to Mr. S, he grew up with six sisters and two brothers. He noted that two of his sisters have passed away, and elaborated that he still feels saddened by this loss from time to time. Mr. S reported that his parents have an excellent relationship. Similarly, he elaborated that his entire family is close, and that the environment while he was growing up was nurturing. Mr. S denied all forms of physical, emotional, and sexual abuse at the hands of family members. Similarly, he denied the presence of substance abuse in the household. Mr. S reported that he married his wife in 1981, and that he has three sons and a daughter. According to Mr. S, he is very close to all of the members of his immediate family. Similarly, he identified his relationships with his immediate and extended family, and his spirituality, as a "great source of strength and support." Mr. S reported that his family is currently in the process of moving, and noted that the process is "somewhat stressful."

Educational History   According to Mr. S, he attended kindergarten through high school in Burlington, New Jersey. Mr. S reported that he graduated from high school in 1975. When asked about his academic achievement and attendance, Mr. S characterized both as good. He elaborated that he received perfect attendance awards throughout his academic career, and was a B average student. Mr. S denied ever repeating a grade, or any involvement in special education. Similarly, Mr. S denied all behavioral difficulties, and described his behavior in school as "perfect." Mr. S did not express future educational goals, but he did note that he studied computer science at a local community college for approximately a year and a half.

Employment History   Mr. S reported an extensive employment history. According to Mr. S, he enlisted in the Marine Corps as a reservist after graduating from high school. He elaborated that he served as a reservist for a year before accepting a job as a general laborer at a fabrics company in June of 1976. According to Mr. S, he was promoted to the examining department within a month of employment. Similarly, he reported that he was promoted again 2 months later to the

position of "knitter." Mr. S reported that he was promoted to a supervisory position 6 months later. He elaborated that held this position until sometime in 1981, when the company declared bankruptcy and eventually closed. According to Mr. S, he moved to Atlanta in 1981 to take a job with a security agency as a security guard in a corporate environment. Mr. S reported that he worked as a security guard until June 1982 when he returned to New Jersey to start a day care service with a friend. According to Mr. S, the day care service fell through, and he worked as a waiter for approximately 1 year before taking a job with an inventory service in 1983. Mr. S stated that he worked as an inventory specialist for approximately 5 months before accepting a position as an assistant manager in the fast food industry. Mr. S elaborated that he was an assistant manager for approximately 3 years before accepting his position with his current employer in 1986.

According to Mr. S, he has never been fired from a job. Similarly, Mr. S denied all forms of disciplinary actions and participation in employee assistance programs. Collateral information obtained from the Human Resources Department suggests that Mr. S was warned at least twice about past behavior in his present work environment. Two incidents were described specifically. The first, in 1996, involved allegations of sexual harassment. The second, in April 1999, involved Mr. S being told to stay out of the security office unless there was a security matter or he had permission to be there. Although Mr. S acknowledged both incidents, he denied the accuracy of both accounts provided by the Human Resources Department. Mr. S did indicate that he had some difficulty with absenteeism on his current job. He attributed this to his wife's medical problems and related surgeries. According to Mr. S, he has collected welfare and other forms of assistance for a total of 3 months during his life. Mr. S noted that he is on unpaid suspension at this time, and is not collecting any type of unemployment compensation. He elaborated that he is under some financial strain as a result of his current situation.

Medical and Psychiatric History   According to Mr. S, he does not have any serious medical problems. It should be noted that Mr. S reported that his wife has had numerous surgeries for various medical conditions. Mr. S identified his wife's medical condition as a source of stress and financial strain. According to Mr. S, regular exercise helps him maintain better control of the impact of such stress. He elaborated that his current situation (moving, his wife's medical condition) has recently made it difficult for him to exercise regularly.

Mr. S denied all involvement with the public or private mental health system. Mr. S denied all familial history of psychiatric illness in his immediate and extended family. According to Mr. B, Mr. S does not have a psychiatric history.

Substance Abuse History   Mr. S reported a limited history of substance use. According to Mr. S, he used marijuana infrequently (approximately two times per year) until approximately 5 years ago, when he reported that he stopped entirely. Mr. S reported that he drinks beer on the weekends about "a six-pack" per weekend. Mr. S denied all other forms of substance use. Mr. B confirmed that Mr. S drinks beer on the weekends and noted that he has never seen Mr. S use any type of illegal or prescription drugs.

Past Antisocial Behavior   Mr. S denied all forms of adolescent and adult antisocial behavior. Similarly, Mr. S denied owning any type of firearm. Mr. B said that, to his knowledge, Mr. S does not own a firearm. Similarly, he indicated that he has never known Mr. S to carry any form of weapon, firearm or otherwise. Mr. B characterized Mr. S as "nonviolent, spiritual and friendly." Mr. B elaborated that he has never seen Mr. S lose his temper, even when he might have been justified in doing so. Similarly, Mr. B indicated that Mr. S will "brush off" things that make Mr. S frustrated or irritated. Further, Mr. B indicated that he has never seen Mr. S overreact to provocation, noting that he has never known Mr. S to engage in provoked or unprovoked physical aggression. To the contrary, Mr. B indicated that Mr. S "always turns the other cheek" in confrontational situations. Mr. B attributed Mr. S's self-control to his "deep spiritual beliefs."

CURRENT CLINICAL CONDITION

Mr. S presented as an African American male of average height and weight who appeared his stated age. He was appropriately dressed and well-groomed when seen for the evaluation on October 21, 1999, at the Department of Clinical and Health Psychology of MCP Hahnemann University. He wore his hair in a ponytail, and carried a book that appeared to be religious; he read from this book whenever there was a break in the evaluation. Initially, he was cooperative and polite, and he remained cooperative and polite throughout the entire evaluation. His speech was clear, coherent, and relevant; Mr. S responded at length to most questions asked of him without encouragement or further questioning. He appeared to give reasonable effort to the tasks involved. His capacity for attention and concentration appeared adequate, and he was able to focus reasonably well on a series of tasks during the 7-hour evaluation without becoming visibly distracted. Therefore, it would appear that this evaluation provides a reasonably good estimate of Mr. S's current functioning.

His mood throughout the evaluation was largely subdued and neutral, but he did display appropriate emotional variability. Mr. S was correctly oriented to time, place, and person. Overall level of intellectual functioning was not formally measured, but appeared to be in the average range.

Mr. S did not report experiencing any perceptual disturbances (auditory or visual hallucinations), and his train of thought was clear and logical. Similarly, Mr. S did not report experiencing delusions (bizarre ideas with no possible basis in reality). On a structured inventory of symptoms of currently experienced mental and emotional disorders (the BSI), Mr. S reported an almost total absence of present symptoms. Mr. S reported that he was distressed "a little bit" by feelings of loneliness and others not giving him proper credit for his achievements. He attributed his feelings of loneliness to intermittent thoughts about his two sisters who passed away. According to Mr. S, he feels that others are not giving him proper credit for his achievements because he was suspended without pay and sent for a psychological evaluation. Although Mr. S reported the presence of significant daily sources of stress in his life—such as financial concerns, his current situation, his family's recent move, decrease in exercise level, and his wife's questionable health—he did not report any symptoms of stress or anxiety. Given Mr. S's current situation, it is possible that he is underreporting, or unaware, of current symptoms or problems.

Consistent with this, Mr. S responded to the items on the MMPI-2 in an unrealistically virtuous manner that suggested an unwillingness or inability to disclose personal information (Welsh Code: 35/87 19 6024: L'+K-/F:). Symptomatically, Mr. S's clinical and content scales were within normal limits. It should be noted that Mr. S omitted 13 items across a number of subscales on the MMPI-2; omitting items may result in an underestimate of the problems measured by the affected scales. Specifically, Mr. S omitted items on scales measuring symptoms of depression, inhibition of aggression, problems with authority, ego inflation, irritability, social imperturbability, and submissiveness. Interpersonally, Mr. S's profile suggests that he is outgoing and sociable, with a strong need to be around others. Mr. S's profile suggests that he usually tries to project a positive attitude about life and typically enters new social relationships in an open and accepting manner. He views his home life in a generally positive and problem-free manner, and tends to feel strong emotional support from those close to him. Individuals with Mr. S's profile, although socialized and responsible, tend not to express anger or verbal hostility in reaction to frustration.

The results of the PCL-R suggest that Mr. S is a low risk for interpersonal violence, and has the capacity to respond favorably to therapeutic intervention. Specifically, Mr. S's responses to the structured interview of the PCL-R do not suggest personality features associated with interpersonal callousness or chronic antisocial behavior.

CONCLUSIONS AND RECOMMENDATIONS

Based on the results of this evaluation, Mr. S does not appear to be a significant risk for workplace violence. There are a number of factors that contribute to this conclusion. Of particular note is the absence of risk factors associated with workplace violence and violence in general. First, based on the account of the incident provided by the Human Resources Department, Mr. S made a general statement out of frustration, without

making specific threats toward a specific individual or individuals. Similarly, there are indications that Mr. S has been involved in disagreements in the workplace (he has received reprimands for harassing another employee and constantly visiting the security office), but neither disagreement escalated into threats or violence, and Mr. S responded to both reprimands by avoiding the individuals involved and not behaving in that way again. Moreover, there are no indications that Mr. S has engaged in aggressive antisocial behavior in the past. There are no indications that Mr. S owns or has immediate access to firearms.

Second, Mr. S does not have a history of mental or emotional disorder that might become acute and contribute to inaccurate perceptions or poor judgment in the present situation. However, he did acknowledge experiencing significant current stress associated with his wife's medical problems, and also indicated that he has been unable to exercise regularly of late, which has been one way Mr. S has coped with stress in the past.

Third, Mr. S has not recently experienced a significant loss or loss of status that might lead him to feel angry or desperate. By contrast, he presents as an individual with a positive outlook toward life.

Fourth, results of the PCL-R suggest that Mr. S does not possess personality traits associated with interpersonal callousness, impulsiveness, and antisocial behavior. While this is not surprising for an individual who has been consistently employed, identified strongly with family, and apparently lacking in antisocial history, it is also consistent with his amenability to respond to interventions (whether made by his employer or perhaps in counseling) in a way that allows him to avoid repeating problem behaviors.

Fifth, there are no indications that Mr. S has a substance abuse problem. The presence of either alcohol or drug abuse could significantly increase his risk for antisocial behavior.

Finally, there are a number of protective factors evident in Mr. S's life that further reduce his risk for workplace violence. Specifically, Mr. S's immediate and extended family appears to provide a strong source of emotional support. Similarly, Mr. S appears to possess strong spiritual beliefs that stand in direct opposition to the commission of violent acts. Also, he has developed coping mechanisms that allow him to respond to frustration without violence, although it seems important that one of his coping mechanisms—regular exercise—has not been used much lately because of the time demands of his wife's illness and his move. The presence of these protective factors, in conjunction with an apparent lack of active risk factors, make Mr. S a low risk for workplace violence. Although Mr. S does not present as a high risk for workplace violence, the results of this evaluation suggest that he tends to overcontrol his emotions, and possesses a number of personality features that make it difficult for him to express feelings of anger or verbal hostility in reaction to frustration, even when such a reaction might be appropriate or justified. In order to reduce further his already low risk for violence, and to improve his overall quality of life, Mr. S would benefit from certain therapeutic interventions.

Mr. S should be referred to a competent cognitive-behavioral psychologist for psychotherapy. The results of this evaluation suggest that Mr. S possesses certain personality traits that make it difficult for him to disclose personal information and express feelings of anger or verbal hostility in reaction to frustration or other environmental stresses. Cognitive-behavioral therapy will not only allow him to address these psychological issues, but it may also provide him with the tools necessary to become more comfortable with the appropriate expression of frustration and anger. Interventions in this area should be highly focused and structured, and they should focus on understanding, and the appropriate expression of frustration and anger in a wide variety of environments. Similarly, interventions in this area should also focus on interpersonal problem solving in general and specifically on interpersonal strategies for the resolution of interpersonal conflict in the face of frustration and anger; role-playing might be a particularly effective intervention. Mr. S should receive counseling on a weekly basis, and the estimated duration of such psychotherapy is approximately 6 months to a year.

As an adjunct to psychotherapy, Mr. S would also benefit from training in stress management. This might be particularly important, given that Mr. S reported a variety of active and significant psychosocial stresses in his current daily life. Mr. S should also be encouraged to increase his physical activity level. Mr. S reported that exercise provides a significant source of stress reduction; he elaborated that exercise makes it significantly easier for him to handle day-to-day stress. Mr. S also reported that recently he has not had the time to exercise as often as he would like. A return to a regular exercise schedule might be particularly important because it will help Mr. S cope more adaptively with stress and frustration while he develops more emotional awareness and problem-solving skills in psychotherapy.

If these interventions can be made successfully, Mr. S's already low risk for violence should be reduced even further. In addition, these interventions should improve his overall quality of life. Mr. S's progress should be monitored in order to ensure the effectiveness and impact of these interventions on the workplace environment. Judgments regarding his progress could be made in a variety of ways, such as regular reports from his therapist, regular discussions with supervisors or representatives of the Human Resources Department, and behavioral monitoring in the workplace itself. Mr. S should receive regular feedback about his progress. Satisfactory progress reports and an absence of concurring incidents should suffice to demonstrate that Mr. S remains a low risk for workplace violence.

Thank you for the opportunity to evaluate Mr. S.

Kirk Heilbrun, Ph.D.
Consulting Psychologist

Geff Marczyk, M.S., M.A.
MCP Hahnemann University
Graduate Student

David DeMatteo, M.A.
MCP Hahnemann University
Graduate Student

Teaching Point: **What are strategies for predicting violent behavior, and others for assessing risk reduction?**

When a forensic clinician is asked to perform any type of FMHA, it is always important to clarify the precise issue to be addressed. This is particularly true, however, when the forensic clinician is asked to perform a FMHA in the area of risk assessment. For example, when a forensic clinician is confronted with a referral in the area of risk assessment, he or she must ascertain whether the purpose of the particular FMHA is to predict future behavior (e.g., provide a classification of risk or a probability of the likelihood of future violence), to identify risk factors and include recommendations for reducing risk, or both. The forensic clinician should also consider that if the referral is focused primarily on one of these areas, it may not be appropriate to address the other.

If the forensic clinician is asked to predict the likelihood of violent behavior, there are several strategies that can be employed to increase the accuracy of the prediction. One particularly effective way to increase accuracy is to use a specialized risk-assessment instrument. It is important, however, that the forensic clinician use a tool that has been developed and validated for a purpose, with a population, and over a period of time comparable to that needed in the evaluation. In this regard, some of the more well-known and useful instruments include the HCR-20 (Webster et al., 1997), the Violence Risk Appraisal Guide (Harris, Rice, & Quinsey, 1993), and the Iterative Classification Tree (Monahan et al., 2000).

It should be noted, however, that these instruments have limitations. Specifically, if they were developed on different populations, or predict outcomes that are different from what is being assessed in the immediate case, or use an outcome period that is not applicable, then they might not be particularly useful in that case.

When compared with the strategies that are currently available for predicting violent behavior, the existing strategies for assessing risk reduction are, at present, less well-developed empirically. In fact, as of this writing, there are no specialized tools that would enable a forensic clinician to make empirically supported judgments regarding the change in an individual's risk of violent behavior. Despite the absence of empirically validated instruments that assess change in risk, there are some tools (e.g., LSI-R, HCR-20) that include an assessment of certain risk factors that may change and, thereby, lower an individual's risk for engaging in violent behavior. However, these aspects of such tools have not been subjected to formal study, so their capacity to gauge risk reduction is not nearly as strong as their capacity to predict violent or antisocial behavior.

Nevertheless, there are specific strategies that a forensic clinician can employ to assess the change in an individual's risk of violent behavior. One could begin by distinguishing the following: (1) level of risk, (2) nature/severity of harm, (3) imminence, (4) contexts of risk, and (5) targets of potential violence. Distinguishing these questions can help the forensic clinician to identify areas with the potential to change, and whose change may affect the individual's risk.

Another step in the strategy for assessing risk reduction is identifying the dynamic risk factors associated with the individual's previous acts of violence, and then determining the status of those risk factors at the time of the assessment. It is important that the forensic clinician assess these dynamic risk factors across time, particularly when they are likely to have changed somewhat (e.g., in response to treatment specifically designed to reduce such risk factors).

In addition to assessing dynamic risk factors, the forensic clinician should consider the protective factors that may have inhibited violence in the past, and then determine the status of those protective factors at the time of the assessment. As with the risk factors, the forensic clinician should periodically assess protective factors, particularly when such factors may have changed in response to treatment or a change in the environment.

Assessing risk reduction can also be facilitated through careful observation of the individual's behavior. This is particularly important if the individual is being moved from a more secure to a less secure setting. If such movement can be implemented gradually, then a "demonstration model," in which the individual has the opportunity to show increasing responsibility under a series of conditions with decreasing monitoring and restrictiveness may be helpful.

It is also important to consider the impact of monitoring, which has been empirically demonstrated to lower an individual's risk for engaging in violent or antisocial behavior. Finally, if the individual's risk is highly context-specific, then the risk can be lowered by changing the individual's environment. For example, if an individual frequently gets into physical altercations when drinking, the individual's risk may be lowered if he or she stops drinking.

Case 2

Principle: Clarify role with attorney

This principle concerns the importance of explicit role clarification in FMHA. Depending on the referral source, a clinician can play one of four roles in the context of FMHA: court-appointed, defense/prosecution/plaintiff's expert, consultant, and "state of the science" expert. A fifth role, that of fact witness, is possible when there has been another professional role played in the case (e.g., treating therapist), but will not be discussed further here because it is not an expert role. The role of court-appointed evaluators is clear and usually requires no further clarification because the court order specifies the legal issues to be evaluated and, therefore, the role to be played by the forensic clinician. In each of the other circumstances, however, competing pressures and the need to remain impartial require the forensic clinician to clarify the role to be played in the evaluation once the forensic issue has been identified.

There is considerable ethical support for the practice of role clarification. The APA *Ethical Principles and Code of Conduct* (APA, 1992) addresses the issue of role selection in two sections. First, the *Ethics Code* notes

> When a psychologist agrees to provide services to a person or entity at the request of a third party, the psychologist clarifies to the extent feasible, at the outset of the service, the nature of the relationship with each party. This clarification includes the role of the psychologist (such as therapist, organizational consultant, diagnostician, or expert witness), the probable uses of the services provided or the information obtained, and the fact that there may be limits to confidentiality.
>
> If there is a foreseeable risk of the psychologist's being called upon to perform conflicting roles because of the involvement of a third party, the psychologist clarifies the nature and direction of his or her responsibilities, keeps all parties appropriately informed as matters develop, and resolves the situation in accordance with this Ethics Code. (1992, p. 1602)

Second, under role clarification in Forensic Activities, the *Ethics Code* notes

> In most circumstances, psychologists avoid performing multiple and potentially conflicting roles in forensic matters. When psychologists may be called on to serve in more than one role in a legal proceeding—for example, as consultant or expert for one party or for the court and as a fact witness—they clarify role expectations and the extent of confidentiality in advance to the extent feasible, and thereafter as changes occur, in order to avoid compromising their professional judgement and objectivity and in order to avoid misleading others regarding their role. (p. 1610)

The *Specialty Guidelines for Forensic Psychologists* (Committee on Ethical Guidelines for Forensic Psychologists, 1991) and the *Principles of Medical Ethics with Annotation Especially Applicable to Psychiatry* (APA, 1998) are indirect in their application to this principle. The *Specialty Guidelines* does describe an "initial consultation with the legal representative of the party seeking services" (p. 658). During this initial consultation, the forensic psychologist is obliged to inform that party of considerations that might affect the decision to contract with the psychologist, and can include issues such as fee structure, prior and current relationships that might produce a conflict of interest, areas of competence and the limits of competence, and the known scientific bases and limitations of the procedures that would be employed. The *Principles of Medical Ethics* states: "Psychiatric services, like all medical services, are dispensed in the context of a contractual arrangement between the patient and the treating physician. The provisions of the contractual agreement, which are binding on the physician as well as on the patient, should be explicitly established" (p. 3). The *Ethical Guidelines for the Practice of Forensic Psychiatry* (AAPL, 1995) does not address the matter of initial role clarification, either directly or indirectly.

This report involves a case in which the clinician assumes the role of evaluator in the context of a threat/risk assessment evaluation. The scope of the forensic clinician's role in this case must be clarified with either the retaining attorney or the court. For example, as a court-appointed evaluator, the court order would specify the role to be played by the forensic clinician. Therefore, no further role clarification is necessary. By contrast, if the forensic clinician is retained by either the prosecution or defense, the forensic clinician bears the responsibility of clarifying the scope and limits of his or her role with the retaining attorney. In such a case, the forensic clinician should clearly indicate what services will be provided, such as testing, report writing, and testimony.

FORENSIC EVALUATION

April 18, 2000

REFERRAL

Joseph Dokes is a 24-year-old African American man who was adjudicated Not Guilty by Reason of Insanity of Assault with Intent to Kill on August 4, 1999. He was committed to the Forensic Unit at Northern State Hospital, where he was admitted on October 22, 1999. He has filed notice of request for conditional release after 6 months of hospitalization. The present evaluation was ordered by the Honorable James Jackson on 4-2-00, for the purpose of assisting the court in determining whether Mr. Dokes continues to meet criteria for involuntary hospitalization as mentally ill and dangerous to himself or others, as set forth in applicable state statutes.

PROCEDURES

Mr. Dokes was interviewed for a total of 3 hours on 4-5-00 and 2 hours on 4-7-00. His hospital records were reviewed, and the results of recently administered psychological testing by hospital staff (including the Brief Symptom Inventory, MMPI-2, and WAIS-III) were also reviewed. Included in the hospital records were his arrest history, police reports from his current offense, and two psychiatric evaluations that were conducted as part of his trial.

Mr. Dokes was informed prior to beginning the first interview about the purpose of the evaluation and the fact that a report would be written and sent to the court, his attorney, and the prosecution. He seemed to understand this notification without problems, and repeated it back clearly.

HISTORY

Mr. Dokes was raised as an only child in a chaotic and violent home, according to his own accounts and confirmed by contemporaneous reports by Child Protective Services. After a reportedly normal birth, he grew up surrounded by a variety of alcoholic adults, including only his mother as a stable member of the household. On his birth certificate, the father is listed as "unknown." Also present were a wide array of her "boyfriends," many of whom were present for only a night, and all of whom were reported by the subject to be drunk. It appears likely that his mother, at least at times, engaged in street prostitution. He reports numerous incidences of severe neglect, all due to his mother's bouts of drunkenness and drug use. As early as he can remember, he was routinely given beer and marijuana in order to "help him sleep," and was felt by one CPS worker to be addicted to alcohol at age 5. CPS personnel eventually investigated these circumstances when the subject was 5 years old, at which time he was permanently removed from the home and sent to a variety of foster care settings.

No extended family of any kind has ever been identified to Mr. Dokes. His mother frequently told him that they were "alone in the world."

Although it is hard to believe, after being removed from the home, Mr. Dokes's life actually became more difficult. His first placement was terminated as a result of sexual abuse suffered at the hands of his foster father, who was arrested and convicted of the crime. A series of other placements typically ended quickly when the subject would physically attack his foster parents, steal alcohol or money, or otherwise behave in an uncontrollable manner. According to CPS, these included some very experienced and well-intentioned foster parents. By age 8, Mr. Dokes was deemed to be "incorrigible," which resulted in a series of placements in juvenile detention facilities. His offenses included simple assault, assault with a deadly weapon, theft, grand theft, and various counts of drug use and drinking by a minor. While in these juvenile placements, Mr. Dokes reports that several times he was the victim of vicious rapes by older boys with whom he was incarcerated, several of which were reportedly brought to the attention of staff (by other anonymous witnesses) but none of which resulted in official action, as the subject steadfastly refused to testify or provide information.

There is no evidence of any psychological or psychiatric evaluations of the subject up to age 11. Finally, at age 11, Mr. Dokes was sent to a forestry camp, where he remained for 2 years. By his own account, this was the first time in his life that he had ever felt safe. Alcohol and drugs were not available, and he learned to read. This individual, who had previously been called mentally retarded, was able to improve from not reading at all to a sixth grade reading level in his first year at the camp. It is also worth noting that the school at this camp was quite nontraditional, in that all of the academic subjects were taught in the context of camping and survival skills training, and formal educational time was often limited to 3 hours per day. Also during this time, Mr. Dokes became a voracious reader. Though there was a psychologist on staff at the camp, Mr. Dokes was doing so well that no evaluation was conducted other than some fairly simple assessments of his educational capacity. These suggested that his previously identified intellectual deficits were entirely due to his socially and educationally impoverished childhood. It was also observed that he responded especially well to the nontraditional style of education that he enjoyed at the forestry camp.

According to official records, during his time at the camp, Mr. Dokes's mother died of unknown causes. He did not find out about her death for some months, and thus was unable to attend his funeral, if indeed one ever occurred.

By age 13, Mr. Dokes was deemed to have "graduated" from the camp, and was moved to a rather traditional orphanage. By now he was extremely physically fit, and willing and able to fight. He reported that he engaged in a number of fights early in this placement, all of which were intended to prevent his being raped by other boys at the orphanage. Staff reports that the subject indeed engaged in a number of fights, many of which were marked by extreme violence by Mr. Dokes. For example, on one occasion he was found banging another boy's head into a concrete floor. For some reason, however, these fights were not prosecuted. It is also interesting to note that the subject was deemed to be quite protective of younger boys at the orphanage, and soon gained a reputation as a positive leader there. There is no evidence that he engaged in any drinking or illegal drug use during his time at the orphanage. He continued to improve academically, and by age 17 he was able to gain acceptance to a state university.

Shortly after arriving on campus, however, things began to unravel rather quickly. Mr. Dokes began drinking heavily, and became surly and combative in his freshman dormitory. He was sent to school counselors, but refused to meet with them. After less than a month of college, he was expelled from school, and in lieu of arrest, he was physically removed by police from the dormitory, with his few belongings in a plastic trash bag. This experience appears to have been very embarrassing and traumatic for Mr. Dokes.

From age 17 until age 21, Mr. Dokes miraculously managed to survive without any stable housing. He reports that he was "drunk for virtually the entire time," but steadfastly claims to have avoided any crimes (especially theft) during this time. Mr. Dokes, who is an otherwise frank and self-critical reporter, is quite moralistic about his unwillingness to commit property crimes. He was arrested on several occasions for simple assault, but his own accounts (and often those of the police) are that these assaults were always in self-defense, though Mr. Dokes would do most of the damage because of his superior strength and ability to fight. Often, when he was intoxicated, the police would arrest him only because he seemed otherwise unwilling or unable to stop after winning a fight. Police report that he is well-liked by them; indeed, they seemed to arrest him rather reluctantly. On many occasions, police, social workers, and others would attempt to assist Mr. Dokes in gaining entry to shelters, mental health and substance abuse programs, or vocational programs. At all times he refused. Indeed, Mr. Dokes appears to take great pride in his ability to survive on the street without stealing.

On June 1, 1999, Mr. Dokes was arrested for assault with intent to kill. The victim was an openly gay homeless man who attempted to fondle Mr. Dokes in his sleep. On awakening, Mr. Dokes quickly overcame the victim, and began to pound the victim's head into the pavement, resulting in apparent severe brain damage. Mr. Dokes was represented by a public defender, and there was a plea bargained insanity defense, which resulted in his placement in a maximum security forensic psychiatric hospital. Apparently, both psychiatrists involved in performing the forensic evaluations in this case (for the defense and for the prosecution, respectively) agreed that he became transiently psychotic on awakening to the unwanted sexual contact, and was unable to control his violent anger until police physically pulled him off the victim. In part, this opinion was based on his failure to stop even after the police arrived, and on some confused and apparently paranoid things that he was saying during the incident. Although these were overheard by police, the reports unfortunately do not include any direct quotes. Despite the fact that all of these incidents involved alcohol or drug intoxication, the psychiatrists agreed that the reason for his inability to conform to the law was not voluntary intoxication, but his transient reactive psychoses. As a result, he was offered a plea of Not Guilty by Reason of Insanity.

CLINICAL CONDITION

Mr. Dokes was polite and cooperative throughout both interviews. Previous psychiatric and psycho-

logical evaluations have consistently described Mr. Dokes as a person with intelligence well above normal, but with serious variability in test scores suggestive of brain damage pursuant to child abuse and years of alcohol and drug abuse. He has been diagnosed as suffering from a number of problems, at times including Borderline Personality Disorder, severe Post Traumatic Stress Disorder, and personality disorder with mixed features. In each case, he was said to be vulnerable to brief psychotic episodes, with or without co-occurring intoxication, always in response to homosexual panic, all of which were in response to real actions by assaultive others. In other words, the threat to which he responds is always real; the psychosis is said to occur after he is attacked. As a result, he becomes homicidally enraged and is unable to stop fighting after he has neutralized the threat. When asked if has ever killed anyone, Mr. Dokes replied "I have no idea," as he reports that he seldom has much memory of these episodes.

Mr. Dokes presented himself in a way consistent with these descriptions. His speech was clear and easily understood. His mood was neutral, and he seemed to be making an effort to respond to all questions asked of him, even in sensitive areas. He was correctly oriented to time, place, and person. Results of the recent WAIS-III indicated that Mr. Dokes is functioning in the average range of intelligence (VIQ = 102, PIQ = 94, FSIQ = 97). He did not describe experiencing any perceptual disturbances (seeing or hearing things not present), nor did he seem to experience any delusions or other disturbances of thought. He has not received psychotropic medication since a low dose of Haldol was discontinued by his attending psychiatrist 3 weeks after Mr. Dokes was admitted to the hospital.

On psychological testing (the BSI and MMPI-2), Mr. Dokes did not describe experiencing any active symptoms of psychosis. He did endorse problems with anger, as described earlier in this section. He also described himself in a way consistent with severe problems with mixed substance abuse, primarily alcohol. Individuals with such profiles are also described as experiencing personality problems consistent with being particularly suspicious toward others and having to deal with severe trauma-related symptoms.

According to his hospital records, Mr. Dokes has been consistently cooperative with hospital staff since his admission. With the exception of involvement in three incidents in which he was apparently protecting another patient from being attacked, there has been no documentation of threats, fights, rule violations, or other incidents of note. He obtained escorted grounds privileges in his third month of hospitalization, and has had unescorted grounds privileges during the last month. He has handled each of these levels of hospital privilege responsibly and without incident.

Mr. Dokes has no observable animosity toward self-identified gay patients or staff. He is, in fact, quite accepting of their right to any sexual orientation of their choosing, as long as they do not impose it on others. There is no record or report of him, drunk or sober, ever initiating an assault on a person because of their sexual orientation.

He is seen as having a number of impressive strengths. He is viewed by all staff as unusually honest and honorable, with a level of candor that is almost unheard of in such institutions. He is completely unwilling to be a "snitch" under any circumstances, but has reportedly been an asset to staff in controlling illegal behavior on the wards. He has continued his impressive record of self-education, and has taught himself to repair and program computers so well that he has been offered jobs in the community, even while hospitalized. His physical health is quite good, and he is a careful eater and avid exercise buff.

Liabilities include a satisfaction with institutional life, and a self-reported acceptance of the inevitability of lifelong incarceration. Further, although Mr. Dokes's extreme violence has occurred while psychotic, he believes that in every case it was a valid response to a sexual crime. He readily espouses the death penalty for sexual offenders, and has no apparent moral context to motivate himself to ameliorate the behaviors that have restricted his freedom. Of course, his long history of alcohol and drug addiction are severe risk factors as well.

It is worth noting that while Mr. Dokes can and does use violence to protect others, he has at all times been able to do so without any accompanying psychosis and without the excessive (and illegal) violence that exceeds the need to protect the victim. This is in stark contrast to his responses when he is the victim of sexual aggression of any kind.

RISK ASSESSMENT

Mr. Dokes's history and current espoused values suggest that he is likely to repeat his pattern of extreme retributive violence if, and only if, he perceives that he is the victim of a sexual assault. So far he has been unable or unwilling to learn how to modulate his violence to conform to the law (i.e., to engage in only that level of violence that is necessary to protect himself and others).

Mr. Dokes's long history of addiction also places him at great peril of living in very unsafe circumstances, which increase the likelihood that he will again be the subject of intrusive and unwanted sexual contact. Further, Mr. Dokes's failure to accept the possibility of an optimistic outcome severely impairs efforts to overcome his addiction and reactive violence. Finally, his uncritical acceptance of institutional values (i.e., a total prohibition of cooperating with authorities or "snitching") prohibits him from relying on legitimate authorities (e.g., hospital staff, police, etc.) to protect him and others, which would otherwise provide an alternative to violence.

Protective factors are equally impressive. Mr. Dokes is a very intelligent and well-educated (indeed self-educated) young man, with vocational skills that are in demand. He is also seen as honorable and having a consistent and prosocial moral code. When he is not the victim of sexual assaults, he is able to modulate his anger and violence. During periods of living in a *safe* structured environment, Mr. Dokes has been able to abstain from alcohol or drugs.

CONCLUSION

Mr. Dokes has made significant progress during his 6 months of hospitalization in a secure forensic setting. His clinical condition is stable, and he has taken important steps toward a graduated release from secure hospitalization into a less restrictive hospital setting. While he has not yet taken all necessary steps that would allow him to return to the community (see next section), and therefore continues to meet the criteria for involuntary hospitalization, he should continue to make good progress if he can take the several necessary steps described in the following section.

RECOMMENDATIONS

In order to allow Mr. Dokes to safely return to the community under condition release, several steps must be successfully negotiated:

1. Mr. Dokes must accept the realistic possibility that the following plan has a reasonable chance of success.

2. He must continue to abstain from alcohol and drug abuse, which experience suggests can only be achieved when he perceives himself to be living in a safe environment. (It is unknown to what extent this environment needs to be structured.) Further, integrated treatment of his addiction and mental illness disorders must begin as soon as possible, and continue throughout his movement through the system to eventual community placement.

3. As it is not possible to preclude any chance of unwanted sexual contact or advances, Mr. Dokes must learn to experience such events without losing control of himself, and to retain his judgment while responding.

    a. Mr. Dokes should first be asked to imagine such events in a safe setting.

    b. He should then be encouraged to create a nonpsychotic, nonexcessive response that includes violence only if necessary to protect himself and that stops as soon as the threat is neutralized. (I doubt seriously that it will be possible to get Mr. Dokes to use authorities as his first response to a direct physical threat.)

    c. He should then be encouraged to imagine responding in this legal and prosocial manner.

    d. Next, Mr. Dokes should verbally describe himself, in a group setting if possible, responding in such an appropriate manner.

    e. Once he is able to successfully imagine and describe a measured response to intrusive sexual contact, Mr. Dokes should be encouraged to role play such events, again if possible in a group setting.

4. Because of his intelligence and integrity, it is likely that Mr. Dokes will be able to form at least an intellectually trusting relationship with a staff person (e.g., a case manager) located in the community to which he will eventually return, and who is respectful of his autonomy. This relationship should begin prior to Mr. Dokes leaving the secure forensic hospital and continue through his time in the state civil hospital and on to his eventual return to freedom.

5. When and only when Mr. Dokes begins to "buy into" this plan, and on successful completion of the behavioral rehearsal in item #3 above, it will be appropriate to allow him progressive steps toward freedom.

    a. First, Mr. Dokes should be moved to a nonsecure hospital, where he will initially (probably a matter of a few weeks) be held on a locked ward. During this time, Mr. Dokes should again rehearse prosocial responses to the situations described above.

    b. Next, Mr. Dokes should begin to move to initially brief, and progressively longer periods of unsupervised time off ward. At the end of each visit, Mr. Dokes should be debriefed by staff, in order to ascertain if and how Mr. Dokes dealt with inappropriate sexual advances (which are frankly not unlikely to occur in a state psychiatric hospital) as well as his continued abstinence from alcohol and nonprescription drugs.

6. As Mr. Dokes self-reports successfully negotiating these situations, it will be appropriate to begin planning for his discharge into the community.

    a. Housing should be selected based on affordability, perceived safety, and Mr. Dokes's preference, which appears to lean toward private as opposed to congregate housing.

    b. Employment seems likely to present little or no problem, as Mr. Dokes's vocational skills are already appropriate for community living. The only exception would be relapse of his addiction disorders.

c. Mr. Dokes's comfort with fellow psychiatric patients, as well as his intellectual generosity and natural leadership, make him an ideal candidate to participate in a Psychosocial Clubhouse or self-help group, where he will buttress his own damaged sense of self-worth by helping others. This will also serve to support his sense of optimism that it might indeed be possible for him to make it in the free world.

7. Ideally, a deal will be struck with Mr. Dokes, whereupon any failure to successfully demonstrate the skills and behaviors contained herein would result in voluntarily moving him back to a more structured situation, but only to the degree necessary to support his continued safe living. Mr. Dokes is highly motivated to cooperate in such a plan, as he openly expresses his wish to avoid such situations that require self-protective violence.

Thank you for the opportunity to evaluate Mr. Dokes.

Joel Dvoskin, Ph.D.

Teaching Point: What are strategies for avoiding dual roles in FMHA?

There are a number of strategies that can be used by the forensic clinician to avoid assuming dual roles in the context of FMHA. Generally, the forensic clinician should decide on a single role from the outset of the evaluation, and clarify that role with the referral source. Similarly, it is important that the referral source understand the limitations and functions of that role in the context of the evaluation. When necessary, the forensic clinician should reclarify his or her role and the contours of the evaluation. The reestablishment of role boundaries can be particularly useful in resisting pressure from referral sources to assume inappropriate dual roles.

More specific strategies are also available. A forensic clinician should not perform a FMHA on an individual where there is a prior personal or professional relationship. The exception to this involves situations in which the prior relationship involved a previous FMHA, with the caveat that subsequent evaluations must be authorized by the same referral source. For example, it would be appropriate to conduct a trial competence evaluation, and subsequently a sentencing evaluation, on the same defendant at the request of his or her defense counsel. Conversely, it would be inappropriate to conduct the trial competence evaluation at the request of defense counsel, and the sentencing evaluation at the request of the prosecution. Any exceptions should be agreed on by all parties or their legal representatives.

By following this simple approach, the forensic clinician should be able to avoid the majority of inappropriate dual roles. When unique or particularly challenging circumstances are involved, and there is doubt about the appropriate course of action, the forensic clinician should consult with a colleague experienced in FMHA.

Case 3

Principle: Use nomothetic evidence in assessing causal connection between clinical condition and functional abilities

This principle is discussed in detail in chapter 2, so we move directly to the case report. This report was conducted as part of an inmate's application for parole. The purpose of the evaluation was to determine what level of violence risk would be presented by the individual being assessed (who was serving a life sentence for murder) if he were released on parole into the community.

During the evaluation, the forensic clinician used several psychological tests and actuarial risk assessment tools, including a standardized rating scale of psychopathic personality traits that is empirically associated with future violence risk (the PCL-R; Hare, 1991), an actuarial instrument used to assess an individual's risk for violence (the Violence Risk Appraisal Guide, or VRAG; Harris et al., 1993), a tool assessing the individual's risk for spousal violence (the Spousal Assault Risk Assessment Guide, or SARA; Kropp & Hart, 2000), and another tool assessing the risk for violence (the HCR-20; Webster et al., 1997). Consistent with this principle, these tests and tools have established psychometric properties. The reliability and validity of the PCL-R is firmly established in the relevant literature (see, e.g., Hare, 1991; Rice, 1997). Similarly, the VRAG (e.g., Harris et al., 1993; Quinsey et al., 1998), SARA (e.g., Kropp & Hart, 2000), and HCR-20 (e.g., Webster et al., 1997) have each undergone validation research that has been presented at professional conferences and is now appearing in the published literature. Such tests are thus reasonably consistent with the guidelines described by Heilbrun (1992) regarding the selection and use of psychological tests in FMHA.

The relationship between the psychological tests and tools used in this evaluation and the forensic issues being addressed is important. A primary consideration in determining whether an individual should be released on parole is whether the individual presents a risk for engaging in future acts of violence and, if so, under what circumstances. Toward that end, the forensic clinician in this case employed several different psychological tests and tools that are directly relevant to the individual's risk of engaging in future acts of violence.

Specifically, the PCL-R measures the degree to which an individual exhibits psychopathic traits that have been shown to be associated with an increased risk for engaging in crime in general and, more specifically, in violent crime against people (Hare, 1991). The VRAG was designed to assess an individual's level of risk for engaging in violence in the community over a relatively long outcome period, averaging over 7 years (Harris et al., 1993). The SARA guidelines are used to assess an individual's risk for engaging in violence against a spouse or partner (Kropp & Hart, 2000); the SARA was used in this case because the inmate was involved in an intimate relationship. Finally, the HCR-20, which is used to assess risk for violence among people with serious psychiatric or personality disorders (Webster et al., 1997), was particularly relevant in this case because the forensic clinician concluded that the inmate was suffering from a severe psychiatric disorder (Psychotic Disorder NOS).

In addition, because each of these measures has an established empirical base, the forensic clinician was able to compare the individual's scores on these tests with the data obtained as part of the test validation process. For example, based on the results of the PCL-R, which placed the inmate in the bottom 5% relative to incarcerated adult male offenders, the forensic clinician concluded that the inmate presented a very low risk for "general violence, especially opportunistic, instrumental violence." Moreover, based on the results of the VRAG, which placed the inmate in the second lowest of nine score categories, the forensic clinician concluded that the inmate's risk of violent recidivism over a relatively long period in the community is low. Finally, based on the results of the HCR-20 and the SARA, the forensic clinician concluded that the inmate presented a moderate risk for both general violence (HCR-20) and spousal violence (SARA). In this case, based partly on the inmate's scores on these tests and tools, the forensic clinician concluded that the inmate would present a moderate risk for future violence if he were to be released on parole.

DEPARTMENT OF CORRECTIONS PSYCHOLOGICAL ASSESSMENT REPORT

Name: Douglas Joseph SMITH
DOB: May 5, 1935
POB: Newcastle, England

REASON FOR REFERRAL

Mr. Smith is a 61-year-old man currently serving a life sentence for murder. He is now eligible for parole, and was referred for a psychological assessment to be submitted as part of his application for release.

METHOD OF ASSESSMENT

Interviews and written communications with Mr. Smith (numerous)

Review of institutional files

Completion of psychological tests and actuarial risk assessment procedures, including the Hare Psychopathy Checklist-Revised (PCL-R), the Violence Risk Appraisal Guide (VRAG), Version 2 of the HCR-20, and the 2nd edition of the Spousal Assault Risk Assessment Guide (SARA).

CURRENT OFFENSE

On April 21, 1989, Mr. Smith was convicted of the second-degree (noncapital) murder of Ms. Emma Jones. The offense took place on or about December 8, 1986.

Ms. Jones was a long-time acquaintance of Mr. Smith. The two first met while employed at an architectural firm. Starting in about 1983, their relationship became intimate in nature. Mr. Smith experienced a very serious disruption in his psychosocial functioning following his affair with Ms. Jones. First, despite a lack of prior history of mental disorder, he became depressed and experienced severe dissociative symptoms (see below), necessitating ongoing inpatient and outpatient psychiatric therapy. Second, the affair put considerable strain on Mr. Smith's marriage, which apparently had been stable since its start in 1959, and the couple subsequently separated. Third, Mr. Smith's employment at a major architectural firm was terminated.

Mr. Smith and Ms. Jones continued their relationship after the onset of his psychiatric problems. They maintained separate residences, however, and it is not clear that Ms. Jones considered the relationship to be committed or exclusive. Indeed, police investigators believed that Ms. Jones "had been anticipating breaking off the relationship with Smith, however was waiting until after the Christmas [1986] season." Also according to the Police, "Mr. Smith's personal diary revealed that he was obsessed with Emma Jones, being very jealous and suspicious of her."

The murder of Ms. Jones occurred in the early morning hours of December 8, 1986. Details of the offense are somewhat sketchy: Mr. Smith claims amnesia for most of the relevant times (something he later attributed to taking the sleeping medication Halcion), and physical evidence did not permit a detailed behavioral reconstruction. It appears Mr. Smith spent the night in question with Ms. Jones at her Vancouver residence. Late in the evening he strangled her manually and removed her body from the residence. Ms. Jones was reported missing on December 8, 1986, but a search of her residence revealed only a small amount of blood on the bed sheets.

Almost a week later, on December 15, 1986, Mr. Smith was apprehended in the interior of British Columbia, several hundred miles from the crime scene. The police spotted Mr. Smith near a car parked on the side of the highway. Mr. Smith was disorganized and incoherent. He had scratch marks on his face and hands, as well as stab wounds on his abdomen—apparently self-inflicted—that were 1 or 2 days old. Inside the car was the body of Ms. Jones, fully dressed, even wearing a coat, toque, and gloves. The car also contained a bag of groceries. An autopsy revealed that the victim was deceased prior to being dressed. There was no evidence that she had been sexually assaulted before or after death.

After his arrest, Mr. Smith was transferred to the Forensic Psychiatric Institute for pretrial psychiatric evaluation. At FPI, he continued to complain of amnesia and to act in a rather disorganized manner. He was diagnosed as suffering from major depression, apparently was involuntarily committed and subsequently treated with medications. Despite thorough examinations by numerous medical and psychological experts, the exact nature of Mr. Smith's psychiatric problems was unclear. Also, although there was good agreement that Mr. Smith suffered from a serious mental disorder, the onset of which predated the offense by some 3 years, psychiatric testimony presented at trial opined that he was criminally responsible.

Mr. Smith still reports amnesia for the events immediately surrounding his offense. On its own, this is not unusual; about 50% of people who commit serious violent crimes report that they cannot recall some details of their offenses. What is unusual, however, is that starting around the time of his trial and continuing to the present day, Mr. Smith has come to believe that he has been the victim of a conspiracy. Specifically, Mr. Smith believes that Ms. Jones was murdered by Irish Republican Army terrorists, who tried to frame him for the crime. The IRA's motive, he says, was revenge: They were trying to punish him for his involvement in antiterrorist activities in Canada on behalf of the government of the United Kingdom (as a member of MI6). His belief in this explanation appears to be sincere and unwavering.

PRIOR CRIMINAL HISTORY

Mr. Smith has no known prior record of convictions for criminal offenses as a juvenile or adult. He was charged with a minor theft (theft under) on April 21, 1986. He says that he was caught leaving a drugstore with goods for which he had not paid—along with some for which he had paid—and was apprehended by private security officers; however, the charge was later dropped after store security and police officers accepted his explanation that he was on medications and suffering from memory lapses. After being treated at FPI, Mr. Smith was granted bail and lived in the community between March 31, 1988, and his conviction on April 21, 1989. There is no indication that he violated the bail conditions imposed on him. However, according to both the police and Mr. Smith, there were several incidents of aggressive behavior during his period of bail supervision, including a verbal altercation with several young men at a pub and a physical confrontation with a man at a restaurant. (Neither of these incidents resulted in suspension of bail, arrest, or criminal charges.) According to Mr. Smith, there were also eight other occasions during his period of bail supervision on which he was accosted by men unknown to him, including one attempted stabbing, two hit-and-runs, and one theft of personal property. He attributes these incidents to continued harassment by IRA and neo-Nazi thugs.

PSYCHIATRIC HISTORY

Apparently Mr. Smith had no history of psychiatric contact prior to 1983. However, he reports a history of multiple (14) closed head injuries between the ages of 15 and 41. These ranged in severity from mild (brief loss of conscious and transient memory difficulties) to severe (skull fractures, major disturbance of orientation and memory, increased irritability, and automatistic aggression). However, extensive neurological and neuropsychological evaluation before and after the current offense failed to reveal any significant, permanent structural or functional brain damage as a result of these accidents. Starting in 1983, around the time that his relationship with Ms. Jones and his marital problems began, Mr. Smith began to experience psychiatric symptoms. These included symptoms of depression, such as dysthymia, anergia, and suicidality; severe dissociative symptoms, including psychogenic fugue, amnesia, and perceptual disturbances (e.g., mood-congruent visual and tactile hallucinations); and exacerbation of his normal personality features, such that he became dramatic in his self-presentation, suspicious, and rigid.

At the peak of his problems in October 1983, Mr. Smith drove from Vancouver to Oregon and made a serious attempt at suicide (by drowning). He was rescued on a beach in Oregon and hospitalized, but could not recall any personal information. Eventually police established his identity and transferred him to hospital in Vancouver, where he was treated with antidepressant medications and electroconvulsive therapy. He received outpatient care after his release from hospital. He was treated primarily on an outpatient basis, with brief inpatient stays in 1984 and 1986, until the time of the offense. His diagnoses at that time included depression and personality disorder, with possible brief psychotic episodes and possible brain damage.

Mr. Smith has undergone numerous evaluations since his offense, both at the FPI (as discussed earlier) and while incarcerated in the Department of Corrections. The consensus among the professionals who evaluated him is that he suffers depression on an episodic basis. There is also consensus that his dramatic, suspicious, and rigid personality style is clinically significant; however, professionals cannot agree whether this reflects exacerbation of his normal personality by severe stress, the presence of a personality disorder, or disruption in personality as a result of severe mental disorder (i.e., psychosis).

SOCIAL HISTORY

Mr. Smith's social history is generally unremarkable. He was born and raised in England. His family life was normal. His school attendance and performance were unremarkable. He does report extrafamilial sexual molestation as a child (a single episode of noncoercive sexual touching by the minister of his church at age 12), but this apparently did not have a significant impact on his subsequent psychosocial functioning. After regular school, he received postsecondary education in architecture for 2 years, got married, and was conscripted into the British army for 2 years of service. After completing his military service, he started working as a designer and draftsman and started raising a family. In 1966 he moved to Canada, and has been employed in a variety of positions in Alberta, British Columbia, and Ontario. He reports frequent job changes, several of which appear to be the result of minor conflicts with employers or coworkers, but no significant periods of unemployment. His work has always been related to architecture, design, and project management; mostly, he worked for firms owned by others (including several prestigious firms), although he has also been self-employed at times.

I emphasize here that from the time that he moved to Canada until the time of the current offense—a period of almost 20 years—Mr. Smith appears to have had a relatively normal work history and family life, and was actively involved in recreational sport as a player and coach. This comment is not meant to imply that his adjustment was perfect or ideal, but simply that it was far superior to that of most federal offenders. Whatever problems Mr. Smith experienced prior to 1983 were sufficiently minor that they did not result in psychiatric or police contacts, they did not leave obvious blemishes on his work record, and they were not reported by coworkers or family members who provided collateral information of events since 1983.

ADJUSTMENT DURING INCARCERATION

Mr. Smith's record of institutional behavior is best described as "mixed" or "spotty." On the one hand, he has obtained evaluations ranging from satisfactory to excellent for his work as a language tutor and, previously, for his work in the cabinet shop. He has completed substance abuse and computer literacy programs, taken university courses, and at his best is a polite, articulate, and well-groomed man who steadfastly avoids involvement in the prison subculture. On the other hand, he rejects the advice and assistance of most correctional staff, who perceive him as critical, suspicious, stubborn, histrionic, and even aggressive at times. His record notes four disciplinary infractions: improper clothing on October 30, 1995 (dismissed); theft of sugar on November 18, 1995; possession of contraband (a memo) on August 16, 1996 (warning only); and use of abusive language to a Correctional Officer on November 10, 1996. He also described to me a series of minor altercations with other inmates who he believed were involved in the institutional drug trade. Mr. Smith's files also contain numerous communications to staff that can only be described as strange. Due to his extreme mistrust of DOC staff, he prefers to record all official conversations in the form of long, rambling memos to which he has added, in many cases, handwritten commentary or appended cartoons or illustrations. The general tenor of these memos is grandi-

ose (highlighting his own abilities and morals, demeaning or berating staff), and he refers repeatedly to his involvement in antiterrorist activities and his career as a professional soccer player. For example, he claims (1) he had 28 years experience in Her Majesty's Secret Service (MI6), (2) he was fired from his work on a construction site because he had knowledge of illegal, covert CIA operations in Columbia, (3) the Canadian Security and Intelligence Service (CSIS) is withholding important information concerning his intelligence work, and instructed his lawyer to sell his story to the media for $150,000, (4) involvement in CSIS operations concerning neo-Nazi groups, and (5) to have special knowledge that IRA and/or neo-Nazi terrorists were planning an attack on the Royal Family during a visit to BC. However, there is absolutely no evidence that these claims are true. Indeed, after Mr. Smith contacted the police in 1992 concerning some of these claims, they reported that the British government denies Mr. Smith has ever worked in an intelligence capacity, and that CSIS has no interest in Mr. Smith's reports.

INTERVIEW AND OBSERVATIONS

I met with Mr. Smith on several occasions and had numerous written communications with him between November 1997 and January 1998. He was informed of the purpose and nonconfidential nature of the assessment. Initially, he was reluctant to participate due to his mistrust of mental health professionals (the reasons for which he explained to me in some detail). However, he later consented after agreeing to submit critical information to me in writing and to keep written records of our interviews.

Despite Mr. Smith's mistrust, we established rapport and Mr. Smith was extremely cooperative in providing information. My impressions of Mr. Smith were generally consistent with those reported by past evaluators: he was articulate, candid, dramatic, suspicious, and angry at times. With respect to his mental status, he was fully oriented. His grooming and hygiene were good. He displayed a full range and depth of affect; indeed, he was emotionally labile at times. There was no evidence of mannerisms, posturing, or bizarre behavior. He denied perceptual disturbances. His speech was mildly pressured at times, and his thought processes were mildly disorganized (circumstantial and tangential). His thought content was moderately disturbed, characterized by high levels of grandiose and persecutory ideation and evidence of full-blown grandiose and persecutory delusions. Although Mr. Smith exaggerates his claims about antiterrorist work and subsequent harassment by the IRA and neo-Nazi organizations at times, and although he recognizes that others perceive (quite reasonably) these claims to be false, his personal belief in their truthfulness is absolute. His insight into his mental state is poor; Mr. Smith does not accept that he suffers from a serious mental disorder, and instead attributes all his problems-in-living to interference by hostile others.

PLANS FOR RELEASE

Mr. Smith provided me with a detailed release plan to accompany the one he submitted previously to the Parole Board (on February 2, 1995). We also had conversations in this regard. Briefly, he has the support of a United Church minister and congregation. The congregation will allow Mr. Smith to reside on church property in a small, rural community close to Vancouver. In exchange, Mr. Smith has agreed to help the congregation with its charity-related activities; he hopes that he will even have the opportunity to use his design and project management skills. He plans to socialize primarily with members of the congregation and with his children. Mr. Smith has no contact with his ex-wife, who has left the country and returned to the UK. He has no intimate partner at the present time and expresses no interest in establishing intimate relations in the future.

Mr. Smith's plans with respect to residence, employment, and associates strike me as reasoned and reasonable. I am concerned, however, that his plans with respect to professional support are inadequate. Mr. Smith's mistrust of DOC corrections and mental health staff is likely to make him difficult to supervise in the community; more specifically, this could be harmful to his mental status. One positive outcome of our conversations was that Mr. Smith indicated a willingness to see a "neutral" (i.e., non-DOC) mental health professional on a regular basis, should he be re-

leased. Two psychiatrists with whom he has established reasonable rapport, and with whom he would be willing to enter treatment, were identified. Although he does not believe that he suffers from a mental illness, he said he was willing to consider the possibility of taking medications after release, but only if these were recommended by a neutral professional.

PSYCHOLOGICAL TESTING AND ACTUARIAL RISK ASSESSMENT

Previous psychological testing, the results of which are summarized in Mr. Smith's institutional files, indicate that he has above average intelligence and intact neuropsychological functions.

The PCL-R is a standardized ratings scale of psychopathic personality traits that is reliably associated with risk for future violence. I completed the PCL-R based on a review of Mr. Smith's institutional files and my interviews with him. His Total score was very low, placing him in the bottom 5% relative to incarcerated adult male offenders. His scores on Factors 1 and 2 were also very low. This finding suggests that, based on the single risk factor of psychopathy, Mr. Smith is at low risk for general violence, especially opportunistic, instrumental violence.

Of course, a comprehensive risk assessment is not limited to consideration of a single risk factor. I therefore evaluated Mr. Smith using an actuarial instrument (the VRAG) and two sets of professional guidelines (the SARA and HCR-20). The VRAG was developed to assess risk for general violence among patients evaluated at a maximum-security forensic psychiatric hospital. The SARA guidelines concern assessment of risk for spousal violence (recall that Mr. Smith had an intimate relationship with Ms. Jones). The HCR-20 guidelines concern assessment of risk for violence among people with serious mental or personality disorders.

On the VRAG, Mr. Smith's score placed him the second lowest of nine score categories. In the original research, people with scores in that category had a violent recidivism rate of 8% over 7 years and 10% over 10 years post-release. The VRAG scores suggest that Mr. Smith's risk of violent recidivism is low in both absolute and relative terms.

On the HCR-20, Mr. Smith definitely had three of 10 Historical risk factors related to psychosocial adjustment (Previous violence, Major mental illness, Relationship instability). There was possible or partial evidence of four other factors (Employment problems, Early maladjustment, Personality disorder, and Prior supervision failure). With respect to Clinical (current) risk factors, he had definite or partial/possible evidence of all five (Lack of insight, Negative attitudes, Active symptoms of major mental illness; and, to a lesser extent, Impulsivity and Unresponsive to treatment). On the Risk Management scale, he had definite or possible/partial evidence of all five factors (Exposure to destabilizers; and, to a lesser extent, Plans lack feasibility, Lack of personal support, Noncompliance with remediation attempts, and Stress). In my opinion, these findings suggest a moderate risk for general violence and that the best way to manage Mr. Smith's risk for violence is to develop a sound program for monitoring and treating his psychiatric symptoms.

On the SARA, Mr. Smith had no risk factors related to past spousal assault or other criminality. He had only one risk factor related to the current offense (Severe assault). However, he had several risk factors relating to psychosocial adjustment (Relationship problems, Employment problems, Victim of child abuse, Homicidal ideation/intent, and Psychotic symptoms). Overall, in my opinion, this pattern suggests that Mr. Smith is a moderate risk for future spousal violence, should he establish a relationship with another woman following release. As was the case with the HCR-20, the results also suggested to me that his risk for spousal violence could be managed easily in the community, provided that his psychiatric problems are properly monitored and treated.

SUMMARY AND RECOMMENDATIONS

Mr. Smith's case is most unusual. It is my opinion, based on a careful review of his institutional records and numerous contacts with him, that he suffers from a major mental illness. Specifically, I believe that he suffers from an atypical psychotic disorder (i.e., Psychotic Disorder NOS), characterized by a combination of major depressive and acute psychotic episodes. At times he appears to have been depressed without exhibiting signs of psychosis; at times he appears to have been psychotic without exhibiting signs of depression; and at times he appears to have been both depressed and psychotic. I do not believe that he suffers from a true personality disorder; rather, it is my opinion that his preexisting personality traits were exacerbated by his acute mental disorder. I also believe that his psychosis is functional, although I cannot rule out the possibility that it is the end result of a series of traumatic brain injuries or some other somatic factor.

It is also my opinion that Mr. Smith's current offense, as well as the numerous altercations he has had in the community (while on bail) and in DOC (while incarcerated), are attributable primarily to his mental disorder. Indeed, with the benefit of hindsight, I find it hard to understand why Mr. Smith was found legally culpable and sentenced to prison, rather than found Not Guilty by Reason of Insanity and committed indefinitely to FPI.

Furthermore, it is my opinion that Mr. Smith is a moderate risk for violence should he be granted parole according to his release plans (including regular visits to a mental health professional). The most likely scenarios for violent reoffending are as follows. First, due to his persecutory delusions, Mr. Smith misperceives as hostile the acts of an adult male stranger and initiates a verbal or physical altercation. Second, Mr. Smith becomes angry at his parole officer (or someone else involved in his community supervision, such as his psychiatrist) for what he perceives as unwarranted interference in his life, and initiates a verbal or physical altercation. Third, Mr. Smith enters into a new intimate relationship that, on actual or threatened dissolution, causes him intense distress, a recurrence of depressive and dissociative symptoms, and automatistic violence.

The first two scenarios have the highest likelihood of occurrence, but the lowest likelihood of causing serious harm (although it is always possible that a minor verbal or physical altercation could escalate into serious violence). Also, there may be few warning signs for violence arising out of these scenarios. In contrast, the third scenario may have the highest likelihood of serious harm, but several events may warn of impending violence (e.g., establishment of and instability in a new intimate relationship, recurrence of depressive symptomatology).

The primary factors related to Mr. Smith's violence risk stem directly from his mental disorder, and the most appropriate strategy to manage his violence risk is to arrange for adequate monitoring and treatment of his mental disorder. Mr. Smith does not appear to be at risk for sexual violence or for nonviolent criminality, and there is no evidence that he has other criminogenic needs (e.g., substance use, antisocial attitudes) that should be addressed through correctional treatment.

Accordingly, I recommend the following: Mr. Smith's release into the community should be contingent on developing a suitable program for monitoring and treating his psychiatric symptomatology. To this end, he should be encouraged to establish a treatment relationship with a non-DOC mental health professional. The mental health professional should be required to report Mr. Smith's attendance to DOC staff, and to inform staff should Mr. Smith become an imminent risk for violence; other aspects of his treatment should remain confidential.

1. If a program similar to that described above is in place and functioning adequately, Mr. Smith's community supervision should be of low intensity. Given his general mistrust of DOC staff, frequent supervision is likely to interfere with rather than assist his reintegration. I would encourage his Parole Officer to consider alternatives to direct, face-to-face supervision (such as telephonic supervision, regular reports from employers or associates, and so forth).

2. Mr. Smith's violence risk should be reevaluated immediately if (a) his psychiatric symptoms become markedly worse, according to either his treatment provider or his Parole Officer, (b) he terminates his relationship with his treatment provider, or (c) he enters into or terminates an intimate relationship.

Please do not hesitate to contact me if I can be of further assistance.

Stephen D. Hart, Ph.D.
Psychologist

Teaching Point: **What are the advantages and disadvantages of using actuarial approaches in risk assessment in forensic contexts?**

The hallmark of the actuarial approach is that, based on the information available to them, evaluators make an ultimate decision according to fixed and explicit rules (Meehl, 1954). It is also generally the case that actuarial decisions are based on specific assessment data, selected because they have been empirically demonstrated to be associated with violence and coded in a predetermined manner. The actuarial approach also has been described as "mechanical" and "algorithmic" (Grove & Meehl, 1996, p. 293).

Although there have been few direct comparisons of the two approaches, there is little doubt that the actuarial approach is superior to unstructured clinical judgment with respect to the reliability (consistency) and validity (accuracy) of decisions regarding violence risk, as well as with respect to specification of the foundation for those decisions (Monahan, 1981). But to make these improvements, actuarial decision making must be procrustean, severely limiting the types of information that can be considered and the types of questions addressed as part of the risk assessment.

A number of limitations of actuarial instruments have been identified (Hart, 1998; Monahan, 1981). First, they tend to focus the evaluation on a small number of risk factors that are thought to predict violence across individuals and settings, thus ignoring factors that may be important but idiosyncratic to the case at hand. Second, they tend to focus attention on (relatively) static or stable features of individuals, such as demographics and criminal history. As a result, actuarial assessments are often passive predictions of limited practical use. How do the results of actuarial tests help clinicians to make treatment or management decisions? Third, especially when their construction is based on empirical research, actuarial instruments may include risk factors that are unacceptable on legal grounds (e.g., sex, race) and exclude factors that are entirely logical but of unknown validity (e.g., threats of violence). Fourth, actuarial instruments constructed using an empirical approach are "high-fidelity" predictors: they are optimized to predict a specific outcome over a specific period of time in a specific population. Without conducting new research, there is no way to ensure that their reliability and validity will generalize to new evaluation contexts. Fifth, actuarial tests have a very restricted definition of violence risk. Typically, risk is defined as the likelihood that an individual will commit an act of criminal violence during some specific period of time. This definition is not concerned with other practically and legally relevant facets of violence risk, such as what kind of violence might occur (nature), what the physical or psychological consequences might be (severity), how often or for how long the violence might occur (frequency or duration), and how soon the violence might occur (imminence). Finally, unless evaluators are sufficiently schooled in psychometric theory to have a healthy respect for (and skepticism of) test data, professionals may tend to grossly over- or underutilize actuarial test findings when making decisions about individuals.

The limitations of actuarial tests are apparent in the case of Mr. Smith. Although the information provided by the VRAG, an actuarial test, is highly specific ("people with scores in that category had a violent recidivism rate of 8% over 7 years and 10% over 10 years postrelease"), it does not help us determine what kinds of violence might occur and why, or what factors might increase or decrease that risk. Neither is there any way of reassuring Parole Board members that the test results are accurate in this particular case. Such information must come from unstructured professional judgment or structured professional judgment (e.g., the results of the SARA and HCR-20). Of course, the problem with the judgment-based approaches is that they are inherently speculative.

The obvious conclusion is that, properly constructed, actuarial tests can play an important role in violence risk assessment. Evaluators who are aware of the limitations of test data (i.e., are familiar with research on the construction, reliability, and validity of the test) are less likely to attach too much or too little importance to test findings. But actuarial tests cannot provide all the information that is relevant to understanding and managing violence risk.

Chapter 24

Malingering

Malingering—the faking of illness or disability for the purpose of escaping criminal responsibility or obtaining secondary gain—is the focus of the report in this chapter. The principle associated with the case—use case-specific (idiographic) evidence in assessing clinical condition, functional abilities, and causal connection—addresses the importance of gathering information specific to the case and the individual to increase accuracy when assessing the relevant domains in forensic mental health assessment. The teaching point provides a more specific discussion on the use of idiographic evidence as it pertains to the assessment of malingering in forensic assessment.

Case 1

Principle: **Use case-specific (idiographic) evidence in assessing clinical condition, functional abilities, and causal connection**

This principle is discussed in chapter 2. Therefore, we turn to the question of how the present report illustrates the application of this principle.

In this case, the forensic clinician was asked to determine whether the individual being evaluated, Ellen T, an attorney, was disabled according to the terms of her Complete Life disability insurance policy. As the report indicates, Ms. T's insurance policy provided that she would be declared disabled if she was "unable to perform the substantial and material duties of her occupation in the usual and customary way." Accordingly, in this case the forensic clinician had to assess whether Ms. T's reported cognitive deficits and other psychological symptoms rendered her disabled based on the above definition. As part of the evaluation, the forensic clinician evaluated Ms. T to determine if she was malingering her reported cognitive deficits (possibly in an effort to obtain secondary financial gain from her insurance company).[1] As will be discussed further, the forensic clinician used idiographic data, obtained through detailed interviewing and a review of case-specific documents, to determine if Ms. T was malingering her reported cognitive deficits. Part of this analysis required the forensic clinician to examine the relationship between Ms. T's reported cognitive deficits and other case-specific information (e.g., the results of clinical interviewing). Significant inconsistences between Ms. T's self-reported cognitive deficits and the results of the clinical interview, for example, would provide support for the hypothesis that Ms. T was malingering.

In this case, the forensic clinician provided a detailed history of Ms. T across several psychosocial domains (e.g., family, education, employment, medical/psychiatric, military). The historical information was obtained partially from a lengthy interview with Ms. T and partially from a review of relevant documents. Of particular importance in this case was the historical information regarding Ms. T's past psychological functioning and her performance on psychological tests that had been previously administered. This information provided important idiographic evidence that was relevant to the issue being addressed (i.e., whether Ms. T was malingering).

For example, the results of previous neuropsychological and intelligence testing conducted by Dr. Womack suggested that Ms. T was exaggerating her reported cognitive deficits. Specifically, Dr. Womack concluded that her performance on the Victoria Symptom Validity Test was "so blatantly faked that there is no doubt that she was intentionally performing poorly in attempting to appear far more impaired than she actually is." Dr. Womack also concluded that Ms. T's Full Scale IQ score of 104 on the Wechsler Adult Intelligence Test-Revised edition was below what might be expected from someone with Ms. T's educational and occupational achievement.

Moreover, the results of previous intellectual and personality testing by Dr. R suggested that Ms. T may be exaggerating her reported cognitive deficits. Specifically, Ms. T's performance on the Kaufman Brief Intelligence Test, on which she scored in the 94th percentile, suggested that Ms. T was functioning intellectually at an extremely high level, which appears to be inconsistent with her subjective complaints regarding cognitive impairment. In addition, Dr. R noted that Ms. T was able to sustain her attention, concentration, and perseverance during the administration of the lengthy Minnesota Multiphasic Personality Inventory, 2nd edition, which, again, appears to be inconsistent with her self-reported cognitive impairment.

In addition to providing a detailed psychosocial history, the forensic clinician gathered a significant amount of information regarding Ms. T's current psychological functioning. As with the historical information, the forensic clinician used this information to help determine if Ms. T was malingering her symptoms. The forensic clinician concluded that Ms. T's ability to sustain her concentration during the 7½-hour interview was inconsistent with her reported cognitive deficits.

The forensic clinician also focused on Ms. T's possible motive for obtaining secondary financial gain. After reviewing case-specific information, the forensic clinician concluded that Ms. T had a substantial financial motive to malinger cognitive deficits to receive disability benefits. For example, the forensic clinician noted that Ms. T experienced significant financial problems from 1996 to 1998. He also noted that Ms. T was sued successfully several times by 1997 and, as a result, owed substantial sums of money on those judgments. The forensic clinician further indicated that Ms. T unsuccessfully filed for bankruptcy in 1999, adding that her disability income would be protected from her creditors if she were ever able to declare bankruptcy successfully. Finally, the forensic clinician noted that Ms. T would receive a tax-free sum of approximately $275,000 per year in disability payments if she were determined to be disabled under her current disability insurance policy. The forensic clinician noted that this amount is substantially more than Ms. T had been earning as an attorney.

Based on the idiographic evidence discussed above, the forensic clinician concluded that Ms. T was malingering her reported cognitive impairment and, therefore, did not have a mental illness that resulted in her being unable to perform the substantial and material duties of being an attorney in the usual and customary way.

June 6, 2000
Ms. Melissa A
[address]
Re: Ellen T
Dear Ms. A:

At your request I performed a psychiatric evaluation of Ellen T for the purpose of assessing whether she was disabled according to the terms of her disability insurance policy. Her policy states that she is disabled "if she is unable to perform the substantial and material duties of her occupation in the usual and customary way. . . . " Ms. T is a 53-year-old white, partnered attorney.

SOURCES OF INFORMATION

1. Interview with Ms. T on 5/1/2000 for 7-1/2 hours.
2. Records of Dr. B, internist. Records of Barbara B, Ph.D.
3. 9/28/98 Letter from Barbara B to VA Regional Office.
4. 10/4/98 Letter from Barbara B to Mr. C.
5. 7/20/98 Letter from Dr. B to Mr. C.
6. 2/16/99 Letter from Dr. B to Dept. of Social Services, State of California.
7. 6/23/99 Letter from Dr. B to Barbara D (vocational rehabilitation specialist).
8. Records of Tracy E, M.D.
9. 10/2/97 Claimant's statement for disability benefits.
10. Records of Dr. S F.
11. Records of G, M.D.
12. Parker H and J, OB/GYN Group Records.
13. Records of Professional Podiatry Group/ Dr. Sherwin F.
14. Records of Tye K, M.D.
15. Records of Enrique L, M.D.
16. Records of Amy H, M.D.
17. Records of Alan M, M.D.
18. Records of Ted N, Ph.D.
19. Records of Anton VA hospital.
20. Records from Blue Cross of California, small group service.
21. Complete Veterans Administration records.
22. Correspondence with the California state bar on disciplinary actions against Ms. T.
23. 4/26/98 Psychiatric evaluation of Ellen T by Dr. Alan O addressed to Mr. C.
24. 5/16/98, 8/22/98, 9/4/98, 9/14/98 Letters to Mr. C by Dr. O.
25. 4/22/98, 5/18/98 Reports of Lynette P, Ph.D.

26. 9/25/98 Letter by Lynette P, Ph.D.
27. 7/24/98 Vietnam Nurse Veteran Psycho-physiology Study Record on Ellen T.
28. 2/3/99 Psychiatric Evaluation by Jack Q, M.D.
29. 2/8/99 Social Security Daily Activities questionnaire.
30. 2/18/99 Daily Activities Questionnaire Completed by V R.
31. 1999 Social Security Administration letter.
32. Psychiatric disability case management log regarding Ellen T (multiple dates), mostly by Mr. C.
33. Records of U.S. Bankruptcy Court regarding Ellen T.
34. Records of continuing legal education of Ms. T.
35. 10/6/97 Insurance Disability Form of occupational information completed by Ms. T.
36. Choice Claim Insurance Services Reports on Ellen T dated 11/14/97, 2/9/98, 2/20/98, 3/20/98, and 11/14/97.
37. National Law journal article dated 9/20/93 regarding settlement of a suit by V R.
38. 1/13/98 letter to David S from V R including Ellen T's 1996 income tax return.
39. 1/13/98 letter to Ms. U by V R.
40. 2/4/98 letter to Ms. U by V R.
41. 3/2/98 letter to Mr. S by V R.
42. 4/29/98 Clinician referral form to Michelle V from David S.
43. May, 1998 *Monitor* Newspaper article entitled "Older Vets Just Now Feeling Pain of War."
44. 6/19/98 letter to Mr. W by Ellen T.
45. 8/28/98 fax of Tokyo *Times* article titled "Retired from Work but not Community."
46. 8/20/98 letter to Mr. W from Ellen T.
47. 6/20/98 letter to Mr. W from Ellen T.
48. 9/8/98 letter to Larry from David X, Ph.D.
49. 10/5/98 letter from V R to Linda Y.
50. 11/24/97 Psychiatric Case Manager Report review by Michelle V, LCSW.
51. Breen investigation of Ellen T dated 3/20/98.
52. Field referral report dated 11/6/97.
53. 1/19/98 Psychiatric assessment form for Paul Z by psychiatrist, Tracy E, M.D.
54. 12/5/97 and 8/17/98 Letters by Dr. S.
55. 3/18/98 Letter to Dr. O from Mr. C
56. 4/29/98 Mason report on MMPI-II referred by Lynette P, Ph.D.
57. 4/21/98 Notes of phone call by Dr. O to Dr. B.
58. 1/5/95: Letter to Dr. Smith from ITT Local Insurance Co.
59. Wounded Healers: A Summary of the Vietnam Nurse Veteran Project by Elizabeth Paul in *Military Medicine*, Vol. 150, 1985.
60. Summary of documents regarding employment search.
61. 3/20–27/98 16-minute surveillance film of Ellen T.
62. 4/26/00 Neuropsychological report of Dr. Charles Womack.

QUALIFICATIONS OF THE EXAMINER

I am enclosing a copy of my curriculum vitae, which states my qualifications to perform this examination.

STATEMENT OF NONCONFIDENTIALITY

Ms. T understood that I was employed by attorneys for the Complete Insurance Company she was suing. She understood that what she told me was not confidential. She agreed to proceed. Both Ms. T and I separately tape recorded the interview.

PERSONAL HISTORY

Ms. T reported she was born 8/5/47 in North Dakota. She is the youngest of four children. Her brothers are respectively 18, 12, and 5 years older than she. Ms. T reported that her father died in 1965, at age 66, when she was 18 years old. She described him as "very outgoing, likeable, and self-educated." She said that he had a great sense of humor. She added that she "got along great with him."

Ms. T reported that her mother died at age 92, on October 1, 1999. Her mother had polio when she was 39 years old and was a paraplegic in a wheelchair throughout Ms. T's life. In fact, the first 15 months of her life, Ms. T was raised by a cousin because of her mother's physical limitations. Ms. T described her mother as "a difficult, very strong-willed woman who was not particularly kind." She said she was "strong, strong, strong." Ms. T indicated that she had a difficult relationship with her mother when she was a young person, but as she grew up she learned to love and respect her mother.

FAMILY HISTORY

Ms. T reported no psychiatric illness in her family.

EDUCATIONAL AND EMPLOYMENT HISTORY

Ms. T reported that she had a difficult time in elementary school because of her relationship with her mother. By the time she was in sixth grade, she liked her teacher and she did well. She had friends in school. She was hardworking in school and had about B+ grades.

She went to City College in Milwaukee, and then transferred to the University of Dakota. She chose nursing because she "liked people and science." She obtained her bachelor's degree in the science of nursing (BSN) in 1969. After 2 years as an army nurse, she went to graduate school and obtained her master's degree in nursing at the University of Missouri. She majored in psychiatric nursing with the goal of providing primary prevention in a mental health clinic setting. She said that she had seen enough "hands-on nursing care" in Vietnam for a lifetime.

Ms. T said that she taught psychiatric nursing in North Dakota from 1974 to 1975. She supervised clinical nurses on inpatient psychiatric wards. She had experience treating patients with depression, but she said that she did not have experience in the treatment of posttraumatic stress disorder (PTSD). Ms. T then moved to teach at the University of Arizona from 1975 to 1978. She was promoted to the head of psychiatric nursing teaching.

Ms. T attended law school from 1978 to 1981 at Legalese University in California. She reported that she did very well in law school. She won awards in moot court competition, in writing, and arguing. She clerked for 6 months.

Ms. T reported that she then went to work for a malpractice defense firm for about 3 years until she went into a solo law practice in 1985. She left the firm because she did not accomplish the advancement that she had hoped to achieve. She felt undervalued there and wanted to make more money. She had also developed a good relationship with a malpractice carrier.

Ms. T worked as a solo practitioner doing civil litigation from 1985 until she became "disabled" in 1997. She did mostly plaintiff's medical malpractice work, but she did an occasional defense case. She also did some business law, toxic torts, and "slip and fall" cases. She stated she had a very successful practice earning $150,000 to $450,000 per year. She said that she loved the work. She enjoyed "the fight and to win." Ms. T was hard to pin down on how much actual trial work she did, but she endorsed the number of about one to five trials or arbitrations each year.

When I asked Ms. T about any financial difficulties, she initially replied that she did not have financial difficulties because her income was good. In fact, she said that 1996 was a good year. When I asked specifically about the foreclosure on her condominium on Street Road, she replied that she let that go back to the bank because the value was less than the mortgage. She said that it was a business decision and not due to any financial problems in her life. On further inquiry, she indicated that she was unable to pay back a line of credit to the bank. The bank sued her and she had begun to make some payments before she became "disabled." She indicated that the difficulty keeping up with payments on the line of credit may have occurred before 1996 due to a year of poor income. She said that her finances were not particularly stressful because, "I thought I'd come out of it."

RELIGIOUS HISTORY

Ms. T stated that she was raised as a Catholic but did not go to parochial school. She got away from her religion during graduate school but returned to religion 2 years ago. She went to a Catholic faith group called "Landings" and a faith-sharing group. She goes to church weekly now. She said that when she was depressed after "falling off my perch," she reached out for religion.

RELATIONSHIP HISTORY

Ms. T reported that she viewed herself as heterosexual until she was 26. She did some dating in high school and was "looking for a guy." She had a 1-year relationship and a marriage offer from one man. While in Vietnam, she fell in love with a married doctor who had two children. This led to her pregnancy and a therapeutic abortion. At the time, she did not want her life disrupted and she did not want to raise a child alone. She has had moral qualms about her decision, particularly in 1982. When she became depressed in 1997, she did not ruminate about her abortion decision.

Ms. T reported that at age 26 she had a dream and concluded that she was attracted to women. She had a serious 7-year relationship with a woman named Alice. Within 6 to 12 months after that relationship ended, she began a sustained monogamous relationship with her current domestic partner, V R. She described her relationship with V as "the best thing that ever happened to me." She said that they have a "beautiful love" together. She commented that they share a strong work ethic, enjoyment of travel, and culture. When I inquired about whether she perceived either of them as dominant, she said that dominance gets switched around depending on the strength of the individual in a particular area. I inquired about any problems in their relationship. She said that the litigation resulting from her leaving her law firm in 1985 was quite stressful to their relationship. She added that her recent disability and financial stresses have tested their relationship; V had never been in the role of a caregiver before.

MEDICAL HISTORY

Ms. T reported that she had a tonsillectomy as a child. In Vietnam she had a back injury resulting in a hospitalization for a few days. In 1992 she had foot surgery due to "hammer toes" and she had a bilateral bunionectomy. She also had a fibroidectomy in 1992. She was placed on Premarin and Provera for menopausal symptoms. She now takes Premarin and Prometrium. She indicated that she had no other significant illnesses and that she had never had any head trauma.

CURRENT MEDICATIONS

Ms. T reported that she is currently taking Wellbutrin 75 mg twice a day. She was prescribed Xanax as necessary, but she took it "only a few times." She stated that the Xanax was "too good." Ms. T also takes Premarin, Promethium, and vitamins.

MILITARY HISTORY

Ms. T reported that she was a Second Lieutenant when she entered the army in 1969 as a nurse. She had not expected the Vietnam war to continue as long as it did when she joined the army. She was initially assigned to Norman Army Hospital in Denver, Colorado, and then spent 11 months in Vietnam. She was assigned to Ft. Riley, Kansas, after Vietnam. She achieved the rank of First Lieutenant before her discharge.

In Vietnam, she was assigned to the 71st evacuation hospital in Pleiku in the Central Highlands. She worked 12-hour shifts, 6 days a week, except during the Cambodian offensive when she worked 7 days a week. She alternated day and night shifts. She spent about 4 months in the emergency room and 7 months on a primarily surgical ward. There was not adequate staffing at the hospital. On one occasion during a shift, she and one corpsman were responsible for 53 patients with IVs. The hospital contained primarily U.S. soldiers, but they took care of some Vietnamese patients, prisoners of war, and even a premature baby.

Ms. T described a number of stressful events in Vietnam. She stated it was upsetting to see traumatic war injuries. She felt helpless and inexperienced in dealing with some major injuries. She was tearful in describing some of her Vietnam experiences. She found it hard to meet her professional responsibilities and deal with her emotions about young people being severely injured and killed. She was upset by seeing dead bodies in body bags. She was overwhelmed at times.

When the hospital went on "red alert," nurses had the duty to protect patients. They were supposed to get patients under their beds if they could; if not, they put mattresses over them. If nurses were off duty, they got under their own beds. Incoming rockets sometimes were aimed at a headquarters building that was near the hospital. On one occasion she saw a plane explode nearby. She got under a small cocktail table. She had to take a defensive posture "many times." The hospital was never actually struck by rockets, but she stated that she never felt safe. She pointed out that women were not issued a weapon. When they went off base, they only went with armed soldiers. She had heard about one nurse who was killed by shrapnel in Vietnam, but she did not know her personally.

Ms. T indicated that it was difficult to trust the South Vietnamese who worked in the hospital. There was stealing in the hospital that was presumed to be by the South Vietnamese. She felt a general foreboding and uneasiness throughout her tour in Vietnam.

In the emergency room she saw people with head injuries who "moaned." She had some responsibility for triage. She recalled one individual who gave her his peace beads and wanted her to be with him before he went to surgery. Because she was so busy, she could not take the time to talk with him. She feels like she failed him. He did not make it out of surgery. She has kept his peace beads. On another occasion Ms. T went into the "morgue hooch" and saw a black man with "horror" on his dead face. One of his limbs was blown off.

Once Ms. T felt a rat next to her foot in bed. She involuntarily kicked her foot and it scurried away. The rat seemed "huge" to her. She said, "It scared me to death." She stated that she slept with the lights on for 3 weeks after that. She was not actually bitten or attacked by the rat. She never experienced any other rats other than the one that was in her bed. However, she had an awareness of rats, since at times she had to lay under her bed when there were incoming rockets.

Ms. T reported that whenever helicopters came in, she dreaded it because it meant new casualties. She stated that the entire physical experience in Vietnam was "pretty bad, especially for a woman." On one occasion she "blew bugs off her tooth brush." She also believed that women were "leaned on" by the soldiers as culture bearers and representatives of home.

LEGAL HISTORY

Ms. T reported that she had never been arrested. She has been named in a number of lawsuits. She volunteered that she was sued by Dr. M. He was a treating doctor in a case in which he was not paid. She believed that she did nothing wrong. She stated that in another lawsuit against her by

Mr. and Mrs. Jones, she prevailed in a jury verdict. She said that she made an error in a third case by failing to file by the time of the deadline. Her insurance carrier settled the suit out of court.

Ms. T added that she was sued by a bank, but she could not recall the year. She said she was sued by business entities and a former tenant. She indicated she was also sued for nonpayment on a piece of property she owned in Hawaii. She said that the bank was foreclosing, and she expected to lose that property. She did not recall being behind in her payments on the Hawaii property before she became disabled. In addition, Ms. T reported a lawsuit by a publisher in a dispute about law books, and a lawsuit by the computer company over a disagreement.

Ms. T also recalled that an expert witness, Dr. Foreman, complained about her in a lawsuit. She believed that he reneged on an agreement to testify and she therefore stopped payment on his check.

When I jogged her memory about a Mr. S, Ms. T stated that he made a state bar claim against her. She said that he was a gay man who panicked near his trial and made inappropriate demands. He did not want to accept a $90,000 settlement, which she thought was fair. There was also a dispute over some of her travel expenses that were "mixed up." He believed that Ms. T breached his confidentiality by revealing his sexual identity and psychological condition to another attorney. Ms. T reported that she was quite distressed that she could not get control of him. He refused to make a court appearance and it was "a huge mess." She received a letter from the California Bar Association warning her about her conduct. She recalled that this warning letter came shortly before her June 24, 1997, appointment with Dr. Barbara B. She said that could have been one of the things that triggered her upset and "pushed me over the edge." On inquiry, she said she believed that she had no more than the ordinary number of lawsuits against her for a solo practitioner.

PSYCHIATRIC HISTORY

Ms. T reported that she was quite upset when she lost her father at age 18. She believed that she adjusted to it by "throwing myself into my school work." On further questioning, Ms. T described ordinary bereavement rather than any true depression at that time.

Ms. T reported that at age 26, when she discovered her homosexual orientation, she went for one or two visits to a University Health Service therapist. She was quite worried at first, but then felt relief because she thought that this was really right for her.

Ms. T reported that in the early 1990s (actually 1985), due to stress with her partner, V R, she sought support from psychologist Dr. Barbara B. She said that she went to some sessions together with V and to some individual sessions. She was concerned that the public disclosure of her lesbian orientation would interfere with how juries and judges perceived her. She stated that her sexual orientation had been "in the closet" throughout law school. It was known by members of her law firm but not by her clients. She reported that she sought therapy at that time primarily because she wanted direction in how to be more supportive to V. She believed that the therapy was quite helpful. She developed insight into the different coping styles that she and V had.

Ms. T reported a number of symptoms related to her Vietnam experience. She said that ever since her experience in Vietnam in 1970–1971, she became upset when helicopters flew overhead. She recalled an incident when she was on her way to law school in 1979. She was driving on a freeway when she reacted to a helicopter with panicky feelings and a racing heart. She had to pull over. Ordinarily when she sees helicopters, it takes her back to feelings she had in Vietnam and she becomes distracted.

Ms. T mentioned that when a car backfired while she was in law school, she reacted as if shots had been fired because it reminded her of Vietnam. She pulled over and pushed her passenger's head down to avoid being shot.

Ms. T reported that since her Vietnam experience she has felt different with people. She is less trusting. Before her Vietnam experience she stated that she "liked a good time and was a good time." Since her Vietnam experience she said that she is less able to get close to people. She feels more emotionally isolated.

Ms. T also described some experiences since Vietnam in which she felt that what was happening to her was "unreal." She found it hard to quantify how often this happened, but she stated that it did not interfere with her life. Since her Vietnam experience, Ms. T said that she was more conscious of death and mortality. She is grateful to be alive each day.

Ms. T reported having some dreams that related to Vietnam over the years. She recalled having only a handful of such dreams from 1971 to 1997. Some dreams involved rats scurrying around her when she was hiding under her bed during a rocket attack. In her dream she was terrified that they would get her. She had the sensation of rats touching her skin while she was on the floor. There were more rats, and she could not scare them off. When she woke up she would be anxious and usually unable to return to sleep. She did not know if she had body movement during her Vietnam dreams. She explained that her partner, V, was a sound sleeper. Furthermore, she is generally a restless sleeper so that her sheets might be in disarray even without a nightmare.

Ms. T reported another dream related to her emergency room responsibilities in Vietnam. She was feeling helpless, and it replicated what happened in Vietnam. This dream did not have any variation. She also reported a dream that replicated the soldier giving her the "peace beads" to keep. She had a few dreams of seeing rows of body bags. She also had a few dreams of the dead black man with horror on his face who she had seen in the morgue. She said that the dreams caused her to be reflective, but they did not cause her concern. Ms. T reported that since her Vietnam experience, she had been a restless sleeper.

After Ms. T had lunch with her partner, V, during my interview; she came back and reported that she had rethought the phenomena of dreams. She then stated that rather than these being dreams they were probably recurrent thoughts that she had experienced. She said that she had not viewed the above noted changes in her since Vietnam as a problem. They did not interfere with her life before June 1997.

Ms. T reported undergoing a number of stressors since 1995. She said that in 1995 or 1996 her mother became debilitated and moved into a nursing home. Her brother developed cancer. Ms. T also became somewhat moody due to menopausal changes before she was given hormones.

Ms. T reported that she became more tired in December 1996 and did not feel refreshed after sleep. She said that she was working fine then. She did not recall feeling clinically depressed until June 1997.

Ms. T reported that when she was given Desyrel in December 1996 (by Dr. S), she thought it was for sleep rather than for its antidepressant effect. From December 1996 until June 1997, Ms. T said that even though she had more to cope with, she believed that she was handling it. She stated that V's ex-son-in-law was ill with cancer and died in February 1997. She said that both she and V were close to V's granddaughter, T, who was being raised by V's ex-son-in-law. They even considered the possibility of taking T into their home. T made a suicide attempt by hanging in March 1997. This was quite upsetting to Ms. T because she viewed it as a serious attempt. They notified T's school staff who got T to see a psychiatrist. T was then moved out of her paternal grandparents' home into a foster home.

Ms. T reported that between December 1996 and June 1997 she also had a series of problems with clients. Two of her cases went badly, and she lost expected fees from those cases. In addition, she was sued by Mr. S and Mr. J. She stated that this "streak of bad luck" caused her to "lose my confidence." She said that things were beginning to get out of her control. She explained that she did not believe that she was depressed because she was still coping. On inquiry, she stated that she did not begin to doubt her choice of the profession of law.

Ms. T reported that she had a single suicidal thought and impulse. She initially thought that she had it in December 1996, but on reflection, she said it occurred in June 1997. While driving on the freeway she had an impulse to switch lanes to cause a head-on crash to end her life. She was fearful that she would not be able to control the impulse if it occurred again. Ms. T was clear in her recollection that this was the only time that she experienced a suicidal thought.

Ms. T said that 1 or 2 days before her 6/24/97 visit with Dr. Barbara B, "I blew out one day." She indicated that what she meant by this was that she could not read something or type something. She felt overwhelmed and "deeply depressed." She said, "I fell off my perch, or into a hole." She felt like she couldn't handle anything.

Ms. T stated that her feelings of depression seemed "all of a sudden" to her. After discussing events with V R at lunch on the day of my evaluation, Ms. T added that she had a better recollection of the precipitating events. She felt overwhelmed by having papers served on her in the Jones suit shortly after she received a warning letter from the California Bar Association.

Ms. T reported that she lost her confidence. She said that the effect of losing her confidence was that she found it hard "to take a risk in a timed situation." She found it hard to put herself out to "create a client opportunity." She lost her alertness to those situations in which she could generate new business.

In June 1997, Ms. T realized that she was depressed because of her increased problems sleeping, suddenly feeling "deeply sad," feeling demoralized and defeated, and having her suicidal thought. She explained that once she acknowledged that she was having problems, "I just deteriorated."

Ms. T said that in her depression she had difficulty focusing, concentrating, and thinking. She became concerned that she could not meet her responsibilities. In July and August 1997, she transferred her clients to other attorneys and did not take new clients.

Ms. T reported that her symptoms included feeling extremely tired and "emotional lability." Ms. T added that she didn't care about her clients or her practice. She had great difficulty doing tasks. She lost interest in her usual activities, such as gardening, genealogy, and reading. At some point she lost her appetite and her taste for food. When she woke up during the night she was unable to go back to sleep.

Ms. T also reported a number of anxiety symptoms, but she was unclear when they began. She indicated that her depression was dominant initially. Her anxiety symptoms included nervousness, panic attacks, and shakiness. She said that her handwriting changed. At my request, she wrote a sentence as a writing sample and said that it was better than she usually wrote.

Ms. T reported that she "reacted adversely to confrontation." For example, once when she was in court, she was so intimidated that she did not speak up. She did not speak up because the judge had yelled at the attorney ahead of her. She said this was quite unusual for her. This confirmed to her that she was going through "something serious." Her failure to speak up resulted in her client not getting a continuance.

Ms. T reported that she did not respond to things set out for her by her secretary. She stated that she was quite distracted: "I was forgetting things." She said that the things that most interfered with her ability to practice law were her inability to concentrate, to think, and to remember things. She added that she felt helpless and overwhelmed.

I asked Ms. T why she declined to take antidepressants on July 1, 1997, when they were offered by Dr. S. She replied that she generally was receptive to medical care and did not recall why she refused.

When I asked Ms. T explicitly about her anxiety symptoms, she replied that she had difficulty concentrating and a short attention span. She said that she was not able to watch a TV show through or read a paper. She said she got distracted easily. She had palpitations and periods where her "mind goes blank." She gave as an example a time that she was yelled at by a client's husband. She stated that her mind went blank and she hung up. She said she had panic attacks manifested by periods of clamminess, pounding heart, inability to see clearly, her mind going blank, and shakiness. She reported that she leaps in response to noises because she startles easily.

She described the shaking of her hands, which interfered with her ability to use a fork in a restaurant. Ms. T volunteered that she had spilled her cereal this morning. I asked Ms. T to rate the current degree of shakiness of her hands on a scale of 1 to 10, with 10 being the worst. She replied that she would rate herself a 7 today. (I examined her hands for tremor and I found a very slight tremor that was within the range of normal.)

When I asked Ms. T about other symptoms, she replied that due to her memory loss she mixed up dates and numbers. She forgot things as fast as people told them to her. "I can't hang on to information." She had trouble making appointments. "I'm not reliable. I can't do more than one thing at a time. I can't prioritize. I give equal weight to doing different things." Ms. T added that she had developed some coping mechanisms for her memory problems. She writes things down and prints out schedules. She no longer keeps things in her head.

I asked Ms. T how her inability to handle stress interfered with her work. She replied that she avoided confrontation. She stated that she had been advised by Dr. E and Dr. B not to go to court. They were afraid that it may make things worse when she was starting to stabilize. She indicated that she knew she could not handle the confrontation or stress. When she tried, she was not able to focus or listen. She lapsed "into my own thinking." She stated that if she is confronted in an adversarial mode, she "tends to shrink. I clam up." She said that she doesn't rise to the situation. She indicated that on two occasions, "I got myself out of the room." The first time occurred in July 1997 when she failed to speak up just so that she could get a hearing over with. The second time occurred in Fall 1999, when she heard one attorney "barking" at another; she pulled back from the conference.

Ms. T reported that she is a lot better now than she was in June 1997. She said that her depressive symptoms were "markedly better." She added that her panic attacks were less frequent because she didn't expose herself to stressful situations. She stated that her memory is no better but she deals with it better. She said that her concentration "is somewhat better."

I asked Ms. T to prepare a graph showing the course of her (1) depression, (2) anxiety symptoms, and (3) memory and concentration problems from June 1997 to the present. Her graph shows that her depression increased from June 1997 to peak from the fall of 1997 to the spring of 1998. Thereafter, her depressive symptoms went down substantially to a small residual level at the present. She attributed the improvement in her depression to Wellbutrin. She reported that her anxiety symptoms and memory and concentration symptoms improved in the fall of 1998 and then reached a plateau at a moderate level. After reflection, she added a peak after July 1998 when she had participated in a Vietnam nurses PTSD research project in New Hampshire. She indicated that all of her symptoms were worse for a few weeks after that.

CURRENT SYMPTOMS REPORTED BY MS. T

Ms. T reported that currently she has trouble concentrating, problems with her memory, and trouble with focusing. She stated that now when she can't concentrate, she gives up on the activity, whereas before her depression, she would "always push." She volunteered that she had been drained by the day of Dr. Womack's testing because of the amount of concentration required.

Ms. T reported that she continued to have disturbed, restless sleep. She stated that it was not like the sleep pattern she had when she was depressed. She added that her sleep pattern has not fully returned to par, which since Vietnam was a mildly restless sleep.

Ms. T reported that she continued to have difficulty with confrontation and with emotional situations that are stressful. She gave as an example that she had attended a roof inspection and was yelled at by an opposing attorney. She stated that she developed a headache, got upset, felt clammy, and had panicky feelings. "I wanted to run but I could not because I was on a roof."

Ms. T reported that she is often inordinately tired. She added that this "does not fit" because her depression was better. She attributed her tiredness to her PTSD and said it was "part of my healing."

Ms. T stated that she had a nightmare in the last week or two about falling down steps. She also jumped off a couch because of a loud noise. She reported that recently she was reminded of the dead black man she had seen in the hooch morgue by a black Federal Express delivery man.

Ms. T said that she has an inability "to be timely responsive." This involves her difficulty with confrontation and running away from things. She gave an example that she has not even read some papers about foreclosure on her property in Hawaii. She said it was this inability to be reliable that caused her "to hook up with other attorneys."

Ms. T explained, "It's like I'm allergic to litigation." She noted that she was unable to do the things that she used to like doing. She said she was not able to draft papers late at night. She was not able to "control my consistency." She gave as an example of her inability to remember things that she had agreed to review some medical records; by the time she finished, she did not recall what the referral question was.

Ms. T stated, "I can't juggle various cases." She said she could do only one thing to completion at a time. As a solo practitioner, she noted that she must be able to take a case from the beginning to the end: "I can't switch gears at all." She said that she felt sad because she was unable to attend a deposition of one of her clients. She said she was not able to handle things by herself anymore.

Ms. T indicated that she has feelings of depersonalization and derealization on occasion. I asked her if those symptoms interfered with her ability to be a trial attorney. She said it interfered when it occurred. She added that she is not allowing it to occur because she now avoids stressful situations. She viewed her failure in legal situations as similar to her failure to be sufficiently helpful in Vietnam.

I specifically reviewed with Ms. T whether she had the explicit symptoms of a major depressive episode as defined in DSM-IV at the peak of her depressive symptoms in December 1997 and whether she had those symptoms at the current time. Ms. T reported that she had the following symptoms in December 1997: depressed mood most of the day, nearly every day; markedly diminished interest and pleasure in activities; loss of appetite and "loss of 20 to 30 pounds;" insomnia; fatigue; difficulty concentrating, and indecisiveness. She did not endorse feelings of worthlessness or excessive guilt, psychomotor retardation (slowing), recurrent thoughts of death, or recurrent suicidal ideation.

Ms. T stated that at the time of my interview, her depressive symptoms were "markedly improved." She still had some sleep disturbance, but her sleep was better; she felt fatigued and had difficulty concentrating, but it was not as bad. She did not currently endorse depressed mood most of the day, nearly every day; markedly diminished interest or pleasure in activities; loss of appetite; psychomotor retardation; feelings of worthlessness or excessive guilt; or thoughts of death.

I asked Ms. T about whether she had the specific symptoms of PTSD at the time she suffered peak distress from those symptoms (after July 1998) and whether she had those symptoms currently. She stated that she witnessed events in Vietnam in which she felt physically threatened and she responded with intense fear, helplessness, and horror. She indicated that she had the following symptoms during the peak of her PTSD: recurrent and intrusive distressing recollections of her Vietnam experiences three to five times a month; occasional recurrent distressing dreams of Vietnam events; occasional flashbacks; intense psychological distress at reminders of Vietnam, such as seeing a helicopter; physiologic reactivity (racing heart, clammy feeling) on exposure to reminders of Vietnam; efforts to avoid thoughts about Vietnam; efforts to avoid activities that remind her of Vietnam, such as going to a Veterans group; inability to recall an important aspect of a trauma, such as which limb was blown off the black man in the morgue; markedly diminished interest in activities (this overlaps with loss of interest due to depression); feelings of detachment from others ever since she returned from Vietnam; restless sleep ever since she returned from Vietnam; irritability ever since she returned from Vietnam; difficulty concentrating only since June 1997; and an exaggerated startle response since she returned from Vietnam, which has been worse since the summer of 1997.

Ms. T reported that she had the following PTSD symptoms currently: flashbacks at seeing a helicopter; intense psychological distress and intense physiologic reactivity to reminders of Vietnam, such as a helicopter; efforts to avoid activities that cause recollections of Vietnam; inability to recall an important aspect of a trauma; feelings of detachment from others; disturbance of her sleep; irritability; and difficulty concentrating. I asked Ms. T which of her residual symptoms of PTSD actually interfered with her ability to practice as a trial attorney. She replied that the only symptoms that interfered were her irritability and difficulty concentrating. She had been successful as a practicing trial attorney in spite of some irritability ever since Vietnam, but she stated that she had experienced an increase in her irritability in 1997.

I asked Ms. T if she had the specific symptoms listed in the *DSM-IV* criteria for panic attacks. Ms. T replied that she did have discrete periods of intense discomfort that developed abruptly in response to some upsetting event or stressor and reached a peak within 10 minutes. During these episodes she reported having the following symptoms: palpitations, sweating, shaking, hyperventilation, feeling of choking, rarely chest discomfort, rarely nausea, feelings of dizziness, derealization, and fear of losing control. Ms. T said that she did not have unexpected panic attacks. She did not

report anxiety about being in places or situations from which escape might be difficult. She said that she did not have excessive anxiety and worry, but she did worry because of her realistic concerns about finances and her employability.

I asked Ms. T whether she had each of the traits of obsessive-compulsive personality disorder. The only symptom that she partially endorsed was excessive devotion to work. I also inquired about the specific traits of dependent personality disorder; Ms. T endorsed none of them.

CURRENT WORK ACTIVITIES

Ms. T reported that she resumed doing some work as an attorney in December 1998. She worked throughout 1999 and to the present. She stated that she has associated herself with other attorneys, and she splits fees with them. At times she does hourly work for other attorneys. She is now practicing law without doing litigation. She is seeking new cases, preparing cases, doing paperwork, doing research, and preparing motions. She does not do trial work, attend depositions, attend arbitration hearings, or take responsibility for any cases on her own. She said that she has met with some opposing attorneys, but due to a recent upsetting experience, she does not intend to continue it. She did work on an appeal. The appeal was complex, and she has "trouble" doing complex things. She gets things mixed up and transposes numbers. When I asked her if it took her longer to carry out the same tasks, she replied that it wasn't simply a matter of taking longer. Instead, she reminded me that she could not do analysis, she needed supervision, and she was not trustworthy to operate alone. She stated that her 1999 earnings were about $25,000–$27,000 for her legal work, separate from her disability income from the Veterans Administration and Social Security Disability.

INQUIRY ABOUT DISABILITY ISSUES

I asked Ms. T when the thought of applying for disability first crossed her mind. She replied that she thought she would get some psychological help and "I'd get over this." She stated that seeking disability benefits did not enter her mind for quite a while. "I don't know if my doctor suggested it." She said she was surprised by the length of the exclusion period before she became eligible. She didn't recall when she filed for disability. She mentioned having three different disability policies. She said that when she had previously filed for disability for her foot surgery, she found the insurance company "very supportive." I raised a question about whether she had a struggle with her insurance company about the extended period that she could not work; she replied that she did not. She explained that she had some conflict with her medical insurer about paying for extended physical therapy. She said she was surprised by the way her insurance companies handled her claim for disability for her depression. She added, "It depressed me."

I asked Ms. T when she first considered filing for bankruptcy. She replied that it was within a few months of when she actually filed in 1999. She added that she was glad that her bankruptcy filing was dismissed.

I asked Ms. T when she took out her disability insurance policies. She was rather uncertain in her answers. She thought she took out the Complete policy in the mid-'80s, and the Z policy in 1992. She stated that the Trust National policy was old. She could not recall when she took out the G policy. When I asked her if she sought any additional disability policies since 1993, she replied, "I don't think so." She then said she might have obtained the G policy since then. I asked her why she sought an additional policy in 1994 or 1995. She did not recall seeking a new policy, but she said that the only reason she bought disability policies was that she was "pushed by brokers." She added that she did seek an increase in policy limits as her income went up.

I asked Ms. T about her statement to Dr. O that she no longer was driving during her examination by him. She said that she never said that she had stopped driving. Instead she suggested a misunderstanding by him because she referred to not driving some of the time.

Ms. T was questioned about whether she saw people as "scary and intimidating." She replied that she saw people as scary if they were confrontational or aggressive. I asked Ms. T if she questioned each decision she made. She stated that she had less indecisiveness now than she did 6 months ago, but that she still had a lot. She added that she had much more confidence now.

I asked Ms. T whether she saw (1) her cognitive deficits or (2) her inability to tolerate stress as more of a problem for her in practicing as a trial attorney. She replied that she was more troubled by her intolerance of stress, but she indicated that she saw each as a fatal flaw.

I asked Ms. T whether she would agree to have blood drawn so that I could check the level of her Wellbutrin. She said she would not submit unless a judge ordered her to do so.

I asked Ms. T why she sought the names of the psychological tests that were to be administered by Dr. Charles Womack. She replied that her attorney had sought the names of the tests, not she. She thought it was done to see if they were the same tests that had been administered to her previously. I asked Ms. T whether she knew the criteria for the DSM-IV diagnosis of PTSD. She replied, "Not really."

I questioned Ms. T regarding how she viewed her degree of cognitive impairment when she was administered the KBIT by Lynette P on 3/28/98. She replied that she was "much worse" then than she is now. I asked Ms. T whether she ever consciously exaggerated her cognitive deficits. She replied that she had not.

MENTAL STATUS EXAMINATION

Ms. T was dressed neatly and appropriately. She was friendly and had a firm handshake. She was cooperative during the examination. When I indicated that I was going to be doing a mental status examination toward the end of my 7.5-hour interview with her, Ms. T said, "I'm tired." She volunteered that she was "not good on dates" so that she had some difficulty giving the sequence of her symptoms. Her thoughts were logical, coherent, and free of disjointed thinking. She was oriented to time, place, and person. When asked to name presidents going backward, she replied, "Clinton, Bush, Reagan . . . I don't recall the others." I asked her to subtract serial sevens from 101. She made only a single error by saying that 7 from 24 was 27. She was able to correctly spell the word "world" forward and backward. She could accurately repeat five digits forward and four digits backward. In an effort to repeat six digits forward, she made errors in two out of three trials. She said that she had never experienced hallucinations. She reported no paranoid ideas or concern about conspiracies. She showed no evidence of delusional thinking. When asked how she would describe her mood, she replied, "pretty good, cooperative." She added she was very anxious when she arrived in the morning but was calm by the afternoon. I did not observe any overt manifestations of anxiety. She showed a full range of emotional expression. She was tearful only when talking about upsetting experiences in Vietnam. When asked to recall three objects after a few minutes, she was able to recall two out of the three. She could not recall the third, which was "ball," but she knew it was "something to play with." Her capacity for abstract thinking was tested by giving her a number of proverbs to interpret. She gave abstract answers to most of the proverbs. She reported that she had no current suicidal or homicidal thoughts.

SUMMARY OF RELEVANT DOCUMENTS

10/2/97 Claimant's Statements for Disability Benefits Ms. T gave the following statement of why she is disabled: "Complete physical health required to function in litigation. Need concentration, reasoning, and use of memory for on-the-spot analysis for argument in court and at depositions. Long drives of 1–4 hours to various courts require judgment and attentiveness . . . [I] have lack of attentiveness; poor concentration, poor judgment, confusion, stress symptoms with memory blackout/loss, periods of inability to function, insomnia, anxiety, flashbacks, distractions. Because my job requires complete mental functioning ability, I am seriously impaired to carry out my responsibilities as a trial lawyer. Limitation of driving because of attentiveness and cannot sustain any duration of standing or sitting."

10/6/97 Insurance Disability Form Occupational Information Completed by Ms. T She described the duties of her occupation in order of importance as "court appearances, preparation for court appearances, legal research, depositions, interviewing clients, telephoning other attorneys, preparing and meeting experts, and supervising staff and managing office."

MEDICAL RECORDS OF DR. S

12/15/92: Complaint of decreased libido. Secondary concern was increased fatigue. Patient works long hours.

12/7/95: Patient with moderate fatigue . . . fatigue is manifested by thinking less clearly and being more forgetful. Height 5'9". Weight went from 162 to 170.

11/26/96: The patient has had a very stressful year. She notes that she is tired all the time and she wakens tired after a full night's sleep. The patient denies depression, but is described as having mood swings, forgetful. The patient was less stressed on vacation.

12/11/96: On Desyrel 50 mg per day. ? less fatigue.

7/1/97: Patient very depressed—discussed with Dr. B who feels this is PTSD from Vietnam coupled into a depression from severe pressure, financial reversals having to do with bogus lawsuits against her. The patient is sleeping poorly and awakening early in the morning unable to return to sleep; thoughts of suicide and depersonalization. Patient feels listless, fragmented, and with no satisfaction.

   Meds: Was on Desyrel but disliked the sensation so stopped. She has no desire to take meds. Antidepressants offered but declined. Assessment: Depression.

8/28/97: For depression, Serzone, 150 mg twice a day. Patient remains severely depressed with tearfulness, forgetfulness, sleeping poorly. She overreacts and has temper tantrums. She has developed a tremor. It is difficult for her to concentrate on her work and she is getting further behind and it is harder to focus.

9/26/97: Remains depressed, tearful, with difficulty concentrating. She comes in with disability forms to sign.

9/26/97: Attending Physician statement by Bruce S, M.D.: Diagnosis: acute situational depression. He suggested Ms. T was unable to practice trial law because of an inability to concentrate, tearful, distracted, memory impaired.

12/5/97: Letter by Dr. S to Insurance Company: Ms. T's depression is very real and very palpable. She sleeps poorly, is frequently tearful, has trouble concentrating, has feelings of depersonalization, and has had suicidal ideation setting the patient back in her depression. Patient is thought to be suffering from a PTSD underlying her depression. Serzone 150 mg twice a day increased to 200 mg twice a day.

12/10/97: On 11/23/97, Ms. T's secretary was mauled by her dog injuring her forearm and leaving the tendon exposed. In the aftermath with shaking, tears, and nightmares, and dissociations setting the patient back in her depression. Patient is felt to be suffering from PTSD underlying her depression. Increase Serzone to 200 mg twice a day.

1/12/98: The patient has stopped driving—the patient drove the wrong way down a one-way street. She feels her concentration is badly compromised. Assessment: Ongoing significant depression.

7/6/98: Depression. Mood and affect improved today and thinking is more logical. However, the patient states that stress situations exacerbate her condition and rekindle her prior symptoms. She is avoiding conflict situations.

3/3/99: In July 1998 the patient partook in a study of Vietnam nurses with PTSD. The psych evaluation was clearly that of PTSD. Meds: Wellbutrin 75 mg three times a day; Xanax as necessary (rare); Buspar, just given, but not used yet.

The patient is persistently shaky, and this is visible in her writing. She is still prone to tears and has trouble focusing her thoughts. Her problems are memory, sleep disturbances off and on, and flashes of anger and panic. She is seeing Dr. E each 3 months and Dr. B weekly.

Parker H and J, OB/GYN Group Records
5/23/96: Complaint of "moody."

10/18/96: Dramatic menopausal symptoms for a number of months.

2/3/97: No libido.

7/28/97: Feels bad, not alive, anorgasmic, irritable, not energized. Work changes, bad time in life. Diagnosis: Menopausal-depression, Provera side effects.

11/24/97: Complains of decreased libido and decreased energy.

Dr. Barbara B's Office Records
6/26/86: Complaints of anxiety, insomnia, irritability since November 85 to present. Diagnosis: Adjustment Disorder with anxious mood. Treatment is psychotherapy to relieve symptoms of stress due to major lawsuits. Notes of sessions were not kept.

6/24/97: Very upset. Feels she is "losing it." Cannot function in court. Flashbacks of Vietnam. Affects work, sleep, mood, anxious all the time.

8/28/97: Insomnia, references to Vietnam.

10/9/97: Attending Physician statement by Dr. B: Diagnosis: Posttraumatic Stress Disorder and Major Depressive Disorder, single episode. Limitations include inability to process clearly, think on her feet, respond to judge. Also has substantial deficits in writing briefs and keeping up with paperwork.

11/11/97: Veterans Day: Upset at newspaper story about MIA. Crying, no sleep. "I can't see the light at the end of the tunnel."

11/12/97: Pulled over by police for going wrong way on a one-way street.

11/12/97: Dr. B completed an insurance form regarding degree of impairment and indicated that Ms. T was moderately impaired in her ability to relate to other people; moderately impaired in her daily activities; moderately impaired in deterioration of personal habits; moderately severe loss of interest; moderately severe impairment in ability to understand, carry out, and remember instructions; moderately severe impairment in ability to perform work requiring regular contact with others; moderately impaired in performing tasks involving minimal intellectual effort; severely impaired in her ability to perform intellectually complex tasks; moderately impaired in performing repetitive tasks; moderately impaired in performing varied tasks; moderately severely impaired in making independent judgments; moderately severely impaired in supervising or managing others; severely impaired in performing under stress; and severely impaired in her ability to work relative to the attached job description.

Dr. B said that Ms. T cannot think, speak, or drive sufficiently to do trial work; do research due to no concentration; meet with prospective clients (cannot plan, confront, problem solve), manage cases or her office (poor judgment, problem solving, concentration). GAF was estimated currently at 42.

11/18/97:   Can't concentrate.

12/8/97:   Haunted by dog bite. Flashbacks to Vietnam. Nervous, shaky, up til 3:30 A.M.

12/9/97:   Figured out how to use phone in office. Then forgot. Nightmares, insomnia, feeling shaky. Feels she is regressing.

1/6/98:   Trouble filling out the form.

1/13/98:   Stopped driving. Not safe. Got a ticket, moving violation. Couldn't even answer interrogatories in her own case. Answered from wrong perspective.

1/20/98:   Lost at least 10 pounds.

1/27/98:   Missed a major court appearance on her behalf. She is defendant. Panic attacks . . . hot, dizzy.

2/12/98:   In court for business debt collection. Anxious, lightheaded.

2/24/98:   Hands shaking today. Had to defend self last week. Was shaky in court. Did not do a good job. Unfocused. Not the old fighter. Depressed, but just did it to end it.

3/5/98:   Went to court this A.M. on own behalf. Forgot what she was supposed to bring up. Two more nights of sleeplessness.

3/18/98:   Still very depressed. Medicine is helping.

3/24/98:   Anhedonia, melancholy, woke up sobbing the other night. She is feeling mistreated by insurance company, just like in Vietnam.

3/31/98:   Is driving again. Is now able to get her insurance forms into me and insurance company. Patient reports more periods of clear thinking. Cried throughout a ceremony for female veterans (at Vietnam memorial).

4/7/98:   Had second part of IME (by Dr. O) yesterday.

4/21/98:   Still not sleeping. Waking up middle of night and early A.M.

7/8/98:   Trying to get VA reimbursement for posttraumatic memories of Vietnam. Went to female Vietnam Memorial three times in 2 days. Cried in session about this. She feels she has lost her confidence. Finds that is what is most important about her job.

7/10/98:   She is not back to normal. She is not thinking as clearly as before. Not focused.

Slow. Avoiding stress and conflict. Turns off the TV if upset. Can't read Vietnam books.

7/22/98:   Went to New Hampshire for Vietnam PTSD nurses project. Brought up many memories.

8/12/98:   Cannot concentrate and focus on getting messages from her answering machine. "Can't get things straight."

9/16/98:   Doing research on possible jobs. Needs to find a job in anything that can pay the mortgage. Gets tired easily, but is thinking more clearly.

9/23/98:   Afraid to bring up old files in garage because of the rat. Looking into nursing jobs.

9/29/98:   Screaming on phone to another attorney. Realizes she can't even answer the phone.

10/7/98:   Went to court, "dressed down." She wasn't paying attention. Felt bad. "Not myself."

2/24/99:   Feeling shaky a lot. Fears she will be unreliable as an employee. Afraid to take on work. Forgetting what she is doing. Can only do one thing at a time (make coffee, put dishes away).

3/3/99:   Partner reported memory losses. Couldn't find an office she had been to before. Went around the block twice. Was crying and upset and walked out of Faith group. Vulnerable, hurt.

3/10/99:   Priority problem, multi-task problems and sequencing problems. Also, can't remember what day she can't park on one side of the street. Trying to file bankruptcy. Can't read the papers.

3/17/99:   Is now getting Social Security, retroactive since December.

3/31/99:   Freaking out because of possible war—more men dying—can't read the papers.

4/14/99:   Upset regarding the Kosovo war. Brought back memories. Looks like Vietnam.

4/21/99:   VA has acknowledged PTSD. Very emotional, tearful, house in foreclosure. Cried all day yesterday. Couldn't move or think. Fall apart.

5/5/99:   Went to answer the door yesterday and had a flashback of a dead guy with hollow eyes in Vietnam. Is going ahead with bankruptcy. Is 50% service connected from VA.

5/29/99: Fell apart from phone call from V's daughter.

6/2/99: Went to vocational rehab this morning but forgot the form. Cannot keep up with details or be organized. Was shaky.

8/20/97: Application for Blue Cross form completed by Ellen T In completing this health questionnaire, Ms. T stated that she had no health history for, and sought no treatment for, a mental or nervous condition. At the time she completed this form, she had been diagnosed as depressed by Dr. S and was reporting symptoms of depression and posttraumatic stress disorder to Dr. B.

Records of Tracy E, M.D.
Dr. E's Record of Summary of prescriptions

12/29/97: Serzone, 200 and 400 discontinued.

1/26/98: Wellbutrin 75 mg twice a day.

3/4/98: 75 mg three times a day.

12/11/98: Buspar, 5 mg three times a day.

3/12/98: Wellbutrin sustained release 150 mg in the morning and 75 at night.

12/29/97: Complains of concentration, attention, depressed, tearful, anxious. End of June depression worsened causing decreased function. Combat memories (helicopters trigger panic). Nurse for 1 year.

Stressor: Client, gay man, sued her. State bar inquiries. Felt being stalked. Still very upsetting, feel out of control. Intermittent, unpredictable, which leads to loss of confidence. Like in Vietnam, could not control the environment.

Lawyer in medical malpractice $150 to $450 thousand. Out of litigation for 6 months.

Plan: Increase Serzone to 200 mg and 400 at night, Xanax .25 each 6 hours. Diagnosis: Major depression, single, moderate; rule out PSTD.

1/12/98: No change with Serzone. Increase from 400 mg to 600 mg for 5 days. Xanax offered good relief from anxiety. Reports decreased tearfulness, sadness, more even, complains of concentration with decreased short-term memory, overreactive. Decreased libido, anorgasmic for 1 year. Libido returned to normal for a few years with Premarin/Provera.

Tearful regarding her failure in coping. Like with Vietnam, out of control—handled in Nam by drinking. Impression: Improved partially.

1/19/98: Psychiatric Assessment Form for Paul Z by Psychiatrist, Tracy E: Diagnosis: Major Depression, rule out PTSD. Current GAF 45. Highest GAF in past year 75. First visit was 12/29/97. Ms. T was then prescribed Serzone 600 mg started in November 1997. Due to no response, it was being tapered. Wellbutrin 75 mg twice a day was to be started after off Serzone. Xanax .25 mg twice a day as necessary has helped anxiety.

Her internist, Dr. Bruce S, placed her on Paxil, but no improvement. She was placed on Serzone increased to 200 mg twice a day without effect. Anxiety presents with intense fear, loss of control, recollections of trauma in combat.

1/26/98: Difficulty with sleep. 2:00 A.M. wake up at times. 3½ out of 10 "Don't feel better." Lost weight, 167 (normal 186—ideal 150), but appetite okay. Had gained weight with depression. Plan: Discontinue Serzone, start Wellbutrin 75 mg twice a day.

2/12/98: Went off Serzone. Increased libido. Reviewing law as career.

3/4/98: Attending Physician Statement by Dr. E: Diagnosis: Major Depression, single episode, moderate. Dates of visits, 12/29/97, 1/12/98, 1/26/98, 2/12/98, 2/26/98 (missed).

Major depression with impaired concentration, loss of energy, interest, sadness. Changes in the patient's condition: Less tearful, improved sleep on Wellbutrin. Occupational restrictions include anergia, anhedonia, impaired concentration, depressive mood.

3/4/98: Complains of lack of energy but sleep is improved. Less teary. But "weight in head." Worse in morning. Anhedonic, lack of enthusiasm, can't problem solve. Still is anxious. Much better sexually.

3/18/98: Less tearful.

4/8/98: Night stimulation with Wellbutrin. Xanax effective. Worried regarding addiction. Wants to avoid clients in litigation. Maybe some other aspect of law. "At least starting to think now." Sometimes injury (illegible) . . . brought back Vietnam dreams. Feels she is being stalked by a client, anxious, like in Vietnam.

4/23/98: Still shaky but depressed. Days with increased clarity. Returns to court as debtor. Increased anxiety. "Observing but not there." (Dissociative type). Avoiding responsibility. "Don't hold together enough to do it." Looking for less stressful legal specialty vs. out of law.

5/13/98: I feel depression better. Fewer down days. Office remains open and partial "wind down" functioning. "Don't see myself resuming litigation. Don't want to face it." Impression: Mood improved on Wellbutrin.

8/17/98: Taking Wellbutrin 225 a day. Improved—more up more of the time. Not as depressed. Still feels tired all the time. Low energy. Feel "right medicine." Complains of difficulty with concentration. Feels depression cleared, but still feels damaged. Can't deal with conflict. Now explained that's PTSD component.

12/11/98: Less depressed with Wellbutrin. Sleeping quite well. Still complains of decreased concentration, decreased memory, makes lists, forgot psychiatric appointment. "Shaking inside" visible still. Not as down. Labile. B believes meds helping. Therapy with B focused on Vietnam—RN. Deaths, blames self. Plan: Continue Wellbutrin. Add Buspar 5 mg three times a day. Return in 3 months.

3/11/99: Trying to deal with deficits in concentration and memory by writing down plans. Overly sensitive. "My confidence poor . . . can't handle litigation." Some legal work, procrastinated, secondary to anxiety. Discussed acceptance of decreased cognitive performance.

1/19/98 Letter from Ted N, Ph.D. He consulted with Ellen T on 12/16/97. She reports a loss of about 10 pounds over the last 3 or 4 months. She has periods of being tearful, which was observed during this appointment. She described feelings of anxiety, shakiness, and intermittent chest discomfort. Psychosocial stressors have included a family member dying in January 1997 and that person's daughter evidently attempting suicide. Ms. T also reported a malpractice lawsuit against her by one of her former clients, which has been highly stressful for her and resulted in allegations against her before the state bar.

Ms. T reports residual symptoms consistent with PTSD, triggered by specific stimuli such as a helicopter. Over the last year she has intermittently experienced feelings of detachment, hypersensitivity, anger, and occasional flashbacks. His impression was a depressive reaction along with symptoms of an anxiety disorder, possibly PTSD.

She currently shows major depression with decreased confidence, self-esteem, poor concentration, and attention span, depressed mood, tearfulness, anxiety with recurrent intense memories. On mental status exam she has depressed mood, impaired concentration and attention, anxious mood.

Summary of Podiatry Records Ms. T claimed disability for foot surgery in 7/91. In a letter by Sherwin F, D.P.M., dated 5/29/92, a recommendation was made for her disability to end on 4/30/92. In a letter by Ms. T to her insurance company dated 12/10/93, she reported that for 1 year she had excruciating foot pain and that she could not drive a car for almost a year after the surgery. She also reported that 2½ years after the surgery, she still had a member of her staff drive her because she was too fatigued to drive after standing for hours in court.

1/5/95: Letter to Dr. S from ITT Local Insurance Co. Mary T was declined a policy for long-term disability because of a history of fatigue.

MS. T'S PRIOR LAWSUITS

Ellen T v. [Law Firm] Intentional Interference with Contractual Relation, Intentional Interference with Prospective Economic Advantage, Intentional Infliction of Emotional Distress, Abuse of Process, Conspiracy, dated February 10, 1987. (Also separate lawsuit by V R against defendants. Ms. R, it was reported, suffered emotional distress and sought psychotherapy as a result. She is a graduate of law school who did not pass the bar exam, and was the chairman of King of the World, a beer manufacturing company).

Ellen T and V R v. Great Life Insurance Co.—Filed Breach of Contract, Fraud, Breach of the Covenant of Good Faith and Fair Dealing, Intentional Infliction of Emotional Distress, Negligent Infliction of Emotional Distress. Bad Faith and Breach of Statutory Duty, Interference with Economic advantage, Declaratory Belief, filed June 8, 1994; filed removal July 18, 1994.

City Bank v. Ellen T: Complaint for Money—Breach of Revolving Note and Loan Revision Agreement, Money Lent, Account Stated, Unjust Enrichment, filed June 12, 1996. Due to Ms. T's failure to make timely payments on an unsecured line of credit, a stipulation for entry of judgment dated 1/27/97 stated that Ms. T was required to repay City Bank $150,000 in principal, daily interest of $49.39, costs of $250, and attorneys' fees of $15,000.

City Bank v. Ellen T: Application for Entry of Judgment Pursuant to Written Stipulation, filed July 3, 1997. Judgment Pursuant to Written Stipulation on July 8, 1997.

National Bank of Boston v. Ellen T, Supplemental Exam of Judgment Debtor, November 9, 1998. Ms. T had a debt based on a revolving line of credit. A stipulation for entry of judgment dated 6/11/97 ordered Ms. T to pay the defendant $50,107.

Carl and Loretta J v. Ellen T, Personal Injury, July 24, 1997 (defendant did not subpoena a chief witness to the case).

11/6/97 Field Referral Report Ms. T reported that on 6/23/97 she received a hearing decision letter from the California State Bar reprimanding the claimant and letting her know she had one year to satisfactorily complete a law ethics class. Ms. T shared that she was stressed by this and promptly made an appointment to see her therapist, Dr. B.

Ms. T reported that two lawsuits were filed against her last month, one by a former client, Paul J and one by Richard M, M.D. Ms. T suggested she works ½ hour to a maximum of 3 hours a day, presently on legal work activities, but not every day. Mostly just monitoring her active "hanging cases."

Ms. R stated that Ms. T earned $200,000 gross for the year 1997, up until her date of loss, and netted $90,000.

Ms. T reads a lot and is presently reading the biography of Gladstone, and other light reading, spending 2 or 3 hours daily.

Ms. T feels she has trouble at times doing work activities such as research, writing, and phoning because her mental abilities to function

have been disrupted. She cannot handle meetings with clients and dealing with legal matters because she has "lost confidence" in her legal abilities.

She acknowledged a bank foreclosure around August 1996 and current malpractice suits filed against her.

11/14/97 Psychiatric Disability Case Management Logs by Larry C He spoke with Dr. S. Dr. S first treated Ms. T for up to 1½ years back in 1985 in conjunction with a lawsuit against the insured. Most recently she saw Ms. T for one session in December 1996 and then began weekly contact in June 1997. Symptoms have included insomnia, irritability, restlessness, tearfulness, panic stricken when attempting to drive (she no longer drives), low concentration, feelings of worthlessness and failure, fatigue, and "cannot write a letter."

Diagnosis is major depression, single episode, severe, current GAF of 42. Also indications of PTSD, delayed as a result of Vietnam duty.

Mr. C indicated that multiple disability policies would total $275,000 a year in tax-free benefits, an increase over her currently reported net income by about $100,000.

11/26/97 Psychiatric Disability Case Management Log by Mr. C Dr. S has treated Ms. T 19 times since 6/24/97, but her clinical notes include only five dated entries.

MARCH 20, 27, AND 30, 1998 BREEN INVESTIGATION OF ELLEN T

Ms. T was observed to drive her Nissan Pathfinder with Ms. R in the passenger seat on two occasions (3/20 and 3/27). She was observed going to high-rise buildings and appeared to be exchanging some paperwork.

4/18/98 Letter to Dr. O from Mr. C As a result of independent surveillance, Ms. T was seen driving on March 20 and March 27, 1998.

4/21/98 Notes of Phone Call by Dr. O to Dr. B All of a sudden everything started crashing in on her. When I saw her in June she was a different person. I think she had three clients suing her, it was way too much for her. It felt like when she was in Vietnam. I think it was inevitable that she would break. She became an entirely different person.

Had seen her 2 years before—very effective person. When I saw her before, Vietnam wasn't a problem. Before the medication started working, it was hard for her to get through a session. Only Axis II would be obsessive-compulsive tendencies. She still seems uncertain and insecure.

4/22/98 Report of Lynette P, Ph.D.   On March 28, 1998 Dr. P conducted a 1-hour clinical interview and administered a Kaufman Brief Intelligence Test and the MMPI-II. Ms. T told Dr. P that she experienced suicidal ideation, which was reflected in her medical records in early December 1996. She reported that she currently was preoccupied with morbid and depressing thoughts. She reported feeling anxious and experiencing distraction, "mental blocks, and having limited organizational ability mentally." She states that she is not able to "analyze." She reported a decrease in appetite and loss of 15 pounds in the last year without an attempt at weight loss.

On the Kaufman Brief Intelligence Test (KBIT) she scored 95 in national percentile rank on the vocabulary section; in the matrices section that measures nonverbal skills that include the ability to solve new problems, she scored in the 87th national percentile rank. Her composite score places her in the 94th national percentile. Her performance on these tests requires attention, concentration, and perseverance. Her performance on the cognitive test suggests that Dr. B's statement that Ms. T was unable to perform occupational duties "of any trial work (cannot think, speak, or drive), research (no concentration), meet with prospective clients (cannot plan, confront, problem solve), manage cases or her office (poor judgment, problem solving, concentration)" is not accurate at the present time.

4/29/98 Mason Report on MMPI- 2   The MMPI-2 was given by Lynette P, Ph.D., on 3/28/98. There were no indications on the Ds scale of any attempt to exaggerate or malinger her level of disturbance. The profile indicates a severe depression with markedly sad moods, crying, acute anxiety, and poignant feelings of inadequacy.

4/26/98 Report of Dr. Alan O   Dr. O examined Ms. T for 5–3/4 hours on March 28, 1998, and April 6, 1998. She reported current symptoms of difficulty falling asleep, early morning awakening, "tremendous sadness," anhedonia, anxiety, poor appetite in the morning, weight loss, difficulty with concentration and judgment, poor attention span, memory impairment, and lack of energy. She described herself as "depressed, lacking in self-confidence, anxious, stressed, helpless, feeling hopeless, despairing, sad, overwhelmed, immobilized, tired."

Ms. T reported both constant and episodic anxiety. She described panic episodes once when in court, and another time when a client yelled at her. She estimates she has had 10 or fewer such episodes. She described a flashback set off by helicopter noise. She recalled three out of four nouns. She did poorly naming the presidents. She made three errors in subtracting serial sevens.

Ms. T denies that she could perform any functions of an attorney: "If I could handle it, I'd be doing it." Ms. T expresses anxiety about returning to law practice: "I'll have to do something less stressful, something that doesn't require the intimate contact with people . . . I don't want to deal with clients. . . . In representing people, you have to be very involved, you take it on, I don't feel that I have the strength or will to carry it forward, I don't feel confident . . . I feel like I'm going to fail again, I don't like failing. Everything I think about the law is stressful." Ms. T feels that she cannot return to work until she regains her self-confidence: "Everything depends on your confidence, your bravado." Ms. T would like to do something "less stressful than litigation, less hostile, like estate planning. I can't see myself going back to the same thing. I want to be on solid ground." At the same time, Ms. T indicates that "I'm not a person to lay around, I get a lot of satisfaction from being a lawyer."

Dr. O made the following diagnoses: Adjustment disorder with mixed anxiety and depressed mood, acute; Dysthymic disorder; Anxiety disorder, NOS; possible Partner Relational Problem; and Occupational Problem. He also made an Axis II diagnosis of Personality disorder NOS with obsessive and dependent features. He estimated her GAF at 60.

Dr. O opined that Ms. T can perform the tasks

of a trial attorney. She did not have any measurable cognitive impairments. He said, "I believe at present she has a limited ability to provide passionate, sophisticated legal argument spontaneously in a courtroom setting. I believe that Ms. T could perform all the other duties of a trial attorney."

7/24/98 Letter to Dr. B regarding Ms. T's Vietnam Nurse Veterans Psychophysiology Study The results of the clinician who administered PTSD scale indicated that Ms. T met the *DSM-IV* criteria for current PTSD related to her service in Vietnam. "The results . . . cannot take the place of any personal, clinical, and/or compensation evaluation the veteran might undergo.

In a self-administered questionnaire, Ms. T stated that she was treated for military PTSD in 1983. She also indicated she was treated for mild depression in 1996 that continued. She said she was currently being treated for depression.

Ms. T checked off that she lost track of what was going on (very true); automatic pilot (somewhat true); what was happening seemed unreal (somewhat true); felt like a spectator (very true); watched as things that I was not aware of (somewhat true); felt confused, difficulty making sense (very true); felt discontented, felt uncertain (very true).

She checked off that she reexperienced the Vietnam intrusive recollections much of the time with severe intensity. Over her lifetime she stated that she suffered intrusive recollections of extreme intensity most of the time. She stated that she currently experienced distressing dreams of Vietnam very little of the time with severe intensity; over the course of her lifetime she had distressing dreams some of the time of extreme intensity. She stated that over the course of her lifetime she acted or felt as if an event were recurring from Vietnam, some of the time with extreme intensity. She reported psychological distress at exposure to cues currently most of the time to a severe degree. Over the course of her lifetime she reported psychological distress at exposure to cues, most of the time to an extreme degree. She reported physiologic activity on exposure to cues currently much of the time to a severe degree; over the course of her lifetime she experienced this much of the time to an extreme degree.

She reported that she currently had no avoidance of thoughts or feelings, but over the course of her lifetime she experienced this most of the time to severe intensity. She reported avoidance of activity/places currently some of the time to a moderate degree; over the course of her lifetime, much of the time to a severe degree. She reported inability to recall important aspects of the trauma currently much of the time to an extreme degree, and the same over the course of her lifetime. She reported diminished interest or participation in activities currently some of the time to a moderate degree; over the course of her lifetime most of the time to a severe degree. She reported a restricted range of affect currently some of the time to a moderate degree; over the course of her lifetime much of the time to an extreme degree. She reported a sense of a foreshortened future currently some of the time to a moderate degree; over the course of her lifetime much of the time to a severe degree.

Ms. T reported difficulty falling or staying asleep currently much of the time to a moderate degree, and over the course of her lifetime much of the time to an extreme degree. She reported irritability or outbursts of anger currently, some of the time to a severe degree; over the course of her lifetime much of the time to a severe degree. She reported currently difficulty concentrating some of the time to a moderate degree; over the course of her lifetime most of the time to an extreme degree. She reported hypervigilance currently some of the time to a moderate degree; over the course of her lifetime much of the time to a severe degree. She reported exaggerated startle response currently some of the time to a severe degree and the same over the course of her lifetime. She reported her overall degree of distress as extreme currently and over the course of her lifetime. Impairment in social functioning severe now and severe over the course of her lifetime. Impairment in occupational functioning extreme now and extreme over the course of her lifetime. Global severity extreme now and extreme over the course of her lifetime.

She reported guilt over commission or omission currently some of the time to a moderate degree; over the course of her lifetime much of the time to a moderate degree. She reported survivor guilt currently some of the time to a moderate degree; over the course of her lifetime most of the time to a severe degree. Ms. T reported confronting a sexual assault to another person when she was 31 years old. She reported experiencing a physical assault when she was 38 years old.

9/28/98 Letter from Barbara B to VA Regional Office Ms. T had "a gradual decline in her emotional state in December 1996 when she complained of depression to her internist." Dr. B saw her for the first time 6/24/97.

She has been confused several times about our appointment time and has had to be called and reminded of the appointment. Even her handwriting changed from strong and steady to consistently shaky.

Ms. T was able to bury her feelings and work for many years but began to experience PTSD symptoms after she stopped working. The course of her illness is similar to that of many nurses in Vietnam: delayed onset; under reporting of symptoms for many years; leading highly functional lives. . . .

On one occasion she scrambled under her bed during an attack and was attacked by a rat. . . . When she was sued by several of her clients, she felt the same feelings of helplessness and despair she felt in Vietnam, and compared her situation as similar to walking in a minefield.

For the last year and one-half, Ms. T has suffered severe cognitive impairment. She was unable to think enough to read, write, answer correspondence, was unable to speak up in the courtroom or to clients.

Ms. T has improved since June 19, 1997, in her cognitive functioning to the extent that she is communicating more clearly and experiencing fewer symptoms of depression and PTSD, partly due to her medication. However, she still cannot function in the courtroom, cannot concentrate enough to focus and write a simple letter, is still having trouble understanding what used to be simple legal language to her, experiences panic attacks while driving, facing court appearances, and speaking to people. When she is in court, she cannot remember why she is there and does not know what to say, and needs the judge to remind her.

Her energy level, while better than in June 1997, is still low and she is easily fatigued, partly due to her continuing insomnia caused by frequent nightmares. She questions every decision she makes including what to eat for dinner.

Ms. T has been 100% disabled since 6/24/97.

2/3/99 Psychiatric Evaluation by Jack Q, M.D. This evaluation was done for the Department of Veterans Affairs. It was based on information obtained from the patient only. Ms. T was described as slightly resistant and cried through a major portion of the interview. She reported that her depression has been responsive to medications, and thus, much better than in the past, although she still does have some feelings of hopelessness, helplessness, some intermittent crying spells, guilt, failure feelings, decreased sleep, decreased concentration, and energy level that is "not as good as it should be." She reports that her appetite is all right. She denies apathy, anhedonia, and suicidal ideation. The patient reports intermittent generalized anxiety, but most of her anxiety accompanies her PTSD symptoms.

She reports that she suffers from nightmares that include generalized themes of death and "that kind of stuff," and an experience she had in Vietnam with a "rat in the bed." She claims that she has flashbacks that vary from once a week to once a month now. They have to do with having to run under bunker beds due to fear from incoming fire, and remembering a plane blowing up and being barely able to hide under a small coffee table. She relives seeing wounded patients, for instance, a guy dead with his arm blown off. Guys who did not come out of surgery, and worst of all, the head injury patients who would continually moan, and the nursing staff could not do anything to help them. Memories are triggered by helicopters and war movies. Physiologic concomitants with her reliving include tachycardia, palpitations, shortness of breath, sweating, and anxiety. The symptoms occurred infrequently in the past, but during June 1997 was pretty much when they exacerbated and took on their present chronic form. She reported that the onset of her depression was at the same time June 24, 1997, when she found herself immobilized for an unknown reason at work.

The diagnosis was posttraumatic stress disorder-delayed and major depressive disorder without psychosis. Global assessment of functioning 68.

VETERANS ADMINISTRATION RECORDS

Ms. T was granted a service-connected 50% disability for posttraumatic stress disorder from 9/8/98. The 50% disability was based on occupational and social impairment with reduced reliability and productivity due to such symptoms as the following: flattened affect; circumstantial, circumlocutory, or stereotyped speech; panic attacks more than once a week; difficulty in understanding complex commands; impairment of short- and long-term memory (e.g., retention of only highly learned material, forgetting to complete tasks); impaired judgment; impaired abstract thinking; disturbance of motivation and mood; difficulty in establishing and maintaining effective work and social relationships.

Ms. T served in Vietnam for 11 months and 5 days as a medical surgical nurse. Her exposure to events outside that of normal human experience is clearly established.

2/8/99 Social Security Daily Activities Questionnaire Ms. T indicated that she has restless sleep, nightmares, wakes easily, often change beds in the middle of the night—"sometimes I go back to sleep, sometimes I don't." In response to the question whether she needs help with shopping, Ms. T replied, "sometimes. I am not organized and I forget things."

In response to the question about activities and hobbies she enjoys and spends time on, Ms. T replied, "Exercise, walks, movies, reading books, TV, visiting friends, attending parties, entertaining."

Ms. T stated that she reads newspapers, "I don't often understand what I read." Sometimes I need someone to drive me because I am nervous and unable to concentrate."

"I have a short fuse—a temper. Sometimes I am too aggressive and get into arguments or disagreements that interfere with what I am trying to accomplish. Sometimes I'm too depressed or upset to socialize at all."

When asked if she had problems concentrating, Ms. T replied, "regularly. I often can't finish or need to reread it. Restless—often unable to finish the newspaper. If it's complicated or new, I often avoid or give up due to lack of confidence."

"I get distracted . . . forget appointments. Often go back two or three times before a job is finished."

"I misconstrue—read teaspoon as tablespoon. Often forget what I am told almost immediately—like driving instructions. I reread instructions . . . could not understand—then forget them."

"I take Wellbutrin 75 mg three times a day. Sometimes I take Xanax."

When asked to explain how her condition keeps her from working, Ms. T replied, "My job as an attorney requires concentration, good memory, understanding of writings, ability to relate closely to people, and respond quickly and aggressively with attorneys and judges. I can't do this consistently enough to be responsible in any job. Too nervous."

When asked if she had tried to work after she became ill and what happened, Ms. T replied "Tried to complete work—needed help. Tried to do a project for another—unable to research and took so long, I was not called back. Too stressed to do what I know and no experience in other things—trying to learn."

2/16/99 Letter from Dr. B to California Department of Social Services (Social Security Disability) Ms. T's depressive symptoms included: anhedonia, insomnia, lack of concentration, indecisive, hopelessness, weight loss, depressed mood, suicidal ideation, and low energy. She was so depressed from 6/97 to 5/98 that she could not think clearly and rambled through much of her psychotherapy sessions. In May 1998 her mind cleared somewhat, and she was able to communicate beginning, middle, and end of her experiences.

She was unable to work in any capacity until November 1998, when she began looking at the classified ads for work and worked on her resume. She began to develop confidence in her thinking ability for the first time since 6/24/97.

In the last year and a half, Ms. T has suffered severe cognitive impairment. She was unable to think enough to read, write, answer correspondence, and was unable to speak up in the courtroom. She experienced an inability to conduct a law practice, a lack of concentration, nightmares, and inability to conduct herself in a court of law, memory problems, panic attacks, and need for psychotropic medication.

Ms. T has improved since May 1998 in her cognitive functioning to the extent that she is communicating more clearly and experiencing fewer symptoms of depression and PTSD, partly due to her medication and treatment. However, she still cannot function in the courtroom, cannot concentrate enough to focus and write a simple letter, is still having trouble understanding what used to be simple legal language to her, experiences panic attacks when driving, and speaking to people. She experiences people as intimidating and scary on phone calls and in person. Her energy level is still low, and she is easily fatigued—partly due to continuing insomnia caused by frequent nightmares. She questions every decision she makes, including what to eat for dinner.

In July 1998, her PTSD symptoms escalated when she took part in a Harvard Medical School study of PTSD in nurses who served in Vietnam. She has experienced suicidal ideation during the past year, but has not acted on it. She has no suicidal ideation at present.

She comes to her sessions with a depressed, anxious attitude and has been tearful, hopeless, and despairing with feelings of guilt and worthlessness. She has experienced severe insomnia, weight loss, decreased energy, and anhedonia. Her intellectual functioning seems to be intact when she is not anxious or depressed.

Her daily activities have changed in that she can accomplish about 10% of what she used to do, including cooking, taking care of the house work, looking for work, paperwork, errands, etc. Socially she is quick-tempered, irritable, and does not trust herself to handle simple telephone calls. Although her mind has cleared somewhat since May 1998, she is still incapable of performing the tasks required for her job as a civil litigator, including court appearances, interactions with clients, legal research, writing briefs or letters, and conducting legal analysis of a case.

Diagnosis: Major Depressive Disorder and Posttraumatic Stress Disorder, GAF 45 to 60 in the past year.

Ms. T has been 100% disabled in her chosen profession of law since 6/24/97. She has been 100% disabled in any occupation from 6/96 to 11/98. She did not work from 6/24/97 to 12/31/98. Her prognosis is very good now, and her mind is functioning better and she has regained some confidence.

2/18/99 DAILY ACTIVITIES QUESTIONNAIRE COMPLETED BY V R

She stated that Ellen volunteers for a nonprofit group. Ellen cooks once or twice a week. When shopping, Ellen buys fruits and vegetables but often forgets items. Ellen often does not finish work. She has to be reminded what day is trash pick up and which days there is street cleaning because cars have to be moved.

Sometimes Ellen needs me to drive her if she feels stressed, is not focused, or has difficulty concentrating. Does not drive long distances.

Ellen reads about 1 hour per day, newspapers and books. Sometimes has difficulty recalling what she has read. Takes her three times longer to read than before her illness. Difficulty concentrating. Misreads words.

Ellen has a short attention span in conversation. Cannot remember past conversations unless reminded. Gets "wrong end of the stick" in conversations. Often irritable and irascible. Loses temper. Often forgets what she is told almost immediately.

Ellen misreads words, for example, "important" for "impotent." She cannot remember phone numbers. Misses appointments—needs to be reminded. Cannot remember deadlines. Can only do one thing at a time. Often leaves a task or job half done.

Ellen is very afraid when police helicopters circle—reminds her of Vietnam experience. Very fearful of flying birds. Frightened by backfiring cars, which sound like gunshot. Afraid of gunshot firing—reminds her of Vietnam.

She is unable to concentrate or perform any complicated task. She has great difficulty writing because her hand shakes, and her handwriting is often illegible.

1999 Social Security Administration letter This indicates that Ms. T became disabled on June 24, 1997. Disability benefits began December 19, 1997.

6/23/99 Letter from Dr. B to Barbara D (vocational rehabilitation) Since September 28, 1998 Ms. T has continued to make slow steady improvement in her functioning. She is more organized, able to complete tasks more efficiently, and can often demonstrate clear thinking and analysis of complicated business issues in her non-compensated capacity as executive director of a nonprofit organization. However, her improvement is inconsistent. She will also misplace files, have days where she cannot complete the simplest task, and does not wish to talk to anyone. She has not recaptured her confidence or tenacious legal attitude and is often intimidated by the most benign people. She cannot handle stressful situations and can break down in tears when a grant does not get funded. Her short-term memory functioning is not as improved as she hoped it would be at this time.

She would have extreme difficulty doing legal research and writing briefs or letters in a timely manner and managing deadlines in general. It is possible that she could be retrained in another area of law, but it is likely that she could not function independently and would need supervision. She could also work in the health administration field with some business training."

NEUROPSYCHOLOGICAL EVALUATION BY CHARLES WOMACK, PH.D., DATED 4/26/00

Dr. Womack evaluated Ms. T on April 19, 2000. I requested his evaluation to assist in evaluating her current level of cognitive functioning. Ms. T told Dr. Womack the following complaints: "difficulty completing tasks; memory problems, trouble with the simplest tasks; trouble sleeping, though she states this has improved as of late; difficulty with conflict and confrontation; difficulty reasoning; slowing; and emotionally volatile, cries easily, gets upset easily, shaky."

Dr. Womack concluded that there was clear evidence to suggest that Ms. T is grossly exaggerating, if not outright fabricating, her complaints of cognitive impairment. The strongest piece of evidence is her performance on the Victoria Symptom Validity Test, which was so blatantly faked that there is no doubt that she was intentionally performing poorly in an attempt to appear far more impaired that she actually is.

Ms. T also failed the Rey 15-word memory test. Additional evidence of symptom exaggeration/malingering was evident on the Wechsler Memory Scale.

Examination of her performance on neuropsychological testing also convincingly converges on the same conclusion. The single most striking example was her abysmally poor performance on the digit span subtest of both the WAIS-R and the WMS-R, on which she was only able to repeat four digits forward and four digits backward. Such profound impairment of attentional ability is simply incompatible with her purported psychological illness. In fact, her digit span is so poor that if truthful, she would have trouble engaging in virtually any of her typical day-to-day behaviors.

Evidence also exists to suggest Ms. T was not responding entirely candidly on measures assessing her mood, personality, and emotional problems. Evidence of misleading responses was revealed on the MMPI-2 on which Ms. T attempted to both present herself as highly moral and virtuous, while at the same time reporting pronounced psychiatric symptoms. Specifically she scored quite high on the F Scale.

Ms. T was administered the Wechsler Adult Intelligence Scale, Revised. She obtained prorated IQs as follows: Full Scale IQ of 101, Verbal IQ of 107, and Performance IQ of 96. These scores fall below what would be expected of someone of her educational and occupational background.

Ms. T achieve a score of 13 on the Beck Depression Inventory, a score that generally reflects only a mild degree of depressive symptomatology.

On the Beck Anxiety Inventory she achieved a score of 23, a score that generally indicates a moderate degree of anxiety.

Dr. Womack concluded that because Ms. T was found to be grossly exaggerating, if not outright fabricating, her neuropsychological deficits, it is not possible to validly determine her actual level of cognitive function. Dr. Womack's conclusion of exaggeration of symptoms was supported by the following data:

1. Ms. T failed several measures specifically designed to detect malingering.
2. She performed in the elevated range of the F Scale of the MMPI-2.
3. Both the level and pattern of cognitive deficits that she evidenced on testing are simply incompatible with the neuropsychological sequelae of mood/anxiety disorder. Her IQ of 101 is highly suspect, especially given her performance on the KBIT 1 year ago when she obtained an IQ equivalent of 123.

4. Ms. T's report that she is writing declarations and performing legal research is not compatible with her impaired performance on neuropsychological testing.

It is possible that Ms. T may actually be experiencing mild cognitive symptoms; but this cannot be currently determined given her present dissimulation. As such, with a reasonable degree of certainty, she now meets *DSM-IV* diagnostic criteria for malingering.

Based on her self-report and her objective psychological test performance, Ms. T no longer suffers from clinically significant depression symptomatology.

Based on the available data, unlike her apparent fabrication of cognitive dysfunction, it does not appear that Ms. T was attempting to grossly exaggerate her psychiatric symptomatology. Many of her psychological test scores are now relatively normal with her primary residual emotional symptoms more anxiety-related than depressive.

In summary, Ms. T appears to have developed a psychiatric disorder in 1997. Successful psychiatric and psychological treatment of this disorder has since transpired. Currently her mood symptoms are, at most, mild. Unfortunately, Ms. T is now attempting to portray herself as having suffered great cognitive losses that now preclude her from being able to function in her previous occupation.

SUMMARY OF DOCUMENTS REGARDING EMPLOYMENT SEARCH

September 16, 1998: Ms. T sent a résumé and a letter to California Medical Audit. She wrote in the cover letter that she is applying for a position as a California Medical Auditor and that she wished to depart from her private law practice, and that she was "currently in the course of activating my nursing license."

December 18, 1998: Ms. T received acknowledgment of her interest in a position at Kaiser Permanente as a neutral arbitrator.

January 5, 1999: Ms. T received acknowledgment of receipt of her résumé at ECS.

January 11, 1999: Ms. T received acknowledgment of receipt of her résumé at ESRI.

January 13, 1999: Ms. T received acknowledgment of her interest in a job position at UCLA as Assistant Vice Chancellor of Government and Community Relations.

February 1, 1999: Ms. T received acknowledgment of receipt of her resume at Esquire Staffing Solutions.

June 4, 1999: Ms. T sent a résumé to American Career College for a position as a Medical Assistant Instructor.

June 14, 1999: Ms. T answered ads in the *L.A. Times* for positions as a planning specialist, an Assistant Administrator, Director of Social Services, and SNF Administrator.

June 15, 1999: Ms. T answered an ad in the *L.A. Times* for a position as an attorney.

June 23, 1999: Ms. T faxed a résumé to Chosen Few for a position as an attorney.

June 25, 1999: Ms. T faxed a résumé to LCC for a position as a program manager, site acquisition zoning and regulatory compliance.

July 9, 1999: Ms. T faxed a résumé to Managed Health Network for a position as an EAP consultant and to Robert Cantrell, Ph.D., as a care manager.

July 14, 1999: Ms. T faxed a résumé to special counsel and e-mailed a résumé.

September 21, 1999: Ms. T sent a résumé to the LA Branch of Major International Firms.

October 21, 1999: Ms. T faxed résumés to Gavin Stilman, Esq. (The Attorney Network Services) and the Law Registry.

Bankruptcy records Ms. T filed for bankruptcy on 5/11/99. She listed total assets of $812,687.92 and total liabilities of $1,031,363.16. She listed current income of $9,207.

PSYCHIATRIC DIAGNOSES

1. Malingering of cognitive impairment.
2. Probable Major Depressive Episode, Mild, in partial remission
3. Probable Posttraumatic Stress Disorder with delayed onset, in partial remission.

The following evidence supports my opinion that Ms. T is malingering cognitive impairment:

1. Ms. T has from the beginning of her disability claim consistently identified cognitive impairment (attention, memory, ability to analyze) as a primary reason that she was unable to work as a trial attorney. Although she reported "marked improvement" in her depression and significant improvement in posttraumatic stress disorder, Ms. T claimed that she continued to have substantial cognitive deficits. The following points illustrate Ms. T's pattern of emphasizing her cognitive impairment as a reason that she could not do trial work.

   A. In Ms. T's original disability claim dated 10/2/97, Ms. T gave the following statement of why she was disabled: "Complete physical health required to function in litigation. Need concentration, reasoning, and use of memory for on the spot analysis for argument in court and at depositions . . . [I] have lack of attentiveness, poor concentration, poor judgment, confusion, stress symptoms with memory blackouts/loss, periods of inability to function, insomnia, anxiety, flashbacks, distractions . . . "

   B. On 9/26/97 Dr. Bruce Smith stated on his attending physician statement that Ms. T was unable to practice trial law because of "inability to concentrate, tearful, distracted, memory impaired."

   C. Based on what Ms. T told her, Dr. B stated on an insurance disability form dated 11/12/97 that Ms. T "cannot think, speak, or drive sufficiently to do trial work; do research due to no concentration; meet with prospective clients (cannot plan, confront, problem solve), manage cases in her office (poor judgment, problem solving, concentration)."

   D. Dr. E reported that in his initial visit with Ms. T on 12/29/97 that she complained of "concentration, attention, depressed, tearful, anxious."

   E. On 9/28/98, Dr. B wrote to the VA Regional office that Ms. T "still cannot function in the courtroom, cannot concentrate enough to focus and write a simple letter; is still having trouble understanding what used to

   be simple legal language to her. . . . When she is in court she cannot remember why she is there and does not know what to say and needs the judge to remind her."

   F. Ms. T reported on a 2/8/99 Social Security daily activity form, "I am not organized and I forget things." She stated that she reads newspapers but, "I don't often understand what I read." She added that she "often forgets what I am told, almost immediately—like driving instructions. I reread instructions . . . could not understand—then forget them."

   G. On 2/16/99, Dr. B wrote to the California Department of Social Services: "In the last year and a half, Ms. T has suffered severe cognitive impairment. She was unable to think enough to read, write, answer correspondence. . . . Ms. T has improved since May 1998 in her cognitive functioning. . . . However, she still cannot function in the courtroom, cannot concentrate enough to focus and write a simple letter. She is still having trouble understanding what used to be simple legal language to her."

   H. Although Ms. T reported significant improvement in her depression by her 8/17/98 appointment with Dr. E, she continued to emphasize her difficulty with concentration in her visits on 8/17/98, 12/11/98, and 3/11/99. In her 3/11/99 appointment with Dr. E, she explicitly indicated that she "can't handle" litigation.

   I. Ms. T emphasized her cognitive impairment as a reason that she was unable to perform as a trial attorney to Dr. O on March 28, 1998.

   J. Ms. T told me on May 1, 2000, that her cognitive impairment was one of the two major reasons that she could not perform as a trial attorney.

2. After doing a battery of neuropsychological tests on April 19, 2000, Dr. Womack concluded that there was clear evidence to suggest that Ms. T is "grossly exaggerating, if not outright fabricating, her complaints of cognitive impairment." The strongest piece of evidence was her performance on the Victoria Symptom Va-

lidity Test which was "so blatantly faked that there is no doubt that she was intentionally performing poorly in attempting to appear far more impaired than she actually is." The fact that she was only able to repeat four digits forward and four digits backward "was not consistent with her performing her typical day to day behaviors." Her (WAIS-R) Full Scale IQ of 101 was below what would be expected of someone with her educational and occupational achievement.

3. Dr. Lynette P administered a Kaufman Brief Intelligence Test (KBIT) to Ms. T on March 28, 1998. Ms. T's composite score placed her in the 94th national percentile. This is equivalent to an IQ on the Weschler Adult Intelligence Scale (WAIS-R) of 123. Ms. T's performance on the KBIT and MMPI 2 on March 28, 1998, required "attention, concentration, and perseverence." Her performance was not consistent with her subjective complaints of having mental blocks and being unable to analyze. Ms. T's performance on the KBIT was not consistent with her subjective complaints to Dr. O on March 28, 1998. She told him that she had "difficulty with concentration and judgment, poor attention span, and memory impairment."

Ms. T's high KBIT score on March 28, 1998 probably reflected her actual cognitive ability. After the denial of her disability claim following her March 1998 psychological testing, Ms. T appeared to change her strategy of deception. When she was administered neuropsychological testing by Dr. Womack on April 19, 2000, she attempted to fake impaired memory and poor attention span on the tests. She scored much lower on tests of intelligence on April 19, 2000, than she did on March 28, 1998. However, the tests designed to detect malingering and a comparison of her intelligence level between the earlier KBIT and the current WAIS-R, showed evidence of conscious faking of cognitive symptoms.

4. Although Ms. T told Dr. B and Dr. O that her difficulties with concentration had caused her to stop driving; a surreptitious surveillance videotape revealed that Ms. T did drive on 3/20/98 and 3/27/98

even though her partner, Ms. R, was in the passenger seat.

5. It is somewhat unusual to have severe cognitive deficits result from PTSD or depression. As Ms. T's symptoms of depression "markedly improved" and her anxiety diminished, it is extremely atypical for severe cognitive deficits to remain.

6. Ms. T's ability to make a well-organized oral presentation at a November 1997 meeting is not consistent with her allegation of severe cognitive deficit.

7. Ms. T reported to a field representative of her disability insurance company on 11/6/97 that "she reads a lot and is presently reading a biography of Gladstone, and other light reading, spending 2 or 3 hours daily." This pattern of reading appears inconsistent with her subjective reports of severe problems in concentration and attention.

8. Although Ms. T reported severe cognitive impairment to the doctors who completed disability forms for her (her internist, Dr. S; her psychologist, Dr. B; and her psychiatrist, Dr. E), when she saw her gynecologist on 7/28/97, she did not mention any difficulty concentrating or other cognitive impairment. She told her gynecologist, "feels bad, not alive, anorgasmic, irritable, not energized."

9. In spite of alleged difficulty with concentration, Ms. T showed sustained attention in her interview with Dr. O on 3/28/98 and in her 7.5-hour interview with me on 5/1/2000.

10. Ms. T's attorney initially declined to allow Ms. T to participate in a neuropsychological evaluation with Dr. Womack unless she was provided with the names of the planned psychological tests in advance. Ms. T did not participate in the neuropsychological evaluation until she was directed to do so by a court order. Although Ms. T told me that seeking the names of the psychological tests was her attorney's idea and not her own, her conduct raises a question about whether Ms. T sought the names of the psychological tests to better prepare herself to fake cognitive deficits.

11. In a 2/16/99 letter to the California Department of Social Services, Dr. B reported that Ms. T "can accomplish about

10% of what she used to do. . . . Although her mind has cleared somewhat since May 1998, she is still incapable of performing the tasks required for her job as a civil litigator, including court appearances . . . legal research, writing briefs or letters, and conducting legal analysis of a case." Dr. B also stated, "her intellectual functioning seems to be intact when she is not anxious or depressed." This last comment suggests that Dr. B relied on Ms. T's subjective statements about her inability to function while her own observations did not show consistent impairment of Ms. T's intellectual functioning.

12. Ms. T had a substantial financial motive to malinger cognitive deficits to receive disability payments.

    A. In June 1996, Ms. T was sued by City Bank because she was unable to keep up payments on a line of credit. A second bank foreclosed on her Street Road condominium in 1996. In her 7/1/97 appointment with Dr. Smith, Ms. T mentioned "financial reversals" as a stressor. Nonetheless, in response to my direct inquiry, Ms. T initially told me that she did not have financial difficulties and that "1996 was a good year." When I specifically reminded her of the foreclosure on her condominium, she said that her decision to let the condominium go back to the bank was a business decision that was not due to any financial problems in her life. She later acknowledged that she was unable to pay back a line of credit to City Bank in 1996. In addition, Ms. T appeared to minimize her financial problems in her interview with Dr. O in March 1998.

    B. If Ms. T was found to be psychiatrically disabled (unable to practice as a trial attorney), she would receive about $275,000 tax free each year. This is substantially more than she had been earning.

    C. Ms. T had several civil suits against her for substantial sums of money by June 1997. Her disability income would be protected from her creditors if Ms. T decided to declare bankruptcy. Ms. T did unsuccessfully file for bankruptcy in 1999.

13. Ms. T was in an unusually knowledgeable position to fake psychiatric disability because she taught psychiatric nursing for several years.

14. Ms. T may have expected her disability insurance companies to make her disability payments without a thorough investigation into the possibility that she was malingering. She told me that when she had her foot surgery, she found her insurance company "very supportive" in making disability payments to her. Ms. T told Dr. O, "Had the insurance done what I expected it to do, and I had a couple of months to soothe myself . . . I might be better now."

15. The fact that Ms. T sought an additional disability policy in late 1994 in spite of substantial preexisting policies raises the possibility that Ms. T planned to seek disability payments in the future.

The following evidence supports Ms. T's diagnosis of Probable Major Depressive Episode, Mild, in partial remission. If Ms. T's account is taken at face value, she met the criteria for major depressive episode in December 1997. She reported that she had a depressed mood most of the day, nearly every day; markedly diminished interest and pleasure in activities; loss of appetite and "loss of 20 to 30 pounds; insomnia; fatigue; difficulty concentrating; and indecisiveness."

The word "probable" is used because there is a possibility that Ms. T exaggerated her symptoms of depression. Although I am not able to say it with reasonable medical certainty, the following evidence suggests that Ms. T may have exaggerated her symptoms of depression in the past:

1. Ms. T told me that she lost 20–30 pounds due to her depression. Records from her treating doctors do not substantiate this degree of weight loss.

2. When I asked Ms. T whether she would be willing to have a blood test to assess her Wellbutrin (antidepressant) level, she stated that she would not have one unless ordered to do so by a judge. This refusal to cooperate raises the possibility that she is not actually taking an antidepressant as prescribed at this time.

I described Ms. T's depression as "in partial remission" because she reported that her depressive symptoms were "markedly improved." The only depressive symptoms she continued to report were: (1) a sleep disturbance, which could be due to anxiety rather than depression; (2) fatigue, which she had reported as far back as 1992; and (3) difficulty concentrating.

The following evidence supports my diagnosis of probable PTSD. If Ms. T's account is taken at face value, she meets the DSM-IV criteria for posttraumatic stress disorder, chronic, with delayed onset, in partial remission. She stated that she witnessed events in Vietnam in which she felt physically threatened and she responded with intense fear, helplessness, and horror. Ms. T reported that she had the following symptoms during the peak of her PTSD: recurrent and intrusive distressing recollections of her Vietnam experiences three to five times a month; occasional recurrent distressing dreams of Vietnam events; occasional flashbacks; intense psychological distress at reminders of Vietnam events; physiologic reactivity on exposure to reminders of Vietnam; efforts to avoid thoughts about Vietnam; efforts to avoid activities that remind her of Vietnam; inability to recall an important aspect of a trauma; markedly diminished interest in activities (this overlaps with loss of interest due to depression); feelings of detachment from others ever since she returned from Vietnam; restless sleep ever since she returned from Vietnam; irritability ever since she returned from Vietnam; difficulty concentrating only since June 1997; and an exaggerated startle response ever since she returned from Vietnam.

The word "probable" is used because there is a possibility that Ms. T exaggerated her PTSD symptoms. Although I cannot say this with reasonable medical certainty, the following evidence supports this possibility:

1. Ms. T reported that she had some symptoms of Posttraumatic Stress Disorder since she got back from Vietnam (psychological and physical distress on seeing helicopters; feelings of detachment from others; restless sleep; and irritability). Nonetheless, Dr. B said that she saw no evidence of posttraumatic stress disorder when she treated Ms. T in 1985.
2. Although PTSD may have a delayed onset, it is less common than developing a full picture of PTSD shortly after traumatic events.
3. If Ms. T were to elect to malinger any mental illness, the choice of combat posttraumatic stress disorder entitled her to Veterans Administration disability benefits in addition to her other disability benefits.

Ms. T's posttraumatic stress disorder is labeled "in partial remission" because she told me that she had a reduction in her symptoms. The PTSD symptoms that she currently reported were flashbacks upon seeing a helicopter; intense psychological distress and intense physiologic reactivity to reminders of Vietnam; efforts to avoid activities that cause recollections of Vietnam; inability to recall an important aspect of a trauma; feelings of detachment from others; disturbance of sleep; irritability; and difficulty concentrating.

I considered the diagnosis of panic disorder because Ms. T reported some symptoms consistent with panic attacks. However, Ms. T did not meet *DSM-IV* criteria for a panic disorder because she did not have any unexpected panic attacks.

OPINION ON DISABILITY

It is my opinion that Ms. T does not have a mental illness that causes her to be unable to perform the substantial and material duties of her occupation as a trial attorney in the usual and customary way.

Ms. T told me that her depressive symptoms were "markedly improved." She stated that her sleep was better, but she still suffered from (1) fatigue and (2) difficulty concentrating. When Ms. T reported fatigue to Dr. Smith in 1992, she was still able to perform as a trial attorney. Ms. T's report of difficulty concentrating is grossly exaggerated as noted earlier. In addition, based on psychological testing, Dr. Womack concluded that Ms. T's depressive symptoms were "mild at most."

Ms. T told me that the only residual symptoms of her PTSD that actually interfered with her ability to practice as a trial attorney were: (1) irritability and (2) difficulty concentrating. Ms. T had been successful as a practicing trial attorney in spite of having irritability ever since she returned from Vietnam. Her reports of difficulty concentrating are grossly exaggerated.

Ms. T reported that she was not able to work as a trial attorney because of symptoms that fell into two major groups: (1) cognitive impairment and (2) anxiety symptoms. Her symptoms related to cognitive impairment were: (a) difficulty concentrating; (b) problems with memory; (c) trouble with focusing; (d) inability to do more than one thing to completion at a time. Her anxiety symptoms resulting from confrontation included: (a) "panicky feelings" and shakiness; (b) inability "to be timely responsive"; (c) inability to read documents that are upsetting to her; (d) feelings of depersonalization or derealization when confronted with stressful situations.

The first group of symptoms (related to impaired cognitive functioning) are not genuine. The evidence that Ms. T is malingering cognitive deficit has been stated earlier. It is my opinion that Ms. T was not unable to practice trial law due to cognitive impairment since at least March, 1998. Her ability to concentrate and sustain attention was demonstrated in her performance on the Kaufman Brief Intelligence Test on March 28, 1998, and her interviews with Dr. Womack and me in April 2000.

It is my opinion that the second group of Ms. T's alleged symptoms (anxiety resulting from confrontation) is exaggerated and does not prevent her from practicing as a trial attorney. The following evidence supports this opinion:

1. Dr. Womack's psychological testing showed that on the MMPI 2, Ms. T attempted to both present herself as "highly moral and virtuous while at the same time reporting pronounced psychiatric symptoms." Specifically, she scored quite high on the Fake Bad Scale (FBS). The Fake Bad Scale is specifically designed to detect claimants in personal injury cases who are exaggerating their emotional damages.

2. Anxiety due to confrontation is not an ordinary manifestation of depression. Anxiety due to confrontation is also not typical for Ms. T's diagnosis of PTSD. I would expect panicky feelings in PTSD to be set off by reminders of a traumatic event, rather than confrontation. Ms. T did describe some panicky feelings on seeing helicopters, but this has never interfered with her ability to practice trial law.

3. Ms. T has a substantial motive to exaggerate her anxiety symptoms due to her financial crisis and generous disability benefits. Ms. T's allegation that she cannot function in a stressful situation, such as in a courtroom or in a confrontation with an opposing attorney, allows her to practice law but not litigation law. This conveniently makes her eligible for extensive disability compensation without requiring her to give up the profession of law.

4. Ms. T's allegations of anxiety symptoms in confrontational situations are subjective and not easy to verify objectively. Although Ms. T reported personal feelings of anxiety, neither Dr. O nor I saw any objective signs of anxiety. Although Ms. T told me that she was shaking (she rated herself as a 7 on a scale of 1–10), I found that she had only a very slight tremor that was within the range of normal. Dr. Womack saw evidence of shakiness at only one point in his lengthy examination.

5. When I confronted Ms. T with inconsistencies, such as her being observed driving after telling Dr. O that she was unable to drive, she did not show any overt anxiety in response to my confrontation of her.

6. In spite of stating that her anxiety symptoms were predictable in court appearances and confrontations, Ms. T has not elected to take Xanax, her antianxiety medication, in anticipation of such events. Ms. T reported that she used Xanax "only a few times" even though she said that it was quite effective in reducing her anxiety.

7. Ms. T used atypical self-serving language to explain to me why she could not perform in court. She said, "It's like I'm allergic to litigation."

8. Ms. T told Dr. O at the end of March 1998 that she could not perform any functions of an attorney. She stated, "I'll have to do something less stessful, something that does not require the intimate contact with people . . . I don't want to deal with clients. . . . In representing people you have to be very involved, you take it on. I don't feel that I have the strength or will to carry it forward. I don't feel confident." Nonetheless, Ms. T informed me that throughout 1999 she did practice law and deal with clients.

9. Ms. T's credibility about her allegation of disabling anxiety symptoms is questionable because of (a) the clear evidence that she is grossly exaggerating her cognitive deficits, and (b) the fact that Ms. T denied any treatment for a mental condition on her 8/20/97 application for Blue Cross health insurance, while she was being treated for depression and Posttraumatic Stress Disorder.

In summary, Ms. T showed symptoms of genuine psychological distress in June 1997. She may have had a true major depressive episode and/or posttraumatic stress disorder at that time. It is also possible that instead, she exaggerated her symptoms of an adjustment disorder with anxiety and depression to receive disability payments. It is clear that by the end of March 1998, Ms. T was malingering severe cognitive deficits. This was shown by the contrast between her subjective complaints and her high performance on the Kaufman Brief Intelligence Test. Ms. T subsequently reported substantial improvement in her depression and some improvement in her posttraumatic stress disorder. She told me that she is unable to practice as a trial attorney because of continued cognitive deficits and inability to handle stressful confrontations. It is my opinion with reasonable medical certainty that Ms. T is grossly exaggerating her cognitive deficits and that she is exaggerating her alleged anxiety in order to receive disability benefits. It is my opinion with reasonable medical certainty that Ms. T is capable of performing the substantial and material duties of her occupation as a trial attorney in the usual and customary way.

Sincerely yours,
Phillip J. Resnick, M.D.

Teaching Point: How does case-specific evidence contribute to the assessment of malingering?

Case-specific, or idiographic, evidence contributes to the assessment of malingering across the three broad domains of history, motivation, and behavior. Case-specific historical evidence can provide data on whether the individual being assessed has ever been diagnosed with a disorder or treated for the kinds of symptoms that are being presented during the current evaluation. Collateral psychiatric records are the prime example of this type of case-specific information, and they can be particularly valuable in documenting signs of malingering, such as rare and improbable symptoms.

From a motivational standpoint, case-specific evidence helps the forensic clinician address the issue of whether the individual being evaluated has an understandable motive to falsify his or her report of experiencing symptoms of psychopathology or cognitive deficits. For example, the motivation to malinger in a civil case involving a potentially large recovery may be greater than in a case where the only potential gain is a meager social security disability payment. Similarly, the motivation to malinger psychiatric symptoms might increase as the severity of criminal penalties increases.

Case-specific behavioral information is also an important data source for the detection of malingering. One example of this is when the individual being evaluated is observed at regular intervals at times when he or she is not being evaluated or interacting with a mental health professional. Of particular importance in this scenario is whether the observed behavior is consistent with the genuine experience of the symptoms they report.

Such case-specific information can be combined with the assessment of how such individuals present during the interview and how they perform on tests with validity scales or specialized inventories, which involves a comparison of how this individual appears relative to others who experience genuine psychopathology, do not experience such psychopathology but report doing so, or do experience it but not in the same fashion or intensity as is reported. This combination of case-specific information with more nomothetic data creates a stronger evaluation of potential malingering.

Note

1. In addition to reporting symptoms of cognitive impairment, Ms. T reported experiencing psychological symptoms associated with Depression and Posttraumatic Stress Disorder (PTSD). The report indicates, however, that Ms. T consistently identified cognitive impairment as the primary reason that she was unable to perform her job as an attorney. Moreover, the report indicates that Ms. T claimed that her symptoms of cognitive impairment remained even after she experienced a "marked improvement" in her symptoms of Depression and PTSD. As a result, the focus of the evaluation was almost exclusively on Ms. T's reported cognitive impairment.

References

CASES CITED

Ake v. Oklahoma, 105 S.Ct. 1087 (1985).
Commonwealth v. Hill, 375 N.E. 2d 1168 (Mass. 1978).
Commonwealth v. Vailes, 275 N.E. 2d 893 (Mass. 1971).
Daubert v. Merrell Dow Pharmaceuticals, Inc., 113 S.Ct. 2786 (1993).
Dusky v. United States, 362 U.S. 402 (1960).
Estelle v. Smith, 451 U.S. 454 (1981).
Ford v. Wainwright, 477 U.S. 399 (1986).
Frendak v. United States, 408 A.2d 364 (1979).
Frye v. United States, 293 F. 1013 (D.C. Cir 1923).
Kumho Tire Company, Ltd. v. Carmichael, 526 U.S. 137 (1999).
Miller v. State, 496 N.E.2d 1297 (Ind. 1986).
Miranda v. Arizona, 384 U.S. 436 (1966).
Rhode Island v. Innis, 446 U.S. 291 (1980).
Tittsworth v. Robinson, 475 S.E. 2d 261 (Va. 1996).
United States ex. rel. Edney v. Smith, 425 F.Supp. 1038 (E.D.N.Y. 1976), aff'd, 556 F.2d 556 (2d Cir. 1977)
United States v. Green, 548 F.2d 1261 (6th Cir. 1977).
United States v. Marble, 949 F.2d 1543 (D.C. Cir. 1991).
United States v. McBroom, 124 F.3d 533 (3d Cir. 1997).
United States v. Velasquez, 885 F.2d 1076 (3d Cir. 1989).

American Academy of Psychiatry and the Law. (1995). *Ethical guidelines for the practice of forensic psychiatry.* Greenfield, CT: Author.
American Bar Association. (1989). *Criminal justice mental health standards.* Washington, DC: Author.
American Psychiatric Association. (1994). *Diagnostic and statistical manual of mental disorders* (4th ed.). Washington, DC: Author.
American Psychiatric Association. (1995). *The principles of medical ethics with annotation especially applicable to psychiatry.* Washington, DC: Author.
American Psychological Association. (1985). *Standards for educational and psychological testing.* Washington, DC: Author.
American Psychological Association. (1992). Ethical principles of psychologists and code of conduct. *American Psychologist, 47,* 1597–1611.
American Psychological Association. (1994). Guidelines for child custody evaluations in divorce proceedings. *American Psychologist, 49,* 677–680.
Anastasi, A. (1988). *Psychological testing* (6th ed.). New York: Macmillan.
Appelbaum, P. S., & Grisso, T. (1988). Assessing patients' capacities to consent to treatment. *New England Journal of Medicine, 319,* 1635–1638.
Appelbaum, P. S., & Grisso, T. (1995). The MacArthur Treatment Competence Study,

I: Mental Illness and competence to consent to treatment. *Law and Human Behavior, 19,* 105–126.

Bagby, R., Gillis, J., Toner, B., & Goldberg, J. (1991). Detecting fake-good and fake-bad responding on the Millon Clinical Multiaxial Inventory-II. *Psychological Assessment, 3,* 496–498.

Bazelon, D. (1975). A jurist's view of psychiatry. *Journal of Psychiatry & Law, 3,* 175–190.

Ben-Porath, Y. S., Shondrick, D., & Stafford, K. (1995). MMPI-2 and race in a forensic diagnostic sample. *Criminal Justice & Behavior, 22,* 19–32.

Bersoff, D. (1995). *Ethical conflicts in psychology.* Washington, DC: American Psychological Association.

Bersoff, D., Goodman-Delahunty, J., Grisso, T., Hans, V., Poythress, N. G., & Roesch, R. (1997). Training in law and psychology: Models from the Villanova Conference. *American Psychologist, 52,* 1301–1310.

Binder, L. M. (1990). Malingering following minor head trauma. *The Clinical Neuropsychologist, 4,* 25–36.

Black, H. C. (1983). *Black's law dictionary.* St. Paul, MN: West Publishing Co.

Blau, T. (1984). *The psychologist as expert witness.* New York: Wiley.

Bonnie, R. (1992). The competence of criminal defendants: A theoretical reformulation. *Behavioral Sciences & the Law, 10,* 291–316.

Borum, R., & Grisso, T. (1996). Establishing standards for criminal forensic reports: An empirical analysis. *Bulletin of the American Academy of Psychiatry and the Law, 24,* 297–317.

Brodsky, S. L. (1991). *Testifying in court: Guidelines and maxims for the expert witness.* Washington, DC: American Psychological Association.

Brodsky, S. L. (1999). *The expert expert witness: More maxims and guidelines for testifying in court.* Washington, DC: American Psychological Association.

Butcher, J., Dahlstrom, W., Graham, J., Tellegen, A., & Kaemmer, B. (1989). *MMPI-2: Manual for administration and scoring.* Minneapolis: University of Minnesota Press.

Butcher, J., Ben-Porath, Y. S., Shondrick, D., Stafford, K., McNulty, J., Graham, J., Stein, L., Whitworth, R., & McBlaine, D. (2000). Cultural and subcultural factors in MMPI-2 interpretation. In J. Butcher (Ed.), *Basic sources on the MMPI-2* (pp. 501–536). Minneapolis: University of Minnesota Press.

Butcher, J. N., Williams, C. L., Graham, J. R., Archer, R. P., Tellegen, A., Ben-Porath, Y. S., & Kaemmer, B. (1992). *Minnesota Multiphasic Personality Inventory-Adolescent (MMPI-A): Manual for administration, scoring, and interpretation.* Minneapolis: University of Minnesota Press.

Butler, R., & Williams, D. (1985). Description of Ohio State Board of Psychology hearings on ethical violations: From 1972 to the present. *Professional Psychology: Research & Practice. 16,* 502–511.

Champagne, A., Shuman, D., & Whitaker, E. (1991). An empirical examination of the use of expert witnesses in American courts. *Jurumetrics Journal of Law, Science, and Technology, 31,* 375–392.

Colbach, E. M. (1981). Integrity checks on the witness stand. *Bulletin of the American Academy of Psychiatry and the Law, 9,* 285–288.

Committee on Ethical Guidelines for Forensic Psychologists. (1991). Specialty guidelines for forensic psychologists. *Law and Human Behavior, 15,* 655–665.

Ekman, P., & O'Sullivan, M. (1991). Who can catch a liar? *American Psychologist, 46,* 913–920.

Emery, R. E., & Rogers, K. C. (1990). The role of behavior therapists in child custody cases. *Progress in Behavior Modification, 26,* 60–88.

Epperson, D. L., Kaul, J. D., & Hesselton, D. (1998, September). *Final report on the development of the Minnesota Sex Offender Screening Tool-Revised (MnSOST-R).*

Paper presented at the Association for the Treatment of Sexual Abusers Conference, Vancouver, British Columbia, Canada.

Federal Rules of Evidence for United States Courts and Magistrates. (1987). St. Paul, MN: West Publishing Company. Sections 401, 402, 702, 703, 704.

Ferguson, G. E., Eidelson, R. J., & Witt, P. H. (1998). New Jersey's sex offender risk assessment scale: Preliminary validity data. *Journal of Psychiatry and Law, 26,* 327–351.

Frederick, R. I. (1997). Validity Indicator Profile manual. Minnetonka, MN: NSC Assessments.

Frederick, R. I. (2000). Mixed group validation: A method to address the limitations of criterion group validation in research on malingering detection. *Behavioral Sciences and the Law, 18,* 693–718.

Frederick, R. I., Carter, M., & Powel, J. (1995). Adapting symptom validity testing to evaluate suspicious complaints of amnesia in medicolegal evaluations. *Bulletin of the American Academy of Psychiatry and the Law, 23,* 231–237.

Frederick, R. I., & Crosby, R. (2000). Development and validation of the Validity Indicator Profile. *Law and Human Behavior, 24,* 59–82.

Frederick, R. I., Crosby, R. D., & Wynkoop, T. F. (2000). Performance curve analysis of invalid responding on the Validity Indicator Profile. *Archives of Clinical Neuropsychology, 15,* 281–300.

Frederick, R. I., & Denney, R. L. (1998). Minding your Ps and Qs when conducting forced-choice recognition tests. *The Clinical Neuropsychologist, 12,* 193–205.

Glassman, J. (1998). Preventing and managing board complaints: The downside risk of custody evaluation. *Professional Psychology: Research and Practice, 29,* 121–124.

Golding, S. G., & Skeem, J. L. (1994). *Adapted Brief Psychiatric Rating Scale–Anchored Rating Manual.* Unpublished manuscript.

Golding, S. L. (1990). Mental health professionals and the courts: The ethics of expertise. *International Journal of Law and Psychiatry, 13,* 261–307.

Greenberg, S., & Brodsky, S. (in press). *The civil practice of forensic psychology: Torts of emotional distress.* Washington, DC: American Psychological Association Press.

Greenberg, S., & Shuman, D. (1997). Irreconcilable conflict between therapeutic and forensic roles. *Professional Psychology: Research and Practice, 1,* 50–57.

Greene, R. L. (1997). Assessment of malingering and defensiveness by multiscale inventories. In R. Rogers (Ed.), *Clinical assessment of malingering and deception* (2nd ed., pp. 169–207). New York: Guilford.

Greiffenstein, M. F., Baker, W. J., & Gola. T. (1996). Comparison of multiple scoring methods for Rey's malingered amnesia measures. *Archives of Clinical Neuropsychology, 11,* 283–293.

Grisso, T. (1981). *Juveniles' waiver of rights: Legal and psychological competence.* New York: Plenum Press.

Grisso, T. (1986). *Evaluating competencies: Forensic assessments and instruments.* New York: Plenum Press.

Grisso, T. (1988). *Competency to stand trial evaluations: A manual for practice.* Sarasota, FL: Professional Resource Exchange.

Grisso, T. (1998a). *Forensic evaluation of juveniles.* Sarasota, FL: Professional Resource Press.

Grisso, T. (1998b). *Instruments for assessing understanding and appreciation of Miranda rights.* Sarasota, FL: Professional Resource Press.

Grisso, T., & Appelbaum, P. S. (1998a). *Assessing competence to consent to treatment: A guide for physicians and other health professionals.* New York: Oxford University Press.

Grisso, T., & Appelbaum, P. S. (1998b). *MacArthur competence assessment tool for treatment (MacCAT-T).* Professional Resource Press: Sarasota, FL.

Grisso, T., & Barnum, R. (1998). *Massachusetts Youth Screening Instrument (MAYSI):*

Preliminary manual and technical report. Worcester: University of Massachusetts Medical School.

Groth, A. N., & Birnbaum, H. J. (1979). *Men who rape.* New York: Plenum.

Grove, W., & Meehl, P. (1996). Comparative efficiency of informal (subjective, impressionistic) prediction procedures: The clinical-statistical controversy. *Psychology, Public Policy, and Law, 2,* 293–323.

Halleck, S. L. (1980). *Law in the practice of psychiatry: A handbook for clinicians.* New York: Plenum Press.

Hanson, R. K. (2000). *Meta-analysis of sex offender recidivism studies: RRASOR; Static-99; SONAR.* Presented for Sinclair Seminars Sex Offender Re-Offense Risk Assessment Videotape Training Program. Madison, WI: Sinclair Seminars.

Hare, R. (1991). *The Hare Psychopathy Checklist-Revised.* Toronto, Ontario, Canada: Multi-Health Systems.

Harris, G., Rice, M., & Quinsey, V. (1993). Violent recidivism of mentally disordered offenders: The development of a standard prediction instrument. *Criminal Justice and Behavior, 20,* 315–335.

Hart, S. (1998). The role of psychopathy in assessing risk for violence: Conceptual and methodological issues. *Legal & Criminological Psychology, 3,* 121–137.

Heilbrun, K. (1992). The role of psychological testing in forensic assessment. *Law and Human Behavior, 16,* 257–272.

Heilbrun, K. (1995). Child custody evaluation: Critically assessing mental health experts and psychological tests. *Family Law Quarterly, 29,* 63–78.

Heilbrun, K. (2001). *Principles of forensic mental health assessment.* New York: Kluwer Academic/Plenum Publishers.

Heilbrun, K., Dvoskin, J., Hart, S., & McNiel, D. (1999). Violence risk communication: Implications for research, policy, and practice. *Health, Risk, & Society, 1,* 91–106.

Heilbrun, K., O'Neill, M., Stevens, T., Strohman, L., Bowman, Q., & Lo, Y. (under review). Normative approaches to communicating violence risk: A national survey of psychologists.

Heilbrun, K., O'Neill, M. L., Strohman, L. K., Bowman, Q., & Philipson, J. (2000). Expert approaches to communicating violence risk. *Law and Human Behavior, 24,* 137–148.

Heilbrun, K., Philipson, J., Berman, L., & Warren, J. (1999). Risk communication: Clinicians' reported approaches and perceived values. *Journal of the American Academy of Psychiatry and the Law, 27,* 397–406.

Hess, A., & Weiner, I. (Eds.). (1999). *The handbook of forensic psychology* (2nd ed.). New York: John Wiley & Sons.

Hoge, R., & Andrews, D. (1996). *Assessing the youthful offender.* New York: Plenum.

Kaufman, A., & Lichtenberger, E. (1999). *Essentials of WAIS-III assessment.* New York: John Wiley & Sons.

Knight, R. A. (1988). A taxonomic analysis of child molesters. In R. A. Prentky and V. Quinsey (Eds.), *Human sexual aggression: Current perspectives* (pp. 2–20). New York: New York Academy of Sciences.

Knight, R. A. (1989). An assessment of the concurrent validity of a child molester typology. *Journal of Interpersonal Violence, 4,* 131–150.

Knight, R. A., & Prentky, R. A. (1987). The developmental antecedents and adult adaptations of rapist subtypes. *Criminal Justice and Behavior, 14,* 403–426.

Knight, R. A., & Prentky, R. A. (1990). Classifying sexual offenders: The development and corroboration of taxonomic models. In W. L. Marshall, D. R. Laws, & H. E. Barbaree (Eds.), *The handbook of sexual assault: Issues, theories, and treatment of the offender* (pp. 23–52). New York: Plenum.

Knight, R., Rosenberg, R., & Schneider, B. (1985). Classification of sexual offenders: Perspectives, methods and validation. In A. Burgess (Ed.), *Rape and sexual assault: A research handbook* (pp. 222–293). New York: Garland.

Kropp, P. R., & Hart, S. D. (2000). The Spousal Assault Risk Assessment (SARA) Guide: Reliability and validity in adult male offenders. *Law and Human Behavior, 24,* 101–118.

Lamb, D., Berry, D., Wetter, M., & Baer, R. (1994). Effects of two types of information on malingering of closed head injury on the MMPI-2: An analog investigation. *Psychological Assessment, 6,* 8–13.

Liebert, D., & Foster, D. (1994). The mental health evaluation in capital cases: Standards of practice. *American Journal of Forensic Psychiatry, 15,* 43–64.

McCann, J. (1998). *Malingering and deception in adolescents: Assessing credibility in clinical and forensic settings.* Washington, DC: American Psychological Association.

Meehl, P. (1954). *Clinical versus statistical prediction.* Minneapolis: University of Minnesota Press.

Meloy, J. R. (Ed.). (1998). *The psychology of stalking: Clinical and forensic perspectives.* San Diego: Academic Press.

Melton, G., Petrila, J., Poythress, N., & Slobogin, C. (1997). *Psychological evaluations for the courts: A handbook for mental health professionals and lawyers* (2nd ed.). New York: Guilford.

Millon, T. (1993). *Millon Adolescent Clinical Inventory: Manual.* Minneapolis, MN: National Computer Systems.

Millon, T. (1994). *Millon Clinical Multiaxial Inventory-III Manual.* Minneapolis, MN: Interpretive Scoring Systems.

Monahan, J. (Ed.). (1980). *Who is the client? The ethics of psychological intervention in the criminal justice system.* Washington, DC: American Psychological Association.

Monahan, J. (1981). *Predicting violent behavior: An assessment of clinical techniques.* Beverly Hills, CA: Sage.

Monahan, J., & Steadman, H. (Eds.). (1994). *Violence and mental disorder: Developments in risk assessment.* Chicago: University of Chicago Press.

Monahan, J., Steadman, H. J., Appelbaum, P., Robbins, P., Mulvey, E., Silver, E., Roth, L., & Grisso, T. (2000). Developing a clinically useful actuarial tool for assessing violence risk. *British Journal of Psychiatry, 176,* 312–319.

Monahan, J., Steadman, H., Silver, E., Appelbaum, P., Robbins, P. C., Mulvey, E., Roth, L., Grisso, T., & Banks, S. (2001). *Rethinking risk assessment: The MacArthur study of mental disorder and violence.* New York: Oxford University Press.

Morse, S. (1978a). Crazy behavior, morals, and science: An analysis of mental health law. *Southern California Law Review, 51,* 527–654.

Morse, S. (1978b). Law and mental health professionals: The limits of expertise. *Professional Psychology, 9,* 389–399.

Morse, S. (1982a). Failed explanations and criminal responsibility: Experts and the unconscious. *Virginia Law Review, 68,* 971–1084.

Morse, S. (1982b). Reforming expert testimony: An open response from the tower (and the trenches). *Law and Human Behavior, 6,* 45–47.

National Research Council. (1989). *Improving risk communication.* Washington, DC: National Academy Press.

Nichols, H., & Molinder, I. (1984). *Multiphasic Sex Inventory Manual.* Tacoma, WA: Author.

Nurcombe, B., & Gallagher, R. (1986). *The clinical process in psychiatry.* Cambridge, England: Cambridge University Press.

Petrella, R. C., & Poythress, N. G. (1983). The quality of forensic evaluations: An interdisciplinary study. *Journal of Consulting and Clinical Psychology, 51,* 76–85.

Pinizzotta, A., & Davis, F. (1992). *Killed in the line of duty: A study of selected felonious killings of law enforcement officers.* Washington, DC: U.S. Department of Justice.

Poythress, N., Monahan, J., Bonnie, R., & Hoge, S. K. (1999). *MacArthur Competence-Assessment Tool-Criminal Adjudication*. Odessa, FL: Psychological Assessment Resources.

Poythress, N. G. (1982). Concerning reform in expert testimony: An open letter from a practicing psychologist. *Law and Human Behavior, 6*, 39–43.

Poythress, N. G., Nicholson, R., Otto, R. K., Edens, J. F., Bonnie, R. J., Monahan, J., & Hoge, S. K. (1999). *Professional manual for the MacArthur Competence Assessment Tool-Criminal Adjudication*. Odessa, FL: Psychological Assessment Resources.

Prentky, R. A., & Burgess, A. W. (2000). *Forensic management of sex offenders*. New York: Kluwer/Plenum.

Prentky, R. A., Knight, R. A., & Lee, A. F. S (1997). Risk factors associated with recidivism among extrafamilial child molesters. *Journal of Consulting and Clinical Psychology, 65*, 141–149.

Prentky, R. A., Knight, R. A., Lee, A., & Cerce, D. (1995). Predictive validity of lifestyle impulsivity for rapists. *Criminal Justice and Behavior, 22*, 106–128.

Quay, H. C. (1975). Classification in the treatment of delinquency and antisocial behavior. In *Issues in the classification of children* (vol 1). San Francisco: Jossey-Bass.

Quinsey, V. L., Harris, G. T., Rice, M. E., & Cormier, C. (1998). *Violent offenders: Appraising and managing risk*. Washington, DC: American Psychological Association.

Rees, L. M., Tombaugh, T. N., Gansler, D. A., & Moczynski, N. P. (1998). Five validation experiments of the Test of Memory Malingering (TOMM). *Psychological Assessment, 10*, 10–20.

Rey, A. (1958). *L'Examen clinique de psychologie*. Paris: Presses Universitaires de France.

Rice, M. E. (1997). Violent offender research and implications for the criminal justice system. *American Psychologist, 52*, 414–423.

Roesch, R., & Golding, S. L. (1980). *Competency to stand trial*. Champaign-Urbana: University of Illinois Press.

Rogers, R. (1984). Towards an empirical model of malingering and deception. *Behavioral Sciences and the Law, 2*, 93–112.

Rogers, R. (Ed.). (1988). *Clinical assessment of malingering and deception*. New York: Guilford Press.

Rogers, R. (1992). *Structured Interview of Reported Symptoms*. Odessa, FL: Psychological Assessment Resources.

Rogers, R. (Ed.). (1997). *Clinical assessment of malingering and deception* (2nd ed.). New York: Guilford Press.

Rogers, R. (2000). The uncritical acceptance of risk assessment in forensic practice. *Law and Human Behavior, 24*, 595–605.

Rogers, R., & Ewing, C. P. (1989). Ultimate opinion proscriptions: A cosmetic fix and a plea for empiricism. *Law and Human Behavior, 13*, 357–374.

Rogers, R., Bagby, R., & Chakraborty, D. (1993). Feigning schizophrenic disorders on the MMPI-2: Detection of coached simulators. *Journal of Personality Assessment, 60*, 215–226.

Rogers, R., & Shuman, D. (2000). *Conducting insanity evaluations* (2nd ed.). New York: Guilford.

Rosenthal, P. (1983). Nature of jury response to the expert witness. *Journal of Forensic Science, 28*, 128–131.

Schacter, D. (1986). Amnesia and crime: How much do we really know? *American Psychologist, 41*, 287–295.

Schetky, D. H., & Benedek, E. P. (in press). *The comprehensive textbook of child and adolescent forensic psychiatry*. Washington, DC: American Psychiatric Press.

Shapiro, D. (1984). *Psychological evaluation and expert testimony*. New York: Van Nostrand Reinhold.

Shapiro, D. (1991). *Forensic psychological assessment: An integrative approach*. Boston: Allyn and Bacon.

Shuman, D., Champagne, A., & Whitaker, E. (1994). An empirical examination of the use of expert witnesses in the courts—Part II: A three-city study. *Jurimetrics Journal of Law, Science and Technology, 34*, 193–208.

Shuman, D., Greenberg, S., Heilbrun, K., & Foote, W. (1998). An immodest proposal: Should treating mental health professionals be barred from testifying about their patients? *Behavioral Sciences & the Law, 16*, 509–523.

Skeem, J., & Golding, S. L. (1998). Community examiners' evaluations of competence to stand trial: Common problems and suggestions for improvement. *Professional Psychology: Research and Practice, 29*, 357–367

Skeem, J., Golding, S. L., Cohn, N., & Berge, G. (1998). The logic and reliability of evaluations of competence to stand trial. *Law and Human Behavior, 22*, 519–548.

Slobogin, C. (1982). *Estelle v. Smith*: The constitutional contours of the forensic evaluation. *Emory Law Journal, 31*, 71–138.

Slobogin, C. (1984). Dangerousness and expertise. *University of Pennsylvania Law Review, 133*, 97–174.

Slovic, P., & Monahan, J. (1995). Probability, danger, and coercion. *Law and Human Behavior, 19*, 49–65.

Slovic, P., Monahan, J., & MacGregor, D. G. (2000). Violence risk assessment and risk communication: The effects of using actual cases, providing instruction, and employing probability versus frequency formats. *Law and Human Behavior, 24*, 271–296.

Thames, H. (1994). *Frye* gone, but not forgotten in the wake of *Daubert*: New standards and procedures for admissibility of scientific expert opinion. *Mississippi Law Journal, 63*, 473–505.

Toch, H. (1970). The care and feeding of typologies and labels. *Federal Probation, 36*, 15–19.

Tombaugh, T. N. (1997). *TOMM: Test of Memory Malingering manual*. Toronto: Multi-Health Systems.

United States Sentencing Commission Guidelines Manual. (1999). Washington, DC: Author.

Van Gorp, W. G., Humphrey, L. A., Kalechstein, A., Brumm, V. L., McMullen, W. J., Stoddard, M., & Pachana, N. A. (1999). How well do standard clinical neuropsychological tests identify malingering? A preliminary analysis. *Journal of Clinical and Experimental Neuropsychology, 21*, 245–250.

Van Zelfde, G., & Otto, R. (1997). *Directory of practicum, internship, and fellowship training opportunities in clinical-forensic psychology*. Pittsburgh: American Academy of Forensic Psychology.

Webster, C., Douglas, K., Eaves, D., & Hart, S. (1997). *HCR-20: Assessing risk for violence* (version 2). Vancouver: Simon Fraser University.

Wechsler, D. (1991). *Manual for the Wechsler Intelligence Scale for Children-Third edition*. San Antonio, TX: Psychological Corporation.

Weiner, I., & Hess, A. (Eds.). (1987). *Handbook of forensic psychology*. New York: John Wiley & Sons.

Wetter, M., Baer, R., Berry, D., Robinson, L., & Sumpter, J. (1993). MMPI-2 profiles of motivated fakers given specific symptom information: A comparison to matched patients. *Psychological Assessment, 5*, 317–323.

Wilkinson, G. S. (1993). *The Wide Range Achievement Test: Administration Manual*. Wilmington, DE: Wide Range, Inc.

Witt, P.H., DelRusso, J., Oppenheim, J., & Ferguson, G. (1996). Sex offender risk assessment and the law. *Journal of Psychiatry and Law, 24*, 343–377.

Woerner, M. G., Mannuzza, S., & Kane, J. M. (1988). Anchoring the BPRS: An aid to improved reliability. *Psychopharmacology Bulletin, 24*(1), 112–118.

Index